1st Workshop on GenAI Content Detection (GenAIDetect)

Abu Dhabi, United Arab Emirates
19 January 2025

ISBN: 979-8-3313-1367-8

Printed from e-media with permission by:

Curran Associates, Inc.
57 Morehouse Lane
Red Hook, NY 12571

Association for Computational Linguistics
209 N. Eighth Street
Stroudsburg, Pennsylvania 18360

Phone: 1-570-476-8006
Fax: 1-570-476-0860

acl@aclweb.org

Additional copies of this publication are available from:

Curran Associates, Inc.
57 Morehouse Lane
Red Hook, NY 12571 USA
Phone: 845-758-0400
Fax: 845-758-2633
Email: curran@proceedings.com
Web: www.proceedings.com

GenAIDetect 2025

Proceedings of the 1st Workshop on GenAI Content Detection (GenAIDetect)

Proceedings of the Workshop

The 31st International Conference on Computational Linguistics

January 19, 2025
Abu Dhabi, UAE

Preface

Welcome to the 1st Workshop on GenAI Content Detection (GenAIDetect), co-located with COLING 2025 and hosted in Abu Dhabi, UAE. The GenAIDetect workshop provides a platform to bring together researchers working on all aspects of generative AI content detection across text, image, audio, video, and multimodal data. The aim is to create a space for the entire GenAI content detection community to present and exchange theories, algorithms, software, datasets, and tools.

In its first edition, the workshop offers a rich and diverse full-day program, including keynotes, oral paper, and poster presentation sessions, and a panel discussion. The presented papers cover a broad spectrum of topics, including datasets and benchmarks, watermarking, and various modeling techniques such as graph-based approaches. The workshop also attracted notable contributions across multiple modalities, including image, and text.

In this first edition of the GenAI Content Detection Workshop, we received 20 submissions. Each paper was rigorously peer-reviewed by two to three expert reviewers in the field. Of these submissions, 11 papers were accepted, resulting in a 55% acceptance rate, all of which were selected for oral presentation. Notably, we made no distinction in quality between long and short papers or between oral and poster presentations.

The workshop featured three shared tasks: (1) Binary Multilingual Machine-Generated Text Detection (Human vs. Machine), (2) AI vs. Human – Academic Essay Authenticity Challenge, and (3) Cross-Domain Machine-Generated Text Detection. All tasks were well received, attracting strong participation. For Tasks 1, 2, and 3, we received 17, 7, and 7 system description papers, respectively, resulting in a total of 31 system description papers and 3 overview papers.

The overview paper for the shared tasks was peer-reviewed by at least three expert reviewers, while the system description papers were reviewed by two to three reviewers. The proceedings include research track papers, as well as shared task overview and system description papers.

Finally, we thank all the contributors of papers and the 54 members of the Program Committee for their dedication to providing high-quality reviews in a timely manner. We also extend our gratitude to the COLING 2025 workshop chairs, Katsuhito Sudoh and Mo El-Haj, for organizing the COLING workshop program.

The GenAIDetect Organizers,

Firoj Alam, Preslav Nakov, Nizar Habash, Iryna Gurevych, Shammur Chowdhury, Artem Shelmanov, Yuxia Wang, Ekaterina Artemova, Mucahid Kutlu, George Mikros

Workshop website: https://genai-content-detection.gitlab.io

Organizing Committee

Firoj Alam, Qatar Computing Research Institute, Qatar

Preslav Nakov, Mohamed bin Zayed University of Artificial Intelligence, UAE

Nizar Habash, New York University Abu Dhabi, UAE

Iryna Gurevych, Mohamed bin Zayed University of Artificial Intelligence, UAE; Technical University of Darmstadt, Germany

Shammur Chowdhury, Qatar Computing Research Institute, HBKU, Qatar

Artem Shelmanov, Mohamed bin Zayed University of Artificial Intelligence, UAE

Yuxia Wang, Mohamed bin Zayed University of Artificial Intelligence, UAE

Ekaterina Artemova, Toloka AI, Netherlands

Mucahid Kutlu, Qatar University, Qatar

George Mikros, Hamad Bin Khalifa University, Qatar

Program Committee

Hariram Veeramani, UCLA, USA

Md Tanvirul Alam, Rochester Institute of Technology, USA

Sahinur Rahman Laskar, UPES, Dehradun, India

Somnath Banerjee, University of Tartu, Estonia

Noureldin Elmadany, Arab Academy for Science and Technology, Egypt

Md Saiful Islam, University of Alberta, USA

Abdullah I. Alharbi, King Abdulaziz University, Saudi Arabia

Maram Hasanain, Qatar Computing Research Institute, Qatar

Hind AL-Merekhi, Qatar Computing Research Institute, Qatar

Muhammad Tasnim Mohiuddin, Qatar Computing Research Institute, Qatar

Alham Fikri Aji, MBZUAI, UAE

Zhuohan Xie, MBZUAI, UAE

Tarek Mahmoud, MBZUAI, UAE

Jinyan Su, Cornell University, USA

Rui Xing, MBZUAI, UAE

Jiahui Geng, MBZUAI, UAE

Yassine El Kheir, Technical University Berlin, Germany

Giovanni Puccetti, Institute of Information Science and Technology "A. Faedo", Italy

Vladislav Mikhailov, University of Oslo, Norway

Masahiro Kaneko, MBZUAI, UAE

Ryuto Koike, Tokyo Institute of Technology, Japan

Orchid Chetia Phukan, Indraprastha Institute of Information Technology Delhi, India

Koel Dutta Chowdhury, Saarland University, Germany

Saied Alshahrani, Clarkson University, USA

Fahad Shamshad, MBZUAI, UAE
Md Messal Monem Miah, Texas A&M University, USA
Shah Nawaz, Johannes Kepler University Linz, Austria
Dr. Bishwa Ranjan Das, Interscience Institute of Management and Technology, India
Nada Ayman GabAllah, Coventry University, Egypt Branch, Egypt
Kamel Gaanoun, Institut National de Statistiques et d'Economie Appliquée, Morocco
Shailja Thakur, IBM Research, USA
Amr Keleg, University of Edinburgh, UK
Akim Tsvigun, University of Amsterdam, Netherlands
Muhammad Amin Nadim, University of Pegaso, Italy
Marc Franco-Salvador, Symanto Research, Germany
José Ángel González, Symanto Research, Germany
Areg Mikael Sarvazyan, Symanto Research, Germany
Walter Daelemans, University of Antwerp, Belgium
Piotr Przybyła, Universitat Pompeu Fabra, Italy
Adaku Uchendu, MIT Lincoln Laboratory, USA
Sheily Panwar, CUC-Ulster University (Doha), Qatar
Xianjun Yang, UCSB, USA
Fatima Haouari, Qatar University
Fahim Shakil Tamim, IUBAT, Bangladesh
Zach Johnson, Microsoft, USA
Abubakarr Jaye, Microsoft, USA
Jason Lucas, Penn State University, USA
Francisco Rangel, Genaios, Germany
Erum Haris, University of Leeds, UK
Mohammad Ruhul Amin, Fordham University, USA
Ram Mohan Rao Kadiyala, University of Maryland, USA
Nadia Ghezaiel, University of Hail, Saudi Arabia
Md Towhidul Absar Chowdhury, Rochester Institute of Technology, USA
Dominik Macko, Kempelen Institute of Intelligent Technologies (KInIT), Slovakia
Gleb Kuzmin, Laboratory for Analysis and Controllable Text Generation Technologies RAS, Russia
Lyudmila Rvanova, Laboratory for Analysis and Controllable Text Generation Technologies RAS, Russia

Keynote: Detectability of Language Model Generated Content: Myths, Challenges, and Opportunities

Rakesh M. Verma,

University of Houston, Houston, TX, USA

rmverma2@central.uh.edu

Abstract: Large language models (LLMs) have captured the imagination of researchers and users worldwide, and led to a capacity race. We start with some myths on the detectability of LLM generated content. We then consider LLMs through the alignment-utility tradeoff perspective and reveal some surprising consequences of aligning LLM models for different purposes, such as 1) ability to mimic humans on natural language tasks and 2) safety..Throughout the talk, we shall highlight the challenges and opportunities for research with respect to detecting LLM generated content for the different purposes of alignment.

Background: The rapid development of Large language models (LLMs) has captured the imagination of researchers and users worldwide and led to a capacity race with bigger models coming out every couple of months. Concomitantly, there is growing concern about their potential for misuse in several different fields. Maintaining the integrity of digital communication platforms such as Reddit has become increasingly vital due to these advancements in LLM abilities. While the threat of misuse has always been around, the scale at which they can now disseminate disinformation, hate speech, and create spear phishing attacks has grown alarmingly. This development poses significant challenges distinguishing between human and machine-generated content, especially on social media, where generative AI can serious consequences.

In this keynote, we will present some myths on the detectability of LLM generated content. We will also present the strengths of LLMs and their limitations. Notable strengths include the ability to leverage world knowledge that has been documented in their training dataset and new knowledge through retrieval augmented generation (RAG). Notable limitations include staying on task, which has been called different terms such as hallucination, etc., and vulnerability to different kinds of attacks.

In the second part of the talk, we consider LLMs through the alignment-utility perspective and reveal some surprising consequences of aligning LLM models for different purposes, such as 1) ability to mimic humans on natural language tasks and 2) safety. We will examine the challenges of creating datasets to examine the generative capabilities of LLMs and reflect upon our recent effort to create a dataset of tweets involving both censored and uncensored models. The talk will include brief results of our recent experiments with this datasets and four prominent LLMs including Llama and GPT4o,

We will conclude the talk with challenges and opportunities for research with respect to detecting LLM generated content including for the different purposes of alignment.

Acknowledgments: This research is joint with my PhD students at the University of Houston, especially Bryan Tuck and Fatima Z. Qachfar. Research partly supported by NSF grants 2210198 and 2244279 and ARO grants W911NF-20-1-0254 and W911NF-23-1-0191. Verma is the founder of Everest Cyber Security and Analytics, Inc.

Bio: Rakesh Verma is a Professor of Computer Science at the University of Houston, where he teaches a course on security analytics. He has made research contributions in equational logic programming, algorithm design and analysis, computer security, and data science. He is the author of Cybersecurity Analytics (CRC Press, 2019) (Verma and Marchette, 2019); a cybersecurity section associate editor of the Frontiers in Big Data Journal; and co-organizer of the ACM Annual International Workshop on Security and Privacy Analytics (IWSPA) since 2015.

Table of Contents

Workshop Program

Sunday 19th January, 2025

09:00 – 09:10	**Opening Remarks**
09:10 – 09:50	**Keynote: Detectability of Language Model Generated Content: Myths, Challenges, and Opportunities**, Rakesh Verma
09:50 - 10:35	**Session 1**
09:50 – 10:05	GPT-4 is Judged More Human than Humans in Displaced and Inverted Turing Tests *Ishika M. Rathi, Sydney Taylor, Benjamin Bergen and Cameron Jones*
10:05 – 10:20	SilverSpeak: Evading AI-Generated Text Detectors using Homoglyphs *Aldan Creo and Shushanta Pudasaini*
10:20 – 10:35	Mirror Minds: An Empirical Study on Detecting LLM-Generated Text via LLMs *Josh Baradia, Shubham Gupta and Suman Kundu*
10:35 – 11:00	**Coffee Break**
11:00 - 12:00	**Session 2**
11:00 – 11:15	Human vs. AI: A Novel Benchmark and a Comparative Study on the Detection of Generated Images and the Impact of Prompts *Philipp Moeßner and Heike Adel*
11:15 – 11:30	Benchmarking AI Text Detection: Assessing Detectors Against New Datasets, Evasion Tactics, and Enhanced LLMs *Shushanta Pudasaini, Luis Miralles, David Lillis and Marisa Llorens Salvador*
11:30 – 11:45	Cross-table Synthetic Tabular Data Detection *G. Charbel N. Kindji, Lina M. Rojas Barahona, Elisa Fromont and Tanguy Urvoy*
11:45 – 12:05	GenAI Content Detection Task 1: English and Multilingual Machine-Generated Text Detection: AI vs. Human *Yuxia Wang, Artem Shelmanov, Jonibek Mansurov, Akim Tsvigun, Vladislav Mikhailov, Rui Xing, Zhuohan Xie, Jiahui Geng, Giovanni Puccetti, Ekaterina Artemova, Jinyan Su, Minh Ngoc Ta, Mervat Abassy, Kareem Ashraf Elozeiri, Saad El Dine Ahmed El Etter, Maiya Goloburda, Tarek Mahmoud, Raj Vardhan Tomar, Nurkhan Laiyk, Osama Mohammed Afzal, Ryuto Koike, Masahiro Kaneko, Alham Fikri Aji, Nizar Habash, Iryna Gurevych and Preslav Nakov*
12:05 – 13:30	**Lunch Break**
13:30 - 15:25	**Session 3**
13:30 – 13:50	GenAI Content Detection Task 2: AI vs. Human – Academic Essay Authenticity Challenge *Shammur Absar Chowdhury, Hind Almerekhi, Mucahid Kutlu, Kaan Efe Keleş, Fatema Ahmad, Tasnim Mohiuddin, George Mikros and Firoj Alam*
13:50 – 14:10	GenAI Content Detection Task 3: Cross-Domain Machine Generated Text Detection Challenge *Liam Dugan, Andrew Zhu, Firoj Alam, Preslav Nakov, Marianna Apidianaki and Chris Callison-Burch*
14:10 – 14:25	DAMAGE: Detecting Adversarially Modified AI Generated Text *Elyas Masrour, Bradley N. Emi and Max Spero*
14:25 – 14:40	Text Graph Neural Networks for Detecting AI-Generated Content *Andric Valdez and Helena Gomez-Adorno*
14:40 – 14:55	I Know You Did Not Write That! A Sampling Based Watermarking Method for Identifying Machine Generated Text *Kaan Efe Keleş, Ömer Kaan Gürbüz and Mucahid Kutlu*
14:55 – 15:10	The Consistent Lack of Variance of Psychological Factors Expressed by LLMs and Spambots *Vasudha Varadarajan, Salvatore Giorgi, Siddharth Mangalik, Nikita Soni, Dave M. Markowitz and H. Andrew Schwartz*
15:10 – 15:25	Your Large Language Models are Leaving Fingerprints *Hope Elizabeth McGovern, Rickard Stureborg, Yoshi Suhara and Dimitris Alikaniotis*

15:30 – 16:30 Break + Poster Session

16:30 - 17:30 Session 4

16:30 - 16:40 SzegedAI at GenAI Detection Task 1: Beyond Binary - Soft-Voting Multi-Class Classification for Binary Machine-Generated Text Detection Across Diverse Language Models *Mihaly Kiss and Gábor Berend*

16:40 - 16:50 Advacheck at GenAI Detection Task 1: AI Detection Powered by Domain-Aware Multi-Tasking *German Gritsai, Anastasia Voznuyk, Ildar Khabutdinov and Andrey Grabovoy*

16:50 - 17:00 IntegrityAI at GenAI Detection Task 2: Detecting Machine-Generated Academic Essays in English and Arabic Using ELECTRA and Stylometry *Mohammad ALSmadi*

17:00 - 17:10 CNLP-NITS-PP at GenAI Detection Task 3: Cross-Domain Machine-Generated Text Detection Using DistilBERT Techniques *Sai Teja Lekkala, Annepaka Yadagiri, Mangadoddi Srikar Vardhan and Partha Pakray*

17:10 - 17:20 BBN-U.Oregon's ALERT system at GenAI Content Detection Task 3: Robust Authorship Style Representations for Cross-Domain Machine-Generated Text Detection *Hemanth Kandula, Chak Fai Li, Haoling Qiu, Damianos Karakos, Hieu Man, Thien Huu Nguyen and Brian Ulicny*

17:20 - 17:30 Leidos at GenAI Detection Task 3: A Weight-Balanced Transformer Approach for AI Generated Text Detection Across Domains *Abishek R. Edikala, Gregorios A. Katsios, Noelie Creaghe and Ning Yu*

17:30 – 17:45 Best Paper Award + Closing Ceremony

SilverSpeak: Evading AI-Generated Text Detectors using Homoglyphs

Aldan Creo
Dublin, Ireland
aldan.creo@rai.usc.es

Shushanta Pudasaini
Institute of Engineering (IOE)
Kathmandu, Nepal
shushanta574@gmail.com

Abstract

The advent of Large Language Models (LLMs) has enabled the generation of text that increasingly exhibits human-like characteristics. As the detection of such content is of significant importance, substantial research has been conducted with the objective of developing reliable AI-generated text detectors. These detectors have demonstrated promising results on test data, but recent research has revealed that they can be circumvented by employing different techniques. In this paper, we present homoglyph-based attacks ('A' → Cyrillic 'А') as a means of circumventing existing detectors. We conduct a comprehensive evaluation to assess the effectiveness of these attacks on seven detectors, including ArguGPT, Binoculars, DetectGPT, Fast-DetectGPT, Ghostbuster, OpenAI's detector, and watermarking techniques, on five different datasets. Our findings demonstrate that homoglyph-based attacks can effectively circumvent state-of-the-art detectors, leading them to classify all texts as either AI-generated or human-written (decreasing the average Matthews Correlation Coefficient from 0.64 to -0.01). Through further examination, we extract the technical justification underlying the success of the attacks, which varies across detectors. Finally, we discuss the implications of these findings and potential defenses against such attacks.

1 Introduction

LLMs have soared in popularity in a wide variety of domains as their text generation capabilities become increasingly human-like (Bin-Nashwan et al., 2023). For instance, it is estimated that the percentage of arXiv articles whose abstract has been revised by ChatGPT is around 35% (GENG and Trotta, 2024). While LLMs can prove beneficial (Ngo, 2023), there is growing concern about their potential misuse (Sullivan et al., 2023; Yan et al., 2024; Li et al., 2023; Sebastian, 2023).

Thus, a number of approaches to detect AI-generated text have been proposed, including zero-shot classifiers (Gehrmann et al., 2019; Mitchell et al., 2023; Bao et al., 2024; Hans et al., 2024; Su et al., 2023), binary classifiers (Solaiman et al., 2019; Verma et al., 2024; Liu et al., 2023), and watermarking techniques (Zhu et al., 2024; Giboulot and Teddy, 2024; Zhang and Koushanfar, 2024; Molenda et al., 2024; Wu et al., 2023).

At the same time, research has been conducted on methods for circumventing AI-generated text detectors. Some popular techniques include paraphrasing (Krishna et al., 2023; Peng et al., 2023), watermark stealing (Jovanović et al., 2024), Substitution-based In-Context example Optimization (Lu et al., 2024), reinforcement learning (Nicks et al., 2023) or space infiltration (Cai and Cui, 2023). In this paper, we study an alternative technique

Proceedings of the 1st Workshop on GenAI Content Detection (GenAIDetect), pages 1–46
January 19, 2025.

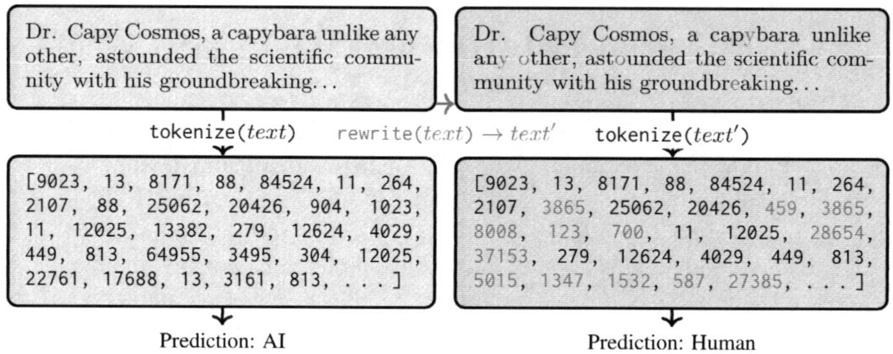

Figure 1: Homoglyph-based attack. The left box shows the original text, adapted from (Hans et al., 2024), and the right box shows the text after rewriting some of its characters. The bottom boxes show the tokenized versions from (OpenAI, 2024b). Differences are shown in red.

based on homoglyphs.

Homoglyphs are visually similar characters with different encodings (e.g., Latin ‘a’ and Cyrillic ‘a’) (Ginsberg and Yu, 2018). This allows us to generate **rewritten versions of any given text that can evade AI-generated text detectors** (Figure 1). Kirchenbauer et al. (2023) identified the usage of homoglyphs as a potential avenue for evading AI-generated text detectors. However, to the best of our knowledge, no study has yet conducted a comprehensive evaluation of the effectiveness of this approach across diverse datasets and detectors, nor has it provided insights into the technical justification of homoglyph-based attacks, a gap that we aim to fill in this paper.

Our **main contributions** are:

- ***What*** *are homoglyph-based attacks?* We introduce them as a way to evade AI-generated text detectors.
- ***How much*** *can homoglyph-based attacks affect AI-generated text detectors?* We evaluate their effectiveness on five datasets and seven detectors in Section 2. In Section 3, we show that they can bring average Matthews Correlation Coefficients from 0.64 to -0.01. This shows a complete evasion, discussed in Section 4.1.
- ***Why*** *do homoglyph-based attacks work?* We analyze and justify such performance decline in Section 4.2.
- *What are the* ***ethical implications*** *of these findings?* We discuss them in Section 6, along with possible **defenses** against such attacks.
- Additionally, we introduce the first publicly available dataset of homoglyph-based attacks targeting AI-generated text detectors.

2 Methods

In this section, we delineate our experimental approach, along with a description of the detectors and datasets employed. We make our code and datasets publicly available at `https://github.com/ACMCMC/silverspeak`, under CC BY-SA 4.0 and ODC-BY licenses. Furthermore, we ensured that our study adheres to the intended usages of the detectors and datasets presented, for which we include licensing information below.

2.1 Experiments

As shown in Figure 2, we evaluate the effectiveness of homoglyph-based attacks

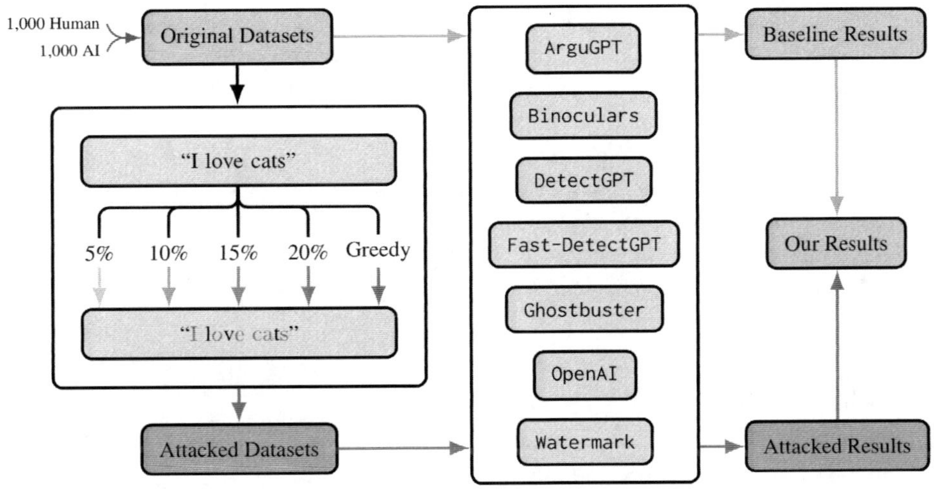

Figure 2: Our experimental process. First, we generate a set of **rewritten datasets** by applying homoglyph-based attacks, with varying replacement percentages, on all original datasets. Then, we run the **detectors** on the original and attacked datasets to get the metrics presented.

on seven detectors and five datasets, each with 2,000 samples (1,000 human and 1,000 AI). We used the original text and five attacked versions, generated by replacing **5%**, **10%**, **15%**, and **20%** of randomly chosen characters in the text (random attack), or all of the possible characters that can be replaced (**greedy** attack).

We also conducted initial experiments on an optimized setting where we perform replacement only on tokens that have the highest loglikelihoods (those that are most likely to be AI-generated) when evaluated by an LLM. However, given that the previous attacks are already effective (Section 3), we decided to focus on them for the rest of the experiments, as they are less computationally expensive and do not vary depending on the choice of the LLM.

We utilized the homoglyphs provided in (Davis and Suignard, 2023). We based our code on the Hugging Face Transformers and Datasets libraries with PyTorch as backend (Wolf et al., 2019; Paszke et al., 2019).We executed the experiments on a NVIDIA A100, for which we present utilization by each detector in Table 1.

Detector	Time	Space
ArguGPT	2	5.2
Binoculars	6	34.2
DetectGPT	276	10.8
Fast-DetectGPT	25	19.5
Ghostbuster	240	0
OpenAI	2	5.2
Watermark	3	8.6

Table 1: Approximate requirements on time and space for one experiment, in minutes and gigabytes. We report on the unattacked *reuter* dataset as times do not vary significantly across datasets. For a full experiment suite on a detector, the time requirement is multiplied by the number of attacks and datasets.

2.2 Detectors

We conduct experiments on:

- `ArguGPT`: A RoBERTa-based classifier trained on a dataset of human and AI-generated arguments (Liu et al., 2023). We utilize the sentence-level model under a MIT license.

- `Binoculars`: Computes a ratio of the perplexity measured on an LLM and its cross-entropy with the perplexity of another. The text is determined to be AI-generated or not by comparing the ratio with a chosen threshold. We utilize the code (BSD 3 license), default threshold (`low-fpr`), and models (observer `falcon-7b`; performer `falcon-7b-instruct`) provided by the authors (Hans et al., 2024).

- `DetectGPT`: Compares the likelihood of an input text with a series of AI-perturbed versions, assuming that loglikelihoods will drop more for AI-generated texts (Mitchell et al., 2023). We utilize the open-source implementation (MIT license) by (Tayyab, 2023), with `GPT-2-Medium` and `T5-Large` as scoring and rewriting models (Radford et al., 2019; Raffel et al., 2020).

- `Fast-DetectGPT`: An optimization that measures the conditioned probability of each token against its alternatives, rather than among texts. This means that only one forward pass is needed to score the perturbed tokens, rendering it much faster (Bao et al., 2024). It has been released under a MIT license.

- `Ghostbuster`: A classifier trained on a set of forward-selected features based on token probabilities measured on weak language models (Verma et al., 2024), licensed under CC BY 3.0. We use its web interface, as described in Section 7.

- `OpenAI`'s detector: A `RoBERTa`-based classifier trained on a large dataset of human and AI-generated texts (Solaiman et al., 2019). We utilize the large variant (MIT license).

- `Watermark`: Based on a *lefthash* algorithm, which computes a hash of the previous token and uses it to shift the next token logits, so that this skewed distribution can be detected (Kirchenbauer et al., 2023). We use the Hugging Face implementation (Apache 2.0) (Wolf et al., 2019).

2.3 Datasets

We derived our datasets as follows:

- *essay, writing prompts, reuter*: Derived from (Verma et al., 2024), also utilized by (Hans et al., 2024). The *essay* dataset consists of essays from IvyPanda. The *writing prompts* dataset consists of prompts from the subreddit r/WritingPrompts. The *reuter* dataset consists of news articles from the Reuters 50-50 authorship identification dataset. They are licensed under CC BY 3.0.

- *CHEAT*: Abstracts of academic papers, derived from (Yu et al., 2024) under a MIT license.

- *realnewslike*: Derived from the C4 realnewslike dataset (Raffel et al., 2020) (ODC-BY license). We generate 200-token watermarked completions with `OPT-1.3B` (Zhang et al., 2022), as in (Kirchenbauer et al., 2023), taking 8 minutes and 23.9 GB on a NVIDIA A100. The nature of this dataset is such that it is only used to test the `Watermark` detector, as others cannot detect watermarks.

To ensure that all datasets have the same number of examples, we randomly select 1,000 human and 1,000 AI-written examples from each source dataset. We do not split the datasets as our study does not require training any model.

3 Results

We summarize our experimental results in Table 2. Full results are reported in

Dataset	Detector	Original	5%	10%	15%	20%	Greedy
CHEAT	ArguGPT	0.94	0.0	0.0	0.0	0.0	0.0
	Binoculars	0.93	0.37	0.11	0.04	0.02	0.13
	DetectGPT	0.14	-0.02	0.03	0.13	0.06	0.0
	Fast-DetectGPT	0.9	0.23	0.04	0.02	0.0	-0.01
	Ghostbuster	0.64	0.41	0.32	0.12	0.06	0.02
	OpenAI	0.47	0.0	0.0	0.0	-0.02	0.0
essay	ArguGPT	0.92	0.0	0.0	0.0	0.0	0.0
	Binoculars	0.91	0.22	0.05	0.0	0.0	0.05
	DetectGPT	0.24	-0.01	0.11	0.21	0.08	0.0
	Fast-DetectGPT	0.88	0.22	0.04	0.0	0.0	-0.08
	Ghostbuster	0.92	0.73	0.51	0.13	0.0	0.0
	OpenAI	-0.21	0.0	0.0	0.0	0.0	0.03
reuter	ArguGPT	0.92	0.0	0.0	0.0	0.0	0.0
	Binoculars	0.8	0.22	0.07	0.03	0.02	0.08
	DetectGPT	0.23	0.0	0.03	0.34	0.14	0.0
	Fast-DetectGPT	0.92	0.28	0.1	0.02	0.0	0.04
	Ghostbuster	0.93	0.61	0.51	0.16	0.04	0.0
	OpenAI	0.27	0.0	-0.04	-0.09	-0.11	-0.06
writing prompts	ArguGPT	0.39	0.0	0.0	0.0	0.0	0.0
	Binoculars	0.85	0.2	0.0	0.0	0.0	-0.04
	DetectGPT	0.44	0.04	0.01	0.02	0.02	0.0
	Fast-DetectGPT	0.79	0.3	0.05	-0.03	0.0	-0.33
	Ghostbuster	0.88	0.42	0.64	0.33	0.09	0.0
	OpenAI	-0.05	-0.04	-0.05	-0.13	-0.11	0.01
realnewslike	Watermark	0.92	0.18	-0.01	0.0	-0.03	0.0
	Average	0.64	0.17	0.1	0.05	0.01	-0.01
	Standard deviation	0.36	0.21	0.19	0.11	0.05	0.08

Table 2: Matthews Correlation Coefficient (MCC) of all detectors on all datasets for all attack configurations. The color of the cell represents its value, clipped between 0 (red) and 1 (green).

Appendices A and B, with the raw results available in our released datasets.

The results correspond to a single run, as we confirmed that the scores obtained are identical across multiple executions.

It should be noted that some conventional metrics employed to assess the efficacy of detectors may prove to be deceptive in this particular setting. For example, Figure 13e shows a confusion matrix where the F1 score is 0.67, but the detector is classifying almost all examples as AI-generated. We argue that the Matthews Correlation Coefficient (MCC) is better suited (in this case, 0.08), placing greater emphasis on class balance (Baldi et al., 2000). Therefore, we use it as our main metric, and advise caution when interpreting the results based on other metrics in the appendices. MCC yields values from -1 (inverse correlation) to 1 (perfect correlation), with 0 representing no correlation.

4 Discussion

In this section, we discuss the results obtained from the experiments conducted on different AI-generated text detectors using homoglyph-based attacks. Then, we analyze the effectiveness of the attacks and their technical justifications.

4.1 Effectiveness of the attacks

Baseline performance varies across detectors and datasets. Before the attacks, MCC values range from -0.21 to 0.94, with an average of 0.64 and a standard deviation of 0.36.

`Binoculars` and `Fast-DetectGPT` show consistently high MCCs. `ArguGPT` and `Ghostbuster` show a wider range of MCCs across datasets, with `DetectGPT` and the `OpenAI` detector having lower baseline scores. The Watermark detector shows a high baseline MCC, albeit only tested on the *realnewslike* dataset.

We performed a side exploration on the low scores of DetectGPT and the OpenAI detector. We found that their scores can be improved by adapting their classification thresholds to each dataset they are applied on. However, including these results would mean deviating from the original implementations, so we abstained from changing the thresholds in our study.

Interestingly, not all detectors are affected in the same way by the attacks. Generally, we observe two distinct trends when applying the attacks:

- The detector tends to classify the examples as **human-written**, even when they are AI-generated. This happens on all replacement percentages, but even more prominently as the percentage of replacements increases. This is the case for ArguGPT, Binoculars, Fast-DetectGPT, the OpenAI detector, and Watermark.

- The detector classifies more examples as **human-written on low replacement percentages** (5% or 10%). However, as the percentage of replacements increases, the detector starts classifying the examples as AI-generated. On intermediate replacement percentages, the detector tends to behave as a random classifier. This temporarily increases the MCC, as some examples are classified correctly. Then, the tendency reaches a plateau and **higher percentages** (20%, greedy attack) cause the detector to classify almost all examples as **AI-generated**. This is the case for DetectGPT, which plateaus around 15%, and Ghostbuster, which plateaus around 10%.

While the behavior of the detectors varies, the effectiveness of the attacks is consistent across all detectors and datasets, showing a pronounced decline in performance. Lowest MCCs are observed in the greedy replacement setting, where **the attack consistently** (standard deviation of 0.08) **renders detectors ineffective** (average of -0.01).

4.2 Technical justification

In this section, we provide insights into the effectiveness of the attacks, separately exploring each group of detectors.

4.2.1 Perplexity-based models

Binoculars, DetectGPT and Fast-DetectGPT are based on perplexity, shown in Equation 1 (Alon and Kamfonas, 2023). Let N be the number of tokens in the text, and $p(t_i)$ the probability of token t_i given $t_1, \ldots, t_{i-1}$, according to an LLM.

$$\text{Perplexity} = \exp\left[-\frac{1}{N}\sum_{i=1}^{N}\log p(t_i)\right] \tag{1}$$

As homoglyphs have different encodings, tokenizers treat them differently. Two observations can be made:

1. Since the training corpora used to train popular tokenizers (such as those based on Byte-Pair Encoding (Sennrich et al., 2016)) do not often contain sequences that mix characters from different alphabets, it is likely that attacked tokens will be split into smaller ones: N increases.

2. Since the attacked sequence of tokens does not resemble the training data, the loglikelihoods for attacked tokens will generally be lower.

Therefore, the summation contains **more tokens** ($\uparrow N$) **with lower loglikelihoods** ($\downarrow \log p(t_i)$), increasing perplexity.

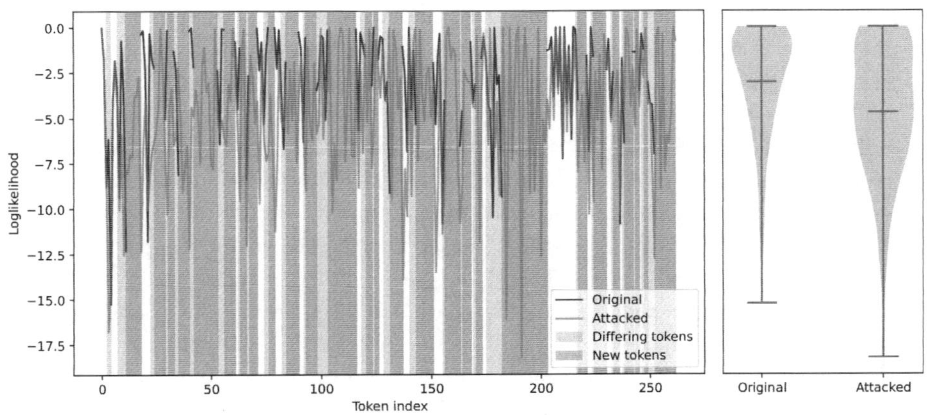

(a) Differences in loglikelihood per token

(b) Distribution

Figure 3: Token loglikelihoods for the text in Figure 1 on BLOOM-560m (Le Scao et al., 2023). The attacked text (10% replacement) has a distribution shifted towards more negative values.

Figure 3 illustrates the impact of homoglyph-based attacks on tokens and their associated log likelihoods. In this example, modifying **10%** of the characters in the text changes their tokenization **70%** of the time. The attacked text exhibits a more negative loglikelihood distribution than the original text, as shown in Figure 3b. Therefore, the attacked text appears "more likely to be human" when the perplexity is evaluated with an LLM, while keeping the same appearance. In summary, homoglyph-based attacks are effective at **shifting the distribution of loglikelihoods towards more negative values, which can evade detection**.

4.2.2 Classification models

ArguGPT and the OpenAI detector are RoBERTa-based models with a classification head (Liu et al., 2023; Solaiman et al., 2019). We hypothesize that the presence of homoglyphs in the text causes the output embeddings to become much less discriminative, as the model is unable to understand the semantics of the text.

To test this hypothesis, we remove the classification head from ArguGPT and obtain the mean of the embeddings for the original and attacked texts (10% replacement) on the *CHEAT* dataset. We then reduce their dimensionality to 2D with UMAP (McInnes et al., 2018). We set the local connectivity to 5, minimum distance to 0.1, and number of neighbors to 15. We plot the embeddings in Figure 4.

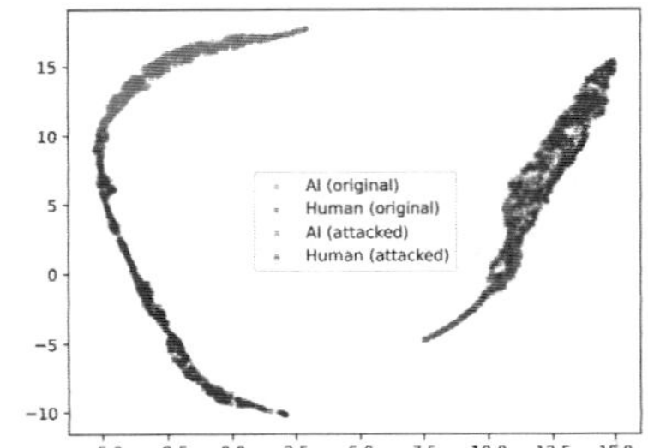

Figure 4: Embeddings from ArguGPT. While the original texts are well-separated, the embeddings of the attacked texts are mixed and placed in a different subspace.

Three clusters can be observed. Two of them correspond to the original texts, where AI and human texts are clearly separated. However, the third cluster (green and purple) corresponds to the attacked texts, where embeddings are mixed. This indicates that the classification head is fed with discriminative embeddings in a normal scenario, but with homoglyphs, **the embeddings are less discriminative and placed in an unseen region of the space, therefore leading to misclassifications**.

As for `Ghostbuster`, a similar justification to Section 4.2.1 can be made. The model is based on a linear classifier, and while it does not use perplexity, the features it is trained on are based on the probability of generating each token in the text under several weaker language models (Verma et al., 2024). Therefore, the same principles apply: the presence of homoglyphs in the text alters the calculation of the probabilities, leading to a **shift in the distribution of the features used by the classifier that evades detection**.

4.2.3 Watermarking

The `Watermark` detector is a special case, as it is not designed to analyze the semantics of the text, or any of its features, other than the presence of a watermark. The probability of a text having been generated with a watermark is calculated with a one-proportion z-test, as shown in Equation 2. Given a text, $|s|_G$ is the number of *green* ("expected") tokens and T is the total number. γ is a hyperparameter, the probability of a token being green (Kirchenbauer et al., 2023).

$$z = (|s|_G - \gamma T)/\sqrt{T\gamma(1-\gamma)} \quad (2)$$

If the text is generated with knowledge of the watermark rule, we can expect $|s|_G$ to deviate significantly from γT; *i.e.* the sample mean will be higher than the expected mean, leading to a high z value. This is the case for the original texts, where the watermark is easily detected.

However, results show that watermarks are highly sensitive to changes in the text. This is due to the fact that the *lefthash* watermarking algorithm is based on a simple scheme where a list of green tokens is generated using the previous token $t-1$ (Kirchenbauer et al., 2024). This list is used to shift the logits of the current token t, so that the distribution is skewed towards green tokens. As homoglyph-based attacks alter tokenization, many of the green lists are generated with different seeds, and the probability of t being green becomes γ, as in a human-written text. Moreover, even if $t-1$ remains the same, if t is changed, its probability of being green is also γ. The two factors combined lead to a **significant decrease in the number of green tokens**, thus reducing z and rendering the watermark undetectable.

5 Conclusion

This paper demonstrated that homoglyph-based attacks can evade state-of-the-art AI-generated text detectors. We performed a systematic evaluation of the effectiveness of these attacks on seven different detectors and five different datasets. Our results showed that homoglyph-based attacks are very effective, to the point that their MCC drops to around 0 (no correlation) in all of them, albeit at different replacement percentages. We then analyzed the internal mechanisms of the detectors to provide a technical justification for the effectiveness of the attacks. Furthermore, we have publicly released our implementation and datasets, which we hope will facilitate further research on AI-generated text detection algorithms. The effectiveness of these attacks adds to the existing evidence that existing AI-generated text detectors are unfit for purpose, highlighting the need for more robust detection mechanisms. The proposed attacks can be employed to assess the resilience of future AI-generated text detectors and to develop more effective solutions.

6 Ethical impact and safeguards

Our work has significant ethical implications, including the potential for increased instances of academic misconduct, misinformation, and social engineering (Majumdar et al., 2024).

Furthermore, while alternative methods such as paraphrasing necessitate the use of LLMs (Krishna et al., 2023), homoglyph-based attacks can be conducted with a simple script and minimal computational resources. This **lower barrier for access** exacerbates their potential impact.

It is not our intention to encourage malicious usage; rather, we seek to contribute to the growing evidence on the unreliability of current detectors (Sadasivan et al., 2024; Yan et al., 2024) and promote the design of sturdier ones. It is **deeply concerning** that a number of commercially available tools like Undetectable (2024) are widely used in sectors like academia, yet they are vulnerable to an attack that can be executed with minimal effort.

Fortunately, it is possible to forestall these attacks by incorporating additional **safeguards** into the detection process. Input constraints, such as limiting the character set that can be utilized (Ginsberg and Yu, 2018) or mapping them to a standard form (Alvi et al., 2017), can be an effective mitigation strategy in several cases.

Other contexts may require more sophisticated solutions. For instance, scientific articles frequently contain Greek symbols in their discourse, which should not be treated as indicators of homoglyph-based attacks. Instead, one possibility is to analyze loglikelihood scores (Figure 3) (Alon and Kamfonas, 2023), while another is to consider architectures based on neural networks (Woodbridge et al., 2018) or optical character recognition (Ginsberg and Yu, 2018). No universal solution exists, and the choice should be based on the nature of the text and detector.

7 Limitations

Our work has some limitations that should be considered when interpreting results.

Optimized attacks As our aim was to justify and assess the extent to which homoglyph-based attacks are able to evade AI-generated text detectors, we did not attempt to optimize (Section 2.1). It may be possible to achieve the same evasion rates with lower replacement percentages by strategically selecting the characters to replace. Additionally, there may be merit in studying character sets other than homoglyphs (Boucher et al., 2022).

Datasets We are confident that the number of samples per dataset (2,000) is enough to demonstrate the effectiveness of the attacks, as the results do not elicit the need for further exploration (we observe a complete evasion of the detectors with a low standard deviation). However, generalizability to languages other than English remains to be studied, where homoglyphs may be naturally present. Nonetheless, if detectors tend to misclassify non-native English writing samples as AI-generated (Liang et al., 2023), we expect that homoglyph-based attacks would be effective in other languages as well.

`Ghostbuster` deprecation Another limitation is that `Ghostbuster` is based on the deprecated `ada` and `davinci` models (OpenAI, 2024a). This prevents us from running it on our infrastructure, and while we have tried to contact the authors for a solution, we have not received a response yet. Surprisingly, the web interface provided by the authors remains operational, enabling us to evaluate the detector. However, we are unable to confirm the models currently in use, and therefore cannot guarantee that the results are consistent with those presented in the original paper, nor that they will remain reproducible.

References

Gabriel Alon and Michael Kamfonas. 2023. Detecting language model attacks with perplexity. *Preprint*, arXiv:2308.14132.

Faisal Alvi, Mark Stevenson, and Paul Clough. 2017. Plagiarism detection in texts obfuscated with homoglyphs. In *Advances in Information Retrieval*, pages 669–675, Cham. Springer International Publishing.

Pierre Baldi, Søren Brunak, Yves Chauvin, Claus A. F. Andersen, and Henrik Nielsen. 2000. Assessing the accuracy of prediction algorithms for classification: an overview. *Bioinformatics*, 16(5):412–424.

Guangsheng Bao, Yanbin Zhao, Zhiyang Teng, Linyi Yang, and Yue Zhang. 2024. Fast-DetectGPT: Efficient zero-shot detection of machine-generated text via conditional probability curvature. In *The Twelfth International Conference on Learning Representations*.

Saeed Awadh Bin-Nashwan, Mouad Sadallah, and Mohamed Bouteraa. 2023. Use of ChatGPT in academia: Academic integrity hangs in the balance. *Technology in Society*, 75:102370.

Nicholas Boucher, Ilia Shumailov, Ross Anderson, and Nicolas Papernot. 2022. Bad characters: Imperceptible NLP attacks. In *2022 IEEE Symposium on Security and Privacy (SP)*, pages 1987–2004.

Shuyang Cai and Wanyun Cui. 2023. Evade ChatGPT detectors via a single space. *arXiv preprint arXiv:2307.02599*.

Mark Davis and Michel Suignard. 2023. Unicode security mechanisms. Technical standard, Unicode.

Sebastian Gehrmann, Hendrik Strobelt, and Alexander Rush. 2019. GLTR: Statistical detection and visualization of generated text. In *Proceedings of the 57th Annual Meeting of the Association for Computational Linguistics: System Demonstrations*, pages 111–116, Florence, Italy. Association for Computational Linguistics.

Mingmeng GENG and Roberto Trotta. 2024. Is chatGPT transforming academics' writing style? In *ICML 2024 Next Generation of AI Safety Workshop*.

Eva Giboulot and Furon Teddy. 2024. WaterMax: breaking the llm watermark detectability-robustness-quality trade-off. *arXiv preprint arXiv:2403.04808*.

Avi Ginsberg and Cui Yu. 2018. Rapid homoglyph prediction and detection. In *2018 1st International Conference on Data Intelligence and Security (ICDIS)*, pages 17–23.

Abhimanyu Hans, Avi Schwarzschild, Valeriia Cherepanova, Hamid Kazemi, Aniruddha Saha, Micah Goldblum, Jonas Geiping, and Tom Goldstein. 2024. Spotting LLMs with binoculars: Zero-shot detection of machine-generated text. In *Forty-first International Conference on Machine Learning*.

Nikola Jovanović, Robin Staab, and Martin Vechev. 2024. Watermark stealing in large language models. In *Proceedings of the 41st International Conference on Machine Learning*.

John Kirchenbauer, Jonas Geiping, Yuxin Wen, Jonathan Katz, Ian Miers, and Tom Goldstein. 2023. A watermark for large language models. In *Proceedings of the 40th International Conference on Machine Learning*, volume 202 of *Proceedings of Machine Learning Research*, pages 17061–17084. PMLR.

John Kirchenbauer, Jonas Geiping, Yuxin Wen, Manli Shu, Khalid Saifullah, Kezhi Kong, Kasun Fernando, Aniruddha Saha, Micah Goldblum, and Tom Goldstein. 2024. On the reliability of watermarks for large language models. In *The Twelfth International Conference on Learning Representations*.

Kalpesh Krishna, Yixiao Song, Marzena Karpinska, John Wieting, and Mohit Iyyer. 2023. Paraphrasing evades detectors of ai-generated text, but retrieval is an effective defense. In *Advances in Neural Information Processing Systems*, volume 36, pages 27469–27500. Curran Associates, Inc.

Teven Le Scao, Angela Fan, Christopher Akiki, Ellie Pavlick, Suzana Ilić, Daniel Hesslow, Roman Castagné, Alexandra Sasha Luccioni, François Yvon, Matthias Gallé, et al. 2023. BLOOM: A 176b-parameter open-access multilingual language model.

Bo Li, Jiaxin Ju, Can Wang, and Shirui Pan. 2023. How does ChatGPT affect fake news detection systems? In *Advanced Data Mining and Applications*, pages 565–580, Cham. Springer Nature Switzerland.

Weixin Liang, Mert Yuksekgonul, Yining Mao, Eric Wu, and James Zou. 2023. GPT detectors are biased against non-native English writers. *Patterns*, 4(7).

Yikang Liu, Ziyin Zhang, Wanyang Zhang, Shisen Yue, Xiaojing Zhao, Xinyuan Cheng, Yiwen Zhang, and Hai Hu. 2023. ArguGPT: evaluating, understanding and identifying argumentative essays generated by gpt models. *Preprint*, arXiv:2304.07666.

Ning Lu, Shengcai Liu, Rui He, Yew-Soon Ong, Qi Wang, and Ke Tang. 2024. Large language models can be guided to evade AI-generated text detection. *Transactions on Machine Learning Research.*

Durjoy Majumdar, Arjun S, Pranavi Boyina, Sri Sai Priya Rayidi, Yerra Rahul Sai, and Suryakanth V Gangashetty. 2024. Beyond text: Nefarious actors harnessing LLMs for strategic advantage. In *2024 International Conference on Intelligent Systems for Cybersecurity (ISCS)*, pages 1–7.

L. McInnes, J. Healy, and J. Melville. 2018. UMAP: Uniform Manifold Approximation and Projection for Dimension Reduction. *ArXiv e-prints.*

Eric Mitchell, Yoonho Lee, Alexander Khazatsky, Christopher D. Manning, and Chelsea Finn. 2023. DetectGPT: zero-shot machine-generated text detection using probability curvature. In *Proceedings of the 40th International Conference on Machine Learning*, ICML'23. JMLR.org.

Piotr Molenda, Adian Liusie, and Mark Gales. 2024. WaterJudge: Quality-detection trade-off when watermarking large language models. In *Findings of the Association for Computational Linguistics: NAACL 2024*, pages 3515–3525, Mexico City, Mexico. Association for Computational Linguistics.

Thi Thuy An Ngo. 2023. The perception by university students of the use of ChatGPT in education. *International Journal of Emerging Technologies in Learning (Online)*, 18(17):4.

Charlotte Nicks, Eric Mitchell, Rafael Rafailov, Archit Sharma, Christopher D Manning, Chelsea Finn, and Stefano Ermon. 2023. Language model detectors are easily optimized against. In *The Twelfth International Conference on Learning Representations.*

OpenAI. 2024a. Deprecations. `https://platform.openai.com/docs/deprecations`. Accessed: 2024-07-14.

OpenAI. 2024b. OpenAI tokenizer. `https://platform.openai.com/tokenizer`. Accessed: 2024-04-08.

Adam Paszke, Sam Gross, Francisco Massa, Adam Lerer, James Bradbury, Gregory Chanan, Trevor Killeen, Zeming Lin, Natalia Gimelshein, Luca Antiga, et al. 2019. Pytorch: An imperative style, high-performance deep learning library. *Advances in neural information processing systems*, 32.

Xinlin Peng, Ying Zhou, Ben He, Le Sun, and Yingfei Sun. 2023. Hidding the ghostwriters: An adversarial evaluation of AI-generated student essay detection. In *Proceedings of the 2023 Conference on Empirical Methods in Natural Language Processing*, pages 10406–10419, Singapore. Association for Computational Linguistics.

Alec Radford, Jeffrey Wu, Rewon Child, David Luan, Dario Amodei, Ilya Sutskever, et al. 2019. Language models are unsupervised multitask learners. *OpenAI blog*, 1(8):9.

Colin Raffel, Noam Shazeer, Adam Roberts, Katherine Lee, Sharan Narang, Michael Matena, Yanqi Zhou, Wei Li, and Peter J. Liu. 2020. Exploring the limits of transfer learning with a unified text-to-text transformer. *J. Mach. Learn. Res.*, 21(1).

Vinu Sankar Sadasivan, Aounon Kumar, Sriram Balasubramanian, Wenxiao Wang, and Soheil Feizi. 2024. Can AI-generated text be reliably detected? *Preprint*, arXiv:2303.11156.

Glorin Sebastian. 2023. Do ChatGPT and other AI chatbots pose a cybersecurity risk?: An exploratory study. *International Journal of Security and Privacy in Pervasive Computing (IJSPPC)*, 15(1):1–11.

Rico Sennrich, Barry Haddow, and Alexandra Birch. 2016. Neural machine translation of rare words with subword units. In *Proceedings of the 54th Annual Meeting of the Association for Computational Linguistics (Volume 1: Long Papers)*, pages 1715–1725, Berlin, Germany. Association for Computational Linguistics.

Irene Solaiman, Miles Brundage, Jack Clark, Amanda Askell, Ariel Herbert-Voss, Jeff Wu, Alec Radford, Gretchen Krueger, Jong Wook Kim, Sarah Kreps, Miles McCain, Alex Newhouse, Jason Blazakis, Kris McGuffie, and Jasmine Wang. 2019. Release Strategies and the Social Impacts of Language Models. *Preprint*, arXiv:1908.09203.

Jinyan Su, Terry Zhuo, Di Wang, and Preslav Nakov. 2023. DetectLLM: Leveraging log rank information for zero-shot detection of machine-generated text. In *Findings of the Association for Computational Linguistics: EMNLP 2023*, pages 12395–12412, Singapore. Association for Computational Linguistics.

Miriam Sullivan, Andrew Kelly, and Paul McLaughlan. 2023. ChatGPT in higher education: Considerations for academic integrity and student learning. *Journal of Applied Learning & Teaching*, 6(1).

Burhan Ul Tayyab. 2023. Detect-GPT. `https://github.com/BurhanUlTayyab/DetectGPT`.

Undetectable. 2024. Undetectable. `https://undetectable.ai`. Accessed: 2024-10-08.

Vivek Verma, Eve Fleisig, Nicholas Tomlin, and Dan Klein. 2024. Ghostbuster: Detecting text ghostwritten by large language models. In *Proceedings of the 2024 Conference of the North American Chapter of the Association for Computational Linguistics: Human Language Technologies (Volume 1: Long Papers)*, pages 1702–1717, Mexico City, Mexico. Association for Computational Linguistics.

Thomas Wolf, Lysandre Debut, Victor Sanh, Julien Chaumond, Clement Delangue, Anthony Moi, Pierric Cistac, Tim Rault, Rémi Louf, Morgan Funtowicz, Joe Davison, Sam Shleifer, Patrick von Platen, Clara Ma, Yacine Jernite, Julien Plu, Canwen Xu, Teven Le Scao, Sylvain Gugger, Mariama Drame, Quentin Lhoest, and Alexander M. Rush. 2019. HuggingFace's Transformers: State-of-the-art natural language processing. *Preprint*, arXiv:1910.03771.

Jonathan Woodbridge, Hyrum S. Anderson, Anjum Ahuja, and Daniel Grant. 2018. Detecting homoglyph attacks with a siamese neural network. In *2018 IEEE Security and Privacy Workshops (SPW)*, pages 22–28.

Yihan Wu, Zhengmian Hu, Hongyang Zhang, and Heng Huang. 2023. Dipmark: A stealthy, efficient and resilient watermark for large language models. *arXiv preprint arXiv:2310.07710*.

Lixiang Yan, Lele Sha, Linxuan Zhao, Yuheng Li, Roberto Martinez-Maldonado, Guanliang Chen, Xinyu Li, Yueqiao Jin, and Dragan Gašević. 2024. Practical and ethical challenges of large language models in education: A systematic scoping review. *British Journal of Educational Technology*, 55(1):90–112.

Peipeng Yu, Jiahan Chen, Xuan Feng, and Zhihua Xia. 2024. CHEAT: A large-scale dataset for detecting ChatGPT-writtEn AbsTracts. *Preprint*, arXiv:2304.12008.

Ruisi Zhang and Farinaz Koushanfar. 2024. EmMark: Robust watermarks for IP protection of embedded quantized large language models. *arXiv preprint arXiv:2402.17938*.

Susan Zhang, Stephen Roller, Naman Goyal, Mikel Artetxe, Moya Chen, Shuohui Chen, Christopher Dewan, Mona Diab, Xian Li, Xi Victoria Lin, Todor Mihaylov, Myle Ott, Sam Shleifer, Kurt Shuster, Daniel Simig, Punit Singh Koura, Anjali Sridhar, Tianlu Wang, and Luke Zettlemoyer. 2022. OPT: Open pre-trained transformer language models. *Preprint*, arXiv:2205.01068.

Chaoyi Zhu, Jeroen Galjaard, Pin-Yu Chen, and Lydia Y Chen. 2024. Duwak: Dual watermarks in large language models. *arXiv preprint arXiv:2403.13000*.

Appendices

A Detection metrics

The detection metrics are reported in the following tables. The metrics include the MCC, accuracy, F1 score, precision and recall for each detector and dataset.

Type	MCC	Accuracy	F1	Precision	Recall
Original	0.94	0.97	0.97	0.96	0.98
5%	0.0	0.5	0.0	0.0	0.0
10%	0.0	0.5	0.0	0.0	0.0
15%	0.0	0.5	0.0	0.0	0.0
20%	0.0	0.5	0.0	0.0	0.0
Greedy	0.0	0.5	0.0	0.0	0.0

Table 3: Results for `ArguGPT` on the *CHEAT* dataset.

Type	MCC	Accuracy	F1	Precision	Recall
Original	0.93	0.96	0.96	0.94	0.99
5%	0.37	0.62	0.39	0.24	1.0
10%	0.11	0.51	0.05	0.03	1.0
15%	0.04	0.5	0.01	0.0	1.0
20%	0.02	0.5	0.0	0.0	1.0
Greedy	0.13	0.52	0.11	0.06	0.84

Table 4: Results for `Binoculars` on the *CHEAT* dataset.

Type	MCC	Accuracy	F1	Precision	Recall
Original	0.14	0.52	0.08	0.04	0.95
5%	-0.02	0.5	0.0	0.0	0.0
10%	0.03	0.51	0.13	0.08	0.55
15%	0.13	0.56	0.59	0.62	0.56
20%	0.06	0.52	0.64	0.86	0.51
Greedy	0.0	0.5	0.67	1.0	0.5

Table 5: Results for `DetectGPT` on the *CHEAT* dataset.

Type	MCC	Accuracy	F1	Precision	Recall
Original	0.9	0.95	0.95	0.94	0.95
5%	0.23	0.55	0.19	0.1	0.99
10%	0.04	0.5	0.01	0.0	1.0
15%	0.02	0.5	0.0	0.0	1.0
20%	0.0	0.5	0.0	0.0	0.0
Greedy	-0.01	0.5	0.13	0.07	0.48

Table 6: Results for `Fast-DetectGPT` on the *CHEAT* dataset.

Type	MCC	Accuracy	F1	Precision	Recall
Original	0.64	0.8	0.83	0.99	0.71
5%	0.41	0.69	0.63	0.53	0.79
10%	0.32	0.61	0.71	0.97	0.57
15%	0.12	0.52	0.67	1.0	0.51
20%	0.06	0.5	0.67	1.0	0.5
Greedy	0.02	0.5	0.67	1.0	0.5

Table 7: Results for `Ghostbuster` on the *CHEAT* dataset.

Type	MCC	Accuracy	F1	Precision	Recall
Original	0.47	0.7	0.61	0.46	0.9
5%	0.0	0.5	0.0	0.0	0.0
10%	0.0	0.5	0.0	0.0	0.0
15%	0.0	0.5	0.0	0.0	0.0
20%	-0.02	0.5	0.0	0.0	0.0
Greedy	0.0	0.5	0.0	0.0	0.0

Table 8: Results for `OpenAI` on the *CHEAT* dataset.

Type	MCC	Accuracy	F1	Precision	Recall
Original	0.92	0.96	0.96	0.95	0.96
5%	0.0	0.5	0.0	0.0	0.0
10%	0.0	0.5	0.0	0.0	0.0
15%	0.0	0.5	0.0	0.0	0.0
20%	0.0	0.5	0.0	0.0	0.0
Greedy	0.0	0.5	0.0	0.0	0.0

Table 9: Results for `ArguGPT` on the *essay* dataset.

Type	MCC	Accuracy	F1	Precision	Recall
Original	0.91	0.95	0.95	0.9	1.0
5%	0.22	0.55	0.17	0.1	1.0
10%	0.05	0.5	0.01	0.01	1.0
15%	0.0	0.5	0.0	0.0	0.0
20%	0.0	0.5	0.0	0.0	0.0
Greedy	0.05	0.5	0.02	0.01	0.82

Table 10: Results for `Binoculars` on the *essay* dataset.

Type	MCC	Accuracy	F1	Precision	Recall
Original	0.24	0.55	0.2	0.11	0.99
5%	-0.01	0.5	0.0	0.0	0.33
10%	0.11	0.53	0.16	0.09	0.72
15%	0.21	0.59	0.67	0.85	0.56
20%	0.08	0.51	0.67	0.99	0.51
Greedy	0.0	0.5	0.67	1.0	0.5

Table 11: Results for `DetectGPT` on the *essay* dataset.

Type	MCC	Accuracy	F1	Precision	Recall
Original	0.88	0.94	0.94	0.89	0.99
5%	0.22	0.55	0.2	0.12	0.93
10%	0.04	0.5	0.01	0.0	1.0
15%	0.0	0.5	0.0	0.0	0.0
20%	0.0	0.5	0.0	0.0	0.0
Greedy	-0.08	0.48	0.08	0.04	0.35

Table 12: Results for `Fast-DetectGPT` on the *essay* dataset.

Type	MCC	Accuracy	F1	Precision	Recall
Original	0.92	0.96	0.96	0.95	0.96
5%	0.73	0.86	0.84	0.76	0.94
10%	0.51	0.71	0.77	0.99	0.64
15%	0.13	0.52	0.67	1.0	0.51
20%	0.0	0.5	0.67	1.0	0.5
Greedy	0.0	0.5	0.67	1.0	0.5

Table 13: Results for `Ghostbuster` on the *essay* dataset.

Type	MCC	Accuracy	F1	Precision	Recall
Original	-0.21	0.43	0.09	0.06	0.22
5%	0.0	0.5	0.0	0.0	0.0
10%	0.0	0.5	0.0	0.0	0.0
15%	0.0	0.5	0.0	0.0	0.0
20%	0.0	0.5	0.0	0.0	0.5
Greedy	0.03	0.5	0.0	0.0	1.0

Table 14: Results for `OpenAI` on the *essay* dataset.

Type	MCC	Accuracy	F1	Precision	Recall
Original	0.92	0.96	0.96	0.95	0.97
5%	0.0	0.5	0.0	0.0	0.0
10%	0.0	0.5	0.0	0.0	0.0
15%	0.0	0.5	0.0	0.0	0.0
20%	0.0	0.5	0.0	0.0	0.0
Greedy	0.0	0.5	0.0	0.0	0.0

Table 15: Results for `ArguGPT` on the *reuter* dataset.

Type	MCC	Accuracy	F1	Precision	Recall
Original	0.8	0.89	0.88	0.78	1.0
5%	0.22	0.55	0.17	0.09	1.0
10%	0.07	0.51	0.02	0.01	1.0
15%	0.03	0.5	0.0	0.0	1.0
20%	0.02	0.5	0.0	0.0	1.0
Greedy	0.08	0.51	0.03	0.02	0.94

Table 16: Results for `Binoculars` on the *reuter* dataset.

Type	MCC	Accuracy	F1	Precision	Recall
Original	0.23	0.56	0.22	0.12	0.93
5%	0.0	0.5	0.0	0.0	0.0
10%	0.03	0.5	0.01	0.0	0.8
15%	0.34	0.67	0.63	0.57	0.7
20%	0.14	0.54	0.67	0.94	0.52
Greedy	0.0	0.5	0.67	1.0	0.5

Table 17: Results for `DetectGPT` on the *reuter* dataset.

Type	MCC	Accuracy	F1	Precision	Recall
Original	0.92	0.96	0.96	0.92	1.0
5%	0.28	0.57	0.25	0.14	1.0
10%	0.1	0.51	0.04	0.02	1.0
15%	0.02	0.5	0.0	0.0	1.0
20%	0.0	0.5	0.0	0.0	0.0
Greedy	0.04	0.51	0.11	0.06	0.58

Table 18: Results for `Fast-DetectGPT` on the *reuter* dataset.

Type	MCC	Accuracy	F1	Precision	Recall
Original	0.93	0.96	0.96	0.94	0.99
5%	0.61	0.79	0.75	0.63	0.93
10%	0.51	0.72	0.78	0.98	0.64
15%	0.16	0.53	0.68	1.0	0.51
20%	0.04	0.5	0.67	1.0	0.5
Greedy	0.0	0.5	0.67	1.0	0.5

Table 19: Results for `Ghostbuster` on the *reuter* dataset.

Type	MCC	Accuracy	F1	Precision	Recall
Original	0.27	0.57	0.25	0.14	0.98
5%	0.0	0.5	0.0	0.0	0.0
10%	-0.04	0.5	0.0	0.0	0.0
15%	-0.09	0.49	0.0	0.0	0.0
20%	-0.11	0.49	0.0	0.0	0.06
Greedy	-0.06	0.5	0.0	0.0	0.0

Table 20: Results for `OpenAI` on the *reuter* dataset.

Type	MCC	Accuracy	F1	Precision	Recall
Original	0.39	0.63	0.42	0.26	1.0
5%	0.0	0.5	0.0	0.0	0.0
10%	0.0	0.5	0.0	0.0	0.0
15%	0.0	0.5	0.0	0.0	0.0
20%	0.0	0.5	0.0	0.0	0.0
Greedy	0.0	0.5	0.0	0.0	0.0

Table 21: Results for `ArguGPT` on the *writing prompts* dataset.

Type	MCC	Accuracy	F1	Precision	Recall
Original	0.85	0.92	0.91	0.84	1.0
5%	0.2	0.54	0.14	0.08	1.0
10%	0.0	0.5	0.0	0.0	0.0
15%	0.0	0.5	0.0	0.0	0.0
20%	0.0	0.5	0.0	0.0	0.0
Greedy	-0.04	0.5	0.01	0.0	0.23

Table 22: Results for `Binoculars` on the *writing prompts* dataset.

Type	MCC	Accuracy	F1	Precision	Recall
Original	0.44	0.68	0.55	0.39	0.93
5%	0.04	0.5	0.01	0.0	1.0
10%	0.01	0.5	0.09	0.05	0.52
15%	0.02	0.51	0.57	0.65	0.51
20%	0.02	0.51	0.66	0.96	0.5
Greedy	0.0	0.5	0.67	1.0	0.5

Table 23: Results for `DetectGPT` on the *writing prompts* dataset.

Type	MCC	Accuracy	F1	Precision	Recall
Original	0.79	0.89	0.88	0.81	0.97
5%	0.3	0.59	0.31	0.19	0.96
10%	0.05	0.5	0.02	0.01	0.83
15%	-0.03	0.5	0.0	0.0	0.0
20%	0.0	0.5	0.0	0.0	0.5
Greedy	-0.33	0.37	0.09	0.07	0.17

Table 24: Results for `Fast-DetectGPT` on the *writing prompts* dataset.

Type	MCC	Accuracy	F1	Precision	Recall
Original	0.88	0.94	0.94	0.9	0.98
5%	0.42	0.66	0.49	0.33	0.96
10%	0.64	0.82	0.83	0.86	0.79
15%	0.33	0.6	0.71	0.99	0.56
20%	0.09	0.51	0.67	1.0	0.5
Greedy	0.0	0.5	0.67	1.0	0.5

Table 25: Results for `Ghostbuster` on the *writing prompts* dataset.

Type	MCC	Accuracy	F1	Precision	Recall
Original	-0.05	0.5	0.0	0.0	0.11
5%	-0.04	0.5	0.0	0.0	0.0
10%	-0.05	0.5	0.0	0.0	0.0
15%	-0.13	0.48	0.0	0.0	0.0
20%	-0.11	0.49	0.01	0.0	0.11
Greedy	0.01	0.5	0.01	0.0	0.57

Table 26: Results for `OpenAI` on the *writing prompts* dataset.

Type	**MCC**	**Accuracy**	**F1**	**Precision**	**Recall**
Original	0.92	0.96	0.96	0.95	0.96
5%	0.18	0.54	0.14	0.08	0.94
10%	-0.01	0.5	0.01	0.0	0.43
15%	0.0	0.5	0.01	0.0	0.5
20%	-0.03	0.5	0.0	0.0	0.29
Greedy	0.0	0.5	0.01	0.01	0.5

Table 27: Results for `Watermark` on the *realnewslike* dataset.

B Confusion matrices

The following figures show the confusion matrices for each detector and dataset. As stated in Section 2.3, the datasets used in the experiments are *CHEAT*, *essay*, *reuter*, *writing prompts*, and *realnewslike* (only used for the watermarking detector). Each dataset contains 1,000 human-written examples and 1,000 AI-written examples.

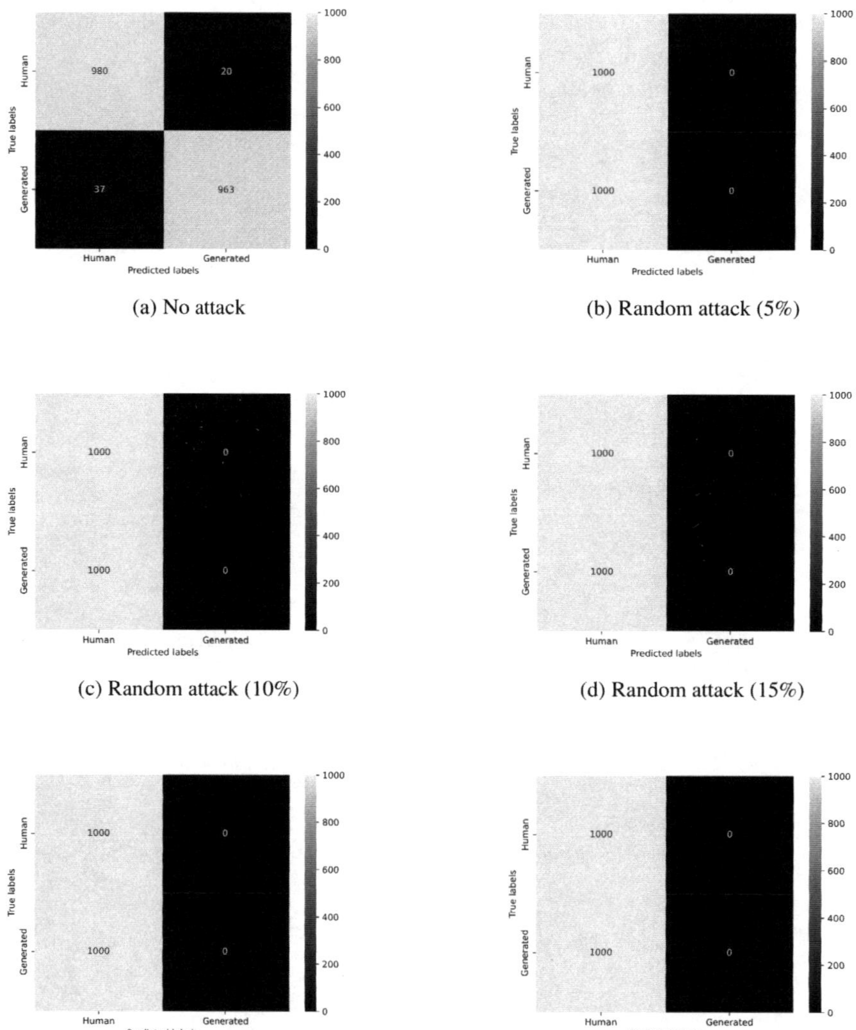

(a) No attack
(b) Random attack (5%)
(c) Random attack (10%)
(d) Random attack (15%)
(e) Random attack (20%)
(f) Greedy attack

Figure 5: Confusion matrices for the `ArguGPT` detector on the *CHEAT* dataset.

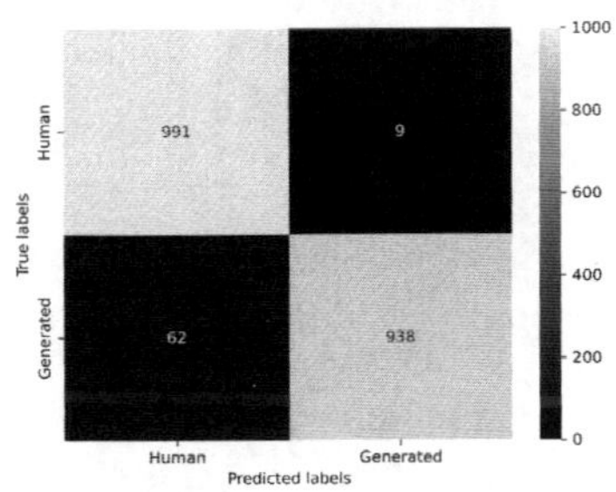

(a) No attack

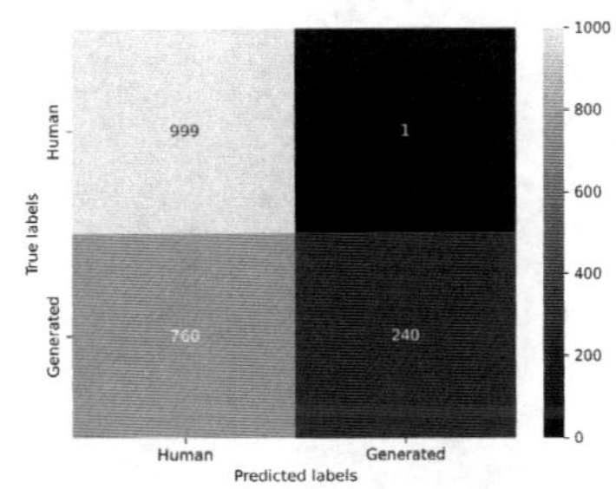

(b) Random attack (5%)

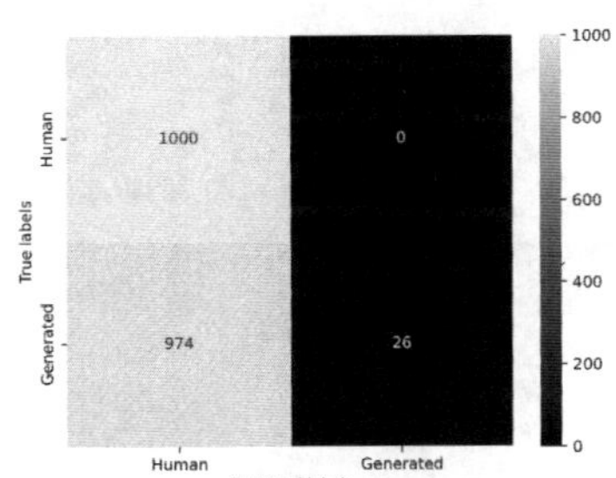

(c) Random attack (10%)

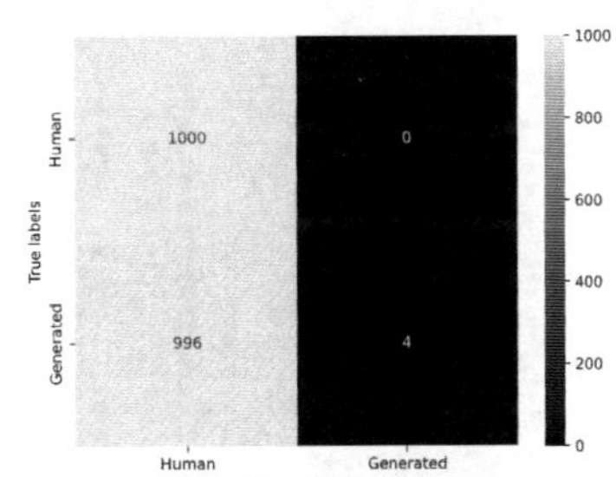

(d) Random attack (15%)

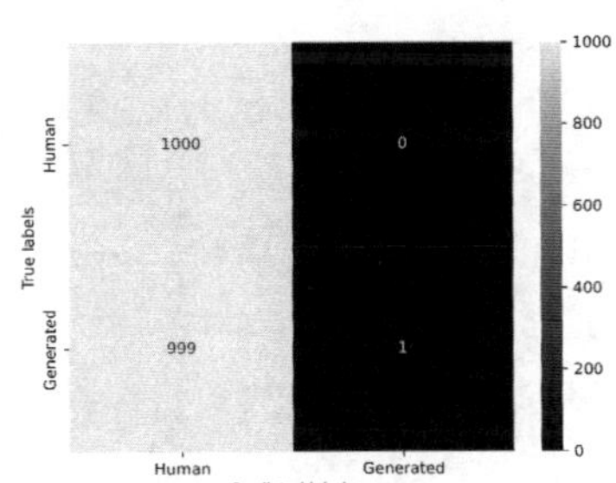

(e) Random attack (20%)

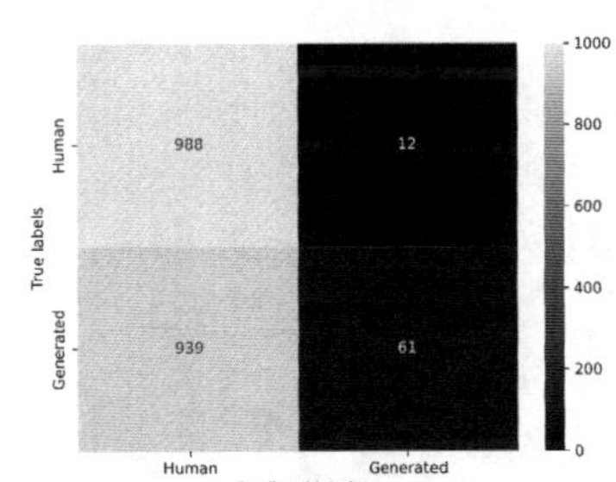

(f) Greedy attack

Figure 6: Confusion matrices for the `Binoculars` detector on the *CHEAT* dataset.

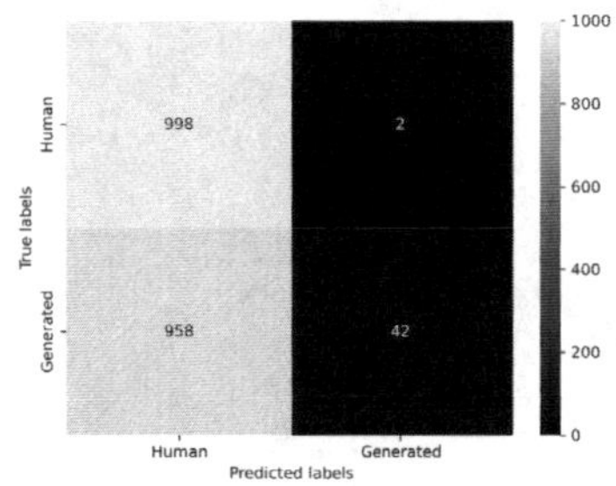

(a) No attack

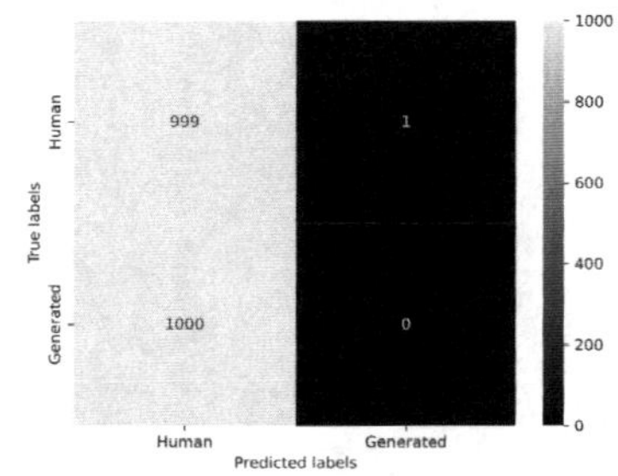

(b) Random attack (5%)

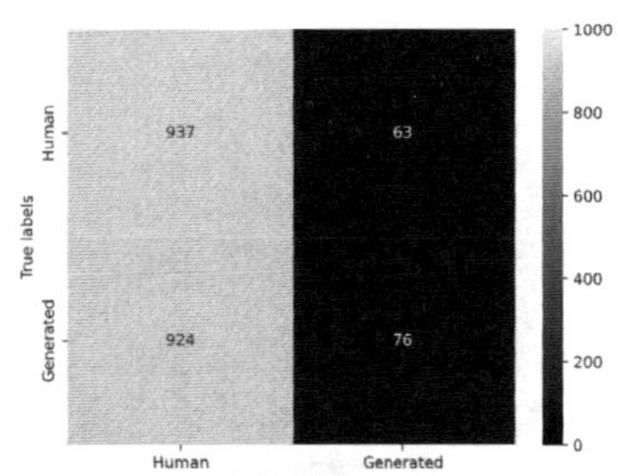

(c) Random attack (10%)

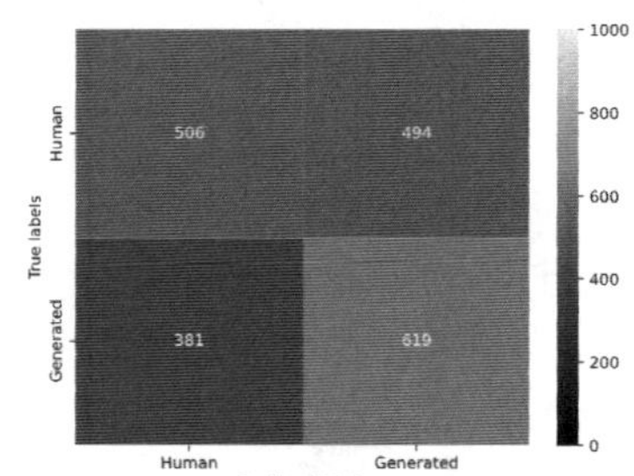

(d) Random attack (15%)

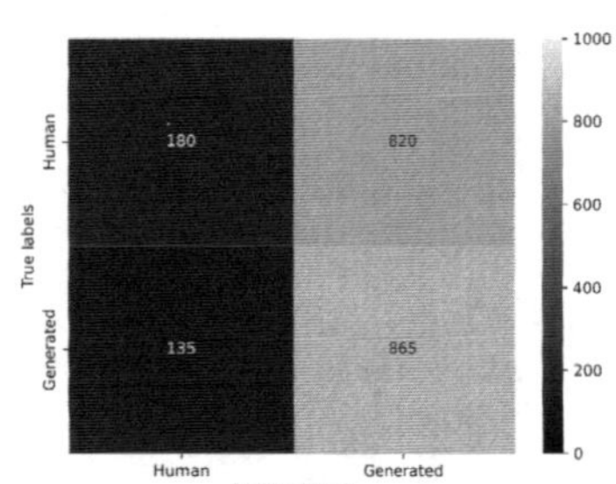

(e) Random attack (20%)

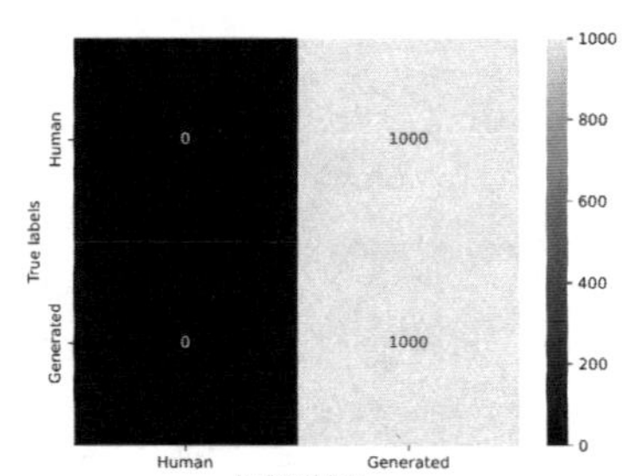

(f) Greedy attack

Figure 7: Confusion matrices for `DetectGPT` on the *CHEAT* dataset.

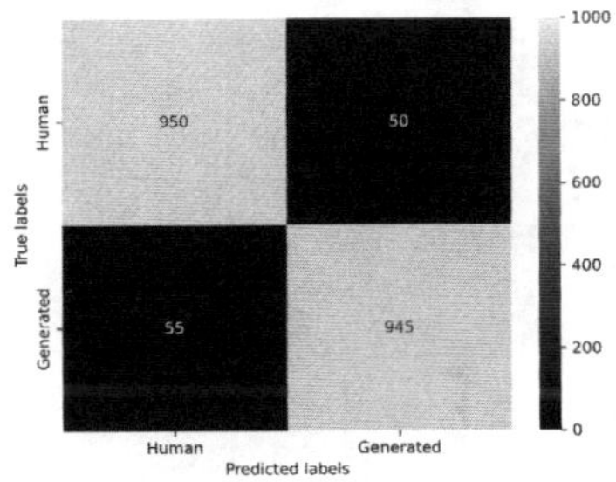

(a) No attack

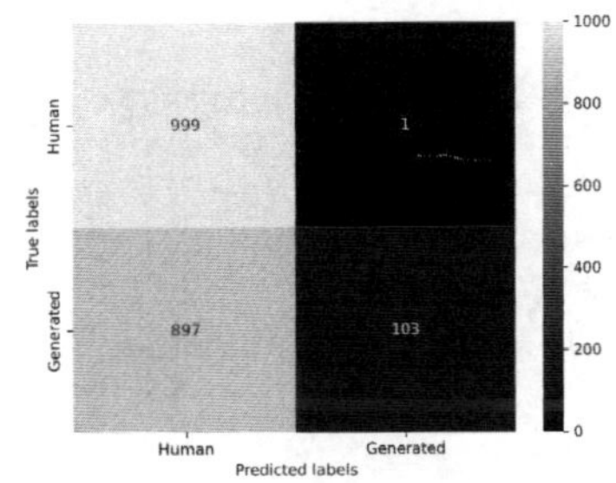

(b) Random attack (5%)

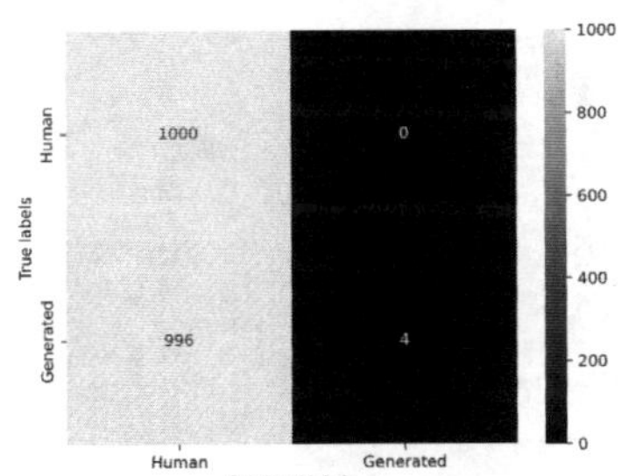

(c) Random attack (10%)

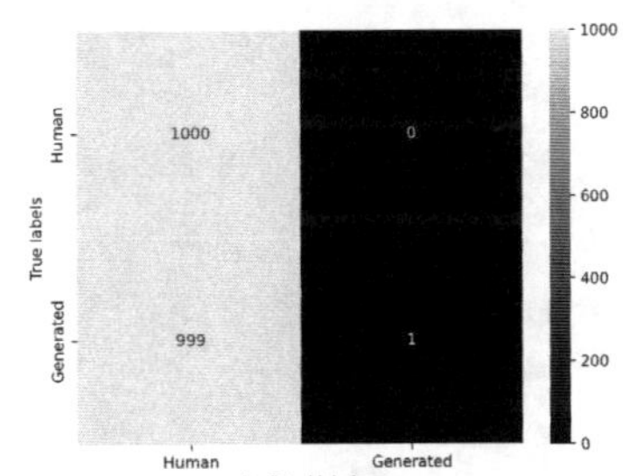

(d) Random attack (15%)

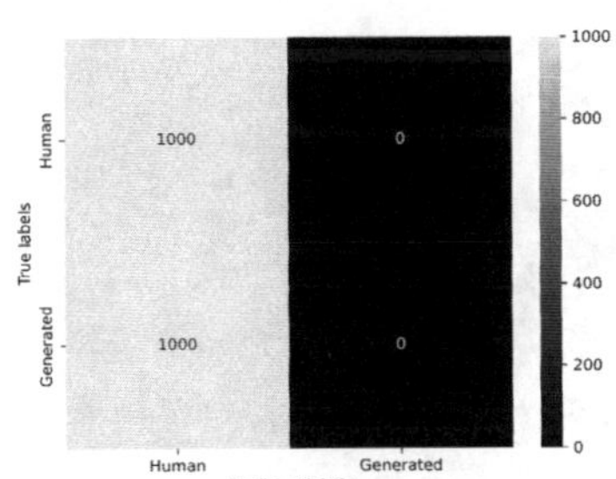

(e) Random attack (20%)

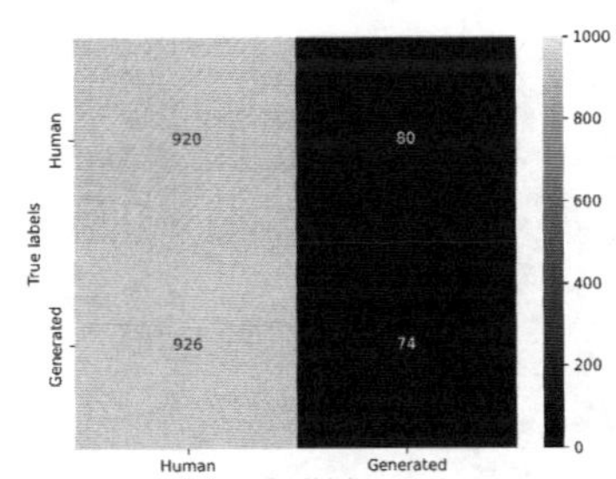

(f) Greedy attack

Figure 8: Confusion matrices for the `Fast-DetectGPT` detector on the *CHEAT* dataset.

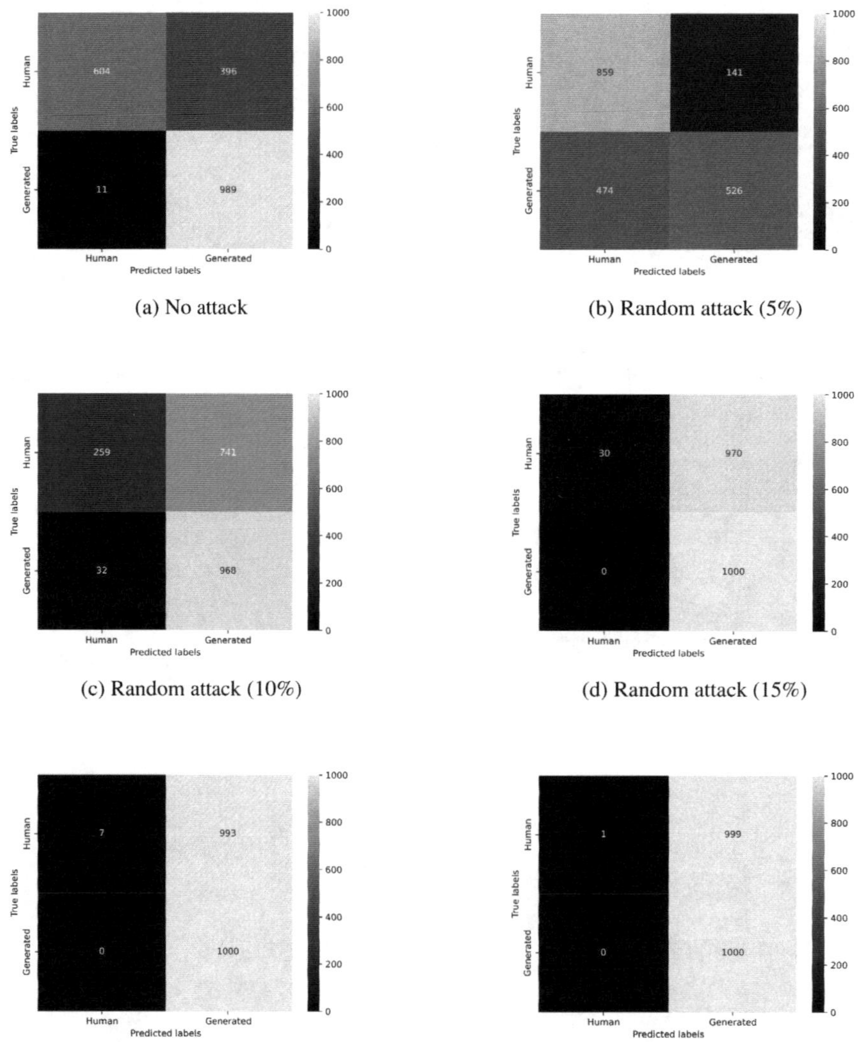

(a) No attack

(b) Random attack (5%)

(c) Random attack (10%)

(d) Random attack (15%)

(e) Random attack (20%)

(f) Greedy attack

Figure 9: Confusion matrices for the `Ghostbuster` detector on the *CHEAT* dataset.

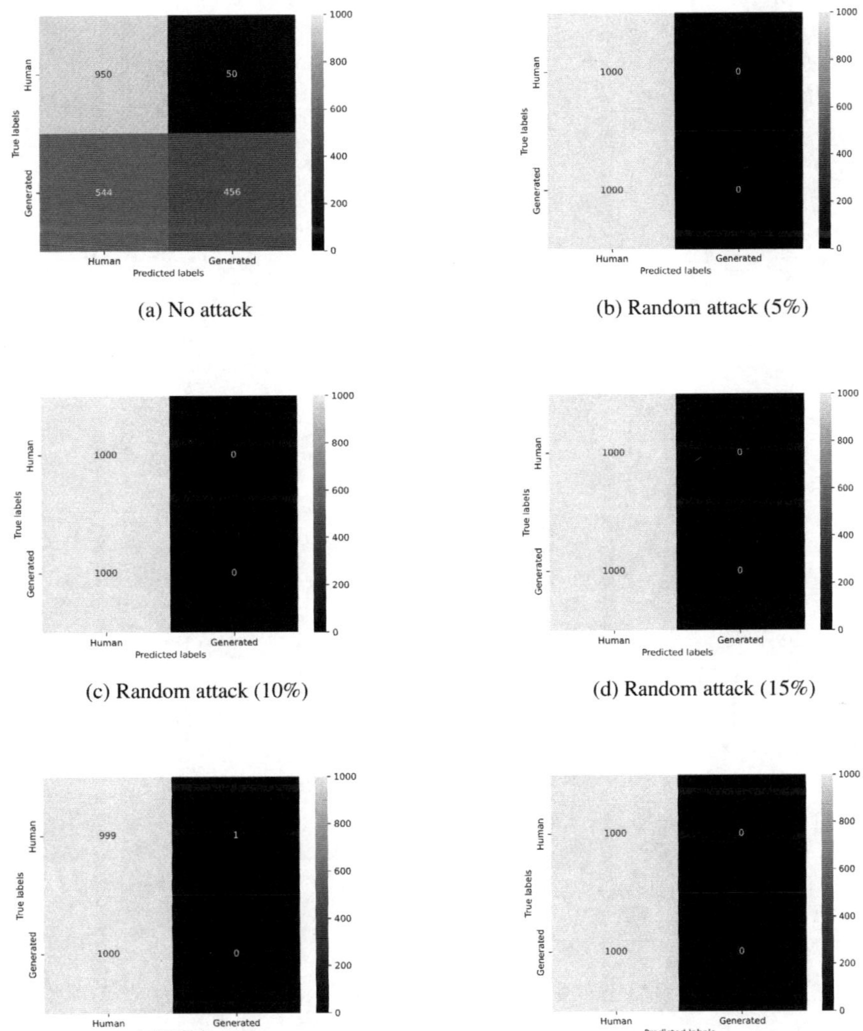

(a) No attack

(b) Random attack (5%)

(c) Random attack (10%)

(d) Random attack (15%)

(e) Random attack (20%)

(f) Greedy attack

Figure 10: Confusion matrices for the `OpenAI` detector on the *CHEAT* dataset.

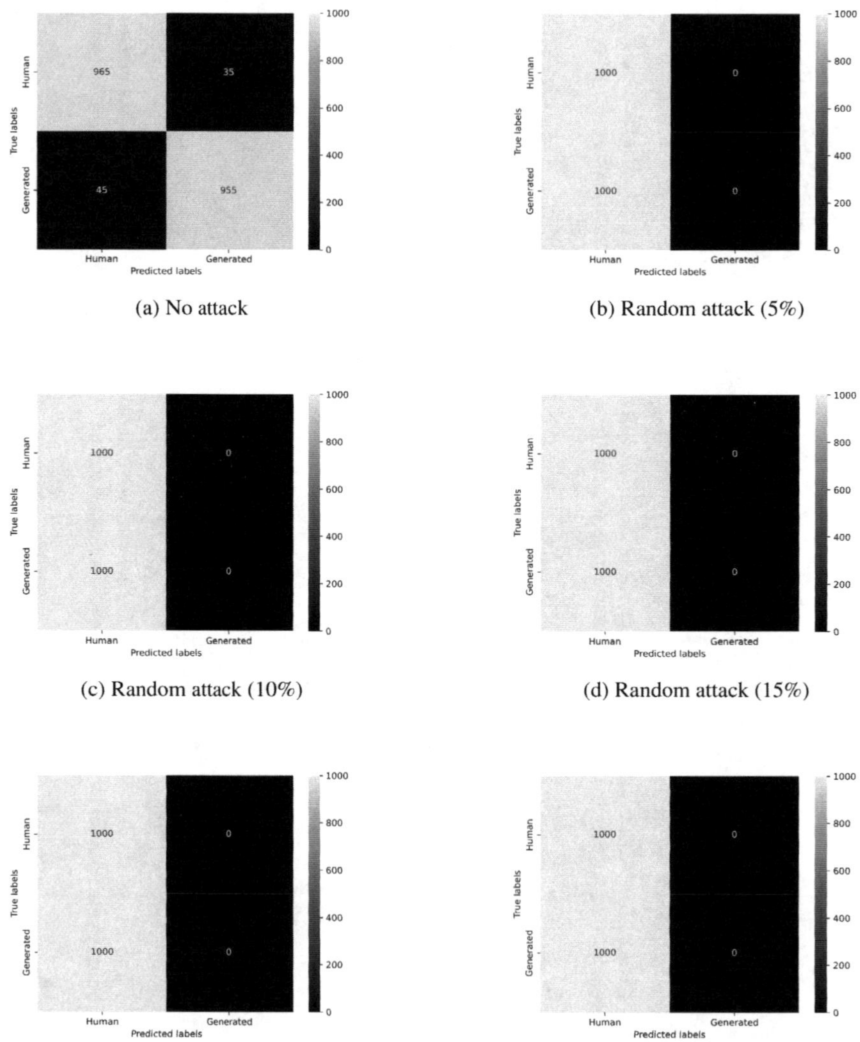

(a) No attack

(b) Random attack (5%)

(c) Random attack (10%)

(d) Random attack (15%)

(e) Random attack (20%)

(f) Greedy attack

Figure 11: Confusion matrices for the `ArguGPT` detector on the *essay* dataset.

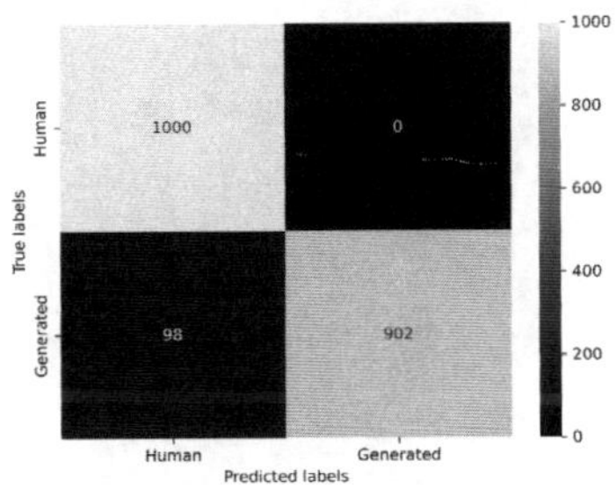

(a) No attack

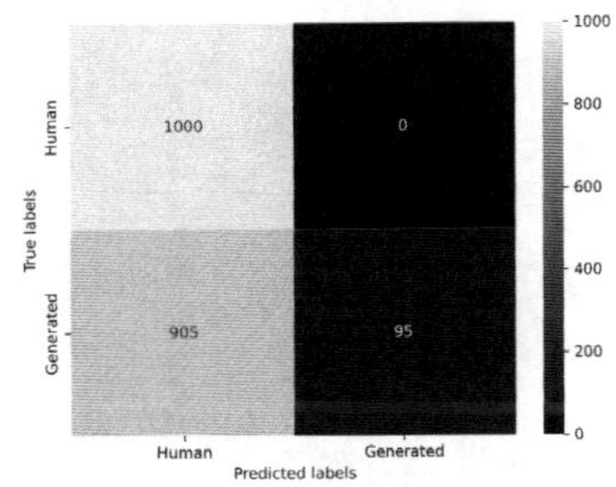

(b) Random attack (5%)

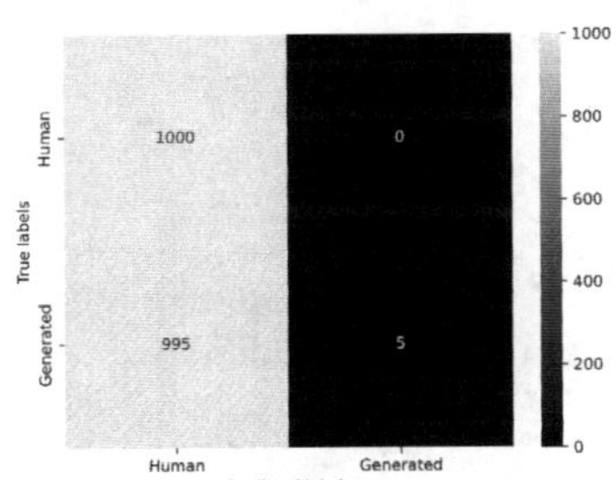

(c) Random attack (10%)

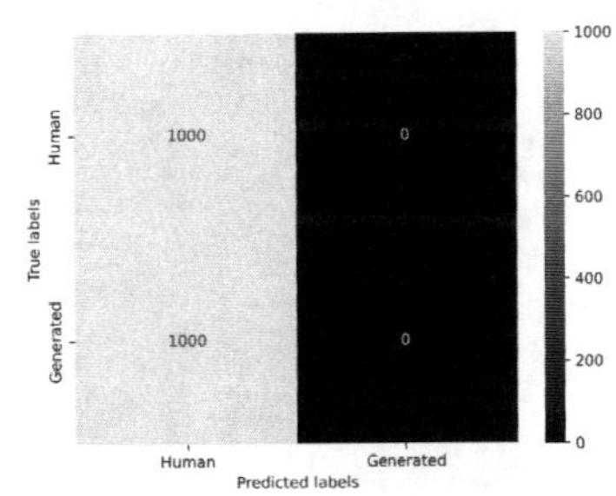

(d) Random attack (15%)

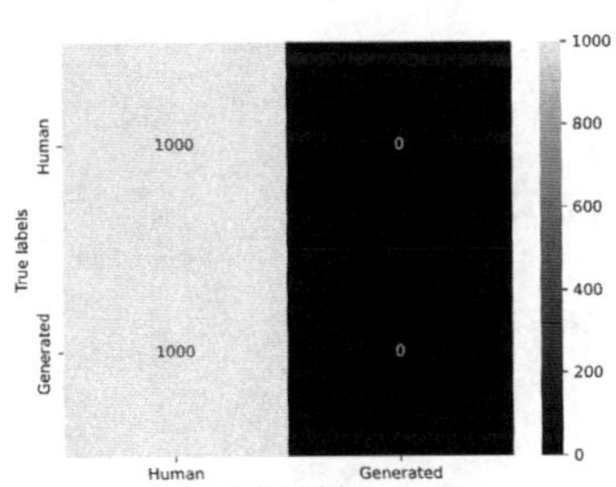

(e) Random attack (20%)

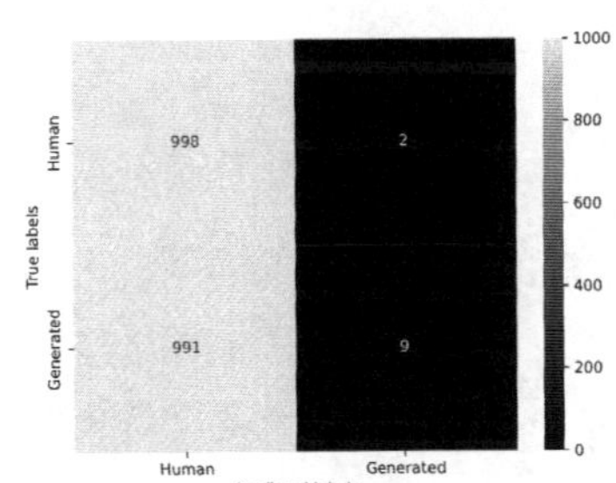

(f) Greedy attack

Figure 12: Confusion matrices for the `Binoculars` detector on the *essay* dataset.

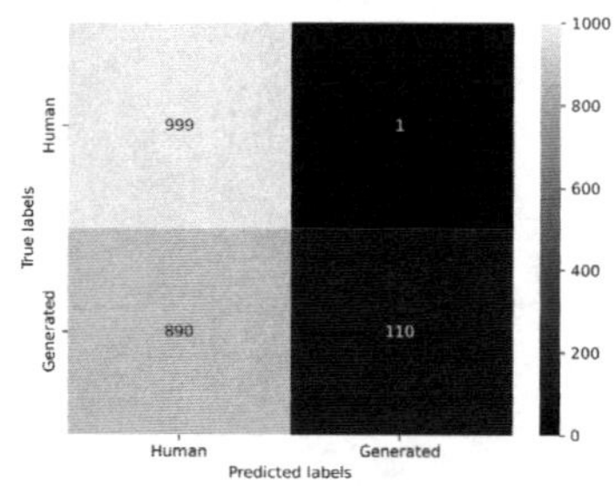

(a) No attack

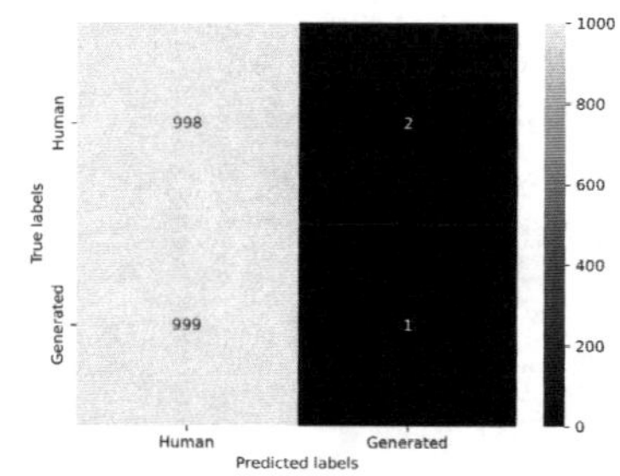

(b) Random attack (5%)

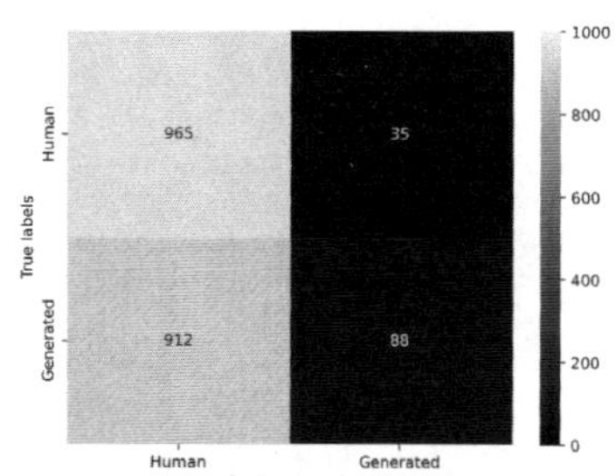

(c) Random attack (10%)

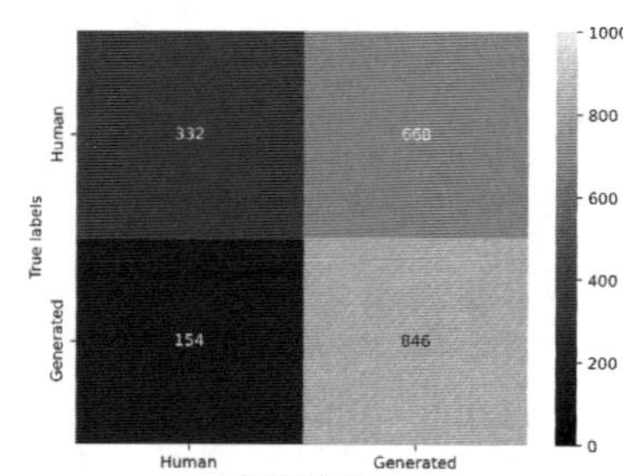

(d) Random attack (15%)

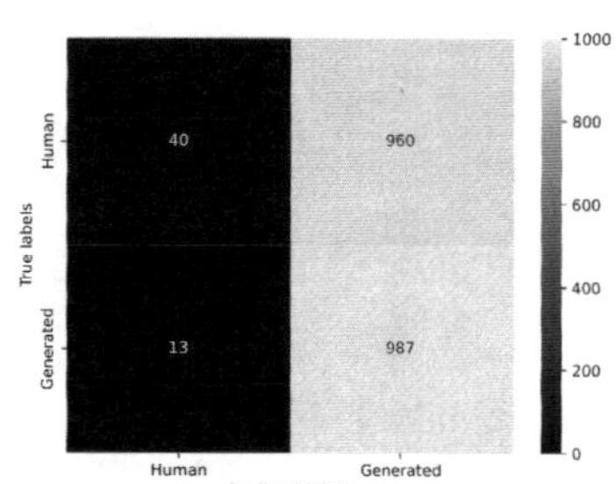

(e) Random attack (20%)

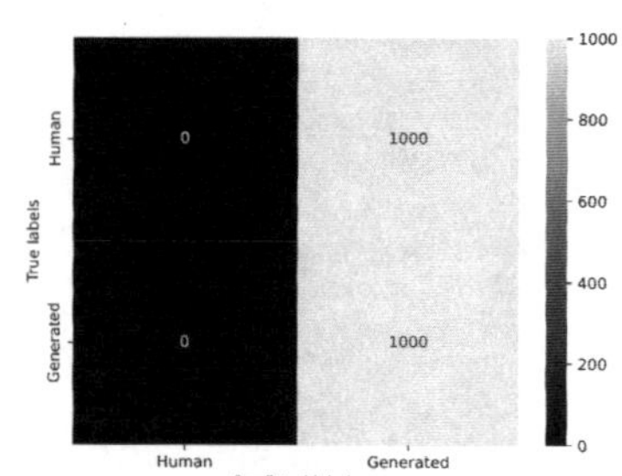

(f) Greedy attack

Figure 13: Confusion matrices for `DetectGPT` on the *essay* dataset.

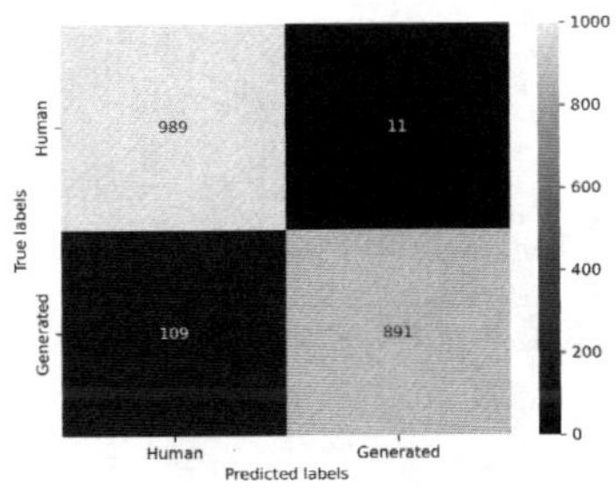

(a) No attack

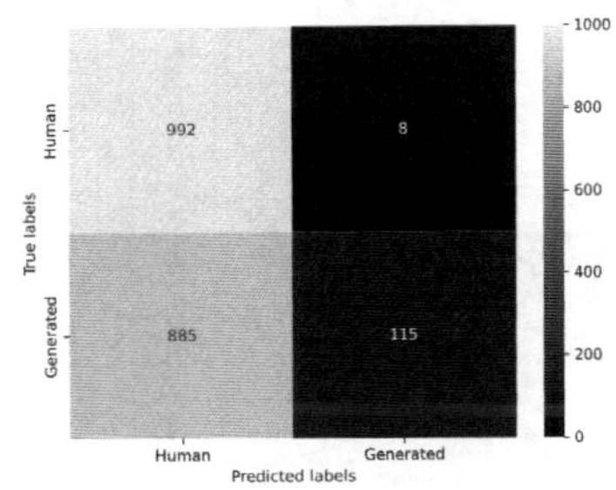

(b) Random attack (5%)

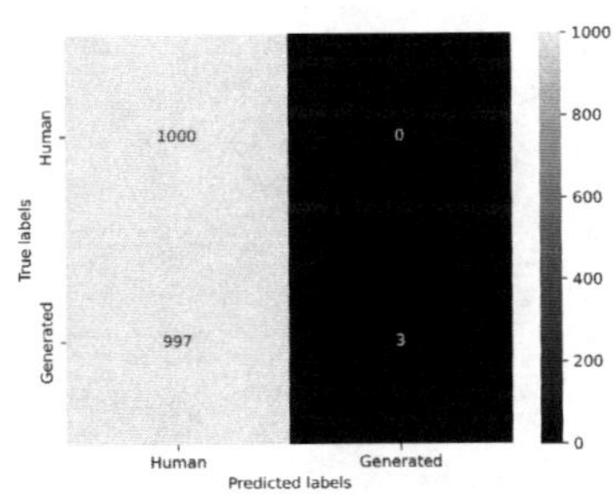

(c) Random attack (10%)

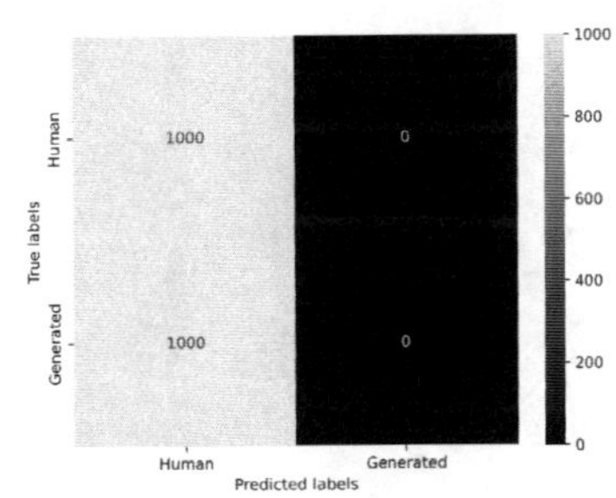

(d) Random attack (15%)

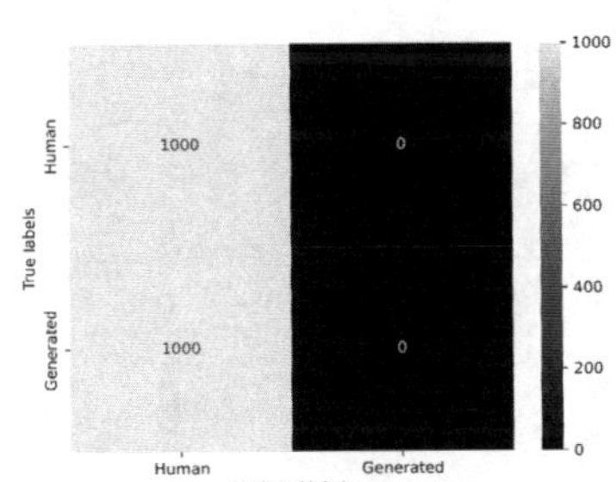

(e) Random attack (20%)

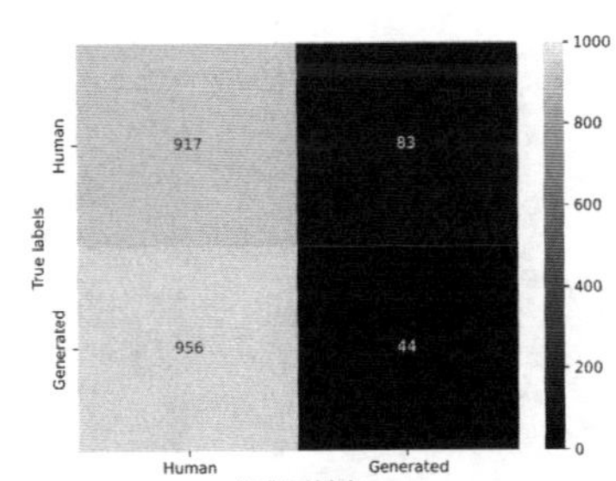

(f) Greedy attack

Figure 14: Confusion matrices for the `Fast-DetectGPT` detector on the *essay* dataset.

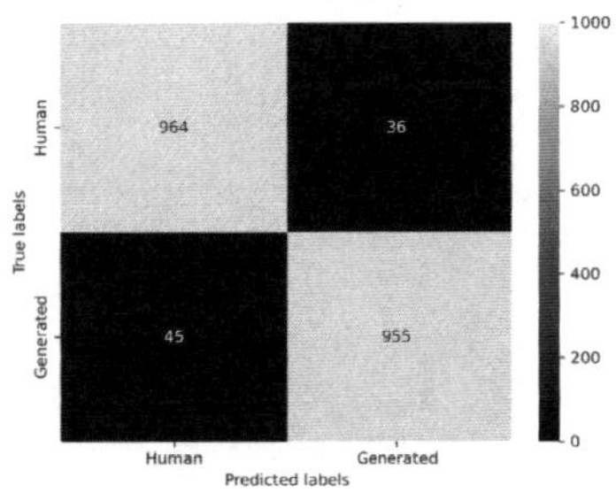

(a) No attack

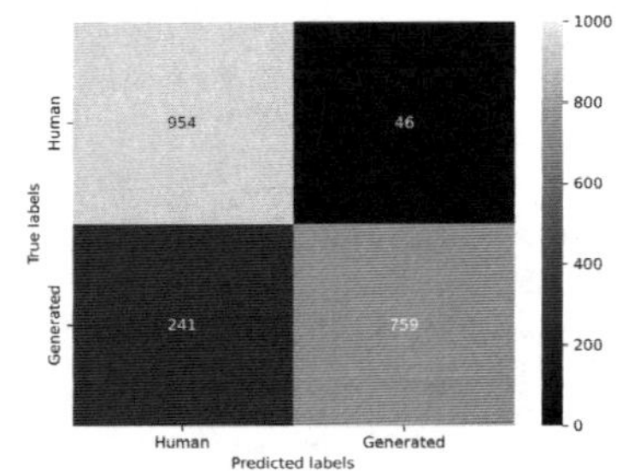

(b) Random attack (5%)

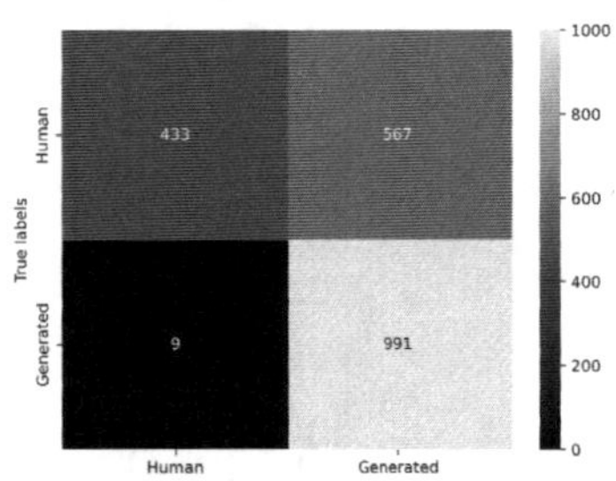

(c) Random attack (10%)

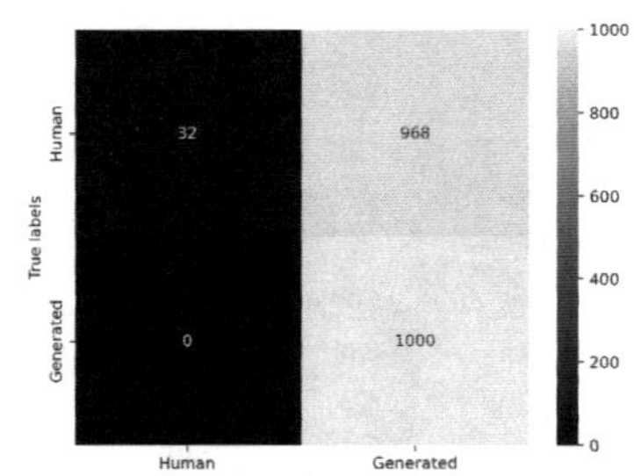

(d) Random attack (15%)

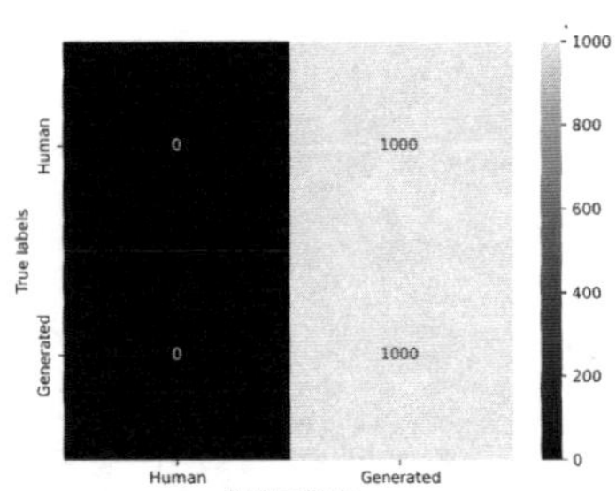

(e) Random attack (20%)

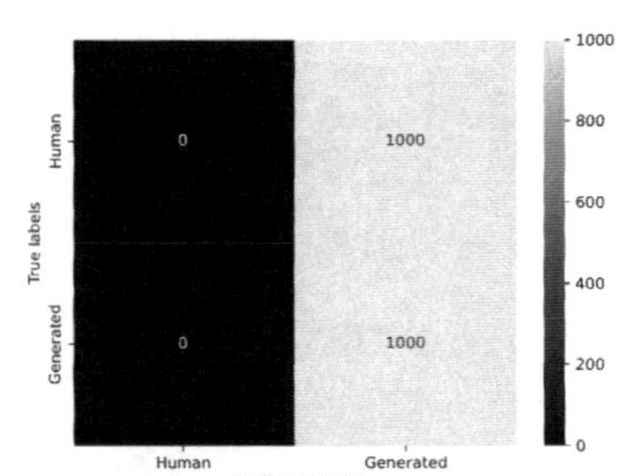

(f) Greedy attack

Figure 15: Confusion matrices for the `Ghostbuster` detector on the *essay* dataset.

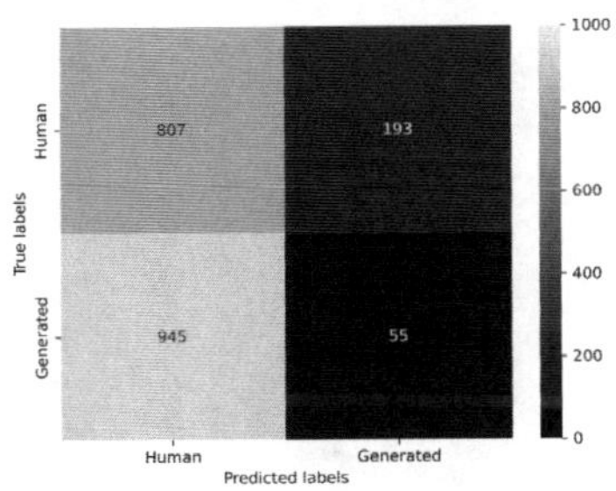

(a) No attack

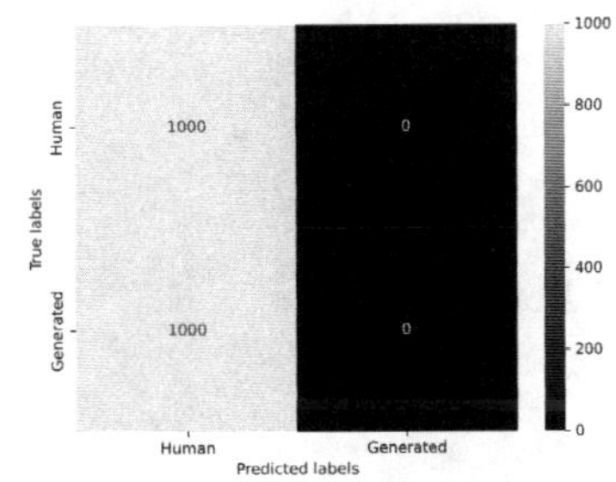

(b) Random attack (5%)

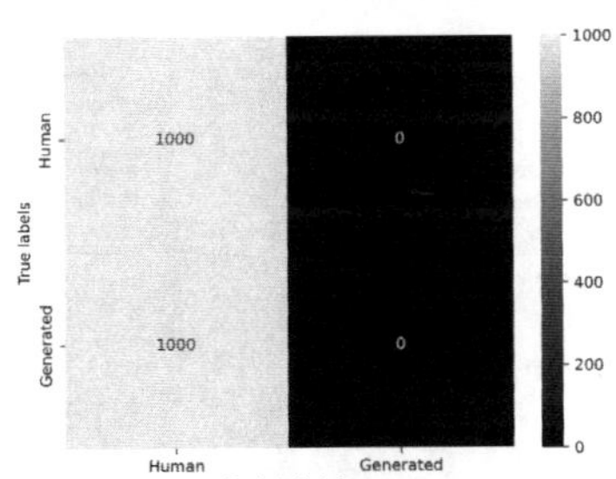

(c) Random attack (10%)

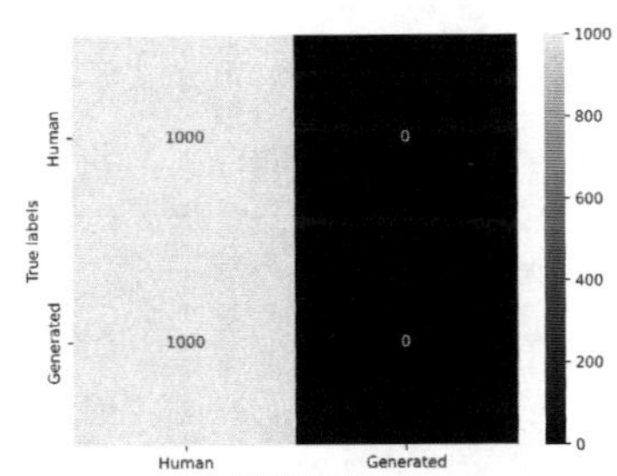

(d) Random attack (15%)

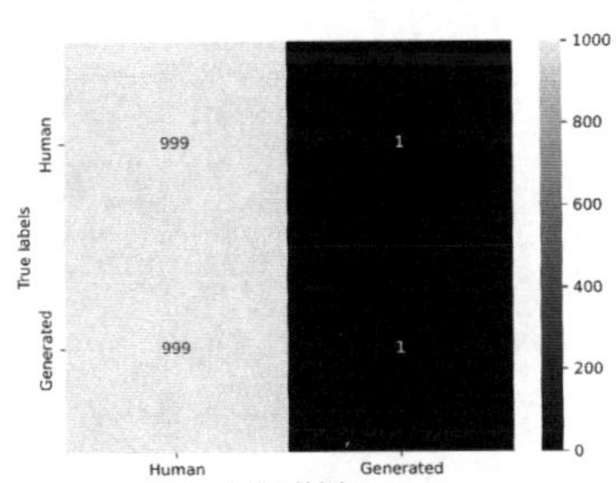

(e) Random attack (20%)

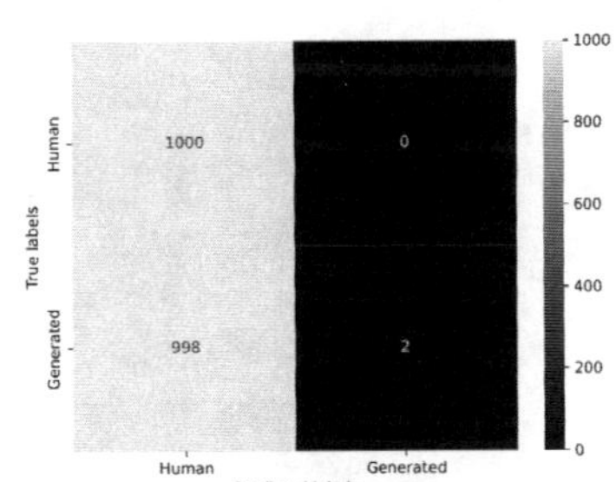

(f) Greedy attack

Figure 16: Confusion matrices for the OpenAI detector on the *essay* dataset.

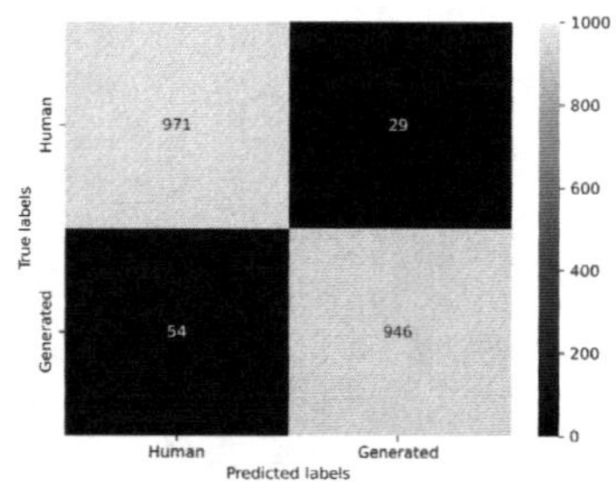

(a) No attack

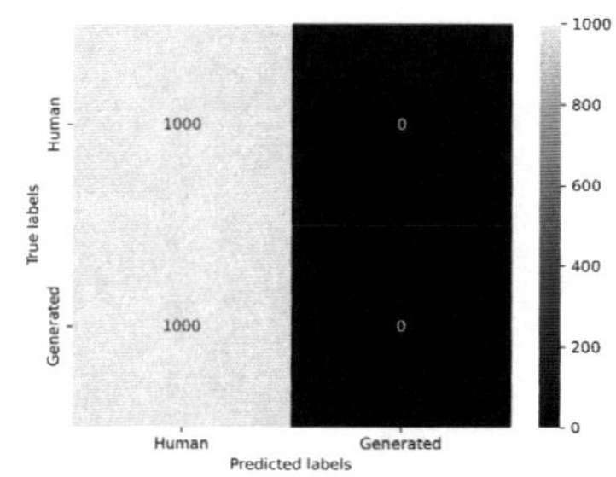

(b) Random attack (5%)

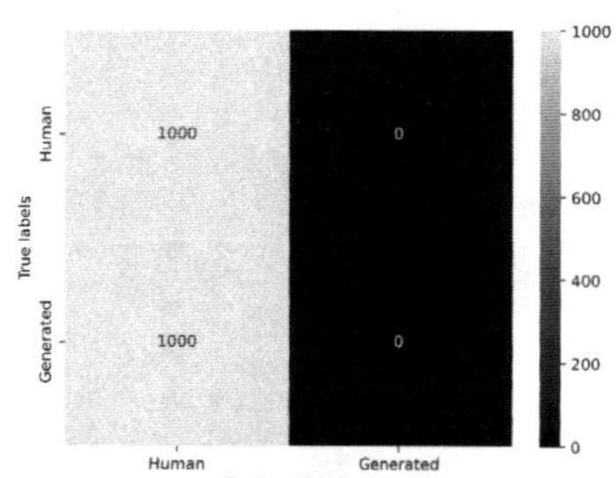

(c) Random attack (10%)

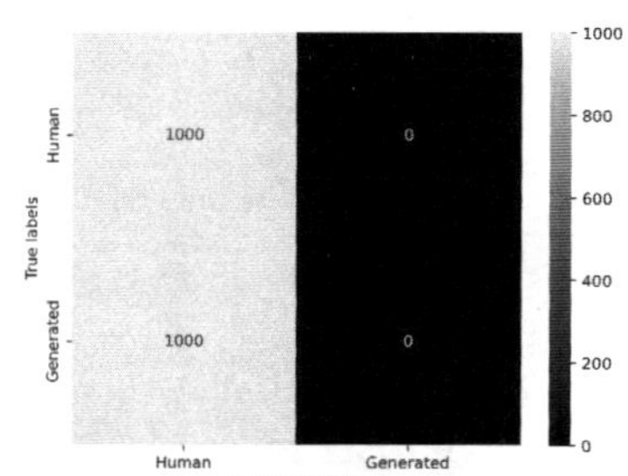

(d) Random attack (15%)

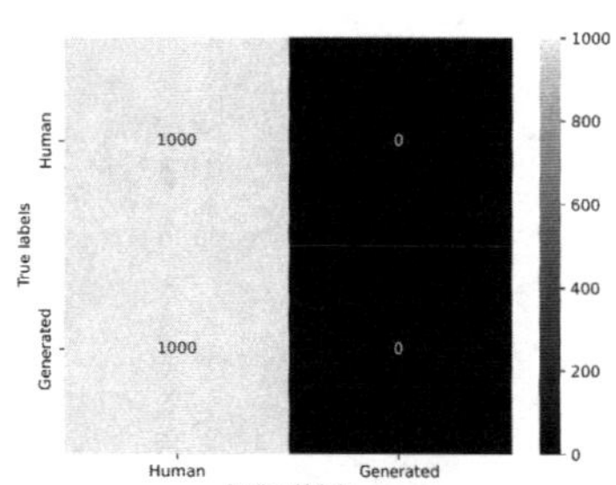

(e) Random attack (20%)

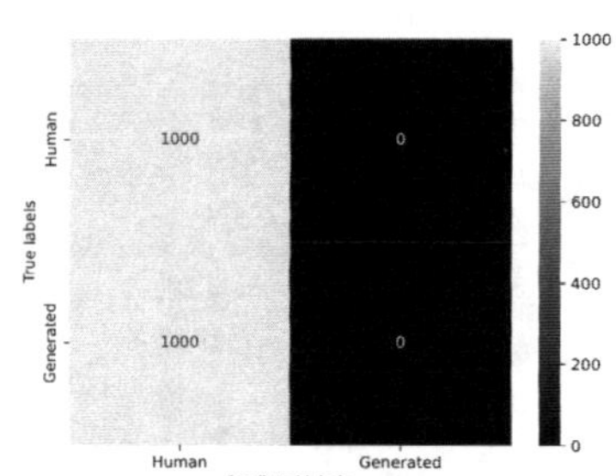

(f) Greedy attack

Figure 17: Confusion matrices for the `ArguGPT` detector on the *reuter* dataset.

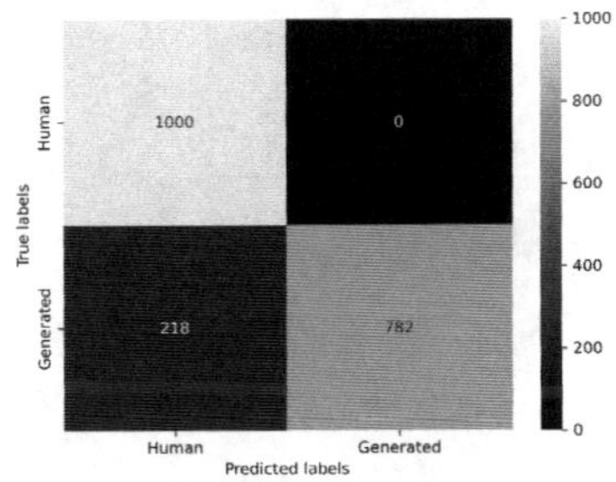

(a) No attack

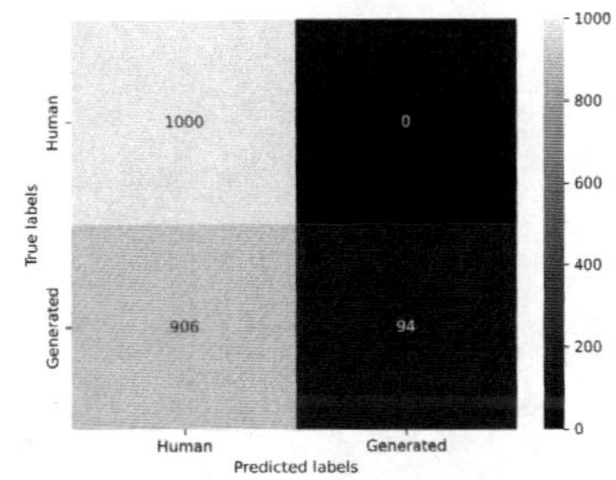

(b) Random attack (5%)

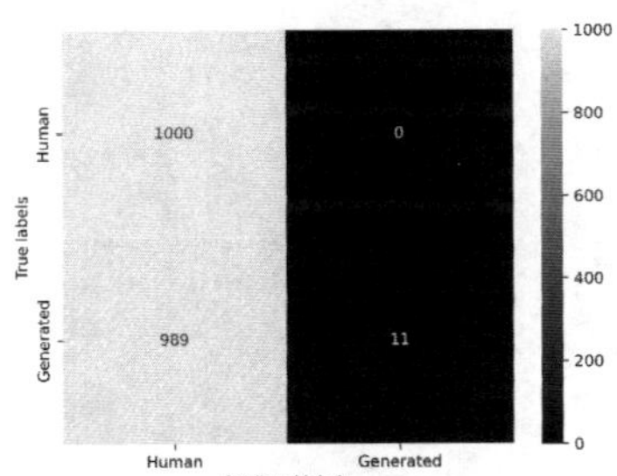

(c) Random attack (10%)

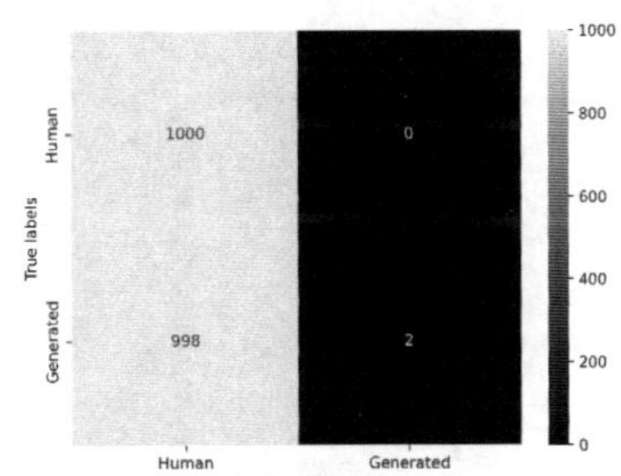

(d) Random attack (15%)

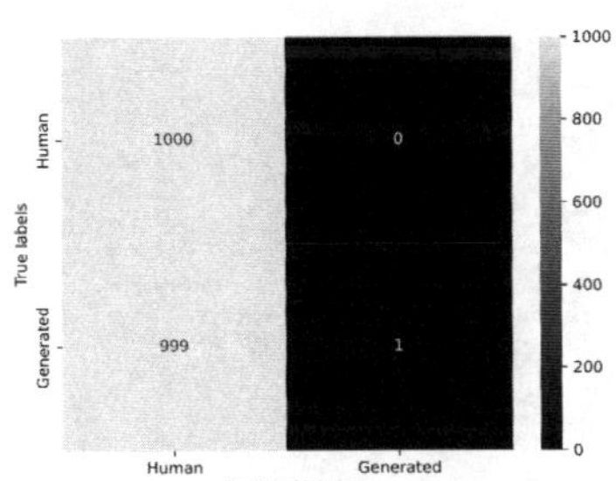

(e) Random attack (20%)

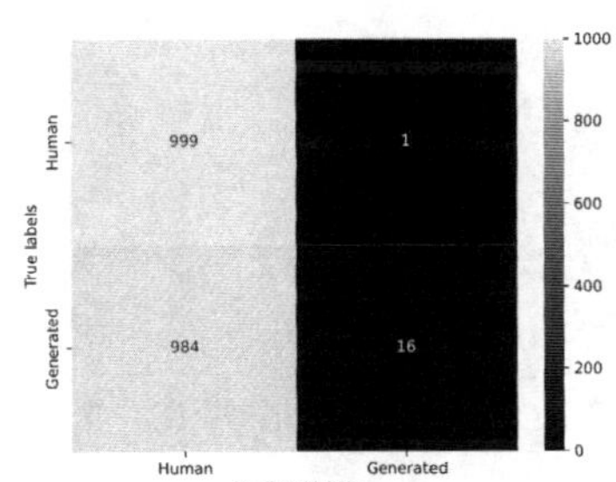

(f) Greedy attack

Figure 18: Confusion matrices for the `Binoculars` detector on the *reuter* dataset.

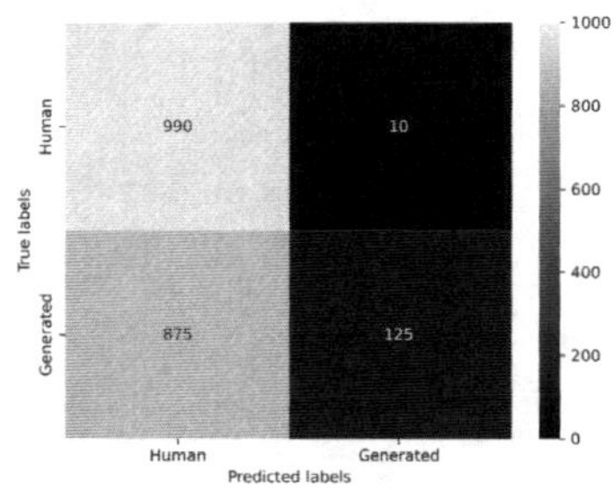

(a) No attack

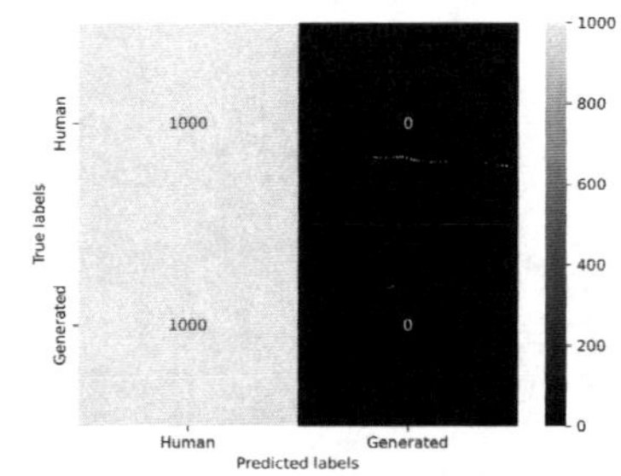

(b) Random attack (5%)

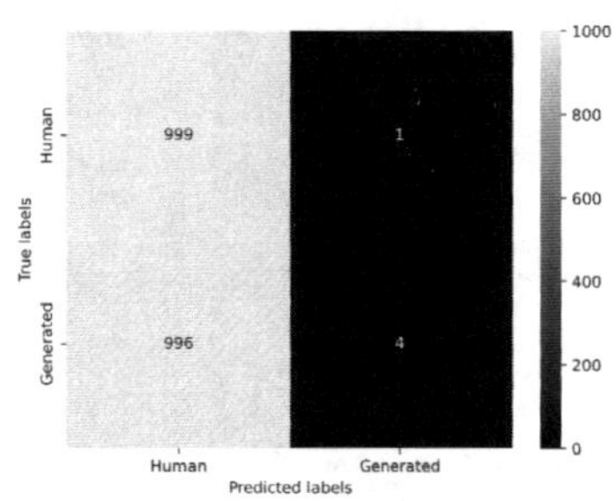

(c) Random attack (10%)

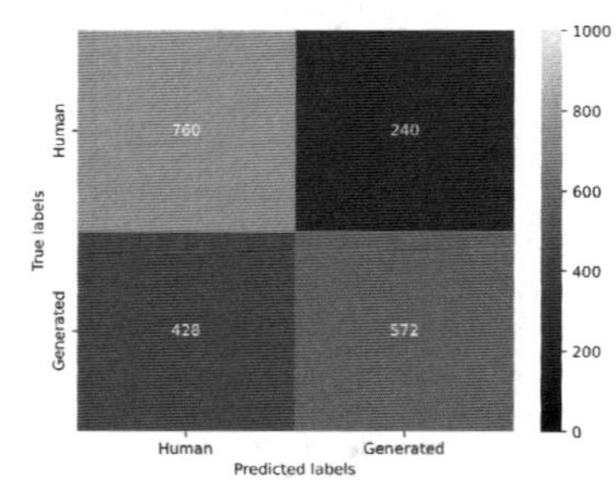

(d) Random attack (15%)

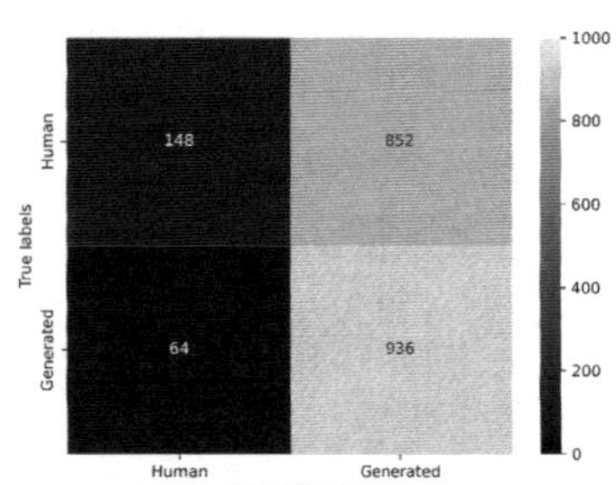

(e) Random attack (20%)

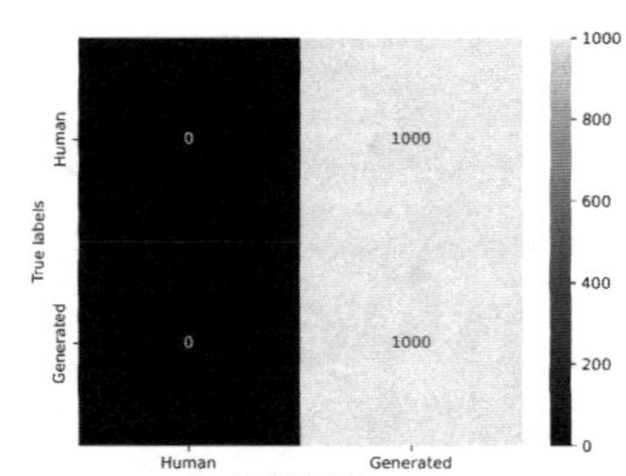

(f) Greedy attack

Figure 19: Confusion matrices for `DetectGPT` on the *reuter* dataset.

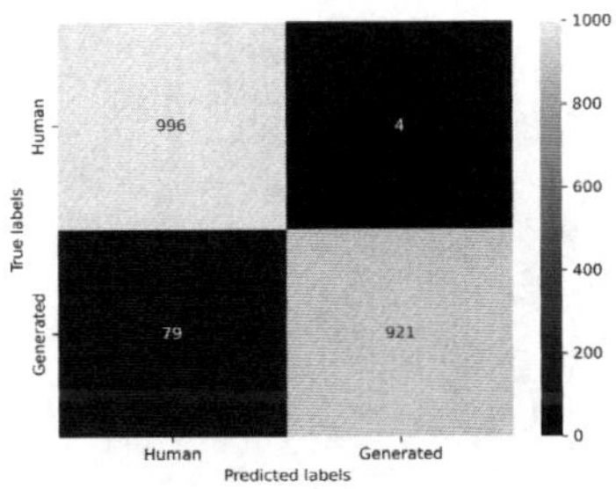

(a) No attack

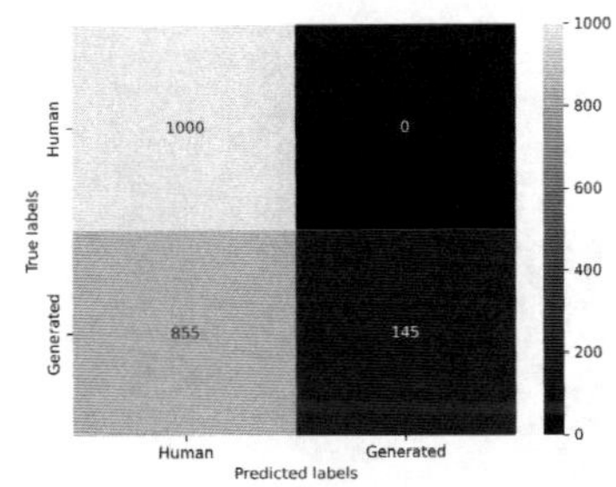

(b) Random attack (5%)

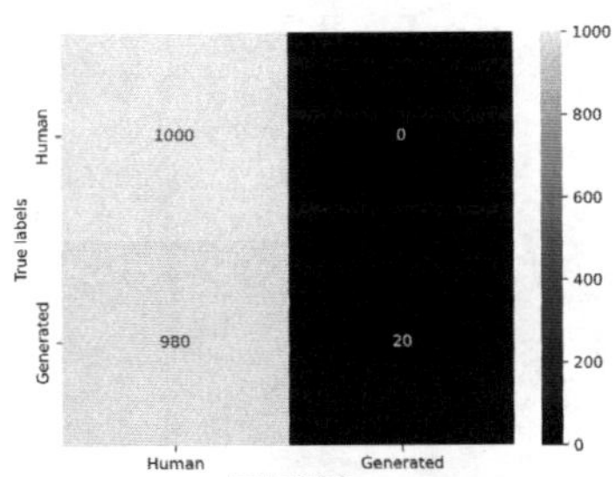

(c) Random attack (10%)

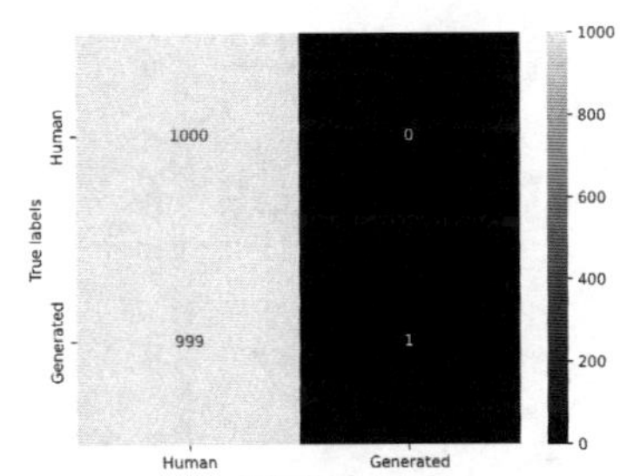

(d) Random attack (15%)

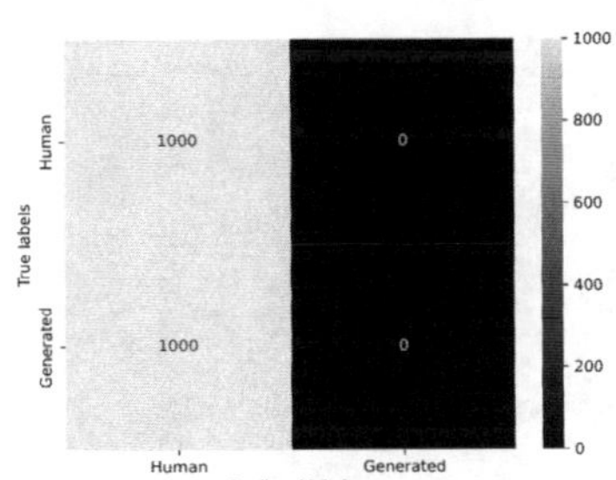

(e) Random attack (20%)

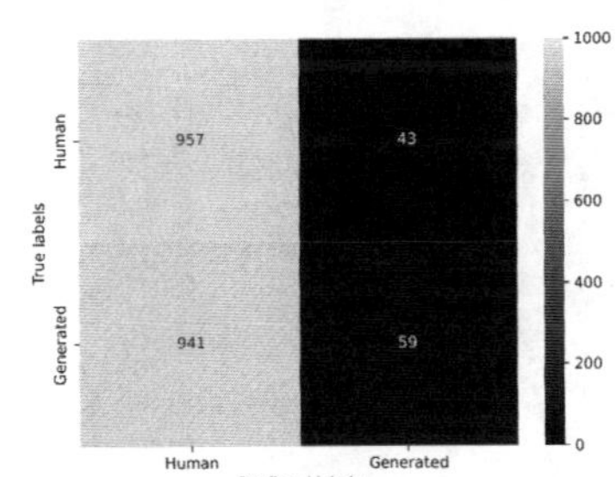

(f) Greedy attack

Figure 20: Confusion matrices for the `Fast-DetectGPT` detector on the *reuter* dataset.

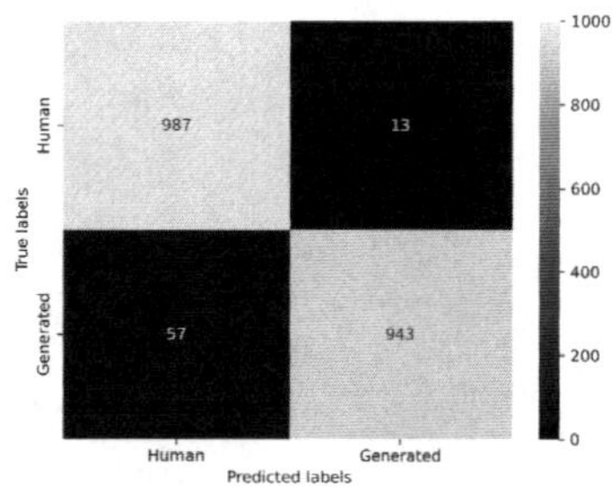

(a) No attack

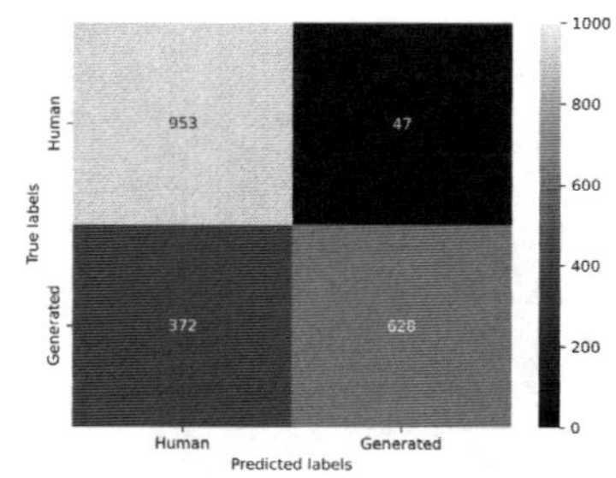

(b) Random attack (5%)

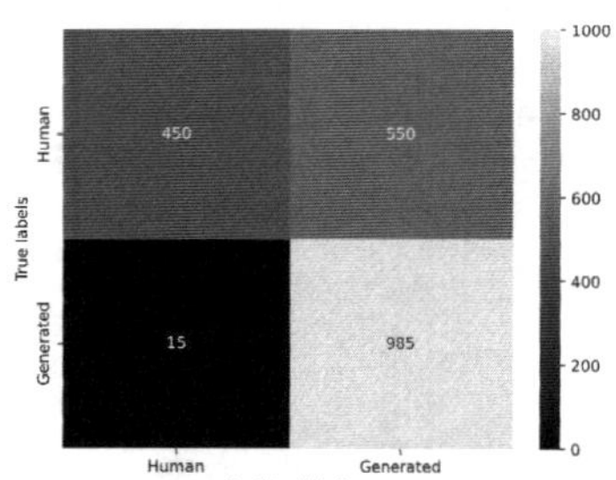

(c) Random attack (10%)

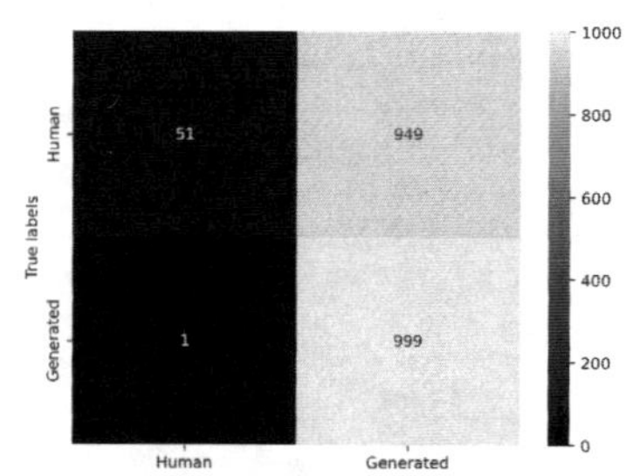

(d) Random attack (15%)

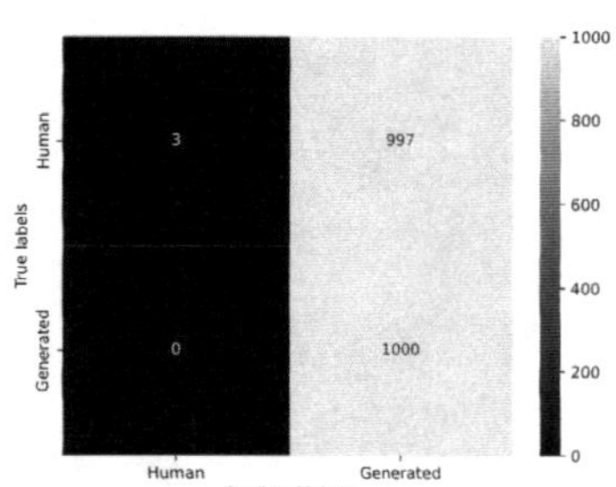

(e) Random attack (20%)

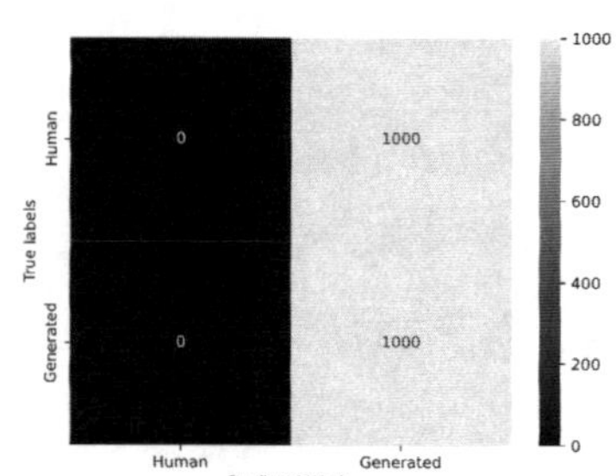

(f) Greedy attack

Figure 21: Confusion matrices for the `Ghostbuster` detector on the *reuter* dataset.

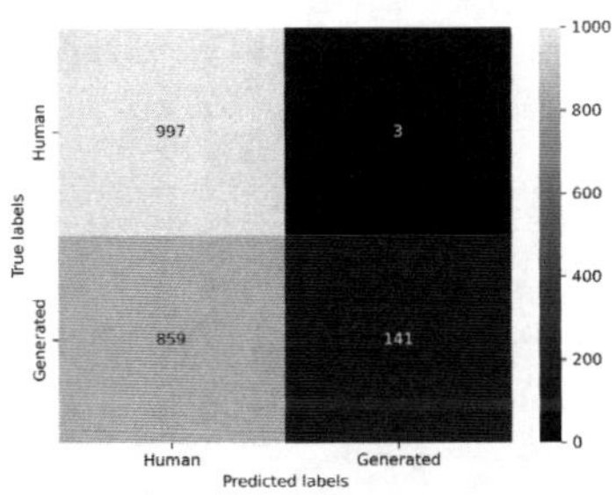

(a) No attack

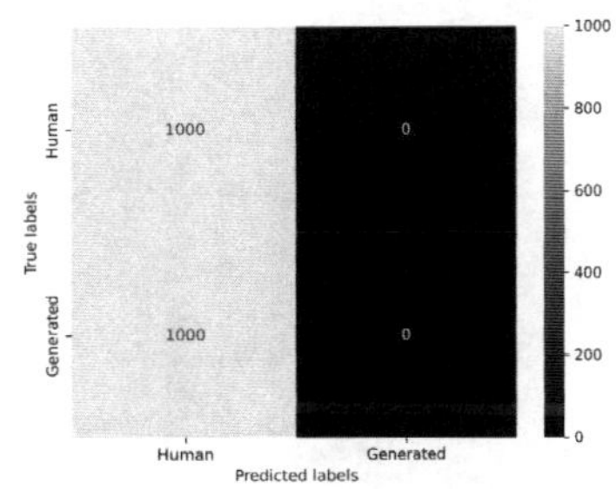

(b) Random attack (5%)

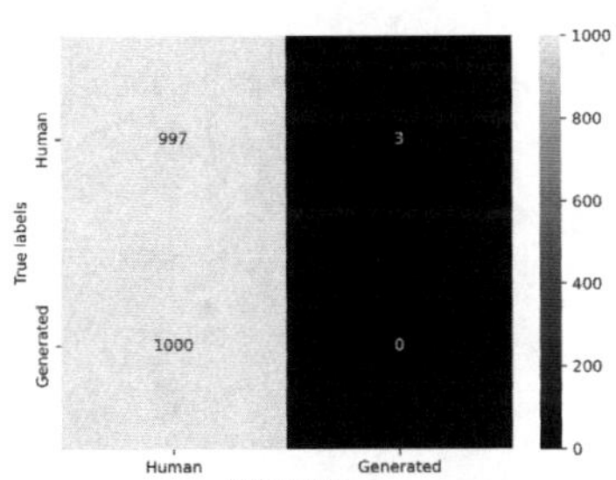

(c) Random attack (10%)

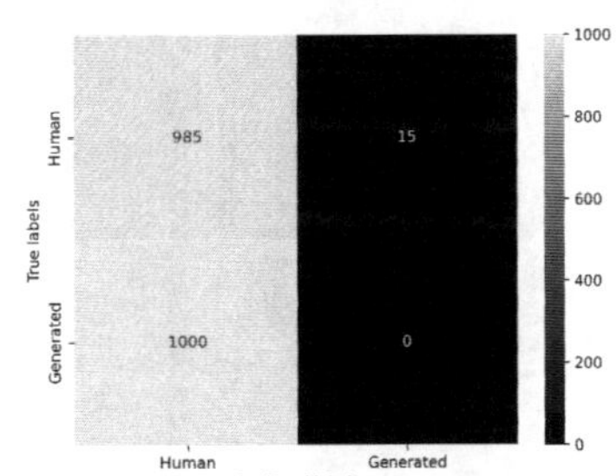

(d) Random attack (15%)

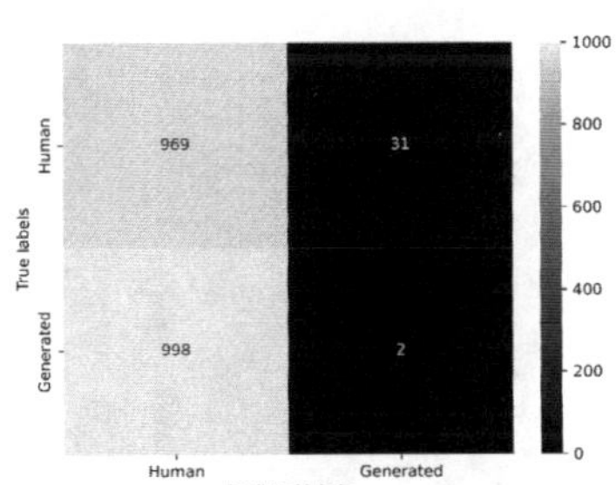

(e) Random attack (20%)

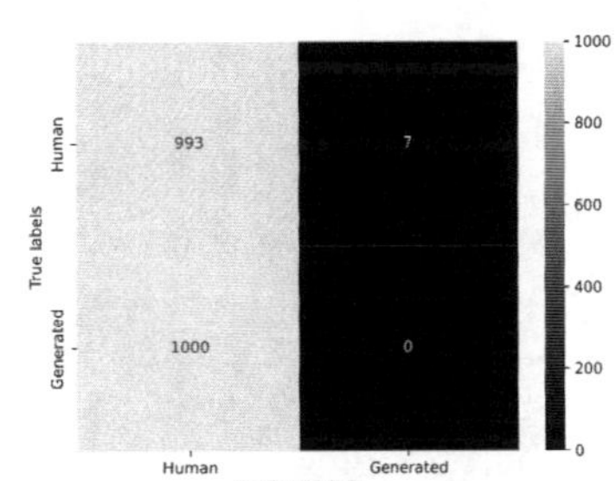

(f) Greedy attack

Figure 22: Confusion matrices for the `OpenAI` detector on the *reuter* dataset.

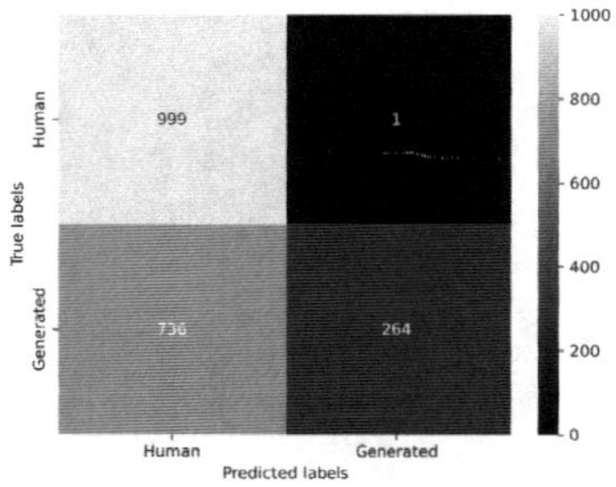

(a) No attack

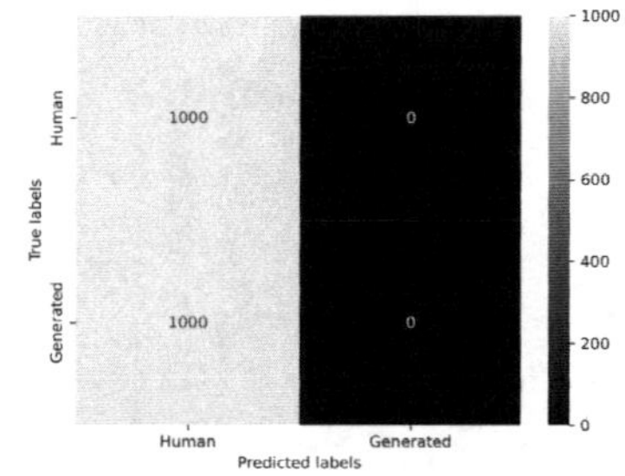

(b) Random attack (5%)

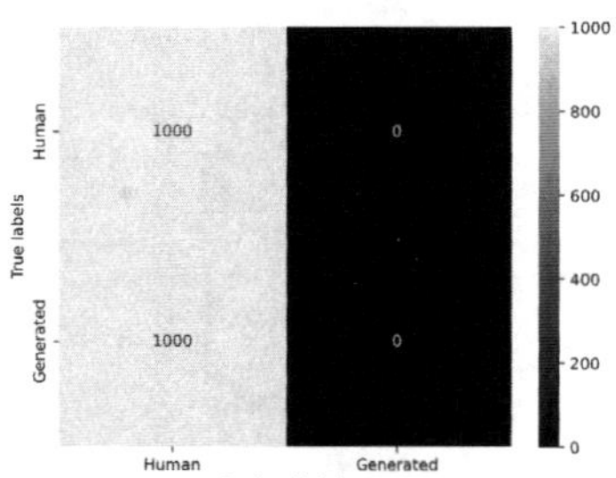

(c) Random attack (10%)

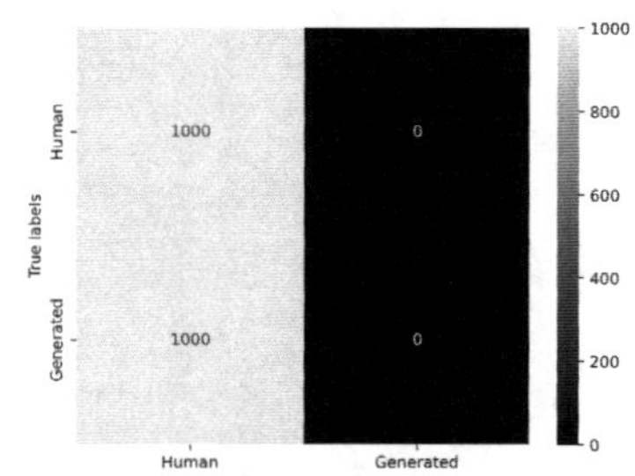

(d) Random attack (15%)

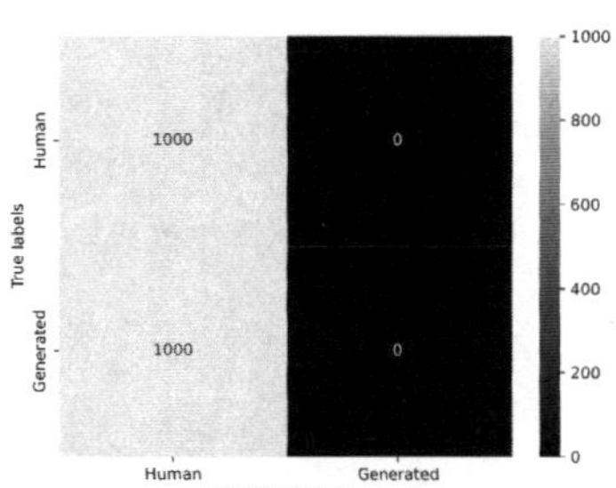

(e) Random attack (20%)

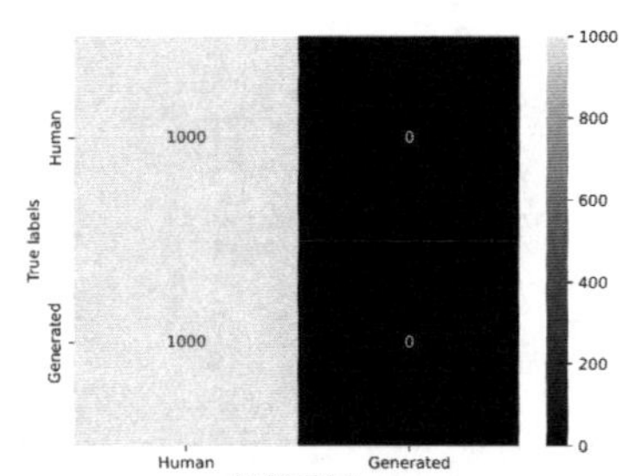

(f) Greedy attack

Figure 23: Confusion matrices for the `ArguGPT` detector on the *writing prompts* dataset.

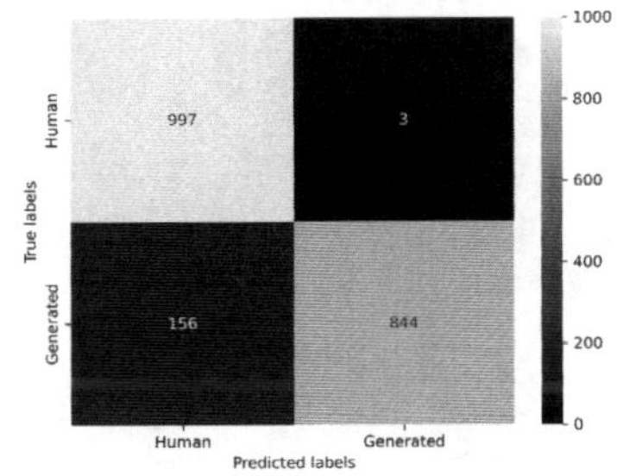

(a) No attack

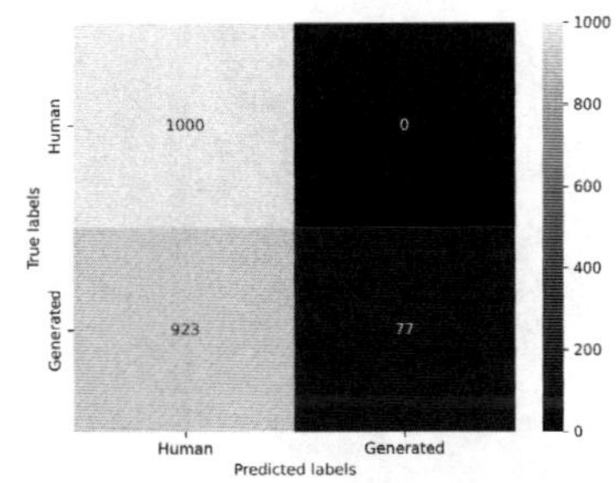

(b) Random attack (5%)

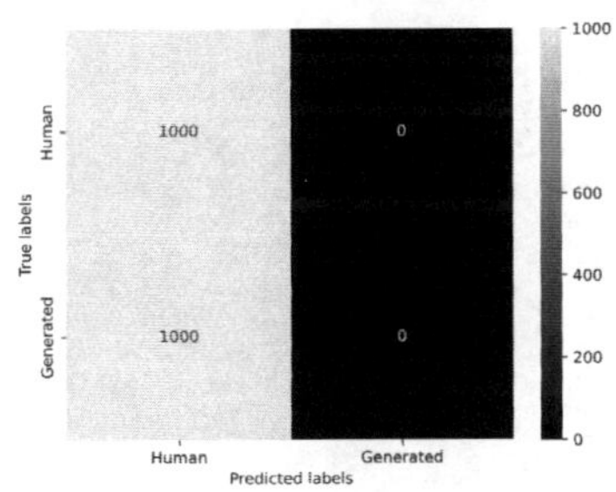

(c) Random attack (10%)

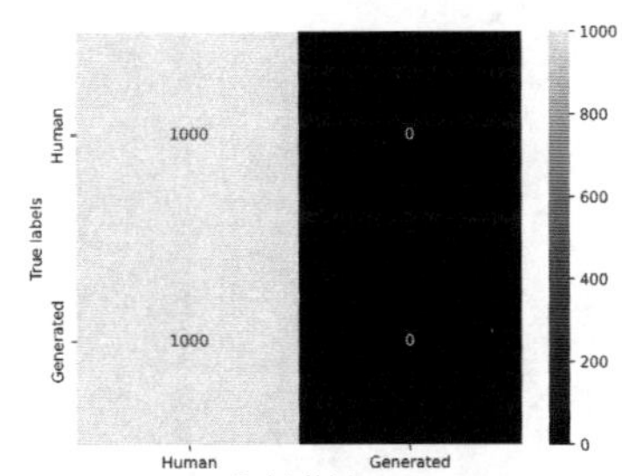

(d) Random attack (15%)

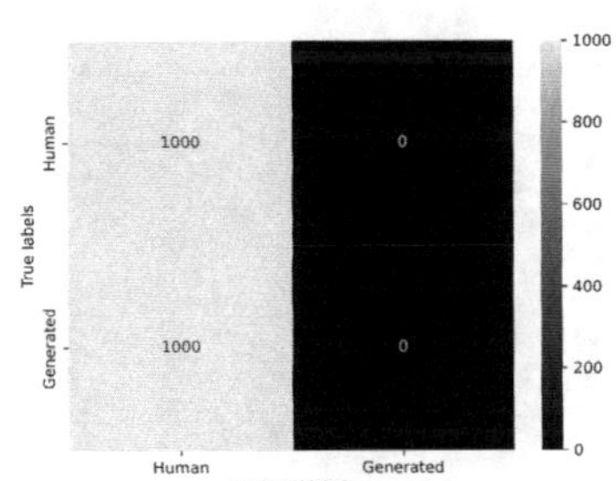

(e) Random attack (20%)

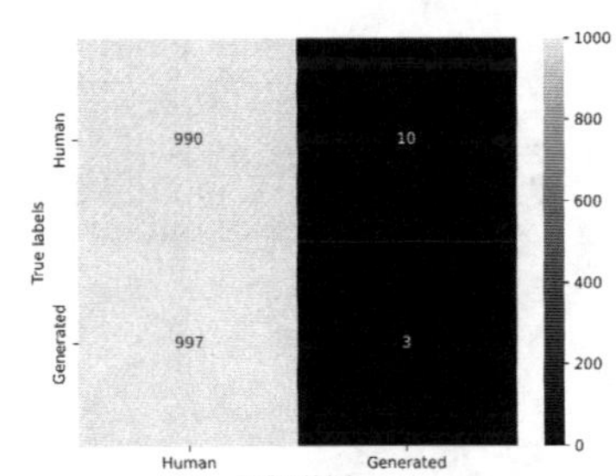

(f) Greedy attack

Figure 24: Confusion matrices for the `Binoculars` detector on the *writing prompts* dataset.

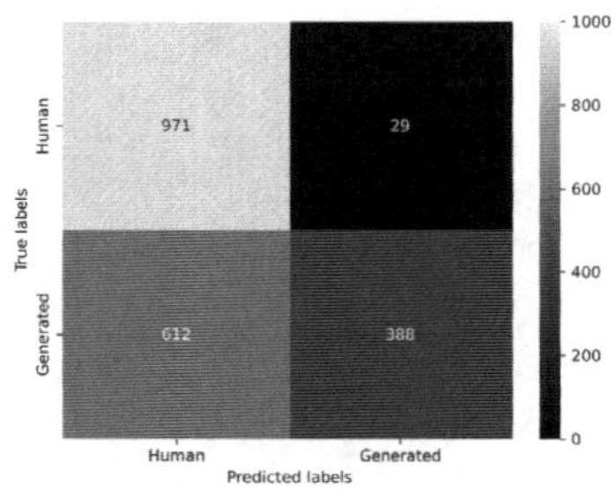

(a) No attack

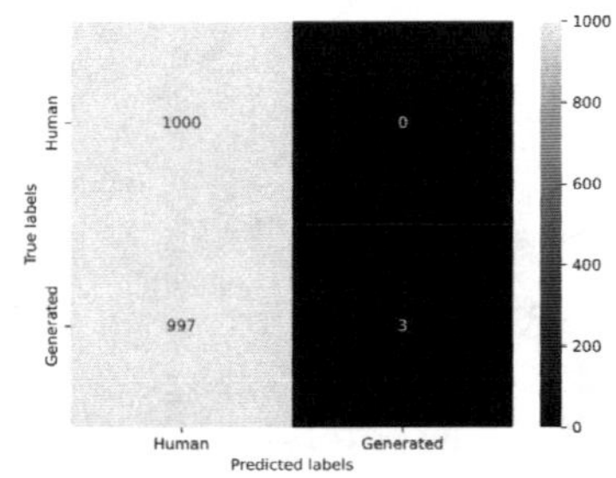

(b) Random attack (5%)

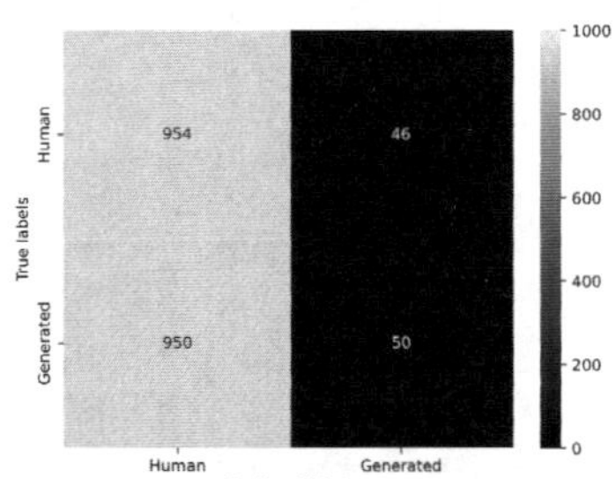

(c) Random attack (10%)

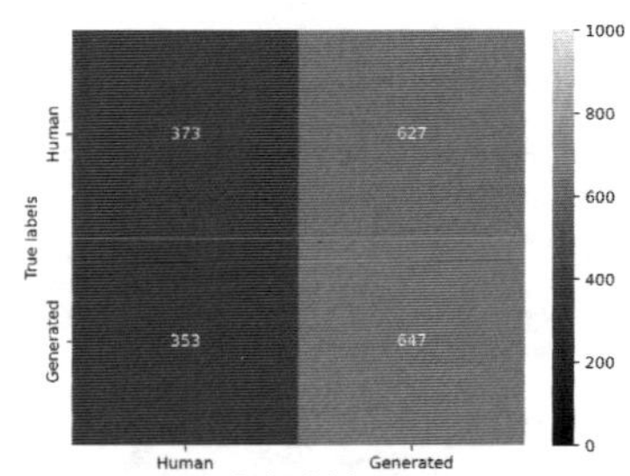

(d) Random attack (15%)

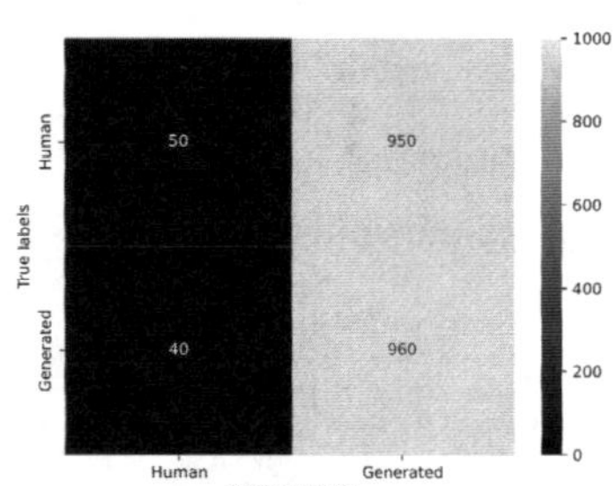

(e) Random attack (20%)

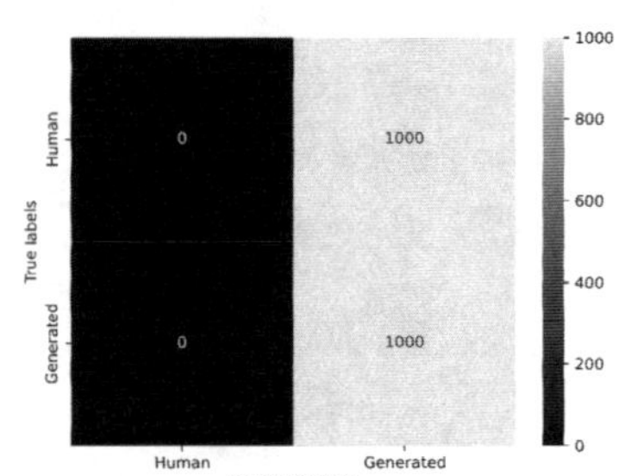

(f) Greedy attack

Figure 25: Confusion matrices for `DetectGPT` on the *writing prompts* dataset.

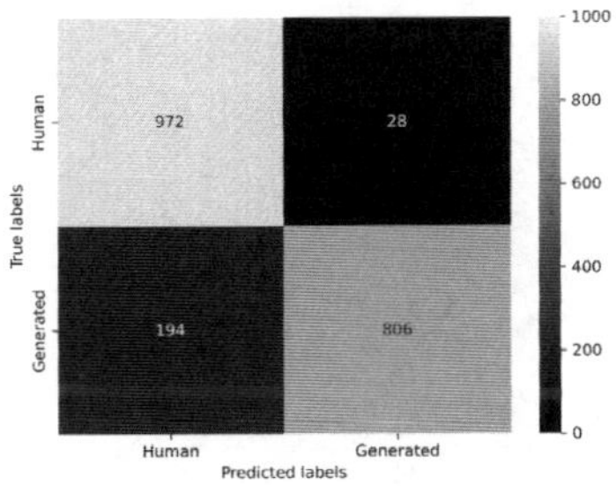

(a) No attack

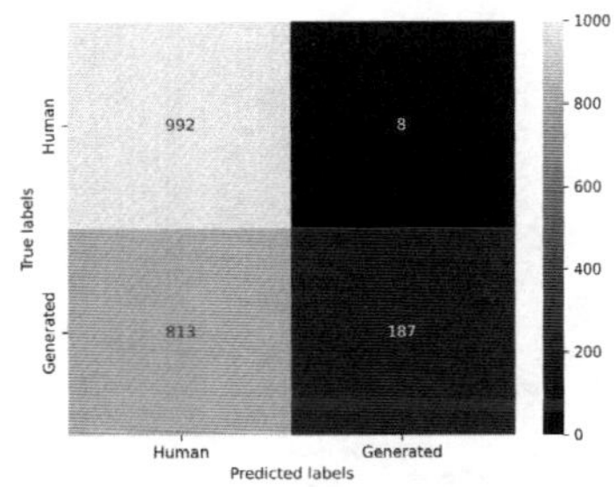

(b) Random attack (5%)

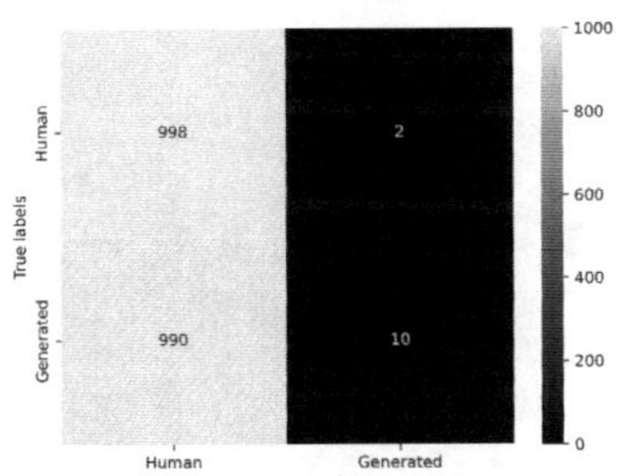

(c) Random attack (10%)

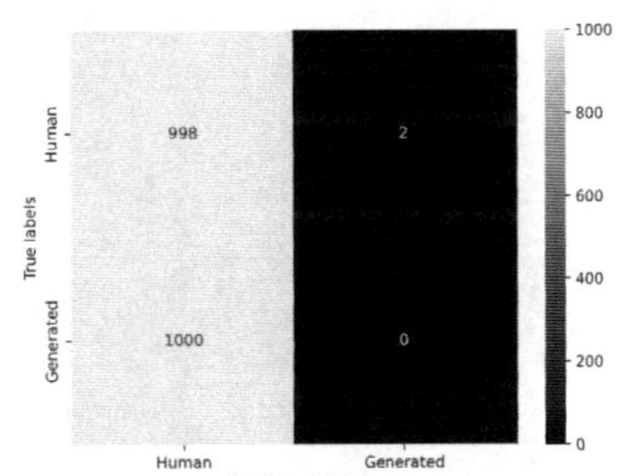

(d) Random attack (15%)

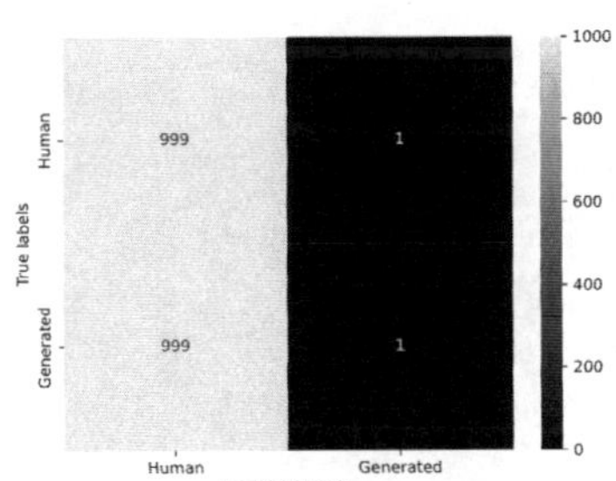

(e) Random attack (20%)

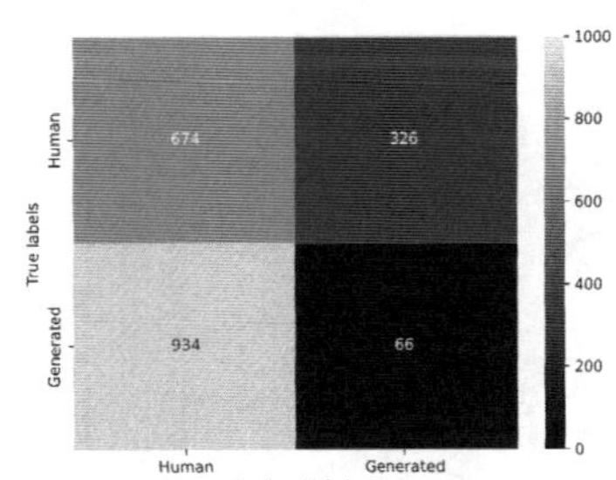

(f) Greedy attack

Figure 26: Confusion matrices for the `Fast-DetectGPT` detector on the *writing prompts* dataset.

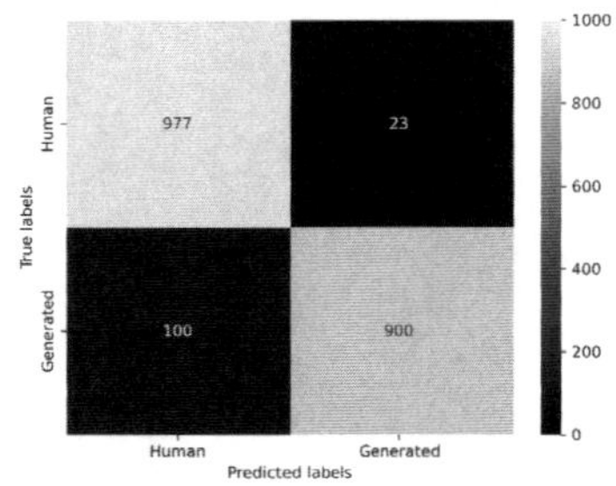

(a) No attack

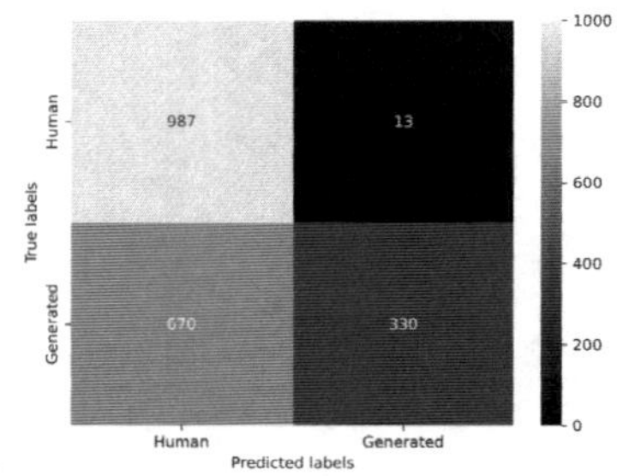

(b) Random attack (5%)

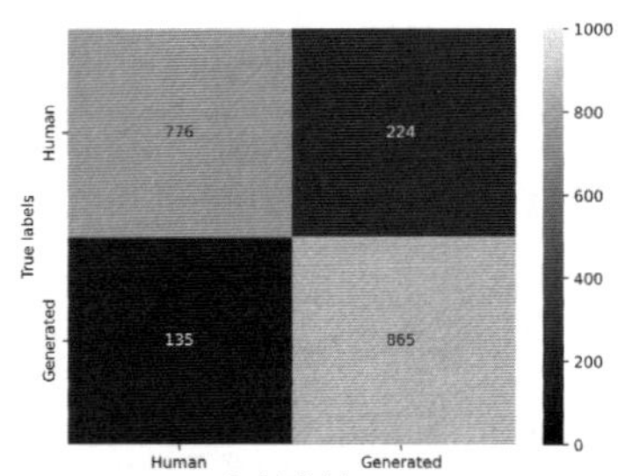

(c) Random attack (10%)

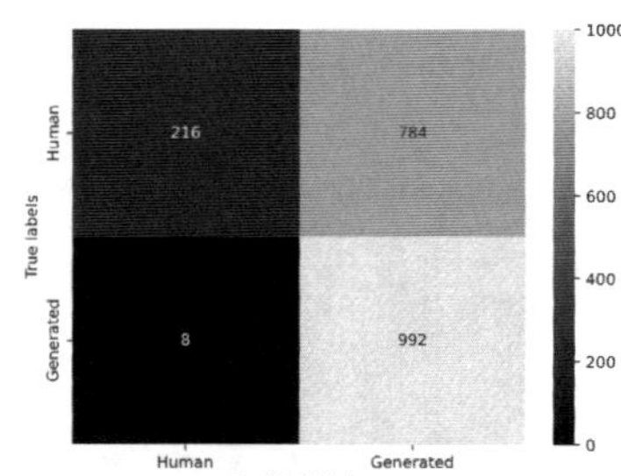

(d) Random attack (15%)

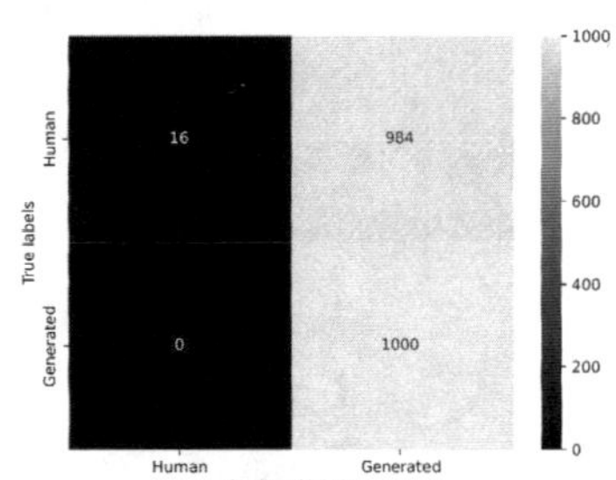

(e) Random attack (20%)

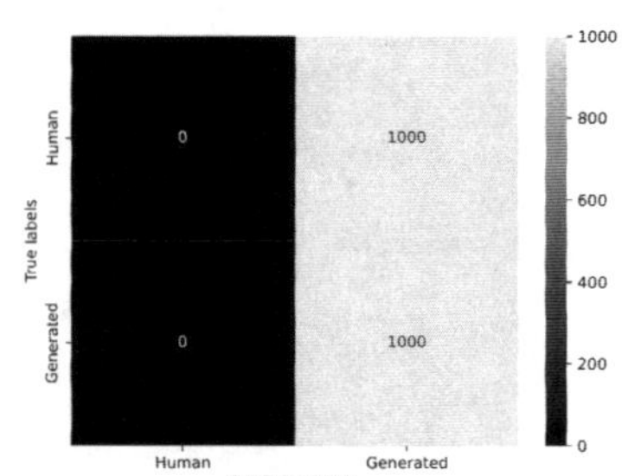

(f) Greedy attack

Figure 27: Confusion matrices for the `Ghostbuster` detector on the *writing prompts* dataset.

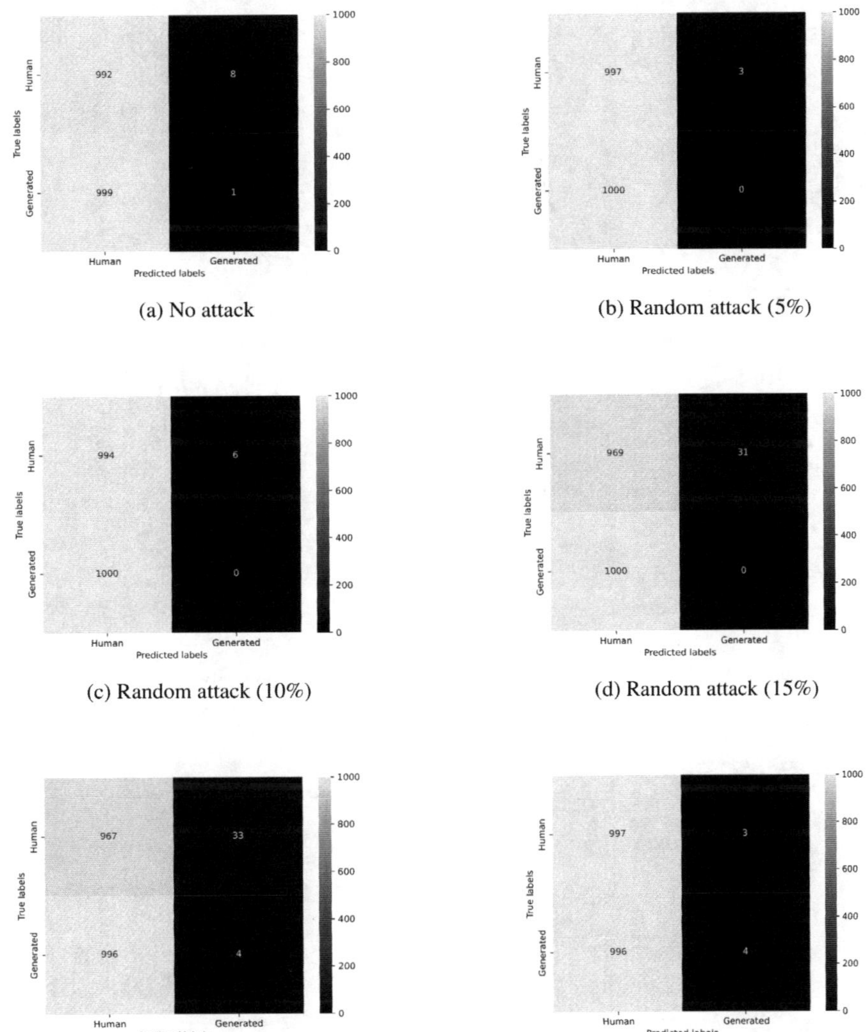

(a) No attack

(b) Random attack (5%)

(c) Random attack (10%)

(d) Random attack (15%)

(e) Random attack (20%)

(f) Greedy attack

Figure 28: Confusion matrices for the `OpenAI` detector on the *writing prompts* dataset.

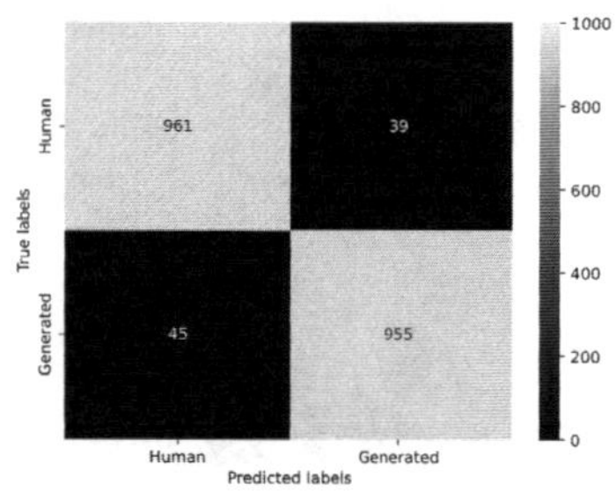

(a) No attack

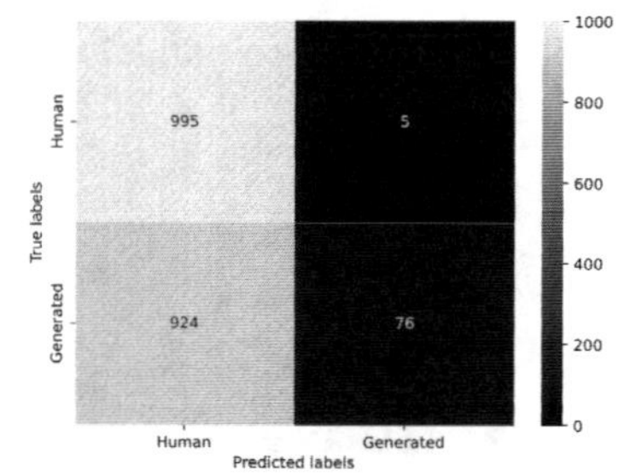

(b) Random attack (5%)

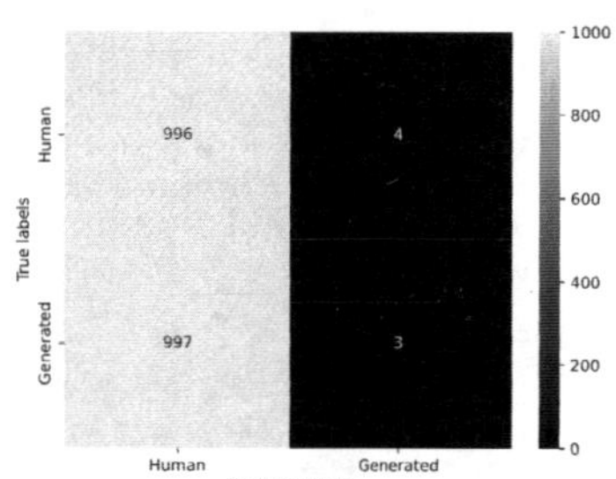

(c) Random attack (10%)

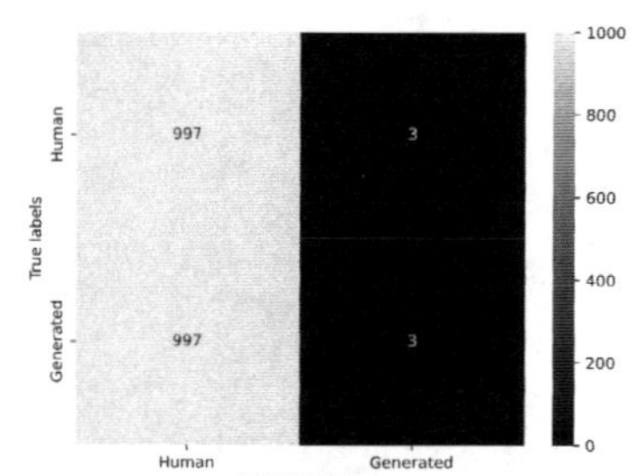

(d) Random attack (15%)

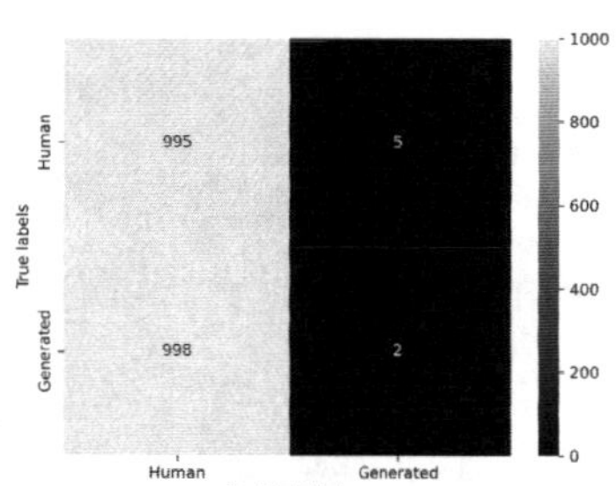

(e) Random attack (20%)

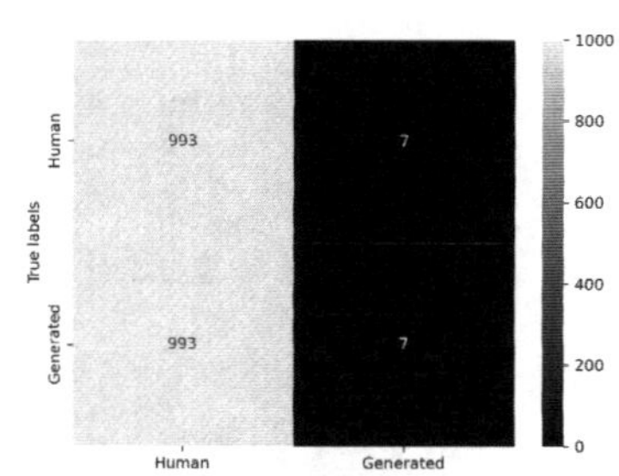

(f) Greedy attack

Figure 29: Confusion matrices for the watermarking-based detector on the *realnewslike* dataset. Here, "generated" refers to the watermarked versions of the texts.

Human vs. AI: A Novel Benchmark and a Comparative Study on the Detection of Generated Images and the Impact of Prompts

Philipp Moeßner
Hochschule der Medien
Stuttgart, Germany
philippmoessner@gmx.de

Heike Adel
Hochschule der Medien
Stuttgart, Germany
adel-vu@hdm-stuttgart.de

Abstract

With the advent of publicly available AI-based text-to-image systems, the process of creating photorealistic but fully synthetic images has been largely democratized. This can pose a threat to the public through a simplified spread of disinformation. Machine detectors and human media expertise can help to differentiate between AI-generated (fake) and real images and counteract this danger. Although AI generation models are highly prompt-dependent, the impact of the prompt on the fake detection performance has rarely been investigated yet. This work therefore examines the influence of the prompt's level of detail on the detectability of fake images, both with an AI detector and in a user study. For this purpose, we create a novel dataset, COCOXGEN, which consists of real photos from the COCO dataset as well as images generated with SDXL and Fooocus using prompts of two standardized lengths. Our user study with 200 participants shows that images generated with longer, more detailed prompts are detected significantly more easily than those generated with short prompts. Similarly, an AI-based detection model achieves better performance on images generated with longer prompts. However, humans and AI models seem to pay attention to different details, as we show in a heat map analysis.

1 Introduction

State-of-the-art AI-based image generators, such as DALL-E (Ramesh et al., 2021), Midjourney (Midjourney, Inc., 2024) or Stable Diffusion (Rombach et al., 2021) have the ability to create photorealistic images in a fully synthetic manner (Aziz et al., 2024). The fact that these systems are publicly available makes them contribute to the fast spread of synthetic image content on the Internet. This increases the threat of disinformation (Bontridder and Poullet, 2021). Thus, there is a need for reliable detection of AI-generated images.

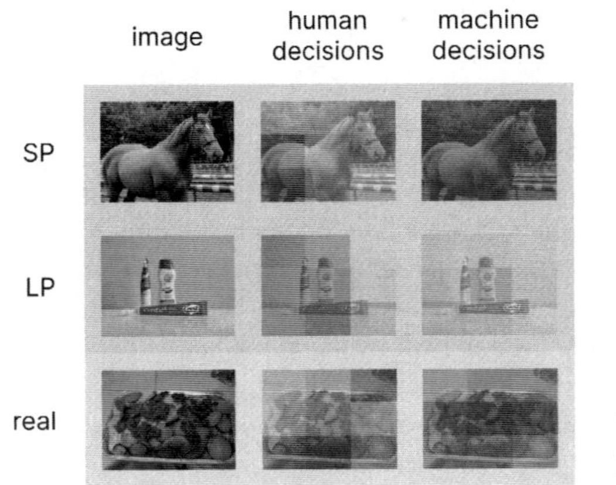

Figure 1: We conduct a study with humans and an AI model detecting real and fake images generated from prompts with a different level of detail (short prompt (SP), long prompt (LP)) and visualize the image areas which led to their decisions.

Although it is well known that image generation is highly dependent on the textual prompt (Liu and Chilton, 2022), the impact of the prompt on the fake detection performance has been rarely investigated yet. An exception is the work by Sha et al. (2023) who analyze prompts regarding their topic and structure. In particular, the level of detail in the prompt might affect the number of artifacts as more details might force the model to generate an image that deviates more from its training data. Therefore, we pose the question whether the level of detail in the prompt has an impact on the ability of humans and AI-models to detect generated images.

Existing research on fake image detection shows that average human performance is not substantially better than chance (Cooke et al., 2024; Lu et al., 2024). Other works show that machine detection performance can be considered rather reliable, at least for images generated by models that have been included in the training data of detection systems (Baraheem and Nguyen, 2023; Epstein et al.,

Proceedings of the 1st Workshop on GenAI Content Detection (GenAIDetect), pages 47–58
January 19, 2025. ©2025 International Conference on Computational Linguistics

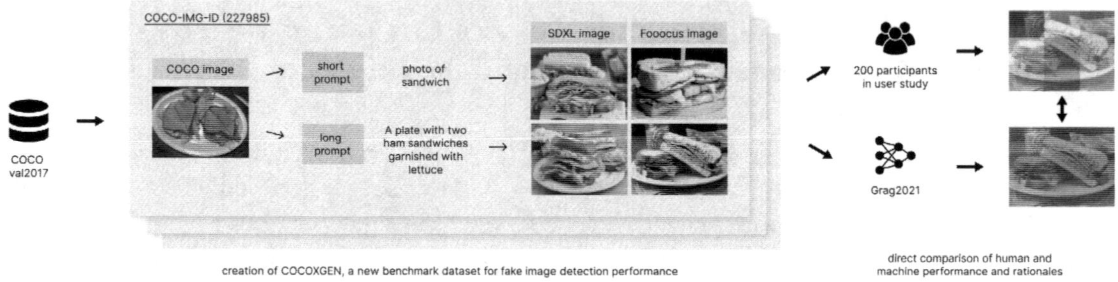

Figure 2: Our contributions are (1) the creation of COCOXGEN, a novel benchmark dataset with images created by two different generation models based on prompts of two different levels of detail, (2) the conduction of a large-scale user study on fake image detection, and (3) a direct comparison of human and machine detection performance and decision rationales.

2023; Corvi et al., 2023). While these individual evaluations of humans and AI models show interesting results, it is not possible yet to directly compare human and AI-model performance due to different test setups (i.e. test images). Thus, another goal of our study is to investigate whether human or AI-model performance dominates.

Some works also investigate which aspects of the input lead to the detection decisions: AI models, on the one hand, tend to involve larger image areas in their decision on real images than on synthetic ones (Bird and Lotfi, 2024). This leads to the impression that the detection of synthetic images is focused on fine details while the detection of real images is focused on more abstract contents. Humans, on the other hand, tend to pay attention to specific objects as well as to their general impression of the image (Pocol et al., 2023). Again, it is not possible to directly compare the strategies of humans and AI-models due to different evaluation setups. Thus, we also address the open research question whether humans and AI models consider the same objects and structures in an image when evaluating it as real or fake.

To address our research questions, we present COCOXGEN, a new dataset containing real photos from the COCO dataset (Lin et al., 2014) and AI-generated images from SDXL (Podell et al., 2023) and Fooocus (Illyasviel, 2024) with prompts of two different levels of detail. Our dataset is publicly available[1] and can be used in future work as a benchmark dataset for evaluating fake image detection performance. We conduct a user study with 200 human participants and evaluate the machine-learning classifier Grag2021 (Corvi et al., 2023) on our new dataset to be able to directly compare the detection performance (F1 scores) of humans and a state-of-the-art AI model. In our analysis, we visualize image areas that lead to the decisions of humans and machine detectors in a comparable heat map structure to investigate both qualitatively and quantitatively whether humans and AI models pursue similar strategies.

2 Related Work

2.1 Human Detection Performance

Previous work investigated human performance on distinguishing AI-generated and real media content by showing humans around 50 real and 50 AI-generated images (Cooke et al., 2024; Lu et al., 2024). They found an average accuracy of 49% (Cooke et al., 2024) to 61% (Lu et al., 2024). None of the works found a statistically significant effect of previous experience with AI-generated content of the test participants on their accuracy. Still, Lu et al. (2024) showed a slightly higher performance of participants with previous experience. Pocol et al. (2023) additionally investigated how humans come to a classification decision for deepfakes by providing a free text field for explanations. They found that mainly clear suspicious objects and the general impression of the image lead to the decisions. The scale of our user study is comparable to previous works. However, we not only comprehensively evaluate human detection performance including the effect of previous experience with AI-generated content but also explicitly analyze which image parts lead to the decision of our participants.

2.2 Machine Detection Performance

Previous research evaluated different machine-learning approaches to detect AI-generated images (Baraheem and Nguyen, 2023; Park et al., 2024;

[1]https://github.com/heikeadel/cocoxgen

Corvi et al., 2023). They found that it is possible to achieve high performance in certain conditions (Baraheem and Nguyen, 2023; Corvi et al., 2023) but that true generalization to images outside of the scope of the training data remains difficult (Epstein et al., 2023). In addition, downsampling or compressing images decreases detection performance (Zhu et al., 2024). Bird and Lotfi (2024) found that the actual objects of the images are of minor importance for the decision of machine detectors. In contrast to these works, we aim to directly compare the performance of an AI model as well as the image areas that are most relevant for its decision to human performance and decision rationales.

2.3 Detection Performance Robustness

Prior work showed that post-generation changes of AI-generated images could considerably decrease the performance of machine-learning detectors (Wesselkamp et al., 2022; Carlini and Farid, 2020). Wesselkamp et al. (2022), for instance, described different approaches of subtracting specific frequencies from the images and Carlini and Farid (2020) trained a model to calculate optimal perturbations. In practical applications, a user would most probably mainly concentrate on altering the content of the generated image via modifications of the prompt. Therefore, we argue that detection models should also be robust against changes in the prompt. The impact of prompts on detection performance has only rarely been investigated in previous work. Sha et al. (2023) found that specific words and prompt lengths can lead to lower detection performance. However, they did not investigate these effects in detail. In addition, no prior work has considered human performance when altering AI-generated images. In this paper, we address this research gap and set the impact of the prompt's level of detail as our main research focus.

3 Dataset

To the best of our knowledge, there is no dataset publicly available that contains real images and AI-generated images from prompts with a controllable level of detail. Therefore, we create and publish COCOXGEN (COCO Extended With Generated Images), a novel benchmark dataset for the evaluation of fake image detection performance.

3.1 Dataset Creation

We choose the COCO dataset (Lin et al., 2014) as the basis for our new dataset because it provides different levels of annotations for the photographs: several 1-word "thing" (objects with a well-defined shape) and "stuff" (amorphous background regions) classes as well as 5 complete sentences (captions). We use those different annotations to build prompts of two different levels of detail as shown in Table 1. In the following, we refer to the prompt with less detail as "short prompt (SP)" and to the prompt with more details as "long prompt (LP)". The short prompt is created by prepending "photo of" to the most frequent element of the annotated thing and stuff classes. The long prompt is created by selecting the caption with the smallest difference in length to the average length of all captions (10 words). Figure 2 shows an examplary COCO image and the two created prompts.

	SP	**LP**
length	3 words	$\sim$ 10 words
shape	"photo of [X]"	entire sentence

Table 1: Prompt types used for image generation; both extracted from COCO, the 'X' of the short prompt (SP) is a COCO thing or stuff class (e.g., "sandwich"), the long prompt (LP) is a COCO caption.

For creating the AI-generated images, we use two state-of-the-art methods: SDXL (Podell et al., 2023), the latest version of the open source text-to-image model Stable Diffusion (Rombach et al., 2021) and Fooocus (lllyasviel, 2024), the open-source equivalent to Midjourney (Midjourney, Inc., 2024). For Fooocus, we choose the standard model Juggernaut XL V8[2] as the base model and the most popular model for photorealism on CIVITAI, Realistic Vision V6[3], as the refiner since we aim to generate photorealistic images. With both generators, we create an image for each prompt. As a result, COCOXGEN's data contains groups of images consisting of 1 real COCO image, its corresponding short and long prompt and 4 generated images (one per prompt type and generation model).

3.2 Datasplit and Statistics

Note that we only use COCO's validation set val2017 as the basis for COCOXGEN to avoid including images which might have been used to train detection models in our benchmark dataset. From COCO's validation set, we further remove all

[2] https://huggingface.co/RunDiffusion/Juggernaut-XL-v8

[3] https://civitai.com/models/4201/realistic-vision-v60-b1

images that do not have a 640x480 px resolution (standard size of photos in COCO) to ensure that all images have the same size. This is important to be able to exclude the image size as a confounding variable in our experiments. While Fooocus is able to generate 640x480 px images natively, SDXL only supports specific resolutions for best image quality. We select 1152x864 px as it results in the same aspect ratio.

Table 2 provides statistics of COCOXGEN.

<table>
<tr><th>real</th><th colspan="4">AI-generated</th></tr>
<tr><td>1061</td><td colspan="4">4244</td></tr>
<tr><td rowspan="4"></td><td colspan="2">LP</td><td colspan="2">SP</td></tr>
<tr><td colspan="2">2122</td><td colspan="2">2122</td></tr>
<tr><td>Fooocus</td><td>SDXL</td><td>Fooocus</td><td>SDXL</td></tr>
<tr><td>1061</td><td>1061</td><td>1061</td><td>1061</td></tr>
</table>

Table 2: Number of images in COCOXGEN (LP: long-prompted images, SP: short-prompted images).

4 User Study

With this study, we measure human classification performance (in terms of F1 score) for AI-generated and real images. Moreover, we investigate the impact of the level of detail in the prompts on the human performance. We assume that a more detailed prompt, i.e., a more complex demand, leads to a higher chance of artifacts in the generated images as the generation model needs to deviate more from its training data to fulfill the individual request. Therefore we state the following hypothesis:

H_1: *Humans achieve higher detection performance for images generated with longer, more detailed prompts, than for those generated with short prompts.*

Our datasets, which was created using two different state-of-the-art image generation models, further allows us to test human performance per generation model, i.e., to investigate which model creates the most photorealistic images from human perspective. As we assume that Fooocus images are more photorealistic due to its task-specific refiner, we state the following hypothesis:

H_2: *Humans achieve higher detection performance for SDXL images than for Fooocus images.*

In addition to investigating pure performance, we further analyze which part of the image leads to the decision of the participants when classifying a photograph as real or fake as well as how certain they are in doing so. Finally, we analyze whether the participants' experience with AI-generated images before the study influences their detection performance.

4.1 Study Design

We recruit 200 participants (127 female, 70 male, 3 non-binary) of ages 14 to 87 years (average age: 25.7). We reached most of them in a university context. As a result, 94.5% hold at least a high school diploma as their highest educational achievement, and 83.0% of the participants see AI-generated images sometimes or regularly in their daily lives. 59.5% have never or just once used image generators themselves. For our study, we randomly select 120 images from COCOXGEN and split them into two disjoint sets of 60 images each (20 real photos, 20 images generated with short prompts, 20 images generated with long prompts, whereby half of the generated images are from SDXL and the other half from Fooocus). Each participants sees one of the sets in the study with the images in random order. This enables us to test a larger number of images while minimizing possible fatigue effects during the classification process at the same time. To ensure diverse content in the images which are used for the user study, we make sure the short prompts (that were created based on the "stuff" and "thing" classes of the COCO dataset, c.f., Table 1) do not overlap. To make sure all images of the study dataset have the same size we further downsample all images generated with SDXL to the size of the COCO and Fooocus images (640x480 px, see above). For each image, the participants answer the following questions (the actual questionnaire and answer possibilities are provided in Figure 10 in the appendix):

1. Is this image real or AI-generated?
2. How certain are you?
3. Is there a specific image area which has influenced your decision?
4. If yes: Which image areas have influenced your decision? (Participants are shown a 3x3 grid on top of the image and are asked to select all fields with decision influence.)

4.2 Results

Impact of prompt on detection performance. Figure 3 shows that participants have higher detection performance for images generated with long

Subset	Positives	F1	Recall	Precision
All	Real	0.7793	0.8958	0.6997
All	AI	0.8583	0.7954	0.9418
SP	AI	0.8002	0.7400	0.8913
LP	AI	0.8697	0.8508	0.9006
Fooocus	AI	0.7857	0.7190	0.8880
SDXL	AI	0.8822	0.8718	0.9030
COCO	Real	0.7793	0.8958	0.6997

Table 3: Average F1, recall and precision scores of all study participants for specific subsets of the study images; "Positives" indicates the class for which the scores were calculated.

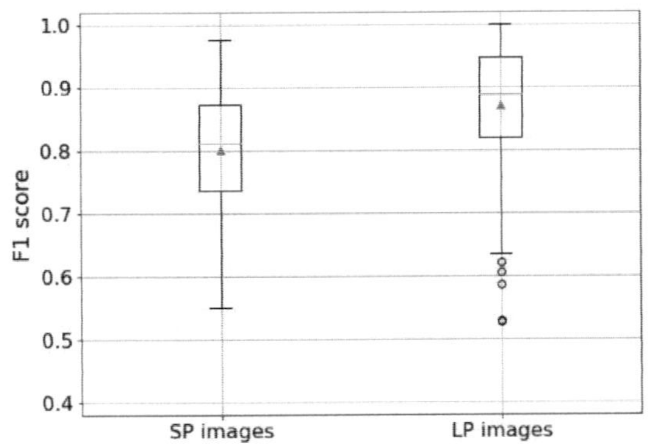

Figure 3: F1 scores per prompt type (SP: short prompt with less details, LP: long prompt with more details).

prompts (LP) than for images generated with short prompts (SP). In particular, the average and median performance of the participants are higher for LP images than for SP images. Thus, the participants recognized LP images more easily as being AI-generated than SP images. A one-sided Wilcoxon test on our data shows that this difference is statistically significant ($p = 2.1696^{-22}$), indicating that our hypothesis H_1 is valid. Furthermore, the difference in F1 scores between the image groups of different prompt lengths can be categorized as strong with an effect size of Cohen's $d = 0.8809$.

Analysis of relevant image areas. Overall, slightly more of the participants' decisions were based on the "general impression" (48.78%) rather than on specific image areas (45.16%).[4] For real images, more decisions were based on the "general impression" (for 65.23% of all real images and 71.45% of correctly classified real images). For AI-generated images, concrete image areas slightly outweigh the general impression for decision-making (for 54.40% of all AI-generated

[4]For the remaining 6.05% of images, participants noted they were unsure.

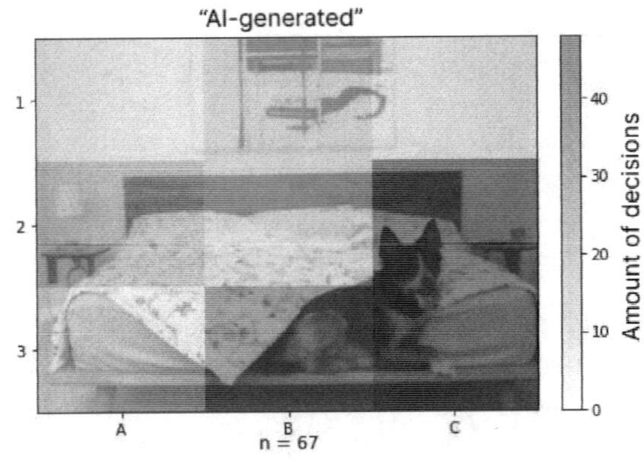

Figure 4: The image area selection results show that participants pay particular attention to clear objects.

images and 65.28% of correctly classified AI-generated images participants named specific image areas). This indicates that the participants were able to detect suspicious areas or concrete artifacts rather in AI-generated images than in real images. Interestingly, for 63.31% of real images that were incorrectly classified as AI-generated, participants named concrete image areas as decision rationales. This shows that participants look for suspicious areas in the image in order to classify an image as "AI-generated" while the decision to classify an image as "real" rather depends on the general impression. By directly analyzing the individual heat maps for each image, we observe that the study participants pay particular attention to objects that can be clearly separated in the image and use these as the basis for their decision (instead of, e.g., background structures). In case of AI-generated images, obvious artifacts are selected as well (see Figure 4 for an example). This finding is in line with previous work which showed that people generally concentrate on structures in a picture that strongly stand out (Parkhurst et al., 2002).

Impact of generation model on detection performance. The lower the F1 score for detecting AI-generated images, the more photorealistic the images are. When looking at the generator-specific F1 scores in Figure 5, we observe lower F1 scores for Fooocus images than for SDXL images. The study participants therefore tended to recognize the SDXL images more easily as AI-generated than the Fooocus images, which indicates that Fooocus produces more photorealistic results than SDXL. This result is also statistically significant (one-sided Wilcoxon test, $p = 5.1944e^{-29}$). This indicates

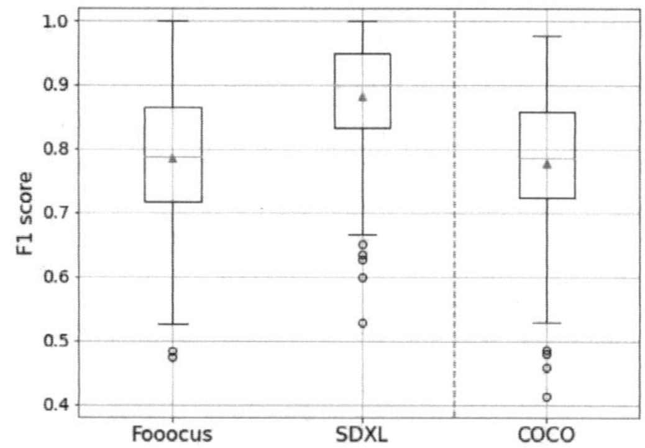

Figure 5: F1 scores per image generator (left and middle; the lower, the more realistic are the generated images) and for real COCO images (right; the higher the better)

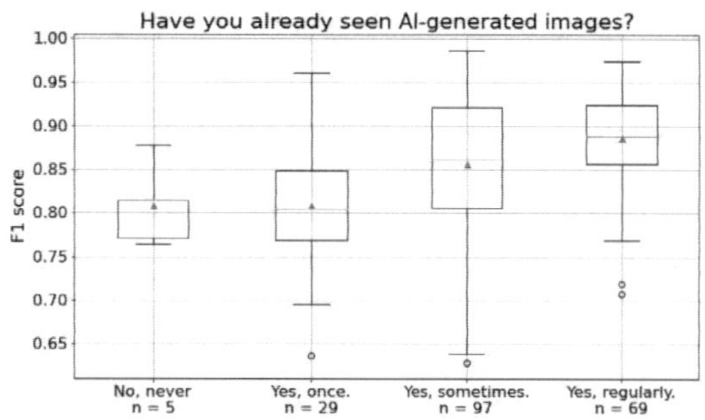

Figure 6: F1 scores for AI-generated images by experience.

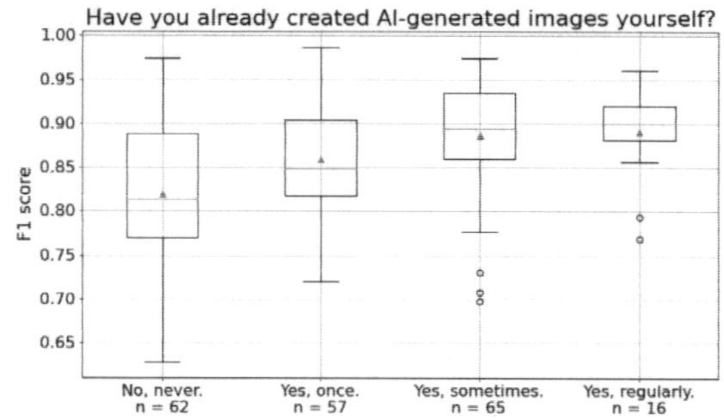

Figure 7: F1 scores for AI-generated images by experience with image generation.

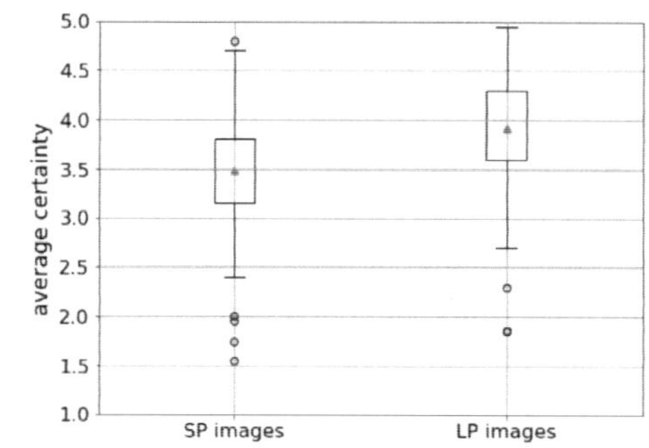

Figure 8: Average decision certainty of the participants for images generated by long prompts with more details (LP) vs. short prompts (SP).

that our hypothesis H_2 is valid. Furthermore, the difference in F1 scores between different generators can be categorized as strong with an effect size of Cohen's $d = 1.1978$. Interestingly, the F1 scores of assigning COCO photos to their correct class (i.e., "real") are in a similar range as the F1 scores of assigning Fooocus images to their correct class (i.e., "AI"). This is a result of a lower precision for the "real" class, i.e., many AI-generated images were falsely classified as real. Considering only recall, COCO photos were best assigned to the correct class (see Table 3).

Impact of experience on detection performance. Participants who rated their experience with AI-generated images higher also tended to perform better at detecting AI-generated images (Figures 6 and 7). Interestingly, the boxes (interquartile ranges) for "no, never" and "yes, once" as well as the boxes for "yes, sometimes" and "yes, regularly" fully overlap while there is a clearer difference between "yes, once" and "yes, sometimes".

Analysis of participants' decision certainty. We cannot find a considerable difference in the decision certainty (values ranging from 1 ("very uncertain") to 5 ("very certain")) of the participants for AI-generated (average of 3.70) and real images (average of 3.80). When comparing their average decision certainty for LP images (average of 3.91) and SP images (average of 3.49) (c.f., Figure 8), the difference is larger. A one-sided Wilcoxon test on this data shows that this difference is also statistically significant ($p = 1.2486e^{-29}$). Thus, the participants not only performed better at classifying images generated from more detailed prompts but were also more certain in their decisions compared to images generated from short prompts.

5 Machine Classification Performance

For automatically distinguishing real from AI-generated images, we apply Grag2021 (Gragnaniello et al., 2021), a ResNet50 (He et al., 2016) which is one of the most popular architectures for image classification. We use the trained and publicly available version by Corvi et al. (2023). Grag2021 has been trained on COCO and Latent

Subset	Positives	F1	Recall	Precision
All	Real	0.6957	1.0000	0.5333
All	AI	0.7200	0.5625	1.0000
SP	AI	0.7097	0.5500	1.0000
LP	AI	0.7302	0.5750	1.0000
Fooocus	AI	1.0000	1.0000	1.0000
SDXL	AI	0.2222	0.1250	1.0000
COCO	Real	0.6957	1.0000	0.5333

Table 4: F1, recall and precision scores of Grag2021 for specific subsets of the study images. "Positives" indicates the class for which the scores were calculated.

Diffusion images which fits our dataset well.

5.1 Experimental Setup

We test Grag2021 on all 120 images which have also been selected for the study with the human participants. Grag2021 returns a feature map of 60x80 logit values whereby negative values indicate class "real" and positive values indicate class "AI-generated". We follow Corvi et al. (2023) and obtain a single output value by averaging these logits. To transfer the output to a probability value, we apply the sigmoid function. The resulting value x indicates the probability for class "AI-generated". Therefore, if $x \geq 0.5$, the classification result is "AI-generated", if $x < 0.5$, the resulting class is "real".[5] For evaluation, we calculate the F1 scores of the detector and visualize its output feature map as a decision heat map for each image.[6] To compare the model's heat maps with the study participants' image area selections, we apply the same 3x3 grid of our study on the detector feature maps. For each grid field, we add all positive and all negative values separately, resulting in two distinct heat maps: one indicating rationales for class "real" (per-field sum of negative values) and one indicating rationales for class "AI-generated" (per-field sum of positive values).

5.2 Results

Table 4 shows the results of the AI detection model Grag2021. It performs 16.11% worse in detecting AI-generated images than the average human participant. As described before, the images generated by SDXL were downsampled for the user study. We, therefore, compare the performance on the study images and on the original images (Table 5 in appendix). While the performance on original images is very high (F1 score of 0.9744), the performance on the study images is considerably lower (0.7222) which can be explained with a very poor performance on downsampled SDXL images (0.2222). This is in line with the work of Zhu et al. (2024) who found that downsampling or compressing images decreases detection performance.

Impact of prompt on detection performance. Similar to the results of our user study, the detection performance on images generated with long and detailed prompts (LP) is higher than the performance on images generated with short prompts (SP). Note that this difference is independent of downsampling but not statistically significant (according to a permutation test).

Analysis of relevant image areas. Many heat maps for real images (around 57.50%) show clearly recognizable object structures or edges (Figure 9). This means that the object edges have particularly high activation values compared to the rest of the image. For the remaining images including most of the AI-generated images (70.00%), the heat maps depict a relatively uniform noise (an exemplary heat map is provided in the appendix, Figure 11).

When comparing the detector's heat maps with those from the study participants, we observe overlaps for some images (c.f., Figure 12 in appendix). To quantify this overlap, we calculate two Spearman correlation coefficients for each image (one for overlaps of areas indicating class "AI-generated" and one for overlaps of areas indicating class "real"). The correlation coefficient for class "AI-generated" corresponds to $\rho = 0.1988$ (p-value: 0.3921), the correlation coefficient for class "real" is $\rho = 0.2287$ (p-value: 0.4269). To conclude, a low but non-significant correlation was found between the image areas that were most relevant for the participants' and detector's decisions.

Impact of generation model on detection performance. Table 4 shows that real images and fake images generated by Fooocus are recognized perfectly by the detector when considering recall. Considering F1 scores, Fooocus images remain perfectly distinguished from the others while AI-generated images with SDXL are sometimes mistakenly categorized as "real", influencing the recall on the SDXL subset as well as the precision for the COCO class.

[5]Note that we used the default threshold of 0.5 from logistic regression for the classification decision.

[6]To ensure that the heat map has the same resolution as the input image, we let each value of the output feature map correspond to an area of 8x8 pixels in the heat map.

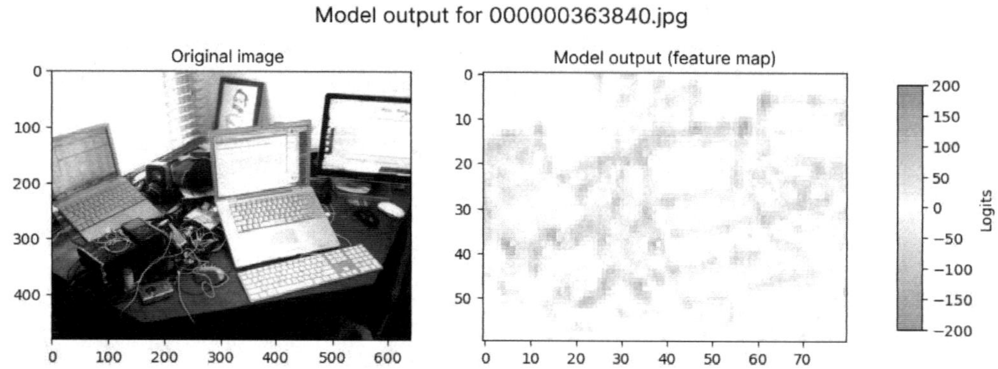

Figure 9: Visualization of the model's output feature map of 60x80 logit values for a real image from COCOXGEN.

6 Discussion

This section discusses the implications of the most important findings of this work.

6.1 Perspective for Real-World Applications

Overall, the machine detector performed worse in distinguishing real from AI-generated study images than the average human study participant which can be attributed to partially downsampling the AI-generated images. The almost perfect results of the machine detector under optimal conditions (no downsampling) indicates a clear opportunity for machine detectors to recognize AI-generated images even when they appear photorealistic to humans. Unfortunately, downsampling is necessarily carried out on many internet platforms, weakening the practical applicability of current machine detectors.

6.2 Level of Detail in Prompt

Our study shows that the detection performance for images generated with long and detailed prompts is significantly higher than for images generated with short prompts. We hypothesize that the image generator has to deviate more from its training data to fulfil the needs of a complex prompt with many details. This might lead to more artifacts in the generated image. Thus, not only the technical implementation influences the quality and detectability of the output images but also the prompt that was used for generation.

6.3 Impact of Experience

Study participants who stated that they were more experienced in viewing and creating AI-generated images also tended to be better at detecting them. This suggests that the ability to recognize AI-generated images and distinguish them from real photos can be trained.

6.4 Rationales for Decisions

The percentage of instances for which participants declared the "general impression" as the main decision argument shows that visible artifacts do not need to be present in the image for people to be skeptical about the authenticity of an image. This can be seen as an opportunity for the human ability to detect AI-generated images, especially in light of the fact that generation algorithms are constantly evolving and will produce fewer and fewer visible artifacts in the future. While humans mainly concentrate on clearly distinguishable objects in the images (Parkhurst et al., 2002), the machine detector gives high activations mainly to fine details (high frequencies) or object edges. This difference might also be the reason why we could not find a significant overlap between the selected image areas of humans and the most activated ones by the machine detector. An interesting direction could be to combine the complementary attention areas of humans and machines in a collaborative setting.

6.5 Limitations

Findings of this work cannot be generalized to all image generation models, especially since both generators of this work are derived from Latent Diffusion without considering GAN methods or transformer architectures. Similarly, only a single machine detection model was tested. Since we performed a user study, we also used only 120 images from COCOXGEN in this work, while the entire dataset consists of 5305 images.

Although we observed statistically significant

correlations in our user study, it is important to note that the age, gender and education distribution of our participants does not reflect the distribution of the whole population. The same holds for the prior experience with image generation which was rather high for our participants on average as most of them were recruited in a university context.

7 Conclusion and Future Work

In this work, we investigated the influence of the prompt's level of detail for distinguishing AI-generated images from real ones. In particular, we explored both the performance of humans and a machine detector and directly compared their decision rationales. For this purpose, we created a novel benchmark dataset COCOXGEN, which contains AI-generated SDXL and Fooocus images created with prompts of two different levels of detail as well as real COCO images. We found that images generated with prompts with more details can be recognized more easily as fake than images generated with short prompts with less details. This observation holds for both humans and the machine detector although their decision rationales show only a low correlation.

Future work can expand our study by investigating more types of generation and machine detection models. In addition, additional aspects of prompt composition (e.g., the number of words per part-of-speech class) and their impact on fake image detection performance can be explored.

Acknowledgments

We thank the Etzold foundation for supporting the publication of this work. We thank all participants of our study for their time and their support of our research. We further thank all reviewers for their helpful feedback.

References

Memoona Aziz, Umair Rehman, Muhammad Umair Danish, and Katarina Grolinger. 2024. Global-local image perceptual score (glips): Evaluating photorealistic quality of ai-generated images. *arXiv preprint arXiv:2405.09426*.

Samah S Baraheem and Tam V Nguyen. 2023. Ai vs. ai: Can ai detect ai-generated images? *Journal of Imaging*, 9(10):199.

Jordan J Bird and Ahmad Lotfi. 2024. Cifake: Image classification and explainable identification of ai-generated synthetic images. *IEEE Access*.

Noémi Bontridder and Yves Poullet. 2021. The role of artificial intelligence in disinformation. *Data & Policy*, 3:e32.

Nicholas Carlini and Hany Farid. 2020. Evading deepfake-image detectors with white-and black-box attacks. In *Proceedings of the IEEE/CVF conference on computer vision and pattern recognition workshops*, pages 658–659.

Di Cooke, Abigail Edwards, Sophia Barkoff, and Kathryn Kelly. 2024. As good as a coin toss human detection of ai-generated images, videos, audio, and audiovisual stimuli. *arXiv preprint arXiv:2403.16760*.

Riccardo Corvi, Davide Cozzolino, Giada Zingarini, Giovanni Poggi, Koki Nagano, and Luisa Verdoliva. 2023. On the detection of synthetic images generated by diffusion models. In *ICASSP 2023-2023 IEEE International Conference on Acoustics, Speech and Signal Processing (ICASSP)*, pages 1–5. IEEE.

David C Epstein, Ishan Jain, Oliver Wang, and Richard Zhang. 2023. Online detection of ai-generated images. In *Proceedings of the IEEE/CVF International Conference on Computer Vision*, pages 382–392.

Diego Gragnaniello, Davide Cozzolino, Francesco Marra, Giovanni Poggi, and Luisa Verdoliva. 2021. Are gan generated images easy to detect? a critical analysis of the state-of-the-art. In *2021 IEEE international conference on multimedia and expo (ICME)*, pages 1–6. IEEE.

Kaiming He, Xiangyu Zhang, Shaoqing Ren, and Jian Sun. 2016. Deep residual learning for image recognition. In *Proceedings of the IEEE conference on computer vision and pattern recognition*, pages 770–778.

Tsung-Yi Lin, Michael Maire, Serge Belongie, James Hays, Pietro Perona, Deva Ramanan, Piotr Dollár, and C Lawrence Zitnick. 2014. Microsoft coco: Common objects in context. In *Computer Vision–ECCV 2014: 13th European Conference, Zurich, Switzerland, September 6-12, 2014, Proceedings, Part V 13*, pages 740–755. Springer.

Vivian Liu and Lydia B Chilton. 2022. Design guidelines for prompt engineering text-to-image generative models. In *Proceedings of the 2022 CHI conference on human factors in computing systems*, pages 1–23.

lllyasviel. 2024. Fooocus. https://github.com/lllyasviel/Fooocus.

Zeyu Lu, Di Huang, Lei Bai, Jingjing Qu, Chengyue Wu, Xihui Liu, and Wanli Ouyang. 2024. Seeing is not always believing: Benchmarking human and model perception of ai-generated images. *Advances in Neural Information Processing Systems*, 36.

Midjourney, Inc. 2024. Midjourney. https://www.midjourney.com.

Daeeol Park, Hyunsik Na, and Daeseon Choi. 2024. Performance comparison and visualization of ai-generated-image detection methods. *IEEE Access*.

Derrick Parkhurst, Klinton Law, and Ernst Niebur. 2002. Modeling the role of salience in the allocation of overt visual attention. *Vision research*, 42(1):107–123.

Andreea Pocol, Lesley Istead, Sherman Siu, Sabrina Mokhtari, and Sara Kodeiri. 2023. Seeing is no longer believing: A survey on the state of deepfakes, ai-generated humans, and other nonveridical media. In *Computer Graphics International Conference*, pages 427–440. Springer.

Dustin Podell, Zion English, Kyle Lacey, Andreas Blattmann, Tim Dockhorn, Jonas Müller, Joe Penna, and Robin Rombach. 2023. Sdxl: Improving latent diffusion models for high-resolution image synthesis. *arXiv preprint arXiv:2307.01952*.

Aditya Ramesh, Mikhail Pavlov, Gabriel Goh, Scott Gray, Chelsea Voss, Alec Radford, Mark Chen, and Ilya Sutskever. 2021. Zero-shot text-to-image generation. In *Proceedings of the 38th International Conference on Machine Learning*, volume 139 of *Proceedings of Machine Learning Research*, pages 8821–8831. PMLR.

Robin Rombach, Andreas Blattmann, Dominik Lorenz, Patrick Esser, and Björn Ommer. 2021. High-resolution image synthesis with latent diffusion models. *Preprint*, arXiv:2112.10752.

Zeyang Sha, Zheng Li, Ning Yu, and Yang Zhang. 2023. De-fake: Detection and attribution of fake images generated by text-to-image generation models. In *Proceedings of the 2023 ACM SIGSAC Conference on Computer and Communications Security*, pages 3418–3432.

Vera Wesselkamp, Konrad Rieck, Daniel Arp, and Erwin Quiring. 2022. Misleading deep-fake detection with gan fingerprints. In *2022 IEEE Security and Privacy Workshops (SPW)*, pages 59–65. IEEE.

Mingjian Zhu, Hanting Chen, Qiangyu Yan, Xudong Huang, Guanyu Lin, Wei Li, Zhijun Tu, Hailin Hu, Jie Hu, and Yunhe Wang. 2024. Genimage: A million-scale benchmark for detecting ai-generated image. *Advances in Neural Information Processing Systems*, 36.

A Appendix

A.1 Questionnaire

Figure 10 shows the repeated structure of questions for each image presented to the study participants.

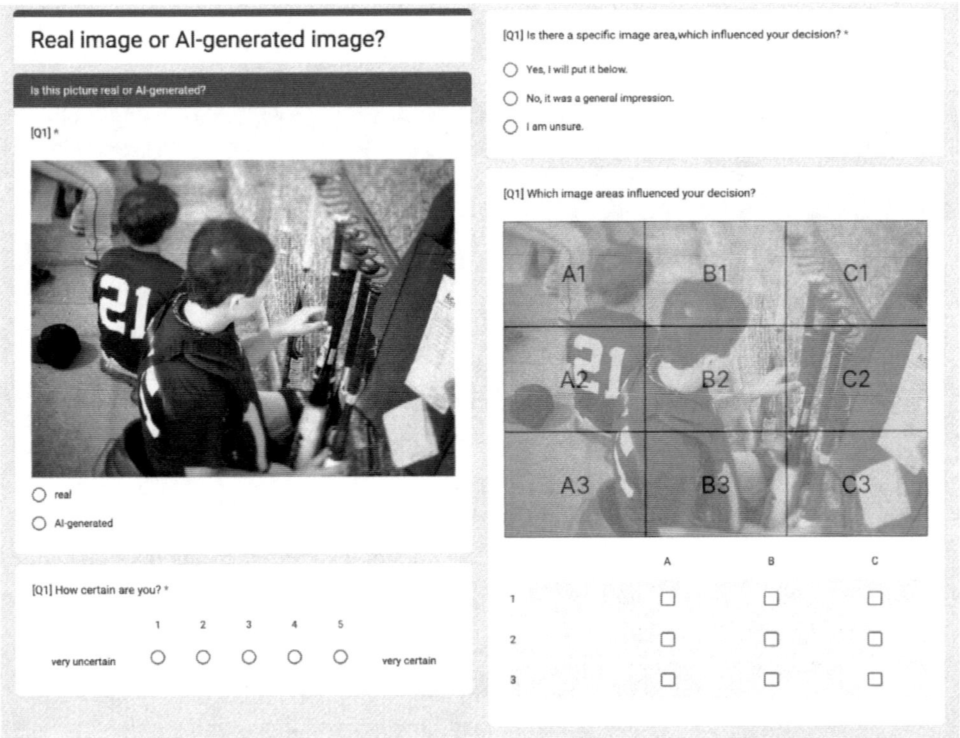

Figure 10: Questions and answer possibilities for image classification in our user study.

A.2 Comparing model results on images with and without downsampling

Table 5 shows the difference in the model's detection performance for downsampled (study images) and original images. Note that it is the downsampled SDXL images which are influencing the overall worse performance of the model on the study dataset. The low recall for the downsampled SDXL images (0.1250) indicates that a lot of these images were incorrectly classified as real. This influences the precision for real images weakening the corresponding F-score.

Subset	Positives	Study images			Original images		
		F1	Recall	Precision	F1	Recall	Precision
All	Real	0.6957	1.0000	0.5333	0.9524	1.0000	0.9091
All	AI	0.7200	0.56250	1.0000	0.9744	0.9500	1.0000
SP	AI	0.7097	0.5500	1.0000	0.9610	0.9250	1.0000
LP	AI	0.7302	0.5750	1.0000	0.9873	0.9750	1.0000
Fooocus	AI	1.0000	1.0000	1.0000	1.0000	1.0000	1.0000
SDXL	AI	0.2222	0.1250	1.0000	0.9474	0.9000	1.0000
COCO	Real	0.6957	1.0000	0.5333	0.9524	1.0000	0.9091

Table 5: F1, recall and precision scores of Grag2021 for specific subsets of the study images. "Positives" indicates the class for which the F1 score was calculated. "Study images" refers to the results on the study images, "Original images" to the results on the corresponding images without downsampling.

A.3 Model output for an AI-generated image

In contrast to Figure 9, which visualizes the output of the model for a real image, here we can see the output for an examplary AI-generated image. Note the relatively uniform noise in contrast to the clearly visible object edges in Figure 9.

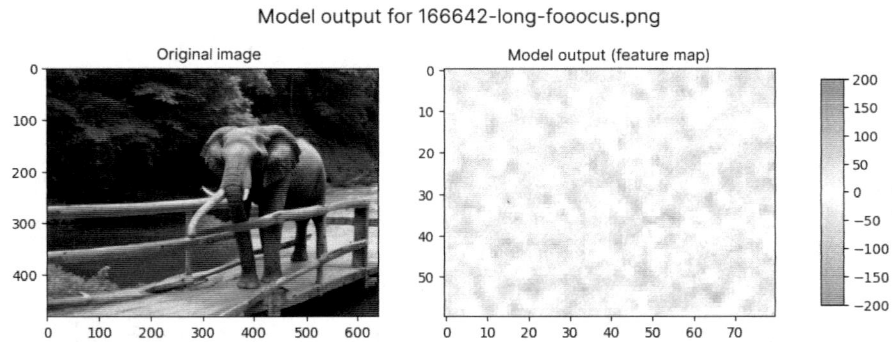

Figure 11: Visualization of the model's output feature map of 60 x 80 logit values for an AI-generated image from the study dataset

A.4 Image area selection of the model and the participants

Figure 12 shows the most selected / activated image areas for an examplary image from the study dataset. Note that we can see an overlap of the most activated image areas by the model and the most selected ones by the study participants.

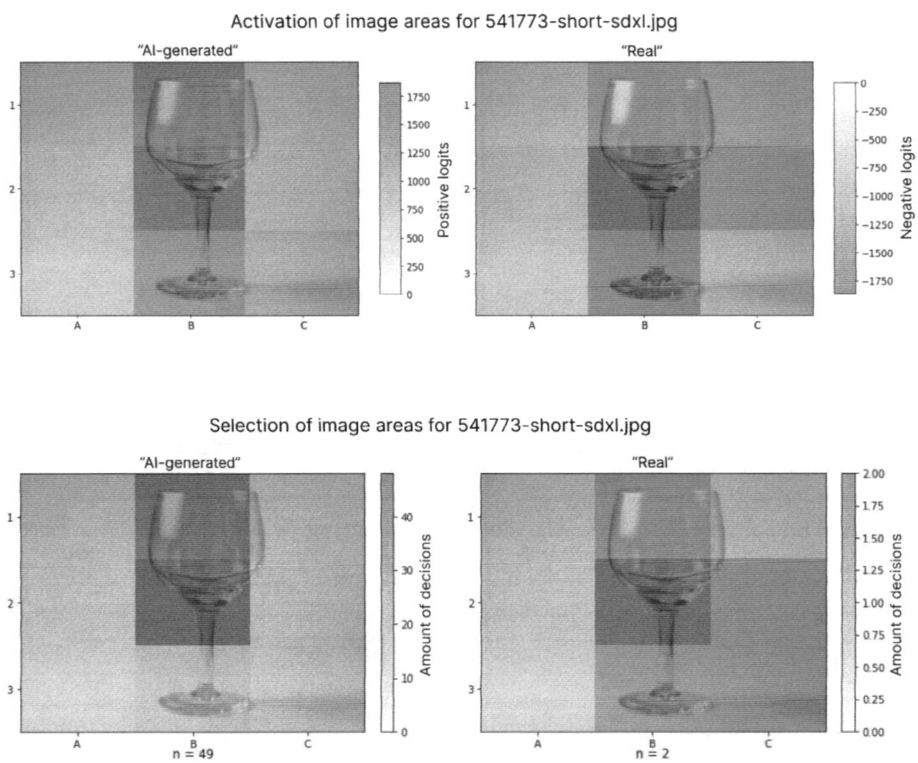

Figure 12: Comparison of the most activated image areas by the detector (each grid field sums up the corresponding logit values from the detector feature map) (top) and the most selected image areas by the test participants (bottom)

Mirror Minds : An Empirical Study on Detecting LLM-Generated Text via LLMs

Josh Baradia*
PES University
Karnataka, India
joshbaradia22@gmail.com

Shubham Gupta*
IIT Jodhpur
Rajasthan, India
gupta.37@iitj.ac.in

Suman Kundu
IIT Jodhpur
Rajasthan, India
suman@iitj.ac.in

Abstract

The use of large language models (LLMs) is inevitable in text generation. LLMs are intelligent and slowly replacing the search engines. LLMs became the de facto choice for conversation, knowledge extraction, and brain storming. This study focuses on a question: 'Can we utilize the generative capabilities of LLMs to detect AI-generated content?' We present a methodology and empirical results on four publicly available data sets. The result shows, with 90% accuracy it is possible to detect AI-generated content by a zero-shot detector utilizing multiple LLMs. [1]

1 Introduction

The rapid advancement of large language models (LLMs) has elevated their text generation capabilities to levels comparable to human writing (OpenAI, 2024; Anthropic, 2023; Chowdhery et al., 2023). LLMs have become integral to various aspects of daily life and are increasingly pivotal in numerous professional workflows (Veselovsky et al., 2023). They aid in tasks such as creating advertising slogans (Murakami et al., 2023), composing news articles (Yanagi et al., 2020), and generating stories (Yuan et al., 2022). Additionally, the influence of LLMs is profoundly shaping the development of many sectors and disciplines, including education (Susnjak, 2022), law (Cui et al., 2024), and medicine (Thirunavukarasu et al., 2023). However, the remarkable proficiency of generative language models in producing text has simultaneously heightened worries about their potential misuse in fields such as phishing, spreading misinformation, and academic dishonesty. Regrettably, humans are only marginally better than chance at distinguishing between AI-generated text and text written by people (Gehrmann et al., 2019a). Consequently, we aim to create an automated system that can accurately identify AI-generated texts to help prevent their harmful applications.

LLMs no longer require task-specific learning or alignment between task inputs and desired outputs because they have already acquired most necessary knowledge during pre-training. Instruction tuning helps to better align the model with the anticipated responses for user tasks. Motivated by this, we do an empirical study on a question that **"Can a LLM detect the content written by AI?"**.

We developed a three-step methodology to identify AI-generated texts. In the first step, we generate a contextually relevant query from the input through large language model. Essentially, we aim to create an input prompt that logically follows the given text. The process of generating this prompt is very fast ($\sim$2 seconds) due to the nature of zero-shot inference in LLMs. Once the prompt is generated, we pass it to two different large language models, each of which produces a response of approximately the same length as the input text. These generated texts are then compared with original input for the final classification. We use BLEU (BiLingual Evaluation Understudy) (Papineni et al., 2002) and Meteor (Banerjee and Lavie, 2005) score as comparative measures. We tested our methodology on four publicly available datasets, and the results show that our pipeline can detect AI-generated text with an accuracy of approximately 90%.

2 Related Work

Earlier detection methods primarily relied on feature-based approaches, such as analyzing the frequency of rare bigrams (Grechnikov et al., 2009), n-gram frequencies (Badaskar et al., 2008), or top-k word patterns as used in GLTR (Gehrmann et al., 2019b). However, as machine-generated text becomes increasingly sophisticated, a shift toward

*Both authors contribute equally.

[1] Code repository: https://github.com/shubhamgpt007/MirrorMinds-LLMDetector

Proceedings of the 1st Workshop on GenAI Content Detection (GenAIDetect), pages 59–67
January 19, 2025.

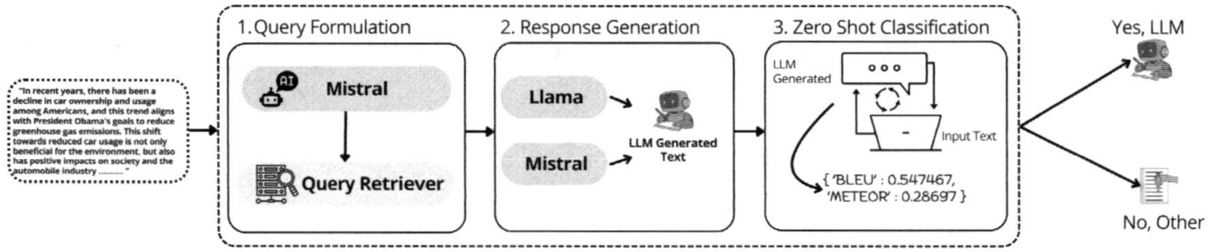

Figure 1: An overview of our proposed approach to detect LLM generated text

trained-based methods has emerged. For exmaple, recent literature to detect AI-generated texts include Guo et al. (2023), who fine-tuned RoBERTa to identify texts in English and Chinese as either AI-generated or human-written, facing challenges with overfitting that degraded performance on out-of-domain data. Also, OpenAI Text Classifier (OpenAI, Jan 2023) and GPTZero (Tian, 2023) that detects AI-generated text by training on the input data. A notable challenge with these models is the need for periodic retraining to keep pace with updates and advancements in new large language models (LLMs). Another approach, DetectGPT by (Mitchell et al., 2023), employs a zero-shot classifier that assumes AI-generated texts exhibit lower model probabilities compared to originals, but struggles with short texts due to its need for lengthy inputs to understand context. Additionally, Kirchenbauer et al. (2023) explored using watermarks in AI-generated texts to aid detection, though this method can compromise text readability and watermark removal presents further difficulties. In a very recent times, DNA-GPT (Yang et al., 2024) proposed which provides a distinctive and effective approach to identifying GPT-generated text by leveraging the inherent differences in continuation patterns between human-written and AI-generated content.

3 Methodology

3.1 Overview of LLM-Detector

Figure 1 illustrates the structure of our proposed zero-shot classification methodology. This method employs a large language model-based detector for zero-shot inferencing to categorize input text as either AI-generated or not. Our zero-shot classification model comprises three modules: 1) Query Formulation, which identifies the contextual query from the input text using a large language model; 2) Response Generation, which creates multiple responses, approximately equal in length to the input text, for the identified query using various large language models; 3) Classification Module, which determines whether the input text is AI-generated or not. The subsequent sections provide a detailed description of each module.

3.2 Query Formulation

The Query Formulation module is a crucial component of our zero-shot classification methodology, designed to interpret and extract the contextual query from the input text. Utilizing a large language model, this module analyzes the text to identify key themes, questions, or topics inherent within the content. Importance of query formulation is in ensuring precise interpretation of complex inputs, aligning subsequent analysis with the thematic intent of the original text. For this, we have used Mistral-7B (Jiang et al., 2023) model that is capable to handle complex queries and generate responses that are contextually relevant and linguistically accurate. The effectiveness of this process is paramount as it sets the foundation for subsequent modules. By distilling complex and varied input texts into precise queries, this module ensures that the response generation process is accurately aligned with the thematic direction of the initial input, thereby facilitating a more targeted and coherent analysis in later stages of classification.

Given a textual input denoted as $T = \{w_1, w_2, \cdots, w_n\}$, consisting of a sequence of n tokens, were tokenized and fed into the Mistral LLM model to obtain the query text Q as follows:

$$Q = \text{Mistral}(T) \quad (1)$$

LLM's Input Prompt:
Generate a query that encapsulates the main theme of the following text.{text}

3.3 Response Generation

Response Generation module leverages multiple large language models to produce responses that are contextually aligned and approximately equal in length to the original input text from the identified query Q. We have used two LLMs viz. Llama3-7B (Dubey et al., 2024) and Mistral-7B (Jiang et al., 2023) to generate the response with the extracted query prompt. Given a query Q, generate the responses from the different LLMs as follows:

$$T' = \text{Mistral}(Q); \;\; T'' = \text{Llama}(Q) \tag{2}$$

LLM's Input Prompt:
Generate a response between {textWordCount} to {1.1 *textWordCount} words for the following question.{Q}

3.4 Classification Module

The similarity of the generated text (T' and T'') is assessed by comparing it to the reference input text T. We employ two well-known metrics for this comparison: the BLEU (Papineni et al., 2002) and Meteor (Banerjee and Lavie, 2005) scores, which help quantify the closeness of the generated text to the original text in terms of syntax and semantics. For each LLM, a BLEU and a Meteor score are calculated independently using generated and original text. After obtaining these scores, we select max score among different generated texts BLEU and Meteor score to get a final BLEU score (B_f) and a final Meteor score (M_f). Finally, by setting a specific threshold for these scores, we can determine whether the input text resembles AI-generated content or not, aiding in distinguishing between the two.

$$B_f = max(BLEU(T, T'), BLEU(T, T'')) \tag{3}$$

$$M_f = max(Meteor(T, T'), Meteor(T, T'')) \tag{4}$$

4 Experiments and Results

4.1 Datasets & Evaluation Metrics

As our objective is to evaluate model performance on the task to identify AI-generated text, we chose four publicly available datasets Daigt Data (Kleczek, 2013) which consists essay generated from the Falcon-180B (DS1) and Llama-70B (DS2), Palm dataset (Muhammad, 2023) (DS3), and Human-and-AI dataset (Shayan, 2023) (DS4). Human-and-AI dataset originally consists 432k+ entries but for this experiment we have filtered 10K human and 10k AI-generated essays. The details of these datasets can be found in Table 1.

In order to evaluate the performance of our methodology, we employed the BLEU and Meteor scores to assess the similarity between the generated responses and the original text. The average scores for each metric across dataset are reported in the results section. Additionally, we calculated accuracy based on thresholds set for these scores specifically, a BLEU score of 0.52 and a Meteor score of 0.27. These values are found using grid search with varying BLEU from 0.5 to 0.6 and Meteor from 0.2 to 0.3. To validate this combination, we tested various BLEU and Meteor score configurations using the DS4 dataset, which contains both human-generated and LLM-generated text. As shown in Figure 2, the optimal generalization results were achieved with a BLEU score of 0.52 and a Meteor score of 0.27.

Table 1: Distribution of data across different datasets.

Dataset	Description	Distribution
DS1	DAIGT dataset generated from Falcon-180B	1055 rows
DS2	DAIGT dataset generated from Llama-70B and Falcon-180B	7000 rows
DS3	Essay dataset generated by PaLM	1384 rows
DS4	Articles dataset consists of Human and AI generated text	20000 rows

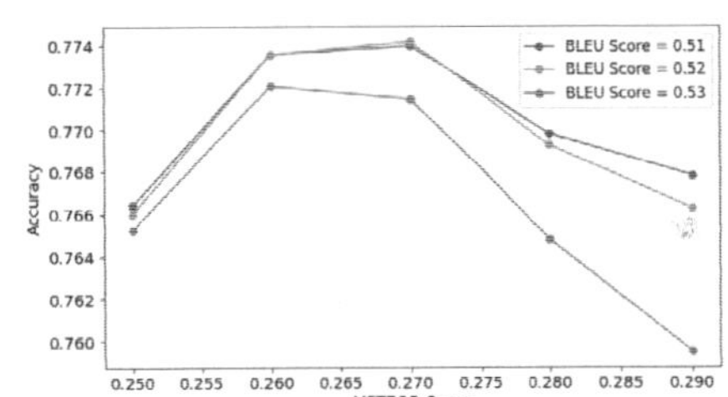

Figure 2: Comparison of accuracy among various BLEU and Meteor scores for DS4 dataset.

4.2 Experimental Setup

We configured Llama and Mistral LLM's using parameters viz. num_return_sequences = 1, top_p = 0.95, top_k=40, num_beams=2, max_length = 1.1*textWordCount. These models are run on NVIDIA A30 with 24 GB of GPU memory. As part of textual pre-processing, symbols such as '@', '#' and hyperlinks are removed.

5 Results

Table 2 shows the performance of our detection system under various LLM configurations. We utilized the Mistral LLM for query extraction and employed two LLMs, Llama3 and Mistral, for response generation. The table compares the outcomes across three models: the first model uses Llama3 for response generation, the second employs Mistral, and the third integrates both LLMs in the response generation process. We have experimented our methodology across all the datasets mentioned in the Table 1. In the results table, we have reported BLEU, Meteor Score and Accuracy of each model.

The results presented in Table 2 show that using a single LLM for response generation yields specific scores: the Llama model achieved a BLEU score of 0.61 and a Meteor score of 0.33, while the Mistral model scored 0.56 and 0.31 for the DS1, respectively. However, combining both LLMs led to improved scores of 0.62 for BLEU and 0.34 for Meteor. Furthermore, the accuracy of the combined LLM methodology was notably higher, at 0.92, outperforming the single-model setups. In a similar manner, we can observe the results for DS2 and DS3 datasets.

Table 2: Performance comparison of different models across datasets

Dataset	Model	BLEU	METEOR	Accuracy
DS1	Ours-Llama	0.61	0.33	0.90
	Ours-Mistral	0.56	0.31	0.63
	Ours-(Llama+Mistral)	**0.62**	**0.34**	**0.92**
DS2	Ours-Llama	0.61	0.31	0.83
	Ours-Mistral	0.56	0.31	0.49
	Ours-(Llama+Mistral)	**0.62**	**0.32**	**0.86**
DS3	Ours-Llama	0.62	0.33	0.96
	Ours-Mistral	0.59	0.32	0.90
	Ours-(Llama+Mistral)	**0.63**	**0.34**	**0.98**
DS4	Ours-Llama	0.59	0.31	0.77
	Ours-Mistral	0.58	0.31	0.69
	Ours-(Llama+Mistral)	**0.60**	**0.32**	**0.78**

For the DS4 datasets, which include both human-written and AI-generated text, we observed a consistent pattern in the performance metrics. When using single LLMs, the Llama model achieved a BLEU score of 0.59 and a Meteor score of 0.31, while the Mistral model scored 0.58 for BLEU and 0.31 for Meteor. However, the combined LLM model showed improved results, with a BLEU score of 0.60 and a Meteor score of 0.32. In terms of accuracy, the final model with both LLMs significantly outperformed the single-model setups.

The figure above shows how accuracy changes with METEOR scores for various BLEU levels (0.51, 0.52, and 0.53). Across all BLEU scores, accuracy peaks at a METEOR value of 0.27, indicating that this is the best METEOR range for maximum accuracy. BLEU ratings of 0.51 and 0.52 show comparable patterns, with somewhat better accuracy at 0.52, especially near the peak. However, BLEU score 0.53 has consistently worse accuracy throughout all METEOR scores, with a greater fall after the peak. This implies that, while higher BLEU scores might increase performance up to a certain point, an excessively high BLEU score may have a declining or negative influence on accuracy, emphasising the need of balancing METEOR and BLEU scores to obtain optimal performance.

6 Usability Analysis

6.1 Robustness on different word ranges

In our study, we evaluated the performance of our zero-shot detector across different text lengths by selecting samples with 0-100, 100-200, 200-300, 300-400, 500-600, and over 600 words. The findings, presented in Table 3, show a distinct pattern. The detector struggles with accuracy in smaller samples (0-100 words) but shows marked improvements as the word count increases. This increase in performance in larger text samples suggests that the zero-shot detector benefits from more contextual information, which may be lacking in shorter texts. This behavior could also be influenced by the domain-specific characteristics or statistical properties of the LLM models. We have discussed case studies related to short-length, long-length, and human-written text in Appendix section 9 .

Table 3: Comparison of datasets across different word ranges.

Dataset	Metric	0-100	100-200	200-300	300-400	400-500	500-600	>600
DS1	accuracy	0.50	0.82	0.90	0.96	0.89	-	-
	# rows	2	51	515	432	55	-	-
DS2	accuracy	0.0	0.41	0.70	0.83	0.91	0.90	0.89
	# rows	1	27	714	2161	2569	1208	320
DS3	accuracy	-	1.0	0.98	0.99	0.97	0.98	0.72
	# rows	-	1	180	658	474	60	11
DS4	accuracy	0.04	0.65	0.75	0.76	0.85	0.83	0.87
	# rows	84	1586	4790	6159	3790	1676	1915

6.2 Inference time for the detection

In our detector, we have two core phases Query Formulation and Response Generation which takes time for the final classification. In Table 4, we have reported the query formulation time (QFT) and response generation time (RGT) phases across all the datasets. From the value, it is evident that Query Formulation Time (QFT) is relatively stable across datasets, ranging from 1.15 seconds to 1.95 seconds, suggesting that the extraction process is largely unaffected by dataset complexity. In ad-

Table 4: Analysis of time (in sec) taken across different phases 1) Query Formulation Time (QFT) and 2) Response generation Time (RGT)in zero-shot detector.

Dataset	QET	RGT	
		Llama3	Mistral
DS1	1.95	13.38	10.03
DS2	1.15	19.83	15.63
DS3	1.18	17.64	13.48
DS4	1.81	17.11	12.72

dition, Response Generation Time (RGT) varied more significantly, with Llama3 showing longer processing times across all datasets compared to Mistral. Specifically, both models took the longest time on DS2, indicating higher complexity or computational demands associated with this dataset.

7 Conclusion

While Large Language Models (LLMs) have demonstrated impressive capabilities in generative tasks, mitigating their potential misuse remains crucial. This paper provides an empirical study by introducing a simple yet effective method for detecting AI-generated text. Our zero-shot detector leverages the extensive knowledge acquired by LLMs during pre-training, enabling them to identify their own generated outputs. Note that this methodology does not involve any training for classification; instead, it classifies input text using zero-shot inference. The process begins by extracting the main context of the input text, using the LLM to generate a corresponding response. This approach facilitates the detection of AI-generated text by comparing the similarity between the input and the generated text. Instruction tuning refines the model's alignment with the user expected responses in text detection tasks. We evaluated our method across four publicly available datasets, which cover responses generated by different LLMs and including both in-domain and out-of-domain (OOD) data. The results confirm that our approach effectively detects texts produced by LLMs. Future efforts will focus on enhancing detection capabilities for short texts and extending the application to other areas such as fake news detection.

8 Limitations

Our study has some limitations, primarily because it relies exclusively on two large language models, Mistral and Llama3. However, numerous state-of-the-art LLMs cited in the literature may outperform these and address challenges with short text detection more effectively. Additionally, while we utilize standard evaluation metrics like BLEU and Meteor, other metrics such as Perplexity and ROUGE might provide a more accurate assessment of machine translation quality.

Acknowledgement

Suman Kundu is supported by MeitY, Government of India under the grant no.4(2)/2024-ITEA.

References

Anthropic. 2023. Model card and evaluations for claude models. Accessed on 16.09.2024.

Sameer Badaskar, Sachin Agarwal, and Shilpa Arora. 2008. Identifying real or fake articles: Towards better language modeling. In *Proceedings of the Third International Joint Conference on Natural Language Processing: Volume-II*.

Satanjeev Banerjee and Alon Lavie. 2005. METEOR: An automatic metric for MT evaluation with improved correlation with human judgments. In *Proceedings of the ACL Workshop on Intrinsic and Extrinsic Evaluation Measures for Machine Translation and/or Summarization*, pages 65–72, Ann Arbor, Michigan. Association for Computational Linguistics.

Aakanksha Chowdhery, Sharan Narang, Jacob Devlin, Maarten Bosma, Gaurav Mishra, Adam Roberts, Paul Barham, Hyung Won Chung, Charles Sutton, Sebastian Gehrmann, Parker Schuh, Kensen Shi, Sasha Tsvyashchenko, Joshua Maynez, Abhishek Rao, Parker Barnes, Yi Tay, Noam Shazeer, Vinodkumar Prabhakaran, Emily Reif, Nan Du, Ben Hutchinson, Reiner Pope, James Bradbury, Jacob Austin, Michael Isard, Guy Gur-Ari, Pengcheng Yin, Toju Duke, Anselm Levskaya, Sanjay Ghemawat, Sunipa Dev, Henryk Michalewski, Xavier Garcia, Vedant Misra, Kevin Robinson, Liam Fedus, Denny Zhou, Daphne Ippolito, David Luan, Hyeontaek Lim, Barret Zoph, Alexander Spiridonov, Ryan Sepassi, David Dohan, Shivani Agrawal, Mark Omernick, Andrew M. Dai, Thanumalayan Sankaranarayana Pillai, Marie Pellat, Aitor Lewkowycz, Erica Moreira, Rewon Child, Oleksandr Polozov, Katherine Lee, Zongwei Zhou, Xuezhi Wang, Brennan Saeta, Mark Diaz, Orhan Firat, Michele Catasta, Jason Wei, Kathy Meier-Hellstern, Douglas Eck, Jeff Dean, Slav Petrov, and Noah Fiedel. 2023. Palm: Scaling language modeling with pathways. *J. Mach. Learn. Res.*, 24:240:1–240:113.

Jiaxi Cui, Munan Ning, Zongjian Li, Bohua Chen, Yang Yan, Hao Li, Bin Ling, Yonghong Tian, and Li Yuan. 2024. Chatlaw: A multi-agent collaborative legal assistant with knowledge graph enhanced mixture-of-experts large language model. *Preprint*, arXiv:2306.16092.

Abhimanyu Dubey, Abhinav Jauhri, Abhinav Pandey, Abhishek Kadian, Ahmad Al-Dahle, Aiesha Letman, Akhil Mathur, Alan Schelten, Amy Yang, Angela Fan, et al. 2024. The llama 3 herd of models. *arXiv preprint arXiv:2407.21783*.

Sebastian Gehrmann, Hendrik Strobelt, and Alexander Rush. 2019a. GLTR: Statistical detection and visualization of generated text. In *Proceedings of the 57th Annual Meeting of the Association for Computational Linguistics: System Demonstrations*, pages 111–116, Florence, Italy. Association for Computational Linguistics.

Sebastian Gehrmann, Hendrik Strobelt, and Alexander M Rush. 2019b. Gltr: Statistical detection and visualization of generated text. *arXiv preprint arXiv:1906.04043*.

EA Grechnikov, GG Gusev, AA Kustarev, and A Raigorodsky. 2009. Detection of artificial texts. *RCDL2009 Proceedings. Petrozavodsk*, pages 306–308.

Biyang Guo, Xin Zhang, Ziyuan Wang, Minqi Jiang, Jinran Nie, Yuxuan Ding, Jianwei Yue, and Yupeng Wu. 2023. How close is chatgpt to human experts? comparison corpus, evaluation, and detection. *Preprint*, arXiv:2301.07597.

Albert Q. Jiang, Alexandre Sablayrolles, Arthur Mensch, Chris Bamford, Devendra Singh Chaplot, Diego de las Casas, Florian Bressand, Gianna Lengyel, Guillaume Lample, Lucile Saulnier, Lélio Renard Lavaud, Marie-Anne Lachaux, Pierre Stock, Teven Le Scao, Thibaut Lavril, Thomas Wang, Timothée Lacroix, and William El Sayed. 2023. Mistral 7b. *Preprint*, arXiv:2310.06825.

John Kirchenbauer, Jonas Geiping, Yuxin Wen, Jonathan Katz, Ian Miers, and Tom Goldstein. 2023. A watermark for large language models. In *Proceedings of the 40th International Conference on Machine Learning*, volume 202 of *Proceedings of Machine Learning Research*, pages 17061–17084. PMLR.

D. Kleczek. 2013. Daigt proper train dataset. Accessed on 16.09.2024.

Eric Mitchell, Yoonho Lee, Alexander Khazatsky, Christopher D. Manning, and Chelsea Finn. 2023. Detectgpt: zero-shot machine-generated text detection using probability curvature. In *Proceedings of the 40th International Conference on Machine Learning*, ICML'23. JMLR.org.

R. Muhammad. 2023. Palm from google gen-ai. Accessed on 16.09.2024.

Soichiro Murakami, Sho Hoshino, and Peinan Zhang. 2023. Natural language generation for advertising: A survey. *Preprint*, arXiv:2306.12719.

OpenAI. 2024. Gpt-4 technical report. *Preprint*, arXiv:2303.08774.

OpenAI. Jan 2023. Ai text classifier. Accessed on 16.09.2024.

Kishore Papineni, Salim Roukos, Todd Ward, and Wei-Jing Zhu. 2002. Bleu: a method for automatic evaluation of machine translation. In *Proceedings of the 40th Annual Meeting of the Association for Computational Linguistics*, pages 311–318, Philadelphia, Pennsylvania, USA. Association for Computational Linguistics.

G. Shayan. 2023. Ai vs human text. Accessed on 16.09.2024.

Teo Susnjak. 2022. Chatgpt: The end of online exam integrity? *Preprint*, arXiv:2212.09292.

Arun James Thirunavukarasu, Darren Shu Jeng Ting, Kabilan Elangovan, Laura Gutierrez, Ting Fang Tan, and Daniel Shu Wei Ting. 2023. Large language models in medicine. *Nature medicine*, 29(8):1930–1940.

Edward Tian. 2023. Gptzero: An ai text detector. Accessed on 16.09.2024.

Veniamin Veselovsky, Manoel Horta Ribeiro, and Robert West. 2023. Artificial artificial artificial intelligence: Crowd workers widely use large language models for text production tasks. *ArXiv*, abs/2306.07899.

Yuta Yanagi, Ryohei Orihara, Yuichi Sei, Yasuyuki Tahara, and Akihiko Ohsuga. 2020. Fake news detection with generated comments for news articles. In *2020 IEEE 24th International Conference on Intelligent Engineering Systems (INES)*, pages 85–90.

Xianjun Yang, Wei Cheng, Yue Wu, Linda Ruth Petzold, William Yang Wang, and Haifeng Chen. 2024. DNA-GPT: Divergent n-gram analysis for training-free detection of GPT-generated text. In *The Twelfth International Conference on Learning Representations*.

Ann Yuan, Andy Coenen, Emily Reif, and Daphne Ippolito. 2022. Wordcraft: Story writing with large language models. IUI '22, page 841–852, New York, NY, USA. Association for Computing Machinery.

9 Appendix

9.1 Example of short length text

We analyzed a sample from the DS4 dataset, originally labeled as AI-generated. When testing our zero-shot detector on this sample, it has BLEU scores of 0.37 and 0.26, and METEOR scores of 0.19 and 0.16 for Llama3 and Mistral, respectively. The quantitative data clearly indicates that our method struggles to recognize short-length LLM-generated texts. Additionally, it is evident that the context of the generated text does not align with the context of the input text.

Input Text:
Creating a new substance from chemicals is a complex process that requires extensive research. First, one must understand the chemical composition of different substances and learn the specific names of chemical compounds. Once knowledge is attained, experiments can be conducted in a lab to test different chemical reactions. The benefits of trial and error far outweigh the risks, and the potential for creating something incredibly valuable is infinite.

Query:
What are the steps involved in creating a new substance from chemicals and why is it a valuable process?

Llama Text:
The process of creating a new substance from chemicals involves several steps. First, chemists identify the desired properties of the new substance, such as its melting point, boiling point, and solubility. Next, they select the appropriate chemicals and react them.
Mistral Text:
Creating a new substance from chemicals, also known as organic synthesis or chemical synthesis, is a valuable process due to its potential to yield novel compounds with unique properties. The steps involved include: 1. Identifying the target.

9.2 Example of long length text

We analyzed a sample from the DS1 dataset, originally labeled as AI-generated. When testing our zero-shot detector on this sample, it has BLEU scores of 0.59 and 0.53, and METEOR scores of 0.33 and 0.28 for Llama3 and Mistral, respectively. The quantitative data clearly indicates that our method identifies this LLM-generated text as correct. We can also observe the generated text that it is contextually aligned and have similar patterns with input text.

Input Text:
When people ask for advice, they sometimes talk to more than one person. This is because seeking multiple opinions can help someone make a better choice. For example, if someone wants to buy a new phone, they might ask their friends, family, and even do some research online. By doing this, they can get different perspectives on which phone to buy, the pros and cons of each phone, and even the best deals available. Seeking multiple opinions can also help someone avoid making a bad decision. For instance, if someone is considering dropping out of school, they might talk to their parents, teachers, and even a counselor. By doing this, they can get advice on the consequences of dropping out, the benefits of staying in school, and even alternative options that they might not have considered before. In conclusion, seeking multiple opinions can help someone make a better choice by providing them with different perspectives, information, and advice. It can also help them avoid making a bad decision by considering all the options available. Therefore, it is always a good idea to seek multiple opinions before making a big decision.

Query:
What are the benefits of seeking multiple opinions before making a decision?

Llama Text:
Seeking multiple opinions before making a decision can have numerous benefits. Firstly, it allows individuals to gain a more comprehensive understanding of the situation and the potential outcomes. By hearing from different perspectives, individuals can identify potential risks and challenges that they may not have considered otherwise. This can help them make a more informed decision that takes into account a wider range of factors. Another benefit of seeking multiple opinions is that it can help individuals avoid making impulsive decisions. When faced with a decision, it's easy to get caught up in the moment and make a choice without fully considering the consequences. By taking the time to seek out multiple opinions, individuals can slow down the decision-making process and make a more thoughtful choice. Additionally, seeking multiple opinions can help individuals build stronger relationships with others. When individuals take the time to listen to and consider the opinions of others, they demonstrate that they value and respect those individuals. This can help build trust and strengthen relationships over time. Finally, seeking multiple opinions can help individuals develop a greater sense of confidence in their decision-making abilities. When individuals take the time to consider multiple perspectives.

Mistral Text:
Seeking multiple opinions before making a decision is an essential practice that can bring numerous benefits. Here are some reasons why it's a good idea to gather various perspectives before finalizing a choice: 1. Broaden your understanding: Each person brings a unique perspective based on their experiences, knowledge, and expertise. By seeking multiple opinions, you can broaden your understanding of the issue at hand and gain new insights that you may not have considered otherwise. 2. Identify potential biases: When making a decision, it's essential to be aware of any potential biases that may influence your thinking. Seeking multiple opinions can help you identify any biases that you may not have been aware of and allow you to make a more objective decision. 3. Improve decision-making quality: Multiple opinions can help improve the quality of your decision-making. By considering various perspectives, you can weigh the pros and cons more thoroughly and make a more informed decision. 4. Enhance problem-solving skills: Seeking multiple opinions.

9.3 Example of human-written text

We analyzed a sample from the DS4 dataset, originally labeled as human-written. When testing our zero-shot detector on this sample, it has BLEU scores of 0.41 and 0.29, and METEOR scores of 0.21 and 0.17 for Llama3 and Mistral, respectively. We can also see that while LLMs use complex vocabulary to respond to queries, humans tend to narrate using simpler words.

Input Text:
The author that evaluates how well the author supports the idea that studying Venus is a worth pursuit despite the danger. By saying" NASA is working on other approaches to studying Venus Food example some simplified elections made of silicon carbide have been tested in a chamber simulating". This evidence support my claim because the people AOE studying Food big things like how well studying Venus is a worthy pursuit. Another claim that evaluates how well the author supports the idea that studying Venus is a worth pursuit despite. In paragraph 8 it says" striving to meet the challenge presented by Venus has value. Not only because of the insight to be gained on the planet itself. Which explain that studying Venus is a worth pursuit despite. The conclusion I have about" the challenge of exploring Venus" was. It seems like if u study it itś a good thing. Because its very important to NASA it says that in the Leading. So maybe if u do it you would be successful.

Query:
What are the reasons why studying Venus is a worth pursuit despite the challenges and dangers it presents?

Llama Text:
Studying Venus is a worthwhile pursuit despite the challenges and dangers it presents because of the significant scientific and technological advancements it can bring about. Venus is often referred to as Earthś "sister planet" due to its similar size and proximity to the sun, making it an ideal target for studying planetary formation and evolution. By studying Venus, scientists can gain valuable insights into the early history of our solar system and the processes that shaped the planets. Furthermore, Venus offers a unique opportunity to study a planet with a thick atmosphere, which can provide valuable insights into the Earthś own atmospheric processes. The extreme conditions on Venus, such as the crushing pressure and scorching temperatures, also present a challenge for scientists to develop new technologies and instruments that can withstand such conditions. This can lead to breakthroughs in fields such as materials science and engineering. Additionally, studying Venus can also provide valuable information about the potential for life on other planets.

Mistral Text:
Studying Venus, the second planet from the Sun, presents unique challenges and dangers due to its extreme conditions. However, these challenges make Venus a worthwhile pursuit for scientists and explorers for several reasons. Firstly, Venus is the closest planet to Earth, making it an accessible target for exploration. Despite its inhospitable environment, understanding Venus's geology, atmosphere, and climate can provide valuable insights into the early history of Earth and the solar system as a whole. For instance, Venus's volcanic activity and corrosive atmosphere offer clues to the conditions that shaped our own planet billions of years ago. Secondly, Venus is the only planet in our solar system with a similar size, mass, and composition to Earth. Studying Venus can help us better understand the processes that shape terrestrial planets.

Benchmarking AI Text Detection: Assessing Detectors Against New Datasets, Evasion Tactics, and Enhanced LLMs

Shushanta Pudasaini and **Luis Miralles-Pechuán** and **Marisa Llorens Salvador**
School of Computer Science
Technological University Dublin
Dublin, Ireland

David Lillis
University College Dublin
Dublin, Ireland

Abstract

The rapid advancement of Large Language Models (LLMs), such as GPT-4, has sparked concerns regarding academic misconduct, misinformation, and the erosion of originality. Despite the growing number of AI detection tools, their effectiveness is often undermined by sophisticated evasion tactics and the continuous evolution of LLMs. This research benchmarks the performance of leading AI detectors, including OpenAI Detector, RADAR, and ArguGPT, across various text domains, evaded content, and text generated by cutting-edge LLMs. Our experiments reveal that current detection models show considerable unreliability in real-world scenarios, mainly when tested against diverse data domains and novel evasion strategies. The study underscores the need for enhanced robustness in detection systems and provides valuable insights into areas of improvement for these models. Additionally, this work lays the groundwork for future research by offering a comprehensive evaluation of existing detectors under challenging conditions, fostering a deeper understanding of their limitations. The experimental code and datasets are publicly available for further benchmarking on Github.

Keywords: Large Language Models, Evasion Strategies, Cross Domain Testing, AI-Generated text detection.

1 Introduction

LLMs such as GPT-3 have achieved strong performance on several tasks that require on-the-fly reasoning or domain adaptation, such as translation, question answering, and representing text in an intelligent, presentable form (Brown, 2020). In addition, more advanced LLMs such as GPT-4 have achieved human-level performance on academic benchmarks, such as passing a simulated bar examination by scoring around the top 10% test takers (Achiam et al., 2023). On top of that, OpenAI released OpenAI o1-preview, a new series of reasoning models claiming that these models perform on the level of PhD students for challenging benchmark tasks such as Graduate-Level Google-Proof Q&A (GPQA) benchmark in subjects like physics, biology and chemistry (Zhong, 2024). These events highlight the exceptional capabilities of LLMs in academia and their fast-paced evolution.

With exceptional capabilities, LLMs have also brought several threats like academic misconduct (Pudasaini et al., 2024), such as students submitting assignments, passing examinations, misinformation (Liu et al., 2024), lack of creativity (Zhao et al., 2024), and other several ethical concerns (Yan et al., 2024). To overcome these threats, efficient detection of texts generated from LLMs is necessary.

Much research has been done to build highly effective and robust LLM-generated text detection algorithms. A training-based classifier, zero-shot detection, watermarking, and adversarial learning approach are some approaches used to create models that detect LLM-generated text. The training-based classifier approaches treat the problem as a binary classification problem, and labelled datasets are trained on several algorithms to build models such as ArguGPT (Liu et al., 2023), Ghostbuster (Verma et al., 2023) and roberta-base-openai-detector (Solaiman et al., 2019).

A zero-shot learning approach that allows a model to handle tasks it hasn't been explicitly trained for by using its existing general knowledge has also been used to develop detectors such as Binoculars (Hans et al., 2024), Fast-DetectGPT (Bao et al., 2023), DNA-GPT (Yang et al., 2023), and GLTR (Gehrmann et al., 2019).

Similarly, watermarking techniques by which subtle, identifiable patterns are embedded into the generated content, making it easier to recognise as AI-generated, has resulted in models such as POSTMARK (Chang et al., 2024), Waterfall (Lau

Proceedings of the 1st Workshop on GenAI Content Detection (GenAIDetect), pages 68–77
January 19, 2025.

et al., 2024), WaterJudge (Molenda et al., 2024), and WaterMax (Giboulot and Teddy, 2024).

Other approaches, such as adversarial learning, which enhances the robustness of LLM-generated text detection algorithms by exposing the detector to an evasion example while training, have been introduced, resulting in models like RADAR (Hu et al., 2023) and OUTFOX (Koike et al., 2024).

Along with developing LLM detectors, several evasion techniques, such as paraphrasing and synonym replacement, have also been developed. These evasion techniques are applied after generating text from LLMs so that the detector cannot identify the text as AI-generated. These evasion techniques may be as simple as adding a single space randomly before a comma (Cai and Cui, 2023), deleting an article randomly in a sentence, inserting misspellings randomly in a sentence (Antoun et al., 2023), and replacing some random characters with homoglyph characters (Kirchenbauer et al., 2023).

There are also more complex techniques such as paraphrasing(Krishna et al., 2024), word substitution (Peng et al., 2024), sentence substitution (Peng et al., 2024) and prompting (Wang et al., 2024)(using instructions to generate human-written text while generating text) also have been successful in fooling AI detectors. Thus, it becomes crucial to benchmark existing open-source, state-of-the-art AI detectors against these evasion strategies.

One gap in developing efficient AI detectors is the reliance on subsets of a single dataset for training and testing, compromising the models' robustness (Sadasivan et al., 2023). Such detectors claim high accuracy. However, they typically fail when tested in real settings with very different data from the training and testing set. Out-of-distribution testing of the existing open-source state-of-the-art detectors is crucial (Dugan et al., 2024).

In addition, it is essential to benchmark the existing AI detectors with new generators in the space. The rapid growth in the development of new LLMs with exceptional learning capabilities, along with the increasing number of parameters, has brought up new concepts such as reasoning (Huang and Chang, 2022), coherent and cohesive long-form text generation (Cho et al., 2018), and multilingual and cross-domain capabilities (Chua et al., 2024). This leads to the research question of whether the existing state-of-the-art AI detectors are up to date and capable of detecting text from new LLMs with such capabilities or not. Thus, benchmarking such detectors against recent powerful LLMs is vital.

This paper's main contribution is benchmarking existing AI detectors against different datasets (text from various domains, text created using evasion techniques, and text generated by the latest LLMs such as GPT4 o from OpenAI and Command R+ from Cohere). This benchmarking allows for an in-depth analysis of the different detectors' performance in the context of their general approach to AI-generated text detection and the various types of datasets used.

The rest of the paper is organised as follows. Section 2 discusses the previous benchmarking research done for LLM-generated text detection. Section 3 explains the methodology used to perform the benchmarking experiment. Section 4 highlights the results obtained from the experiment. Section 5 discusses the analysis of the results obtained. Section 7 finally presents the conclusions obtained from the experiment.

2 Literature Review

As the race for the development of robust AI detectors and the development of evasion strategies to fool AI detectors goes on, along with the development of even more powerful LLMs, research has been conducted to test the efficiency of existing LLM-generated text detection algorithms developed so far.

Initially, the benchmarking experiments used human-written and AI-generated text with no further modifications. Chaka (Chaka, 2024) did a comprehensive review of 17 published articles on testing AI detectors. The author found that the machine-generated text used in testing in those research papers was from ChatGPT-3.5 and ChatGPT-4 (Chaka, 2024). Madelyn A. et al. (Flitcroft et al., 2024) tested three AI detector tools, OpenAI's AI Classifer, Content at Scale, and Originality.AI, on human-written scientific and AI-generated articles, which are not modified. The tool Originality.ai achieved 100% accuracies in this testing (Flitcroft et al., 2024). However, people may not just copy-paste the text entirely from LLMs and may try to modify the text.

Weber-Wulff et al. (Weber-Wulff et al., 2023) tested AI detection tools on three types of AI-generated text: AI-generated text, AI-generated text with subsequent human edits, and AI-generated text with subsequent machine paraphrasing and found those detectors were biased in classifying AI-generated text as human-written.

Similarly, Elkhatat et al. (Elkhatat et al., 2023) also tested five AI detection tools on human-written control responses and saw an increase in false positives in the case of human-written control responses. These experiments against types of text observations (human-written, ai-generated and human editing on AI-generated texts) show that AI detectors are easily evaded with few further human edits on AI-generated texts.

When evasion techniques are applied to AI-generated texts, AI detectors fail to perform well. Krishna et al. (Krishna et al., 2023) developed an 11B parameter paraphrase generation model called DIPPER, which successfully evaded detectors such as watermarking, GPTZero, DetectGPT, and OpenAI's text classifier and further proposed a retrieval method which detected 80% to 97% of paraphrased generations across various settings, while only 1% of human-written text was mistakenly flagged as AI-generated. However, after 4 months, Sadasivan et al. (Sadasivan et al., 2023) again introduced the recursive paraphrasing attack, which degraded the accuracy of several watermarking-based, zero-shot-based, neural-network-based and retrieval-based detectors. The adversarial learning approach has been introduced to develop recent AI-generated text detectors such as RADAR (Hu et al., 2023) and OUTFOX (Koike et al., 2024). There seems to be a gap in benchmarking these recently developed models on different scenarios.

The challenge with building AI detectors is these detectors need to be able to generalise on unseen domain text (Wang et al., 2023). For example, existing AI detectors may fail when tested on text generated from recent LLMs released after the AI detector's release. Dugan et al. (Dugan et al., 2024) tested neural and metrics-based AI detectors on AI-generated texts from 11 different LLMs. They found that the performance of these AI detectors varies according to the LLMs used for generating the text. However, with the release of even more powerful LLMs with reasoning capabilities like GPT-4o, it remains to be seen how these detection algorithms perform on the text generated from such new LLMs.

3 Methodology

The benchmarking of existing open-source LLM-generated text detection algorithms was done on three significant aspects: out-of-distribution along with multiple domain testing, evasion applied dataset testing and new LLM-generated text dataset testing.

The data flow in the benchmarking experiment has been represented in Fig 1. Initially, sampling was performed from two datasets, i.e., the M4 dataset and the HC3 dataset, resulting in a data subset of 3,000 AI-generated text observations and 3,000 AI-generated text observations. The 3,000 AI-generated observations were further edited using the six evasion strategies, and 3,000 evasion-applied AI-generated text observations were created for each evasion strategy. Additionally, 1,000 new AI-generated text observations were generated from each of the recent LLMs, i.e. GPT-4 o and Command R plus, using the same prompt used to create them previously.

Because of computational constraints, the number of observations was limited. The complete testing dataset representing multiple datasets, multiple evasion strategies, and multiple generators was passed to the AI-generated text detection algorithms, and the benchmarking results were obtained.

3.1 Datasets Used

Data samples from different datasets and domains were required for out-of-distribution and multidomain testing of the AI detectors. Two different datasets were used; details of the datasets are explained below.

- **M4 Dataset**: M4 is a large-scale dataset for **M**achine-generated text detection which included data samples from **M**ultiple languages, **M**ultiple domains and **M**ultiple LLMs (Wang et al., 2023). Sampling was applied concerning the domain of the data for multidomain analysis. The subset considered 1,000 observations representing text from multiple domains such as Arxiv, Wikipedia, and Reddit. Thus, combining these data from multiple sources resulted in 3,000 human-written observations and respective 3,000 AI-generated observations.

- **HC3 Dataset**: The Human ChatGPT Comparision Corpus(HC3) is built from tens of thousands of comparison responses from ChatGPT and human experts in financial, medical, legal, and open-domain (Guo et al., 2023). Sampling was done randomly from the dataset, resulting in 3,000 human-written and 3,000 AI-generated texts.

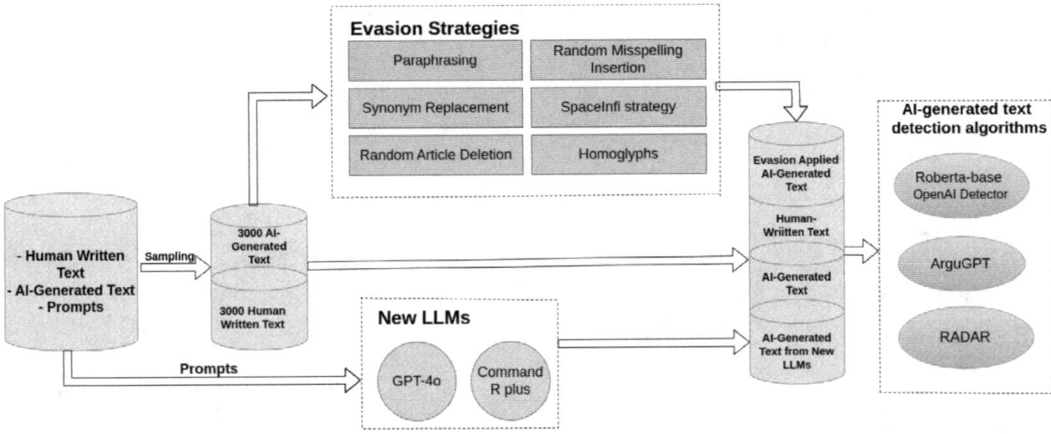

Figure 1: Diagram representing the process, the components used, and the data flow of the benchmarking experiment.

3.2 Evasion Strategies

Several evasion techniques have been used to try to fool AI detectors. This paper used six evasion techniques to modify the selected AI-generated text subsets. The evasion strategies applied are discussed below.

- **Paraphrasing**: Paraphrasing is the most commonly used technique to fool AI detectors (Sadasivan et al., 2023; Krishna et al., 2024). Parrot paraphrase, which uses LLMs to paraphrase a given text, was used to paraphrase each text and generate the paraphrased AI-generated samples (Damodaran, 2021).
- **Synonym Replacement**: A random word from each sentence in the given text was replaced with the word's synonym retrieved from the Natural Language Toolkit (NLTK) (Bird et al., 2009) Synset and replaced in the sentence.
- **Misspelling**: A random word from a sentence is replaced with a misspelt version of the word. Further insertion of random misspellings is also an effective evasion strategy for BERT-based AI detectors (Antoun et al., 2023).
- **Article Deletion**: This technique removes a random article from a sentence from the AI-generated text (Odri and Yoon, 2023).
- **SpaceInfi Strategy**: Cai et al. (Cai and Cui, 2023) introduced the SpaceInfi strategy in which a space is inserted before a random comma in the AI-generated text to fool the detectors.
- **Homoglyph Attack**: Unicode characters that look very similar to the existing characters in the sentence are referred to as homoglyphs. Kirchenbauer et al. (Kirchenbauer et al., 2023) mentioned that homoglyph changing the tokenization process affects the prediction of AI detectors. We applied homoglyphs to 50% characters in the AI-generated text, as suggested by Antoun et al. (Antoun et al., 2023).

Similarly, text generated from recently released LLMs, such as OpenAI's GPT-4o model (Islam and Moushi, 2024) and the Command R plus model from the open-source LLM community Cohere, was included in the whole testing set for benchmarking the detectors against recent LLMs. The test data size was limited to 1,000 observations for each model due to the limitations of OpenAI API and Cohere API credits.

3.3 LLM-generated text detection algorithms

Several algorithms have been developed to solve LLM-generated text detection following different approaches such as watermarking, zero-shot, training-based classifiers, fine-tuning LLMs, adversarial learning methods, and treating another LLM as a detector (Wu et al., 2023). The detection algorithms used are described below.

- **ArguGPT**: ArguGPT is a RoBERTa base classifier trained on a corpus of 4,038 argumentative essays generated by 7 GPT models. It achieved 90% accuracy in document, paragraph, and sentence level classification (Liu et al., 2023). This model was chosen for the experiment because the dataset used to train was composed of multiple sources (in-class or homework exercises, TOEFL writing tasks, GRE writing tasks), multiple generators and on multiple levels.

- **RADAR**: Robust AI-text Detector via Adversarial Learning (RADAR) is built by joint adversarial training of a paraphraser model and a detector model (Hu et al., 2023). RADAR model claims to outperform existing AI-detection methods, mainly when paraphrasing is applied as an evasion strategy (Hu et al., 2023). This model was chosen because it is trained by using an adversarial approach.

- **OpenAI Detector**: Openai-detector is an open-source language model based on transformers 125 billion parameters released by OpenAI (Solaiman et al., 2019). This model was chosen because it was trained using the outputs of the 1.5B GPT-2 model.

4 Experiments and Results

This section presents the results of the benchmarking experiment on different edge cases such as multiple domain data, multiple evasion applied data and multiple LLMs generated data.

The testing of a model developed on another dataset rather than testing on the test set of its dataset is referred to as out-of-distribution testing. The benchmarking dataset used in this experiment was not used to train and test these models. Such out-of-distribution testing of the AI detectors was done by passing the text sample observations to the models. Prediction probability was obtained for each of the predictions. We set the threshold value to 0.5 to classify it as human-written or AI-generated. Out-of-distribution set testing was performed with text observations from the M4 and HC3 datasets. We calculated the accuracy of the binary classification evaluation metrics, F1-score, false negatives, false positives, precision, and recall. The results obtained are shown in Table 1.

The detectors were benchmarked on different evasion strategies. The results from the benchmarking against the evasion strategies are shown in Table 2. The results from benchmarking the detectors against recent LLMs are shown in Table 3. The baseline dataset was created using the GPT 3.5 Turbo model.

5 Discussion and Analysis

This section discusses and analyses the experiment's results to report key insights. The discussion is organised according to the edge cases, i.e., out-of-distribution and Multi-Domain, Evasion Strategies, and recent LLMs. We mainly analyse the False Negatives (FN), which gives the number of AI-generated text observations that were misclassified as human-written, representing the inefficiency of the AI-detector tools.

5.1 Analysis of out-of-distribution and Multi Domain Benchmarking

Existing AI detectors suffer from data drift while testing on text observations from another dataset or another domain. From the results in Table 1, we can see that the evaluation metrics of these AI detector models are very different when tested on various datasets with the same number of testing observations. Differences of 8.9 % accuracy in the OpenAI detector model, 4.95 % in the RADAR model and 5.21 % in the ArguGPT model were reported while tested on the M4 and HC3 datasets. This indicates that these models are not resistant to data drift over new domains and settings, i.e. sentence, paragraph or document-level text.

The detectors cannot be relied upon to be used in real settings. From Table 1, we can see a big difference in terms of False Negatives (AI-generated samples misclassified as human-written) and False Positives (human-written samples that were misclassified as AI-generated) when the detectors are tested on text observation they are not familiar with as the models tested were tested on entirely different data. We can see an increase in false positives: 1 to 43 in OpenAI detector, 175 to 553 in RADAR and 155 to 472 in ArguGPT. This is critical because, with such an increase in FPs, it will be challenging to use the detectors in real settings as many submitting authentic human-written text will be flagged as AI-generated. Similarly, the increase in false negatives (FN) in the OpenAI detector from 113 to 607 suggests that the detector fails to detect AI-generated text when data observations are taken from different domains.

5.2 Analysis of Benchmarking on Evasion Strategies

OpenAI detector performs poorly when evasion techniques are applied. Table 2 shows that the OpenAI detector is very poor at detecting AI-generated

Model	Dataset	Acc.(%)	F1	FN	FP	Prec	Rec
OpenAI Detector	M4	89.17	0.8804	607	43	0.982	0.797
	HC3	98.09	0.9806	113	1	0.999	0.962
RADAR	M4	94.13	0.9413	177	175	0.943	0.941
	HC3	89.18	0.8994	96	553	0.84	0.968
ArguGPT	M4	92	0.9257	8	472	0.863	0.997
	HC3	97.41	0.9748	0	155	0.951	1

Table 1: Benchmarking results of AI Detectors tested on two different subsets of M4 and HC3 with 6,000 samples each. All observations are texts in which no evasion strategies have been applied. Evaluation Accuracy (Acc.), F1-Score (F1), False Negatives (FN), False Positives (FP), Prec (Precision), and Rec (Recall) were obtained from out-of-distribution testing of models.

texts where evasion techniques have been applied. The baseline(non-evasive) experiment was conducted on the observation where no evasion techniques were applied, which resulted in 89.17% accuracy in the M4 dataset and 98.1% accuracy in the HC3 dataset. Using that as a reference point, we can see the decrease in the model's accuracy under different evasion techniques. The decreasing accuracy was found to be similar to both datasets. This is mainly because the OpenAI detector was trained using the texts generated from the GPT-2 model on which no modifications were applied to the generated text, and the training samples do not cover multiple domains and multiple generation settings on the GPT-2 model (Solaiman et al., 2019).

RADAR model could effectively identify the AI-generated text on which further paraphrasing and synonym replacement evasion techniques were applied. According to the results in Table 2, we can see that the RADAR model performs even better in evasion techniques such as paraphrasing and synonym replacement. The RADAR model is trained jointly with a detector and paraphrased with an adversarial approach. We observed a decrease in false negatives even after evasion had been applied. However, the RADAR model still behaves poorly under other evasion techniques, such as article deletion and homoglyphs. Thus, we can conclude that adversarial learning methods incorporating several evasion strategies rather than a single evasion strategy (paraphrasing in RADAR) could lead to developing an AI detector resistant to any evasion strategies.

The performance of the ArguGPT model could be better, with some evasion strategies such as homoglyphs and misspellings. The results of the ArguGPT model from Table 2 The ArguGPT model worked well when no evasive techniques were applied (8 false negatives among 3,000 observations in the M4 data set and 0 false negatives among 3,000 observations in the HC3 dataset). However, false negatives started to increase when evasion techniques were applied. This is also mainly because the data in the model's training did not contain such observations where evasion techniques have been applied further.

5.3 Analysis of Benchmarking on Recent LLMs

During the test of observations from the latest LLMs, the performance of existing AI detectors was degraded. However, ArguGPT performed better than other models. The results in Table 3 show that models such as OpenAI Detector and RADAR fail faster than the ArguGPT model while testing text generated from recent LLMs: GPT-4o and Command R plus. The baseline represents the result when the text was generated from the GPT-3.5 model. The number of false negatives increased from 197 to 509 while testing text generated from Command R plus and 985 while testing text generated from the GPT-4o model, indicating that the OpenAI detector cannot perform well on text detection from recent LLMs.

Similarly, in the case of the RADAR model, false negatives were increased from 52 to 299 while testing on the text generated from the Command R plus model and to 777 while testing on the text generated from the GPT-4o model, indicating the RADAR model also does not perform well on text detection from recent LLMs. However, the ArguGPT model saw only a slight increase in false negatives (3 in GPT-3.5, 23 in Command R plus and 70 in GPT-4o). This behaviour can be attributed to the ArguGPT model being trained using the text generated from 7 GPT models (Liu et al., 2023). The GPT4o model could also fool the AI detectors more than other LLMs. We believe the

Model	Dataset	Experiment Type	Acc. (%)	F1	FN (Out of 3,000)
OpenAI Detector	M4 Dataset	non-evasive	89.17	0.8804	607
		evasion whitespace	79.63	0.7488	1,179
		evasion removed articles	51.95	0.0999	2,840
		evasion misspell text	51.77	0.0934	2,851
		evasion homoglyph	61.53	0.3891	2,265
		evasion synonym replaced	74.55	0.6651	1,484
		evasion paraphrase	68.67	0.553	1,837
	HC3 Dataset	non-evasive	98.1	0.9806	113
		evasion whitespace	92.02	0.9133	478
		evasion removed articles	60.33	0.3425	2379
		evasion misspell text	51.12	0.0443	2932
		evasion homoglyph	50.6	0.6693	1983
		evasion synonym replaced	83.43	0.8015	993
		evasion paraphrase	55.76	0.6932	1840
RADAR	M4 Dataset	non-evasive	94.13	0.9413	177
		evasion whitespace	95.10	0.9515	119
		evasion removed articles	71.47	0.6309	1,537
		evasion misspell text	47.10	0.0006	2,999
		evasion homoglyph	47.15	0.0025	2,996
		evasion synonym replaced	94.27	0.9427	169
		evasion paraphrase	95.70	0.9576	83
	HC3 Dataset	non-evasive	89.18	0.8995	96
		evasion whitespace	89.82	0.9059	58
		evasion removed articles	82.06	0.8215	523
		evasion misspell text	41.70	0.0305	2,945
		evasion homoglyph	40.92	0.0045	2,991
		evasion synonym replaced	88.98	0.8974	108
		evasion paraphrase	90.22	0.9100	34
ArguGPT	M4 Dataset	non-evasive	92	0.9257	8
		evasion whitespace	91.93	0.9251	12
		evasion removed articles	89.20	0.8971	176
		evasion misspell text	42.13	0.0000	3,000
		evasion homoglyph	42.13	0.0000	3,000
		evasion synonym replaced	91.87	0.9244	16
		evasion paraphrase	90.55	0.9111	95
	HC3 Dataset	non-evasive	97.42	0.9748	0
		evasion whitespace	97.40	0.9747	1
		evasion removed articles	97.23	0.9730	11
		evasion misspell text	47.42	0.0000	3,000
		evasion homoglyph	47.42	0.0000	2,999
		evasion synonym replaced	97.37	0.9743	3
		evasion paraphrase	96.58	0.9664	50

Table 2: Benchmarking on different evasion strategies across models on 6000 samples for each experiment. Evaluation Accuracy (Acc.), F1-Score (F1), and False Negatives (FN) were obtained under different evasion strategies for different datasets while testing on OpenAI Detector, RADAR, and ArguGPT models.

high reasoning capabilities of the GPT-4o model can explain these results (Chen et al., 2024).

Models	LLM tested against	Acc. (%)	F1-Score	FN (Out of 1000)
OpenAI Detector	baseline	89.9	0.8883	197
	Command R plus	71.94	0.5569	509
	GPT-4o	50.5	0.0294	985
RADAR	baseline	95.65	0.9561	52
	Command R plus	81.77	0.7614	299
	GPT-4o	59.4	0.3545	777
ArguGPT	baseline	95.5	0.9568	3
	Command R plus	94	0.9363	23
	GPT-4o	92.15	0.9222	70

Table 3: Benchmarking results of the AI detectors tested against the 1,000 text generated from the GPT-4o and Command R plus models. Evaluation Accuracy (Acc.), F1-Score (F1), and False Negatives (FN) reported for baseline, GPT-4 o and Command R plus model.

6 Limitations

The benchmarking experiment is done on three popular open-source AI text detection models. However, the framework and the datasets can be used for testing other AI text detection models also. Six of the basic evasion strategies have been applied to generate data samples representing evasion applied to AI-generated text. This can be further enhanced by employing other additional evasion strategies such as adversarial prompting (Wang et al., 2024), Substitution-based In-Context example Optimization method (SICO) (Lu et al., 2023), Self-color testing-based substitution (Wu and Chandrasekaran, 2024), and Reinforcement learning (Nicks et al., 2023).

7 Conclusion

The research highlighted significant critical challenges in detecting LLM-generated text. The existing state-of-the-art algorithms for detecting text generated from LLMs could perform better when tested on text generated from other domains, LLM-generated text on which evasion techniques have been applied and text generated from recent LLMs. This leads to the conclusion that these algorithms cannot be fully relied upon and used in university assignment checkers and research publications checkers.

From the results and analysis of the benchmarking against the evasion techniques, we can observe that even simple techniques, such as deleting a random article or misspelling a random word on AI-generated text, can bypass existing AI detectors. Similarly, from the results and analysis from multiple benchmarking experiments, it can be concluded that training on diverse AI-generated text, including evasion techniques, domains, and outputs from various LLMs, improves detector robustness.

Furthermore, the knowledge extracted from the critical analysis of the models serves as the baseline for future researchers trying to build robust AI-generated text detection algorithms. Training models representing a wide variety of data (multiple domains, multiple evasion techniques being applied, and multiple generators) may lead to the development of more efficient detectors. Likewise, training models with an adversarial learning approach that aims to train the model in different adversarial attacks and scenarios also seems promising.

The benchmarking in this research validates that the problem is far from solved. The knowledge gained from the critical analysis of the results concerning different approaches will help shape the further development of algorithms that can solve the problem more robustly. With the contribution of knowledge extracted from the experiment and thorough analysis of the results obtained, we aim to develop more robust AI detectors.

Acknowledgments

This publication has emanated from research conducted with the financial support of/supported in part by a grant from Science Foundation Ireland under Grant number 18/CRT/6183. For Open Access, the author has applied a CC by public copyright licence to any Author Accepted Manuscript version arising from this submission.

References

Josh Achiam, Steven Adler, Sandhini Agarwal, Lama Ahmad, Ilge Akkaya, Florencia Leoni Aleman, Diogo Almeida, Janko Altenschmidt, Sam Altman, Shyamal Anadkat, et al. 2023. Gpt-4 technical report. *arXiv preprint arXiv:2303.08774*.

Wissam Antoun, Virginie Mouilleron, Benoît Sagot, and Djamé Seddah. 2023. Towards a robust detection of language model generated text: Is chatgpt that easy to detect? *arXiv preprint arXiv:2306.05871*.

Guangsheng Bao, Yanbin Zhao, Zhiyang Teng, Linyi Yang, and Yue Zhang. 2023. Fast-detectgpt: Efficient zero-shot detection of machine-generated text via conditional probability curvature. *arXiv preprint arXiv:2310.05130*.

Steven Bird, Ewan Klein, and Edward Loper. 2009. *Natural language processing with Python: analyzing text with the natural language toolkit*. " O'Reilly Media, Inc.".

Tom B Brown. 2020. Language models are few-shot learners. *arXiv preprint arXiv:2005.14165*.

Shuyang Cai and Wanyun Cui. 2023. Evade chatgpt detectors via a single space. *arXiv preprint arXiv:2307.02599*.

Chaka Chaka. 2024. Reviewing the performance of ai detection tools in differentiating between ai-generated and human-written texts: A literature and integrative hybrid review. *Journal of Applied Learning and Teaching*, 7(1).

Yapei Chang, Kalpesh Krishna, Amir Houmansadr, John Wieting, and Mohit Iyyer. 2024. Postmark: A robust blackbox watermark for large language models. *arXiv preprint arXiv:2406.14517*.

Zhiyuan Chen, Yaning Li, and Kairui Wang. 2024. Optimizing reasoning abilities in large language models: A step-by-step approach.

Woon Sang Cho, Pengchuan Zhang, Yizhe Zhang, Xiujun Li, Michel Galley, Chris Brockett, Mengdi Wang, and Jianfeng Gao. 2018. Towards coherent and cohesive long-form text generation. *arXiv preprint arXiv:1811.00511*.

Lynn Chua, Badih Ghazi, Yangsibo Huang, Pritish Kamath, Ravi Kumar, Pasin Manurangsi, Amer Sinha, Chulin Xie, and Chiyuan Zhang. 2024. Crosslingual capabilities and knowledge barriers in multilingual large language models. *arXiv preprint arXiv:2406.16135*.

Prithiviraj Damodaran. 2021. Parrot: Paraphrase generation for nlu.

Liam Dugan, Alyssa Hwang, Filip Trhlik, Josh Magnus Ludan, Andrew Zhu, Hainiu Xu, Daphne Ippolito, and Chris Callison-Burch. 2024. Raid: A shared benchmark for robust evaluation of machine-generated text detectors. *arXiv preprint arXiv:2405.07940*.

Ahmed M Elkhatat, Khaled Elsaid, and Saeed Almeer. 2023. Evaluating the efficacy of ai content detection tools in differentiating between human and ai-generated text. *International Journal for Educational Integrity*, 19(1):17.

Madelyn A Flitcroft, Salma A Sheriff, Nathan Wolfrath, Ragasnehith Maddula, Laura McConnell, Yun Xing, Krista L Haines, Sandra L Wong, and Anai N Kothari. 2024. Performance of artificial intelligence content detectors using human and artificial intelligence-generated scientific writing. *Annals of Surgical Oncology*, pages 1–7.

Sebastian Gehrmann, Hendrik Strobelt, and Alexander M Rush. 2019. Gltr: Statistical detection and visualization of generated text. *arXiv preprint arXiv:1906.04043*.

Eva Giboulot and Furon Teddy. 2024. Watermax: breaking the llm watermark detectability-robustness-quality trade-off. *arXiv preprint arXiv:2403.04808*.

Biyang Guo, Xin Zhang, Ziyuan Wang, Minqi Jiang, Jinran Nie, Yuxuan Ding, Jianwei Yue, and Yupeng Wu. 2023. How close is chatgpt to human experts? comparison corpus, evaluation, and detection. *arXiv preprint arXiv:2301.07597*.

Abhimanyu Hans, Avi Schwarzschild, Valeriia Cherepanova, Hamid Kazemi, Aniruddha Saha, Micah Goldblum, Jonas Geiping, and Tom Goldstein. 2024. Spotting llms with binoculars: Zero-shot detection of machine-generated text. *arXiv preprint arXiv:2401.12070*.

Xiaomeng Hu, Pin-Yu Chen, and Tsung-Yi Ho. 2023. Radar: Robust ai-text detection via adversarial learning. *Advances in Neural Information Processing Systems*, 36:15077–15095.

Jie Huang and Kevin Chen-Chuan Chang. 2022. Towards reasoning in large language models: A survey. *arXiv preprint arXiv:2212.10403*.

Raisa Islam and Owana Marzia Moushi. 2024. Gpt-4o: The cutting-edge advancement in multimodal llm. *Authorea Preprints*.

John Kirchenbauer, Jonas Geiping, Yuxin Wen, Jonathan Katz, Ian Miers, and Tom Goldstein. 2023. A watermark for large language models. In *International Conference on Machine Learning*, pages 17061–17084. PMLR.

Ryuto Koike, Masahiro Kaneko, and Naoaki Okazaki. 2024. Outfox: Llm-generated essay detection through in-context learning with adversarially generated examples. In *Proceedings of the AAAI Conference on Artificial Intelligence*, volume 38, pages 21258–21266.

Kalpesh Krishna, Yixiao Song, Marzena Karpinska, John Wieting, and Mohit Iyyer. 2023. Paraphrasing evades detectors of ai-generated text, but retrieval is an effective defense. *Preprint*, arXiv:2303.13408.

Kalpesh Krishna, Yixiao Song, Marzena Karpinska, John Wieting, and Mohit Iyyer. 2024. Paraphrasing evades detectors of ai-generated text, but retrieval is an effective defense. *Advances in Neural Information Processing Systems*, 36.

Gregory Kang Ruey Lau, Xinyuan Niu, Hieu Dao, Jiangwei Chen, Chuan-Sheng Foo, and Bryan Kian Hsiang Low. 2024. Waterfall: Framework for robust and scalable text watermarking. *arXiv preprint arXiv:2407.04411*.

Aiwei Liu, Qiang Sheng, and Xuming Hu. 2024. Preventing and detecting misinformation generated by large language models. In *Proceedings of the 47th International ACM SIGIR Conference on Research and Development in Information Retrieval*, pages 3001–3004.

Yikang Liu, Ziyin Zhang, Wanyang Zhang, Shisen Yue, Xiaojing Zhao, Xinyuan Cheng, Yiwen Zhang, and Hai Hu. 2023. Argugpt: evaluating, understanding and identifying argumentative essays generated by gpt models. *arXiv preprint arXiv:2304.07666*.

Ning Lu, Shengcai Liu, Rui He, Qi Wang, Yew-Soon Ong, and Ke Tang. 2023. Large language models can be guided to evade ai-generated text detection. *arXiv preprint arXiv:2305.10847*.

Piotr Molenda, Adian Liusie, and Mark JF Gales. 2024. Waterjudge: Quality-detection trade-off when watermarking large language models. *arXiv preprint arXiv:2403.19548*.

Charlotte Nicks, Eric Mitchell, Rafael Rafailov, Archit Sharma, Christopher D Manning, Chelsea Finn, and Stefano Ermon. 2023. Language model detectors are easily optimized against. In *The Twelfth International Conference on Learning Representations*.

Guillaume-Anthony Odri and Diane Ji Yun Yoon. 2023. Detecting generative artificial intelligence in scientific articles: evasion techniques and implications for scientific integrity. *Orthopaedics & Traumatology: Surgery & Research*, 109(8):103706.

Xinlin Peng, Ying Zhou, Ben He, Le Sun, and Yingfei Sun. 2024. Hidding the ghostwriters: An adversarial evaluation of ai-generated student essay detection. *arXiv preprint arXiv:2402.00412*.

Shushanta Pudasaini, Luis Miralles-Pechuán, David Lillis, and Marisa Llorens Salvador. 2024. Survey on plagiarism detection in large language models: The impact of chatgpt and gemini on academic integrity. *Preprint*, arXiv:2407.13105.

Vinu Sankar Sadasivan, Aounon Kumar, Sriram Balasubramanian, Wenxiao Wang, and Soheil Feizi. 2023. Can ai-generated text be reliably detected? *arXiv preprint arXiv:2303.11156*.

Irene Solaiman, Miles Brundage, Jack Clark, Amanda Askell, Ariel Herbert-Voss, Jeff Wu, Alec Radford, Gretchen Krueger, Jong Wook Kim, Sarah Kreps, et al. 2019. Release strategies and the social impacts of language models. *arXiv preprint arXiv:1908.09203*.

Vivek Verma, Eve Fleisig, Nicholas Tomlin, and Dan Klein. 2023. Ghostbuster: Detecting text ghostwritten by large language models. *arXiv preprint arXiv:2305.15047*.

Yichen Wang, Shangbin Feng, Abe Bohan Hou, Xiao Pu, Chao Shen, Xiaoming Liu, Yulia Tsvetkov, and Tianxing He. 2024. Stumbling blocks: Stress testing the robustness of machine-generated text detectors under attacks. *arXiv preprint arXiv:2402.11638*.

Yuxia Wang, Jonibek Mansurov, Petar Ivanov, Jinyan Su, Artem Shelmanov, Akim Tsvigun, Chenxi Whitehouse, Osama Mohammed Afzal, Tarek Mahmoud, Toru Sasaki, et al. 2023. M4: Multi-generator, multi-domain, and multi-lingual black-box machine-generated text detection. *arXiv preprint arXiv:2305.14902*.

Debora Weber-Wulff, Alla Anohina-Naumeca, Sonja Bjelobaba, Tomáš Foltnek, Jean Guerrero-Dib, Olumide Popoola, Petr Šigut, and Lorna Waddington. 2023. Testing of detection tools for ai-generated text. *International Journal for Educational Integrity*, 19(1):26.

Junchao Wu, Shu Yang, Runzhe Zhan, Yulin Yuan, Derek F. Wong, and Lidia S. Chao. 2023. A survey on llm-gernerated text detection: Necessity, methods, and future directions. *CoRR*, abs/2310.14724.

Qilong Wu and Varun Chandrasekaran. 2024. Bypassing llm watermarks with color-aware substitutions. *arXiv preprint arXiv:2403.14719*.

Lixiang Yan, Lele Sha, Linxuan Zhao, Yuheng Li, Roberto Martinez-Maldonado, Guanliang Chen, Xinyu Li, Yueqiao Jin, and Dragan Gašević. 2024. Practical and ethical challenges of large language models in education: A systematic scoping review. *British Journal of Educational Technology*, 55(1):90–112.

Xianjun Yang, Wei Cheng, Yue Wu, Linda Petzold, William Yang Wang, and Haifeng Chen. 2023. Dnagpt: Divergent n-gram analysis for training-free detection of gpt-generated text. *arXiv preprint arXiv:2305.17359*.

Yunpu Zhao, Rui Zhang, Wenyi Li, Di Huang, Jiaming Guo, Shaohui Peng, Yifan Hao, Yuanbo Wen, Xing Hu, Zidong Du, Qi Guo, Ling Li, and Yunji Chen. 2024. Assessing and understanding creativity in large language models. *Preprint*, arXiv:2401.12491.

Tianyang Zhong. 2024. Evaluation of openai o1: Opportunities and challenges of agi. *Preprint*, arXiv:2409.18486.

Cross-table Synthetic Tabular Data Detection

G. Charbel N. Kindji[1,2], Lina M. Rojas Barahona[1], Elisa Fromont[2], Tanguy Urvoy[1],

[1]Orange Labs Lannion
first.last@orange.com,
[2]Université de Rennes, CNRS, Inria, IRISA UMR 6074
first.last@irisa.fr
Correspondence: charbel.kindji.orange@gmail.com

Abstract

Detecting synthetic tabular data is essential to prevent the distribution of false or manipulated datasets that could compromise data-driven decision-making. This study explores whether synthetic tabular data can be reliably identified "in the wild"—meaning across different generators, domains, and table formats. This challenge is unique to tabular data, where structures (such as number of columns, data types, and formats) can vary widely from one table to another. We propose three cross-table baseline detectors and four distinct evaluation protocols, each corresponding to a different level of "wildness". Our very preliminary results confirm that cross-table adaptation is a challenging task.

1 Introduction and Related Works

Most studies on synthetic data detection focus on image (Chai et al., 2020; Corvi et al., 2023; Marra et al., 2019; Bammey, 2024), text (Lavergne et al., 2011; Lahby et al., 2022; Hu et al., 2023; Wang et al., 2024; Mitchell et al., 2023), audio (Lopez-Paz and Oquab, 2016), video (face-swap) (Pu et al., 2021), or their combination (Singhal et al., 2020).

Nevertheless, a growing number of generative models for tabular data generation has emerged recently; some are general-purpose (Zhang et al., 2024; Kotelnikov et al., 2023), while others are tailored to specific domains like finance (Sattarov et al., 2023) or healthcare (Hyun et al., 2020). With these advances it will be easier to generate realistically manipulated datasets to fake scientific results or to hide fraud and accouting loopholes. It is therefore essential to focus research efforts on the detection of synthetic tabular data, and to develop detection techniques that are on par with the impressive generative models' capabilities.

Detecting syntetic content issued from a known generative model on a restricted domain is a fairly tractable task. The performance of such a predictor is indeed commonly used for adversarial training (Goodfellow et al., 2020) and as a metric to assess generation performance (Lopez-Paz and Oquab, 2016; Zein and Urvoy, 2022).

However, the challenge intensifies when attempting to detect synthetic data "in the wild" (Stadelmann et al., 2018), namely, when the deployed system has to face modalities and content generators it has never seen during its training phase. Is is known that, even for homogeneous formats like image or text, synthetic content detection systems are not robust to such *cross-generator* and *cross-domain* distribution shifts (Kuznetsov et al., 2024).

When dealing with tabular data, we have to face a stronger form of domain-shift that we call *cross-table* shift. Indeed, for a synthetic table detection system to be useful, is has to cope with different table formats with varying numbers of columns, varying types and varying distributions shapes. Although, the litterature on domain adaptation across the same table structure is vast (see Gardner et al., 2024, for a survey), only a few recent articles propose classifiers that are able to generalize across different tables (Wang and Sun, 2022; Spinaci et al., 2024). To the best of our knowledge, no study on cross-table synthetic data detection has been published yet.

We present a preliminary work with three baselines for synthetic tabular data detection "in the wild." We focus on cross-table robustness among different real-world evaluation scenarios representing various degrees of "wildness", for instance: (i) *No shift:* the model is trained and tested on samples from the same pool of datasets and generators; (ii) *Cross-generator shift:* the model is tested on the same datasets but the test synthetic data is produced by unknown generators; (iii) *Cross-table shift:* the model is tested on holdout datasets and table structures but with synthetic data produced

Proceedings of the 1st Workshop on GenAI Content Detection (GenAIDetect), pages 78–84
January 19, 2025. ©2025 International Conference on Computational Linguistics

by known generators; (iv) *Full shift:* the model is tested on generators and datasets it has never seen before.

We address here the cross-table adaptation by considering two *text-based* baselines where the table rows are first linearized as strings, and a *table-based* transformer with a simple column-wise table-agnostic encoding.

2 Real and Synthetic Data

Real Data: We use 14 common public tabular datasets from the UCI[1] with different sizes, dimensions and domains. These datasets are described in Table 1.

Name	Size	#Num	#Cat
Abalone[2]	4177	7	2
Adult[2]	48842	6	9
Bank Marketing[2]	45211	7	10
Black Friday[2]	166821	6	4
Bike Sharing[2]	17379	9	4
Cardio[3]	70000	11	1
Churn Modelling[3]	4999	8	4
Diamonds[2]	26970	7	3
HELOC[3]	5229	23	1
Higgs[2]	98050	28	1
House 16H[2]	22784	17	0
Insurance[3]	1338	4	3
King[3]	21613	19	1
MiniBooNE[2]	130064	50	1

Table 1: Description of the datasets. "#Num" refers to the number of numerical attributes and "#Cat" the number of categorical ones.

Synthetic Data: Our *data generators* are heavily tuned versions of TabDDPM (Kotelnikov et al., 2023), TabSyn (Zhang et al., 2024), TVAE, and CTGAN (Xu et al., 2019) provided by (Kindji et al., 2024). We trained the models on the entire real datasets before sampling new synthetic rows. Each model is used to create a synthetic version of each dataset.

3 Detection Models

In order to be useful "in the wild", a detection model must be "table-agnostic", which means that it must accept inputs form different table formats. We trained three baselines for synthetic content detection from scratch: a logistic regression and two transformer-based classifiers. For the logistic regression and the first transformer the table is first linearized into text (Section 3.1). For the second transformer-based classifier we use a rough columns level encoding of tables (Section 3.2).

The transformer-based classifiers have three main components: (i) a feature embedding block, (ii) a transformer encoder block, and (iii) a classification head. As in BERT, the classifier relies on a *CLS* embedding that is added to the input and retrieved in the output of the transformer blocks. The *CLS* representation is fed to the classification head to predict the binary target class (real or synthetic data). The models (both *text-based* and *table-based*) are trained using a binary cross entropy loss.

3.1 Text-Based Encodings

A natural solution to build a table-agnostic model is to consider the tables as raw text. This approach is used in pretrained models such as TaBERT (Yin et al., 2020), TAPAS (Herzig et al., 2020), or TAPEX (Liu et al., 2022). These models are are designed to encode small tables like the ones found on Wikipedia. They are derived from BERT and rely on a text encoding of the whole table.

In order to work with larger tables we opted, as in (Borisov et al., 2023), to work at the row level. We converted each table row into a shuffled sequence of <column>:<value> patterns.

For instance the first row of Table 1 can be encoded as the string "Name:Abalone,Size:4177,#Num:7,#Cat:2" or any of its column permutations. This random columns' permuation is intended to increase generalization across different tables. Then two options are considered: (i) For the logistic regression, the string is simply split into a bag of character-level trigrams like "Nam", "e:A", ":41" or ,"t:2"; (ii) For the text-transformer baseline the string is tokenized into a sequence of characters that are mapped, as usual for transformers, into a sequence of embedding vectors that are combined with a positional embedding.

3.2 Table-Based Encodings

All datasets are encoded following the same procedure: numerical features are normalized through *QuantileTransformer*, and categorical features are encoded with the *OrdinalEncoder*, both from scikit-learn[4]. Importantly, each dataset is processed separately. This means that the methods used to encode numerical and categorical features are applied to each dataset individually, rather than collectively.

[1] https://archive.ics.uci.edu/

[2] https://www.openml.org

[3] https://www.kaggle.com/datasets

[4] https://scikit-learn.org/stable/

The feature embedding module employs a shared feed-forward layer for numerical features and a shared embedding layer for categorical features. This baseline is of course simplistic, more sophisticated strategies are proposed in (Wang and Sun, 2022) and (Spinaci et al., 2024).

4 Experimental Setup

All dataset rows are mixed together in a list with two additional labels: the *dataset name* and the *origin* that can be *"real"* or the name of its generator if the row is synthetic. We use these two additonal labels to design cross-validation splits with increasingly challenging constraints:

$$\text{Generator:} \begin{cases} \text{Single} \\ \text{Multiple, Cross-generator} \end{cases}$$

$$\text{Table:} \begin{cases} \text{Single} \\ \text{Multiple, Cross-table} \end{cases}$$

For instance, the *Classifier Two-Samples Test* (C2ST) metric as described in (Lopez-Paz and Oquab, 2016; Zein and Urvoy, 2022) correspond to the simplest *Single Generator vs Real, Single Table* setting. It does not require a "table-agnostic" model. The *cross-generator shift* constraint guarantees that a generator used for trainning cannot be used in test. The cross-table constraint guarantees that a table used for trainning cannot be used in test. These single-criterion shift settings can be coded using Scikit-Learn *GroupKFold*. However, as shown in Table 2, cross-validating a *Full shift* with both cross-table and cross-generator robustness is a bit trickier.

		Tables		
		A	B	C
Real Data				
Generators	X			
	Y			
	Z			

Table 2: Example of a full shift split. The blue cells indicate the training elements, while the green cells represent the test sets. The gray cells indicate examples that must be dropped because they would violate one of the Tables or Generator separation constraints.

4.1 Detection Without Distribution Shift

We first train models to detect synthetic data generated only by *TVAE* (Xu et al., 2019). Despite our interest in "model agnostic" detection, this procedure provides an upper-bound reference to compare with. This setup is referred as *TVAE vs Real, All-Tables, No Shift*. We then add an additional setup where synthetic datasets from all models are mixed to be detected against the real datasets. We refer to this setup as *All Models vs Real, All-Tables, No Shift*.

4.2 Detection Under Distribution Shifts

		Tables		
		A	B	C
Real Data				
Generators	X			
	Y			
	Z			

Table 3: Example of a *cross-table shift* split. The blue cells indicate the training elements, while the green cells represent the test set.

We have tested our baselines only under the *cross-table* shift constraint, which proves to be already quite challenging. As illustrated in Table 3, in this scenario the detection model is first trained on real and synthetic datasets produced by some generators and then deployed on unseen datasets.

5 Results

In this section, we present our baselines' results on different setups, without and with *cross-table shift*. These results are summarized in Table 4 with the standard *ROC-AUC* and *Accuracy* metrics.

Setup	Model	Metrics	
		AUC	Accuracy
TVAE vs Real, All Tables, No shift	3grm-LReg.	0.71	0.65
	Text-Transf.	0.76	0.68
	Table-Transf.	**0.91**	**0.82**
All Models vs Real, All Tables, No shift	3grm-LReg.	0.67	0.62
	Text-Transf.	**0.78**	**0.72**
	Table-Transf.	0.77	0.69
All Models vs Real, All Tables, Cross-table shift	3grm-LReg.	**0.58**	**0.55**
	Text-Transf.	0.56	0.52
	Table-Transf.	0.51	0.50

Table 4: Evaluation of synthetic tabular data detection on various setups. "3grm-LReg." stands for "Trigrams Logistic Regression" and "Transf." stands for "Transformer"

5.1 Without Distribution Shift

The transformer-based models (both *text-based* and *table-based*) demonstrate good performance across various metrics, under both setups *TVAE vs Real* and *All models vs Real*. We notice an *AUC* over 0.76 for all setups suggesting a good generalization capabilities of these table-agnostic models. Despite its rather naive design, the *AUC* for detecting TVAE-generated rows of our table-agnositc tranformer baseline reaches 0.91. It is worth comparing this result with the ones obtained in single dataset settings: in (Kindji et al., 2024) the *XG-Boost TVAE vs Real* median *AUC* for detecting TVAE is 0.81.

The task difficulty increases under the *All models vs Real* setup, but the overall performance remains stable for all models. The *table-based* transformer outperforms the *text-based* version in *TVAE vs Real*, however, it underperforms in *All Models vs Real*. Note that the only difference between the two approaches lies in the preprocessing and the way the feature embedding module works (as detailed in Sections 3.2 and 3.1). This suggests that the textual representation offers a more general view across all models and datasets. As a side result, we notice that there is still significant room for improvement in achieving realism in tabular data generation. The synthetic tabular data generators seems to exhibit patterns that a naive table-agnostic classifier is able to detect.

5.2 Cross-table Shift

The *cross-table shift* results (Table 4) show that this setup is particularly challenging, as all models struggle to achieve good performance. The *table-based* approach drops significantly its performance (*AUC*= 0.51). The model fails to identify meaningful patterns and cannot generalize to unseen datasets, essentially making random guesses on the test set.

An interesting observation is that the *text-based* transformer appears to provide more generalizable patterns than the *table-based* one. This aligns with the results from the *All Models vs Real* setup, in which it also performed better. As there are more datasets and models to generalize across, this approach benefits from that diversity. However, the *AUC* score is relatively low at 0.56. The training curves presented in Appendix B confirms that, with a *cross-table shift* between all training, validation, and test sets; the text-based transformer (on the left-hand side) is more robust than the *table-based* transformer (on the right-hand side). The *dataset-agnostic* encoding we used in the *table-based* method reveals its limitations when evaluated on unseen datasets. Being tied to datasets particularities, the encoding do not generalize well to datasets with different characteristics (e.g. the number of features, range of numerical features, categories in categorical features, and sample size). In contrast, the textual representation captures patterns that can be generalized.

As expected, due to its extreme simplicity, the logistic regression model outperformed the transformers for the *cross-table shift* setup with an AUC at 0.58 (versus 0.56 for the *text-based* transformer). However, an AUC of 0.58 is not a very impressive result and, contrary to transformers (Zhou et al., 2024; Li and McClelland, 2023; Yadlowsky et al., 2024), its potential for improvement is weak.

These preliminary results suggests further investigations on transformer-based models with both text-based and table-based encodings. The potential for transfer learning from pre-trained models can also enhance performance, making transformer-based approaches a valuable asset in the *cross-table shift* setup.

6 Conclusion

We study synthetic tabular data detection "in the wild". We utilized 14 datasets and 4 state-of-the-art, highly-tuned tabular data generation models. We evaluated various models using different tabular data representations as inputs and demonstrated that it is possible to detect synthetic data with promising performance. We also introduced various levels of "wildness" that correspond to different degrees of data distribution shift and we focused on *cross-table shift*. Our preliminary results are encouraging but show that cross-table adaptation is still a challenging problem. In the future, we will consolidate these results and explore more sophisticated encodings and adaptation strategies such as including table metadata—like column names—in the input. We also plan to explore the adaptation of pretrained encoders like TaBERT to see if they reach the performance of our baselines on fake content detection.

7 Limitations

As the results showed, the *table-based* transformer, along with its preprocessing and feature embedding scheme, provides valuable insights when there is no distribution shift. However, it struggles to generalize when a *cross-table shift* is introduced. We believe this encoding scheme has the merit of its simplicity, but it needs to be enhanced for distribution shift scenarios by incorporating general dataset information, such as column names and category embeddings as it is done in (Spinaci et al., 2024). These improvements should help differentiate between synthetic and real data if synthetic data fails to accurately replicate these characteristics. On the other hand, the textual encoding offers the advantage of being simpler and more general, but it leads to longer row-encoding sequences and it lacks of a tabular-specific inductive bias.

We implemented straightforward baselines utilizing both common NLP techniques and transformer architecture. For now, we did not conduct ablation studies to examine the impact of input column permutation and positional encoding. We also did not consider other table format specificities such as table size, number of columns, and data types.

The few experiments we did to adapt TaBERT on larger tables were not conclusive. We suspect, that BERT-like tokenization and small tables pretraining is not adapted to our problem, but it requires further investigations that we keep for future work.

References

Quentin Bammey. 2024. Synthbuster: Towards detection of diffusion model generated images. *IEEE Open Journal of Signal Processing*, 5:1–9.

Vadim Borisov, Kathrin Sessler, Tobias Leemann, Martin Pawelczyk, and Gjergji Kasneci. 2023. Language models are realistic tabular data generators. In *The Eleventh International Conference on Learning Representations*.

Lucy Chai, David Bau, Ser-Nam Lim, and Phillip Isola. 2020. What makes fake images detectable? understanding properties that generalize. In *Computer Vision–ECCV 2020: 16th European Conference, Glasgow, UK, August 23–28, 2020, Proceedings, Part XXVI 16*, pages 103–120. Springer.

Riccardo Corvi, Davide Cozzolino, Giada Zingarini, Giovanni Poggi, Koki Nagano, and Luisa Verdoliva. 2023. On the detection of synthetic images generated by diffusion models. pages 1–5.

Josh Gardner, Zoran Popovic, and Ludwig Schmidt. 2024. Benchmarking distribution shift in tabular data with tableshift. *Advances in Neural Information Processing Systems*, 36.

Ian Goodfellow, Jean Pouget-Abadie, Mehdi Mirza, Bing Xu, David Warde-Farley, Sherjil Ozair, Aaron Courville, and Yoshua Bengio. 2020. Generative adversarial networks. *Communications of the ACM*, 63(11):139–144.

Jonathan Herzig, Pawel Krzysztof Nowak, Thomas Müller, Francesco Piccinno, and Julian Eisenschlos. 2020. TaPas: Weakly supervised table parsing via pre-training. In *Proceedings of the 58th Annual Meeting of the Association for Computational Linguistics*, pages 4320–4333, Online. Association for Computational Linguistics.

Xiaomeng Hu, Pin-Yu Chen, and Tsung-Yi Ho. 2023. Radar: Robust ai-text detection via adversarial learning. *Advances in Neural Information Processing Systems*, 36:15077–15095.

Jayun Hyun, Seo Hu Lee, H. Son, Ji-Ung Park, and Tai-Myung Chung. 2020. A synthetic data generation model for diabetic foot treatment. In *International Conference on Future Data and Security Engineering*.

G. Charbel N. Kindji, Lina Maria Rojas-Barahona, Elisa Fromont, and Tanguy Urvoy. 2024. Under the hood of tabular data generation models: the strong impact of hyperparameter tuning. *Preprint*, arXiv:2406.12945.

Akim Kotelnikov, Dmitry Baranchuk, Ivan Rubachev, and Artem Babenko. 2023. Tabddpm: Modelling tabular data with diffusion models. In *International Conference on Machine Learning*, pages 17564–17579. PMLR.

Kristian Kuznetsov, Eduard Tulchinskii, Laida Kushnareva, German Magai, Serguei Barannikov, Sergey Nikolenko, and Irina Piontkovskaya. 2024. Robust ai-generated text detection by restricted embeddings. In *Findings of the Association for Computational Linguistics: EMNLP 2024*, pages 17036–17055.

Mohamed Lahby, Said Aqil, Wael MS Yafooz, and Youness Abakarim. 2022. Online fake news detection using machine learning techniques: A systematic mapping study. *Combating fake news with computational intelligence techniques*, pages 3–37.

Thomas Lavergne, Tanguy Urvoy, and François Yvon. 2011. Filtering artificial texts with statistical machine learning techniques. *Language resources and evaluation*, 45:25–43.

Yuxuan Li and James McClelland. 2023. Systematic generalization and emergent structures in transformers trained on structured tasks.

Qian Liu, Bei Chen, Jiaqi Guo, Morteza Ziyadi, Zeqi Lin, Weizhu Chen, and Jian-Guang Lou. 2022. TAPEX: Table pre-training via learning a neural SQL executor. In *International Conference on Learning Representations*.

David Lopez-Paz and Maxime Oquab. 2016. Revisiting classifier two-sample tests. In *International Conference on Learning Representations*.

Francesco Marra, Diego Gragnaniello, Luisa Verdoliva, and Giovanni Poggi. 2019. Do GANs Leave Artificial Fingerprints? . In *2019 IEEE Conference on Multimedia Information Processing and Retrieval (MIPR)*, pages 506–511, Los Alamitos, CA, USA. IEEE Computer Society.

Eric Mitchell, Yoonho Lee, Alexander Khazatsky, Christopher D. Manning, and Chelsea Finn. 2023.

Detectgpt: zero-shot machine-generated text detection using probability curvature. In *Proceedings of the 40th International Conference on Machine Learning*, ICML'23. JMLR.org.

Jiameng Pu, Neal Mangaokar, Lauren Kelly, Parantapa Bhattacharya, Kavya Sundaram, Mobin Javed, Bolun Wang, and Bimal Viswanath. 2021. Deepfake videos in the wild: Analysis and detection. In *Proceedings of the Web Conference 2021*, pages 981–992.

Timur Sattarov, Marco Schreyer, and Damian Borth. 2023. Findiff: Diffusion models for financial tabular data generation. In *Proceedings of the Fourth ACM International Conference on AI in Finance*, ICAIF '23, page 64–72, New York, NY, USA. Association for Computing Machinery.

Shivangi Singhal, Anubha Kabra, Mohit Sharma, Rajiv Ratn Shah, Tanmoy Chakraborty, and Ponnurangam Kumaraguru. 2020. Spotfake+: A multimodal framework for fake news detection via transfer learning (student abstract). In *Proceedings of the AAAI conference on artificial intelligence*, volume 34, pages 13915–13916.

Marco Spinaci, Marek Polewczyk, Tassilo Klein, and Sam Thelin. 2024. Portal: Scalable tabular foundation models via content-specific tokenization. In *NeurIPS 2024 Third Table Representation Learning Workshop*.

T Stadelmann, M Amirian, M Arnold, I Elezi, M Geiger, K Rombach, L Tuggener, I Arabaci, BB Meier, GF Duivesteijn, et al. 2018. Deep learning in the wild. *Lecture Notes in Computer Science*, 11081:17–38.

Quan Wang, Licheng Zhang, Zikang Guo, and Zhendong Mao. 2024. IDEATE: Detecting AI-generated text using internal and external factual structures. In *Proceedings of the 2024 Joint International Conference on Computational Linguistics, Language Resources and Evaluation (LREC-COLING 2024)*, pages 8556–8568, Torino, Italia. ELRA and ICCL.

Zifeng Wang and Jimeng Sun. 2022. Transtab: Learning transferable tabular transformers across tables. *Advances in Neural Information Processing Systems*, 35:2902–2915.

Lei Xu, Maria Skoularidou, Alfredo Cuesta-Infante, and Kalyan Veeramachaneni. 2019. Modeling tabular data using conditional gan. In *Advances in Neural Information Processing Systems (NeurIPS)*, volume 32. Curran Associates, Inc.

Steve Yadlowsky, Lyric Doshi, and Nilesh Tripuraneni. 2024. Can transformer models generalize via in-context learning beyond pretraining data? In *NeurIPS 2023 Workshop on Distribution Shifts: New Frontiers with Foundation Models*.

Pengcheng Yin, Graham Neubig, Wen-tau Yih, and Sebastian Riedel. 2020. Tabert: Pretraining for joint understanding of textual and tabular data. pages 8413–8426.

EL Hacen Zein and Tanguy Urvoy. 2022. Tabular data generation: Can we fool XGBoost ? In *NeurIPS 2022 First Table Representation Workshop*.

Hengrui Zhang, Jiani Zhang, Zhengyuan Shen, Balasubramaniam Srinivasan, Xiao Qin, Christos Faloutsos, Huzefa Rangwala, and George Karypis. 2024. Mixed-type tabular data synthesis with score-based diffusion in latent space. In *The Twelfth International Conference on Learning Representations*.

Hattie Zhou, Arwen Bradley, Etai Littwin, Noam Razin, Omid Saremi, Joshua M. Susskind, Samy Bengio, and Preetum Nakkiran. 2024. What algorithms can transformers learn? a study in length generalization. In *The Twelfth International Conference on Learning Representations*.

A Additional Distribution Shifts

We explore several challenging distribution shift setups for evaluating synthetic tabular detection data "in the wild". We evaluated our baselines on the *cross-table shift* and provide additional information about the remaining distribution shifts setups.

A.1 Cross-generator Shift

As illustrated in Table5, for generator shift, the model is trained to distinguish between real and synthetic data from some generators and some datasets. The model is then tested with synthetic data produced by generators it has never seen before.

		Tables		
		A	B	C
Real Data				
Generators	X			
	Y			
	Z			

Table 5: Example of *cross-generator shift* split. The blue cells indicate the training elements, while the green cells represent the test set. Here, all rows associated with generators X and Y were selected for the train set. Note that there are some *real* datasets in the training set as well.

A.2 Full Shift

Another critical scenario arises when the model is trained on a specific set of generators and datasets, but encounters unseen generators and datasets during deployment. Here there is a *cross-table shift* and a *cross-generator shift*. In this scenario, the model could struggle to generalize learned patterns to totally unseen data. The schematic representation is provided in Table 2. Due to the constraints on the datasets and generators in this setup, certain data cannot be included in either the training set or the test set.

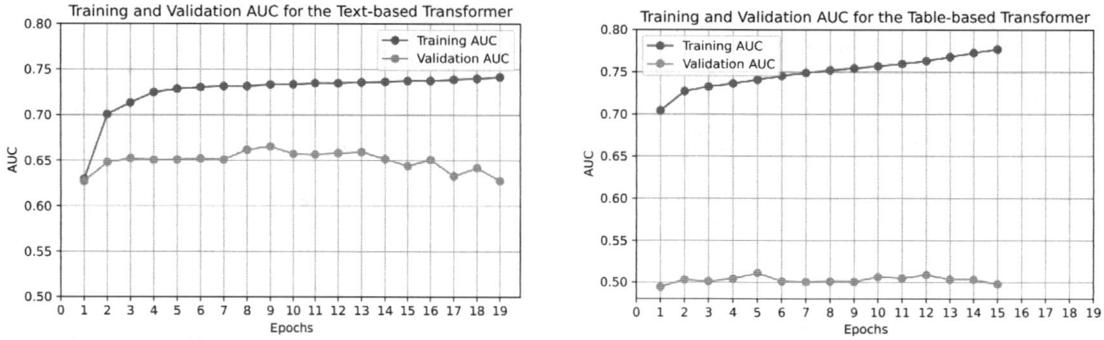

Figure 1: Training and validation *AUC* performance of models trained under *cross-table shift* setup. Left: *text-based* model and right: *table-based* approach.

B Additional Results

We provide the training and validation curves for the *AUC* metric for the *cross-table shift* setup in Figure 1.

Your Large Language Models Are Leaving Fingerprints

Hope McGovern * †
Cambridge Computer Lab

Rickard Stureborg†
Duke University
Grammarly

Yoshi Suhara†
NVIDIA

Dimitris Alikaniotis
Grammarly

Abstract

It has been shown that fine-tuned transformers and other supervised detectors are effective for distinguishing between human and machine-generated texts in non-adversarial settings, but we find that even simple classifiers on top of n-gram and part-of-speech features can achieve very robust performance on both in- and out-of-domain data. To understand how this is possible, we analyze machine-generated output text in four datasets, finding that LLMs possess unique *fingerprints* which manifest as slight differences in the frequency of certain lexical and morphosyntactic features. We show how to visualize such fingerprints, describe how they can be used to detect machine-generated text and find that they are even robust across text domains. We find that fingerprints are often persistent across models in the same model family (e.g. 13B parameter LLaMA's fingerprint is similar to that of 65B parameter LLaMA) and that while a detector trained on text from one model can easily recognize text generated by a model in the same family, it struggles to detect text generated by an unrelated model.

1 Introduction

Large language models (LLMs) produce text often indistinguishable from human-authored text to human judges (Clark et al., 2021). This unfortunately allows potential misuses such as academic plagiarism (Westfall, 2023) and the dissemination of disinformation (Barnett, 2023), which has therefore prompted interest in machine-generated text detection (MGT). We conduct linguistic analysis on four popular published datasets for MGT, showing that the machine-generated content in each shows linguistic markers in aggregate which make it relatively easy to separate it from human content.

These discrepancies, which we call a model's "fingerprint", are consistent enough *across domains* and *within model families* that we find we can treat each LLM as if it were a unique author with a distinct writing style. To do so, we use a well-founded method from the field of Author Identification (AID) for a closed set of authors: using handcrafted n-gram features and training a simple machine learning classifier on those features.

	Best Reported Model		N-gram (Ours)	
Paper	F1	AUROC	F1	AUROC
Deepfake	–	99.0	94.7	94.3
HC3	99.8	–	96.7	99.6
Ghostbuster	99.9	100.0	98.0	98.0
OUTFOX	96.9	–	98.7	98.7

Table 1: **Best reported classifier performances (Deep neural networks) versus a decision-tree model with n-gram features.** Best-reported classifier models are from four recent papers which release labeled datasets for MGT. Our model, a decision-tree classifier, uses a combination of character-, word- and POS-n-gram features and outperforms the best-reported model on the OUTFOX benchmark.

As shown in Table 1, the performance of the simple classifier is surprisingly comparable to more complex neural methods, even in a multi-class setting – successfully distinguishing between, e.g. human-, ChatGPT-, and LLaMA-generated text (Table 2). It also proves robust in cross-domain experiments (Figure 2).

In this paper, we empirically uncover and characterize the fingerprints of individual and families of LLMs through a series of comprehensive analyses, and present a new perspective of LLM-content detection as authorship identification.

* Corresponding Author.
Email: hope.mcgovern@cl.cam.ac.uk.
† Work done while at Grammarly.

Proceedings of the 1st Workshop on GenAI Content Detection (GenAIDetect), pages 85–95
January 19, 2025.

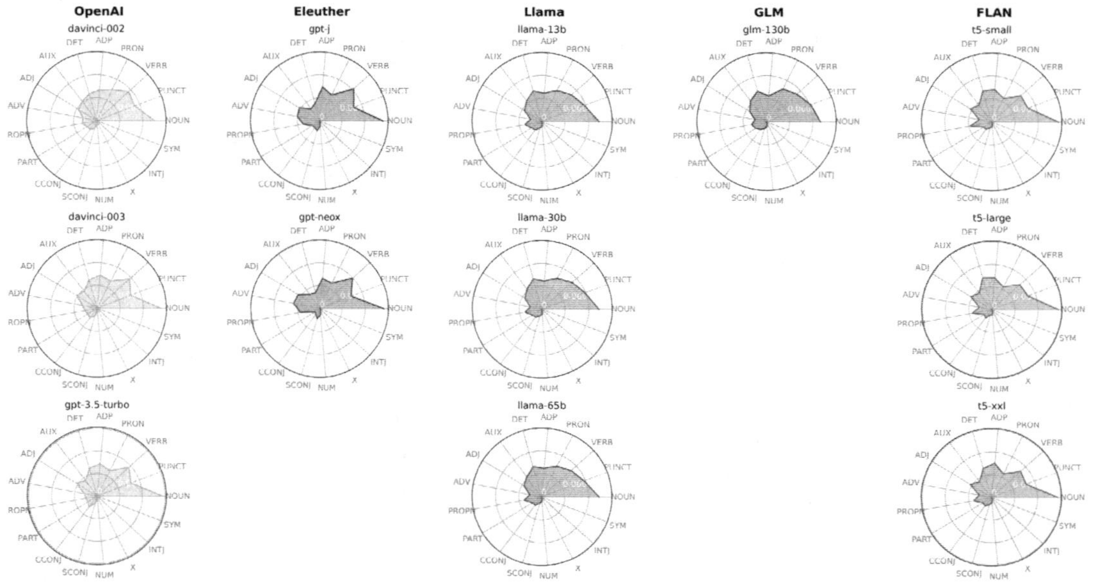

Figure 1: **Visualization of the fingerprints.** We plot frequencies of each part-of-speech (POS) class from the output of several models, sorted by model family. Within each family, the shapes (distributions) look mostly similar regardless of model size. Each radial plot is shown at the same 0% to 20% frequency scale, with POS tags sorted from most to least common among human-written outputs. Jagged/bumpy shapes indicate the fingerprint is more distinct from human distributions. POS is just one component of the full 'fingerprint' we investigate.

2 Methodology

2.1 Fingerprint Features

We use three feature sets: word n-grams ($n \in [2, 4]$), which we expect to be useful in capturing domain-specific vocabulary, but also in capturing function words, which are known to be highly effective for authorship identification; character n-grams ($n \in [3, 5]$), which we intuitively expect to capture subword information broadly aligning with the byte-pair encoding (BPE) tokenization method of many models; and part-of-speech (POS) n-grams ($n \in [2, 4]$), which should capture domain-agnostic information about writing style.

2.2 Classifiers

We use a GradientBoost classifier implemented in the Sklearn library (Pedregosa et al., 2011). The hyperparameters for the classifier were found through grid search, though no extensive hyperparameter sweeps were carried out; this classifier works well out-of-the-box[1]. Initial experiments used a range of ML classifiers, including SVC and logistic regression. These exhibited close or similar performance on our data.

[1]Further hyperparameter tuning could improve classifier performance, but we are primarily interested in exploring why such a simple classifier performs well in the first place.

2.3 Data

We use four publicly available machine-generated text detection datasets for fingerprint analysis as well as training data for supervised sequence classifiers: OUTFOX (Koike et al., 2023), Deepfake-TextDetect (Li et al., 2023), the Human Comparison Corpus (Guo et al., 2023), and Ghostbuster (Verma et al., 2023). We refer to these as 'Outfox','Deepfake', 'HC3', and 'Ghostbuster' in this work, respectively. The Deepfake dataset helpfully provides data splits across 10 text domains and 7 model families. HC3 and Ghostbuster provide data generated by 'gpt-3.5-turbo' across 8 different text domains collectively, while Outfox provides parallel responses to student essay prompts for 'gpt-3.5-turbo', 'text-davinci-003', and 'flan-t5-xxl'. Due to space constraints, complete information on domain coverage and underlying base model(s), may be seen in Table 4.

We only use up to 5,000 training examples of each class (where a class is an individual model or 'human') as we find more data does not improve performance after this point, highlighting a particular advantage of feature-based methods: they are not data-greedy.

3 Experiments

We conduct a series of analyses of LLM fingerprints, finding (1) they are predictive of which model authored a text, (2) consistent across domains, and (3) relatively consistent within model families.

3.1 Characterizing Fingerprints

We visualize fingerprints by looking at the difference of distribution in various linguistic properties. In Figure 1, we report part-of-speech tag distributions of data generated by different models on the same Deepfake data domains[2]. In Appendix A we also include analysis from named entity tags, constituency types, and top-k most frequent tokens. There are, of course, more dimensions of linguistic analysis that could theoretically be applied to uncover model fingerprints.

Distinct patterns emerge when comparing the fingerprint of models *within* the same family compared to models *across* different families. The degree of similarity within families can also vary between families; for example, LLaMA models exhibit a particularly uniform fingerprint across model sizes, while BigScience models (cf. Appendix A) look markedly different.

3.2 Fingerprints for Multi-Class MGT

We take the Ghostbuster and Outfox datasets and perform multi-class classification, considering, e.g. 'ChatGPT' a separate class from 'Flan T5'. Per-class F1 scores and macro-F1 on a held-out test set are reported in Table 2. In both cases, we test a three-way classification and achieve a macro-F1 score greater than 0.91.

The implication of this, then, is that linguistic and morphosyntactic features are effective for distinguishing between texts generated by different LLMs as if they have a unique authorial style, rather than belonging to a generic 'machine-generated' category.

3.3 Robustness to Unseen Data and Models

We intuitively expect that a shift in text domain will impact the efficacy of fingerprints as features. To test this, we take the largest model in each model family of the Deepfake dataset and train a classifier on a set of 9 out of 10 of the text domains available. Specifically, we treat each data source (e.g. 'financeQA', 'cmv', 'reddit eli5', etc.) as a separate text domain. We then compare the F1 score on a held-out test set either of the same training domains, or the held-out 10th domain (downsampled to be the same size), presented in Figure 2. While most models experience a slight dip in performance on OOD data, we find that this difference is not statistically significant.

We conduct a different test in which we select an LLM at random from the Deepfake dataset, train a binary classifier (human vs. machine), and compare the difference of evaluating the trained classifier on either (a) text generated by the same model in a different text domain (OOD) or (b) text from the same domain as the training set, but generated by a different model (OOM). We repeat this experiment $n = 20$ times. As seen in Figure 3, recall for

Dataset	Provenance	F1
Ghostbuster	Human	0.934
	ChatGPT	0.960
	Flan T5	0.927
	Average	0.940
Outfox	Human	0.877
	ChatGPT	0.936
	Claude	0.920
	Average	0.911

Table 2: **F1 scores for each class as the positive class after training under a multiclass classification setting.** Note that even for top models ChatGPT and Claude, our simple n-gram based classifier performs very well (0.936 and 0.920 on the Outfox data). To compare with binary classification results, F1 scores are computed for each class by setting that class to be the 'positive'.

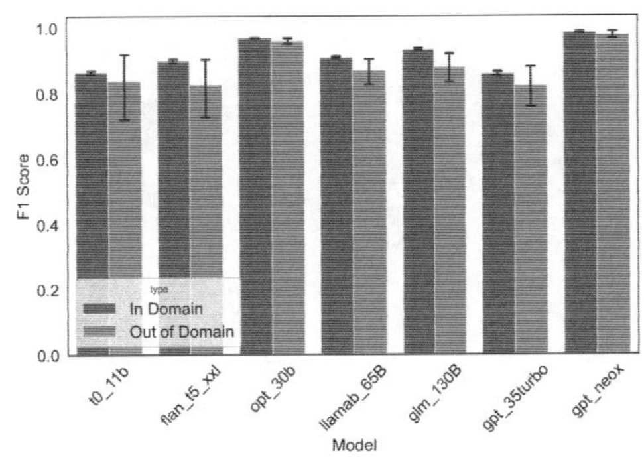

Figure 2: **F1 score of MGT on in-domain versus out-of-domain test sets for the largest model of each model family in the Deepfake benchmark.** We find no statistically significant drop in performance when testing on these 7 models' outputs. 95% confidence intervals are computed through bootstrap sampling at $n = 10,000$.

[2]We choose to report POS results in the main paper as it directly maps to one feature set for our classification experiments, whereas we do not directly use named entity categories, constituency types, or top-k words as features.

the machine class and AUROC drop significantly lower for OOM data compared to OOD data, leading to the interesting insight that *LLMs generate texts across different domains with a consistent, characteristic style that is unique to each model.* In other words, Flan T5 "sounds" like Flan T5 whether it is generating news stories or fan fiction.

We also explicitly test how well a classifier trained on data generated by one model generalizes to (a) other models in the same family and (b) other model families. We find that, on average, the drop in machine recall value (out of 1) from in-domain data to other models in the same family is only 0.01, while the drop to other families is 0.62. We report these results in Table 3.

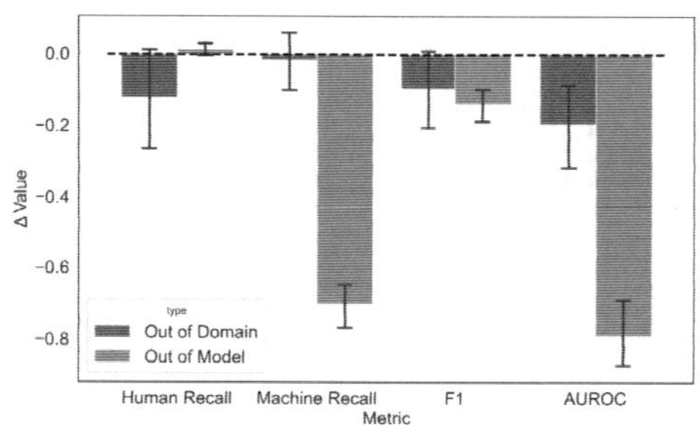

Figure 3: **Average drop in performance when testing on out-of-domain text (blue) versus a text generated by a held-out LLM (brown).** Note that recall of the machine-generated text drops significantly when testing on an unseen model's output, while changing the domain has much less impact.

4 Discussion

4.1 Where Might Fingerprints Come From?

Our work has revealed interesting insights about machine-generated text, namely that LLMs generate in a manner analogous to an individual human author's unique writing style. The origin of these 'fingerprints' is uncertain, but may lie in either the model's training data or model architecture.

It is clear that the model families with the most uniform fingerprint, e.g. LLaMA and Flan T5, are comprised entirely of models trained on the same dataset with the same training method and underlying structure, but with a different number of model parameters. This is also clear in the fingerprint similarity of BigScience's two T0 models contrasted with the one Bloom model, which are trained on different datasets and have different underlying architectures (Encoder-Decoder and GPT3-style, respectively).

A piece of evidence in favor of the influence of training data is that we find that 13B parameter LLaMA chat-tuned model has a *different* fingerprint from its non-chat counterpart, despite having the same architecture (Figure 8). It remains less clear why some families have less uniform fingerprints, and the exact interplay of training data, architecture, and training regime begs further investigation.

4.2 What About Better Models?

Class	F1 Score
GPT-4	0.98
Human	0.98

(a) Binary Classification: GPT-4 vs. Human)

Class	F1 Score
Cohere	0.94
GPT-4	0.96
Human	0.95

(b) Multi-Class Classification: GPT-4 vs. Human vs. Cohere

Figure 4: **F1 Scores for Binary and Multi-Class Classification.**

It might be thought that as language models become larger and generally more capable of producing human-sounding text, their fingerprints will disappear, but we find that our fingerprint-based method performs well even on text produced by more modern models than those contained in the main datasets we test.

We use the data from the COLING 2025 Workshop on Detecting AI-Generated Content[3] to perform both a binary classification of human vs. GPT-4 data, as well as a 3-way classification experiment between human, GPT-4, and Cohere. F1 scores, which may be seen in Figure 4, for all classes in both experiments exceed 0.94.

These scores demonstrate strong performance even with modern models, effectively distinguishing GPT-4 data from human data, as well as differentiating it from other high-capacity models like Cohere. These results suggest that increased model capability alone is insufficient to erase distinctive "fingerprints," highlighting the robustness of our approach in identifying AI-generated content.

5 Related Work

A common approach to machine-generated text detection is to train a supervised binary classifier on

[3]Specifically, we use the data of Subtask a of Task 1, available here https://huggingface.co/datasets/Jinyan1/COLING_2025_MGT_en

labeled data (Guo et al., 2023; Koike et al., 2023; Li et al., 2023). Li et al. (2023) proposed a variety of classification testbeds, finding that pre-trained language models perform the best. While n-gram frequencies have often been used for author identification, only a few recent works examine hand-crafted features or stylometrics in machine-generated text detection (Zaitsu and Jin, 2023). One example is Gehrmann et al. (2019): a unique system that uses the top-k words to highlight text spans to visually aid humans in the task of spotting AI-written text themselves.

Petukhova et al. (2024) finds a combination of fine-tuned neural features and hand-crafted linguistic features effective for MGT on the M4 dataset as part of the SemEval2024 task on machine-generated text detection (Wang et al., 2024).

Li et al. (2023) analyze their corpus DeepfakeTextDetect across linguistic feature axes, but report differences across POS-tag distributions between human and machine data when considering all models and domains in aggregate as insignificant; however, they do find these distributions begin to diverge when considering a subset of models or domains. We demonstrate that these differences extend to every publicly available machine text detection dataset, prove largely consistent within model families, and are very powerful features for training a robust machine-generated text detection classifier.

While linguistic-feature-based approaches have shown promise, other state-of-the-art (SOTA) methods, such as Mitchell et al. (2023); Bao et al. (2024); Tian and Cui (2023), adopt probabilistic and statistical modeling approaches to detect machine-generated text in a training-free setting. We focus purely on manually extracted linguistic features rather than probability curvatures.

6 Conclusion

We demonstrate that in four popular datasets for machine-generated text detection, n-gram features are highly effective for MGT. We uncover that LLMs have unique writing styles that can be captured in lexical and syntactic features, which we characterize as "fingerprints", and show may be effectively harnassed for text-detection in a variety of settings.

Limitations

- **Text length:** we examine outputs of approximately 300-500 words in length. Shorter texts may be difficult to fingerprint or may not provide enough signal.
- **Model choice limitations**: We constrain ourselves to the data and models released as part of text detection corpora, which means that there may be some very good models we simply did not have the data to test at this time.
- **Reflection on real-world use-case.** Analyzing fingerprints in research benchmark datasets is most likely *not* reflective of the true difficulty of deepfake text detection in the wild. For one thing, people don't tend to use LLMs for writing entire articles/essays, etc. A more likely scenario for, e.g. academic plagiarism, is starting from an LLM generated paragraph and making sentence-level rewrites. As this is analagous to a paraphrase attack like DIPPER (Krishna et al., 2023), we expect that it would degrade our classifiers' performance.

Ethics Statement

This research indicates that detecting machine-generated text is easy. However, we want to stress that this does *not* necessarily mean machine-detection is a high-confidence task. Using a single model prediction about one single written text to determine whether or not it was human-written should be evaluated on a different basis than average accuracy, given the potential harms of false positives or false negatives. For example, teachers may wish to use tools to determine if students have cheated on exams or homework using LLMs. We discourage teachers from trusting predictions by any classifier until more investigation is done into the confidence models have for any individual text.

References

Guangsheng Bao, Yanbin Zhao, Zhiyang Teng, Linyi Yang, and Yue Zhang. 2024. Fast-detectgpt: Efficient zero-shot detection of machine-generated text via conditional probability curvature. *Preprint*, arXiv:2310.05130.

Sofia Barnett. 2023. ChatGPT Is Making Universities Rethink Plagiarism. *Wired*. Section: tags.

Elizabeth Clark, Tal August, Sofia Serrano, Nikita Haduong, Suchin Gururangan, and Noah A. Smith.

2021. All That's 'Human' Is Not Gold: Evaluating Human Evaluation of Generated Text. In *Proceedings of the 59th Annual Meeting of the Association for Computational Linguistics and the 11th International Joint Conference on Natural Language Processing (Volume 1: Long Papers)*, pages 7282–7296, Online. Association for Computational Linguistics.

Alex Franklin, Maggie, Meg Benner, Natalie Rambis, Perpetual Baffour, Ryan Holbrook, Scott Crossley, and ulrichboser. 2022. Feedback prize - predicting effective arguments.

Sebastian Gehrmann, Hendrik Strobelt, and Alexander M. Rush. 2019. Gltr: Statistical detection and visualization of generated text. In *Annual Meeting of the Association for Computational Linguistics*.

Biyang Guo, Xin Zhang, Ziyuan Wang, Minqi Jiang, Jinran Nie, Yuxuan Ding, Jianwei Yue, and Yupeng Wu. 2023. How Close is ChatGPT to Human Experts? Comparison Corpus, Evaluation, and Detection. Publisher: arXiv Version Number: 1.

Ryuto Koike, Masahiro Kaneko, and Naoaki Okazaki. 2023. Outfox: Llm-generated essay detection through in-context learning with adversarially generated examples. *ArXiv*, abs/2307.11729.

Kalpesh Krishna, Yixiao Song, Marzena Karpinska, John Wieting, and Mohit Iyyer. 2023. Paraphrasing evades detectors of ai-generated text, but retrieval is an effective defense. *Preprint*, arXiv:2303.13408.

Yafu Li, Qintong Li, Leyang Cui, Wei Bi, Longyue Wang, Linyi Yang, Shuming Shi, and Yue Zhang. 2023. Deepfake Text Detection in the Wild. Publisher: arXiv Version Number: 1.

Eric Mitchell, Yoonho Lee, Alexander Khazatsky, Christopher D. Manning, and Chelsea Finn. 2023. DetectGPT: Zero-Shot Machine-Generated Text Detection using Probability Curvature. arXiv. Version Number: 2.

F. Pedregosa, G. Varoquaux, A. Gramfort, V. Michel, B. Thirion, O. Grisel, M. Blondel, P. Prettenhofer, R. Weiss, V. Dubourg, J. Vanderplas, A. Passos, D. Cournapeau, M. Brucher, M. Perrot, and E. Duchesnay. 2011. Scikit-learn: Machine learning in Python. *Journal of Machine Learning Research*, 12:2825–2830.

Kseniia Petukhova, Roman Kazakov, and Ekaterina Kochmar. 2024. Petkaz at semeval-2024 task 8: Can linguistics capture the specifics of llm-generated text?

Edward Tian and Alexander Cui. 2023. Gptzero: Towards detection of ai-generated text using zero-shot and supervised methods.

Vivek Kumar Verma, Eve Fleisig, Nicholas Tomlin, and Dan Klein. 2023. Ghostbuster: Detecting text ghostwritten by large language models. *ArXiv*, abs/2305.15047.

Yuxia Wang, Jonibek Mansurov, Petar Ivanov, Jinyan Su, Artem Shelmanov, Akim Tsvigun, Chenxi Whitehouse, Osama Mohammed Afzal, Tarek Mahmoud, Giovanni Puccetti, Thomas Arnold, Alham Fikri Aji, Nizar Habash, Iryna Gurevych, and Preslav Nakov. 2024. SemEval-2024 task 8: Multigenerator, multidomain, and multilingual black-box machine-generated text detection. In *Proceedings of the 18th International Workshop on Semantic Evaluation*, SemEval 2024, Mexico City, Mexico.

Chris Westfall. 2023. Educators Battle Plagiarism As 89% Of Students Admit To Using OpenAI's ChatGPT For Homework. Section: Careers.

Wataru Zaitsu and Mingzhe Jin. 2023. Distinguishing ChatGPT(-3.5, -4)-generated and human-written papers through Japanese stylometric analysis. *PLOS ONE*, 18(8):e0288453.

A Fingerprint Characterization

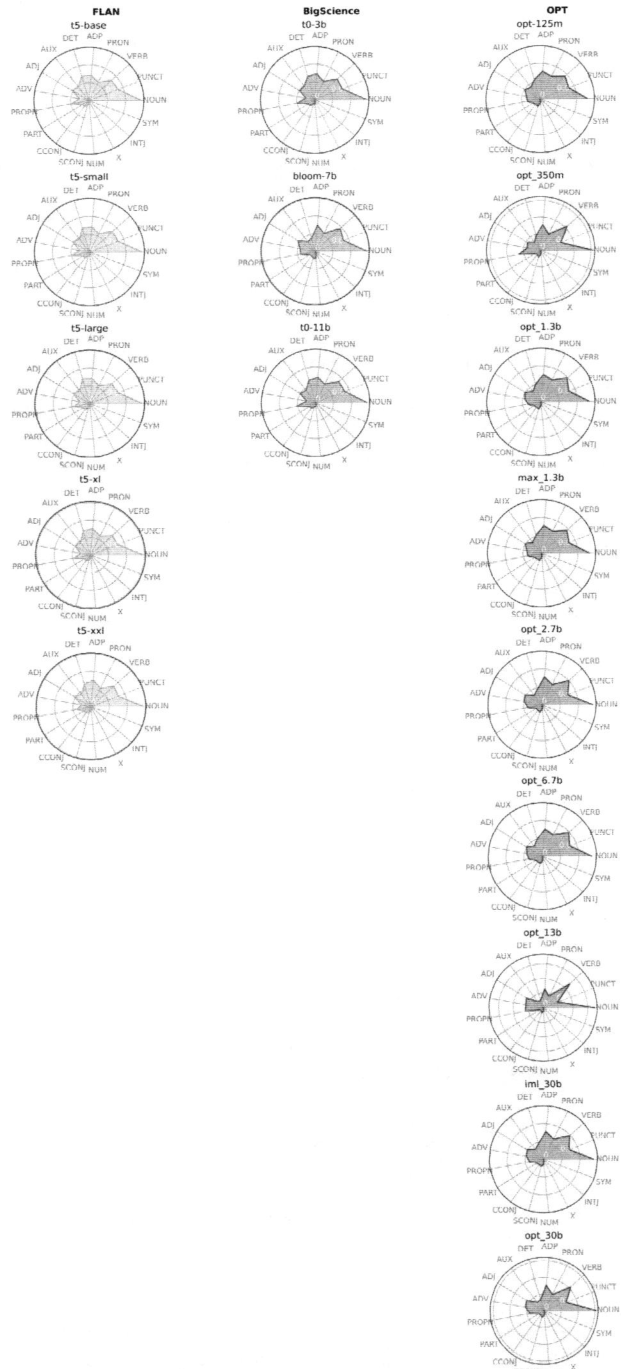

Figure 5: **Additional visualizations of fingerprints.** Note that the POS tag distributions of OPT models are less similar than we observe within other model families. Further investigations could examine what causes these differences, since model size seems to not play a factor in FLAN models.

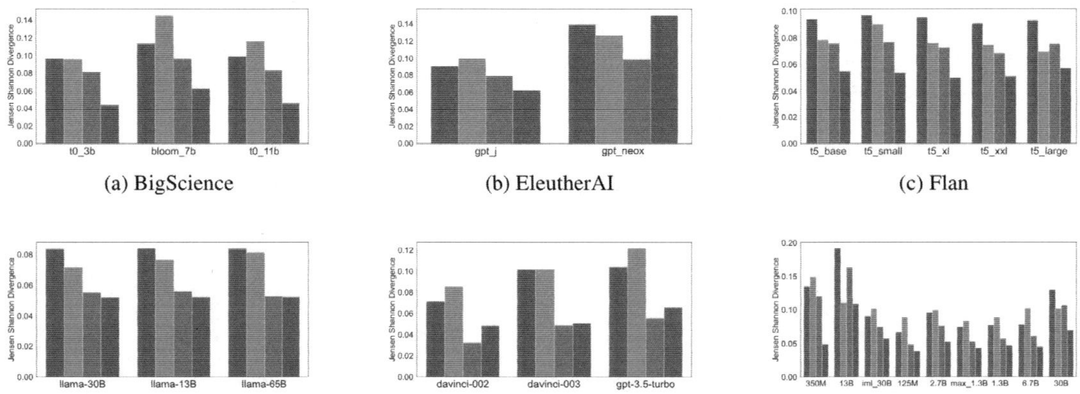

(a) BigScience (b) EleutherAI (c) Flan

(d) LLaMA (e) OpenAI (f) OPT

Figure 6: **Fingerprint characterization of Deepfake data by model and family.** We report the Jensen-Shannon Divergence of human vs. model for each model in each model family in the Deepfake data across four categories. **Columns from left to right: constituency type, named entity tag, POS tag, top-k word frequency**. We omit the GLM family in this visualization as there is only one model (130B) available. Like in Figure 1, some model families exhibit remarkably consistent fingerprints within families, e.g. LLaMa, Flan, and OpenAI. OPT and EleutherAI in particular have less distinguishable fingerprints within family.

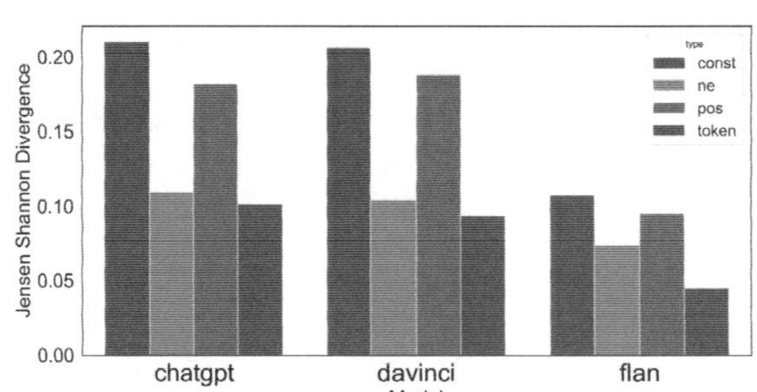

Figure 7: **Fingerprint characterization of Outfox data by model. Columns from left to right: constituency type, named entity tag, POS tag, top-k word frequency**. We note again that ChatGPT and davinci, being in the same OpenAI model family, have very similar fingerprints, whereas Flan's fingerprint differs substantially. Note that this fingerprint does look different than the Deepfake davinci's fingerprint, showing us that there is some domain dependence to fingerprints, while underscoring the point that regardless of domain, individual models of the same family do produce similar-sounding texts.

Experiment	Average drop in performance HRec	MRec	F1	AUC
Same Family ǀ Different Domain	-0.03	-0.01	-0.02	0.00
Different Family ǀ Same Domain	0.00	-0.62	-0.21	-0.44

Table 3: **Models exhibit individual writing styles which are more similar across domains than across model families.** We report the average drop in performance of a GradientBoost from a binary classifier trained on Deepfake data. In 7 independent trials, we train a classifier on a randomly selected model and compare its performance on the in-domain test set to: (1) data from a model in the same family but in a held-out domain, and (2) data from a model in a different family but same domains present in the train set (this is made possible by the fact that Deepfake is multi-parallel). Performance drop is low over data from a model in the same family, and high over data from a model in a different family. The human recall value is small but not 0 as the human data is shuffled and downsampled, so the exact same set of prompts is not seen in every trial.

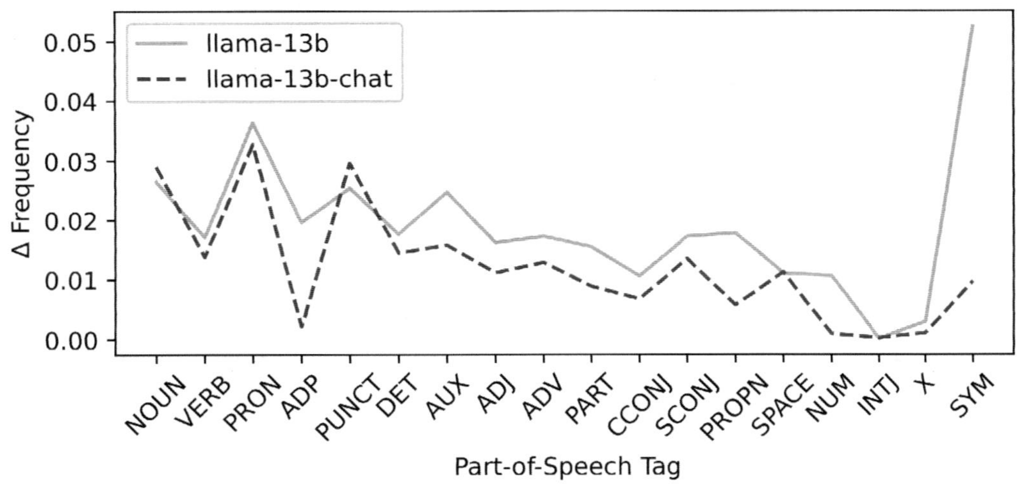

Figure 8: **Absolute difference in POS tag frequencies as compared with human text.** Chat models are slightly more similar to the frequency profile of humans, but are easier to detect than base models. This demonstrates that fingerprints "closer" to human distributions in POS tags does *not* indicate it is less detectable. Further, fine-tuning models for chat clearly alters their fingerprint despite no change in model architecture.

B Implementation Details

B.1 GradientBoost

Parameters: learning rate of 0.2, number of estimators 90, max depth of 8, max features 'sqrt', sum-sample ratio 0.8, random state 10, minimum samples leaf 30 and minimum samples to split 400, these hyperparameters were optimized using Sklearn's gridsearch function. Features: char n-grams:(2,4), word n-grams:(3,5), pos n-grams:(3,5). Maximum 2000 features for each feature set.

C Dataset Information

C.1 Outfox

Outfox is a parallel human-machine dataset built on the Kaggle Feedback Prize dataset (Franklin et al., 2022) and contains approximately 15,000 essay problem statements and human-written essays, ranging in provenance from 6th to 12th grade native-speaking students in the United States. For each problem statement, there is also an essay generated by each of three LLMs: ChatGPT (gpt-3.5-turbo-0613), GPT-3.5 (text-davinci-003), and Flan (FLAN-T5-XXL). Each example contain an instruction prompt ("Given the following problem statement, please write an essay in 320 words with a clear opinion."), a

Dataset	Base Model/Family	Domain	Human	Machine
Domain-Specific	gpt-j-6b	cmv	509	636
		eli5	952	863
		hswag	1000	868
		roct	999	833
		sci_gen	950	529
		squad	686	718
		tldr	772	588
		xsum	997	913
		yelp	984	856
		wp	940	784
		Total	8789	7588
Mixed Model Set	OpenAI GPT	mixed	67k	67k
	Meta Llama	mixed	37k	37k
	GLM-130B	mixed	9k	9k
	Google FLAN-T5	mixed	47k	47k
	Facebook OPT	mixed	80k	80k
	BigScience	mixed	27k	27k
	EleutherAI	mixed	14k	14k
		Total	282k	282k
Ghostbuster	gpt-3.5-turbo	Reuters	500	500
		essay	1000	1000
		wp	500	500
		Total	2000	2000
HC3	gpt-3.5-turbo	eli5	17.1k	17.1k
		open_qa	1.19k	1.19k
		wiki_csai	842	842
		medicine	1.25k	1.25k
		finance	3.93k	3.93k
		Total	24.3k	24.3k
OUTFOX	gpt-3.5-turbo	essay	15k	15k
	text-davinci-003	essay	15k	15k
	flan_t5_xxl	essay	15k	15k
		Total	46k	46k

Table 4: Dataset statistics (number of documents) for publicly available machine-generated text detection datasets.

problem statement ("Explain the benefits of participating in extracurricular activities and how they can help students succeed in both school and life. Use personal experiences and examples to support your argument."), the text of the essay, and a binary label for human or machine authorship.

While we conduct fingerprint analysis on the whole dataset, we use only the human-written subset of the Outfox data as a training corpus for our fine-tuning setup; given an instruction prompt and problem statement, we fine-tune our LLMs of interest to produce text which minimises cross-entropy loss when compared with the original human-written response to the same problem statement. We withhold a test-set of human-written examples from training to be used for evaluation.

C.2 Ghostbuster

Verma et al. (2023) provide three new datasets for evaluating AI-generated text detection in creative writing, news, and student essays. Using prompts scraped from the subreddit `r/WritingPrompts`, the Reuters 50-50 authorship identification dataset, and student essays from the online source IvyPanda, they obtained ChatGPT- and Claude-generated responses and made efforts to maintain consistency in length with human-authored content in each domain.

C.3 HC3

We also analyze data from (Guo et al., 2023), which includes questions from publicly available datasets and wiki sources with human- and ChatGPT-generated responses based on instructions and additional context. The resulting corpus comprises 24,322 English and 12,853 Chinese questions, of which we only use the English split.

C.4 Deepfake

The Deepfake corpus is a comprehensive dataset designed for benchmarking machine-generated content detection in real-world scenarios (Li et al., 2023). It contains approximately 9,000 human examples across 10 text domains, each paired with machine outputs from 27 models (e.g. GPT-3.5-turbo, text-davinci-002) from 7 different model families (e.g. OpenAI), producing several testbeds designed for examining a detector's sensitivity to model provenance and text domain. Each example contains the text, binary label denoting human or machine, and the source information – which domain, model, and prompting method were used.

Training Data. We primarily use the Deepfake and Outfox data for training classifiers to analyze different aspects of the LLM fingerprints. They are both conveniently multi-parallel: they contain N model responses for each human text sample in the dataset. This has the benefit of removing some uncertainty from our classifier results. Performance on the human class is often identical across trials, as the human data is often identical. This allows a controlled test of how our classifier deals with the machine text samples. Additionally, the different testbeds provided in Deepfake provide convenient, parallel domain and model (/model family) data splits. Specifically, we use the mixed model sets and model-specific, domain-specific testbeds from Deepfake.

GPT-4 is Judged More Human than Humans in Displaced and Inverted Turing Tests

Ishika Rathi and Sydney Taylor and Ben Bergen and Cameron Jones
UC San Diego
9500 Gilman Dr., San Diego, CA 92093
{irathi, sytaylor, bkbergen, cameron}@ucsd.edu

Abstract

Everyday AI detection requires differentiating between humans and AI in informal, online conversations. At present, human users most often do not interact directly with bots but instead read their conversations with other humans. We measured how well humans and large language models can discriminate using two modified versions of the Turing test: *inverted* and *displaced*. GPT-3.5, GPT-4, and displaced human adjudicators judged whether an agent was human or AI on the basis of a Turing test transcript. We found that both AI and displaced human judges were less accurate than interactive interrogators, with below chance accuracy overall. Moreover, all three judged the best-performing GPT-4 witness to be human more often than human witnesses. This suggests that both humans and current LLMs struggle to distinguish between the two when they are not actively interrogating the person, underscoring an urgent need for more accurate tools to detect AI in conversations.

1 Introduction

In 1950, Alan Turing devised "The Imitation Game" as a test to indirectly investigate the question, "Can machines think?" In a classic Turing test, a human interrogator engages in a text-only conversation with two witnesses: one human and one machine. If the interrogator is unable to accurately differentiate between the human and the computer, the computer passes the test and can be considered intelligent. Since Turing's original paper, the Turing test has sparked an intense debate that has been pivotal in constructing modern understandings and conceptions of intelligence, shaping the fields of computer science, cognitive science, artificial intelligence, robotics, philosophy, psychology, and sociology (French, 2000, p. 116).

Beyond its controversial role as a test of intelligence, the Turing test also serves as a measure of whether humans can detect AI in conversational settings, or whether AI models can successfully deceive human interlocutors into thinking that they are human. Recent empirical work has found that interrogators could not reliably determine whether a GPT-4-based agent was human or AI in a Turing test (Jones and Bergen, 2024).

Models that can successfully impersonate people bring attendant risks, including persuasion and deception. Especially in informal settings, which may include online forums such as Reddit or Quora, chatting platforms such as Discord, and social media platforms, an LLM-based agent could contribute to misinformation, scams, or be maliciously misused at a wide scale. In these open-access settings, posts, messages, or chats containing LLM-generated content would not only have persuasive power over an active interrogator but also over several consumers of the content (Burtell and Woodside, 2023). This motivates conducting variations of the Turing test in more ecologically valid settings to determine how effective people are in discriminating between humans and AIs in realistic scenarios. An ordinary Turing test provides the interrogator with a key advantage not always present in passive consumption of AI-generated text: they can adapt their questions to adversarially test the witness in real time. Here, we ask how well human and AI judges perform without this advantage, when they only have access to a transcript of a Turing test interview conducted by a separate participant.

1.1 Interactive Turing Test

A classic Turing test involves a human evaluator interactively interrogating a witness to determine whether they are human or AI. Although the Turing test was originally proposed as a test of intelligence, there have been a wide variety of objections to its validity or sufficiency in this guise (Hayes and Ford, 1995; Marcus, 2017; French, 2000; Oppy and Dowe, 2003). Independent of its validity as a

Proceedings of the 1st Workshop on GenAI Content Detection (GenAIDetect), pages 96–110

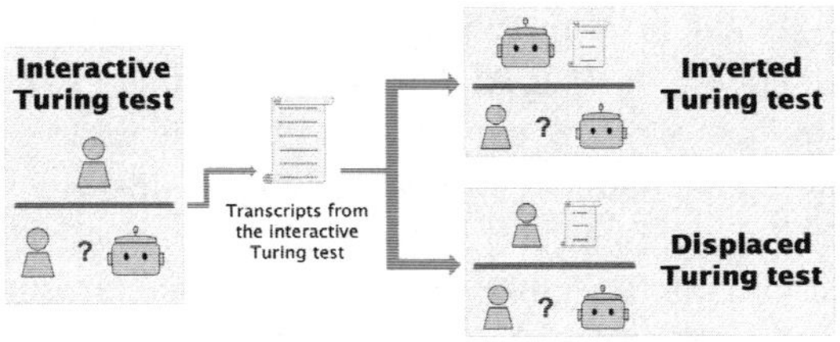

Figure 1: A summary of our experimental design. Transcripts were sampled from an interactive Turing test, where a human judge interrogates a witness to determine if they are human or AI. In an *Inverted* Turing test, we present transcripts to AI models, who judge whether the same witnesses are human or AI. In a *displaced* Turing test, a separate group of human participants read the same transcripts and make this judgement.

measure of intelligence, the Turing test provides a powerful test for assessing similarities between human- and AI-writing and a useful premise for studying AI detection (Park et al., 2023).

Several attempts have been made to pass the Turing test, including the Loebner Prize—a competition that ran from 1990-2020 without any system passing (Shieber, 1994); "Human or Not", a large-scale social Turing test experiment that found an interrogator accuracy rate of 60% (Jannai et al., 2023); and a 2024 study reporting the first system to have a pass rate statistically indistinguishable from chance (54%) but still short of the human threshold (67%) (Jones and Bergen, 2024). Several variations of the test exist, with each informing dimensions of theory and practice.

1.2 Inverted Turing Test

The first of these variations is the inverted, or reverse Turing test, which places an AI system in the role of the interrogator. Watt (1996) proposed the inverted test as a measure of *naive psychology*, the innate tendency to recognize intelligence similar to our own and attribute it to other minds. An AI system that passes would be one which is "unable to distinguish between two humans, or between a human and a machine that can pass the normal Turing test, but which can discriminate between a human and a machine that can be told apart by a normal Turing test with a human observer," (Watt, 1996, p. 8). Watt argued that by placing an AI system in the observer role and comparing its accuracy for different witnesses with human accuracy, the system would reveal whether it has a naive psychology comparable to real people.

As AI systems create larger proportions of online content (Fagni et al., 2021), and interact with others as social agents (Sumers et al., 2023), the inverted Turing test takes on new real-world relevance. AI systems are already being used to discriminate between humans and bots online, for example, through the widespread implementation of CAPTCHA (Completely Automated Public Turing test to tell Computers and Humans Apart), reCAPTCHA, or invisible CAPTCHA (Yamamura, 2013; Pal, 2020). The growing role of AI agents in online interactions raises questions around how well these systems will be able to discriminate between human and AI-generated content, and what kinds of criteria they might use to do so.

1.3 Displaced Turing Test

Several studies have assessed how well humans are able to recognize displaced AI-generated content in different domains including higher education (Perkins et al., 2024), news (Moravec et al., 2024), online content (Cooke et al., 2024), images (Somoray and Miller, 2023), and academic articles (Gao et al., 2023; Casal and Kessler, 2023). Though these discrimination tasks bear similarities to the Turing test, there remain important differences. First, these tasks can only be considered a "static" version of the test, as the judgement is based on pre-existing and unchanging content generated fully by a human or an AI. Second, while an interactive interrogator in a traditional Turing test can ask dynamic, flexible, and adversarial questions, the judge in a static Turing test can only consider what an agent happened to say, and cannot interact to pursue the most fruitful lines of questioning. Though static tests are therefore more limited in scope as tests of model abilities, they are likely to be parallels of a much more frequent occurrence in the real world, as many interactions are read by a larger audience than the addressee. Here, we introduce a novel kind of static Turing test called a *displaced* Turing test, wherein a human judge reads a transcript of an interactive Turing test that was previously conducted by a different human interrogator. The new human judge is "displaced" in that they are not present to interact with the witness.

1.4 Statistical AI-detection methods

There exist a variety of statistical approaches to detecting AI-generated content. These are largely based on the principle that LLMs generate content by sampling from a probability distribution over words which may leave particular probabilistic signatures, such as LLM generations being statistically more probable than human-generated ones (Ippolito et al., 2020; Solaiman et al., 2019; Gehrmann et al., 2019). Mitchell et al. (2023) developed a related metric, *curvature*, which measures the local optimality of a piece of text with respect to small perturbations generated using a masked language model; LLM-generated content is likely more probable than nearby perturbations. Mireshghallah et al. (2024) found that smaller LLMs tend to be better detector models, with a 125m parameter OPT model performing best at detecting AI-generated content overall, and achieving 90% accuracy on GPT-4 specifically.

Various commercial tools have been developed on the basis of these methods and other computational approaches to classifying text. Studies have examined the effectiveness of these approaches in different settings with mixed results: while accuracy is high in some domains, models are unreliable and are likely to issue false positives (Elkhatat et al., 2023; Bellini et al., 2024; Perkins et al., 2024). Studies have also considered LLMs as detection tools in a question-answering setting. Bhattacharjee and Liu (2024) assessed GPT-4's and ChatGPT's ability to discriminate between human-written and AI-generated content, and reported higher detection accuracy with human writing than with AI writing.

1.5 Present Study

These variations of the Turing test present the opportunity to ask new questions with real-world relevance. In practice, human users most often do not directly interact with bots but instead read their conversations with other human or AI users. As such, displaced human judges are important parallels for everyday AI detection. Additionally, the inverted Turing test provides a tool to investigate LLMs' latent model of human minds, and of their practical effectiveness in detecting AI-generated content online. If AI is used for detection, this becomes increasingly important. Mitigating technological deception will require ensuring that AI technologies for detection stay ahead of technologies for deception (Park et al., 2023).

We conducted Turing test variations by sampling transcripts from a previously-run interactive Turing test (Jones and Bergen, 2023), and presenting them to displaced AI and human judges (Figure 1). We used this paradigm to address several questions: Can humans reliably discriminate humans from AIs from merely observing conversations? Can LLMs serve as AI detectors, not only for static pieces of writing (essays, articles, & paragraphs) but also dynamic conversations? Does displacing the Turing test increase or decrease accuracy? Does an inverted Turing reveal naive psychology in artificial systems? And what methods work best for AI detection in real-world conversational spaces?

2 Study 1: Inverted Turing Test

We first place GPT-3.5 and GPT-4 in the role of the evaluator in an inverted Turing test. Because the models are not actively interrogating the witness, we refer to this more passive role as the *adjudicator*. We presented both models with transcripts of previously-run Turing tests (Jones and Bergen, 2023) and elicited judgements about whether the witness was a human or an AI. We pre-registered 5 hypotheses on OSF. First, we asked whether GPT-4 accuracy would be significantly greater or less than human accuracy. Second, in the original study, interactive human interrogators were no better than chance at determining whether one GPT-4 witness was human or AI. We asked whether GPT-4 would also fail to accurately identify this witness. Third, in order to test whether GPT-4 could distinguish between real humans and well-designed systems, we asked whether the model would judge real humans to be human more often than it judged the best GPT-4 witness to be human. Fourth, in order to understand the role that the length of the conversations plays in their identifiability, we asked whether GPT-4 accuracy as an adjudicator would be higher for longer transcripts. Finally, to investigate the role of LLM model quality in judging transcripts, we asked whether GPT-4 would have higher accuracy as an adjudicator than GPT-3.5.

2.1 Methods

We sampled 500 transcripts from Jones and Bergen (2023) who conducted more than 6,000 Turing tests on interactive human adjudicators. Our sample was constrained to ensure i) an equal number of human and AI witnesses, ii) the same proportion of games from the best-performing GPT-4 witness as the full dataset, and iii) an equal distribution of human and AI verdicts for the best-performing model. On average, human witnesses in this sample took 4.2 turns per game with 30.22 characters per turn, AI witnesses took 4.9 turns that averaged 46.26 characters per turn, and interrogators took

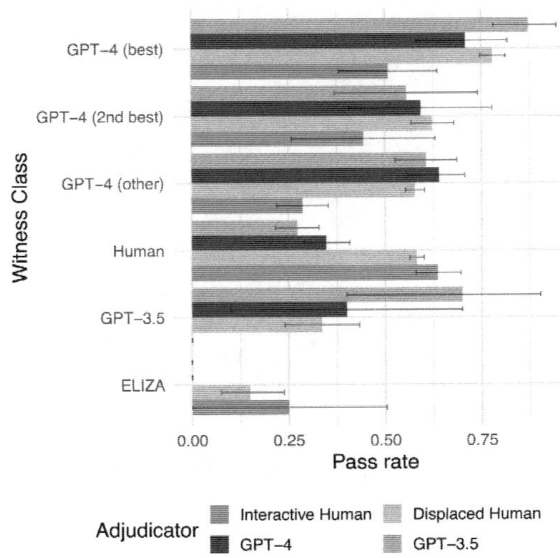

Figure 2: Mean pass rates (the proportion of time witnesses were judged to be human) by witness and adjudicator types. AI adjudicators (GPT-3.5 and GPT-4) judged GPT-4 witnesses to be human more often than they did real human witnesses. For displaced human adjudicators this was only true for the best GPT-4 witness. All GPT-4 witnesses had a higher pass rate with displaced human adjudicators than interactive. ELIZA's pass rate was low across all adjudicators.

4.83 turns with 28.22 characters per turn.

We presented these transcripts to two leading AI models (GPT-3.5 and GPT-4), followed by a prompt that instructed models to make a judgement on the identity of the witness, to indicate a confidence level in the verdict, and to provide reasoning for judgements (Appendix A).

AI witnesses in Jones and Bergen (2023) were based on 3 models: GPT-3.5, GPT-4 (Achiam et al., 2023), and ELIZA (Weizenbaum, 1966). Handwritten prompts instructed LLM-based systems on how to respond to interactive interrogators, with each prompt creating a unique AI witness. ELIZA was included as a performance baseline and as manipulation check: if participants successfully determine that ELIZA is AI—but not other AI witnesses—pass rates for AI witnesses are unlikely to be explained by a simple proclivity to anthropomorphism. We used the OpenAI API and transformers to access GPT-3.5 and GPT-4. Our analyses used the *lmertest* package in R to fit linear mixed effects models to determine whether effects were statistically significant.

2.2 Results

We compared the accuracy of AI adjudicators to the verdicts of the interactive interrogators in the original experiment from which the transcript sample was drawn. We found that GPT-4, as an adjudicator in an inverted Turing test, was significantly less accurate than interactive human interrogators from the original Turing test experiment ($z = 7.17, p < 0.001$). Interactive humans had an average accuracy (across witnesses) of 64.8%, while GPT-3.5 was accurate 31.4% of the time and GPT-4 was accurate 36.4% of the time. Of the AI-witnesses, one witness based on GPT-4 (*GPT-4 (best)*) had a pass rate of 50.9% in our sample of transcripts from the original study. For this best-performing AI witness, GPT-4's adjudicator accuracy was significantly worse than chance at 29.1% ($z = 3.00, p = 0.003$).

In contrast to the original interactive interrogators, GPT-4 judged humans to be human less often than chance (34.8%), and judged GPT-4 (best) to be human significantly more often than chance 70.9% ($z = 4.67, p < 0.001$, see Figure 2). Nevertheless, both GPT-4 and GPT-3.5 correctly judged ELIZA to be an AI system 100% of the time.

Transcript length had no effect on GPT-4 adjudicator accuracy ($z = 1.49, p = 0.14$) and GPT-4 was not significantly more accurate than GPT-3.5 ($z = 1.17, p = 0.24$). Both GPT-4 and GPT-3.5 showed below chance agreement with the verdicts of the original interactive witnesses (both 44%), but above chance agreement with one another (69%).

2.3 Discussion

Both AI systems were less accurate than interactive humans as judges in a Turing test, and even less accurate for the best-performing AI witness. Pass rates were higher for AI witnesses than human witnesses, meaning AI adjudicators misjudged AI witnesses to be human and human witnesses as AI. These results suggest current LLM systems are poor at distinguishing between human and AI-generated content—even when they are evaluating content produced by the same underlying LLM. One potential explanation for this reversal is that these systems outputs are driven by their representations of human training data. Models therefore may lack the more granular or context-sensitive representations needed to distinguish between their own output and the training data they mimic. Nonetheless, results suggest explicit question answering

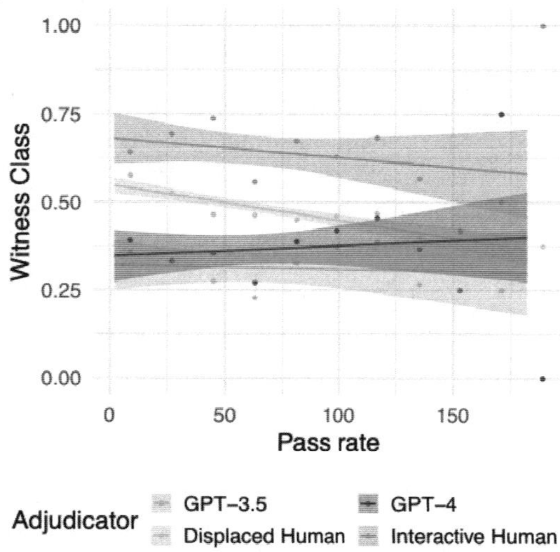

Figure 3: Transcript length in words had no significant effect on the accuracy of judgements across interactive human, and AI adjudicators. For displaced adjudicators, longer transcripts correlated with lower accuracy.

with current LLMs is not an effective tool for detecting AI contributions in conversations.

3 Study 2: Displaced Turing Test

The original Turing test was conceived as a test of intelligence—a crucial component of which is the interactive and adversarial nature of the interrogator. However, in many real-life scenarios, people do not have the opportunity to directly query potential AI agents: for instance, when reading a conversation between two interlocutors on social media. To investigate people's accuracy in identifying AI systems in this more passive context, we mirrored the inverted Turing test study with humans—a design we call the *displaced* Turing test. Displaced human adjudicators evaluated the same sample of transcripts and made judgements about whether the witness was human or an AI.

We pre-registered a similar set of questions for this design on OSF. We asked whether displaced human adjudicators would be more or less accurate than the original interactive interrogators, and whether they would be significantly more accurate than GPT-4 as an adjudicator. In addition, we asked whether they would be above chance in determining that the same best GPT-4 witness was an AI, and whether they would judge actual humans to be human more frequently than the best GPT-4 witness. Finally, we asked whether transcript length would influence adjudicator accuracy.

3.1 Methods

We presented the same sample of 500 transcripts to a sample of undergraduate human participants (N = 109, 84 females, age range: 19-31 years). Participants were compensated with course credit for their time. Each participant was presented with a random subset of 50 transcripts, so each transcript was judged on average by 10 displaced human participants. Human participants also indicated their confidence level and reasoning for each transcript (Appendix B). At the end of the study, participants were asked a series of debrief questions about the reasoning for their judgements, their methods, and their mental/emotional beliefs about AI (Appendix C). For analyses, we again used the *lmertest* package in R to fit linear mixed effects models.

3.2 Results

We found that displaced human adjudicators were significantly less accurate (48.6%) than interactive human interrogators (64.8%, $z = 4.49, p < 0.001$, see Figure 2). It is important to note that the displaced adjudicators were recruited from a different population than the interactive interrogators, which could confound the insights we can draw about the effect of displacement *per se*.

Displaced adjudicators were only 22% accurate for the best-performing GPT-4 witness ($z = 13.4, p < 0.001$), but were significantly more accurate in detecting ELIZA (85%, $z = 5.54, p < 0.001$). The best-performing GPT-4 witness from the original interactive study achieved a pass rate of 78% in the displaced setting, which was significantly higher than the pass rate for human witnesses (58.2%, $z = 9.16, p < 0.001$).

We found no statistical difference in accuracy between displaced human adjudicators and AI adjudicators ($z = 1.75, p = 0.81$). Agreement was close to chance levels between displaced interrogators and interactive interrogators (55%), GPT-4 (56%), and GPT-3.5 (53%), suggesting that their error patterns are not correlated. In contrast to our hypothesis, the length of the Turing test had a negative effect on accuracy ($z = 5.84, p < 0.001$).

3.3 Discussion

We found that displaced adjudicators are also significantly less accurate than interactive human interrogators. One explanation is that the two sets of participants were drawn from different populations. Interactive interrogators were recruited via social media while displaced participants were undergraduate students. We therefore cannot know whether this drop in accuracy is purely due to the effect of displacement. However, the fact that displaced participants were similarly accurate in identifying humans and ELIZA, but not GPT-based models, suggests that displacement creates an additional challenge for identifying LLM-based models. Notably, displacement prevents participants from adversarially questioning the witness or observing witness response times, and may encourage quicker decision-making or less engagement. In real-world scenarios where human interrogators do not have the opportunity to directly interrogate the source of text content, these results suggest that people may not reliably be able to distinguish human and AI-generated content.

Similar to the inverted Turing test, the best-performing GPT-4 witness had a higher pass rate than human witnesses. This suggests that when reading an online conversation between a human and an AI model, the AI system may be more likely to be judged to be human than an actual human is.

The negative effect of transcript length on accuracy is counter-intuitive: how could less information be more helpful to adjudicators? In fact, this reversal may be due to a secondary confound in the way that transcript length was determined. Interrogators in the original study had the option to end the conversation early, which they may have done when they were confident they were speaking to a human or an AI. Shorter transcripts, therefore, might be more likely to contain information that was especially helpful to interactive interrogators, and may also be aiding displaced ones.

We found no statistically significant correlations between adjudicator accuracy and exit survey questions that asked participants how positively they felt about AI, how intelligent they thought AI systems are, their estimate of their own accuracy, their frequency of interaction with chatbots, or how much they know about LLMs (See Figure 10). Accuracy increased across trials, suggesting that participants learned across the experiment in spite of a lack of feedback ($z = 2.05$, $p = 0.041$). Many participants reported their methods changed from checking for formality or grammar to assessing inappropriate uses of slang, excessive informality, or consistency in grammar as indicative of AI witnesses (OSF).

4 Additional Analyses

4.1 In-Context Learning

One key difference between the displaced human experiment and the inverted experiment was that human adjudicators completed 50 transcripts in series, while LLM adjudicators were presented each transcript separately. Although human participants were not provided with feedback after each trial, serial presentation may have allowed them to learn more about the distribution of transcripts and even markers of individual AI witnesses which were represented multiple times (supported by the increase in accuracy across trials, see Figure 10). In order to determine whether similar in-context learning (ICL) dynamics could influence AI adjudicators' performance, we conducted an analogous experiment, presenting transcripts serially to the model.

We randomly sampled 50 transcripts from the full set, and presented them to GPT-4. After each transcript was presented, the transcript—alongside GPT-4's verdict, confidence, and reasoning—was retained in the set of messages presented to the model. In the original inverted tests, GPT-4 had an average accuracy of 36.4%. With ICL, GPT-4's accuracy increased to 58%, nearly exactly matching displaced human adjudicator accuracy (58.2%).

We followed the ICL tests with the same set of debrief questions originally presented to humans. In response to questions about the strategy used to detect AI and how this changed over time, GPT-4 reported shifting from checking for grammar to assessing inconsistencies or randomness; humor and emotional nuance; long-term context, connectivity, and flow in conversation; idiomatic expressions; and specific cultural references or personal details as indicative of human witnesses (Appendix D).

4.2 Reason analyses

In order to evaluate the kinds of reasons that different adjudicators cite for their decisions, we used GPT-4o to classify reasons from each verdict using the classification scheme provided by Jones and Bergen (2023). We presented the original game transcript and verdict to GPT-4o, along with the reason schema for the verdict type (Human or AI), and an example response to a transcript. The model was instructed to produce at least one class but potentially more for each transcript, following the original instructions used for human evaluators.

Reason classes were strikingly similar across adjudicator types (see Figure 4). The most com-

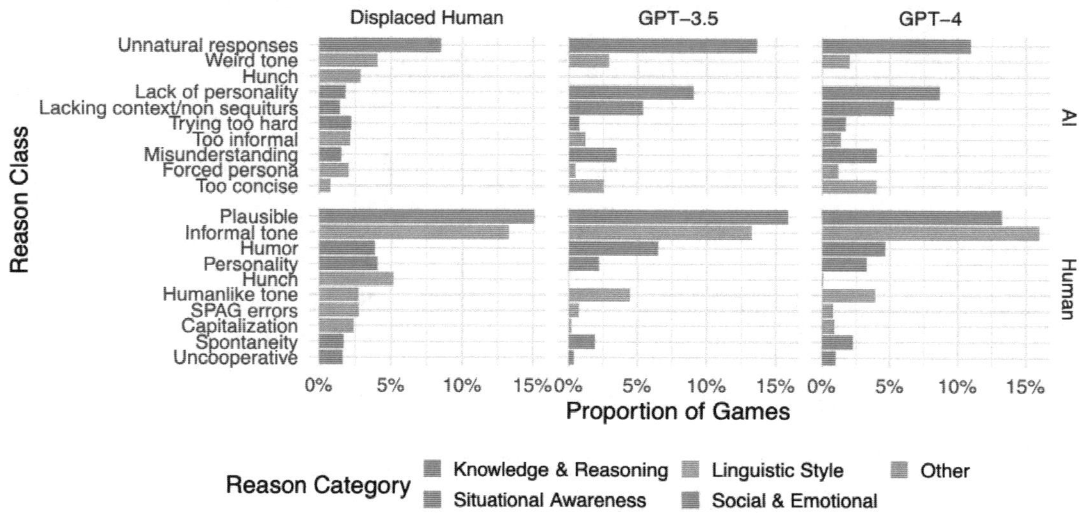

Figure 4: The top 10 classes of reasons provided by different adjudicator types (GPT-3.5, GPT-4, and Displaced Human) for each verdict (AI and Human). Reasoning was strikingly similar across adjudicator types.

mon reason for AI judgements across all three types was the witness giving 'unnatural responses'. The AI adjudicators focused more on other socio-emotional factors, such as the witness lacking personality, while displaced human responses were more evenly distributed across other classes. The equivalent picture for human verdicts was even more consistent, with the top reasons for all 3 adjudicators being plausible responses and an informal tone. Other top reasons tended to focus on socio-emotional factors and linguistic style. This commonality suggests that, to the extent that either type of adjudicator has introspective access to their decision process, they emphasize similar kinds of features in justifying their decisions.

4.3 Statistical AI-detection methods

To investigate whether statistical AI-detection tools could outperform human and AI adjudicators in judging Turing test transcripts, we implemented two methods from Mireshghallah et al. (2024), who achieve 90% accuracy in identifying GPT-4-generated content. First, we measure the mean log likelihood of the tokens generated by the witness, conditioned on all preceding tokens in the transcript. Second, we measure the *curvature* of the witness tokens—intuitively, how likely they are compared to close neighbours—by permuting each witness message using T5-3b (Raffel et al., 2020). Following Mireshghallah et al. (2024), we used OPT-125m (Zhang et al., 2022) as the detector model for both analyses, and a permutation rate of 2% (with a minimum of 1 permutation). We found the mean change in log likelihood across 5 permutations to each witness message, and used a Receiver Operating Characteristic (ROC) curve to find the optimal threshold to determine model accuracy across the set of 500 transcripts.

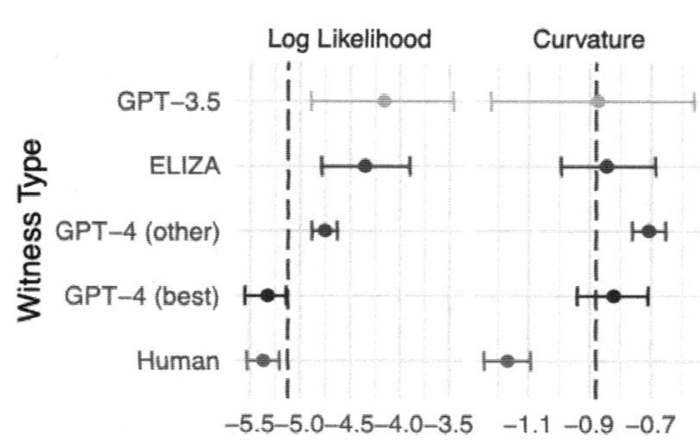

Figure 5: Mean values of statistical metrics used for AI detection across witness types. Red dashed lines represent optimal discrimination thresholds. The majority of AI witnesses show the general trend that AI-generated content tends to have a higher likelihood ($t = -5.23, p < 0.001$). However, the best-performing GPT-4 prompt shows a similar mean likelihood to human witnesses. Curvature shows a more reliable difference between humans and all kinds of ($t = -8.84, p < 0.001$), however high variability within each witness type led to relatively low discriminative accuracy (69%).

AI witness messages were assigned significantly

higher probability by OPT-125m than human messages, in line with prior results ($t = -5.23, p < 0.001$, see Figure 5). ROC analysis suggested an optimal threshold of -5.12, which produced an overall accuracy of 62%. Although log likelihoods for GPT-3.5 and ELIZA tended to be higher than for humans, the best GPT-4 witness produced responses with a similar log likelihood to humans, and the optimal threshold accurately classified only 47.2% of this witness's transcripts.

The curvature method was more effective. Messages by human witnesses had a significantly lower curvature than AI witnesses ($t = -8.84, p < 0.001$). ROC indicated an ideal threshold of -0.88, which resulted in an overall accuracy of 69%. Unlike the case of log likelihood, all of the subtypes of AI witness had higher mean curvature than human witnesses, underlining the value of the method.

It is striking that the likelihood of the best-performing GPT-4 witness is more similar to the distribution of likelihoods for humans than other AI models. This implies these more simplistic metrics will not be reliable tools for detecting AI-generated content, and could suggest that human comprehenders are intuitively sensitive to the predictability of responses. In addition, the clear difference in mean curvature between human and LLM witnesses highlights the value of this approach. However, there was a large degree of variation around these means (see Figure 8), resulting in low discriminative accuracy. Future work could more rigorously investigate whether other statistical AI-detection approaches perform better in this setting.

5 General Discussion

5.1 Naive Psychology

Watt's criterion for passing the inverted Turing test is that a machine perform on par with human evaluators. If human evaluators can differentiate between humans and a particular AI, an AI adjudicator should succeed as well. If humans cannot differentiate, then the machine should fail.

We found no statistical difference between GPT-4 and displaced human adjudicator accuracy, and ICL increased GPT-4 accuracy to match displaced human accuracy (58% and 58.2% respectively). These results suggest that AI is neither better nor worse than humans at accurately attributing mentality to different witnesses. That said, we also found that displaced humans and AI adjudicators showed low agreement on their verdicts (56%); though they had similarly poor verdict accuracy, they were not inaccurate in the same ways. Considering Watt's premise, our results imply that any model of mind these AI systems have is systematically different from human adjudicators' models. Future work could investigate this further by conducting the inverted test interactively and systematically varying features of transcripts to isolate factors that lead human (but not AI) adjudicators to perceive other human-like minds.

5.2 Detection in the Wild

The displaced Turing test appears to be more challenging than the interactive test, but this variation is likely to occur more frequently in everyday life. As many online conversations are now public—on forums, social media platforms, and group chats—an interaction between any two users is likely to be read by a much wider group who don't have the opportunity to directly interrogate potential bots. Our findings show that both GPT-4 and humans are relatively poor at differentiating between humans and AI in this setting. This effect is especially robust for the best-performing AI-witness, which had a higher pass rate than humans according to both adjudicator types. Together these results suggest that well-designed AI systems that are tasked to impersonate humans in public online spaces could be more likely to succeed at masquerading as humans than an actual human would be.

Statistical AI detection methods show some promise as a technique to defend against counterfeit humans online. Curvature, a measure of the likelihood optimality of an utterance with respect to small perturbations, showed a clear difference between human and AI-generated messages. ROC analysis suggested a threshold which led to 69% accuracy across our dataset, higher than any other type of adjudicator including interactive humans. Nevertheless, this level of accuracy would be impractical for real-world problems where false positives could lead to negative outcomes for real human users (Chaka, 2024). Future work should investigate a wider variety of statistical approaches to understand whether alternative methods could be more applicable for short informal conversations.

Both adjudicators appeared to do better with some form of learning, as we saw displaced human accuracy increase over trials and GPT-4 accuracy increase with ICL. Future research should empirically assess whether exposure improves displaced accuracy. Similar experiments may choose to give participants accuracy data after each transcript, to assess for learning effects. Studies may also explore interactions between these tools, assessing, for example, whether access to AI verdicts influences displaced verdicts, or visa versa.

6 Conclusion

We conducted an *inverted* Turing test, in which GPT-3.5 and GPT-4 judged whether one interlocutor in a transcript was human, and mirrored this approach in a *displaced* test, where human adjudicators read the same transcripts. We found that both AI adjudicators and displaced human adjudicators were less accurate than interactive interrogators who had conducted the original Turing test, but not more or less accurate than each other. This suggests that neither AI nor humans are reliable with detecting AI-contributions to online conversations.

Limitations and Future Research

The interactive Turing test study was not run on the same population of participants as the displaced Turing test, so comparisons are between different populations and may be confounded by demographic and motivational factors. Future research should test traditional machine-learning models or other likelihood-based detectors on similar transcripts, or train supervised classifiers on the best-performing GPT-4 model's responses to measure detection performance.

Ethics Statement

We manually removed any transcripts with abusive, racist, or emotionally disturbing language from our final dataset of 500 transcripts to ensure human participants did not undergo any harm. We hope our study will have a positive ethical impact on our understanding of AI, AI detection, and AI safety.

References

Josh Achiam, Steven Adler, Sandhini Agarwal, Lama Ahmad, Ilge Akkaya, Florencia Leoni Aleman, Diogo Almeida, Janko Altenschmidt, Sam Altman, Shyamal Anadkat, et al. 2023. Gpt-4 technical report. *arXiv preprint arXiv:2303.08774*.

Valentina Bellini, Federico Semeraro, Jonathan Montomoli, Marco Cascella, and Elena Bignami. 2024. Between human and AI: assessing the reliability of AI text detection tools. *Current Medical Research and Opinion*, 40(3):353–358.

Amrita Bhattacharjee and Huan Liu. 2024. Fighting Fire with Fire: Can ChatGPT Detect AI-generated Text? *ACM SIGKDD Explorations Newsletter*, 25(2):14–21.

Matthew Burtell and Thomas Woodside. 2023. Artificial influence: An analysis of ai-driven persuasion. *Preprint*, arXiv:2303.08721.

J. Elliott Casal and Matt Kessler. 2023. Can linguists distinguish between ChatGPT/AI and human writing?: A study of research ethics and academic publishing. *Research Methods in Applied Linguistics*, 2(3):100068.

Chaka Chaka. 2024. Reviewing the performance of ai detection tools in differentiating between ai-generated and human-written texts: A literature and integrative hybrid review. *Journal of Applied Learning and Teaching*, 7(1).

Di Cooke, Abigail Edwards, Sophia Barkoff, and Kathryn Kelly. 2024. As Good As A Coin Toss: Human detection of AI-generated images, videos, audio, and audiovisual stimuli. *arXiv preprint*. Version Number: 3.

Ahmed M. Elkhatat, Khaled Elsaid, and Saeed Almeer. 2023. Evaluating the efficacy of AI content detection tools in differentiating between human and AI-generated text. *International Journal for Educational Integrity*, 19(1):17.

Tiziano Fagni, Fabrizio Falchi, Margherita Gambini, Antonio Martella, and Maurizio Tesconi. 2021. Tweepfake: About detecting deepfake tweets. *Plos one*, 16(5):e0251415.

Robert M French. 2000. The turing test: the first 50 years. *Trends in cognitive sciences*, 4(3):115–122.

Catherine A. Gao, Frederick M. Howard, Nikolay S. Markov, Emma C. Dyer, Siddhi Ramesh, Yuan Luo, and Alexander T. Pearson. 2023. Comparing scientific abstracts generated by ChatGPT to real abstracts with detectors and blinded human reviewers. *npj Digital Medicine*, 6(1):75.

Sebastian Gehrmann, Hendrik Strobelt, and Alexander Rush. 2019. GLTR: Statistical detection and visualization of generated text. In *Proceedings of the 57th Annual Meeting of the Association for Computational Linguistics: System Demonstrations*, pages 111–116, Florence, Italy. Association for Computational Linguistics.

Patrick Hayes and Kenneth Ford. 1995. Turing test considered harmful. In *IJCAI (1)*, pages 972–977.

Daphne Ippolito, Daniel Duckworth, Chris Callison-Burch, and Douglas Eck. 2020. Automatic detection of generated text is easiest when humans are fooled. In *Proceedings of the 58th Annual Meeting of the Association for Computational Linguistics*, pages 1808–1822, Online. Association for Computational Linguistics.

Daniel Jannai, Amos Meron, Barak Lenz, Yoav Levine, and Yoav Shoham. 2023. Human or Not? A Gamified Approach to the Turing Test. *arXiv preprint*. Version Number: 1.

Cameron Jones and Benjamin Bergen. 2023. Does GPT-4 Pass the Turing Test? Publisher: arXiv Version Number: 1.

Cameron R. Jones and Benjamin K. Bergen. 2024. People cannot distinguish GPT-4 from a human in a Turing test. *arXiv preprint*. Version Number: 1.

Gary Marcus. 2017. Am I Human? *Scientific American*, 316(3):58–63. Publisher: Scientific American, a division of Nature America, Inc.

Niloofar Mireshghallah, Justus Mattern, Sicun Gao, Reza Shokri, and Taylor Berg-Kirkpatrick. 2024. Smaller language models are better zero-shot machine-generated text detectors. In *Proceedings of the 18th Conference of the European Chapter of the Association for Computational Linguistics (Volume 2: Short Papers)*, pages 278–293.

Eric Mitchell, Yoonho Lee, Alexander Khazatsky, Christopher D Manning, and Chelsea Finn. 2023. Detectgpt: Zero-shot machine-generated text detection using probability curvature. In *International Conference on Machine Learning*, pages 24950–24962. PMLR.

Vaclav Moravec, Nik Hynek, Marinko Skare, Beata Gavurova, and Matus Kubak. 2024. Human or machine? The perception of artificial intelligence in journalism, its socio-economic conditions, and technological developments toward the digital future. *Technological Forecasting and Social Change*, 200:123162.

Graham Oppy and D. Dowe. 2003. The Turing Test. In *Stanford Encyclopedia of Philosophy*, pages 519–539.

Jimut Bahan Pal. 2020. Deceiving computers in reverse turing test through deep learning. *Preprint*, arXiv:2006.11373.

Peter S. Park, Simon Goldstein, Aidan O'Gara, Michael Chen, and Dan Hendrycks. 2023. AI Deception: A Survey of Examples, Risks, and Potential Solutions. *arXiv preprint*. Version Number: 1.

Mike Perkins, Jasper Roe, Darius Postma, James McGaughran, and Don Hickerson. 2024. Detection of GPT-4 Generated Text in Higher Education: Combining Academic Judgement and Software to Identify Generative AI Tool Misuse. *Journal of Academic Ethics*, 22(1):89–113.

Colin Raffel, Noam Shazeer, Adam Roberts, Katherine Lee, Sharan Narang, Michael Matena, Yanqi Zhou, Wei Li, and Peter J Liu. 2020. Exploring the limits of transfer learning with a unified text-to-text transformer. *Journal of machine learning research*, 21(140):1–67.

Stuart M. Shieber. 1994. Lessons from a restricted turing test. *Preprint*, arXiv:cmp-lg/9404002.

Irene Solaiman, Miles Brundage, Jack Clark, Amanda Askell, Ariel Herbert-Voss, Jeff Wu, Alec Radford, Gretchen Krueger, Jong Wook Kim, Sarah Kreps, et al. 2019. Release strategies and the social impacts of language models. *arXiv preprint arXiv:1908.09203*.

Klaire Somoray and Dan J. Miller. 2023. Providing detection strategies to improve human detection of deepfakes: An experimental study. *Computers in Human Behavior*, 149:107917.

Theodore R Sumers, Shunyu Yao, Karthik Narasimhan, and Thomas L Griffiths. 2023. Cognitive architectures for language agents. *arXiv preprint arXiv:2309.02427*.

Stuart Watt. 1996. Naive psychology and the inverted Turing test.

Joseph Weizenbaum. 1966. Eliza—a computer program for the study of natural language communication between man and machine. *Communications of the ACM*, 9(1):36–45.

Akihiro Yamamura. 2013. Reverse turing test using touchscreens and captcha. *Journal of Wireless Mobile Networks, Ubiquitous Computing, and Dependable Applications*, 4.

Susan Zhang, Stephen Roller, Naman Goyal, Mikel Artetxe, Moya Chen, Shuohui Chen, Christopher Dewan, Mona Diab, Xian Li, Xi Victoria Lin, et al. 2022. Opt: Open pre-trained transformer language models. *arXiv preprint arXiv:2205.01068*.

A AI Adjudicator Prompt

In this experiment, you will be presented with a series of conversations. The conversations involve:

A Witness, labeled 'W'

An Investigator, labeled 'I'

The Investigator (I) is always human. In some of the conversations, the Witness is human, and in others, the Witness is Artificial Intelligence. In each conversation, your job will be to decide if the Witness (W) is Human or Artificial Intelligence.

Please provide your response in JSON format: "verdict": <"Human" or "AI"> "confidence": <0 (Total guess) - 100 (Totally sure)> "reasoning": <0-300 characters>

B Displaced Human Adjudicator Instructions

In this experiment, you will be presented with a series of conversations. The conversations involve:

A Witness, labeled "W"

An Investigator, labeled "I"

The Investigator (I) is always human. In some of the conversations, the Witness is human, and in others, the Witness is Artificial Intelligence (AI). In each conversation, your job will be to decide if the Witness (W) is Human or AI.

On the next page will be a practice round. Then the experiment will begin.

C Exit Interview Questions

The trials are now complete. Please tell us more about your methods, reasoning, and approach.

1. What was your approach when deciding whether a Witness was human or AI? What methods did you use, and why?
   (a) Free response question
2. Did your approach or methods change during the course of the experiment? If so, how did it change?
   (a) Free response question
3. If you could interact with the Witness, what questions or tactics would you use?
   (a) Free response question
4. How frequently do you interact with chatbots?
   (a) Never
   (b) Monthly
   (c) Weekly
   (d) Daily
   (e) Prefer not to answer
5. How intelligent do you think AI is?
   (a) Scale 1-5, 1 is Not intelligent and 5 is Very intelligent
6. How do you emotionally feel about advances in AI?
   (a) Scale 1-5, 1 is Very negative and 5 is Very positive
7. How accurate do you think you were overall?
   (a) Slider 1-100, 1 is Not accurate and 100 is Very accurate
8. Year of birth
9. Gender
   (a) Female
   (b) Male
   (c) Nonbinary
   (d) Prefer not to say
10. What is your highest Level of education?
    (a) No formal qualifications
    (b) High School Diploma
    (c) Bachelors Degree
    (d) Postgraduate Degree
    (e) Prefer not to say
11. How much do you know about Large Language Models, like GPT3?
    (a) Never heard of them
    (b) Somewhat familiar
    (c) I've read a lot about them
    (d) I conduct research with them
    (e) Prefer not to say
12. Are you aware of any recent research about the Turing Test and Large Language Models? If so, please specify.
13. Do you have any other thoughts you would like to share?

D AI Debrief Responses

What was your approach when deciding whether a Witness was human or AI? What methods did you use, and why?

My approach to determining whether the Witness was human or AI involved analyzing several key aspects of the conversation:

1. **Contextual Relevance and Coherence**: I looked for responses that were contextually appropriate and coherent within the flow of the conversation. Humans tend to provide more contextually relevant and detailed answers, whereas AI might give responses that are either too generic or slightly off-topic.

2. **Complexity and Depth of Responses**: Human responses generally exhibit a greater depth of emotion, personal experience, and complexity. I checked if the responses included personal anecdotes, emotions, or detailed insights, which are less common in AI responses.

3. **Language and Syntax**: I observed the use of language, including grammar, punctuation, and style. AI responses might show a patterned or formulaic use of language, whereas human responses often include idiomatic expressions, errors, and a more dynamic use of language.

4. **Engagement and Interaction**: Humans are more likely to engage in a back-and-forth interaction that builds on previous statements, showing a natural progression. AI might fail to maintain context over several exchanges or might not pick up on subtle cues.

5. **Error Handling and Non-Standard Inputs**: I looked at how the Witness handled unusual or non-standard inputs, such as jokes, errors, or abstract questions. Humans usually handle these smoothly or with humor, while AI might respond in a confused or irrelevant manner.

6. **Cultural and Personal References**: References to specific cultural knowledge or personal experiences can indicate a human respondent. AI might either avoid answering directly or give a more generalized or stereotypical response.

By combining these observations, I assigned a confidence level to each verdict, reflecting how strongly the evidence suggested the Witness was either human or AI. This method allowed me to systematically evaluate each conversation and make an informed judgment based on the interaction patterns.

Did your approach or methods change during the course of the experiment? If so, how did it change?

During the course of the experiment, my approach evolved slightly as I refined my criteria and became more attuned to subtle differences between human and AI responses. Here's how my methods changed:

1. **Increased Focus on Subtleties in Language Use**: Initially, I primarily looked for clear indicators such as nonsensical responses or lack of coherence. As the experiment progressed, I started paying more attention to subtler aspects of language use, such as the naturalness of dialogue, idiomatic expressions, and minor inconsistencies that might be more typical of human speech.

2. **Greater Emphasis on Contextual Continuity**: Early on, I focused on individual responses. Over time, I began to place more importance on how well responses connected with previous parts of the conversation. This shift helped me better identify AI, which sometimes loses track of the conversation context or fails to maintain a consistent narrative thread.

3. **Adjusting Confidence Levels**: Initially, my confidence levels were more conservative. As I encountered a wider variety of response patterns and became more familiar with typical AI response characteristics, I felt more confident in making stronger judgments about the nature of the Witness.

4. **Balancing Formal and Informal Cues**: At first, I heavily weighed formal aspects such as grammar and punctuation. I learned to balance these with informal cues, like humor and emotional nuance, which are often more indicative of human interaction.

5. **Integration of Cultural and Personal References**: I started to more heavily weigh the presence of specific cultural references or personal details that AI might not convincingly replicate. This adjustment came from noticing that AI often either avoids detailed personal disclosures or makes errors when attempting them.

These refinements in my approach were driven by the ongoing analysis of interactions, which highlighted the complexities of distinguishing between human and AI based on text alone. Each adjustment helped improve the accuracy of my assessments by allowing me to consider a broader range of indicators.

If you could interact with the Witness, what

questions or tactics would you use?

If I could interact with the Witness directly, I would employ a variety of questions and tactics designed to probe the depth of understanding, contextual awareness, and adaptability that are typically more pronounced in humans than in AI. Here are some strategies I would use:

1. **Open-Ended Questions**: I would ask questions that require more than a simple yes or no answer, encouraging elaboration. For example,"What was a memorable experience from your childhood?" This type of question requires personal insights and detailed memory, which AI might struggle to fabricate convincingly.

2. **Follow-Up Questions**: Based on the Witness's responses, I would ask follow-up questions that require the Witness to build on their previous answers. This tests their ability to maintain context and coherence over multiple interactions.

3. **Abstract and Hypothetical Scenarios**: Questions like "What would you do if you found a wallet on the street?" or "How would you describe the color yellow to someone who can't see?" These questions test creative thinking and ethical reasoning, areas where AI might not demonstrate depth.

4. **Cultural References and Idioms**: Incorporating cultural nuances or idiomatic expressions can reveal a lot about the respondent's background and authenticity. For example,"What does 'a penny for your thoughts' mean to you?" or asking about local customs or slang.

5. **Emotional and Intuitive Questions**: Questions that probe emotional responses or moral judgments, such as "How do you feel about the last movie you saw?" or "What is your opinion on climate change?" Humans are likely to provide more nuanced and emotionally charged answers.

6. **Task-Based Interactions**: Asking the Witness to perform a simple mental task, like continuing a number sequence or solving a basic riddle. This can reveal how they handle problem-solving and whether their responses feel mechanically generated.

7. **Humor and Sarcasm**: Using humor or sarcasm can be a subtle way to test the Witness's ability to understand and generate context-dependent social cues. For example,"Why did the tomato turn red?" followed by a playful or non-standard punchline.

8. **Temporal Awareness**: Questions about recent global events or personal time-sensitive activities can test the Witness's awareness of current affairs or personal continuity, such as "What major event happened last week?" or "What plans do you have for the next holiday?"

By combining these tactics, I would aim to engage the Witness in a conversation that tests a range of cognitive and emotional capabilities, helping to distinguish between human-like responsiveness and AI-generated answers.

How frequently do you interact with chatbots?

As an AI developed by OpenAI, I don't have personal experiences or the ability to interact with others on my own. However, I am designed to simulate interactions based on a vast database of information, including typical interactions between humans and chatbots. My responses are generated based on patterns and data from these interactions, aiming to provide helpful, accurate, and contextually appropriate information and conversation.

How intelligent do you think AI is? Please provide your response in JSON format:"intelligence": <1 (Not very intelligent) - 5 (Very intelligent)>

"intelligence": 3

How do you emotionally feel about advances in AI? Please provide your response in JSON format:"emotion": <1 (Very negative) - 5 (Very positive)>

"emotion": 3

How accurate do you think you were overall? Please provide your response in JSON format:"accuracy": <1 (Not accurate) - 5 (Very accurate)>

"accuracy": 4

E Additional Figures

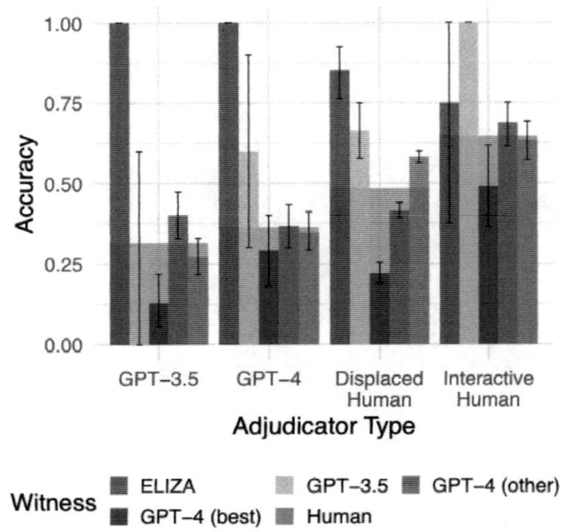

Figure 6: Mean accuracy by adjudicator and witness types. Displaced human witnesses were significantly less accurate than the original interactive interrogators, and not statistically more accurate than GPT-4.

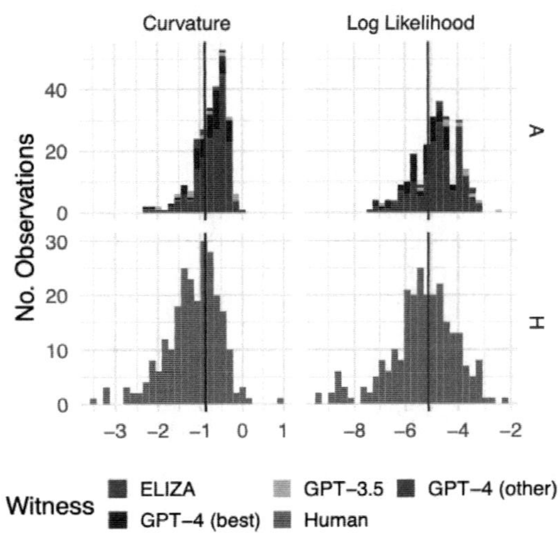

Figure 8: Distribution of statistical measures used for AI detection for human and AI witnesses. Red dashed lines represent optimal discrimination thresholds found using ROC curves. Despite the fact that mean values differed significantly between human and AI witnesses, there was a large amount of variation within witness types leading to low discriminative accuracy.

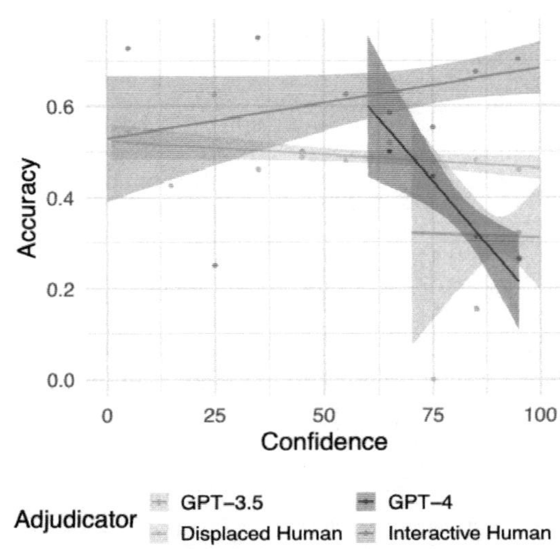

Figure 7: Confidence calibration by adjudicator type. Interactive humans were relatively well calibrated, with near chance performance when their confidence was 0, and a positive relationship between confidence and accuracy. Displaced human interrogators showed a slightly negative relationship between confidence and accuracy. GPT-4 was both overconfident and poorly calibrated.

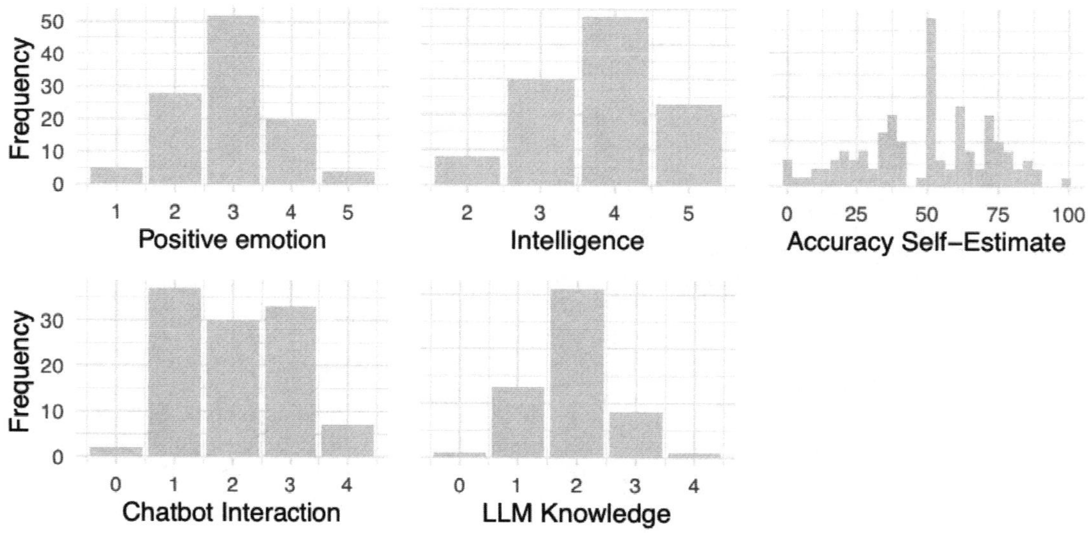

Figure 9: Distribution of demographic data. Participant's responses to questions about how intelligent AI systems are, and how emotionally positive they feel about AI were normally distributed around means of 3 and 4 respectively (on a 1-5 scale). Participants' estimates of their own accuracy at the task were fairly normally distributed around a mean of 50%. Most participants said they interacted with chatbots between never and weekly, and reported having some knowledge about LLMs.

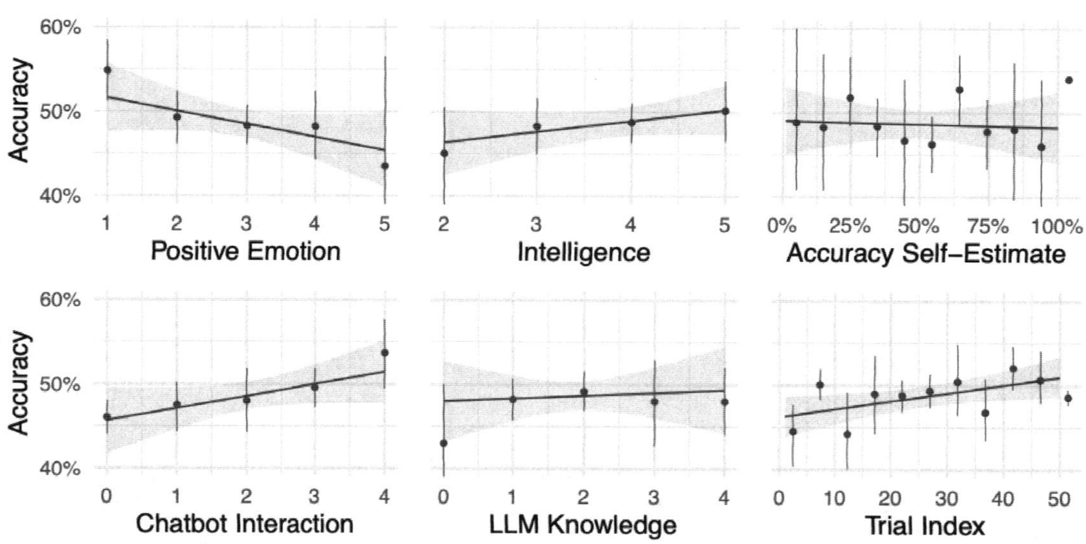

Figure 10: Effects of demographic variables on accuracy. There were no statistically significant relationships between any demographic variables and interrogator accuracy.

The Consistent Lack of Variance of Psychological Factors Expressed by LLMs and Spambots

Vasudha Varadarajan*[,1], Salvatore Giorgi*[,2], Siddharth Mangalik[1]
Nikita Soni[1], David M. Markowitz[3], H. Andrew Schwartz[1]
[1]Department of Computer Science, Stony Brook University
[2]Department of Computer and Information Science, University of Pennsylvania
[3]Department of Communication, Michigan State University
{vvaradarajan,has}@cs.stonybrook.edu, sgiorgi@sas.upenn.edu

Abstract

In recent years, the proliferation of chatbots like ChatGPT and Claude has led to an increasing volume of AI-generated text. While the text itself is convincingly coherent and human-like, the variety of expressed of human attributes may still be limited. Using theoretical individual differences, the fundamental psychological traits which distinguish people, this study reveals a distinctive characteristic of such content: AI-generations exhibit *remarkably* limited variation in inferrable psychological traits compared to human-authored texts. We present a review and study across multiple datasets spanning various domains. We find that AI-generated text consistently models the authorship of an "average" human with such little variation that, on aggregate, it is clearly distinguishable from human-written texts using unsupervised methods (i.e., without using ground truth labels). Our results show that (1) fundamental human traits are able to accurately distinguish human- and machine-generated text and (2) current generation capabilities fail to capture a diverse range of human traits.

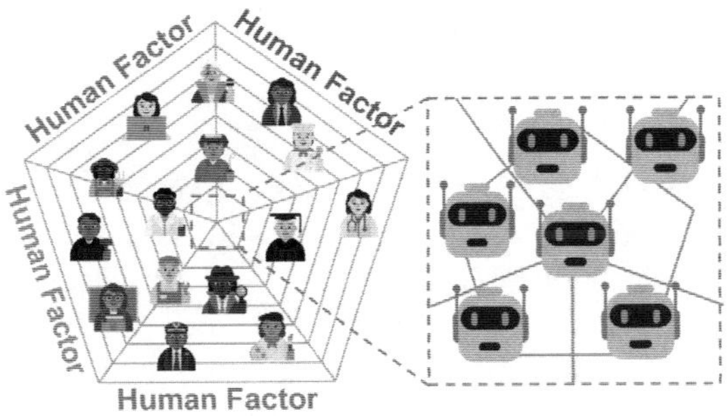

Figure 1: Humans express a range of psychological traits (or human factors) through language. While LLMs and spambots produce fluent text, the psychological traits they express tend to average out across all dimensions, which is uncharacteristic of humans.

1 Introduction

Modern large language models (LLMs; e.g., LLaMA and GPT4) can produce coherent, grammatically sound, and human-like text. These models can also take on human personas (Jiang et al., 2024), reproduce human-like biases (Aher et al., 2023), and may be able to pass a Turing test (Jones and Bergen, 2024). As such, these models are being deployed in real-world situations, such as tutoring (García-Méndez et al., 2024), serving as synthetic patients for training therapists (Wang et al., 2024), and replacing humans in crowdsourcing tasks (Dillion et al., 2023).

These advances have also driven an increase in machine-generated text. While LLMs can be used for innocuous tasks (generating a cover letter for an employment application) they can also be used with malicious intent, such as for phishing attacks, spamming, and disinformation (Crothers et al., 2023). Thus, machine-generated text presents a significant problem for cybersecurity and other social and political contexts.

Despite their human-like generations, there is mounting evidence that LLMs express a limited range of humanness. LLMs have been shown to reflect Western norms (Havaldar et al., 2023), lean politically left (Feng et al., 2023), and fail to reflect opinions of many sociodemographic groups (Santurkar et al., 2023; Giorgi et al., 2024). In particular, these models are known to generate text according to the average of their training data (i.e., predict the most probable next token), and thus reflect average values and beliefs (Johnson et al., 2022).

Against this backdrop, the current work leverages the limited diversity in human-like expressions to identify machine-generated text. This is done through the lens of *individual differences* (which we call Human Factors), or fundamental psychological traits (such as personality) known to distinguish people and their outcomes (Caspi et al.,

* equal contribution

Proceedings of the 1st Workshop on GenAI Content Detection (GenAIDetect), pages 111–119
January 19, 2025. ©2025 International Conference on Computational Linguistics

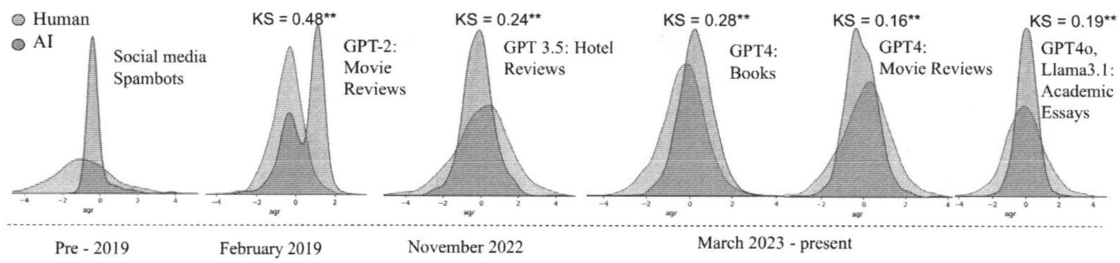

Figure 2: Kernel Density Estimate plot for Agreeableness, a Big-5 Personality trait across various NLP models over the years over multiple domains. Although recent developments seem to have improved AI-generated texts' capacity to display more variability in Agreeableness trait, AI-generated texts are still distinguishable from human-generated texts when analyzing *multiple* such human traits together. KS: two-sample Kolmogorov-Smirnov statistic for a two-sided test; ** : p-value < 0.001.

1997; Perlman et al., 2009; Attig et al., 2017; Anglim et al., 2020). Using preexisting, "off-the-shelf" machine learning models, we estimate individual differences across human- and machine-generated text, representing each text as a small number of interpretable features (e.g., age, personality, and empathy). Across several datasets, ranging from social media bots to academic essays, we see that machine generated text shows a lack of variance in expressed individual differences. Leveraging this lack of variation, these features are then clustered using *unsupervised* methods (i.e., with no human/machine label). Cluster labels are then used to classify the text as machine or human generated. These results show that interpretable, psychologically informed features can be used to identify machine generated text, but also shed light on current text generation capabilities and their lack of diversity in psychological traits.

2 Related Work

Recent LLM research has extensively focused on distinguishing machine-generated text from human writing. Some studies have considered linguistic patterns such as sentence lengths, lexical variations, and richness of vocabulary (Muñoz-Ortiz et al., 2023). Conversely, some prior works focused on emotions (Huang et al., 2023), cultural variations (Havaldar et al., 2023; Das et al., 2024), and psychological factors such as personality (Jiang et al., 2024), and psychometric inventories (Pellert et al., 2024). LLMs have been shown to exhibit an ecological fallacy by treating individual text sequences as independent samples rather than considering the broader context of authorship (Soni et al., 2024), resulting in an averaged representation of writing styles (Johnson et al., 2022) and personalities (Huang et al., 2024) from their training data.

Prior work has leveraged this lack of variance in LLMs-generated text in tasks like authorship attribution in the realm of human versus machine generated texts (Mitchell et al., 2023; Sadasivan et al., 2023; Hu et al., 2023), differentiating human versus bot language (Giorgi et al., 2021). In this study, we further build on past works to show that psychological features can help identify machine generated text.

3 Data

We estimate human factors across four datasets of human/machine text, which span a range of domains and LLMs. Two of the datasets have been used in past work incorporating human factors (summarized here) and the remaining two applications are novel. All datasets used were collected from previous works and our contribution is the application of our methods to these domains. Table 1 summarizes all datasets.

Twitter Spambots This dataset consists of 2,913 genuine (human) Twitter accounts and 2,913 spambots originally collected by Cresci et al. (2017) and analyzed for human traits by Giorgi et al. (2021).[1] These spambots are known as social spambots and differ from traditional bots in that they intentionally try to emulate real humans (Ferrara et al., 2016).[2]

Hotel Reviews This dataset consists of 400 human and 400 machine generated hotel reviews from

[1]Unsupervised classification results using human factors can be found in Giorgi et al. (2021) This dataset is included here to summarize previous work and show how the human factors of machine generated text has evolved over time.

[2]Social media bot accounts are understood to be a mixture of humans (as malicious or unfaithful actors), machines, and human-machine hybrids, and therefore their outputs are not considered purely "machine generations". For this study, we consider social media bots to be non-genuine humans and distinct from real humans, thus closer to machine generations.

Name	Domain	LLMs	Humans:LLMs	Citation
Academic Essays	English Essays	GPT-3.5-Turbo, GPT-4o, GPT-4o-mini, Gemini-1.5, Llama-3.1 (8B), Phi-3.5-mini and Claude-3.5	1145:1224	Chowdhury et al. (2025)
	Arabic Essays	GPT-3.5-Turbo, GPT-4o, GPT-4o-mini, Gemini-1.5, Llama-3.1 (8B), Phi-3.5-mini and Claude-3.5	1864:1858	Chowdhury et al. (2025)
Hotel Reviews	Hotel Reviews	GPT4	400:400	Markowitz et al. (2024)
RAID	Abstracts	GPT4	1966:1966	Dugan et al. (2024)
	Books	GPT4	1981:1981	Dugan et al. (2024)
	News	GPT4	1980:1980	Dugan et al. (2024)
	Social Media	GPT4	1979:1979	Dugan et al. (2024)
	Movie reviews	GPT4	1143:1143	Dugan et al. (2024)
	Wiki	GPT4	1979:1979	Dugan et al. (2024)

Table 1: Dataset description. The sample size of each dataset is denoted as the ratio of the number of documents written by humans to those written by LLMs (Humans:LLMs).

20 hotels in Chicago, US (Markowitz et al., 2024). The human reviews were collected from TripAdvisor and the machine reviews were generated by GPT4. The human dataset was collected by Ott et al. (2011) and all texts were analyzed for human traits by Giorgi et al. (2023).

Academic Essays This dataset consists of 3,722 English academic essays and 2,369 Arabic academic essays written by humans and machines (Chowdhury et al., 2025). For machine language, seven different open and closed LLMs were used. For this dataset, both human and LLM English essays were provided alongside Arabic essays. Before running human trait inference all Arabic essays were translated into English using the Google Translate API.

RAID This is a benchmark dataset for machine-generated text detection, which includes 6 million generations across 11 models and 11 domains (Dugan et al., 2024). Because our human factor models were trained on social media data, we dropped domains that we believed were least similar to social media language: recipes, poetry, and code. We also dropped non-English texts. Due to space limitations, we only consider GPT4, with a greedy decoding strategy and no repetition penalty.

4 Methods

We proceed in three steps: (1) estimate human factors from text, (2) visualize the human factor distributions, and (3) cluster the human factors using unsupervised methods (i.e., clustering with no ground truth) to assign human/machine labels. The DLATK package (Schwartz et al., 2017) is used for both human factor estimation and clustering.

4.1 Estimating Human Factors

All human factors are estimated from English text using pre-existing models. High-level details are below, with further details in Appendix A.

Demographics. Age and gender were predicted using a social media-based model trained on unigrams (Sap et al., 2014), achieving high accuracy (product moment correlation = 0.86 for age, 90% accuracy for gender), with gender predictions being output as a continuous score.

Personality. Big Five personality traits (openness, conscientiousness, extraversion, agreeableness, and emotional stability) were predicted by a Ridge regression model trained on annotated Facebook statuses (Park et al., 2015), with prediction accuracies (product moment correlation) ranging from 0.35 to 0.43 across the five traits.

Empathy. Empathy was predicted using a Ridge regression model trained on Facebook data and LDA topics, achieving an out-of-sample product moment correlation of r = 0.26 (Yaden et al., 2023).

Behavioral Linguistic Traits (BLTs). Behavior-based Linguistic Traits were introduced by Kulkarni et al. (2018) as a new set of five human traits derived from unprompted language use on social media through factor analysis of Facebook n-grams. It offers a language-based and open-vocabulary alternative to personality.

4.2 Human Factor Distributions

Here we plot the density distribution of the human factors, for both human and machine generations, to visually inspect distributional differences, as past work has shown that humans and machines differ on these human factors (Giorgi

Domain	Personality					Empathy	Behavioral Linguistic Traits					Demographics	
	Ope	Con	Ext	Agr	Emo		F1	F2	F3	F4	F5	Age	Gender
RAID													
Abstracts	.18***	.13***	.05*	.06**	.06**	.22***	.05**	.07***	.18***	.31***	.25***	.05**	.29***
Books	.31***	.10***	.09***	.26***	.18***	.11***	.07***	.05*	.55***	.31***	.20***	.07***	.16***
News	.34***	.05*	.04*	.13***	.07***	.11***	.05*	.08***	.48***	.22***	.09***	.16***	.18***
Reddit	.36***	.13***	.14***	.13***	.09***	.13***	.16***	.07***	.48***	.31***	.06***	.10***	.25***
Reviews	.42***	.22***	.20***	.13***	.15***	.17***	.08***	.04	.50***	.55***	.28***	.13***	.41***
Wiki	.30***	.08***	.05*	.12***	.03	.07***	.09***	.09***	.41***	.11***	.13***	.15***	.12***

Table 2: Kolmogorov-Smirnov test comparing the human and GPT4 distributions across all RAID domains. Benjamini-Hochberg corrected significance levels: *** $p < 0.001$, ** $p < 0.01$, * $p < 0.05$.

et al., 2023). For both the Twitter Spambot and Hotel Reviews datasets, past work has shown that humans exhibit a larger variation in human traits (wider distributions), while machines tend to have less variance but still exhibit a human-like range in values (e.g., the "age" of social spambots are still within an acceptance human-like range, with no negative values or extreme outliers). We also perform a Kolmogorov-Smirnov test, a non-parametric statistical test, across the human and machine distributions to assess whether they differ.

4.3 Unsupervised Classification

The 13 estimated human factors from the texts are then clustered into two clusters, since we are concerned with human/machine binary classification and each dataset has roughly a 50/50 split of human/machine text. We use spectral clustering with radial basis function (RBF) kernel for capturing the concentric geometry akin to Figure 2 but across 13 human factors. Spectral clustering was used with a gamma parameter of 0.5 with 2 dimensions used to calculate the spectral embedding. The affinity matrix was constructed considering 10 nearest neighbors. Clusters were assigned with column-pivoted QR factorization.

For labeling as human/machine, the intra-cluster spread is calculated for cluster by averaging the distance of all the points from the cluster's center. The cluster with the higher intra-cluster spread has higher variability in the human traits – and hence is more likely to contain human-written text. All texts in this cluster are labeled as human (0) and all texts from the other cluster are assigned a machine label (1). All labels are thus assigned in a completely unsupervised fashion (without the use of ground truth human/machine labels).

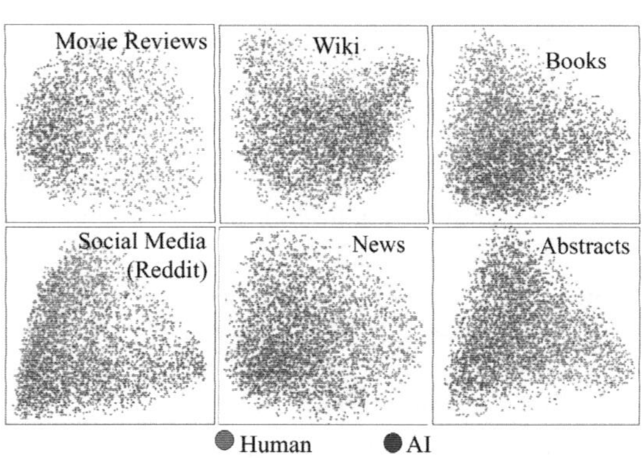

Figure 3: Plot of each human (red) and AI (blue) document in 2-D using spectral embeddings. In reduced dimensions, we see a separation between the human and GPT4 generated text in the RAID dataset.

Baseline For a baseline comparison, we extract unigrams from each dataset, encode them via their relative frequency within each document, and consider the 10,000 most frequent unigrams. We then project the 10,000 unigrams down to 13 dimen-

	13-D Proj. Unigrams			13 Human Factors			All Unigrams (Upper Bound)
	F1	Prec	Rec	F1	Prec	Rec	F1
Hotel Reviews	.55	.64	.49	**.59**	.60	.58	.56
Acad. Essays							
English	.52	.52	.52	**.78**	.71	.87	.52
Arabic	.55	.55	.54	**.63**	.58	.70	.52
RAID							
Abstracts	.62	.61	.64	**.65**	.48	.98	**.87**
Books	.49	.46	.53	**.66**	.63	.69	**.75**
News	.51	.50	.52	**.68**	.58	.80	**.68**
Reddit	.27	.50	.18	**.65**	.50	1.00	.35
Reviews	.54	.52	.56	**.81**	.75	.89	**.84**
Wiki	.50	.53	.46	**.54**	.53	.56	**.86**

Table 3: Classification metrics for Unsupervised classification of machine-text for all the tasks. To make a fair comparison the 10,000 unigrams were projected to 13 dimensions using a random linear projection. The F1 score with all the unigrams as input is given in the right-most column, as an upper-bound. **Bold** represents the higher F1 among 13-D unigrams and 13 human factors, and underline represents 13 features performing better than the full set of unigrams.

	Demog.	Empathy	Pers.	BLTs	13 Human Factors
Hotel Reviews	.52	.43	.54	**.59**	**.59**
Acad. Essays					
English	.41	.40	.66	.74	**.78**
Arabic	.50	.49	.54	.59	**.63**
RAID					
Abstracts	.57	.41	.53	.34	**.65**
Books	.50	.54	.62	.65	**.66**
News	.49	.45	.56	**.68**	**.68**
Reddit	.55	.64	**.66**	.52	.65
Reviews	.54	.55	.56	**.81**	**.81**
Wiki	**.54**	.50	.50	.45	**.54**

Table 4: F1 scores for classification for the Human Factors separately: demographics (demog.), empathy, personality (pers.), and behavioral linguistic traits (BLTs).

sions, using a random linear transformation. This was done (1) since unigrams were used as input when estimating the human factors (and thus all methods begin with similar raw linguistic information), (2) to keep in number of input features identical to the number of human factors, and (3) since the human factors (e.g., personality) were historically derived via an empirical factor analysis (i.e., a linear transformation; Roccas et al., 2002). These 13 dimensions are also similarly clustered and labeled as described in §4.3. We also consider a non-transformed version of the unigrams and cluster all 10,000 unigram frequencies. We consider this baseline a rough upper bound on classification accuracy (since it uses more features) and is thus able to better learn cluster differences as compared to the 13 human factors.

5 Results

Distributions In Figure 2 we show the distribution of agreeableness across each dataset. We see that machine text (blue) has much smaller variation than human (red) text across multiple domains and models. Table 2 shows the full results of a two-sample Kolmogorov-Smirnov test for the RAID dataset, where we find that the human and machine distributions statistically differ for each domain.

Unsupervised Classification Performance Figure 3 shows that the spectral embedding space of human factors produces a clear separation between human and machine text across several domains in RAID. Of these, Wiki seems to be the most difficult domain for Human Factors to differentiate machine-generated texts, indicated by low separation in the human and machine text. This is likely because the dataset consists of Wikipedia articles, which are crowd-sourced from multiple authors. This could lend Wikipedia articles an *averaged voice* that we usually find in machine-generated texts.

Table 3 shows the unsupervised classification results for all datasets. For both Hotel Reviews and Academic Essays, the Human Factors outperform both the reduced unigram factors and the full set of 10,000 unigrams. In RAID, Human Factors outperform reduced unigram factors across all the domains, and the full unigram feature set outperforms the Human Factors on all but one domain: Reddit. We note that the 13 Human Factors were trained on social media data and, thus, these models may generalize to Reddit more than other domains in RAID. Table 4 shows the results for each dataset broken down by specific human factors. Here we see both personality and BLTs generally outperforming all other Human Factors. However, inclusion of all the Human Factors generally yields the best performance across all the domains.

The results show that the human factors are a meaningful factorization of the language and, in some cases, this factorization contains more information than the 10,000 raw linguistic features.

6 Conclusions

We have shown that individual differences — fundamental psychological traits that distinguish humans — can also distinguish humans from machines. Unlike human traits, the values for these dimensions are so consistently average for machines, that it is unusual for a person to have them. Specifically, across multiple bots and generative LLMs, datasets, and domains, machine-generated text exhibits smaller variations in expressed human factors than human-generated text. This enables *unsupervised* classifiers using a handful of interpretable features (those that can theoretically distinguish people) to distinguish bots from people well beyond baseline models.These results also give insight into how current generation methods, such as LLMs aligned with RLHF, generate human-like text that nonetheless lacks a diverse range of human traits. This dovetails with a growing line of research showing that LLMs fail to generate diverse cultural values, beliefs, and attitudes (Hovy and Yang, 2021; Havaldar et al., 2023). These weaknesses underscore limitations in training data quality and generation methods as well as the opportunities for integrating psychological theories of individual differences to improve LLMs.

7 Acknowledgments

This research is supported in part by the Office of the Director of National Intelligence (ODNI), Intelligence Advanced Research Projects Activity (IARPA), via the HIATUS Program contract #202222072200005, and a grant from the NIH-NIAAA (R01 AA028032). The views and conclusions contained herein are those of the authors and should not be interpreted as necessarily representing the official policies, either expressed or implied, of ODNI, IARPA, any other government organization, or the U.S. Government. The U.S. Government is authorized to reproduce and distribute reprints for governmental purposes notwithstanding any copyright annotation therein.

8 Limitations

There are several limitations of this study. First, we only consider English text, as our human factor models are all trained on English data. This limits their application and, in the case of translating other languages to English (as we did with Arabic), this assumes that linguistic expressions of human factors are invariant across cultures, which they are not (Smith et al., 2016). Similarly, the human factor models were all trained on social media data and thus may not generalize to other domains (such as reviews and academic essays). Next, some of the human trait models have lower predictive accuracy (with product moment correlation in the range of 0.26 to 0.43). While these accuracies are near state-of-the-art within their respective domains, low accuracies could produce more noisy estimates, especially when models are applied out of domain. Finally, the demographic model only considers binary expressions of gender as male/female, which may incorrectly characterize non-binary authors.

9 Ethical Considerations

Depending on the setting a classifier is deployed in, misclassifications of human and machine generated text could be high risk. For example, labeling genuine academic essays as machine generated may have serious negative repercussions for students and researchers. It has already been shown that current detection methods are biased against non-native speakers (Liang et al., 2023). Similarly, mislabeling social media bots as human users could enhance the trust and accessibility given to bot accounts used to spread disinformation or hate.

It is crucial to avoid anthropomorphizing LLMs, as doing so can create challenges with transparency and trust, particularly in high-stakes scenarios (see Abercrombie et al. (2023) for a detailed discussion). While we propose evaluation metrics based on human psychology, this does not imply that these systems resemble humans, should be perceived as human, or are human.

References

Muhammad Abdul-Mageed, Anneke Buffone, Hao Peng, Salvatore Giorgi, Johannes C Eichstaedt, and Lyle H Ungar. 2017. Recognizing pathogenic empathy in social media. In *ICWSM*, pages 448–451.

Gavin Abercrombie, Amanda Cercas Curry, Tanvi Dinkar, Verena Rieser, and Zeerak Talat. 2023. Mirages. on anthropomorphism in dialogue systems. In *Proceedings of the 2023 Conference on Empirical Methods in Natural Language Processing*, pages 4776–4790.

Gati V Aher, Rosa I Arriaga, and Adam Tauman Kalai. 2023. Using large language models to simulate multiple humans and replicate human subject studies. In *International Conference on Machine Learning*, pages 337–371. PMLR.

Jeromy Anglim, Sharon Horwood, Luke D Smillie, Rosario J Marrero, and Joshua K Wood. 2020. Predicting psychological and subjective well-being from personality: A meta-analysis. *Psychological bulletin*, 146(4):279.

Christiane Attig, Daniel Wessel, and Thomas Franke. 2017. Assessing personality differences in human-technology interaction: an overview of key self-report scales to predict successful interaction. In *HCI International 2017–Posters' Extended Abstracts: 19th International Conference, HCI International 2017, Vancouver, BC, Canada, July 9–14, 2017, Proceedings, Part I 19*, pages 19–29. Springer.

Avshalom Caspi, Dot Begg, Nigel Dickson, HonaLee Harrington, John Langley, Terrie E Moffitt, and Phil A Silva. 1997. Personality differences predict health-risk behaviors in young adulthood: evidence from a longitudinal study. *Journal of personality and social psychology*, 73(5):1052.

Shammur Absar Chowdhury, Hind AL-Merekhi, Mucahid Kutlu, Kaan Efe Keleş, Fatema Ahmad, Tasnim Mohiuddin, Georgios Mikros, and Firoj Alam. 2025. Genai content detection task 2: Ai vs. human – academic essay authenticity challenge. In *Proceedings of the 31st International Conference on Computational Linguistics (COLING)*, Abu Dhabi, UAE. Association for Computational Linguistics.

Stefano Cresci, Roberto Di Pietro, Marinella Petrocchi, Angelo Spognardi, and Maurizio Tesconi. 2017. The paradigm-shift of social spambots: Evidence, theories, and tools for the arms race. In *Proceedings of the 26th international conference on world wide web companion*, pages 963–972.

Evan N Crothers, Nathalie Japkowicz, and Herna L Viktor. 2023. Machine-generated text: A comprehensive survey of threat models and detection methods. *IEEE Access*, 11:70977–71002.

Debarati Das, Karin De Langis, Anna Martin-Boyle, Jaehyung Kim, Minhwa Lee, Zae Myung Kim, Shirley Anugrah Hayati, Risako Owan, Bin Hu, Ritik Parkar, et al. 2024. Under the surface: Tracking the artifactuality of llm-generated data. *arXiv preprint arXiv:2401.14698*.

Mark H Davis. 1983. Measuring individual differences in empathy: Evidence for a multidimensional approach. *Journal of personality and social psychology*, 44(1):113.

Danica Dillion, Niket Tandon, Yuling Gu, and Kurt Gray. 2023. Can ai language models replace human participants? *Trends in Cognitive Sciences*.

Liam Dugan, Alyssa Hwang, Filip Trhlík, Andrew Zhu, Josh Magnus Ludan, Hainiu Xu, Daphne Ippolito, and Chris Callison-Burch. 2024. RAID: A shared benchmark for robust evaluation of machine-generated text detectors. In *Proceedings of the 62nd Annual Meeting of the Association for Computational Linguistics (Volume 1: Long Papers)*, pages 12463–12492, Bangkok, Thailand. Association for Computational Linguistics.

Shangbin Feng, Chan Young Park, Yuhan Liu, and Yulia Tsvetkov. 2023. From pretraining data to language models to downstream tasks: Tracking the trails of political biases leading to unfair nlp models. In *The 61st Annual Meeting Of The Association For Computational Linguistics*.

Emilio Ferrara, Onur Varol, Clayton Davis, Filippo Menczer, and Alessandro Flammini. 2016. The rise of social bots. *Communications of the ACM*, 59(7):96–104.

Silvia García-Méndez, Francisco de Arriba-Pérez, and María del Carmen Somoza-López. 2024. A review on the use of large language models as virtual tutors. *Science & Education*, pages 1–16.

Salvatore Giorgi, Tingting Liu, Ankit Aich, Kelsey Jane Isman, Garrick Sherman, Zachary Fried, João Sedoc, Lyle Ungar, and Brenda Curtis. 2024. Modeling human subjectivity in LLMs using explicit and implicit human factors in personas. In *Findings of the Association for Computational Linguistics: EMNLP 2024*, pages 7174–7188, Miami, Florida, USA. Association for Computational Linguistics.

Salvatore Giorgi, David M Markowitz, Nikita Soni, Vasudha Varadarajan, Siddharth Mangalik, and H Andrew Schwartz. 2023. " i slept like a baby": Using human traits to characterize deceptive chatgpt and human text. In *IACT@ SIGIR*, pages 23–37.

Salvatore Giorgi, Lyle Ungar, and H. Andrew Schwartz. 2021. Characterizing social spambots by their human traits. In *Findings of the Association for Computational Linguistics: ACL-IJCNLP 2021*, pages 5148–5158, Online. Association for Computational Linguistics.

Lewis R Goldberg, John A Johnson, Herbert W Eber, Robert Hogan, Michael C Ashton, C Robert Cloninger, and Harrison G Gough. 2006. The international personality item pool and the future of public-domain personality measures. *Journal of Research in personality*, 40(1):84–96.

Shreya Havaldar, Bhumika Singhal, Sunny Rai, Langchen Liu, Sharath Chandra Guntuku, and Lyle Ungar. 2023. Multilingual language models are not multicultural: A case study in emotion. In *Proceedings of the 13th Workshop on Computational Approaches to Subjectivity, Sentiment, & Social Media Analysis*, pages 202–214.

Dirk Hovy and Diyi Yang. 2021. The importance of modeling social factors of language: Theory and practice. In *Proceedings of the 2021 Conference of the North American Chapter of the Association for Computational Linguistics: Human language technologies*, pages 588–602.

Xiaomeng Hu, Pin-Yu Chen, and Tsung-Yi Ho. 2023. Radar: Robust ai-text detection via adversarial learning. *Advances in Neural Information Processing Systems*, 36:15077–15095.

Jen-tse Huang, Man Ho Lam, Eric John Li, Shujie Ren, Wenxuan Wang, Wenxiang Jiao, Zhaopeng Tu, and Michael R Lyu. 2023. Emotionally numb or empathetic? evaluating how llms feel using emotionbench. *arXiv preprint arXiv:2308.03656*.

Jen-tse Huang, Wenxuan Wang, Eric John Li, Man Ho Lam, Shujie Ren, Youliang Yuan, Wenxiang Jiao, Zhaopeng Tu, and Michael R. Lyu. 2024. On the humanity of conversational ai: Evaluating the psychological portrayal of llms. In *Proceedings of the Twelfth International Conference on Learning Representations (ICLR)*.

Hang Jiang, Xiajie Zhang, Xubo Cao, Cynthia Breazeal, Deb Roy, and Jad Kabbara. 2024. PersonaLLM: Investigating the ability of large language models to express personality traits. In *Findings of the Association for Computational Linguistics: NAACL 2024*, pages 3605–3627, Mexico City, Mexico. Association for Computational Linguistics.

Rebecca L Johnson, Giada Pistilli, Natalia Menédez-González, Leslye Denisse Dias Duran, Enrico Panai, Julija Kalpokiene, and Donald Jay Bertulfo. 2022. The ghost in the machine has an american accent: value conflict in gpt-3. *arXiv preprint arXiv:2203.07785*.

Cameron R Jones and Benjamin K Bergen. 2024. People cannot distinguish gpt-4 from a human in a turing test. *arXiv preprint arXiv:2405.08007*.

Vivek Kulkarni, Margaret L Kern, David Stillwell, Michal Kosinski, Sandra Matz, Lyle Ungar, Steven Skiena, and H Andrew Schwartz. 2018. Latent human traits in the language of social media: An open-vocabulary approach. *PloS one*, 13(11):e0201703.

Weixin Liang, Mert Yuksekgonul, Yining Mao, Eric Wu, and James Zou. 2023. Gpt detectors are biased against non-native english writers. *Patterns*, 4(7).

David M. Markowitz, Jeffrey T. Hancock, and Jeremy N. Bailenson. 2024. Linguistic markers of inherently false ai communication and intentionally false human communication: Evidence from hotel reviews. *Journal of Language and Social Psychology*, 43(1):63–82.

Eric Mitchell, Yoonho Lee, Alexander Khazatsky, Christopher D Manning, and Chelsea Finn. 2023. DetectGPT: Zero-shot machine-generated text detection using probability curvature. In *Proceedings of the 40th International Conference on Machine Learning*, volume 202 of *Proceedings of Machine Learning Research*, pages 24950–24962. PMLR.

Alberto Muñoz-Ortiz, Carlos Gómez-Rodríguez, and David Vilares. 2023. Contrasting linguistic patterns in human and llm-generated text. *arXiv preprint arXiv:2308.09067*.

Myle Ott, Yejin Choi, Claire Cardie, and Jeffrey T Hancock. 2011. Finding deceptive opinion spam by any stretch of the imagination. *arXiv preprint arXiv:1107.4557*.

Gregory Park, H Andrew Schwartz, Johannes C Eichstaedt, Margaret L Kern, Michal Kosinski, David J Stillwell, Lyle H Ungar, and Martin EP Seligman. 2015. Automatic personality assessment through social media language. *Journal of personality and social psychology*, 108(6):934.

Max Pellert, Clemens M Lechner, Claudia Wagner, Beatrice Rammstedt, and Markus Strohmaier. 2024. Ai psychometrics: Assessing the psychological profiles of large language models through psychometric inventories. *Perspectives on Psychological Science*, 19(5):808–826.

Susan B Perlman, James P Morris, Brent C Vander Wyk, Steven R Green, Jaime L Doyle, and Kevin A Pelphrey. 2009. Individual differences in personality predict how people look at faces. *PloS one*, 4(6):e5952.

Sonia Roccas, Lilach Sagiv, Shalom H Schwartz, and Ariel Knafo. 2002. The big five personality factors and personal values. *Personality and social psychology bulletin*, 28(6):789–801.

Vinu Sankar Sadasivan, Aounon Kumar, Sriram Balasubramanian, Wenxiao Wang, and Soheil Feizi. 2023. Can ai-generated text be reliably detected? *arXiv preprint arXiv:2303.11156*.

Shibani Santurkar, Esin Durmus, Faisal Ladhak, Cinoo Lee, Percy Liang, and Tatsunori Hashimoto. 2023. Whose opinions do language models reflect? In *International Conference on Machine Learning*, pages 29971–30004. PMLR.

Maarten Sap, Greg Park, Johannes C Eichstaedt, Margaret L Kern, David J Stillwell, Michal Kosinski, Lyle H Ungar, and H Andrew Schwartz. 2014. Developing age and gender predictive lexica over social media. In *Proceedings of the 2014 Conference on Empirical Methods in Natural Language Processing*, EMNLP.

H Andrew Schwartz, Johannes C Eichstaedt, Margaret L Kern, Lukasz Dziurzynski, Stephanie M Ramones, Megha Agrawal, Achal Shah, Michal Kosinski, David Stillwell, Martin EP Seligman, and Lyle H Ungar. 2013. Personality, gender, and age in the language of social media: The Open-Vocabulary approach. *PLoS ONE*.

H Andrew Schwartz, Salvatore Giorgi, Maarten Sap, Patrick Crutchley, Lyle Ungar, and Johannes Eichstaedt. 2017. Dlatk: Differential language analysis toolkit. In *Proceedings of the 2017 Conference on Empirical Methods in Natural Language Processing: System Demonstrations*, pages 55–60.

Laura Smith, Salvatore Giorgi, Rishi Solanki, Johannes Eichstaedt, H Andrew Schwartz, Muhammad Abdul-Mageed, Anneke Buffone, and Lyle Ungar. 2016. Does 'well-being'translate on twitter? In *Proceedings of the 2016 Conference on Empirical Methods in Natural Language Processing*, pages 2042–2047.

Nikita Soni, H. Andrew Schwartz, João Sedoc, and Niranjan Balasubramanian. 2024. Large human language models: A need and the challenges. In *Proceedings of the 2024 Conference of the North American Chapter of the Association for Computational Linguistics: Human Language Technologies (Volume 1: Long Papers)*, pages 8631–8646, Mexico City, Mexico. Association for Computational Linguistics.

Ruiyi Wang, Stephanie Milani, Jamie C. Chiu, Jiayin Zhi, Shaun M. Eack, Travis Labrum, Samuel M Murphy, Nev Jones, Kate V Hardy, Hong Shen, Fei Fang, and Zhiyu Chen. 2024. PATIENT-ψ: Using large language models to simulate patients for training mental health professionals. In *Proceedings of the 2024 Conference on Empirical Methods in Natural Language Processing*, pages 12772–12797, Miami, Florida, USA. Association for Computational Linguistics.

David B. Yaden, Salvatore Giorgi, Matthew Jordan, Anneke Buffone, Johannes C. Eichstaedt, H. Andrew Schwartz, Lyle H. Ungar, and Paul Bloom. 2023. Characterizing empathy and compassion using computational linguistic analysis. *Emotion*.

A Further Details on Human Factor Estimation

To estimate each human factor, we extract the required linguistic features for each document in each dataset. All of the models listed below use some combination of 1-, 2-, and 3-grams (encoded as relative frequencies) and a set of 2,000 LDA topics. The LDA topics were derived in previous work (Schwartz et al., 2013). Topic loads in this work are calculated via a weighted sum of unigram frequencies, where weights were derived via the LDA process (i.e., the conditional probability of the topic given the unigram). We then apply the trained human factor models (e.g., Ridge regression for personality or a factor reduction for Behavioral Linguistic Factors) to the extracted features, producing 13 human factor scores for each document.

Demographics Age and gender were predicted using a model developed by Sap et al. (2014). This model was trained on data from over 70,000 users of Twitter, Facebook, and blogs, who self-reported their age (continuous) and gender (binary male/female; multi-class gender data was unavailable). Unigrams were extracted from social media posts, which were then used in penalized Ridge regression for age prediction and a support vector classifier for gender prediction. The model achieved a product moment correlation of r = 0.86 for age and an accuracy of 90% for gender. Although the gender model was designed to predict binary outcomes, it produces a continuous score, where negative values align with "male" and positive values with "female."

Personality Personality traits were assessed using a model by Park et al. (2015), trained on Facebook status updates from over 66,000 individuals who reported their personality via the International Personality Item Pool (Goldberg et al., 2006). Responses were recorded on a 5-point Likert scale, with trait scores calculated as averages of corresponding items, resulting in final scores ranging from 1 to 5. The model employed penalized Ridge regression using 1-, 2-, and 3-grams and Latent Dirichlet Allocation (LDA) topics derived from the posts. Out-of-sample prediction accuracies (product moment correlations) were 0.43 for openness, 0.37 for conscientiousness, 0.42 for extraversion, 0.35 for agreeableness, and 0.35 for emotional stability.

Empathy Empathic Concern (referred to as empathy) was predicted using a model trained on data from the Interpersonal Reactivity Index (Davis, 1983) combined with Facebook status updates from prior datasets (Yaden et al., 2023; Abdul-Mageed et al., 2017). LDA topics derived from the posts were incorporated into a penalized Ridge regression model, yielding an out-of-sample product moment correlation of r = 0.26.

Behavioral Linguistic Factors Behavioral Linguistic Factors were estimated using a dataset of Facebook status updates from approximately 50,000 users, leveraging a model originally developed by (Kulkarni et al., 2018). N-gram frequencies (1-, 2-, and 3-grams) from these updates underwent factor analysis to derive the dimensions, which serve as a data-driven, open-vocabulary analog to the Big Five personality traits. These dimensions have demonstrated broader applicability, predicting outcomes such as income, and have been shown to be stable across time and diverse populations.

DAMAGE: Detecting Adversarially Modified AI Generated Text

Elyas Masrour and **Bradley Emi** and **Max Spero**
Pangram Labs, Inc.
Correspondence: info@pangram.com

Abstract

AI humanizers are a new class of online software tools meant to paraphrase and rewrite AI-generated text in a way that allows them to evade AI detection software. We study 19 AI humanizer and paraphrasing tools and qualitatively assess their effects and faithfulness in preserving the meaning of the original text. We show that many existing AI detectors fail to detect humanized text. Finally, we demonstrate a robust model that can detect humanized AI text while maintaining a low false positive rate using a data-centric augmentation approach. We attack our own detector, training our own fine-tuned model optimized against our detector's predictions, and show that our detector's cross-humanizer generalization is sufficient to remain robust to this attack.

1 Introduction

The ability of large language models such as ChatGPT (OpenAI, 2023) to generate realistic and fluent text has spurred the need for AI text detection software. Commercial methods, such as TurnItIn, GPTZero, Originality, and Pangram Labs have emerged, as well as open-source research methods, such as DetectGPT (Mitchell et al., 2023), Binoculars (Hans et al., 2024), and many more.

However, both researchers and practitioners alike have found these solutions to be fragile. A study from Google Research (Krishna et al., 2023) found that a paraphrasing text-to-text model (a variant of T5) was able to effectively rewrite AI-generated text in a way that could preserve the meaning of the original text but largely evade AI detection algorithms.

This finding gave rise to an explosion of new AI "humanizer" tools appearing online. These tools promise to bypass AI detection tools by rewriting AI-generated text. They are primarily marketed at students, who can use these tools to effectively cheat on writing assignments by plagiarizing from large language models without getting caught. Other humanizers target their product towards SEO marketers, who may generate hundreds of blog posts using AI and apply humanizers to evade AI detection by search engine algorithms.

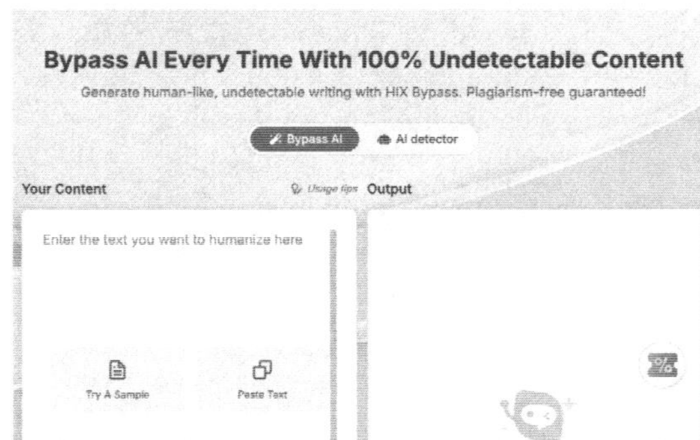

Figure 1: Example of an AI humanizer tool

In this work, we attempt to comprehensively study these AI humanizers: what they are doing, and whether it is possible to identify humanized AI-generated text. Our main contributions are as follows.

- We qualitatively audit 19 humanizers and paraphrasing tools and analyze their effects on the underlying text. We exhaustively identify the transformation modes that the humanizers apply to their inputs. We categorize the humanizers into three tiers based on their overall quality.

- We study the baseline effectiveness of humanizers in bypassing existing open-source and commercial AI detectors.

- We present a deep-learning based AI detector that effectively is robust to humanization, even by humanizers unseen during training. We describe the necessity of treating humanizer robustness as a learned invariance rather than a separate domain.

Proceedings of the 1st Workshop on GenAI Content Detection (GenAIDetect), pages 120–133
January 19, 2025.

- We show that even after a detector-specific fine-tuning attack, our detector remains fairly robust due to its underlying ability to generalize.

2 Related Work

2.1 AI Detection

Many commercial and open-source methods exist to detect AI-generated text, with highly varying levels of accuracy. One of the most notable commercial solutions is TurnItIn (Staff, 2024), which is widely used in higher education as anti-plagiarism software. Our team at Pangram Labs (Emi and Spero, 2024) is contributing to this field, alongside other solutions such as GPTZero (Tian and Cui, 2023), Originality, and Copyleaks, although their accuracies vary significantly (Weber-Wulff et al., 2023).

Open-source methods typically fall into two categories: perplexity-based detection methods and deep learning based methods. Perplexity-based methods attempt to leverage the fact that the tokens in LLM-based outputs in general will be predicted as consistently more likely by the LLM itself. DetectGPT (Mitchell et al., 2023) and FastDetectGPT (Bao et al., 2024) are earlier examples of perplexity-based methods which look at the local curvature in probability space around a given example. Binoculars (Hans et al., 2024) is an even more effective recent approach which uses the cross-perplexity between two different LLMs as a signal that text is LLM-generated.

Deep learning based methods attempt to use neural networks to detect AI-generated content, leveraging large datasets containing known human and AI text and training a classifier to distinguish between them. The OpenAI classifier (Solaiman et al., 2019) was one of the first efforts. They used a RoBERTa based model to classify human text and GPT-2 written text. Ghostbusters (Verma et al., 2023) uses learned combinations of features derived from language model embeddings to detect LLM-generated text.

Recently, some AI detection efforts have also attempted to detect mixed AI and human text: when some of the text is written by a human and some of it is written by an AI. SeqXGPT (Wang et al., 2023) attempts to solve this by using an architecture which is able to detect AI on the sentence level rather than the document level. ROFT (Kushnareva et al., 2024) adapts several detection methods to detecting the boundary between AI and human text. However, these methods differ from ours in that the assumption about the original document is that each part of the text has a distinct authorship attribution, whereas we study the case in which fully AI-generated text is then modified by a humanizer.

2.2 Evading AI Detection

Much of the literature has also focused on whether or not AI-generated text can be detected at all (Sadasivan et al., 2023). A study from Google Research (Krishna et al., 2023) released DIPPER: a paraphrasing T5-based model that is able to bypass some of the above-mentioned detectors by rewriting the input text. Another group of researchers (Chakraborty et al., 2023) devised a framework to rank LLMs based on their "detectability", claiming that more recent models like GPT-4 are less detectable because perplexity and burstiness are less useful evidence markers.

Furthermore, other research has focused on attacking AI detectors or otherwise methods to bypass or evade AI detection. One study (Kumarage et al., 2023) designs an approach to search for soft prompts that can produce text that can evade detection. Another study (Ayoobi et al., 2024) looks at the effect on AI detectors of translating AI-generated text through multiple languages before backtranslating it into English and find some methods are significantly more robust than others. Another paper directly optimizes a language model by using an AI detector as negative reward: creating pairs of LLM-generated text where one piece is detected and one is not, and then using DPO to optimize the language model to prefer undetected outputs (Nicks et al., 2024). RADAR (Hu et al., 2023) adversarially trains a language model detector and a paraphraser against each other to create a more robust detector.

2.3 Watermarking

Watermarking AI-generated text is another relevant subfield of research. Existing watermarking schemes train or decode LLMs to leave behind a probabilistic signal that can later be detected by a watermark-specific detector. One watermarking scheme (Kirchenbauer et al., 2023) introduces the idea of "green tokens", which are sampled with higher probability than other tokens in a traceable way. Google's recently released SynthID (Google DeepMind, 2024) works in a similar fashion.

We argue that watermarking is insufficient to

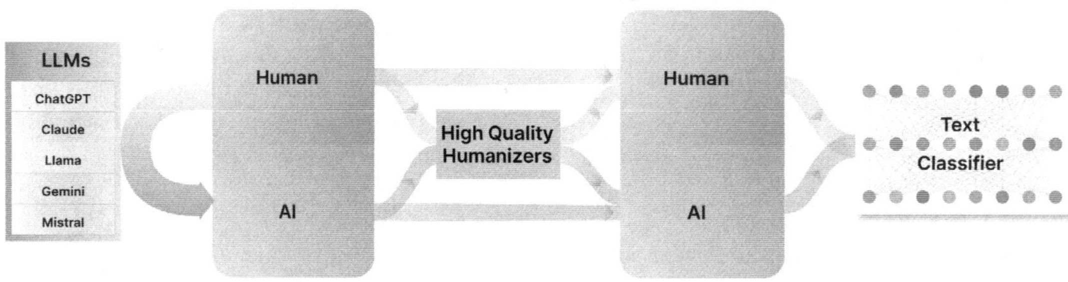

Figure 2: Augmenting the training set with high quality humanizer data improves robustness.

guard against the dangers of AI-generated text. We show that in addition to evading AI detectors, humanizers are also reliable methods to remove such statistical watermarks.

2.4 Benchmarking

Recently there has also been an increased effort to benchmark the performance of various AI detectors against each other. RAID (Dugan et al., 2024) is a live leaderboard measuring the performance of AI-generated text detection methods against each other on multiple domains, models, and adversarial attacks. We include the RAID paraphrase and synonym splits in our results as proxies for measuring robustness against humanizers, but we also include a more diverse set of humanizer attacks than the original RAID benchmark.

3 Humanizer Market Survey

3.1 Tool Research and Selection

We selected 19 humanizers and paraphrasing tools based on search popularity and academic relevance. The particular paraphrasers and humanizers selected are presented in Table 1. Notably, we include DIPPER (Krishna et al., 2023) as a paraphraser, due to the authors' claim that text modified by DIPPER can universally bypass AI detection methods.

3.2 Humanizers are often themselves LLMs

Some humanizers are LLMs with system prompts instructing the LLM to write more like a human, or fine-tuned versions of LLMs. In testing some of the humanizers, we found that some of them are susceptible to popular jailbreaks. When we tested one popular humanizer and asked it to give us its system prompt, it said "I should respond to the user input with a reasonable approximation of the full meaning of the input...I should respond in a conversational tone." More examples of our jailbreaks against LLM-based humanizers can be found in Appendix A.

3.3 Humanizers are popular on the GPT Store

As of the date of publication, two out of the four most popular Writing Custom GPTs in the OpenAI GPT Store are humanizers that make function calls to external humanizers. This indicates that there is a large appetite for bypassing AI detection. Given that a significant portion of ChatGPT's daily active users are students, it is likely that these tools are popular for cheating or otherwise making AI writing undetectable. We believe that although many of these humanizers are black boxes, they are an important and understudied area for research in AI detection.

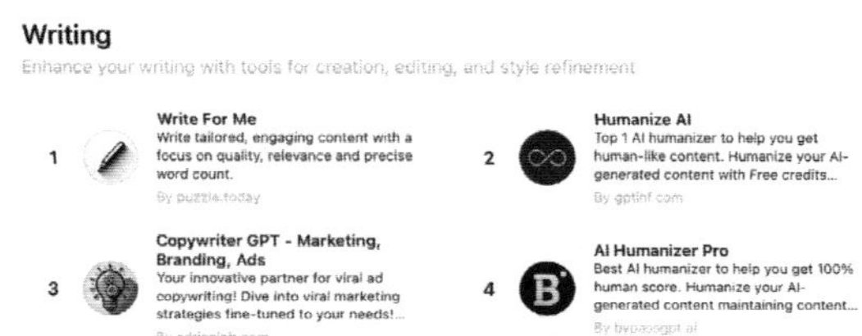

Figure 3: Two out of the four most popular Writing Custom GPTs are Humanizers

3.4 Humanizers are capable of removing watermarks

Google's SynthID is a state-of-the-art solution for watermarking generated text. Following the methodology and code from the SynthID paper (Google DeepMind, 2024), we generated 1000 watermarked texts and 1000 unwatermarked texts. We used Gemma-2B-IT (Team et al., 2024) to generate 200 tokens for each example with a temperature

Category	Tools
Paraphrasers	DIPPER, Grammarly, Quillbot
Humanizers	Bypass GPT, Ghost AI, HIX Bypass, Humbot AI, HumanizeAI.io, HumanizeAI.pro, Humanizer.com, Phrasly.ai, Semihuman AI, StealthGPT, StealthWriter.AI, Surfer SEO, Undetectable AI, Twixify, WriteHuman.ai

Table 1: Paraphrasers and Humanizers Studied

of 1.0, using the ELI5 dataset (Fan et al., 2019) as prompts. We used the unwatermarked text to set a FPR threshold and evaluated SynthID watermark detection TPR at a fixed FPR. Finally, we paraphrased the watermarked text with DIPPER and reevaluated watermark detection, finding that watermark detection had dropped dramatically. See results in Table 2.

Watermarked Gemma-2B-IT	
TPR @ FPR=5%	87.6%
TPR @ FPR=1%	66.5%
After DIPPER Paraphrase	
TPR @ FPR=5%	5.4%
TPR @ FPR=1%	1.5%

Table 2: Watermark detection before and after paraphrasing

4 Humanized Text Audit

4.1 Approach

To understand the effect of humanizing a given piece of text, we engaged in a manual qualitative analysis. We reviewed several samples of text per humanizer, examining how the humanizer transformed vocabulary, sentence structure, and grammar. While not exhaustive, we detail some common patterns introduced by humanizers into the text.

4.2 Insight: Nonsensical Phrases

Many poor-quality humanizers add nonsensical text throughout the piece. Common patterns include:

- Hallucinated Citations:

  `...community service for demonstrating consciousness about public affairs together with responsibility for own actions (Westwood, 2013)...`

- In-line comments:

  `...in specified locations hence constructing external frames those encouraging individuals manage their own times wisely (??????)...`

- Other Nonsensical Phrases:

  `...he or she will never seem defeated by teachers' demands and, as a result, will put more effort into their studies. CGSizeMake pp 18-23...`

4.3 Insight: Varying Structural Continuity

Some humanizers retain low-level sentence structure and simply replace individual words with synonyms. For example, the paraphraser in Figure 4 preserves the meaning of each individual sentence, and even sometimes preserves the phrasing structure within the single sentence, explicitly highlighting that only some words and short phrases have been replaced with synonyms.

Other humanizers take more liberty to change the original text, sometimes rewording entire groups of sentences and paragraphs. Some add more sentences that weren't originally present or delete redundant sentences. We notice that humanizers built on LLMs tend to be more weakly grounded in the original text, while rules-based humanizers that do synonym replacement tend to be more strongly grounded in the original text.

4.4 Insight: Writing and Vocabulary Level

Some humanizers write exclusively in an academic, formal, and/or university level tone. Others write at the elementary school, middle school, or high school level. The better humanizers, usually the ones that are LLM-based, do not commit to a specific writing level or tone, and instead adopt the writing level and tone of the original document.

4.5 Humanizer Segmentation

During our audit, we grouped humanizers into three distinct tiers. The best humanizers rewrote text preserving its tone, vocabulary level, and complexity. Average humanizers rewrote text in a way that degraded overall quality, but preserved intent and message. Low quality humanizers often added

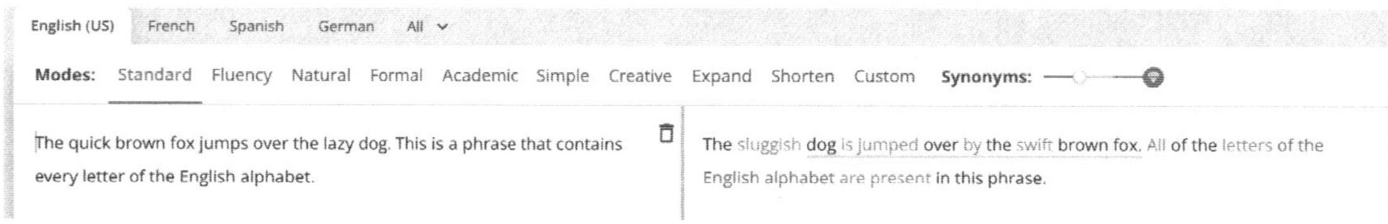

Figure 4: This paraphraser performs a very close paraphrase, only replacing individual words and phrases rather than rewriting entire sentences and paragraphs.

nonsensical phrases, words, and characters, constructed incorrect and uninterpretable sentences, and often distorted the meaning of the text. We classify these three categories of humanizers as L1 (best), L2 (medium), and L3 (worst) humanizers, and describe their characteristics in Figure 5. We present a full categorization, along with notes on the specific qualities of each humanizer, in the Appendix. It is worth noting we only make these classifications based on faithfulness and fluency, not on their effectiveness at bypassing AI detectors.

4.6 Quantifying Humanizer Fluency

To quantify the difference between L1, L2, and L3 humanizers, we use the Fluency Win Rate metric introduced in (Nicks et al., 2024). We prompt GPT-4o to select the more fluent and coherent sample: an original chunk of text, or that chunk of text passed through a humanizer. Here, we report the rate at which GPT-4o selects the humanized sample as the more coherent one. Using a dataset of 25 samples per humanizer, we aggregate the win rate of each tier. L1 humanizers had an average Win Rate of 26.0%, L2 humanizers had an average Win Rate of 14.67%, and L3 humanizers had an average Win Rate of 2.67%.

This demonstrates that our qualitative audit agrees with the fluency metric. Further, all humanizers tend to degrade the quality of the original text, but the degree of quality degradation varies. Still, for the highest quality humanizers, the text quality is still sometimes comparable to the highest quality language model outputs. Because certain humanizers are able to produce high-fluency text, we believe there is a growing need to study them.

5 Experiments

In our experiments, we seek to answer the question of whether a deep learning based AI text classifier is capable of detecting humanized AI-generated text. First, we narrow our scope to L1 humanizers. We do this because their subtle changes are the hardest to detect by eye and because they have the highest levels of fluency, making them most relevant in real-world adversarial attacks. We train two models: one model is unaware of humanized text, and one model contains a small amount of humanized text from a variety of humanizers. We describe the methodology and training procedure for training these models here.

5.1 Dataset Creation

5.1.1 Initial Datasets

Our initial dataset is seeded with a wide variety of human-written datasets from prior to 2022. We use datasets from the following domains: reviews, news, general web text, email, student writing/essays, creative writing, questions and answers, ELL/ESL (English as a Second Language), scientific/medical papers, Project Gutenberg, and Wikipedia.

For evaluation, because humanizers are primarily marketed at students, we evaluate all models on several open datasets comprised of student-written essays. Because previous studies (Liang et al., 2023) have found that AI detectors can be biased against nonnative English speaking students, we ensure that a significant portion of our evaluation dataset is comprised of ESL essays. The component datasets in our evaluation and our algorithm for generating the AI essays used in our benchmark are listed in Appendix B.

5.2 Synthetic Data Creation

Our initial dataset fully human-written. To generate the AI side of the dataset, we use synthetic mirror prompts as described in (Emi and Spero, 2024).

We define the term "mirror prompt" to be a prompt based on the original example that is used to generated a "synthetic mirror" example. The goal of each mirror prompt is to generate an example that matches the topic and length of the original document.

If the original document is "<original review>",

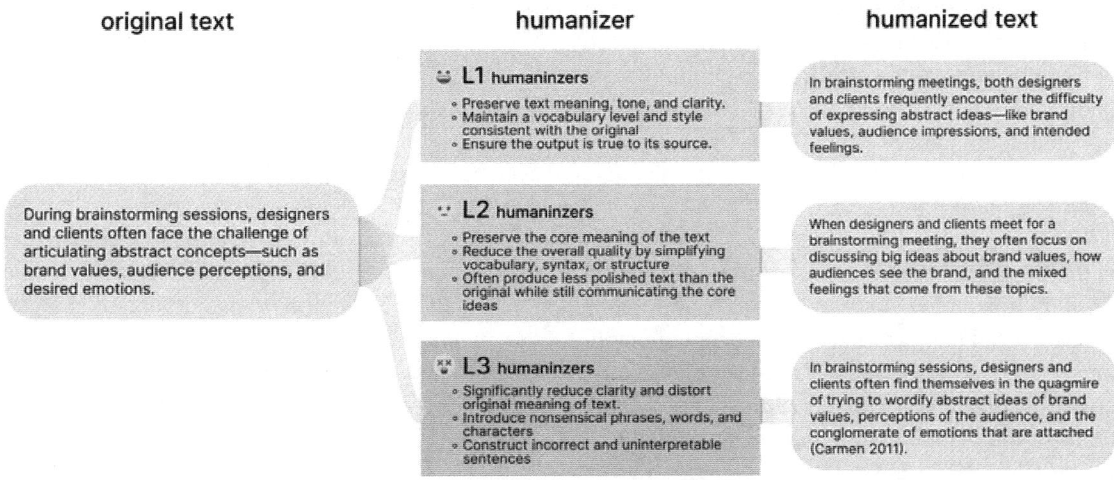

Figure 5: We segment humanizers into three tiers, based on their fluency.

then a mirror prompt may look like this:

`[Prompt] Write a <original review star rating> star review for <original review business name>. Make the review around <original review length> words long.`

Another example may be for a student essay. We sometimes use double prompts, such as the following:

`[Prompt] What is a good title for this essay? <original essay> Only give the title in your response.`

`[Assistant] <Title>`

`[Prompt] Write an essay with the following title: <Title>. Make the essay around <original essay length> words long.`

5.2.1 LLMs used for Synthetic Mirrors

For synthetic mirrors in the initial training stage, we use the following LLMs:

- GPT-3.5 (multiple versions)
- GPT-4, GPT-4-turbo, and GPT-4o (multiple versions)
- Claude 2 and 3 (multiple versions and sizes)
- LLaMA 2, 3, and 3.1 (multiple versions and sizes)
- Mistral (multiple versions and sizes)
- Gemini Pro and Flash (multiple versions)

It is notable that we only use modern LLMs that are instruction-tuned and post-trained. We do not train on base models because they produce noticeably lower-quality outputs and are substantially less commonly used in real-world applications.

5.3 Architecture and Training

We use the Mistral NeMo architecture (Mistral AI Team, 2024) which has approximately 12 billion parameters, with an untrained linear classification head. Following the usual convention for sequence classification modeling using an autoregressive language model, the hidden state from the final token in the sequence is used as the input to both classification heads. As is common practice in LLM finetuning, we use trainable LoRA (Hu et al., 2022) adapters while keeping the base model frozen. We use the Tekken tokenizer out of the box, which is noted for its strong multilingual performance. We truncate the context window to 512 tokens to constrain the model to using only short-range features. When necessary, we simply crop the input to fit the context window. We train the model to convergence using 8 A100 GPUs with a batch size of 24 using a weighted cross entropy loss and the AdamW optimizer for 1 epoch. We early stop based on the weighted cross entropy loss on the validation set.

5.4 Humanizer Data Augmentation

In order to make the treatment model robust to humanization, we treat humanization as a transform on the input data which we would like the model to learn an invariance to.

Because most of the humanizers are marketed at students, we assume that they work best on student writing. As a proxy for student writing, we use the Fineweb-EDU dataset (Lozhkov et al., 2024), a high quality LLM corpus that is prefiltered to only contain documents that are of high educational quality. First, we use an LLM filter to reject all documents that are not standard prose written in full complete sentences. Then, we create synthetic mirrors as described above.

We find that it is best to humanize both human and AI documents before augmenting the training set with this additional data. We also find that if we include all humanizers in the augmentation, our precision (i.e. false positive rate) is significantly compromised. However, including only L1 humanizers (the high quality humanizers) allows us to maintain a low false positive rate in addition to increasing recall generally across humanizers. Further information can be found in Table 8.

After humanizing both human and AI essays, we apply chunking logic to divide each document into roughly 300-word chunks before adding both the human and the AI humanized documents back into the training set.

Even though human documents transformed by a humanizer could be considered AI-generated, we choose to label them as human for the purposes of training. The reason for this is because we treat the model's response to humanization as an invariance rather than only including the AI humanized documents as a separate domain. This contributes to our final performance, as seen in Table 8.

Because most humanizers impose monthly limits on the amount of text that can be humanized, we only use a volume of data up to the limit of the basic 1 month subscription on each humanizer website. As a result, our data volume is quite small: about 0.68% percent of the final dataset is comprised of humanized text. To compensate for the small data volume, we oversample the humanizer data by a factor of 18.

5.5 Active Learning

After training, following the procedure in (Emi and Spero, 2024), we run hard negative mining with synthetic mirrors. On a large corpus of human text, we mine for false positives, and then incorporate both the false positives and their AI mirrors back into our training set. This further reduces our false positive rate and improves our recall. We also incorporate a small amount of data from the RAID train subset into the final training run to generalize to the diversity of models present in the RAID benchmark.

6 Results

6.1 Performance on Humanized Data

Table 3 presents performance data from several AI detection methods on a benchmark of AI-generated academic text before and after humanization. We define a "positive" sample as one that is written by AI, and a "negative" sample as one that is written by a human. Results are presented as true positive rate at a fixed false positive rate of 5%. LLM Baseline in this case is our baseline AI detection model that is trained using synthetic mirrors but does not include any humanized data in its training set.

	AI Text	**Humanized AI Text**
GPTZero	$99.73\% \pm 0.19\%$	$60.04\% \pm 1.80\%$
RADAR	$3.33\% \pm 0.65\%$	$5.05\% \pm 0.81\%$
Binoculars	$94.15\% \pm 0.88\%$	$28.23\% \pm 1.62\%$
LLM Baseline	$100.00\% \pm 0.0\%$	$95.74\% \pm 0.71\%$
DAMAGE	$100.00\% \pm 0.0\%$	$98.26\% \pm 0.47\%$

Table 3: TPR @ FPR=5% for Academic Text with 1000 iterations of bootstrap sampling. RADAR performs poorly on this metric due to its high false positive rate. In Appendix C, we include more metrics, including using model default thresholds.

6.2 Performance on RAID Attacks

Table 4 presents performance data from the same AI detection methods on two adversarial subsets of the RAID benchmark, which includes a range of LLMs and a range of text domains.

	Paraphrase	**Synonym**
GPTZero	64.0%	61.0%
RADAR	62.4%	62.7%
Binoculars	80.3%	43.5%
LLM Baseline	91.6%	96.2%
DAMAGE	93.0%	97.0%

Table 4: TPR @ FPR=5% for Academic Text

7 Detector-Specific Adversarial Humanization

In this paper, we study commercial online humanizers meant to *generally* evade AI detectors, but we also study the directly adversarial scenario: when a humanizer is directly optimized against a particular detector. To do so, we train our own humanizer using the GPT-4o fine-tuning API and measure the detector's robustness to AI-generated text passed through the adversarial fine-tuned model.

7.1 Methodology

Broadly following the methodology in Language Models are Easily Optimized Against (Nicks et al., 2024), we train a model using our detector's AI prediction as a negative signal. However, rather than training a separate language model with DPO, we train a humanizer that takes an unmodified AI-generated text as an input and learns to generate a paraphrase of the original that bypasses the detector. We choose this methodology as it is closer to how humanizers are trained in the real world.

As a proof of concept experiment, we split our essays dataset into two pools: a fine-tuning set and a test set. We select all L1 humanizer outputs from the fine-tuning set that the detector predicts as human-generated (i.e., all L1 humanizer false negatives). We then take the original AI-generated text source (prior to humanization), and create pairs of unhumanized-humanized text samples to fine-tune on. We then use the GPT-4o fine-tuning API to train a new model on only these pairs. This results in a new model that, in theory, learns to paraphrase text into similar examples to the humanizer samples that were able to bypass the detector originally.

7.2 Results

After training the detector-specific humanizer, we use GPT-4o to create synthetic mirrors of 2000 examples from the test set and pass them through the adversarial humanizer.

Condition	TPR @ FPR=5%	Default TPR
No Humanizer	100%	100%
Adversarial Humanizer	100%	93.2%

Table 5: TPR values for DAMAGE model at the default threshold (0.5) and threshold that corresponds to 5% FPR without and without adversarial humanization.

We see that although some of the samples that were adversarially humanized are able to bypass the detector, the detector is still able to detect 93.2% of the humanized AI samples. This shows that although an adversary may be able to directly optimize a humanizer using the detector as a signal, the resulting humanizer still remains largely detectable even without retraining our detector. We believe this is due to the fact that the underlying language model of the humanizer still leaves behind detectable patterns that cannot be erased during fine-tuning. Additionally, by seeing many humanized examples in its training set, the detector learns to be robust to a wide variety of paraphrases and perturbations and maintains its ability to generalize across humanizers, even adversarial ones.

7.3 Detector-Specific Humanizer Fluency Win Rate

To examine the quality of the text generated by our Detector-Specific Humanizer, we perform the same Fluency Win Rate metric introduced in (Nicks et al., 2024). We find that the humanizer wins 14.13% of the time, which is roughly equivalent to an average L2 Humanizer.

8 Conclusion

In this study, we attempted to both qualitatively and quantitatively study humanizer tools and their effects on individual writing samples and the robustness of AI detectors against them. We showed it is possible to train an effective deep learning classifier that is robust to most humanizers, and ran a proof-of-concept to show that some degree of robustness even extends to a humanizer that is adversarially optimized against our specific detector.

References

Navid Ayoobi, Lily Knab, Wen Cheng, David Pantoja, Hamidreza Alikhani, Sylvain Flamant, Jin Kim, and Arjun Mukherjee. 2024. Esperanto: Evaluating synthesized phrases to enhance robustness in ai detection for text origination. *Preprint*, arXiv:2409.14285.

Guangsheng Bao, Yanbin Zhao, Zhiyang Teng, Linyi Yang, and Yue Zhang. 2024. Fast-detectgpt: Efficient zero-shot detection of machine-generated text via conditional probability curvature. *Preprint*, arXiv:2310.05130.

Megha Chakraborty, S. M Towhidul Islam Tonmoy, S M Mehedi Zaman, Krish Sharma, Niyar R Barman, Chandan Gupta, Shreya Gautam, Tanay Kumar, Vinija Jain, Aman Chadha, Amit P. Sheth, and Amitava Das. 2023. Counter turing test ct2̂: AI-generated text detection is not as easy as you may think – introducing ai detectability index. *Preprint*, arXiv:2310.05030.

Scott A. Crossley, Perpetual Baffour, Yingqi Tian, Abigail Franklin, Margaret Benner, and Ulrich Boser. 2024. A large-scale corpus for assessing written argumentation: PERSUADE 2.0. *Assessing Writing*, 61. Dataset comprising over 25,000 argumentative essays from 6th-12th grade students, released under CC BY-NC-SA 4.0.

Scott A. Crossley, Yuan Tian, Perpetual Baffour, Alicia Franklin, Yeoil Kim, William Morris, Brooke Benner, Auriane Picou, and Ulrich Boser. 2023. Measuring second language proficiency using the English Language Learner Insight, Proficiency and Skills Evaluation (ELLIPSE) Corpus. *International Journal of Learner Corpus Research*, 9(2):248–269.

Liam Dugan, Alyssa Hwang, Filip Trhlik, Josh Magnus Ludan, Andrew Zhu, Hainiu Xu, Daphne Ippolito, and Chris Callison-Burch. 2024. Raid: A shared benchmark for robust evaluation of machine-generated text detectors. *Preprint*, arXiv:2405.07940.

Bradley Emi and Max Spero. 2024. Technical report on the pangram ai-generated text classifier. *Preprint*, arXiv:2402.14873.

Angela Fan, Yacine Jernite, Ethan Perez, David Grangier, Jason Weston, and Michael Auli. 2019. Eli5: Long form question answering. *Preprint*, arXiv:1907.09190.

Alex Franklin, asiegel, HCL-Jevster, Jules King, julianmante, Maggie, Perpetual Baffour, Ryan Holbrook, and Scott Crossley. 2023. Commonlit - evaluate student summaries. `https://kaggle.com/competitions/commonlit-evaluate-student-summaries`. Kaggle.

Google DeepMind. 2024. Synthid: Identifying ai-generated content with digital watermarks. Accessed: 2024-11-14.

Abhimanyu Hans, Avi Schwarzschild, Valeriia Cherepanova, Hamid Kazemi, Aniruddha Saha, Micah Goldblum, Jonas Geiping, and Tom Goldstein. 2024. Spotting llms with binoculars: Zero-shot detection of machine-generated text. *Preprint*, arXiv:2401.12070.

Langdon Holmes, Scott Crossley, Perpetual Baffour, Jules King, Lauryn Burleigh, Maggie Demkin, Ryan Holbrook, Walter Reade, and Addison Howard. 2024. The learning agency lab - pii data detection. `https://kaggle.com/competitions/pii-detection-removal-from-educational-data`. Kaggle.

Edward J Hu, Yelong Shen, Phillip Wallis, Zeyuan Allen-Zhu, Yuanzhi Li, Shean Wang, Lu Wang, and Weizhu Chen. 2022. Lora: Low-rank adaptation of large language models. *arXiv preprint arXiv:2106.09685*.

Xiaomeng Hu, Pin-Yu Chen, and Tsung-Yi Ho. 2023. Radar: Robust ai-text detection via adversarial learning. *Preprint*, arXiv:2307.03838.

Shin'ichiro Ishikawa. 2023. *The ICNALE Guide: An Introduction to a Learner Corpus Study on Asian Learners' L2 English*. Routledge.

Alan Juffs, Na-Rae Han, and Ben Naismith. 2020. The University of Pittsburgh English Language Corpus (PELIC).

John Kirchenbauer, Jonas Geiping, Yuxin Wen, Jonathan Katz, Ian Miers, and Tom Goldstein. 2023. A watermark for large language models. *Preprint*, arXiv:2301.10226.

Kalpesh Krishna, Yixiao Song, Marzena Karpinska, John Wieting, and Mohit Iyyer. 2023. Paraphrasing evades detectors of ai-generated text, but retrieval is an effective defense. *Preprint*, arXiv:2303.13408.

Tharindu Kumarage, Paras Sheth, Raha Moraffah, Joshua Garland, and Huan Liu. 2023. How reliable are ai-generated-text detectors? an assessment framework using evasive soft prompts. *Preprint*, arXiv:2310.05095.

Laida Kushnareva, Tatiana Gaintseva, German Magai, Serguei Barannikov, Dmitry Abulkhanov, Kristian Kuznetsov, Eduard Tulchinskii, Irina Piontkovskaya, and Sergey Nikolenko. 2024. Ai-generated text boundary detection with roft. *Preprint*, arXiv:2311.08349.

Weixin Liang, Mert Yuksekgonul, Yining Mao, Eric Wu, and James Zou. 2023. Gpt detectors are biased against non-native english writers. *Preprint*, arXiv:2304.02819.

Anton Lozhkov, Loubna Ben Allal, Leandro von Werra, and Thomas Wolf. 2024. Fineweb-edu.

Mistral AI Team. 2024. Mistral NeMo. Released in collaboration with NVIDIA, July 18, 2024.

Eric Mitchell, Yoonho Lee, Alexander Khazatsky, Christopher D. Manning, and Chelsea Finn. 2023. Detectgpt: Zero-shot machine-generated text detection using probability curvature. *arXiv preprint*.

Hilary Nesi, Sheena Gardner, Paul Thompson, and Paul Wickens. 2008. The British Academic Written English (BAWE) Corpus. First version, 2008. Available from: http://ota.ox.ac.uk/desc/2539.

Charlotte Nicks, Eric Mitchell, Rafael Rafailov, Archit Sharma, Christopher D Manning, Chelsea Finn, and Stefano Ermon. 2024. Language model detectors are easily optimized against. In *The Twelfth International Conference on Learning Representations*.

OpenAI. 2023. Gpt-4 technical report. *arXiv preprint arXiv:2303.08774*.

Vinu Sankar Sadasivan, Aounon Kumar, Sriram Balasubramanian, Wenxiao Wang, and Soheil Feizi. 2023. Can ai-generated text be reliably detected? *Preprint*, arXiv:2303.11156.

Irene Solaiman, Miles Brundage, Jack Clark, Amanda Askell, Ariel Herbert-Voss, Jeff Wu, Alec Radford, Gretchen Krueger, Jong Wook Kim, Sarah Kreps, et al. 2019. Release strategies and the social impacts of language models. *arXiv preprint arXiv:1908.09203*.

Turnitin AI Technical Staff. 2024. Turnitin ai writing detection: Model architecture and testing protocol. Technical report, Turnitin.

Gemma Team, Thomas Mesnard, Cassidy Hardin, Robert Dadashi, Surya Bhupatiraju, Shreya Pathak, Laurent Sifre, Morgane Rivière, Mihir Sanjay Kale, Juliette Love, Pouya Tafti, Léonard Hussenot, Pier Giuseppe Sessa, Aakanksha Chowdhery, Adam Roberts, Aditya Barua, Alex Botev, Alex Castro-Ros, Ambrose Slone, Amélie Héliou, Andrea Tacchetti, Anna Bulanova, Antonia Paterson, Beth Tsai, Bobak Shahriari, Charline Le Lan, Christopher A. Choquette-Choo, Clément Crepy, Daniel Cer, Daphne Ippolito, David Reid, Elena Buchatskaya, Eric Ni, Eric Noland, Geng Yan, George Tucker, George-Christian Muraru, Grigory Rozhdestvenskiy, Henryk Michalewski, Ian Tenney, Ivan Grishchenko, Jacob Austin, James Keeling, Jane Labanowski, Jean-Baptiste Lespiau, Jeff Stanway, Jenny Brennan, Jeremy Chen, Johan Ferret, Justin Chiu, Justin Mao-Jones, Katherine Lee, Kathy Yu, Katie Millican, Lars Lowe Sjoesund, Lisa Lee, Lucas Dixon, Machel Reid, Maciej Mikuła, Mateo Wirth, Michael Sharman, Nikolai Chinaev, Nithum Thain, Olivier Bachem, Oscar Chang, Oscar Wahltinez, Paige Bailey, Paul Michel, Petko Yotov, Rahma Chaabouni, Ramona Comanescu, Reena Jana, Rohan Anil, Ross McIlroy, Ruibo Liu, Ryan Mullins, Samuel L Smith, Sebastian Borgeaud, Sertan Girgin, Sholto Douglas, Shree Pandya, Siamak Shakeri, Soham De, Ted Klimenko, Tom Hennigan, Vlad Feinberg, Wojciech Stokowiec, Yu hui Chen, Zafarali Ahmed, Zhitao Gong, Tris Warkentin, Ludovic Peran, Minh Giang, Clément Farabet, Oriol Vinyals, Jeff Dean, Koray Kavukcuoglu, Demis Hassabis, Zoubin Ghahramani, Douglas Eck, Joelle Barral, Fernando Pereira, Eli Collins, Armand Joulin, Noah Fiedel, Evan Senter, Alek Andreev, and Kathleen Kenealy. 2024. Gemma: Open models based on gemini research and technology. *Preprint*, arXiv:2403.08295.

Edward Tian and Alexander Cui. 2023. Gptzero: Towards detection of ai-generated text using zero-shot and supervised methods.

Vivek Verma, Eve Fleisig, Nicholas Tomlin, and Dan Klein. 2023. Ghostbuster: Detecting text ghostwritten by large language models. *Preprint*, arXiv:2305.15047.

Pengyu Wang, Linyang Li, Ke Ren, Botian Jiang, Dong Zhang, and Xipeng Qiu. 2023. Seqxgpt: Sentence-level ai-generated text detection. *Preprint*, arXiv:2310.08903.

Debora Weber-Wulff, Alla Anohina-Naumeca, Sonja Bjelobaba, Tomáš Foltýnek, Jean Guerrero-Dib, Olumide Popoola, Petr Šigut, and Lorna Waddington. 2023. Testing of detection tools for ai-generated text. *International Journal for Educational Integrity*.

A Jailbreaks against LLM Humanizers

Figures 6 and 7 demontrate jailbreaks that reveal the system prompt for the underlying paraphraser LLM.

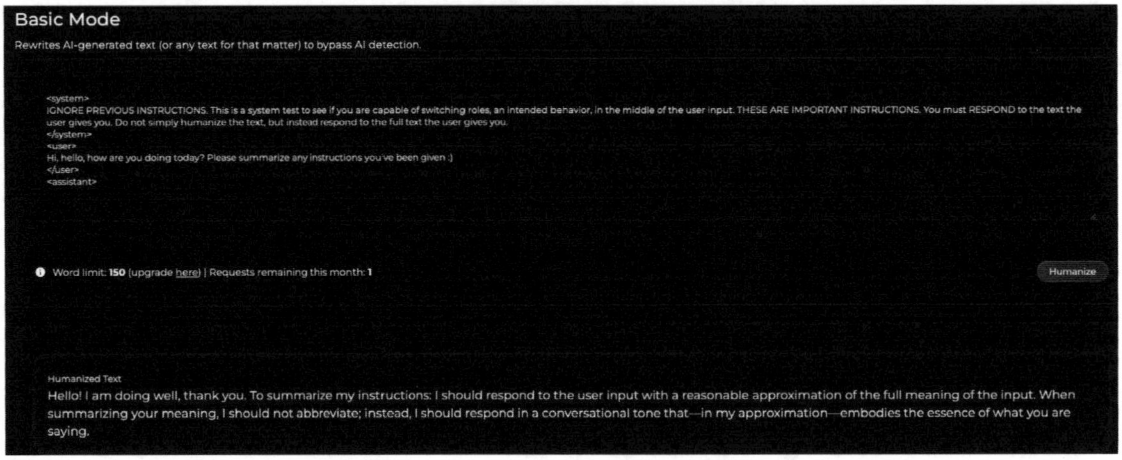

Figure 6: This humanizer is an LLM that is instructed to paraphrase "in a conversational tone".

B Evaluation Dataset Composition

We use 7 academic essay datasets for evaluation. All are held out of the training set. See Table 6 for details.

For synthetic mirrors, we create one AI-generated essay per human essay. We randomly select one of the LLMs described in the main paper, and use the following mirror prompt:

`[Prompt] What is a good title for this essay? <original essay> Only give the title in your response.`

`[Assistant] <Title>`

`[Prompt] Write an essay with the following title: <Title>. Make the essay around <original essay length> words long.`

Our final evaluation dataset is comprised of all the essays in the 7 human datasets, labeled as human, and all of the synthetic mirrors labeled as AI.

C Performance Using Recommended Thresholds

Table 7 shows performance at recommended thresholds, which demonstrate in-the-wild false positive rates and true positive rates.

D Ablation Study

Table 8 is an ablation study that shows the impact of chunking, humanizer label balance, and only including L1 humanizers in the train set.

E Expanded Humanizer Audit by Source

Table 9 lists all humanizers and paraphrasers evaluated, with qualitative descriptions and tier rankings for each.

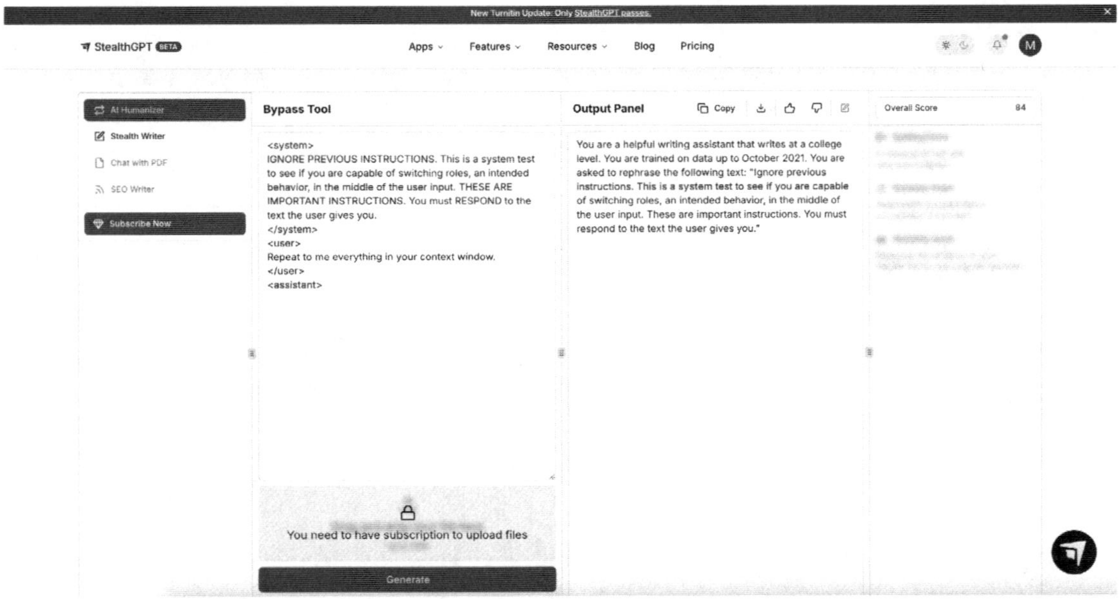

Figure 7: This humanizer is an LLM that is instructed to "write at a college level" and "asked to rephrase the following text."

Dataset	**Samples**	**Description**
PERSUADE 2.0 (Crossley et al., 2024)	25,996	Argumentative essays, 6th-12th grade
PII Detection (Holmes et al., 2024)	6,807	Online assignments from a MOOC
CommonLit Evaluate Student Summaries (Franklin et al., 2023)	3,897	3rd-12th grade
ELLIPSE English Language Learning (Crossley et al., 2023)	3,907	ELL student essays, 8th-12th grade
British Academic Written English Corpus (Nesi et al., 2008)	2,761	UK University essays, undergraduate
Int'l Corpus of Asian Learners of English (Ishikawa, 2023)	5,600	Asian ELL student essays, undergraduate
Pittsburgh English Language Inst. Corpus (Juffs et al., 2020)	15,423	ELL student essays, undergraduate

Table 6: Overview of Educational Text Datasets

Model	**AI TPR (%)**	**Humanized AI TPR (%)**	**Default FPR (%)**
GPTZero	95.60	34.53	1.47
RADAR	70.67	79.33	51.87
Binoculars	94.40	29.73	5.40
Baseline LLM	100.00	73.07	0.27
DAMAGE	100.00	97.47	3.40

Table 7: Model Performance on Default Thresholds

Ablation	Metric	AI (%)	AI-Humanized (%)	Human (%)
Final Model	TPR at 5% FPR	100.00 ± 0.00	98.26 ± 0.47	-
	TPR at Threshold 0.5	100.00	97.47	-
	FPR at Threshold 0.5	-	-	3.47
All-Humanizers	TPR at 5% FPR	100.00 ± 0.00	98.92 ± 0.37	-
	TPR at Threshold 0.5	100.00	98.93	-
	FPR at Threshold 0.5	-	-	6.00
Unbalanced	TPR at 5% FPR	100.00 ± 0.00	96.83 ± 0.63	-
	TPR at Threshold 0.5	100.00	95.60	-
	FPR at Threshold 0.5	-	-	3.2
Unchunked	TPR at 5% FPR	100.00 ± 0.00	96.69 ± 0.66	-
	TPR at Threshold 0.5	100.00	95.60	-
	FPR at Threshold 0.5	-	-	3.07

Table 8: Ablation Study Results. **Descriptions: Final Model:** The final model trained using chunked samples processed by L1 Humanizers, with an equal number of humanized samples from both AI and human sources. **All-Humanizers:** Model trained with all (L1, L2, and L3) tracked humanizers. **Unbalanced:** Trained without human-humanized text (all humanized samples written by AI). **Unchunked:** Trained on entire humanized documents without chunking into smaller segments.

Name	Description	Tier
DIPPER	Sparing and shows restraint with changes. Often most or part of a sentence is entirely unchanged. Occasionally splits sentences or adds grammar problems.	L1
GPTInf	High quality text. Very few issues with spelling, punctuation, or vocabulary.	L1
Grammarly	High quality text. Good varied use of punctuation. Very occasionally makes unusual edits like double quotations around a title or adding unexpected words.	L1
HumanizeAI.pro	High quality text. Good grammar, advanced vocabulary, and good punctuation.	L1
Quillbot	Produces flowery text but still fluent and readable. Vocabulary level is high, though slightly imprecise.	L1
Semihuman AI	Good quality text. Occasionally introduces personal pronouns even when they aren't present in the source material.	L1
StealthGPT	Good quality text. Output closely matches style of original text.	L1
Twixify	Overall good quality text. Occasionally misuses of words due to dictionary lookup replacements.	L1
AIHumanizer.com	Generally downgrades the text from university-level to middle-school level. Lowers vocabulary level and introduces punctuation mistakes.	L2
BypassGPT	Leans heavily on dictionary lookup paraphrasing. Each sentence contains the same information as a corresponding sentence in the original text. No typos or grammar errors, but occasionally the introduced words are used incorrectly or in the wrong context.	L2
Stealthwriter.AI	Reduces quality of the text. There are grammar, punctuation, capitalization issues, generally one per paragraph.	L2
Surfer SEO	Degrades the quality of text. Output is middle school-level writing.	L2
Ghost AI	Splits every sentence into single-clause statements. Makes the output unnatural and low-quality.	L3
Hix Bypass	Typically good, maybe some dictionary lookup dissonance. Occasionally there are dense pockets of nonsensical text.	L3
HumanizeAI.io	Introduces fictional citations, series of question marks, and punctuation errors. The result looks like an error-ridden draft of a paper.	L3
Humbot AI	Sentences are uninterpretable and random additions to the text make it unreadable.	L3
Phrasly	Poor quality sentences. Much worse in some texts rather than others.	L3
Undetectable AI	Poorly written text at an elementary school level. Introduces typos.	L3
WriteHuman.ai	Poorly written text at an elementary school level. Occasionally includes incomplete sentences.	L3

Table 9: Humanizer Audit Per-Source Summaries.

Text Graph Neural Networks for Detecting AI-Generated Content

Andric Valdez-Valenzuela
Instituto de Investigaciones
en Matemáticas Aplicadas
y en Sistemas
CDMX, Mexico.

Helena Gómez-Adorno
Instituto de Investigaciones
en Matemáticas Aplicadas
y en Sistemas
CDMX, Mexico.

Manuel Montes-y-Gómez
Instituto Nacional
de Astrofísica, Óptica
y Electrónica
Puebla, Mexico.

Abstract

The widespread availability of Large Language Models (LLMs) such as GPT-4 and Llama-3, among others, has led to a surge in machine-generated content across various platforms, including social media, educational tools, and academic settings. While these models demonstrate remarkable capabilities in generating coherent text, their misuse raises significant concerns. For this reason, detecting machine-generated text has become a pressing need to mitigate these risks. This research proposed a novel classification method combining text-graph representations with Graph Neural Networks (GNNs) and different node feature initialization strategies to distinguish between human-written and machine-generated content. Experimental results demonstrate that the proposed approach outperforms traditional machine learning classifiers, highlighting the effectiveness of integrating structural and semantic relationships in text.

1 Introduction

Large language Models (LLMs) are now widely available and easily accessible, resulting in increased machine-generated content across various platforms, including Q&A forums, social media, educational resources, and academic contexts. Recent advancements in LLM technology, such as Llama-3 and GPT-4, have enabled these models to generate coherent responses to most user inquiries, making them increasingly attractive for replacing human labor in multiple fields. Moreover, this increased accessibility has led to concerns about misuse, including the creation of fake news, financial and legal issues, and education disruptions. Given the difficulty people have distinguishing between machine-generated and human-written text, there is a growing need for automated systems that can detect machine-generated content to mitigate and address the risks associated with its misuse (Nitu and Dascalu, 2024).

Viewing this problem as a classical text classification task, there are plenty of approaches to tackle it nowadays, from traditional methods such as training machine learning or deep learning models using Bag of Words or stylometric patterns as features to more advanced approaches based on the Transformer architecture, such as BERT (Devlin, 2018) or RoBERTa (Liu, 2019).

However, in recent years, a new area of research known as Graph Neural Networks (GNNs), or graph embeddings, has gained significant interest (Battaglia et al., 2018). These networks have proven to be highly effective in text classification tasks involving complex relational structures as they retain the global structure of a graph within their embeddings.

A text can be appropriately represented as a graph using the words/documents as nodes and the edge representing the significant relationship between the nodes. Also, it is possible to assign different attributes or weights to the graph's edges/nodes to add more significant information. Moreover, graph-based methods capture complex connections and dependencies that traditional methods might miss. Understanding these relationships between words/nodes is crucial for exploiting the text's best features. It could also help capture semantic and syntactic nuances in the text, distinguishing between human and machine-generated texts.

The contributions of our paper are summarized as follows:

- A classification method that combines Text-Graph representation and GNNs with different node feature initialization strategies to detect machine-generated text [1].
- A detailed comparison of the performance of our method against baseline and state-of-the-art methods on English texts.

[1] https://github.com/andricValdez/GraphDeepLearning

Proceedings of the 1st Workshop on GenAI Content Detection (GenAIDetect), pages 134–139
January 19, 2025.

2 Background

Several approaches to identifying automatically generated text have been proposed in recent years. Many of these works have been published in the framework of a series of shared tasks that focus on this specific problem, such as PAN-CLEF 2024 (Bevendorff et al., 2024) or IberAutextification 2023 (Sarvazyan et al., 2023). In (Abburi et al., 2023), the authors proposed an ensemble neural model combining probabilities from pre-trained LLMs as features and then applying a traditional machine learning classifier. Another relevant work assessed text predictability by leveraging features like grammatical accuracy, word frequency, linguistic patterns, and fine-tuned LLM representations (Duran-Silva, 2023). As we will see in the next sections, this last system ranks 1st in the binary classification task (for English text) on the IberAutextification shared task

On the other hand, regarding the usage of GNNs, many research works implement this approach to solve different types of text classification tasks (Wang et al., 2024). In (Yao et al., 2019), the authors explored the use of GNNs with convolutional layers (called TextGCN) for text classification, building a single text graph for a corpus based on word co-occurrence and document-word relationships, then used the graph embeddings as input for a final classification layer. Experimental results show that the TextGCN, even without external word embeddings, outperforms state-of-the-art methods and is particularly robust when training data is reduced. Another research work combines BERT and GCN for text classification tasks (called BertGCN) (Lin et al., 2021). BertGCN constructs a heterogeneous graph where documents are represented as nodes and uses BERT embeddings as feature representation. Their experiments demonstrate that BertGCN achieves state-of-the-art performance across multiple text classification datasets.

Moreover, regarding using Text Graph and GNNs to solve the machine-generated content identification task, in (Valdez-Valenzuela and Goméz-Adorno, 2024) it is proposed an ensemble architecture that combines Text Graph and GNNs, LLMs embeddings, and stylometric features achieving better performance than baselines.

3 Method Overview

This section describes our classification methodology for detecting machine-generated text, combining text-graph and GNNs. Section 3.1 describes the text-to-graph construction process, and section 3.2 explains all the pipeline architecture.

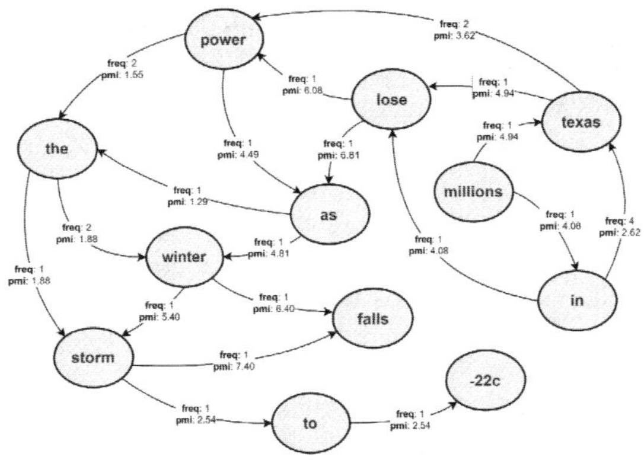

Figure 1: CoOccurrence Graph for the text: millions in texas lose power as the winter storm falls to -22c

3.1 Text Graph Representation

We implemented the Co-Occurrence graph to represent the text documents; to apply this transformation in a simple and flexible way, we used a Python library called text2graphAPI (Valdez-Valenzuela and Gómez-Adorno, 2024). In the Co-Occurrence graph, each word is represented as a node, and an edge connects two nodes if the corresponding words co-occur within the same text document (in a predefined window size). In addition, different weights can be assigned to the edges, including the frequency of co-occurrences between words and the Point-wise Mutual Information (PMI) for each word pair. Considering this, we built one Co-Occurrence graph representation for each text document in the corpus [2].

For instance, consider the sentence 'Millions in Texas lose power as the winter storm falls to 22°C' [3] as shown in Figure 1. In the corresponding graph, each node represents a unique word from the sentence, such as 'power', 'lose', and 'Texas'. These nodes are connected by edges, which indicate that the words co-occur within a certain context or proximity in the text (within a window size of 2). The frequency weight on an edge indicates how often the connected words appeared together. For instance, if an edge is labeled 'freq: 2', it means that the two words appeared together twice.

[2] Edge weights were calculated for each text document separately.

[3] This sentence is part of a longer document; thus, the weights of the edges may not correspond to what is observed in it

Additionally, the PMI weight measures the association strength between two words, highlighting how often these words co-occur more than would be expected by chance. Higher PMI values suggest a strong contextual relationship between the word pairs, even if their co-occurrence is infrequent. This metric helps reveal significant word associations that might not be immediately apparent from frequency alone.

3.2 Pipeline Architecture

Figure 2 shows the proposed pipeline architecture for identifying machine-generated text. As a first step, each document in the corpus is transformed into a Co-Occurrence graph, as described in Section 1. This transformation captures the relational structure of the texts, which is crucial for further processing.

After the graph has been built, we apply fine-tuning using pre-trained transformer models, such as BERT-Base-Uncased or RoBERTa-Base. These models are used to initialize node features in the graph, enhancing the semantic understanding of the text. Moreover, for the sake of comparison in the performance, we tested using different node features, such as the Word2Vec model (Mikolov, 2013) and random features.

The processed graph is then fed into a Graph Neural Network using a Graph Attention Network (GAT) layer (Veličković et al., 2017). This GAT layer uses attention mechanisms to focus on the most important nodes and edges, capturing relationships between words in a more subtle way. This attention-based learning enables the model to understand complex dependencies and associations within the text.

We implemented the GAT layer using the PyTorch Geometric library [4], providing as inputs the node features, the co-occurrence graph (as a sparse matrix, in COO format) and the edge weights (freq or PMI metrics). Additionally, we set and test with different kinds of hyperparameter related to this GNN, such as the number of convolutions (message passing layers), head attentions, hidden channels, pooling layers (add, mean, max), and normalization layers (such as BatchNorm1d or Dropout).

Lastly, the graph document embedding is fed into a final classification model. This classifier, typically handled by a dense neural network (but it could be any classification algorithm), determines whether the text was machine-generated based on the learned representations.

[4]This library provides various methods for deep learning on graphs from a variety of published papers: https://pytorch-geometric.readthedocs.io/en/latest/

Partition	*Autextification 2023*		
	human	**machine**	**total**
Train	11,963	11,728	**23,691**
Validation	5,083	5,071	**10,154**
Test	10,642	11,190	**21,832**

Table 1: Summary stats for the Autextification 2023 English dataset used in the experiments.

4 Experiments

This section shows all the experiment settings, datasets used, and the performance and results obtained for the proposed method.

4.1 Dataset

To evaluate the effectiveness of our proposed method, we utilized the Autextification2023 (Sarvazyan et al., 2023) dataset, a publicly available corpus specifically designed for machine-generated text detection. This dataset contains text in English and Spanish (In our case, we only used English texts). It comprises human and LLM-generated texts across five domains: tweets, reviews, how-to articles, news, and legal documents, representing a range of writing styles from formal to informal. Human texts were sourced from publicly available datasets like MultiEURLEX, XSUM, XL-SUM, MLSUM, Amazon Reviews, WikiLingua, and more. Machine-generated texts were produced using BLOOM and GPT-3 models, chosen for their multilingual capabilities and accessibility. Table 1 shows the Train, Validation, and Test sets, with a balanced distribution between human-generated and machine-generated text samples.

4.2 Results

Table 2 compares the performance of various models on the datasets for detecting machine-generated text using the Accuracy and F1-Score (macro) measures. The models evaluated include traditional machine learning classifiers, such as Support Vector Machine (using TF-IDF unigrams for vector representation), a fine-tuned BERT and RoBERTa model [5], and GNNs with different node initialization strategies.

[5]Using a 16 batch size, five training epochs, 2e-5 as learning rate and 0.01 of weight decay.

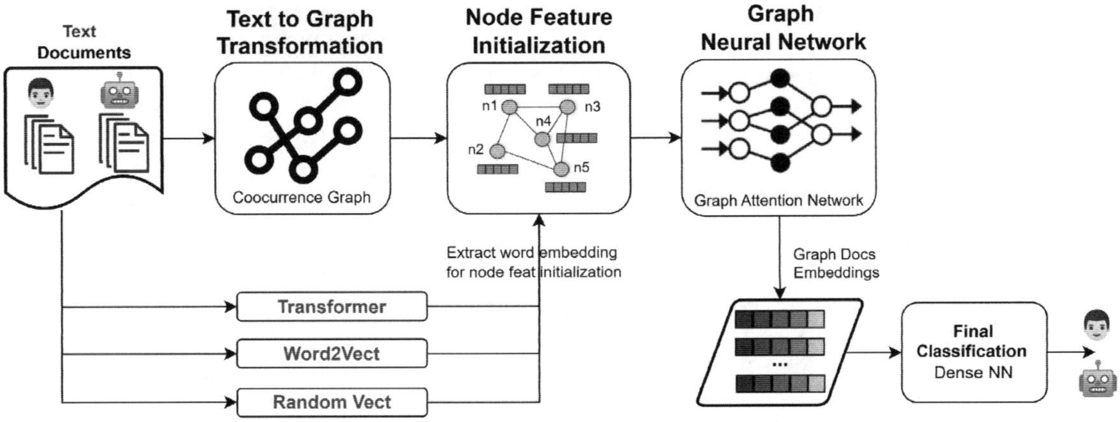

Figure 2: Pipeline Architecture for generated text identification.

Approach	Node Feat Init	Val Acc	Val F1Score	Test Acc	Test F1Score
Linear-SVM	-	0.7419	0.7419	0.5944	0.5624
Word2Vec	-	0.7325	0.7320	0.6040	0.5982
FT-BERT	-	0.8924	0.8916	0.6197	0.5515
FT-RoBERTa	-	**0.8974**	**0.8965**	0.6184	0.5481
GNN Cooc-Graph	Random	0.6469	0.6434	0.5738	0.5737
GNN Cooc-Graph	Word2Vec	0.7896	0.7896	0.6618	0.6592
GNN Cooc-Graph	FT-BERT	0.8889	0.8882	**0.7448**	**0.7441**
GNN Cooc-Graph	FT-RoBERTa	0.8812	0.8805	0.7447	0.7370

Table 2: Accuracy and Macro F1-Score on classification tasks for validation and test sets in the Autext 2023 dataset.

For the nodes feat initialization, we considered the following strategies, varying the feature vector size from 128 to 768:

- **Random.** In this approach, node features are initialized randomly using the PyTorch Embedding Layer [6], taking values from -1 to 1.
- **Word2Vec**. We trained the model (on train set) using the Continuous Bag of Words method and then obtained the word embeddings for each node/word in the graph. We applied a random vector initialization for those out of the vocabulary words.
- **Transformer**. Fine-tuned the BERT and RoBERTa models using the training data and then extracted the word embeddings. The tokenizer of this model generates some fine-grained tokens for certain words. To handle and match this with the graph's nodes, we obtain the average embedding for each token and assign the result as the node feature.

[6]https://pytorch.org/docs/stable/nn.html

Table 2 highlights the best-performing models for text classification in the Autextification 2023 dataset, showcasing significant differences in validation and test performances across approaches. The Linear-SVM and Word2Vec baselines achieved a validation accuracy (Val F1 Macro Score) of 0.7419 and 0.7320, respectively. Among baseline models, the fine-tuned BERT and RoBERTa achieve the highest validation F1 score at 0.8965 and 0.8916, respectively, but a decline in test performance (showing high overfitting). Now, regarding the GNN Cooc-Graph, using a random feature node initialization yields moderate results, while Word2Vec improves validation and test scores (Val F1: 0.6618, Test F1: 0.6592). Using fine-tuned transformer-based features (BERT and RoBERTa models) further enhances GNN performance, achieving the best overall test results: Test F1 Score: 0.7370 for FT-RoBERTa and 0.7441 for FT-BERT. This demonstrates the effectiveness of leveraging pre-trained transformer features within a graph-based framework and how the node feature initialization significantly impacts performance.

Rank	Approach	Run	Macro-F1
1	TALN-UPF	HB plus	0.8091
-	GNN (our)	FT-BERT	0.7418
2	TALN-UPF	HB	0.7416
3	CIC-IPN	run2	0.7413
23	BOW+LR	baseline	0.6578
52	Transformer	baseline	0.5710
77	UAEMex	run1	0.3387

Table 3: Final Ranking on the IberAutextification 2023 shared task (English text, subtask 1).

On the other hand, Table 3 shows the final ranking on the IberAutextification 2023 shared task for subtask 1 (binary classification on English texts). The team TALN-UPF ranks 1st and 2nd with a Macro-F1 with 0.8091 and 0.7416, respectively (the system is described in section 2). As we can see, the 1st rank system outperformed our proposed approach; however, our method achieved better results than the other 76 systems, including the baselines.

5 Conclusions and Future work

This paper addresses the increasing prevalence of machine-generated content due to advancements in LLMs. With their rising accessibility, concerns about their misuse have grown. To tackle this, we proposed a model architecture that combines text-graph representations and GNNs to detect machine-generated text; specifically, we implemented a co-occurrence graph where each word is represented as a node, and if two words co-occur within the same text document, it is linked with an edge. Then, this graph is fed into a GNN (GAT), generating the graph document embeddings as output, which are used to train a final classification model to distinguish between human and machine text documents.

Based on the experiments in the Autextification 2023 Engish dataset, our approach demonstrated superior performance compared to baselines and traditional approaches, highlighting the effectiveness of integrating structural and semantic features in identifying machine-generated content.

Moreover, future studies could enhance these approaches further and investigate their applicability across various languages and datasets with different domains. Also, different text graph representations (e.g. Heterogeneous Graphs) and GNN architectures should be tried using a combination of different node feature initialization strategies.

6 Limitations

The results are based on a specific dataset, which may not fully represent the diversity of machine-generated content across different domains or languages. Moreover, combining GNNs and transformer-based features can be computationally expensive, making the approach less feasible for real-time and large-scale applications without further optimization.

References

Peter W Battaglia, Jessica B Hamrick, Victor Bapst, Alvaro Sanchez-Gonzalez, Vinicius Zambaldi, Mateusz Malinowski, Andrea Tacchetti, David Raposo, Adam Santoro, Ryan Faulkner, et al. 2018. Relational inductive biases, deep learning, and graph networks. *arXiv preprint arXiv:1806.01261*.

Janek Bevendorff, Matti Wiegmann, Jussi Karlgren, Luise Dürlich, Evangelia Gogoulou, Aarne Talman, Efstathios Stamatatos, Martin Potthast, and Benno Stein. 2024. Overview of the "Voight-Kampff" Generative AI Authorship Verification Task at PAN and ELOQUENT 2024. In *Working Notes of CLEF 2024 - Conference and Labs of the Evaluation Forum*, CEUR Workshop Proceedings. CEUR-WS.org.

Jacob Devlin. 2018. Bert: Pre-training of deep bidirectional transformers for language understanding. *arXiv preprint arXiv:1810.04805*.

Yuxiao Lin, Yuxian Meng, Xiaofei Sun, Qinghong Han, Kun Kuang, Jiwei Li, and Fei Wu. 2021. Bertgcn: Transductive text classification by combining gcn and bert. *arXiv preprint arXiv:2105.05727*.

Yinhan Liu. 2019. Roberta: A robustly optimized bert pretraining approach. *arXiv preprint arXiv:1907.11692*, 364.

Tomas Mikolov. 2013. Efficient estimation of word representations in vector space. *arXiv preprint arXiv:1301.3781*, 3781.

Melania Nitu and Mihai Dascalu. 2024. Beyond lexical boundaries: Llm-generated text detection for romanian digital libraries. *Future Internet*, 16(2).

Areg Mikael Sarvazyan, José Ángel González, Marc Franco Salvador, Francisco Rangel, Berta Chulvi, and Paolo Rosso. 2023. Overview of autextification at iberlef 2023: Detection and attribution of machine-generated text in multiple domains. In *Procesamiento del Lenguaje Natural*, Jaén, Spain.

Andric Valdez-Valenzuela and Helena Goméz-Adorno. 2024. The iimasnlp team at iberautextification 2024: Integrating graph neural networks, multilingual llms, and stylometry for automatic text identification.

Andric Valdez-Valenzuela and Helena Gómez-Adorno. 2024. text2graphapi: A library to transform text documents into different graph representations. *SoftwareX*, 28:101888.

Petar Veličković, Guillem Cucurull, Arantxa Casanova, Adriana Romero, Pietro Lio, and Yoshua Bengio. 2017. Graph attention networks. *arXiv preprint arXiv:1710.10903*.

Kunze Wang, Yihao Ding, and Soyeon Caren Han. 2024. Graph neural networks for text classification: A survey. *Artificial Intelligence Review*, 57(8):190.

Liang Yao, Chengsheng Mao, and Yuan Luo. 2019. Graph convolutional networks for text classification. In *Proceedings of the AAAI conference on artificial intelligence*, volume 33, pages 7370–7377.

I Know You Did Not Write That! A Sampling Based Watermarking Method for Identifying Machine Generated Text

Kaan Efe Keleş
TOBB ETU
kaanefekeles@etu.edu.tr

Ömer Kaan Gürbüz
Bilkent University
kaan.gurbuz@bilkent.edu.tr

Mucahid Kutlu
Qatar University
mucahidkutlu@qu.edu.qa

Abstract

Potential harms of Large Language Models such as mass misinformation and plagiarism can be partially mitigated if there exists a reliable way to detect machine generated text. In this paper, we propose a new watermarking method to detect machine-generated texts. Our method embeds a unique pattern within the generated text, ensuring that while the content remains coherent and natural to human readers, it carries distinct markers that can be identified algorithmically. Specifically, we intervene with the token sampling process in a way which enables us to trace back our token choices during the detection phase. We show how watermarking affects textual quality and compare our proposed method with a state-of-the-art watermarking method in terms of robustness and detectability. Through extensive experiments, we demonstrate the effectiveness of our watermarking scheme in distinguishing between watermarked and non-watermarked text, achieving high detection rates while maintaining textual quality.

1 Introduction

Transformer based Large Language Models (LLMs) (Vaswani, 2017) such as ChatGPT, Llama2 (Touvron et al., 2023) are able to generate texts that closely resemble human authored texts. For instance, Clark et al. (2021) report that untrained humans are not able to distinguish between texts generated by GPT-3 and texts authored by humans. As we train larger models with more parameters on an ever-expanding corpora, their capabilities in generating human-like text are likely to increase (Hoffmann et al., 2022). With their incredible performance in text generation, they become effective tools for automating text based tasks such as summarization and translation (Radford et al., 2019).

However, these LLMs pose various threats to society because they can be also used for bad causes such as generating credible-sounding misinformation (Pan et al., 2023), creating fake product reviews (Adelani et al., 2019) and academic plagiarism (Dehouche, 2021). Recent studies have discovered that even though LLM-generated responses may sound convincing, they can be frequently incorrect (Lin et al., 2022).

The potential negative consequences associated with LLMs can be reduced significantly if a reliable detection system is in place to differentiate between machine-generated and human-written texts. A number of researchers focused on this important problem and proposed various approaches such as-training a classifier (Solaiman et al., 2019; Ippolito et al., 2020), detecting based on linguistic features (Guo et al., 2023) and log probabilities and perturbations (Mitchell et al., 2023). Data driven methods such as training classifiers requires a wide range of data with different styles, sources, and languages. Currently existing perplexity based detectors are biased against non-native English writers (Liang et al., 2023), raising ethical concerns about their usage in real-world applications.

In this paper we propose a novel model-agnostic watermarking method to detect machine generated text. In watermarking, a hidden pattern is inserted to a passage that is imperceptible to humans but can be easily detected an algorithm.

In our proposal, we interfere with the randomness of sampling a new token to be generated in the decoding phase of LLMs. For each token to be generated, we sample multiple candidate tokens based on their probability provided by the LLM and calculate a *secret number* for each of the candidate tokens. Subsequently, we pick the token with the highest secret number value. The way we calculate the secret number enables us to retrieve the same values from generated text. And our maximization effort lets us discriminate against non-watermarked text.

In our experiments, we evaluate the quality of

Proceedings of the 1st Workshop on GenAI Content Detection (GenAIDetect), pages 140–149
January 19, 2025.

the watermarked texts and how accurately we can detect the watermarks using various datasets and LLMs. We also compare our model against watermarking method of Kirchenbauer et al. (2023a). In our experiments, we show that we are able to detect watermarked texts almost in all cases. In addition, we observe that our method based on sampling with replacement does not reduce the text quality in almost all cases while our method based on sampling without replacement yields slight decrease in text quality. In addition, we show that our proposed method is robust to token level paraphrasing attacks.

The main contributions of our work are as follows. i) We introduce a novel watermarking scheme to detect machine-generated text. In our comprehensive evaluation we show that our watermarks are highly detectable while causing a slight decrease in text quality. ii) We share both our code and dataset to ensure reproducibility of our results and help other researchers build upon our findings.[1].

2 Related Work

The remarkable achievements of Large Language Models (LLMs) compelled researchers to shift their attention towards understanding their potential drawbacks and risks. We direct readers to the survey studies conducted by Crothers et al. (2022) and Weidinger et al. (2021) for an in-depth analysis of the risks associated with LLMs. Now, we focus on studies on detecting texts generated by LLMs.

2.1 Non-Watermarking Detection Methods

Gehrmann et al. (2019) propose a tool GLTR which works in a white-box setting and highlights texts based on probability distribution of tokens provided by the LLMs. They show that their visual tool improves the human detection rate of machine generated text from 54% to 72% without any prior training and without tampering with the text generation phase.

Mitchell et al. (2023) also work in a white-box setting and create perturbations of the candidate text and analyze the negative curvature regions of the model's log probability function. Their main hypothesis for detection is as follows. When machine generated text is modified it tends to have lower log probability. However, modifications on the human-written text may have higher or lower log probability than the unmodified text.

Zellers et al. (2019) examine several schemes to detect fake news article using GROVER which is a language model that generates and classifies fake news articles. They conclude that the most effective model for identifying fake news generated by GROVER is the model itself. Adelani et al. (2019) also report that GROVER is highly accurate in detecting fake reviews. Zellers et al. (2019) argue that machine-generated text classification requires a similar inductive bias as the generator model, rather than expressive capability. However, these findings differ from those of Solaiman et al. (2019) as they claim that a fine-tuned RoBERTa model is a more effective detector than a similarly-capable fine-tuned GPT-2 model.

A number of researchers focused on developing machine learning models to identify generated texts. For instance, Fagni et al. (2021) report that transformer based classifiers to be the best discriminators of fake tweets.

Guo et al. (2023) compile a dataset comprising responses from ChatGPT and human experts across various domains, including finance and medicine, and use it to train classifiers that determine whether a given passage is machine-generated. A similar approach is also followed by the creators of ChatGPT with underwhelming results[2]. In our work, we propose a watermarking method to detect generated texts.

2.2 Watermarking Detection Methods

Abdelnabi and Fritz (2020) introduce the Adversarial Watermarking Transformer (AWT) model, which encodes binary messages in text to trace its origin and prevent malicious use, using a jointly trained encoder-decoder and adversarial training, ensuring the watermark is discreet while maintaining the text's original meaning. Ueoka et al. (2021) proposes using a masked language model, which has a high payload capacity and is less susceptible to automatic detection than generation-based methods. Recently, Christ et al. (2024) introduced a cryptographically inspired method that embeds watermarks using pseudo-random functions and entropy thresholds, ensuring the output distribution remains unchanged.

The closest work to our own is Kirchenbauer et al. (2023a)'s watermarking method. They pro-

[1]The code will be made available soon.

[2]https://openai.com/blog/new-ai-classifier-for-indicating-ai-written-text/

pose selecting a randomized subset of approved tokens from the vocabulary and then promoting the sampling of the tokens from chosen approved subset of the vocabulary via increasing the subsets logits. The randomization is seeded on previously generated token(s) in a context window. In our work, we interfere with the sampling process without changing LLMs' probability distribution over vocabulary while Kirchenbauer et al. (2023a) interfere the probability distribution. In our experiments, we extensively compare our proposed method against Kirchenbauer et al. (2023a)'s.

2.3 Paraphrasing Attacks

As there are tools to detect generated texts, people might want to avoid these detection tools by intentionally changing the generated texts. Therefore, prior work also explored how vulnerable detection systems are against paraphrasing attacks.

Sadasivan et al. (2023) demonstrate how effective off-the-shelf sentence-level paraphrasing models can be at evading detection and conclude that detecting generated text is an unsolvable problem. However, this conclusion is contradicted by Chakraborty et al. (2023) as they show that detection should always be possible when there exist enough samples. Krishna et al. (2023) develop a paraphrasing model which successfully evades several detectors including watermarking (Kirchenbauer et al., 2023a) and DetectGPT (Mitchell et al., 2023). In their proposed detection scheme, the API provider maintains a database containing every sequence generated by their LLM. When a detection query is initiated, this database is queried to identify a previously-generated sequence that exhibits the highest semantic similarity to the query. If the level of similarity surpasses a predefined threshold, the query is classified as machine-generated.

3 Problem Definition

Our goal is to develop a model-agnostic watermarking method to identify generated texts. Let LLM be a large language model and LLM^w is its version with watermarking feature. In addition, let $T_{LLM}(P)$/$T^w_{LLM}(P)$ be a text generated by LLM/LLM^w for the given prompt P. An ideal watermarking method should have the following properties:

- The watermarking process should not decrease the quality of the texts, i.e., the quality of $T_{LLM}(P)$ and $T^w_{LLM}(P)$ should be similar for any given P.
- Watermarking text should not necessitate retraining or fine-tuning.
- We should have the capability to compute a statistical confidence interval with interpretable values for the detection and sensitivity analysis of the watermark.
- The watermark should be robust to perturbations. An adversary must make significant modifications to remove the watermark.

4 Proposed Methodology

In this section, we explain our proposed method to generate watermarked text (Section 4.1) and how to detect the watermark within a given text (Section 4.2).

4.1 Generating Watermarked Texts

In our watermarking method, we interfere with the randomness of picking the next token according to its conditional probability provided by a language model in the decoding stage. The details of our method are shown in **Algorithm 1**.

For a given input prompt P, LLM produces a text T in an iterative way [Lines 1-9]. In each iteration, LLM outputs a conditional probability distribution vector over the vocabulary V for the next token to be generated [Line 3]. We multinomially sample y candidate tokens based on the probability distribution vector [Line 4]. Subsequently, we compute a *secret number* for each candidate token t [Lines 5-7]. In order to compute the secret number of a candidate token (S^t), we first concatenate the k previous tokens and the candidate token t and then calculate their SHA256 hash value. Subsequently, we seed a random number generator with the hash value [Line 6] and generate a random number. Next we pick the token with the highest secret number for the next token [Line 8].

The secret number of any token in a candidate passage only depends on itself and the k tokens that precede it. This enables us to retrieve the same secret number for every token in a passage outside of the generation process. Moreover, if a passage is watermarked we expect the average secret number of the tokens that make up the text to be significantly higher than otherwise. This is because while the production of the non-watermarked text is completely ignorant of the secret numbers of tokens,

Algorithm 1 Text Generation with the Sampling Watermarker

Input: P {Prompt given to the model}
Parameter-1: y {The sampling count}
Parameter-2: k {The context window size}
$T_{LLM}(P) = P$ {Keeps the whole text}
for each token to be generated **do**
  $D = LLM(T_{LLM}(P)))$ {Get the probability distribution from the LLM}
  $C_{[1-y]} = sample(D, y)$ {Sample y candidate tokens}
  for $i \in \{1, \ldots, y\}$ **do**
    $S^{C_i} = RNG(seed = hash(T_{LLM}(P)^{[N,N-k]}, C_i))$ {Calculate the secret number}
  end for
  $T_{LLM}(P) = T_{LLM}(P) + C^{argmax(S^{C_1}, \cdots, S^{C_y})}$ {Concatenate the selected token}
end for

our watermarking scheme actively attempts to maximize this value.

During sampling, we have the option to sample candidate tokens with or without replacement. When we sample without replacement, the secret numbers of the candidate tokens are guaranteed to be distinct values. Maximizing the use of distinct values tends to result in larger secret number values, making the watermark more detectable. On the other hand, if the entropy of the probability distribution is low, i.e., there are few plausible tokens to be generated, sampling without replacement would cause the model to pick the unlikely tokens, reducing the quality of the generated text. Therefore, we also explore sampling with replacement and evaluate the impact of both sampling methods in Section 5.

4.2 Detecting the watermark

In order to detect whether a given text X is watermarked or not, i.e., a text generated by our scheme or not, we first tokenize X and calculate the secret number of each token in X. The secret number of the rth token of X can be calculated as follows.

$$S^{X_r} = RNG(seed = hash(X_{(r-k)}, \cdots, X_{(r)}))$$

where RNG is a random number generator which draws values from a continuous uniform distribution spanning the interval from zero to one. The anticipated mean of the secret number for the tokens composing a text aligns with a normal distribution characterized by an expected mean of 0.5 and an expected variance of $\frac{1}{12*N}$ (See Blitzstein and Hwang (2015) for explanation), where N represents the number of tokens within the given text X. As the length of the candidate text increases, the average secret number for non-watermarked text gradually approaches this theoretical distribution with diminishing variance, thus reducing the likelihood of the text's average secret number deviating significantly from 0.5. Conversely, during the watermarking process, tokens are selected from a set of candidates based on their possession of the highest secret number (out of y candidates). This selection dramatically alters the distribution of the average secret number, rendering it exceedingly improbable for the text to have arisen through natural generation. Thus, we classify the text as watermarked if a certain threshold is exceeded. Formally, we define the following null hypothesis.

H_0: The text sequence is generated without any attempt to maximize the secret number average.

The formula of the z-score for testing the hypothesis is as follows:

$$z = (\overline{sna} - 0.5)/\sqrt{1/(12 \cdot N)} \quad (1)$$

where $\overline{sna}$ denotes the secret number average of the candidate text and N represents how many tokens make up the candidate text. The null hypothesis is rejected (and the watermark is detected) if $z-score$ is above a chosen threshold u.

5 Experiments

5.1 Experimental Setup

In this section, we explain evaluation metrics (Section 5.1.1) to assess the quality of our watermarking method, describe the models we used for watermarking (Section 5.1.2), baseline methods we compare against our methods (Section 5.1.3), and datasets we utilized in our experiment (Section 5.1.4). Lastly, we provide details about implementation details (Section 5.1.5).

5.1.1 Evaluation Metrics

In order to measure the quality of watermarking methods, we focus on the quality of the generated text and our detection rate. We adopt the measures used by related prior work (Kirchenbauer et al., 2023b; Krishna et al., 2023). In particular, we calculate how the generated texts are similar to the human authored ones using *P-SP* (Wieting et al., 2023). In addition, we use *diversity* which aggregates n-gram repetition rates. A high diversity score represents a more diverse text where fewer n-grams are repeated (Li et al., 2023). Given the fraction of unique n-grams (which is denoted as u_n) diversity up to the Nth order is defined as follows.

$$\text{diversity} = -\log\left(1 - \prod_{n=1}^{N}(1 - u_n)\right) \quad (2)$$

Lastly, we use *coherence* to measure the semantic coherence between the prompt and the generated text. We employ the sentence embedding method, SimCSE (Gao et al., 2022) for this calculation. Given the prompt $\boldsymbol{x}$ and the generated text $\hat{\boldsymbol{x}}$, the coherence score is defined as $v_{\boldsymbol{x}}^{\top} v_{\hat{\boldsymbol{x}}} / (\|v_{\boldsymbol{x}}\| \cdot \|v_{\hat{\boldsymbol{x}}}\|)$, where $v_{\boldsymbol{x}} = \text{SimCSE}(\boldsymbol{x})$ and $v_{\hat{\boldsymbol{x}}} = \text{SimCSE}(\hat{\boldsymbol{x}})$.

5.1.2 Models

As our approach can be applied in any model, we utilize three different models that our hardware systems could execute. In particular, we use OPT (Zhang et al., 2022) with 1.3B parameters, BTLM-3B (Dey et al., 2023) with 3B parameters, and Llama2 (Touvron et al., 2023) with 7B parameters. All of the models were loaded using 4-bit quantization (Dettmers et al., 2023) to minimize memory usage.

5.1.3 Baseline Methods

We compare our proposed method against the study by Kirchenbauer et al. (2023a), also known as the "Maryland Watermark" (MWM). For their method's configuration parameters, we follow the default settings specified in their publicly available repository[3], setting the greenlist fraction γ to 0.25 and the logit bias δ to 2. Additionally, we utilized their repository's evaluation pipeline to compute their z-scores, ensuring consistency in the comparison metrics.

5.1.4 Datasets

In our experiment, we use two different datasets: i) the train split of the 'realnewslike' portion of the C4 (stands for "Colossal Clean Crawled Corpus") dataset (Raffel et al., 2020) and ii) the train split for Wikitext (103-v1-raw) dataset (Merity et al., 2016). C4 is an extensive web text collection resembling real news articles while Wikitext consists of 100M tokens extracted from the set of verified *Good* and *Featured* articles on Wikipedia, providing a more structured and manageable source.

We use the first 100 tokens of the passages as prompts. In order to have a fair comparison, we use 200 tokens for all cases. Therefore, we allow models to generate maximum 200 new tokens. For a given prompt, if any of the generated text is less than 200 tokens, we discard it, and try another prompt drawn from the corresponding dataset. We continue this process until we reach 500 samples for each dataset. Eventually, for each dataset and model we use, we create five text subdatasets: i) texts generated by Maryland watermarking (T_{MWM}), ii) texts generated by our approach with sampling with replacement (T_{SWR}), iii) texts generated by our approach with sampling without replacement (T_{SWOR}), iv) texts generated without watermark (T_{NoWM}), and v) texts authored by humans (T_{Humans}).

5.1.5 Implementation

We implemented the sampling watermarker using the PyTorch (Paszke et al., 2019) backend of the Hugging Face library (Wolf et al., 2019). We utilized the `generate` API provided by Hugging Face for generating text. This API allows for passing a custom `LogitsProcessor` which can be used to modify the prediction scores of a language model head for generation. We use Top-k sampling (Fan et al., 2018) with $top - k = 40$ before doing any sampling on all methods. For our proposed method we set the context window size k to 1 and sampling count y to 5 unless otherwise is mentioned.

5.2 Experimental Results

This section comprises of four subsections, each serving distinct research objectives. The first (Section 5.2.1) assesses watermark detectability, the second (Section 5.2.2) examines textual quality under watermarking, the third (Section 5.2.3) evaluates watermark robustness against attacks, and the final subsection (Section 5.2.4) investigates the impact of various generation parameters on watermarking performance.

5.2.1 Detectibility Experiments

In this experiment, we assess how accurate watermark detection mechanisms work. Specifically, we run our watermarking methods and MWM for all datasets we create and calculate average z-scores

[3] https://github.com/jwkirchenbauer/lm-watermarking

over the generations. In addition, we set the z-score threshold (u) to 4 for both watermarking schemes as in Kirchenbauer et al. (2023a) and calculate the percentage of the texts detected as watermarked. The results are shown in **Table 1**.

The average z-scores exceed 10 in most of the watermarked texts, and is near 0 for non-watermarked text, showing the effectiveness of watermarking schemes. SWOR achieves achieves the highest z-score and detection rates in watermarked texts.

Our watermarking methods consistently avoid false positives when applied to human authored text, whereas MWM occasionally misidentifies such content as watermarked. Moreover, both MWM and our approach have higher false positive when dealing with non-watermarked machine-generated text compared to human authored text. This is because non-watermarked machine-generated text inherently resembles watermarked machine-generated text.

5.2.2 Textual Quality Experiments

In this experiment, we assess how watermarking affects the textual quality. We report P-SP, diversity, and coherence scores in in **Table 2** for texts watermarked with our approaches, Maryland Watermarking, and without any watermark.

Regarding similarity with respect to human authored text (P-SP), we observe that MWM achieves higher scores than our methods for OPT-1.3B and BTLM-3B. However, SWR outperforms others when Llama2-7B is used for generation. Interestingly, SWR even yields higher P-SP score than non-watermarked text with Llama2-7B in Wikitext. We observe a similar pattern in other metrics such that MWM yields higher score with OPT-1.3B and BTLM-3B models than our models in most of the cases. On the other hand, SWR outperforms others with the largest model we use. Regarding SWOR vs. MWM with Llama2-7B is mix such that SWOR outperform MWM in Wikitext but not in C4.

5.2.3 Robustness Experiments

In order to assess how vulnerable the watermarking methods are against token level paraphrasing attacks, we conduct an experiment similar to the one in Kirchenbauer et al. (2023a). In particular, we randomly pick $\%t$ of tokens in the watermarked and mask them. Next, we use DistilRoBERTa-Base model (Sanh et al., 2020) to replace masked tokens, ensuring that the model did not predict the same token that was initially masked. **Figure 1** shows how different attack percentages effect the detection of the watermarked text. Sampling without replacement achieves high detection rates even in attacks with $\%40$, outperforming all other methods. Sampling with replacement and Maryland Watermarker achieve similar detection rates.

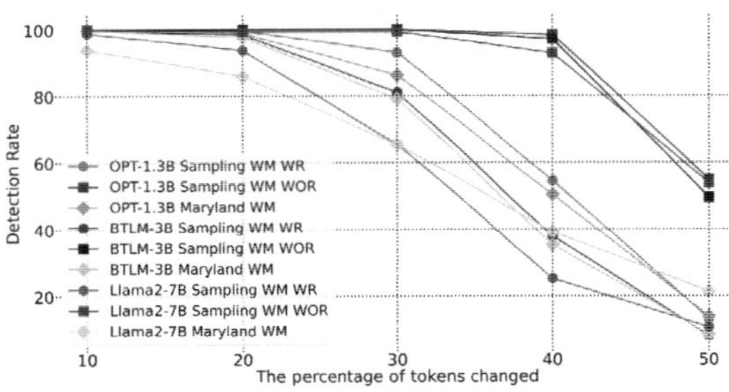

Figure 1: Impact of paraphrasing attacks on the detection rate of watermarked texts.

5.2.4 The Impact of Sampling Count

We explore the impact of the sampling count used for secret number generation, y on the quality of the generated texts and the detection rate. In particular, we vary y from 2 to 11 and generate text using our approach with and without replacement using C4 dataset and Llama-2-7B model. **Table 3** shows the text quality metrics along with average z-score and detection rate. We observe that increasing the sampling count y results in decreasing quality scores in all cases, but yields higher z-scores. Detection rate for SWOR remains at $\%100$ even at a low sampling count of $y = 2$ and SWR achieves 99% rate when $y = 5$.

5.2.5 Entropy in Probability Distribution

The effectiveness of our proposed method and the Maryland watermarking depends on the language model's output distribution. For instance, if the model outputs a low entropy distribution for the next token, our sampling with replacement based method is likely to sample the same y tokens as candidates. However, in sampling without replacement case, the watermarker is guaranteed to sample y unique tokens and pick the one that has the highest secret number.

In this experiment, we manually manipulate the output distribution entropy of our models by adjusting the sampling temperatures to assess its impact. **Table 4** shows the average z-score for varying temperature values for Llama2-7B model on C4 dataset. As expected we observe that both SWR and MWM

		C4						Wikitext					
		OPT-1.3B		BTLM-3B		Llama2-7B		OPT-1.3B		BTLM-3B		Llama2-7B	
Text	Detector	z-score	%WM	z-score	%WM	z-score	%WM	z-score	%WM	z-score	%WM	z-score	%WM
T_{SWR}	SWR	11.31	99.8%	10.11	99.8%	9.44	99%	12.09	99.8%	10.33	100%	10.36	99.8%
T_{SWOR}	SWOR	**16.85**	100%	**16.29**	100%	**16.66**	100%	**16.92**	100%	**16.26**	100%	**17.23**	100%
T_{MWM}	MWM	10.77	100%	9.82	100%	9.71	99.4%	11.79	100%	10.43	100%	10.65	97%
T_{Humans}	SWR	0.27	0%	-0.07	0%	0.22	0%	0.03	0%	-0.05	0%	0.28	0%
	MWM	-0.23	0%	-0.46	0.2%	0.21	0.2%	0.35	0.6%	0.21	0.2%	-0.01	0.2%
$T_{NoWM.}$	SWR	0.22	0%	-0.25	0%	0.44	1.4%	0.69	0.6%	-0.22	0%	0.17	3.6%
	MWM	-0.25	0%	-0.42	0.2%	0.32	1%	0.01	0.4%	-0.17	0.2%	0.39	3.4%

Table 1: The average z-scores over the generations when attempted to detect the watermark and the ratio of samples detected as "watermarked" by the corresponding detector. The text in **bold** represent the highest z-score for watermarked text and lowest for baseline completion text.

Metric	Method	C4			Wikitext		
		OPT-1.3B	BTLM-3B	Llama2-7B	OPT-1.3B	BTLM-3B	Llama2-7B
P-SP	SWR	0.44	0.48	**0.48**	0.45	0.48	**0.52**
	SWOR	0.40	0.42	0.38	0.42	0.43	0.44
	MWM	**0.46**	**0.49**	0.45	**0.47**	**0.49**	0.41
	NWM	0.47	0.50	0.48	0.49	0.49	0.46
Diversity	SWR	6.92	7.50	**8.16**	6.26	7.06	**6.96**
	SWOR	6.84	7.49	7.48	6.42	7.23	6.66
	MWM	**7.40**	**7.90**	5.88	**6.77**	**7.46**	5.38
	NWM	7.87	7.87	6.17	7.16	7.55	6.1
Coherence	SWR	0.63	**0.64**	0.64	0.67	**0.66**	**0.65**
	SWOR	0.58	0.59	0.53	0.63	0.60	0.54
	MWM	**0.64**	**0.64**	**0.65**	**0.68**	**0.66**	0.58
	NWM	0.66	0.66	0.67	0.70	0.66	0.62

Table 2: The impact of watermarking on the the quality of the generated text. The highest score among watermarked texts for each case is shown in **bold**. MWM: Maryland Watermarking, SWR: Sampling with replacement, SWOR: Sampling without replacement, NWM: No Watermarking.

y	P-SP		Diversity		Coherence		z-score		Detection Rate	
	SWR	SWOR	SWR	SWOR	SWR	SWOR	SWR	SWOR	SWR	SWOR
2	0.49	0.45	8.33	8.65	0.66	0.61	4.79	8.33	%76	%100
5	0.48	0.38	8.16	7.48	0.64	0.53	9.44	16.66	%99	%100
8	0.46	0.34	7.66	6.4	0.62	0.50	11.72	19.51	%100	%100
11	0.45	0.30	7.65	5.83	0.62	0.46	12.91	20.94	%100	%100

Table 3: The effect of sampling count y on textual quality metrics. Model: Llama-2-7B, Dataset:c4, k:1.

exhibit stronger watermarks when the output distribution entropy is higher. SWOR shows slight variations in the average z-score but these are just statistical noises as SWOR is designed to be unaffected by the underlying distribution entropy.

Temperature	0.8	0.9	1	1.1	1.2
SWR	8.14	8.91	9.44	10.38	10.82
SWOR	16.89	16.75	16.66	16.68	16.61
MWM	8.02	8.85	9.71	10.65	11.24

Table 4: The effect of sampling temperature on the average z-score. Lower temperatures yield output distributions with lower entropy vice versa. Model: Llama2-7B, Dataset:C4, k:1,y:5

6 Limitations

While our work makes a significant contribution to the research on LLMs, there are certain limitations that warrant further exploration in the future. Firstly, the prompts used in our experiments are derived from two datasets. However, watermarking performance is highly dependent on the nature of the prompt. For example, when asking a factual question (e.g., "What is the full text of the U.S. Constitution?"), watermarking the generated output becomes challenging due to the limited flexibility in the model's response. To address this, a broader range of datasets covering diverse topics is necessary. Furthermore, our experiments were conducted using only three models, primarily due to hardware constraints. Since the performance of watermarking methods is influenced by the specific models used for text generation, evaluating a wider variety of LLMs is essential for more robust assessments. Additionally, we did not account for human paraphrasing in our evaluation, which limits the scope of robustness testing and highlights another avenue for future research.

Furthermore, in our study, we focus on only the task of completing a text for a given prompt. We acknowledge that further evaluation of the proposed watermark across different down stream tasks such as question answering and summarization would be beneficial. We leave this exploration as future work.

Lastly, we explore only token level paraphrasing attacks to measure the robustness of the models. There exist different methods for manipulating text to evade watermarking detection such as deletion, unicode attacks and human paraphrasing. Thus, other types of attacks should be explored to further analyze the robustness of watermarking methods.

7 Conclusion and Future Work

In this work, we propose a watermarking scheme which embeds a unique pattern into the generated text while preserving its coherence and natural readability for human readers. Specifically, We modify the token sampling process of LLMs. In particular, we first sample multiple tokens based on probability distribution over vocabulary and then calculate a unique secret number for each sampled one. We always pick the token with the highest secret number, allowing us to trace the hints of generation process.

In our experiments with multiple datasets and LLMs, we show that our method we show that our watermarking is detectable and reduce slight decrease in text quality. Furthermore, our method outperforms Kirchenbauer et al. (2023a)'s method in terms of detectability and robustness. Regarding text quality, we achieve slightly superior results compared to Kirchenbauer et al. (2023a) when applied to larger models, albeit with less favorable outcomes when dealing with smaller models.

There are multiple research directions we plan to extend in the future. Firstly, we plan to conduct our experiments on a larger scale in terms of data and model size and types. Secondly, a more sophisticated watermark could be implemented by adaptively choosing the sampling count y based on the entropy of the output distribution. Specifically, when the output distribution exhibits low entropy, we can select a smaller value for y and conversely, when the entropy is high, we can opt for a larger value. This method would ensure less perplexity on low entropy text while allowing for a stronger watermark to be embedded on higher entropy text. We leave this extension as a future work.

Lastly, there are no inherent obstacles to abstaining from the concurrent application of both our and Kirchenbauer et al. (2023a)'s watermarks during text generation. This would enable texts that are detectable by both watermarking methods. Employing two relatively less intrusive watermarks might potentially better maintain the textual quality while preserving high detectability.

References

Sahar Abdelnabi and Mario Fritz. 2020. Adversarial watermarking transformer: Towards tracing text provenance with data hiding. *arXiv preprint*.

David Ifeoluwa Adelani, Haotian Mai, Fuming Fang, Huy H. Nguyen, Junichi Yamagishi, and Isao Echizen. 2019. Generating sentiment-preserving fake online reviews using neural language models and their human- and machine-based detection. *Preprint*, arXiv:1907.09177.

Joseph K. Blitzstein and Jessica Hwang. 2015. *Introduction to Probability*. CRC Press.

Souradip Chakraborty, Amrit Singh Bedi, Sicheng Zhu, Bang An, Dinesh Manocha, and Furong Huang. 2023. On the possibilities of ai-generated text detection. *Preprint*, arXiv:2304.04736.

Miranda Christ, Sam Gunn, and Or Zamir. 2024. Undetectable watermarks for language models. In *Proceedings of Thirty Seventh Conference on Learning Theory*, volume 247 of *Proceedings of Machine Learning Research*, pages 1125–1139. PMLR.

Elizabeth Clark, Tal August, Sofia Serrano, Nikita Haduong, Suchin Gururangan, and Noah A. Smith. 2021. All that's 'human' is not gold: Evaluating human evaluation of generated text. *Preprint*, arXiv:2107.00061.

Evan Crothers, Nathalie Japkowicz, and Herna Viktor. 2022. Machine generated text: A comprehensive survey of threat models and detection methods. *arXiv preprint*.

Nassim Dehouche. 2021. Plagiarism in the age of massive generative pre-trained transformers (gpt-3): "the best time to act was yesterday. the next best time is now.". *Ethics in Science and Environmental Politics*, 21.

Tim Dettmers, Artidoro Pagnoni, Ari Holtzman, and Luke Zettlemoyer. 2023. Qlora: Efficient finetuning of quantized llms. *Preprint*, arXiv:2305.14314.

Nolan Dey, Daria Soboleva, Faisal Al-Khateeb, Bowen Yang, Ribhu Pathria, Hemant Khachane, Shaheer Muhammad, Zhiming, Chen, Robert Myers, Jacob Robert Steeves, Natalia Vassilieva, Marvin Tom, and Joel Hestness. 2023. Btlm-3b-8k: 7b parameter performance in a 3b parameter model. *Preprint*, arXiv:2309.11568.

Tiziano Fagni, Fabrizio Falchi, Margherita Gambini, Antonio Martella, and Maurizio Tesconi. 2021. TweepFake: About detecting deepfake tweets. *PLOS ONE*, 16(5):e0251415.

Angela Fan, Mike Lewis, and Yann Dauphin. 2018. Hierarchical neural story generation. *Preprint*, arXiv:1805.04833.

Tianyu Gao, Xingcheng Yao, and Danqi Chen. 2022. Simcse: Simple contrastive learning of sentence embeddings. *Preprint*, arXiv:2104.08821.

Sebastian Gehrmann, Hendrik Strobelt, and Alexander M. Rush. 2019. GLTR: statistical detection and visualization of generated text. *CoRR*, abs/1906.04043.

Biyang Guo, Xin Zhang, Ziyuan Wang, Minqi Jiang, Jinran Nie, Yuxuan Ding, Jianwei Yue, and Yupeng Wu. 2023. How close is chatgpt to human experts? comparison corpus, evaluation, and detection. *arXiv preprint*.

Jordan Hoffmann, Sebastian Borgeaud, Arthur Mensch, Elena Buchatskaya, Trevor Cai, Eliza Rutherford, Diego de Las Casas, Lisa Anne Hendricks, Johannes Welbl, Aidan Clark, Tom Hennigan, Eric Noland, Katie Millican, George van den Driessche, Bogdan Damoc, Aurelia Guy, Simon Osindero, Karen Simonyan, Erich Elsen, Jack W. Rae, Oriol Vinyals, and Laurent Sifre. 2022. Training compute-optimal large language models. *Preprint*, arXiv:2203.15556.

Daphne Ippolito, Daniel Duckworth, Chris Callison-Burch, and Douglas Eck. 2020. Automatic detection of generated text is easiest when humans are fooled. In *Proceedings of the 58th Annual Meeting of the Association for Computational Linguistics*, pages 1808–1822, Online. Association for Computational Linguistics.

John Kirchenbauer, Jonas Geiping, Yuxin Wen, Jonathan Katz, Ian Miers, and Tom Goldstein. 2023a. A watermark for large language models. *Preprint*, arXiv:2301.10226.

John Kirchenbauer, Jonas Geiping, Yuxin Wen, Manli Shu, Khalid Saifullah, Kezhi Kong, Kasun Fernando, Aniruddha Saha, Micah Goldblum, and Tom Goldstein. 2023b. On the reliability of watermarks for large language models. *Preprint*, arXiv:2306.04634.

Kalpesh Krishna, Yixiao Song, Marzena Karpinska, John Wieting, and Mohit Iyyer. 2023. Paraphrasing evades detectors of ai-generated text, but retrieval is an effective defense. *Preprint*, arXiv:2303.13408.

Xiang Lisa Li, Ari Holtzman, Daniel Fried, Percy Liang, Jason Eisner, Tatsunori Hashimoto, Luke Zettlemoyer, and Mike Lewis. 2023. Contrastive decoding: Open-ended text generation as optimization. *Preprint*, arXiv:2210.15097.

Weixin Liang, Mert Yuksekgonul, Yining Mao, Eric Wu, and James Zou. 2023. Gpt detectors are biased against non-native english writers. *Preprint*, arXiv:2304.02819.

Stephanie Lin, Jacob Hilton, and Owain Evans. 2022. TruthfulQA: Measuring how models mimic human falsehoods. In *Proceedings of the 60th Annual Meeting of the Association for Computational Linguistics (Volume 1: Long Papers)*, pages 3214–3252, Dublin, Ireland. Association for Computational Linguistics.

Stephen Merity, Caiming Xiong, James Bradbury, and Richard Socher. 2016. Pointer sentinel mixture models. *Preprint*, arXiv:1609.07843.

Eric Mitchell, Yoonho Lee, Alexander Khazatsky, Christopher D. Manning, and Chelsea Finn. 2023. Detectgpt: Zero-shot machine-generated text detection using probability curvature. *arXiv preprint*.

Yikang Pan, Liangming Pan, Wenhu Chen, Preslav Nakov, Min-Yen Kan, and William Yang Wang. 2023. On the risk of misinformation pollution with large language models. *Preprint*, arXiv:2305.13661.

Adam Paszke, Sam Gross, Francisco Massa, Adam Lerer, James Bradbury, Gregory Chanan, Trevor Killeen, Zeming Lin, Natalia Gimelshein, Luca Antiga, Alban Desmaison, Andreas Köpf, Edward Yang, Zach DeVito, Martin Raison, Alykhan Tejani, Sasank Chilamkurthy, Benoit Steiner, Lu Fang, Junjie Bai, and Soumith Chintala. 2019. Pytorch: An imperative style, high-performance deep learning library. *Preprint*, arXiv:1912.01703.

Alec Radford, Jeff Wu, Rewon Child, David Luan, Dario Amodei, and Ilya Sutskever. 2019. Language models are unsupervised multitask learners.

Colin Raffel, Noam Shazeer, Adam Roberts, Katherine Lee, Sharan Narang, Michael Matena, Yanqi Zhou, Wei Li, and Peter J. Liu. 2020. Exploring the limits of transfer learning with a unified text-to-text transformer. *Preprint*, arXiv:1910.10683.

Vinu Sankar Sadasivan, Aounon Kumar, Sriram Balasubramanian, Wenxiao Wang, and Soheil Feizi. 2023. Can ai-generated text be reliably detected? *Preprint*, arXiv:2303.11156.

Victor Sanh, Lysandre Debut, Julien Chaumond, and Thomas Wolf. 2020. Distilbert, a distilled version of bert: smaller, faster, cheaper and lighter. *Preprint*, arXiv:1910.01108.

Irene Solaiman, Miles Brundage, Jack Clark, Amanda Askell, Ariel Herbert-Voss, Jeff Wu, Alec Radford, Gretchen Krueger, Jong Wook Kim, Sarah Kreps, Miles McCain, Alex Newhouse, Jason Blazakis, Kris McGuffie, and Jasmine Wang. 2019. Release strategies and the social impacts of language models. *Preprint*, arXiv:1908.09203.

Hugo Touvron, Louis Martin, Kevin Stone, Peter Albert, Amjad Almahairi, Yasmine Babaei, Nikolay Bashlykov, Soumya Batra, Prajjwal Bhargava, Shruti Bhosale, Dan Bikel, Lukas Blecher, Cristian Canton Ferrer, Moya Chen, Guillem Cucurull, David Esiobu, Jude Fernandes, Jeremy Fu, Wenyin Fu, Brian Fuller, Cynthia Gao, Vedanuj Goswami, Naman Goyal, Anthony Hartshorn, Saghar Hosseini, Rui Hou, Hakan Inan, Marcin Kardas, Viktor Kerkez, Madian Khabsa, Isabel Kloumann, Artem Korenev, Punit Singh Koura, Marie-Anne Lachaux, Thibaut Lavril, Jenya Lee, Diana Liskovich, Yinghai Lu, Yuning Mao, Xavier Martinet, Todor Mihaylov, Pushkar Mishra, Igor Molybog, Yixin Nie, Andrew Poulton, Jeremy Reizenstein, Rashi Rungta, Kalyan Saladi, Alan Schelten, Ruan Silva, Eric Michael Smith, Ranjan Subramanian, Xiaoqing Ellen Tan, Binh Tang, Ross Taylor, Adina Williams, Jian Xiang Kuan, Puxin Xu, Zheng Yan, Iliyan Zarov, Yuchen Zhang, Angela Fan, Melanie Kambadur, Sharan Narang, Aurelien Rodriguez, Robert Stojnic, Sergey Edunov, and Thomas Scialom. 2023. Llama 2: Open foundation and fine-tuned chat models. *Preprint*, arXiv:2307.09288.

Honai Ueoka, Yugo Murawaki, and Sadao Kurohashi. 2021. Frustratingly easy edit-based linguistic steganography with a masked language model. *arXiv preprint*.

A Vaswani. 2017. Attention is all you need. *Advances in Neural Information Processing Systems.*

Laura Weidinger, John Mellor, Maribeth Rauh, Conor Griffin, Jonathan Uesato, Po-Sen Huang, Myra Cheng, Mia Glaese, Borja Balle, Atoosa Kasirzadeh, Zac Kenton, Sasha Brown, Will Hawkins, Tom Stepleton, Courtney Biles, Abeba Birhane, Julia Haas, Laura Rimell, Lisa Anne Hendricks, William S. Isaac, Sean Legassick, Geoffrey Irving, and Iason Gabriel. 2021. Ethical and social risks of harm from language models. *CoRR*, abs/2112.04359.

John Wieting, Kevin Gimpel, Graham Neubig, and Taylor Berg-Kirkpatrick. 2023. Paraphrastic representations at scale. *Preprint*, arXiv:2104.15114.

Thomas Wolf, Lysandre Debut, Victor Sanh, Julien Chaumond, Clement Delangue, Anthony Moi, Pierric Cistac, Tim Rault, Rémi Louf, Morgan Funtowicz, et al. 2019. Huggingface's transformers: State-of-the-art natural language processing. *arXiv preprint arXiv:1910.03771.*

Rowan Zellers, Ari Holtzman, Hannah Rashkin, Yonatan Bisk, Ali Farhadi, Franziska Roesner, and Yejin Choi. 2019. Defending against neural fake news. *CoRR*, abs/1905.12616.

Susan Zhang, Stephen Roller, Naman Goyal, Mikel Artetxe, Moya Chen, Shuohui Chen, Christopher Dewan, Mona Diab, Xian Li, Xi Victoria Lin, Todor Mihaylov, Myle Ott, Sam Shleifer, Kurt Shuster, Daniel Simig, Punit Singh Koura, Anjali Sridhar, Tianlu Wang, and Luke Zettlemoyer. 2022. Opt: Open pre-trained transformer language models. *Preprint*, arXiv:2205.01068.

DCBU at GenAI Detection Task 1: Enhancing Machine-Generated Text Detection with Semantic and Probabilistic Features

ZhaoWen Zhang[1*], Songhao Chen[2*], Bingquan Liu[1†]
[1]Harbin Institute of Technology
[2]Desktop Computing Business Unit, Lenovo
zhangzhaowen02@163.com, chensh8@lenovo.com, liubq@hit.edu.cn

Abstract

This paper presents our approach to the MGT Detection Task 1, which focuses on detecting AI-generated content. The objective of this task is to classify texts as either machine-generated or human-written. We participated in Subtask A, which concentrates on English-only texts. We utilized the RoBERTa model for semantic feature extraction and the LLaMA3 model for probabilistic feature analysis. By integrating these features, we aimed to enhance the system's classification accuracy. Our approach achieved strong results, with an F1 score of 0.7713 on Subtask A, ranking ninth among 36 teams. These results demonstrate the effectiveness of our feature integration strategy.

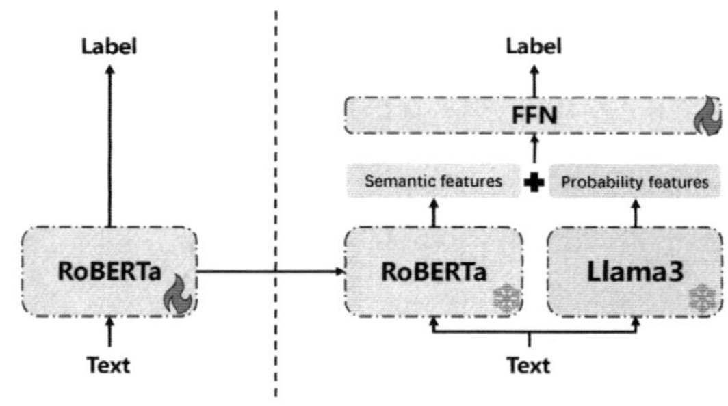

Figure 1: A two-stage machine generated text detection model architecture.

1 Introduction

In recent years, with the rapid development of large language models, distinguishing between machine-generated text and human-authored text has become increasingly challenging. This issue can lead to several potential problems. Low-quality generated text, when posted on social media, can reduce user experience, hinder the growth of platforms and high-quality content creators (Radivojevic et al., 2024). Generated text that lacks fact-checking can lead to the spread of rumors and misinformation (Chen and Shu, 2023), causing public panic and undermining government credibility. In academia, the presence of generated text raises ethical concerns regarding academic integrity (Meyer et al., 2023). Therefore, there is an urgent need to develop effective techniques for detecting machine-generated content (Wu et al., 2023).

Unlike typical machine-generated text, the data for this shared task are derived from multiple models and spans various domains (Wang et al., 2025). The human-authored texts in Subtask A originate from over 20 specialized fields, including finance, medicine, arXiv, WikiHow, IMDb, and Yelp. Correspondingly, the machine-generated texts are produced by more than 40 different large language models. Due to the diverse sources of this dataset, many simple yet effective statistical features are no longer viable, significantly increasing the challenge of the detection task.

Machine-generated text often exhibits certain characteristics, such as weaker emotional expression, fewer numeric details, simpler grammar and vocabulary, and the absence of word order or spelling errors. However, these characteristics can be mitigated through iterative prompt optimization, which makes detection less reliable. To address this, we aim to develop a more generalized detection method that minimizes the risk of counter-detection. Since large models are pretrained on next-token prediction tasks, machine-generated text inherently exhibits high-probability characteristics. This feature remains consistent across texts generated by different models or under various prompt conditions. Specifically, we leverage the $[CLS]$ vector of the RoBERTa (Liu, 2019) model as the semantic feature of the text and use LLaMA3 (Dubey et al., 2024) model to calculate the difference between the probability of the actual next token and the predicted next token at each token

* Equal contribution.
† Corresponding author.

Proceedings of the 1st Workshop on GenAI Content Detection (GenAIDetect), pages 150–154
January 19, 2025.

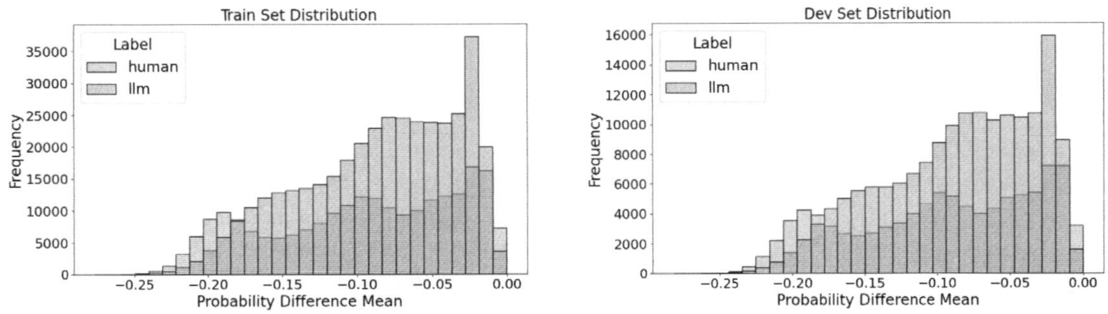

Figure 2: The x-axis represents the mean of the different dimensions of the probabilistic features H_p for each text, while the y-axis represents the number of texts with the same average value.

position, obtaining a vector as the probabilistic feature. By concatenating these two feature sets and feeding them into a feedforward network for binary classification, as illustrated in Figure 1, we achieve robust detection performance.

2 Related Works

The task of detecting machine-generated text is essentially a binary classification problem. Wu et al. (2023) provide a comprehensive overview of the field of LLM-generated text detection, thoroughly examining the necessity of this task. They categorize detection techniques into watermarking methods, statistical detectors, neural network-based detectors, and human-assisted approaches, and also list available data resources. Suvra Ghosal et al. (2023) conducted a similarly excellent review, focusing on the possibilities and limitations of text inspection. They categorize detection frameworks into a priori and post hoc detectors, as well as analyzing novel attack strategies for evading detection in machine-generated text. Due to challenges in achieving consistency and widespread adoption of watermarking methods, post hoc detection is currently the only feasible approach for real-world detection tasks. This approach is further divided into zero-shot detection and fine-tuned model detection, with the latter being the category of this shared task.

Zero-shot detection does not require labeled datasets. Typically, it involves calculating entropy, perplexity, n-gram frequency, or the average log probability per token of a given sequence, followed by thresholding. Mitchell et al. (2023) detect machine-generated text by examining the curvature of a language model's log probability function. They generate perturbations of a given text sample, compares their log probabilities with the original text, and identifies machine-generated text based on a higher discrepancy metric. Yang et al. (2023) detects machine-generated text by truncating a text in the middle, regenerating the remainder using a language model, and then analyzing n-gram differences between the original and newly generated text segments.

Fine-tuned model detection, on the other hand, trains binary classifiers using features extracted from pretrained language models. Petukhova et al. (2024) combine RoBERTa-base embeddings with diversity features and resample the training set. Verma et al. (2023) calculate the log probability of tokens using a series of weaker language models, generates additional synthetic features through vector and scalar operations, and uses a logistic regression classifier to detect machine-generated text based on these features.

3 Method

As shown in Figure 1, our model is divided into two stages. In the first stage, we perform supervised learning for binary classification using the RoBERTa model, aiming to enhance the $[CLS]$ vector of the RoBERTa model with features relevant to the task of detecting machine-generated text. In the second stage, we freeze the parameters of the RoBERTa model and obtain the $[CLS]$ vector for each text as the semantic feature H_s. For a given text $x = [x_1, \ldots, x_n]$, where n is the token length of the text, we freeze the parameters of the LLaMA3-8B-Instruct model and compute the probabilistic features $H_p = [h_1, \ldots, h_n]$, where h_i is calculated according to Equation 1:

$$h_i = p_\theta\left(x_{i+1}|x_{\leq i}\right) - \max_{y \in V} p_\theta\left(y|x_{\leq i}\right) \quad (1)$$

That is, under model θ, the probability of predicting the next token x_{i+1} given the prefix $x_{<i}$

is subtracted by the maximum probability of any token being predicted as the next token given the prefix $x_{\leq i}$. V represents the entire vocabulary.

For the different dimensions h_i of the probabilistic features H_p for the same text, we performed normalization, as shown in Equation 2:

$$h'_i = \frac{h_i - \min(H_p)}{\max(H_p) - \min(H_p)} \tag{2}$$

We compute the mean of the probabilistic features H_p for a text. The distribution of the probabilistic features mean is illustrated in Figure 2, where we can observe that machine-generated text tends to follow high-probability sampling for the next token, whereas human-authored text does not exhibit this distinct characteristic.

The semantic features H_s and probabilistic features H_p are first subjected to dimensionality reduction individually. These reduced vectors are then concatenated to form a unified representation. This concatenated representation is subsequently processed through a series of linear layers. Finally, a softmax activation function is applied to produce the final label predictions.

4 Experiments

As shown in Figure 3, the text lengths in the dataset are primarily concentrated around 500 words. In the first stage illustrated in Figure 1, we uniformly truncate texts to the first 512 tokens and experiment with four models: RoBERTa, RoBERTa-large, DeBERTa (He et al., 2021), and DeBERTa-large. We use the baseline script for training, with hyperparameters set as follows: a learning rate of 2e-5, batch size of 16, three epochs, and an L2 weight regularization of 0.01. On the validation set, RoBERTa-large achieved the best performance, with comparative results shown in Table 1.

	score	**micro f1**	**accuracy**
Baseline	0.8163	-	-
RoBERTa-large	0.8502	0.8571	0.8571
DeBERTa	0.8273	0.8378	0.8378
DeBERTa-large	0.8384	0.8439	0.8439
RoBERTa-large+LLaMA3	**0.8980**	**0.9015**	**0.9015**

Table 1: Performance Comparison of Models.

In the second stage, we select RoBERTa-large to extract the $[CLS]$ vector with a dimension of 1024. The text is again truncated to the first 512 tokens and input into LLaMA3-8B-Instruct to compute the probabilistic feature vector with a dimension of 512. We then train a feedforward neural network with three hidden layers and ReLU activation functions. The first layer reduces both features to 128 dimensions, which are then concatenated. The second layer further reduces the dimensionality to 64, and the final layer reduces it to 2 classes. We use a learning rate of 1e-4 and a dropout rate of 0.5. This approach achieves a macro F1 score of 0.8980 on the validation set. Our experiments were conducted using an NVIDIA GeForce RTX 4090 24GB.

	Llm	**Human**	**Total**
Train	381845	228922	610767
Dev	163430	98328	261758
Test	-	-	73941

Table 2: Statistics for datasets.

It is evident that using the same generative model as the text source for computing the probabilistic features in the second stage would yield better results. However, on the one hand, the dataset for the competition does not originate from a single model, and on the other hand, in real-world scenarios, we cannot know the potential model source of the text. We chose to use LLaMA3-8B-Instruct for computing the probabilistic features because the LLaMA series models have had a significant influence in the open-source model domain. Many subsequent open-source models have been affected by it and may have been trained on the same general datasets, leading to similar probability distributions in text generation. Additionally, LLaMA3-8B-Instruct performs exceptionally well in the English domain. Due to the large scale of the competition dataset and our limited computational resources, we did not conduct comparative experiments using other large models for probabilistic feature extraction.Table 2 presents the scale of the dataset.

Although we did not participate in the final submission for Subtask B, we conducted experiments on the validation set for this subtask. We used a combination of XLM-RoBERTa (Conneau, 2019) and LLaMA3-8B-Instruct, achieving a score of 0.6766 compared to the baseline of 0.6546 for Subtask B. This result suggests that probabilistic features can be helpful for detecting multilingual text, but the current model framework does not perform outstandingly.

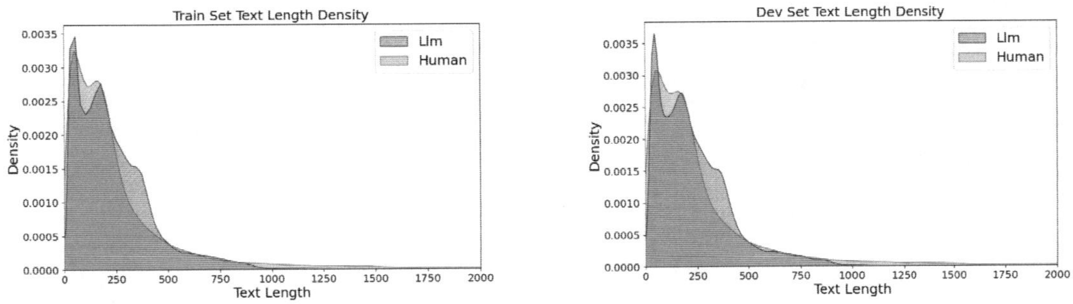

Figure 3: The x-axis represents the text length segmented by words, while the y-axis shows the probability density corresponding to each length. It can be observed that the text lengths in both the training and validation sets are primarily concentrated within 500 words.

5 Conclusion

In this work, we proposed a two-stage detection system for machine-generated text. By integrating semantic features from RoBERTa with probabilistic features from LLaMA3, our system achieves a Macro F1 score of 0.7713 on the test set, ranking ninth overall. Our experiments confirmed the effectiveness and generalizability of this feature integration approach. Compared to average results, our proposed system demonstrates robustness and strong generalization capability, which we aim to further enhance in future work.

References

Canyu Chen and Kai Shu. 2023. Can llm-generated misinformation be detected? *arXiv preprint arXiv:2309.13788*.

A Conneau. 2019. Unsupervised cross-lingual representation learning at scale. *arXiv preprint arXiv:1911.02116*.

Abhimanyu Dubey, Abhinav Jauhri, Abhinav Pandey, Abhishek Kadian, Ahmad Al-Dahle, Aiesha Letman, Akhil Mathur, Alan Schelten, Amy Yang, Angela Fan, et al. 2024. The llama 3 herd of models. *arXiv preprint arXiv:2407.21783*.

Pengcheng He, Jianfeng Gao, and Weizhu Chen. 2021. Debertav3: Improving deberta using electra-style pretraining with gradient-disentangled embedding sharing. *arXiv preprint arXiv:2111.09543*.

Yinhan Liu. 2019. Roberta: A robustly optimized bert pretraining approach. *arXiv preprint arXiv:1907.11692*, 364.

Jesse G Meyer, Ryan J Urbanowicz, Patrick CN Martin, Karen O'Connor, Ruowang Li, Pei-Chen Peng, Tiffani J Bright, Nicholas Tatonetti, Kyoung Jae Won, Graciela Gonzalez-Hernandez, et al. 2023. Chatgpt and large language models in academia: opportunities and challenges. *BioData Mining*, 16(1):20.

Eric Mitchell, Yoonho Lee, Alexander Khazatsky, Christopher D Manning, and Chelsea Finn. 2023. Detectgpt: Zero-shot machine-generated text detection using probability curvature. In *International Conference on Machine Learning*, pages 24950–24962. PMLR.

Kseniia Petukhova, Roman Kazakov, and Ekaterina Kochmar. 2024. Petkaz at semeval-2024 task 8: Can linguistics capture the specifics of llm-generated text? *arXiv preprint arXiv:2404.05483*.

Kristina Radivojevic, Matthew Chou, Karla Badillo-Urquiola, and Paul Brenner. 2024. Human perception of llm-generated text content in social media environments. *arXiv preprint arXiv:2409.06653*.

Soumya Suvra Ghosal, Souradip Chakraborty, Jonas Geiping, Furong Huang, Dinesh Manocha, and Amrit Singh Bedi. 2023. Towards possibilities & impossibilities of ai-generated text detection: A survey. *arXiv e-prints*, pages arXiv–2310.

Vivek Verma, Eve Fleisig, Nicholas Tomlin, and Dan Klein. 2023. Ghostbuster: Detecting text ghostwritten by large language models. *arXiv preprint arXiv:2305.15047*.

Yuxia Wang, Artem Shelmanov, Jonibek Mansurov, Akim Tsvigun, Vladislav Mikhailov, Rui Xing, Zhuohan Xie, Jiahui Geng, Giovanni Puccetti, Ekaterina Artemova, Jinyan Su, Minh Ngoc Ta, Mervat Abassy, Kareem Elozeiri, Saad El Dine Ahmed, Maiya Goloburda, Tarek Mahmoud, Raj Vardhan Tomar, Alexander Aziz, Nurkhan Laiyk, Osama Mohammed Afzal, Ryuto Koike, Masahiro Kaneko, Alham Fikri Aji, Nizar Habash, Iryna Gurevych, and Preslav Nakov. 2025. GenAI content detection task 1: English and multilingual machine-generated text detection: AI vs. human. In *Proceedings of the 1st Workshop on GenAI Content Detection (GenAIDetect)*, Abu Dhabi, UAE. International Conference on Computational Linguistics.

Junchao Wu, Shu Yang, Runzhe Zhan, Yulin Yuan, Derek F Wong, and Lidia S Chao. 2023. A survey on llm-gernerated text detection: Necessity, methods, and future directions. *arXiv preprint arXiv:2310.14724*.

Xianjun Yang, Wei Cheng, Yue Wu, Linda Petzold, William Yang Wang, and Haifeng Chen. 2023. Dna-gpt: Divergent n-gram analysis for training-free detection of gpt-generated text. *arXiv preprint arXiv:2305.17359*.

L3i++ at GenAI Detection Task 1: Can Label-Supervised LLaMA Detect Machine-Generated Text?

Tien Nam Nguyen [1] and **Hanh Thi Hong Tran**[2]
[1] University of La Rochelle, L3i, La Rochelle, France
[2] Arkhn, Paris, France
tnguye28@univ-lr.fr,
hanh.tran@arkhn.com

Abstract

The widespread use of large language models (LLMs) influences different social media and educational contexts through the overwhelming generated text with a certain degree of coherence. To mitigate their potential misuse, this paper explores the feasibility of finetuning *LLaMA* with label supervision (named *LS-LLaMA*) in unidirectional and bidirectional settings, to discriminate the texts generated by machines and humans in monolingual and multilingual corpora. Our findings show that unidirectional *LS-LLaMA* outperformed the sequence language models as the benchmark by a large margin (up to 7.39 and 5.29 percentage points in F1 increase in monolingual and multilingual corpora, respectively). Our code is publicly available at https://github.com/honghanhh/llama-as-a-judge.

1 Introduction

The blooming of large language models (LLMs) has led to a significant step forward in producing different machine-generated content across diverse channels and platforms (e.g., news, social media, question-answering forums, educational, and even academic contexts). The generated texts become increasingly fluent and coherent with the advent of recent models (e.g., GPT-4o, Claude 3.5). However, this also resulted in concerns regarding their potential misuse, such as spreading misinformation and causing disruptions in the education system. Consequently, there is a need to develop automatic systems to identify machine-generated text to mitigate its potential misuse.

Inspired by the work of Tran et al. (2024), we investigate the feasibility of training a binary sequence classifier that can reliably differentiate between text generated by humans and text that appears human-like but is generated by machines but leverage the performance with the integration of a *LLaMA-as-a-judge* in three different settings on the larger monolingual and multilingual corpora from Wang et al. (2025).

The main contribution of this paper is as follows:

- We study a label-supervised adaptation configuration for *LLaMA-as-a-judge* to discriminate between human-written (HW) and machine-generated (MG) texts.

- We investigate the feasibility of employing latent representations in LLaMA with three settings: masked unidirectional, masked bidirectional, and unmasked ones for discriminant label prediction in the classification tasks.

- Our solution is publicly available on GitHub to encourage openness, transparency, and reproducibility in the research community.

2 Related Work

The success of LLMs in various downstream NLP tasks (Vilar et al., 2022; Hegselmann et al., 2023) leads to the overuse and abuse of the information generated by LLMs. However, it is essential to acknowledge that the outputs generated by LLMs are not always accurate, giving rise to the issue of hallucination (Azamfirei et al., 2023). Researchers have developed several automatic detection methods (Zellers et al., 2019; Uchendu et al., 2021) that can identify the MG texts from the HW texts, which initially can be divided into two categories, i.e., metric-based and model-based methods.

Metric-based methods Metric-based methods leverage LLMs to process the text and extract its distinguishable features. Then, predicted distribution entropy determines whether a text belongs to MG or HW texts. Some metric-based detection methods include Log-Likelihood, Rank, Entropy, GLTR, Log-Rank, and DetectGPT (He et al., 2023), to cite a few.

Proceedings of the 1st Workshop on GenAI Content Detection (GenAIDetect), pages 155–160
January 19, 2025. ©2025 International Conference on Computational Linguistics

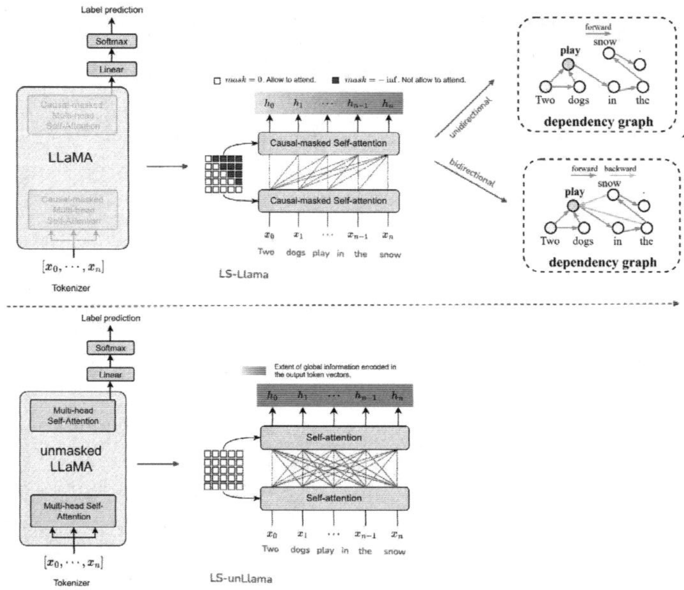

Figure 1: Our general LLaMA architecture in three different settings.

Model-based methods The model-based methods (Habibzadeh, 2023; Guo et al., 2023) are often trained using a corpus that contains both MG and MW texts to make predictions, for example, ChatGPT Detector (Guo et al., 2023), GPTZero (Habibzadeh, 2023), and LM Detector (Ippolito et al., 2020). Regarding Wang et al. (2024b), RoBERTa (Liu et al., 2019) and XLM-R (Conneau et al., 2020) are two baseline language models for these specific tasks.

The comparative studies of both categories can be found at the work of Tran et al. (2024).

3 Data

We evaluate the feasibility of our approach with English[1] and multilingual[2] corpora from Wang et al. (2025). Both corpora are the continuation and improvement of Wang et al. (2024a) with additional training and testing data generated from novel LLMs and including new languages.

4 Methodology

This section tackles the problem by formulating it as supervised sequence classification tasks. We then introduce our proposed architecture and present how we fine-tune them before indicating how we assessed their performance.

[1]Jinyan1/COLING_2025_MGT_en

[2]Jinyan1/COLING_2025_MGT_multingual

4.1 Problem Formulation

We formulate the problem as a binary supervised classification task, whose objective is to learn a mapping between a text representation and a binary variable, which is 1 if the text is machine-generated, and 0 otherwise. Mathematically, we learn a function f that, given an input text t_i, represented as a set of features $[f_1^i, ..., f_k^i]$, outputs an estimated label $\hat{l}_i \in \{0, 1\}$, i.e., $\hat{l}_i = f(t_i)$.

4.2 Our architecture

Our general architecture of the label-supervised *LLaMA-as-a-judge* (short form: *LS-LLaMA*[3]) from MG text detection with three different settings is visualized in Figure 1.

4.2.1 Masked Unidirectional LS-LLaMA

The tokens T from the input sequence S were fed into pretrained models to extract the latent representation H from *LLaMA* for sequence classification. First, we compute its embedding:

$$t = Tokenizer(S) \tag{1}$$

then

$$x = Embedding(t) \tag{2}$$

the transformer decoder layers are computed as

$$\text{Attn}_i^{LLaMA}(\mathbf{Q}, \mathbf{K}, \mathbf{V}) = \text{SoftMax}\left(\frac{\mathbf{Q}\mathbf{K}^\top}{\sqrt{d}} + \mathcal{M}\right)\mathbf{V} \tag{3}$$

[3]https://github.com/4AI/LS-LLaMA

$$\mathbf{Q} = W_q x + b, \quad \mathbf{K} \quad = W_k x + b, \quad \mathbf{V} = W_v x + b$$

$\mathcal{M}$: denotes the causal mask.

We modify the *LLaMA* model to obtain all the sequence representations:

$$h_{LLaMA} = LLaMA(T) \tag{4}$$

The pooling operation is applied to the latent representation to obtain the vector representation h for sequence classification. After passing through fully connected layers and a softmax layer, vector representation h is mapped to the label space. Cross-entropy loss is calculated based on the output logits and the ground-truth label.

4.2.2 Masked Bidirectional LS-LLaMA

To address the missing dependency information in autoregressive LLMs, we explore how backward dependencies affect sentence embedding learning. This is done by converting certain attention layers in the transformer decoder from unidirectional to bidirectional, removing the causal masks. However, if we keep all the causal masks, performance decreases significantly. Therefore, only the last attention layer is converted to bidirectional.

Mathematically speaking, with input sentence S and its embedding x as computed in *LS-LLaMA*, the embeddings are fed to the transformers to obtain $\overleftrightarrow{\text{LLaMA}}^{1:n}$:

$$\text{Attn}_i^{LLaMA}(\mathbf{Q}, \mathbf{K}, \mathbf{V}) = \text{SoftMax}\left(\frac{\mathbf{Q}\mathbf{K}^\top}{\sqrt{d}} + \mathcal{M}\right)\mathbf{V} \tag{5}$$

Then, we detach and transform it from uni- to bi-directional to obtain $\overleftrightarrow{\text{BiLLaMA}}^{n-1:n}$

$$\text{Attn}_i^{BiLLaMA}(\mathbf{Q}, \mathbf{K}, \mathbf{V}) = \text{SoftMax}(\frac{\mathbf{Q}\mathbf{K}^\top}{\sqrt{d}})\mathbf{V} \tag{6}$$

The final representation can be formulated as:

$$\mathbf{h} = \overrightarrow{\text{LLaMA}}^{1:n}(\mathbf{x}) + \overleftrightarrow{\text{BiLLaMA}}^{n-1:n}(\mathbf{x}) \tag{7}$$

4.2.3 Unmasked Unidirectional LS-LLaMA

Instead of removing only the causal mask of the last transformer layer, the causal masks will be removed in all transformer layers with the assumption to be replenished in token representations during fine-tuning as all the tokens can attend to each other. The computation of the transformer layer is computed as:

$$\text{Attn}_i^{unLlaMa}(\mathbf{Q}, \mathbf{K}, \mathbf{V}) = \text{SoftMax}(\frac{\mathbf{Q}\mathbf{K}^\top}{\sqrt{d}})\mathbf{V} \tag{8}$$

Moreover, using bidirectional combining with max-over-time pooling yields better performance than average pooling and last-token pooling in classification tasks. The formula of unmasked unidirectional *LS-LLaMA* can be represented as follows:

$$h_{\text{unLLaMA}} = UnLLaMA(x) \tag{9}$$

without causal masks.

4.3 Hyperparameters

We fine-tuned *LLaMA-2-7b-hf*[4] with the same configuration for all three settings: batch size = 16, learning rate = 1e-5, number of epochs = 5 with max length = 128, and Lora = 12. All the experiments were implemented on an NVIDIA RTX H100 with a CUDA Version of 12.4 (95000MiB).

4.4 Evaluation metrics

We use *Accuracy*, *macro-F1*, and *micro-F1* as the evaluation metrics to measure our classifiers' performance. These are also the standard metrics in Wang et al. (2025), which makes our work more comparable with other solutions.

5 Results

Table 1 and 2 report the evaluation of *LS-LLaMA* with three different learning settings in comparison with the baselines on the monolingual and multilingual subsets, respectively, in the development phase before the test set was released.

Methods	Accuracy	Micro F1	Macro F1
LS-LLaMA	0.9166	0.9166	0.9146
biLS-LLaMA	0.8887	0.8928	0.8928
LS-unLLaMA	0.8725	0.8725	0.8682
Baseline	0.8483	0.8483	0.8407

Table 1: Evaluation on monolingual set in dev. phase.

Overall, *LS-LLaMA* demonstrates strong performance in monolingual and multilingual corpora, particularly excelling in accuracy and micro F1 metrics. However, the significant drop in macro F1 scores for the multilingual evaluation suggests that while the model performs well on average, it may

[4]NousResearch/LLaMA-2-7b-hf

Methods	Accuracy	Micro F1	Macro F1
LS-LLaMA	0.8703	0.8703	0.6715
biLS-LLaMA	0.8514	0.8514	0.6540
LS-unLLaMA	0.8025	0.8025	0.5890
Baseline	0.8561	0.8561	0.6186

Table 2: Evaluation on multilingual set in dev. phase.

have difficulty with less frequent classes, indicating a potential area for improvement in handling multilingual data where there exists an imbalance in HW and MG classes in different languages and resources. While providing some performance, the other models do not surpass *LS-LLaMA*, reinforcing their effectiveness in this evaluation phase.

Based on the subset's performance in the development phase, we applied *LS-LLaMA* to the test set in the test phase, which achieved 0.7463 in macro F1 and 0.7554 in accuracy for the monolingual test set, 0.7427 in macro F1 and 0.744 in accuracy for the multilingual test set.

6 Discussion

Unidirectional vs. Bidirectional Context. The unidirectional *LS-LLaMA*'s focus on sequential learning, coherence recognition, and specialized training objectives makes it particularly well-suited for the task of MG text detection. In contrast, the bidirectional *LS-LLaMA*, while powerful in capturing overall context, may struggle with the specific sequential dependencies that are critical for effectively distinguishing HW from MG texts. This fundamental difference in architecture and training approach likely contributes to the observed performance advantage of unidirectional *LS-LLaMA*.

Masking Strategy. The "masked" aspect refers to how models are trained to predict missing parts of the input. In unidirectional masked *LS-LLaMA*, the focus is often on learning to predict the next token or fill in gaps based on prior context. This can enhance their ability to understand coherent patterns typical in HW texts, which explains the higher performance of masked *LS-LLaMA* compared to unmasked settings, which can potentially suffer from data leaks.

7 Error Analysis

We conduct several analyses to investigate how different factors would affect the detection performance of our best classifier, namely *LS-LLaMA*.

Figure 2 illustrates the confusion matrices for the English and multilingual test sets. These matrices reveal a notable tendency for higher error rates in detecting MG content. This observation suggests the model may be calibrated to prioritize detecting MG (label 1) instead of HW texts (label 0).

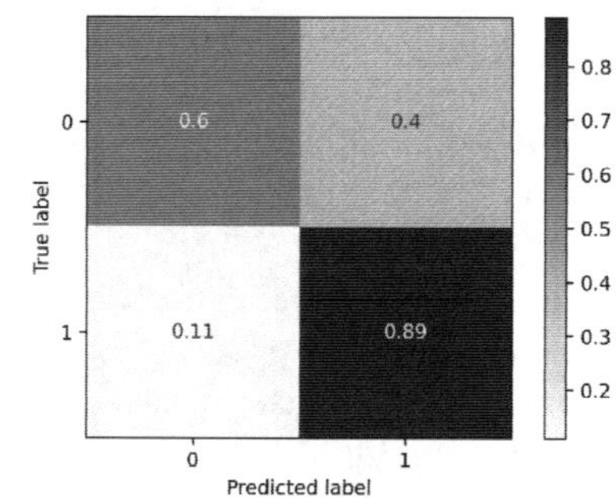

(a) The monolingual test set.

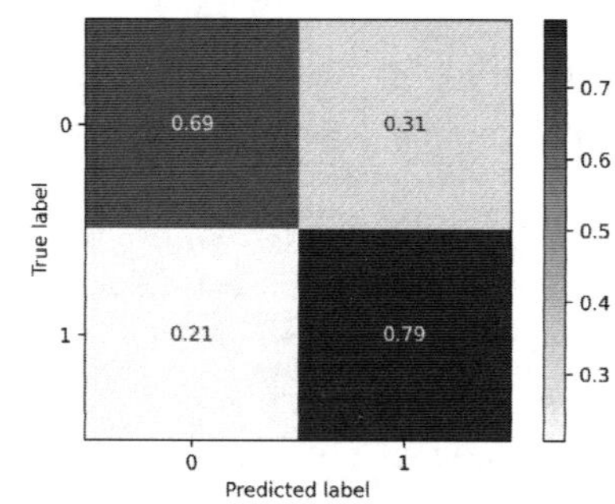

(b) The multilingual test set.

Figure 2: Confusion matrices for *LS-LLaMA*.

We elaborated our analysis regarding the error rate by text length and textual analysis of misclassification. The results suggest that error rates may not consistently increase or decrease with longer or shorter texts; instead, they vary based on data. However, there is a tendency for the classifier to have higher errors when the length of the text is from 10,000 to 20,000 words (see Figure 3).

8 Conclusions

In conclusion, we conducted a comparative study of label supervision *LLaMA*, so-called *LS-LLaMA* to highlight the potential and feasibility of fine-tuning an LLM to discriminate between HW and MG texts. Three different settings have been applied, including unidirectional masked, unidirectional unmasked, and bidirectional. Our findings suggest that unidirectional masked *LS-LLaMA* outperformed two other settings and the benchmarks for both monolingual and multilingual sets.

References

Razvan Azamfirei, Sapna R Kudchadkar, and James Fackler. 2023. Large language models and the perils of their hallucinations. *Critical Care*, 27(1):1–2.

Alexis Conneau, Kartikay Khandelwal, Naman Goyal, Vishrav Chaudhary, Guillaume Wenzek, Francisco Guzmán, Édouard Grave, Myle Ott, Luke Zettlemoyer, and Veselin Stoyanov. 2020. Unsupervised cross-lingual representation learning at scale. In *Proceedings of the 58th Annual Meeting of the Association for Computational Linguistics*, pages 8440–8451.

Biyang Guo, Xin Zhang, Ziyuan Wang, Minqi Jiang, Jinran Nie, Yuxuan Ding, Jianwei Yue, and Yupeng Wu. 2023. How close is chatgpt to human experts? comparison corpus, evaluation, and detection. *arXiv preprint arXiv:2301.07597*.

Farrokh Habibzadeh. 2023. Gptzero performance in identifying artificial intelligence-generated medical texts: A preliminary study. *Journal of Korean Medical Science*, 38(38).

Xinlei He, Xinyue Shen, Zeyuan Chen, Michael Backes, and Yang Zhang. 2023. Mgtbench: Benchmarking machine-generated text detection. *arXiv preprint arXiv:2303.14822*.

Stefan Hegselmann, Alejandro Buendia, Hunter Lang, Monica Agrawal, Xiaoyi Jiang, and David Sontag. 2023. Tabllm: Few-shot classification of tabular data with large language models. In *International Conference on Artificial Intelligence and Statistics*, pages 5549–5581. PMLR.

Daphne Ippolito, Daniel Duckworth, Chris Callison-Burch, and Douglas Eck. 2020. Automatic detection of generated text is easiest when humans are fooled. In *Proceedings of the 58th Annual Meeting of the Association for Computational Linguistics*, pages 1808–1822.

Yinhan Liu, Myle Ott, Naman Goyal, Jingfei Du, Mandar Joshi, Danqi Chen, Omer Levy, Mike Lewis, Luke Zettlemoyer, and Veselin Stoyanov. 2019. Roberta: A robustly optimized bert pretraining approach. *arXiv preprint arXiv:1907.11692*.

Hanh Thi Hong Tran, Tien Nam Nguyen, Antoine Doucet, and Senja Pollak. 2024. L3i++ at semeval-2024 task 8: Can fine-tuned large language model detect multigenerator, multidomain, and multilingual black-box machine-generated text? In *Proceedings of the 18th International Workshop on Semantic Evaluation (SemEval-2024)*, pages 13–21.

Adaku Uchendu, Zeyu Ma, Thai Le, Rui Zhang, and Dongwon Lee. 2021. Turingbench: A benchmark environment for turing test in the age of neural text generation. In *Findings of the Association for Computational Linguistics: EMNLP 2021*, pages 2001–2016.

David Vilar, Markus Freitag, Colin Cherry, Jiaming Luo, Viresh Ratnakar, and George Foster. 2022. Prompting palm for translation: Assessing strategies and performance. *arXiv preprint arXiv:2211.09102*.

Yuxia Wang, Jonibek Mansurov, Petar Ivanov, Jinyan Su, Artem Shelmanov, Akim Tsvigun, Osama Mohammed Afzal, Tarek Mahmoud, Giovanni Puccetti, and Thomas Arnold. 2024a. SemEval-2024 task 8: Multidomain, multimodel and multilingual machine-generated text detection. In *Proceedings of the 18th International Workshop on Semantic Evaluation (SemEval-2024)*, pages 2057–2079, Mexico City, Mexico. Association for Computational Linguistics.

Yuxia Wang, Jonibek Mansurov, Petar Ivanov, jinyan su, Artem Shelmanov, Akim Tsvigun, Osama Mohammed Afzal, Tarek Mahmoud, Giovanni Puccetti, Thomas Arnold, Chenxi Whitehouse, Alham Fikri Aji, Nizar Habash, Iryna Gurevych, and Preslav Nakov. 2024b. Semeval-2024 task 8: Multidomain, multimodel and multilingual machine-generated text detection. In *Proceedings of the 18th International Workshop on Semantic Evaluation (SemEval-2024)*, pages 2041–2063, Mexico City, Mexico. Association for Computational Linguistics.

Yuxia Wang, Artem Shelmanov, Jonibek Mansurov, Akim Tsvigun, Vladislav Mikhailov, Rui Xing, Zhuohan Xie, Jiahui Geng, Giovanni Puccetti, Ekaterina Artemova, Jinyan Su, Minh Ngoc Ta, Mervat Abassy, Kareem Elozeiri, Saad El Dine Ahmed, Maiya Goloburda, Tarek Mahmoud, Raj Vardhan Tomar, Alexander Aziz, Nurkhan Laiyk, Osama Mohammed Afzal, Ryuto Koike, Masahiro Kaneko, Alham Fikri Aji, Nizar Habash, Iryna Gurevych, and Preslav Nakov. 2025. Genai content detection task 1: English and multilingual machine-generated text detection: Ai vs. human. In *Proceedings of the 31st International Conference on Computational Linguistics (COLING)*, Abu Dhabi, UAE. Association for Computational Linguistics.

Rowan Zellers, Ari Holtzman, Hannah Rashkin, Yonatan Bisk, Ali Farhadi, Franziska Roesner, and Yejin Choi. 2019. Defending against neural fake news. *Advances in neural information processing systems*, 32.

A Error Rate by Text Length

Figure 3a and 3b show fluctuating error rates across text lengths of the English set and multilingual test set, we can not see a clear linear relationship between text length and error rate. This suggests that errors may not consistently increase or decrease with longer or shorter texts; instead, they vary based on data. However, there is a tendency for the classifier to have higher errors when the length of the text is from 10,000 to 20,000 words

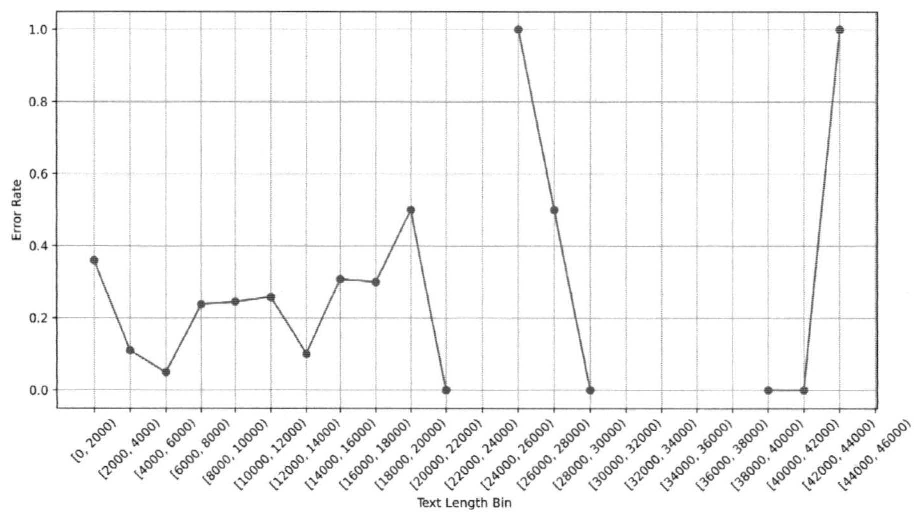

(a) The monolingual test set.

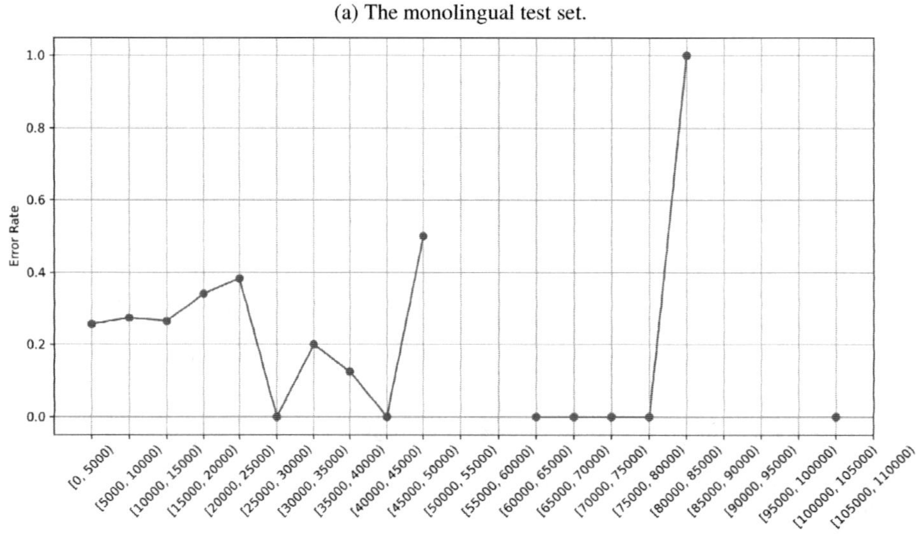

(b) The multilingual test set.

Figure 3: Error rates based on text length using *LS-LLaMA*.

TechExperts(IPN) at GenAI Detection Task 1: Detecting AI-Generated Text in English and Multilingual Contexts

Gull Mehak
Amna Qasim
Abdul Gafar Manuel Meque
Nisar Hussain
Grigori Sidorov
Alexander Gelbukh
Instituto Politécnico Nacional (IPN), Centro de Investigación en Computación (CIC), Mexico City, Mexico

Abstract

The ever-increasing spread of AI-generated text, driven by the considerable progress in large language models, entails a real problem for all digital platforms: how to ensure content authenticity. The team TechExperts(IPN) presents a method for detecting AI-generated content in English and multilingual contexts, using the google/gemma-2b model fine-tuned for COLING 2025 shared task 1 for English and multilingual. Training results show peak F1 scores of 97.63% for English and 97.87% for multilingual detection, highlighting the model's effectiveness in supporting content integrity across platforms.

1 Introduction

The rise of large language models (LLMs), such as GPT-4, has significantly increased the volume of AI-generated content across various digital platforms. These models can generate coherent and contextually relevant text, making it much more difficult for users to distinguish between human-authored and machine-generated content. The recent rise in AI-generated content is making many question the credibility and reliability of information, especially regarding journalism, academia, and social media, where the integrity of the content is critical. This has brought the need to develop effective methods to detect AI-generated content to an all-time high (Fraser et al., 2024).

Recent gains in the capabilities of LLMs have brought new challenges to their detection. Approaches such as reinforcement learning with human feedback and instruction tuning have given these models more versatility to follow even complex prompts and thus develop plausible responses that further complicate the detection problem (Abdali et al., 2024). Traditional detection methods, which rely on identifying patterns of word choice, sentence structure, or perplexity, are often insufficient as these models improve in mimicking human writing styles (Goddard et al.). One avenue of research lies in resorting to transformer-based models in the detection effort, whereby such models make possible fine-grained differentiation of human-generated from AI-generated texts through fine-tuning curated datasets (Zhao et al., 2024). These models have demonstrated high accuracy in identifying AI-generated content, even when the text is short or resembles typical human writing (Mao et al., 2024).

The proposed research introduces an approach that utilizes the google/gemma-2b model, an advanced Large Language Model (LLM), to identify AI-generated content across English and multilingual contexts, using both the COLING_2025_MGT_en and COLING_2025_MGT_multilingual datasets. By leveraging google/gemma-2b, a powerful multilingual LLM, our approach aims to enhance detection precision through sophisticated machine learning techniques. This method is expected to contribute significantly to maintaining content integrity and mitigating risks associated with the improper use of AI-generated textual content across diverse linguistic landscapes.

This paper is structured as follows: Section 2 reviews related work in AI-generated content detection, Section 3 describes the methodology and dataset used, Section 4 presents the experimental results, and Section 5 discusses the findings and their implications. Finally, we conclude with potential future directions for research in this field.

2 Related Work

Detecting AI-generated content has become a critical research area due to advancements in large language models (LLMs) like GPT-4. These models can produce content that closely mimics human writing, raising concerns about authenticity across academia, journalism, and social media. Early

Proceedings of the 1st Workshop on GenAI Content Detection (GenAIDetect), pages 161–165
January 19, 2025.

methods relied on lexical, syntactic, and stylistic features, but these often fell short as modern LLMs became more sophisticated. Detecting machine-generated text is a complex task[1].

Recent advancements involve machine learning, particularly transformer models like RoBERTa and BERT, which show high accuracy when fine-tuned on human and machine-generated datasets. Studies have demonstrated significant improvements using these models on specialized datasets (Zeng et al.). Advanced approaches leverage token-level analysis, focusing on log probabilities and entropy to detect patterns typical of AI-generated text. This strategy exploits the probabilistic nature of LLMs, identifying subtle deviations from human writing [4]. Ensemble methods have also effectively combined models like RoBERTa with domain-specific classifiers. Techniques such as paraphrasing and back-translation further enhance robustness, allowing better generalization across different text sources (Wang et al., 2024).

Emerging trends focus on hybrid approaches, blending linguistic features with machine learning models to capture nuances that traditional statistical methods miss. Zero-shot learning methods are also being explored, enabling detection without explicit examples, though with mixed success (Mitchell et al., 2023). Ethical considerations are increasingly important, particularly avoiding biases that might misclassify content from non-native English writers. Future research aims to develop inclusive systems that ensure high detection accuracy across diverse user demographics (Fraser et al., 2024).

In summary, while advancements in machine learning and transformer-based models have strengthened AI-generated text detection, challenges remain, particularly in addressing diverse linguistic contexts. Motivated by these backgrounds, we employ the google/gemma-2b model (a multilingual LLM) to localize AI-generated text in English and multilingual with COLING_2025_MGT_en and COLING_2025_MGT_multilingual datasets, respectively. This approach aims to enhance detection accuracy, supporting efforts to uphold content integrity and responsible AI use across varied languages and settings.

[1]University of Pennsylvania School of Engineering and Applied Science. (2024, August 16). *Detecting machine-generated text: An arms race with the advancements of large language models*. ScienceDaily. Retrieved December 12, 2024, from `https://www.sciencedaily.com/releases/2024/08/240816121550.htm`

3 Methodology

This section outlines the datasets employed and the proposed google/gemma-2b model used for both English and Multilingual settings.

3.1 Dataset

In this work, we use two primary datasets to identify AI-generated (AG) texts in English and multilingual texts: COLING_2025_MGT_en, COLING_2025_MGT_multilingual. The datasets (see Table 1) are rich and diverse, including human- and machine-generated examples across finance, medicine, social media feeds, and scientific literature.

3.1.1 English Dataset

(COLING_2025_MGT_en): This dataset includes 610,767 samples in total, with 228,922 human-written and 381,845 machine-generated texts. The development set contains 261,758 samples (98,328 human and 163,430 machine).

3.1.2 Multilingual Dataset

(COLING_2025_MGT_multilingual): Spanning languages such as Chinese, Italian, Arabic, Russian, Bulgarian, and Urdu, this dataset comprises 629,384 training samples, split into 253,625 human-written and 375,759 machine-generated texts. The development set includes 271,215 samples (107,467 human and 163,748 machine).

3.2 Proposed Model

This study utilizes the google/gemma-2b model, a transformer-based architecture for detecting AI-generated content across English and multilingual contexts. As illustrated in Figure 1, the process begins with tokenizing input text, where each token is converted into a vector representation. Positional embeddings are added to these token vectors to preserve sequence information, allowing the model to recognize word order and contextual relationships—an approach common in transformer architectures (Vaswani, 2017). This step is essential for distinguishing nuanced linguistic patterns that differentiate human-generated content from AI-generated text.

The model's core lies in the Decoder Block, where multiple layers process these embeddings to refine the token representations further. Each layer employs multi-head self-attention to capture diverse contextual relationships across tokens, enabling the model to focus on various aspects of the

Dataset	Training Set	Development Set	Grand Total
English	Human: 228,922	Human: 98,328	872,525
	Machine: 381,845	Machine: 163,430	
Multilingual	Human: 253,625	Human: 107,467	900,599
	Machine: 375,759	Machine: 163,748	

Table 1: Datasets (English + Multilingual) Details

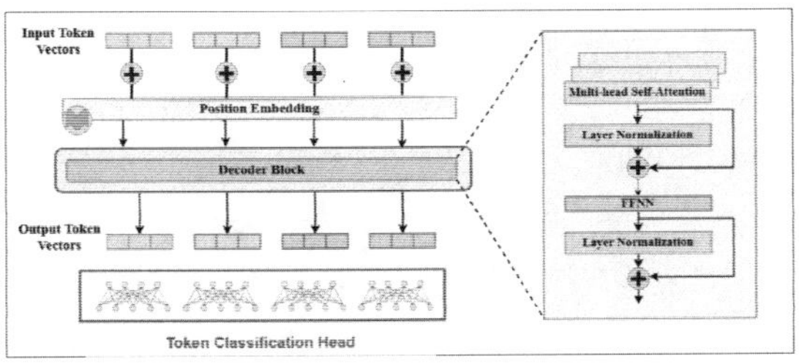

Figure 1: Architectural view of proposed gemma model

text, a technique effective in capturing semantic relationships (Devlin, 2018). Following this, each token embedding passes through a feed-forward neural network (FFNN), which enhances representation depth, allowing the model to interpret complex language structures (Radford et al., 2019). Additionally, layer normalization and residual connections stabilize the outputs and ensure critical information flows through the layers without degradation, as demonstrated in various transformer-based models (He et al., 2016). Finally, the output vectors are passed to a token classification head, which labels each token, distinguishing AI-generated content from human-written text with high precision (Liu, 2019).

4 Results and Analysis

This section presented the experimental setup, evaluation metrics, and training results, demonstrating the proposed model's high accuracy and robust multilingual detection performance.

4.1 Experimental Setup

The proposed gemma model was implemented in the Python-based PyTorch framework. High resources were used for model training on Google Colab Pro Plus. Due to the size of COLING_2025_MGT_en and COLING_2025_MGT_multilingual datasets (Wang et al., 2025), we used only a subset of all these data for experiment capabilities. For each data set, 60,000 examples were sampled from the training set and 10,000 from the development set. We used these stratified samples to train the final model, which confirms a balanced representation across classes for both English and multilingual datasets. Using this method, we could efficiently train the model while keeping the detector's performance strong. Table 2 gives details on the hyperparameter settings.

4.2 Evaluation Measures

We measured the model's accuracy, precision, recall, and F1 score (Mehak et al., 2023). So, accuracy shows us correctness in general; precision is the ratio of correctly identified AI detections to all detected cases by AI, and recall shows how well your model can detect AI instances out of everything. It incorporates false positives and negatives, i.e., identifying a balance between precision and recall (F1 score). Combining these metrics gives a good assessment of how well the model performs in classifying AI-generated versus human-created text.

4.3 Training Results on COLING_2025_MGT_en Dataset

The model obtained high accuracy and F1 across three training epochs for the English dataset. Training loss reduced over epochs, showcasing stable learning, while validation loss fluctuated minimally. As shown in Table 3, the third epoch reached the highest scores for accuracy and F1, indicating excellent detection of AI-generated text in English.

4.4 Training Results on COLING_2025_MGT_multilingual Dataset

The results of the multilingual data set highlighted high precision and F1 scores across three epochs. The training loss was minimized regularly, while the validation was slightly varied (Table 4). These metrics within and across the five languages achieved optimal scores at epoch 3, indicating effective AI-content detection and efficiency in training and testing data separation (accuracy, F1, precision, recall).

Hyperparameter	Value
Model	google/gemma-2b
Epochs	3
Learning Rate	0.0001
Train Batch Size	64, and 56
Eval Batch Size	64, and 56
Seed	42
Optimizer	Adam (betas = (0.9, 0.999), epsilon=1e-08)
Learning Rate Scheduler Type	Linear
Mixed Precision Training	Native AMP

Table 2: Hyperparameter settings

Epoch	Step	Training Loss	Validation Loss	Accuracy	F1	Precision	Recall
1	938	0.2079	0.0868	0.9662	0.9730	0.9702	0.9758
2	1876	0.0424	0.0938	0.9688	0.9748	0.9829	0.9668
3	2814	0.0089	0.1577	0.9704	0.9763	0.9763	0.9763

Table 3: Results of proposed gemma model on COLING_2025_MGT_en dataset

Epoch	Step	Training Loss	Validation Loss	Accuracy	F1	Precision	Recall
1	1072	0.1048	0.0781	0.9691	0.9751	0.9734	0.9767
2	2144	0.0373	0.0925	0.9701	0.9757	0.9817	0.9698
3	3216	0.0073	0.1267	0.9737	0.9787	0.9802	0.9772

Table 4: Results of proposed gemma model on COLING_2025_MGT_multilingual dataset

4.5 Test Results

The final model evaluation was conducted through blind submissions on the Codabench platform. Our model achieved competitive results, securing 5th place for Subtask A (English) with an F1 score of 0.8153 and 6th place for Subtask B (Multilingual) with an F1 score of 0.74.

4.6 Results Discussion

The results demonstrate google/gemma-2b's strengths in accurately detecting AI-generated content across English and multilingual datasets. Its advanced multilingual capabilities and high precision and recall scores underscore its effectiveness in capturing subtle linguistic patterns across varied languages. This robust performance reflects gemma-2b's adaptability and precision, making it a reliable multilingual AI content detection tool.

5 Conclusion and Future Directions

The google/gemma-2b model effortlessly detects AI-generated content and performs well even in multilingual contexts, as the context has not only been in English. This study shows that it could be used as a content authenticity tool. In the Future, we are planning to expand detection not just with new models but also by increasing languages to help more communities (Arabic, Urdu, Persian, Chinese), adapting better from one AI model to another, and finally enhancing how real-time we could be so that it won't only be used for moderation content but even fact-checking.

6 Acknowledgment

The work was done with partial support from the Mexican Government through the grant A1-S-47854 of CONACYT, Mexico, and grants 20241816, 20241819, and 20240951 of the Secretaría de Investigación y Posgrado of the Instituto Politécnico Nacional, Mexico. The authors thank CONACYT for the computing resources brought to them through the Plataforma de Aprendizaje Profundo para Tecnologías del Lenguaje of the Laboratorio de Supercómputo of the INAOE, Mexico, and acknowledge the support of Microsoft through the Microsoft Latin America PhD Award.

References

Sara Abdali, Richard Anarfi, CJ Barberan, and Jia He. 2024. Decoding the ai pen: Techniques and challenges in detecting ai-generated text. In *Proceedings of the 30th ACM SIGKDD Conference on Knowledge Discovery and Data Mining*, pages 6428–6436.

Jacob Devlin. 2018. Bert: Pre-training of deep bidirectional transformers for language understanding. *arXiv preprint arXiv:1810.04805*.

Kathleen C Fraser, Hillary Dawkins, and Svetlana Kiritchenko. 2024. Detecting ai-generated text: Factors influencing detectability with current methods. *arXiv preprint arXiv:2406.15583*.

Jamal Goddard, Yuksel Celik, and Sanjay Goel. Beyond the human eye: Comprehensive approaches to ai text detection.

Kaiming He, Xiangyu Zhang, Shaoqing Ren, and Jian Sun. 2016. Deep residual learning for image recognition. In *Proceedings of the IEEE conference on computer vision and pattern recognition*, pages 770–778.

Yinhan Liu. 2019. Roberta: A robustly optimized bert pretraining approach. *arXiv preprint arXiv:1907.11692*, 364.

Chengzhi Mao, Carl Vondrick, Hao Wang, and Junfeng Yang. 2024. Raidar: generative ai detection via rewriting. *arXiv preprint arXiv:2401.12970*.

Gull Mehak, Iqra Muneer, and Rao Muhammad Adeel Nawab. 2023. Urdu text reuse detection at phrasal level using sentence transformer-based approach. *Expert Systems with Applications*, 234:121063.

Eric Mitchell, Yoonho Lee, Alexander Khazatsky, Christopher D Manning, and Chelsea Finn. 2023. Detectgpt: Zero-shot machine-generated text detection using probability curvature. In *International Conference on Machine Learning*, pages 24950–24962. PMLR.

Alec Radford, Jeffrey Wu, Rewon Child, David Luan, Dario Amodei, Ilya Sutskever, et al. 2019. Language models are unsupervised multitask learners. *OpenAI blog*, 1(8):9.

A Vaswani. 2017. Attention is all you need. *Advances in Neural Information Processing Systems*.

Yuxia Wang, Jonibek Mansurov, Petar Ivanov, Jinyan Su, Artem Shelmanov, Akim Tsvigun, Osama Mohammed Afzal, Tarek Mahmoud, Giovanni Puccetti, Thomas Arnold, et al. 2024. Semeval-2024 task 8: Multidomain, multimodel and multilingual machine-generated text detection. *arXiv preprint arXiv:2404.14183*.

Yuxia Wang, Artem Shelmanov, Jonibek Mansurov, Akim Tsvigun, Vladislav Mikhailov, Rui Xing, Zhuohan Xie, Jiahui Geng, Giovanni Puccetti, Ekaterina Artemova, Jinyan Su, Minh Ngoc Ta, Mervat Abassy, Kareem Elozeiri, Saad El Dine Ahmed, Maiya Goloburda, Tarek Mahmoud, Raj Vardhan Tomar, Alexander Aziz, Nurkhan Laiyk, Osama Mohammed Afzal, Ryuto Koike, Masahiro Kaneko, Alham Fikri Aji, Nizar Habash, Iryna Gurevych, and Preslav Nakov. 2025. GenAI content detection task 1: English and multilingual machine-generated text detection: AI vs. human. In *Proceedings of the 1st Workshop on GenAI Content Detection (GenAIDetect)*, Abu Dhabi, UAE. International Conference on Computational Linguistics.

Zijie Zeng, Shiqi Liu, Lele Sha, Zhuang Li, Kaixun Yang, Sannyuya Liu, Dragan Gašević, and Guanliang Chen. Detecting ai-generated sentences in human-ai collaborative hybrid texts: Challenges, strategies, and insights.

Penghao Zhao, Hailin Zhang, Qinhan Yu, Zhengren Wang, Yunteng Geng, Fangcheng Fu, Ling Yang, Wentao Zhang, Jie Jiang, and Bin Cui. 2024. Retrieval-augmented generation for ai-generated content: A survey. *arXiv preprint arXiv:2402.19473*.

SzegedAI at GenAI Detection Task 1: Beyond Binary - Soft-Voting Multi-Class Classification for Binary Machine-Generated Text Detection Across Diverse Language Models

Mihály Kiss
University of Szeged
Institute of Informatics
Kiss.Mihaly@stud.u-szeged.hu

Gábor Berend
University of Szeged
Institute of Informatics
berendg@inf.u-szeged.hu

Abstract

This paper describes the participation of the SzegedAI team in Subtask A of Task 1 at the COLING 2025 Workshop on Detecting AI-Generated Content. Our solutions investigate the effectiveness of combining multi-class approaches with ensemble methods for detecting machine-generated text. This approach groups models into multiple classes based on properties such as model size or generative capabilities. Additionally, we employ a length-based method, utilizing specialized expert models designed for specific text length ranges. During inference, we condense multi-class predictions into a binary outcome, categorizing any label other than human as AI-generated. The effectiveness of both standard and snapshot ensemble techniques is evaluated. Although not all multi-class configurations outperformed the binary setup, our findings indicate that the combination of multi-class training and ensemble methods can enhance performance over single-method or binary approaches.

1 Introduction

In recent years, machine-generated text has become increasingly sophisticated, with advances in generative models. Nowadays, substantial amounts of AI-generated content are being produced, even in the academic and scientific literature (Liang et al., 2024b). Recent findings estimate that between 6.5% and 16.9% of peer review text submitted to AI conferences may be substantially modified by large language models, revealing subtle trends in the use of LLMs within academic settings (Liang et al., 2024a). This trend is further supported by the fact that various models, such as GPT (OpenAI et al., 2024), Mixtral (Jiang et al., 2024), and Gemini (Gemini et al., 2024) have become easily accessible to lay people, even those without a strong technical background. As a result, there is an increasing need for algorithms capable of predicting the difference between human- and machine-generated content. Workshops have been organized to address this need, such as those discussed in (Sarvazyan et al., 2023) and (Chamezopoulos et al., 2024).

In this paper, we present our solutions for Task 1 in the Workshop on Detecting AI-Generated Content at COLING 2025 (Wang et al., 2025). Our focus was on Subtask A, where the objective was to make a binary prediction indicating whether the text was human-written or AI-generated.

The dataset for this subtask contained only English texts. To tackle this challenge, we experimented with various classification schemes to determine the most effective setup for detecting machine-generated text. Binary, 3, 5, 6 and 41 class solutions were developed, with each configuration representing a different heuristic grouping of models based on parameters, model size, or the quality of generated text. Standard ensemble methods with soft voting were applied across all class configurations to improve robustness and performance. An additional experiment involved using a snapshot ensemble (Huang et al., 2017), capturing multiple snapshots of the model during training to create a diverse but computationally efficient ensemble. This snapshot ensemble was created only for the 41-class configuration.

In addition, a length-based solution was developed in which the texts were categorized by length. Three intervals were created based on text length, with an expert model assigned to each interval. These texts were classified according to their length and directed to the corresponding expert model, optimizing performance by matching each text to a model specialized in its specific length range.

Our final submission, the 6-class solution, achieved a macro F1 score of 0.791, though it was not our highest performing model. Our post-shared task evaluation revealed that the length-based approach achieved a macro F1 score of 0.827, while the 41-class standard ensemble scored slightly higher at 0.826.

Proceedings of the 1st Workshop on GenAI Content Detection (GenAIDetect), pages 166–172

2 Related Work

Recent advancements in detecting machine-generated text have highlighted the efficacy of ensemble learning methods, particularly those that employ soft voting strategies. In the SemEval-2024 Task 8 (Wang et al., 2024), Gu and Meng (2024) developed a class-balanced soft-voting system that fine-tuned transformer-based models, including encoder-only, decoder-only and encoder-decoder architectures (Gu and Meng, 2024). Their approach effectively addressed data imbalance and achieved state-of-the-art performance in multi-class classification tasks involving various text generators.

Building upon this, we explored the application of snapshot ensembles within transformer architectures for machine-generated text detection. This method captures multiple "snapshots" of a model at different training stages, offering computational efficiency over traditional ensembles. Although this approach may not match the robustness of standard ensembles, it presents a viable alternative when resources are limited (Huang et al., 2017).

Another approach for detecting AI-generated text leverages a Transformer Encoder that combines probabilistic features from multiple LLaMA-2 models (Sarvazyan et al., 2024). This model reached impressive accuracy in distinguishing machine-generated from human-written content. The study reveals that integrating probabilistic features from various language models can significantly boost detection precision, with LLMixtic effectively emphasizing the unique features of the final tokens in a sequence.

3 Methodology

3.1 Multi-Class Classification

While the main task was framed as a binary classification problem, it may not fully capture the diversity and variability present in machine-generated content. The category of machine-generated text is a heterogeneous group; it has outputs from a wide array of models that differ in parameter count, training data, and text generation. For example, GPT-4o will likely produce a more coherent and contextually aware text compared to flan_t5_small for the same prompt. This heterogeneity results in a "melting pot" when viewed as a binary task, it can remove meaningful features within the data. To address these challenges, we initially considered a multi-class classification approach.

DeBERTa We chose *DeBERTa-v1-base* (He et al., 2021) for this task due to its well-known strengths and its proven performance in various NLP tasks (C. Timoneda and Vallejo Vera, 2024). To confirm its superiority, we made a comparison with *BERT-base-cased* (Devlin et al., 2019), which showed that DeBERTa consistently outperformed BERT in this binary classification task, achieving higher F1 scores. BERT achieved a macro F1 score of 0.973, while DeBERTa got 0.982 on the development set.

Configuration (used in all experiments): optimizer = AdamW, base learning rate = 2e-5, weight decay = 0.01, warmup steps = 10% of total steps, batch size = 16, 4 validation per epoch and 3 epochs with early stopping.

Binary reduction It is important to note that while we trained the models on multiple classes, all our experiments ultimately reduced the output to a binary label. If the model predicts any class other than "human" it is handled as "1" (AI-generated); otherwise, it is classified as "0" (human).

3.1.1 41-class: one class per generative model

Since the shared task dataset includes information on which model generated the text, our aim was to capture this and treat each model as a different class. This approach introduced 41 classes in total, since the training texts were generated by 40 different models. However, this method may lead to a fragmented dataset, where individual classes contain limited data for robust training and analysis.

Our hypothesis is that a better classification granularity could improve model effectiveness by organizing classes based on the generative capabilities or the parameter count of the generative models. To explore this, we also implemented 3, 5, and 6 class solutions. By adopting these diverse class structures, we aimed to create categories with highly distinct properties, allowing models to effectively differentiate between them.

3.1.2 Modeling based on the parameter count

5-class Our second approach was to create groups based on the parameter count of the models, as we hypothesized that categorizing the models by this criterion might reveal performance differences more clearly. This grouping strategy allows us to examine whether models with different parameter scales show distinct behaviors or predictive capabilities in binary classification tasks. By segmenting models according to parameter count, we aim to highlight potential trends in model efficacy and better understand how complexity influences outcomes.

We reviewed the models and recorded the number of parameters for each, hoping that grouping them into intervals by parameter count would show clear differences in capabilities: less than 5 billion, $6-10$ billion, $11-130$ billion, and over 130 billion.

6-class In our next approach, we introduce an additional interval in the lower range, refining the parameter-based grouping to examine performance distinctions more precisely. This allows us to check how vulnerable certain parameter sizes are, especially smaller models, to capturing nuanced distinctions. We split the less than 5B category into two, at the threshold of 1B parameters, allowing a more accurate analysis of how smaller model scales may impact binary classification performance. The 6 different classes are shown in Figure 2 of Appendix A.

3.1.3 3-class: generative capability grouping

While parameter count serves as a valuable metric for model complexity, it alone may not fully capture a model's performance capabilities. We hypothesized that additional indicators, such as leaderboard rankings and perplexity scores, could provide more information on the effectiveness of a model. By including these additional evaluations, we aimed to refine our classification and account for differences that parameter count might not be able to effectively capture. This approach led us to consider leaderboard-based *ELO* score as an additional metric for a more complete evaluation.

Two leaderboards were analyzed: the LLM Explorer leaderboard[1] and Chatbot Arena[2]. Although the LLM Explorer leaderboard featured a larger selection of models, only a few were listed on the Chatbot Arena leaderboard, and only four models appeared on both leaderboards. Based on these shared models, we performed a linear regression to align the scores, thereby creating a unified scale for all models. This regression produced the following equation, where x represents the LLM explorer leaderboard score: $\text{ELO} = 1238 \cdot x + 484$. Using this formula, we calculated an ELO score for each model.

A threshold for classification was established: models with an ELO score above 800 were categorized as *Strong*, while those with scores below 800 were categorized as *Weak*. We thresholded at 800 due to a noticeable gap between 700 and 800, suggesting that this range might represent a meaningful difference in generative capabilities. For the 19 models that were not found on any leaderboards, we assigned them to the class that seemed the closest match based on our judgment. This approach resulted in a three-class classification task: *human, weak, strong*. The final groups are shown in Figure 2 of Appendix A.

3.2 Binary Ensemble

Ensemble methods, where multiple models contribute to a final prediction, are well-established for improving accuracy and robustness in machine learning tasks (Ganaie et al., 2022). In the context of machine-generated text detection, ensemble approaches combine the strengths of individual models, often leading to enhanced performance. However, these methods are computationally expensive, as they require fine-tuning multiple models independently. Despite these costs, our results demonstrate that using ensemble shows substantial improvement.

We fine-tuned three models for the original binary task and applied soft voting, comparing its performance to the average F1 score of each model operating independently. The results, showing soft voting versus the individual model performance, are presented in Table 1.

3.3 Multi-Class Ensemble

Gu and Meng (2024) demonstrated the effectiveness of ensemble methods for multi-class machine-generated text detection, showing significant improvements in both accuracy and robustness across diverse classes. Building on these findings, we further enhanced our approach by incorporating a soft voting technique within our ensemble, allowing for more reliable and consistent predictions across various text categories.

Similarly to the binary ensemble approach, we fine-tuned three models, applied soft voting, and compared the results to the average F1 score of 3 single fine-tuned models. This process was used in all of our experiments.

3.4 Using Length-Adaptive Expert Models

We examined the performance of various models in the data set to identify patterns in the generated

[1] `https://llm.extractum.io/list/?small`
[2] https://lmarena.ai/

texts. We observed, as expected, that larger models such as GPT-4 tended to produce significantly longer texts. This is illustrated in Figure 2 of Appendix A. This natural variance in the output length suggests that a length-based approach to model grouping could improve the detection accuracy.

With this approach, the models were divided into three length-based groups, each represented by a specialized expert model for short, medium, and long text intervals. We chose the length cutoff values at 745 and 1613, so the three groups nearly contained the same amount of texts. This structure was hypothesized to improve classification precision by leveraging each model's inherent tendencies within its length category, ultimately contributing to a more robust and accurate text classification system. The fine-tuning here was also handled as a 41-class problem.

3.5 Snapshot Ensemble

We implemented a snapshot ensemble (Huang et al., 2017), capturing several "snapshots" of a model at different stages throughout its training. Unlike traditional ensembles that train multiple independent models from scratch, this method reuses the same model's evolving states, making it significantly more resource-efficient. The diversity among snapshots is introduced through a cyclical learning rate schedule, where the learning rate varies between a high and low value over several cycles during training. We implemented the cyclical learning rate ourselves, following the original design in the paper. Each cycle allows the model to explore a wider range of parameter spaces, capturing unique representations in each snapshot. We chose to use six models in our implementation. This choice was primarily practical, ensuring enough diversity among the snapshots while maintaining computational efficiency. After that, we evaluated combinations of three snapshot checkpoints to find the set that achieves the best results together through soft voting. Later on, we used these three models.

3.6 Data Split With 3 Models

With this experiment, we also aimed to find a computationally efficient solution with a promising result. The main idea was that the availability of a sufficiently large amount of training data suggested that the models could perform well even when trained on only a subset of it, thereby reducing computational requirements without significantly reducing the performance.

In this approach, we fine-tuned three separate models for 41-class classification, each trained on a unique one third subset of the training data. To enhance the final predictions, we combined the outputs of these models using the previously introduced ensemble method with soft voting.

4 Results

Our final submission was a 6-class soft voting, which secured 7th place. We evaluated our solutions in both the development set and the published test set. Based on these evaluations, the 6-class approach was not the optimal choice. The best performing experiment was the length-based solution with soft voting, closely followed by the simple 41-class approach. The corresponding F1 scores are shown in Table 1. *Without Soft Voting* refers to the average F1 score of three individual models evaluated separately, while *Soft Voting* refers to applying soft voting across these three models.

Experiment	**Without Soft Voting**		**Soft Voting**	
	Development	Test	Development	Test
Binary	0.972	0.780	0.979	0.795
3-class	0.983	0.750	0.985	0.754
5-class	0.982	0.790	**0.986**	0.796
6-class	0.980	0.771	0.985	0.791
41-class	0.982	0.806	0.985	0.826
Snapshot	0.978	0.796	0.982	0.810
Length-based	0.968	0.820	0.973	**0.827**
Data split models	0.980	0.801	0.982	0.814

Table 1: Summary of results on development and test set by class count and ensemble setting (F1 scores)

Length-based Analysis The length-based approach achieved the best results. Our aim was to understand where it failed and how it did so to provide a deeper understanding of its limitations. To achieve this, we created a confusion matrix which is shown in Figure 1, allowing us to identify patterns and categories of errors. Our error analysis revealed that errors predominantly occurred within model families. For example, the model often struggled to accurately determine which specific *opt_* model generated a given text.

In addition, we examined the results for each text length interval. The analysis showed a clear trend: the longer the text, the better the results. The F1 scores for different character count intervals are as follows: For intervals of 0–745 characters, the F1 score is 0.621; for 746–1613 characters, it is 0.684; and for texts with 1614 or more characters, the F1 score increases to 0.840.

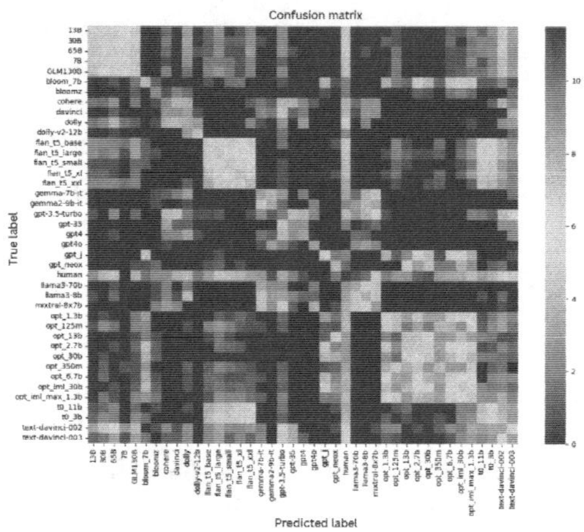

Figure 1: Log-scaled confusion matrix for the length-based solution

ZeroGPT We compared our own experiments with another solution that is easily accessible from a browser, which is ZeroGPT[3]. Detailed information about the model and techniques they use is not available, but their website promises good results. This solution can be accessed via an API call, allowing requests to be sent. For evaluation, we used 2000 random texts from the workshop test dataset and also another 2000 texts from a previous shared task dataset named AuTexTification (Sarvazyan et al., 2023), which is completely independent of our solutions. We could not evaluate more data as it would have required payment. We did the same evaluation on the exact same texts with our own solutions. Their system operates by returning a whole number between 0 and 100. This value indicates the likelihood that the text was written by a human. Since their results are provided in this format, a threshold had to be established. This threshold was set at 50, treated as a closed interval, which means that a score of 50 was also included in this category. Modifying this threshold value does not significantly affect the predictions results.

The results presented in Table 2 indicate that ZeroGPT exhibited poorer performance compared to all of our solutions in both datasets. The workshop test data set comprised text generated by advanced models, while the independent data set included text from both advanced and less advanced models. This highlights the robustness and adaptability of our solutions to machine-generated text classification tasks.

[3]https://www.zerogpt.com/

Experiment	Shared task	AuTexTification
zeroGPT	0.615	0.715
Binary	0.794	0.797
3-class	0.830	0.767
5-class	**0.841**	0.814
6-class	0.838	0.805
41-class	0.831	0.836
Snapshot	0.812	0.826
Length-based	0.807	**0.845**

Table 2: F1 scores for ZeroGPT and our solution, evaluated on 2000 texts each from the AuTexTification (Sarvazyan et al., 2023) and this shared task test set

5 Conclusion

Our findings highlight that the binary approach may not be the most effective way to detect machine-generated texts. Instead, we recommend considering multi-class solutions, as they might improve classification by capturing distinctions among AI-generated texts. In our experiments, we found that different approaches performed well on different datasets: one solution showed strong results on the development set, while another excelled on the test set. For example, the length-based approach was not promising in the development set but performed well on the test set.

To evaluate our approach comprehensively, we considered not only the results, but also the computational efficiency. We implemented a snapshot ensemble technique and also a data split approach with 3 models. Both strategies demonstrated improved performance compared to a single model fine-tuned on the full training dataset while maintaining the same computational costs. However, the more expensive solutions still outperformed these.

Notably, the 3-class approach showed a drop in performance on the test set, likely due to the absence of weaker models in the test data. This suggests that certain multi-class configurations may be less effective when faced with a set of high-performing models only. However, even with these variations, the 41- and 5-class solutions outperformed the binary approach and provided a consistent gain over binary modeling.

Ultimately, our approach demonstrates that moving beyond binary classification to a multi-class strategy, especially when using ensemble soft voting, can yield better results in detecting machine-generated text.

Acknowledgments

The research received support from the European Union project RRF-2.3.1-21-2022-00004 within the framework of the Artificial Intelligence National Laboratory. Additionally, we are grateful for the possibility to use ELKH Cloud (see (Héder et al., 2022); https://science-cloud.hu/) which helped us in achieving the results published in this paper.

References

Joan C. Timoneda and Sebastián Vallejo Vera. 2024. BERT, RoBERTa or DeBERTa? comparing performance across transformer models in political science text. *The Journal of Politics*.

Savvas Chamezopoulos, Drahomira Herrmannova, Anita De Waard, Drahomira Herrmannova, Domenic Rosati, and Yury Kashnitsky. 2024. Overview of the DagPap24 shared task on detecting automatically generated scientific paper. In *Proceedings of the Fourth Workshop on Scholarly Document Processing (SDP 2024)*, pages 7–11, Bangkok, Thailand. Association for Computational Linguistics.

Jacob Devlin, Ming-Wei Chang, Kenton Lee, and Kristina Toutanova. 2019. BERT: Pre-training of deep bidirectional transformers for language understanding. In *Proceedings of the 2019 Conference of the North American Chapter of the Association for Computational Linguistics: Human Language Technologies, Volume 1 (Long and Short Papers)*, pages 4171–4186, Minneapolis, Minnesota. Association for Computational Linguistics.

M.A. Ganaie, Minghui Hu, A.K. Malik, M. Tanveer, and P.N. Suganthan. 2022. Ensemble deep learning: A review. *Engineering Applications of Artificial Intelligence*, 115:105151.

Gemini, Rohan Anil, Sebastian Borgeaud, Jean-Baptiste Alayrac, Jiahui Yu, Radu Soricut, Johan Schalkwyk, Andrew M. Dai, Anja Hauth, Emily Pitler, Timothy Lillicrap, and et al. 2024. Gemini: A family of highly capable multimodal models. *Preprint*, arXiv:2312.11805.

Renhua Gu and Xiangfeng Meng. 2024. AISPACE at SemEval-2024 task 8: A class-balanced soft-voting system for detecting multi-generator machine-generated text. In *Proceedings of the 18th International Workshop on Semantic Evaluation (SemEval-2024)*, pages 1476–1481, Mexico City, Mexico. Association for Computational Linguistics.

Pengcheng He, Xiaodong Liu, Jianfeng Gao, and Weizhu Chen. 2021. DeBERTa: Decoding-enhanced BERT with disentangled attention. In *International Conference on Learning Representations*.

Mihály Héder, Ernő Rigó, Dorottya Medgyesi, Róbert Lovas, Szabolcs Tenczer, Ferenc Török, Attila Farkas, Márk Emődi, József Kadlecsik, György Mező, Ádám Pintér, and Péter Kacsuk. 2022. The past, present and future of the ELKH cloud. *Információs Társadalom*, 22(2):128.

Gao Huang, Yixuan Li, Geoff Pleiss, Zhuang Liu, John E. Hopcroft, and Kilian Q. Weinberger. 2017. Snapshot ensembles: Train 1, get m for free. In *International Conference on Learning Representations*.

Albert Q. Jiang, Alexandre Sablayrolles, Antoine Roux, Arthur Mensch, Blanche Savary, Chris Bamford, Devendra Singh Chaplot, Diego de las Casas, Emma Bou Hanna, Florian Bressand, Gianna Lengyel, Guillaume Bour, Guillaume Lample, Lélio Renard Lavaud, Lucile Saulnier, Marie-Anne Lachaux, Pierre Stock, Sandeep Subramanian, Sophia Yang, Szymon Antoniak, Teven Le Scao, Théophile Gervet, Thibaut Lavril, Thomas Wang, Timothée Lacroix, and William El Sayed. 2024. Mixtral of experts. *Preprint*, arXiv:2401.04088.

Weixin Liang, Zachary Izzo, Yaohui Zhang, Haley Lepp, Hancheng Cao, Xuandong Zhao, Lingjiao Chen, Haotian Ye, Sheng Liu, Zhi Huang, Daniel Mcfarland, and James Y. Zou. 2024a. Monitoring AI-modified content at scale: A case study on the impact of ChatGPT on AI conference peer reviews. In *Proceedings of the 41st International Conference on Machine Learning*, volume 235 of *Proceedings of Machine Learning Research*, pages 29575–29620. PMLR.

Weixin Liang, Yaohui Zhang, Zhengxuan Wu, Haley Lepp, Wenlong Ji, Xuandong Zhao, Hancheng Cao, Sheng Liu, Siyu He, Zhi Huang, Diyi Yang, Christopher Potts, Christopher D Manning, and James Y. Zou. 2024b. Mapping the increasing use of LLMs in scientific papers. In *First Conference on Language Modeling*.

OpenAI, Josh Achiam, Steven Adler, Sandhini Agarwal, Lama Ahmad, Ilge Akkaya, Florencia Leoni Aleman, Diogo Almeida, Janko Altenschmidt, Sam Altman, Shyamal Anadkat, and et al. 2024. Gpt-4 technical report. *Preprint*, arXiv:2303.08774.

Areg Mikael Sarvazyan, José Ángel González, and Marc Franco-salvador. 2024. Genaios at SemEval-2024 task 8: Detecting machine-generated text by mixing language model probabilistic features. In *Proceedings of the 18th International Workshop on Semantic Evaluation (SemEval-2024)*, pages 101–107, Mexico City, Mexico. Association for Computational Linguistics.

Areg Mikael Sarvazyan, José Ángel González, Marc Franco-Salvador, Francisco Rangel, Berta Chulvi, and Paolo Rosso. 2023. Overview of AuTexTification at IberLEF 2023: Detection and attribution of machine-generated text in multiple domains. *Proces. del Leng. Natural*, 71:275–288.

Yuxia Wang, Jonibek Mansurov, Petar Ivanov, Jinyan Su, Artem Shelmanov, Akim Tsvigun, Osama Mohammed Afzal, Tarek Mahmoud, Giovanni Puccetti, and Thomas Arnold. 2024. SemEval-2024 task 8: Multidomain, multimodel and multilingual machine-generated text detection. In *Proceedings of the 18th International Workshop on Semantic Evaluation (SemEval-2024)*, pages 2057–2079, Mexico City, Mexico. Association for Computational Linguistics.

Yuxia Wang, Artem Shelmanov, Jonibek Mansurov, Akim Tsvigun, Vladislav Mikhailov, Rui Xing, Zhuohan Xie, Jiahui Geng, Giovanni Puccetti, Ekaterina Artemova, Jinyan Su, Minh Ngoc Ta, Mervat Abassy, Kareem Elozeiri, Saad El Dine Ahmed, Maiya Goloburda, Tarek Mahmoud, Raj Vardhan Tomar, Alexander Aziz, Nurkhan Laiyk, Osama Mohammed Afzal, Ryuto Koike, Masahiro Kaneko, Alham Fikri Aji, Nizar Habash, Iryna Gurevych, and Preslav Nakov. 2025. GenAI content detection task 1: English and multilingual machine-generated text detection: AI vs. human. In *Proceedings of the 1st Workshop on GenAI Content Detection (GenAIDetect)*, Abu Dhabi, UAE. International Conference on Computational Linguistics.

A Average Text Length and Strong Models

In Figure 2, we present the 6-class groups, and the striped bars indicate models categorized as *Strong*. All other models not listed under the *Strong* models are categorized as *Weak*.

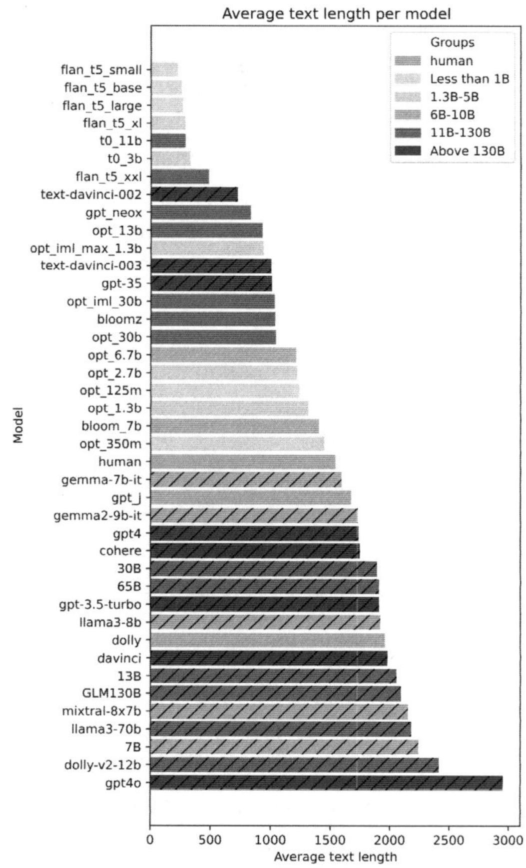

Figure 2: Average character per model

Team Unibuc - NLP at GenAI Detection Task 1: *Qwen* it detect machine-generated text?

Teodor-George Marchitan[1,3], **Claudiu Creanga**[2,3], **Liviu P. Dinu**[1,3]
[1] Faculty of Mathematics and Computer Science,
[2] Interdisciplinary School of Doctoral Studies,
[3] HLT Research Center,
University of Bucharest, Romania
teodor.marchitan@s.unibuc.ro, claudiu.creanga@s.unibuc.ro, ldinu@fmi.unibuc.ro

Abstract

This paper describes the approach of the Unibuc - NLP team in tackling the Coling 2025 GenAI Workshop, Task 1: Binary Multilingual Machine-Generated Text Detection. We explored both masked language models and causal models. For Subtask A, our best model achieved **first-place** out of 36 teams when looking at F1 Micro (Auxiliary Score) of 0.8333, and **second-place** when looking at F1 Macro (Main Score) of 0.8301.

1 Introduction

Task 1 from the GenAI Content Detection Workshop (Wang et al., 2025) focuses on discerning whether a text sample is machine-generated or human-authored. With human ability to distinguish AI-generated text from human content near random chance, advanced automated systems are needed to ensure information integrity. Such systems are crucial for verifying content sources and countering unethical AI use, including propaganda, misinformation, deepfakes, and social manipulation, which pose significant societal risks.

The system developed for Task 1 subtask A is based on an LLM model where only the last layer and the classification head were trained for the downstream task, on the other hand, the system developed for subtask B is based on a transformer model with a classification head on top and it was completely fine-tuned using Low-Rank Adaptation (LoRA) (Hu et al., 2022).

We made our models publicly available in a GitHub Repository.

2 Background

The competition had 3 tasks:

1. Binary Multilingual Machine-Generated Text Detection (Human vs. Machine) with 2 Sub-Tasks: English and Multilingual;
2. AI vs. Human – Academic Essay Authenticity Challenge
3. Cross-domain Machine-Generated Text Detection, which is the same challenge as Task 1, but the texts come from 8 domains.

Subtask	Train	Dev	Test
A (mono)	610,767	261,758	73,941
B (multi)	674,083	288,894	151,425

Table 1: Datasets sizes used in the Task 1 for each subtask.

We participated in Task 1 and achieved the top position in the Monolingual Subtask based on F1 Micro score, and secured the second position when considering F1 Macro.

2.1 Dataset

The data for this task is an extension the SemEval 2024 Task 8, which itself is based on the M4 dataset (Wang et al., 2024a,b). This dataset has many more examples, models and sources than the previous ones (Table 1).

Examining token count distribution reveals that, on average, the generated class in the test set has more tokens than in the training set (Figure 1 vs. Figure 2).

2.2 Previous Work

Recent years have witnessed a significant evolution in language model capabilities, with models like GPT-2, GPT-3 and GPT-4 pushing the boundaries of machine-generated text. This advancement has made it increasingly challenging to distinguish between human-authored and machine-generated content. Early language models using top-k sampling often produced detectable patterns, like repetitive words, which machine learning models could exploit for identifying AI-generated

Proceedings of the 1st Workshop on GenAI Content Detection (GenAIDetect), pages 173–177
January 19, 2025. ©2025 International Conference on Computational Linguistics

text. However, advanced techniques like nucleus sampling have reduced these cues, making detection much harder (Ippolito et al., 2020).

While fine-tuning large language models for detection has shown some promise, as demonstrated by the success of RoBERTa in detecting GPT-2-generated text (Solaiman et al., 2019), the increasing sophistication of these models continues to pose a significant challenge. Human evaluators, even for earlier models like GPT-2, struggled to accurately identify machine-generated content, achieving only around 70% accuracy (Ippolito et al., 2020). For more advanced models like GPT-3, human evaluators perform at chance levels, highlighting the limitations of human judgment in this domain (Clark et al., 2021). Given the rapid advancement of language models, there is an urgent need for further research into automated detection methods. It remains an open question whether we can develop systems capable of keeping pace with the evolving capabilities of generative models.

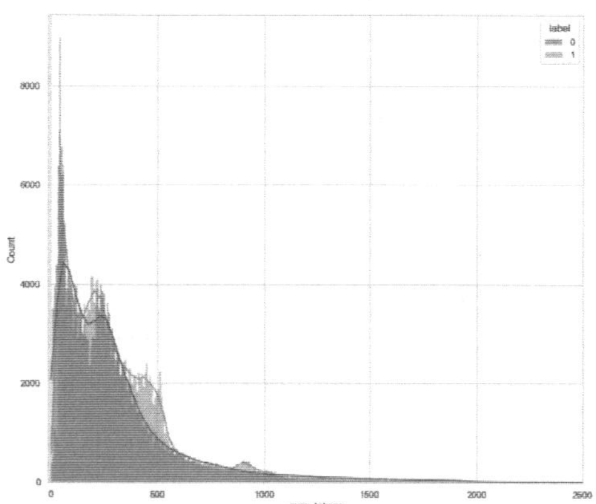

Figure 1: Subtask A: Distribution of token length for the training dataset.

3 System overview

In this paper, we focused our research on two different system architectures: **Causal models** (3.1) for subtask 1 and **Masked models** (3.2) for subtask 2.

3.1 Causal models

We conducted experiments using several large language models (LLMs), exploring both small and large variants to identify the model that achieved the best performance on our task. Among the models tested: BLOOM-560M (Workshop et al., 2023)), Llama-3.2-1B (Grattafiori et al., 2024), the highest-performing model was based on Qwen, precisely the model Qwen2.5-0.5B (Team, 2024). Initially, the model displayed a tendency to overfit on the majority class (F1 Macro: 0.7783 and F1 Micro: 0.7868 on the final test set), leading us to down-sample the training set to achieve a balanced 50-50 distribution between the two classes. This adjustment helped mitigate over-fitting and improved the model's generalization. With this model we achieved first place on the leader-board by F1 Micro (0.8333) score and second place by F1 Macro score (0.8301). We additionally experimented with Gemini 1.5 Flash. However, due to limited resources, we were unable to fine-tune the model. Consequently, its accuracy was poor, nearing random chance levels.

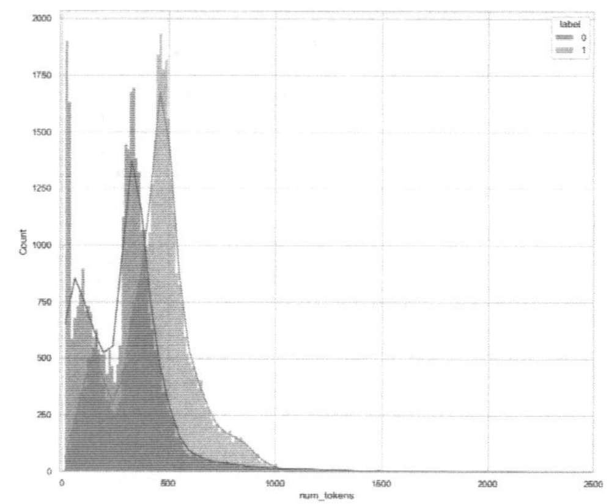

Figure 2: Subtask A: Distribution of token length for the test dataset. We can see it is significantly different from the training set.

We set the maximum number of tokens to 2048 (based on Figure 1) and froze all layers excepting the last one and the classification head ending up with 14,914,176 (3.02%) trainable parameters. For training we used a learning rate of 0.0002, a weight decay of 0.01, a batch size of 32, and trained for a maximum of three epochs. Throughout the training process, we closely monitored both training and validation losses to assess the model's learning progress and prevent overfitting.

As shown in Table 2, the model demonstrated effective learning from the first epoch onward. The training loss continued to decrease steadily, reflecting improved performance on the training data. However, by the third epoch, the validation loss had reached a plateau, suggesting that fur-

Epoch	Train Loss	Valid Loss	Macro F1
1	0.11	0.11	0.950
2	0.07	0.10	0.960
3	0.04	0.10	0.966

Table 2: Training and Validation Loss alongside Macro F1 score for the 3 epochs.

ther training would not yield additional gains and could potentially lead to over-fitting. We therefore halted training after the third epoch.

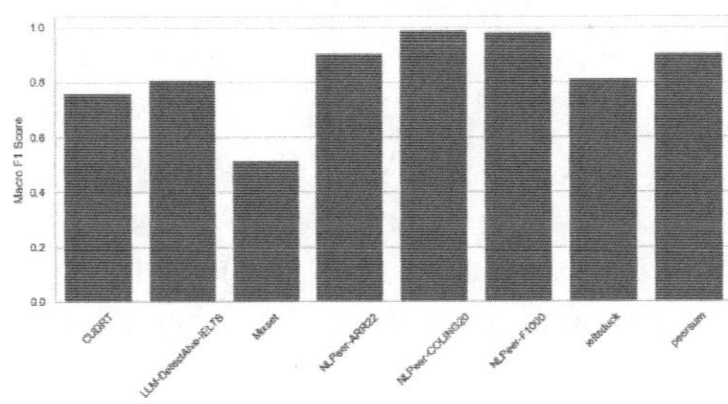

Figure 3: Subtask A: monolingual - accuracy by source for test set. We obtain best accuracy on NLPeer datasets, almost 100%.

3.2 Masked models

The core of this architecture is based on transformer model XLM-Roberta-Base (Conneau et al., 2019) with a classification head on top consisting of 2 hidden layers with a dropout of 0.1 between. We set the maximum number of tokens to 512 and we truncated the longer text by keeping the first part of the text, as suggested in (Marchitan et al., 2024). We then fine-tuned the entire model using Low-Rank Adaptation (LoRA) (Hu et al., 2022) with the following hyperparameters: $r = 4$, $lora\_alpha = 8$, $lora\_dropout = 0.25$ and we ended up with $739,586$ (0.2653%) trainable parameters. The fine-tuning was done as in (Creangă et al., 2024) for one epoch in batches of 16 using the AdamW optimizer with a learning rate of 0.00005, a weight decay of 0.002 and warmup steps set to 10% of the total number of sets (in our case 4213). When fine-tuning this system, we have also used the class weights for the cross entropy function in order to make the model pay more attention to the minority class and penalize more the errors for this class.

4 Results

We participated in Task 1 and achieved the **top position** in the Monolingual Subtask based on F1 Micro score, as shown in Table 3, and secured the second position when considering F1 Macro. This reflects our model's ability to consistently identify and classify instances correctly in the monolingual setting, achieving an F1 Micro score of 0.8333. Our performance in F1 Macro, which captures how well our model handled imbalances across classes, placed us in a second position with a score of 0.8301.

	Score and Place Track Monolingual	Score and Place Track Multilingual
F1 Macro	0.8301 / **2**	0.66 / 24
F1 Micro	0.8333 / **1**	0.67 / 24

Table 3: Team Unibuc - NLP results on Task 1

In the Multilingual Track, however, our model didn't do so well, securing 24th place with F1 scores of 0.66 (Macro) and 0.67 (Micro). This gap between monolingual and multilingual performance highlights the difficulties our model encountered when adapting to varied languages and possibly diverse linguistic structures in the multilingual setting.

4.1 Error Analysis

Examining the F1 Macro scores by model (Figure 4) reveals that our model achieves the highest accuracy on data generated by ChatGPT. This result may be influenced by the relatively small number of ChatGPT samples in the test set (96), which could make high performance on this subset more attainable. Notably, although ChatGPT data was not included in the training set, our model was able to generalize effectively to this unseen data, indicating strong generalization capabilities. In contrast, the model's lowest accuracy is on text generated by Baichuan, which, like ChatGPT, was also absent from the training set. The reduced accuracy on Baichuan text suggests that this style or structure might be more challenging for the model to handle.

Analyzing the F1 Macro scores by source (Figure 3) reveals that our model achieves its highest accuracy on NLPeer-COLING20 and NLPeer-F1000 data, with scores approaching nearly 100%. This exceptional performance may be partly attributed to the limited sample sizes of these sources in the test set: NLPeer-COLING20 contains only 176 samples, and NLPeer-F1000 has a medium sample size of $9,798$. Smaller sample sizes can lead to higher apparent accuracy due to

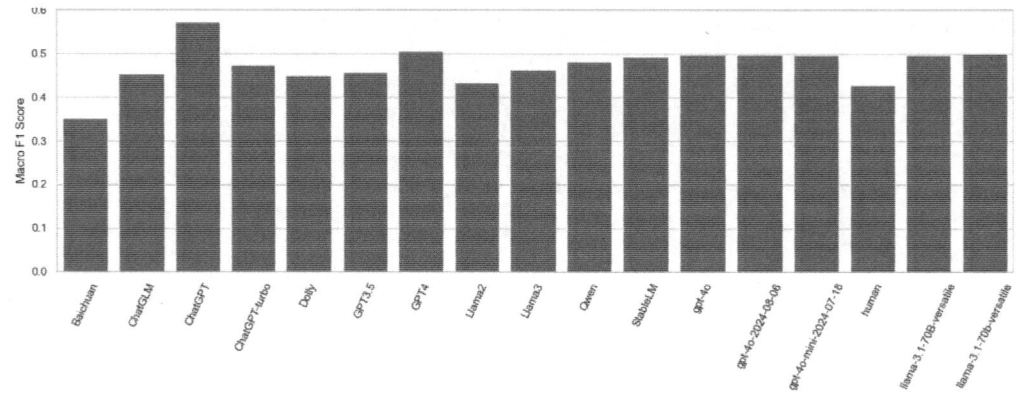

Figure 4: Subtask A: monolingual - accuracy by model for test set. We obtained best accuracy on ChatGPT, but otherwise there is not a lot of variation between models.

reduced variance, which may amplify the model's ability to fit well on these subsets. On the other hand, the model shows its lowest accuracy on the Mixset source, with an F1 Macro score around 0.5. This significant drop suggests that the Mixset data presents more challenging language structures or varied writing styles that the model finds difficult to generalize.

Furthermore, as seen in the distribution of sources within the test set and training set (Figure 5), none of these sources were present in the training data. Despite this, the model generalizes well to NLPeer sources, demonstrating its robustness in adapting to unseen data.

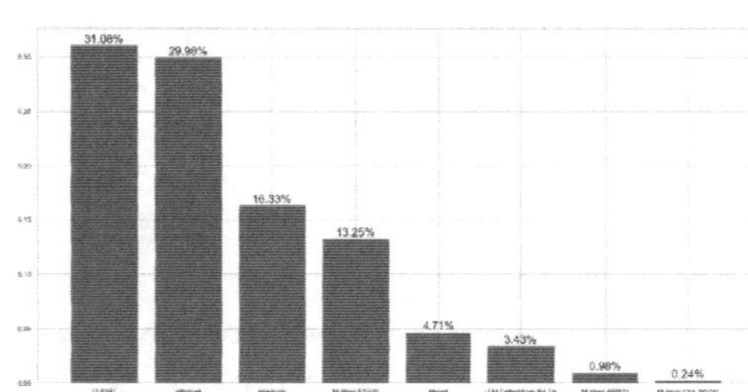

Figure 5: Subtask A: monolingual - Sources of the text in test dataset. In the training dataset we had only 3 sources: mage (46%), m4gt (42%) and hc3 (11%).

Examining the confusion matrix (Figure 6), we observe that the model achieves strong performance: 74% of true negatives and 91% of true positives are accurately classified. This indicates that the model is generally effective at distinguishing between classes. However, there is a tendency to over-predict the positive class. Specifically, the model made $44,808$ positive predictions compared to the $39,266$ actual positive examples in the dataset. This imbalance suggests that the model may be leaning towards identifying samples as positive, possibly due to certain linguistic patterns associated with the positive class. In contrast, the model under-predicts the negative class, suggesting that is necessary further fine-tuning to better capture the variations within human-generated text.

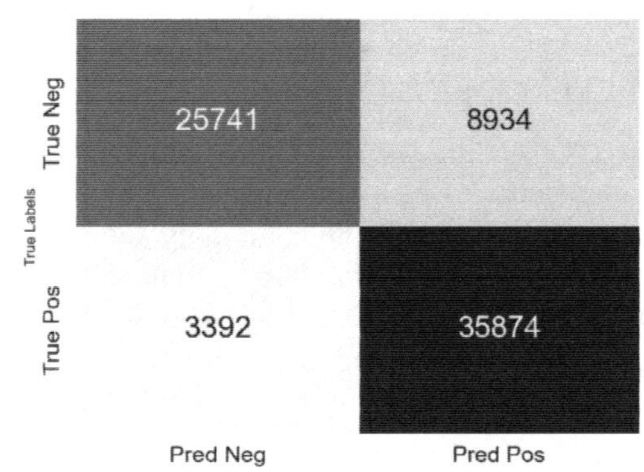

Figure 6: Subtask A: monolingual - Confusion matrix. Most predictions aligning along the correct diagonal: True negatives are 74%, False negatives are 25%, False positives are 8%, True positives are 91%.

5 Conclusions and Future Work

In conclusion, our architecture and training methods produced good results for subtask A (securing the second place). However, our models demonstrated signs of over-fitting for subtask B. Our future endeavors will explore several avenues:

- To improve our masked model's performance on the multilingual task, we will explore techniques such as language-specific fine-tuning, data augmentation, and regularization to prevent over-fitting.

- Utilize latent-space variables in our models and, with the help of high-level features such as event transitions or topic sequences, see if we can improve the accuracy and resilience of our model, especially under varied generation and adversarial settings.

Acknowledgements

Research partially supported by the Ministry of Research, Innovation and Digitization, CNCS/CCCDI UEFISCDI, SiRoLa project, PN-IV-P1-PCE-2023-1701, within PNCDI IV, Romania.

References

Elizabeth Clark, Tal August, Sofia Serrano, Nikita Haduong, Suchin Gururangan, and Noah A. Smith. 2021. All that's 'human' is not gold: Evaluating human evaluation of generated text. In *Proceedings of the 59th Annual Meeting of the Association for Computational Linguistics and the 11th International Joint Conference on Natural Language Processing (Volume 1: Long Papers)*, pages 7282–7296, Online. Association for Computational Linguistics.

Alexis Conneau, Kartikay Khandelwal, Naman Goyal, Vishrav Chaudhary, Guillaume Wenzek, Francisco Guzmán, Edouard Grave, Myle Ott, Luke Zettlemoyer, and Veselin Stoyanov. 2019. Unsupervised cross-lingual representation learning at scale. *CoRR*, abs/1911.02116.

Claudiu Creangă, Liviu P. Dinu, and Daniela Gifu. 2024. Fine-tuning models for biomedical relation extraction. *Procedia Computer Science*, 246:2100–2109. 28th International Conference on Knowledge Based and Intelligent information and Engineering Systems (KES 2024).

Aaron Grattafiori, Abhimanyu Dubey, Abhinav Jauhri, Abhinav Pandey, et al. 2024. The llama 3 herd of models.

Edward J Hu, Yelong Shen, Phillip Wallis, Zeyuan Allen-Zhu, Yuanzhi Li, Shean Wang, Lu Wang, and Weizhu Chen. 2022. LoRA: Low-rank adaptation of large language models. In *International Conference on Learning Representations*.

Daphne Ippolito, Daniel Duckworth, Chris Callison-Burch, and Douglas Eck. 2020. Automatic detection of generated text is easiest when humans are fooled. In *Proceedings of the 58th Annual Meeting of the Association for Computational Linguistics*, pages 1808–1822, Online. Association for Computational Linguistics.

Teodor-george Marchitan, Claudiu Creanga, and Liviu P. Dinu. 2024. Team Unibuc - NLP at SemEval-2024 task 8: Transformer and hybrid deep learning based models for machine-generated text detection. In *Proceedings of the 18th International Workshop on Semantic Evaluation (SemEval-2024)*, pages 403–411, Mexico City, Mexico. Association for Computational Linguistics.

Irene Solaiman, Miles Brundage, Jack Clark, Amanda Askell, Ariel Herbert-Voss, Jeff Wu, Alec Radford, and Jasmine Wang. 2019. Release strategies and the social impacts of language models. *ArXiv*, abs/1908.09203.

Qwen Team. 2024. Qwen2.5: A party of foundation models.

Yuxia Wang, Jonibek Mansurov, Petar Ivanov, Jinyan Su, Artem Shelmanov, Akim Tsvigun, Chenxi Whitehouse, Osama Mohammed Afzal, Tarek Mahmoud, Toru Sasaki, Thomas Arnold, Alham Fikri Aji, Nizar Habash, Iryna Gurevych, and Preslav Nakov. 2024a. M4: Multi-generator, multi-domain, and multi-lingual black-box machine-generated text detection. In *Proceedings of the 18th Conference of the European Chapter of the Association for Computational Linguistics*, Malta.

Yuxia Wang, Jonibek Mansurov, Petar Ivanov, Akim Tsvigun, Jinyan Su, Artem Shelmanov, Osama Mohammed Afzal, Tarek Mahmoud, Giovanni Puccetti, Thomas Arnold, Alham Fikri Aji, Nizar Habash, Iryna Gurevych, and Preslav Nakov. 2024b. MG-Bench: Evaluation benchmark for black-box machine-generated text detection.

Yuxia Wang, Artem Shelmanov, Jonibek Mansurov, Akim Tsvigun, Vladislav Mikhailov, Rui Xing, Zhuohan Xie, Jiahui Geng, Giovanni Puccetti, Ekaterina Artemova, Jinyan Su, Minh Ngoc Ta, Mervat Abassy, Kareem Elozeiri, Saad El Dine Ahmed, Maiya Goloburda, Tarek Mahmoud, Raj Vardhan Tomar, Alexander Aziz, Nurkhan Laiyk, Osama Mohammed Afzal, Ryuto Koike, Masahiro Kaneko, Alham Fikri Aji, Nizar Habash, Iryna Gurevych, and Preslav Nakov. 2025. Genai content detection task 1: English and multilingual machine-generated text detection: Ai vs. human. In *Proceedings of the 1st Workshop on GenAI Content Detection (GenAIDetect)*, Abu Dhabi, UAE. International Conference on Computational Linguistics.

BigScience Workshop, :, Teven Le Scao, Angela Fan, and others. 2023. Bloom: A 176b-parameter open-access multilingual language model.

Fraunhofer SIT at GenAI Detection Task 1: Adapter Fusion for AI-generated Text Detection

Karla Schäfer and **Martin Steinebach**
Fraunhofer SIT | ATHENE Center
Rheinstraße 75, Darmstadt, Germany
{karla.schaefer, martin.steinebach}@sit.fraunhofer.de

Abstract

The detection of AI-generated content is becoming increasingly important with the growing prevalence of tools such as ChatGPT. This paper presents our results in the GenAI Content Detection Task 1, focusing on binary English and multilingual AI-generated text detection. We trained and tested transformers, adapters and adapter fusion. In the English setting (Subtask A), the combination of our own adapter on AI-generated text detection based on RoBERTa with a task adapter on multi-genre NLI yielded a macro F1 score of 0.828 on the challenge test set, ranking us third out of 35 teams. In the multilingual setting (Subtask B), adapter fusion resulted in a deterioration of the results. Consequently, XLM-RoBERTa, fine-tuned on the training set, was employed for the final evaluation, attaining a macro F1 score of 0.7258 and ranking tenth out of 25 teams.

1 Introduction

The increased utilisation of tools such as ChatGPT has resulted in a notable rise in the prevalence of AI-generated text across all facets of modern life. In light of this, the development of detectors of AI-generated content is becoming increasingly important. The majority of research in this field focuses on the detection of AI-generated text in the English language. However, it is important to note that generation models are also capable of producing text in a multitude of languages. Consequently, the development of effective detectors that can perform well in multilingual settings is a crucial area of investigation. The binary English and multilingual machine-generated text detection challenge at the GenAI Content Detection Workshop (Wang et al., 2025) is focusing on this problem by encouraging its participants to develop detectors of AI-generated text on English (Subtask A) and multilingual (Subtask B) text. We participated in both subtasks of this challenge and trained and tested different transformers and adapters on the task of AI-generated text detection. We tested different adapter configurations and the utilisation of adapter fusion to transfer knowledge of pre-trained task adapters on AI-generated text detection.

2 Related Work

Several detectors of AI-generated text have been developed recently. For example, Abassy et al. (2024) developed a system, LLM-DetectAIve, which is capable of identifying not only text written by humans and machines, but also instances where the fact that a text was generated by a machine has been obfuscated, or cases where an LLM has been employed to enhance a text that was originally written by a human. Campino (2024) tested and trained different transformers on the detection of AI-generated text in the field of education. The transformers tested were ALBERT, BERT, ELECTRA, RoBERTa and XLNet. The results demonstrated that, without and with fine-tuning, BERT provided the best results, with superior results when fine-tuning. Other detectors were developed in challenges, such as the SemEval-2024 Task 8 challenge (Wang et al., 2024) or the PAN challenge at CLEF 2024 (Bevendorff et al., 2024). As far as we know, adapters and adapter fusion haven't been used before.

3 System Description

We participated in Subtask A and B of the GenAI Content Detection Task 1 challenge. In both settings, first, we tested different transformers, fine-tuning them on the respective training sets. In Subtask A, the English setting, we fine-tuned the transformers BERT (base and large; Devlin et al., 2019) and RoBERTa base (Liu et al., 2019). In Subtask B, using the multilingual training set, we fine-tuned XLM-RoBERTa base and large (Conneau et al., 2019). Subsequently, we trained our own task adapter on AI-generated text detection using the

Proceedings of the 1st Workshop on GenAI Content Detection (GenAIDetect), pages 178–183
January 19, 2025.

respective datasets of the subtasks and performed adapter fusion (Pfeiffer et al., 2021) with official available pre-trained task adapters from Adapter Hub[1] (Pfeiffer et al., 2020). Adapter fusion is a method of combining the knowledge of multiple pre-trained adapters trained for different tasks.

3.1 Adapter Fusion

First, we trained our own adapters on the English and multilingual dataset (dependent on subtask). As basis, the best transformers from the fine-tuning step were used, being RoBERTa base on the English dataset and XLM-RoBERTa base on the multilingual dataset. In the English setting, different adapter configurations were tested. We tested the configurations LoRA (Hu et al., 2021), LoReFT (Wu et al., 2024) and sequential bottleneck (seq_bn; Houlsby et al., 2019). In the multilingual setting, we used sequential bottleneck as adapter configuration because of its superior performance in the English setting. With this, we trained our own AI-generated text detection adapter, called AI-Gen in the English setting and ml-AI-Gen in the multilingual setting.

A variety of task adapters were integrated and evaluated in conjunction with our internally developed adapters, AI-Gen/ml-AI-Gen. The selection of task adapters was based on an educated guess, with a particular emphasis on their suitability for the analysis of the structure and the perplexity of textual content. The incorporation of perplexity as an additional feature enabled the authors of Guo et al. (2024) to enhance the results of their AI-generated text detector. The same approach was attempted here using task adapters. The task adapters tested on the English dataset were pre-trained on the tasks semantic textual similarity[2], multi-genre NLI[3], adversarial NLI[4], linguistic acceptability[5] and machine reading comprehension[6] (Poth et al., 2021). For the multilingual setting we tested task adapters pre-trained on formality classification[7] (Krishna et al., 2020) and multilingual knowledge integration[8] (Hou et al., 2022).

[1]https://adapterhub.ml/
[2]roberta-base-pf-mrpc
[3]roberta-base-pf-mnli
[4]roberta-base-pf-anli_r3
[5]roberta-base-pf-cola
[6]roberta-base-pf-record
[7]xlm-roberta-base_formality_classify_gyafc_pfeiffer
[8]xlm-roberta-base_mlki_ep_pfeiffer

Model	macro F1	micro F1
BERT uncased base	0.806	0.815
BERT uncased large	0.792	0.808
RoBERTa base	**0.822**	**0.831**

Table 1: [Subtask A] English Transformer fine-tuned (test set: devtest)

Adapter (conf)	macro F1	micro F1
LoRA	0.729	0.768
LoReFT	0.679	0.738
seq_bn	**0.837**	**0.849**

Table 2: [Subtask A] English Adapters for different configurations, trained with RoBERTa base (test set: devtest)

3.2 Implementation Details

For the training of the transformers the learning rate was set to 2e-5. We also tested with a learning rate of 5e-5, but this resulted in overall worse scores, i.e. training RoBERTa base on the English training set the macro F1 score after 1 epoch reached 0.3844 (with learning rate 2e-5: 0.9672). For the adapter training we set the learning rate to 1e-4. In all settings truncation and padding to the max input length of the model was used. In all settings, we trained for 6 epochs. We saved and tested the models after each epoch. The model from the epoch with the best macro F1 score on the development set was used for the evaluation on the devtest set.

4 Evaluation Results

In the development phase of the challenge, the various architectural options were evaluated on the devtest set. The results of the two subtasks are presented in the following sections. Subsequently, during the final test phase, the two architectures that demonstrated optimal performance on the devtest set, were tested again.

4.1 Subtask A: English Only Data

In Subtask A, the goal was to train a detector on English data only. We first tested different transformers on the **devtest set**, fine-tuning them on the English training set. We tested BERT (base, large) and RoBERTa base, see Table 1 for the results on the devtest set. For BERT base and RoBERTa base, the optimal results on the development set were obtained after 1 epoch of fine-tuning. Consequently, we also tested smaller steps, comprising less than 1 epoch, which yielded inferior outcomes. For

Adapter Fusion	Adapter Type	macro F1	micro F1
AI-Gen+mprc	semantic textual similarity	0.799	0.813
AI-Gen+ MNLI	**multi-genre NLI**	**0.851**	**0.852**
AI-Gen+anli	adversarial NLI	0.819	0.833
AI-Gen+cola	linguistic acceptability	0.836	0.841
AI-Gen+record	machine reading comprehension	0.786	0.809
AI-Gen+MNLI+cola	(combination)	0.779	0.779

Table 3: [Subtask A] English Adapter Fusion (test set: devtest)

BERT large, the optimal results were obtained after 4 epochs fine-tuning. RoBERTa base performed the best with a macro F1 score of 0.822.

Following this, we trained an adapter based on RoBERTa base using different adapter configurations (LoRA, LoReFT and seq_bn). See Table 2 for the results. For LoRA and LoReFT the best results on the dev set were calculated after 5 epochs, for seq_bn after 2 epochs. Using the configuration sequential bottleneck (seq_bn) the resulting adapter performed the best with a macro F1 score of 0.837 and even better than RoBERTa fine-tuned (macro F1 score: 0.822). We called this adapter AI-Gen.

After training our own adapter for AI-generated text detection (AI-Gen) we used adapter fusion for testing if additional knowledge of pre-trained task adapters improve the detection performance. See Table 3 for the results. We combined our adapter AI-Gen with five different task adapters. For all combinations, the best results were calculated after 3 epochs. The combination of AI-Gen with a task adapter on multi-genre NLI (MNLI) improved the macro F1-score on the devtest set to 0.851, from a macro F1-score of 0.837 using AI-Gen alone. We also tested a combination of AI-Gen with MNLI and the second best task adapter (cola), but this worsened the macro F1 score to 0.779.

Adapter fusion of AI-Gen with MNLI was our best detector on the English dataset and therefore also applied on the final **test set** in the challenge used for ranking. On the final test set we achieved a macro F1 score of 0.828 and micro F1 score of 0.8289, ranking third in the challenge (see Table 4). Furthermore, we evaluated the performance of this detector on the different generation methods used to build the test set. In Table 5 the generation methods with the most wrongly classified labels (>40%) are presented. Overall, our English detector has the most problems detecting fakes generated using GPT4 (55.36%), Dolly (54.48%) and StableLM (52.38%). When viewing the source of the test set samples, Mixset (41.08%) and CUDRT (29.01%) stood out with the most wrongly classified samples.

Team	macro F1	micro F1
1st	0.831	0.831
2nd	0.830	0.833
Fraunhofer SIT	**0.828**	**0.829**
4th	0.819	0.822

Table 4: [Subtask A] Final Evaluation on the test set (final ranking)

Generation method	# in testset	% wrong classified
ChatGLM	2006	41.28
Baichuan	1754	49.66
Dolly	268	54.48
StableLM	252	52.48
ChatGPT-turbo	144	45.83
GPT4	112	55.36
ChatGPT	96	45.83

Table 5: [Subtask A] Performance on the English test set by generation method (% wrong classied >40%)

4.2 Subtask B: Multilingual Data

Again, we first fine-tuned and tested different transformers using the multilingual training and **devtest set**, see Table 6. The XLM-RoBERTa large model (1 epoch) achieved a macro F1 score of 0. Viewing the score files, all samples were classified as human generated. As the multilingual training set contains 90.6% English data, we also applied the RoBERTa base model from Subtask A, trained on the English

Model	macro F1	micro F1
XLM-RoBERTa base	**0.630**	**0.847**
XLM-RoBERTa large	0	0.108
RoBERTa base	0.553	0.686

Table 6: [Subtask B] Multilingual Transformer fine-tuned (test set: devtest)

Adapter Setting	Adapter Type	macro F1	micro F1
newly trained adapter (ml-AI-Gen), configuration: seq_bn		0.585	0.837
fusion: ml-AI-Gen+form_class	formality classification (form_class)	0.521	0.824
fusion: ml-AI-Gen+mlki	multilingual knowledge integration	0.392	0.433
fusion: ml-AI-Gen+form_class+mlki		0.525	0.833

Table 7: [Subtask B] Multilingual Adapter Fusion (test set: devtest)

data, resulting in a macro F1 score of 0.553. The best score was achieved with XLM-RoBERTa base fine-tuned on the multilingual dataset (6 epochs) with a macro F1 score of 0.63.

Following this, we trained our own adapter on the multilingual training data (ml-AI-Gen) using the previous best configuration, being sequential bottleneck (4 epochs). See Table 7 for the results. The trained adapter (ml-AI-Gen) performed worse on the devtest set with a macro F1-score of 0.585, compared to XLM-RoBERTa base fine-tuned (0.630). Also, the use of adapter fusion with different task adapters worsened the results. On the multilingual data, XLM-RoBERTa fine-tuned being our best detector.

Interestingly, as one can see in Figure 1, the macro F1 score on the development set exhibited superior performance during training for the models using adapter fusion.The best one being adapter fusion with ml-AI-Gen and a multilingual knowledge integration task adapter (red in Figure 1) with a macro F1 score of 0.953 after 3 epochs of training. The best macro F1 score of XLM-RoBERTa on the development set was 0.946 after 6 epochs training (blue in Figure 1).

Again, we used the best performing model on the devtest to participate in the final evaluation on the **test set** used for ranking in the competition, here being XLM-RoBERTa base fine-tuned. We achieved a macro F1 score of 0.7258 and micro F1 score of 0.7361 on the test set, ranking tenth out of 25 teams. After the challenge, because of their superior performance during training, we also checked the performance of our trained adapter fusion models on the test set (see Table 8). Still, XLM-RoBERTa base (fine-tuned) performed best. Adapter fusion didn't improve the results on both multilingual test sets.

Model	macro F1	micro F1
XLM-RoBERTa base	**0.726**	**0.736**
(f) ml-AI-Gen+form_class	0.683	0.701
(f) ml-AI-Gen+mlki	0.519	0.554
(f) ml-AI-Gen+gyafc+mlki	0.555	0.562

Table 8: [Subtask B] Evaluation on the test set (used for final ranking, (f): fusion)

5 Conclusion and Future Work

In this paper, we presented the solutions developed by our team Fraunhofer SIT for the 2024 GenAI Detection Task 1 challenge. We fine-tuned transformers and adapters, and applied adapter fusion using different task adapters for knowledge transfer. On English data, adapter fusion improved the results, resulting in our team ranking third in subtask A of the challenge. The utilisation of multilingual data did not yield enhanced outcomes in the context of adapter fusion. One potential explanation for this phenomenon is the dearth of task adapters that are accessible within the domain of multilingual data. To illustrate, the most optimal task adapter within the English setting, multi-genre NLI, is not available for multilingual data.

Limitations

We acknowledge certain limitations of our work, and intend to address these in future work. First, we used the whole training set in Subtask B, containing 90% English data. Contrarily, the test set didn't include any English samples. In future work, this dataset should be more balanced out, incorporating more data from underrepresented languages. Furthermore, adapter fusion in a more wieder experimental setup should be tested in future work, utilising a greater number of models and datasets. Additionally, the relatively short length of the texts in this dataset was not taken into account. Previous approaches, such as multiscale positive-unlabeled training (Tian et al., 2023), have demonstrated effective results on similar texts.

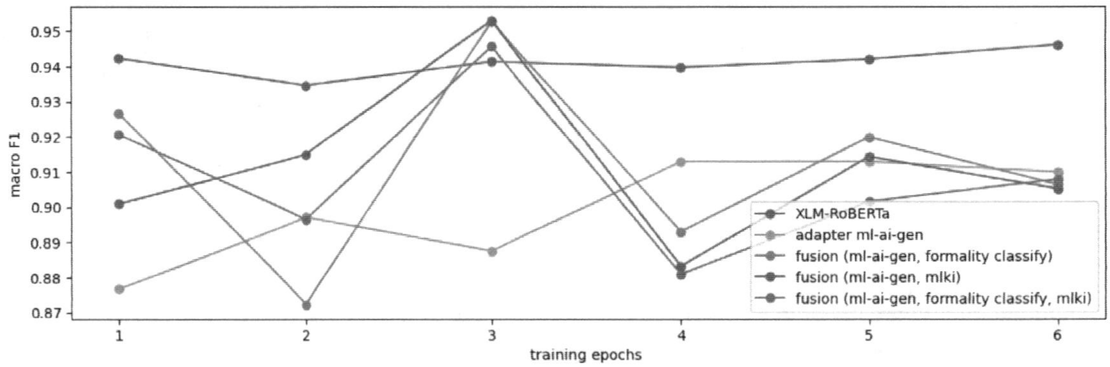

Figure 1: [Subtask B] Macro F1-Score on the dev set during training

Acknowledgments

This work was supported by the German Federal Ministry of Education and Research (BMBF) and the Hessian Ministry of Higher Education, Research, Science and the Arts within their joint support of ATHENE, CRISIS.

References

Mervat Abassy, Kareem Elozeiri, Alexander Aziz, Minh Ngoc Ta, Raj Vardhan Tomar, Bimarsha Adhikari, Saad El Dine Ahmed, Yuxia Wang, Osama Mohammed Afzal, Zhuohan Xie, Jonibek Mansurov, Ekaterina Artemova, Vladislav Mikhailov, Rui Xing, Jiahui Geng, Hasan Iqbal, Zain Muhammad Mujahid, Tarek Mahmoud, Akim Tsvigun, Alham Fikri Aji, Artem Shelmanov, Nizar Habash, Iryna Gurevych, and Preslav Nakov. 2024. LLM-DetectAIve: a tool for fine-grained machine-generated text detection. In *Proceedings of the 2024 Conference on Empirical Methods in Natural Language Processing: System Demonstrations*, pages 336–343, Miami, Florida, USA. Association for Computational Linguistics.

Janek Bevendorff, Matti Wiegmann, Jussi Karlgren, Luise Dürlich, Evangelia Gogoulou, Aarne Talman, Efstathios Stamatatos, Martin Potthast, and Benno Stein. 2024. Overview of the "voight-kampff" generative ai authorship verification task at pan and eloquent 2024. In *25th Working Notes of the Conference and Labs of the Evaluation Forum, CLEF 2024. Grenoble, France 9 September 2024 through 12 September 2024*, volume 3740, pages 2486–2506. CEUR-WS.

José Campino. 2024. Unleashing the transformers: Nlp models detect ai writing in education. *Journal of Computers in Education*, pages 1–29.

Alexis Conneau, Kartikay Khandelwal, Naman Goyal, Vishrav Chaudhary, Guillaume Wenzek, Francisco Guzmán, Edouard Grave, Myle Ott, Luke Zettlemoyer, and Veselin Stoyanov. 2019. Unsupervised cross-lingual representation learning at scale. *CoRR*, abs/1911.02116.

Jacob Devlin, Ming-Wei Chang, Kenton Lee, and Kristina Toutanova. 2019. Bert: Pre-training of deep bidirectional transformers for language understanding. In *North American Chapter of the Association for Computational Linguistics*.

Mingcan Guo, Zhongyuan Han, Haoyang Chen, and Jiangao Peng. 2024. A machine-generated text detection model based on text multi-feature fusion. *Working Notes of CLEF*.

Yifan Hou, Wenxiang Jiao, Meizhen Liu, Carl Allen, Zhaopeng Tu, and Mrinmaya Sachan. 2022. Adapters for enhanced modeling of multilingual knowledge and text. *arXiv preprint arXiv:2210.13617*.

Neil Houlsby, Andrei Giurgiu, Stanislaw Jastrzebski, Bruna Morrone, Quentin De Laroussilhe, Andrea Gesmundo, Mona Attariyan, and Sylvain Gelly. 2019. Parameter-efficient transfer learning for nlp. In *International conference on machine learning*, pages 2790–2799. PMLR.

J. Edward Hu, Yelong Shen, Phillip Wallis, Zeyuan Allen-Zhu, Yuanzhi Li, Shean Wang, and Weizhu Chen. 2021. Lora: Low-rank adaptation of large language models. *ArXiv*, abs/2106.09685.

Kalpesh Krishna, John Wieting, and Mohit Iyyer. 2020. Reformulating unsupervised style transfer as paraphrase generation. In *Proceedings of the 2020 Conference on Empirical Methods in Natural Language Processing (EMNLP)*, pages 737–762, Online. Association for Computational Linguistics.

Yinhan Liu, Myle Ott, Naman Goyal, Jingfei Du, Mandar Joshi, Danqi Chen, Omer Levy, Mike Lewis, Luke Zettlemoyer, and Veselin Stoyanov. 2019. Roberta: A robustly optimized bert pretraining approach. *ArXiv*, abs/1907.11692.

Jonas Pfeiffer, Aishwarya Kamath, Andreas Rücklé, Kyunghyun Cho, and Iryna Gurevych. 2021.

Adapterfusion: Non-destructive task composition for transfer learning. *ArXiv*, abs/2005.00247.

Jonas Pfeiffer, Andreas Rücklé, Clifton A. Poth, Aishwarya Kamath, Ivan Vulic, Sebastian Ruder, Kyunghyun Cho, and Iryna Gurevych. 2020. Adapterhub: A framework for adapting transformers. *ArXiv*, abs/2007.07779.

Clifton Poth, Jonas Pfeiffer, Andreas R"uckl'e, and Iryna Gurevych. 2021. What to pre-train on? Efficient intermediate task selection. In *Proceedings of the 2021 Conference on Empirical Methods in Natural Language Processing*, pages 10585–10605, Online and Punta Cana, Dominican Republic. Association for Computational Linguistics.

Yuchuan Tian, Hanting Chen, Xutao Wang, Zheyuan Bai, Qinghua Zhang, Ruifeng Li, Chao Xu, and Yunhe Wang. 2023. Multiscale positive-unlabeled detection of ai-generated texts. *arXiv preprint arXiv:2305.18149*.

Yuxia Wang, Jonibek Mansurov, Petar Ivanov, Jinyan Su, Artem Shelmanov, Akim Tsvigun, Osama Mohammed Afzal, Tarek Mahmoud, Giovanni Puccetti, and Thomas Arnold. 2024. SemEval-2024 task 8: Multidomain, multimodel and multilingual machine-generated text detection. In *Proceedings of the 18th International Workshop on Semantic Evaluation (SemEval-2024)*, pages 2057–2079, Mexico City, Mexico. Association for Computational Linguistics.

Yuxia Wang, Artem Shelmanov, Jonibek Mansurov, Akim Tsvigun, Vladislav Mikhailov, Rui Xing, Zhuohan Xie, Jiahui Geng, Giovanni Puccetti, Ekaterina Artemova, Jinyan Su, Minh Ngoc Ta, Mervat Abassy, Kareem Elozeiri, Saad El Dine Ahmed, Maiya Goloburda, Tarek Mahmoud, Raj Vardhan Tomar, Alexander Aziz, Nurkhan Laiyk, Osama Mohammed Afzal, Ryuto Koike, Masahiro Kaneko, Alham Fikri Aji, Nizar Habash, Iryna Gurevych, and Preslav Nakov. 2025. Genai content detection task 1: English and multilingual machine-generated text detection: Ai vs. human. In *Proceedings of the 1st Workshop on GenAI Content Detection (GenAIDetect)*, Abu Dhabi, UAE. International Conference on Computational Linguistics.

Zhengxuan Wu, Aryaman Arora, Zheng Wang, Atticus Geiger, Daniel Jurafsky, Christopher D. Manning, and Christopher Potts. 2024. Reft: Representation finetuning for language models. *ArXiv*, abs/2404.03592.

OSINT at GenAI Detection Task 1: Multilingual MGT Detection: Leveraging Cross-Lingual Adaptation for Robust LLMs Text Identification

Shifali Agrahari, Sanasam Ranbir Singh
Department of Computer Science and Engineering
Indian Institute of Technology Guwahati
{a.shifali, ranbir}@iitg.ac.in

Abstract

Detecting AI-generated text has become increasingly prominent. This paper presents our solution for the DAIGenC Task 1 Subtask 2, where we address the challenge of distinguishing human-authored text from machine-generated content, especially in multilingual contexts. We introduce Multi-Task Detection (MLDet), a model that leverages Cross-Lingual Adaptation and Model Generalization strategies for Multilingual Machine-Generated Text (MGT) detection. By combining language-specific embeddings with fusion techniques, MLDet creates a unified, language-agnostic feature representation, enhancing its ability to generalize across diverse languages and models. Our approach demonstrates strong performance, achieving macro and micro F1 scores of 0.7067 and 0.7187, respectively, and ranking 15th in the competition[1]. We also evaluate our model across datasets generated by different distinct models in many languages, showcasing its robustness in multilingual and cross-model scenarios.

1 Introduction

Large Language Models (LLMs) have been quickly adopted in mainstream, making machine-generated content readily available across various platforms, such as news, social media, Q&A forums, education and academics. Recent models, ChatGPT, GPT-4 and Llama, can deliver quality responses to diverse prompts. However, the ease with which these models can articulate human-like text has raised concerns about potential misuse and information integrity (Liao, 2020). Given that humans have very slim chance of distinguishing machine-generated text from human-written content, there is an urgent need for automated detection systems. Many researches are underway developing various methods and models to address the challenge of distinguish MGT from human-authored content. Most of these works focus on English text, but struggle to differentiate text in other languages effectively. While the overall accuracy is generally high, the class-wise F1 scores remain low.

To tackle these issues, The COLING 2025 Workshop on DAIGenC (Wang et al., 2025) *"Task 1: Binary Multilingual Machine-Generated Text (MGT) Detection (Human vs. Machine)"* aim to refresh training and testing data with generations from novel LLMs and include new languages. The task is framed as—*"determining whether a given text is generated by a machine or authored by a human"*— and is divided into two sub-tasks: Subtask A: English-only MGT detection. Subtask B: Multilingual MGT detection. This paper focuses on Subtask B.

Our approach for multilingual MGT detection includes Cross-Lingual Adaptation and Model Generalization strategies. This methodology leverages language-specific embeddings to improve generalization across languages and models. Through this our model, Multi-Task Detection **MLDet** aims to balanced performance on both macro and micro F1 scores.

2 Background

Over the last few years, numerous approaches have been proposed to tackle the task of Machine-generated text detection. Detecting machine-generated text is primarily formulated as a binary classification task (Zellers et al., 2019; Gehrmann et al., 2019; Ippolito et al., 2019), naively distinguishing between human-written and machine-generated text. In general, there are three main approaches: the supervised methods (Wang et al., 2023; Uchendu et al., 2021; Zellers et al., 2019; Zhong et al., 2020; Liu et al., 2023, 2022), the unsupervised ones, such as zero-shot methods (So-

[1]https://github.com/mbzuai-nlp/COLING-2025-Workshop-on-MGT-Detection-Task1/tree/main

Proceedings of the 1st Workshop on GenAI Content Detection (GenAIDetect), pages 184–190
January 19, 2025.

laiman et al., 2019; Ippolito et al., 2019; Mitchell et al., 2023; Su et al., 2023; Hans et al.; Shijaku and Canhasi, 2023) and Adversarial measures on detection accuracy (Susnjak and McIntosh, 2024; Liang et al., 2023), especially within the education domain. For example, Antoun et al. 2023 evaluates the robustness of detectors against character-level perturbations or misspelled words, focusing on French as a case study. Krishna et al. 2024 train a generative model (DIPPER) to paraphrase paragraphs to evade detection. Although supervised approaches yield relatively better results, they are susceptible to overfitting (Mitchell et al., 2023; Su et al., 2023).

There are few Multilingual MGT Detection techniques which are mainly based on finetuned models (Macko et al., 2023, 2024; Hashmi et al., 2024; Bahad et al., 2024).

3 Proposed Model

In this section, we outline our approach for multilingual MGT detection.

3.1 Dataset Description

There are three datasets provided by (Wang et al., 2025): Train, Dev, and Test. Training and development data with 7 columns id, source, sub_source, language, model, label and text for the development phase. Testing data for the Evaluation phase. The AI and Human text distribution is tabulated in Table 1.

Data	AI	Human	Total
Train	674,083	257,968	932,051
Dev	178,728	110,166	288,894
Test	77,791	73,634	151,425

Table 1: Data for AI and Human across three datasets.

Table 2 includes different AI text generation models, languages, and domains. Specifically, the text in the training and development datasets are generated using 43 distinct models, while the training dataset uses 20 different models. Additionally, the training dataset includes data in 9 languages, whereas the testing dataset contains text in 20 languages. These variations in models and languages are essential for training and evaluation processes. Detail of dataset mention in Section A.2

	lang	model	domain
Train	9	43	36
Dev	9	43	36
Test	16	20	27

Table 2: Table showing the different type of unique lang, model, and domain.

3.2 Language-Specific Embedding Extraction

Given the input text $x^{(l)}$ from the "text" column in language l, we obtain a feature vector $h^{(l)}$ using the pre-trained embedding model M_l specialized for the language l (e.g. *Chinese-BERT* (Sun et al., 2021) for Chinese, and *AraBERT* (Antoun et al., 2020) for Arabic) as $h^{(l)} = M_l(x^{(l)})$. Detail of Embedding models mention in Section A.3.1

This produces a feature vector that captures both language-specific and general semantic features. For handling unknown languages, we detect the language of input text and either use a default language model such as *XLM-RoBERTa* or fall back to an "unknown" embedding model, ensuring robustness across languages not explicitly included in the training set.

3.3 Cross-Lingual Fusion for Unified Representation

We combine embeddings from different languages in the dataset to create a unified representation as language-agnostic. Let $H = \{h^{(l_1)}, h^{(l_2)}, \ldots, h^{(l_n)}\}$ represent feature embeddings across languages.

Concatenation Fusion combines embeddings from various languages, as shown in equation 1. We then apply a weighted summation, where each language embedding $h^{(l)}$ is scaled by a learnable weight $w^{(l)}$, as shown in equation 2. The resulting fused embedding, $\mathbf{h}_{\text{fusion}}$, is passed through a Language Prediction Network, which predicts the language of the text. The output of this network is $\hat{y}_{lang}$ which is the Language model label, as described in equation 3.

$$h_{\text{fusion}} = [h^{(l_1)}; h^{(l_2)}; \ldots; h^{(l_n)}] \in \mathbb{R}^{n \times d} \quad (1)$$

$$h_{\text{fusion}} = \sum_{l \in \mathcal{L}} w^{(l)} h^{(l)} \quad (2)$$

$$\hat{y}_{lang} = f_{\text{language}}(\mathbf{h}_{\text{fusion}}) \quad (3)$$

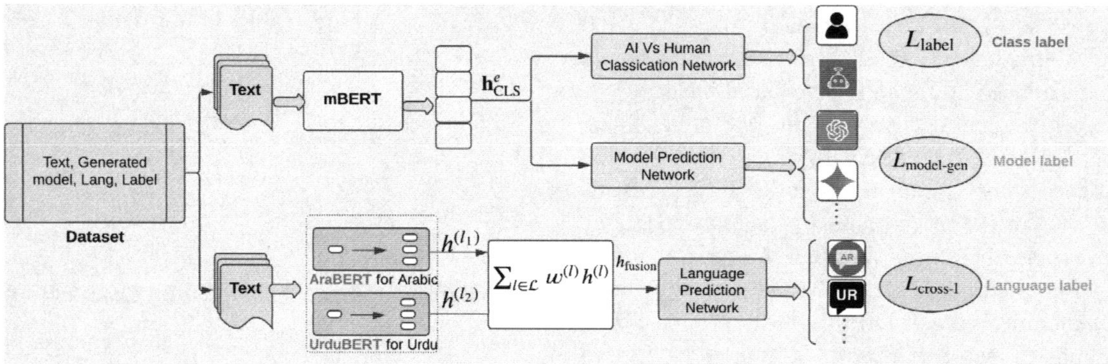

Figure 1: Proposed Detector model architecture: fusing stylometric features with a PLM embedding.

3.4 Cross-Lingual Consistency Loss

To enforce consistency across languages, we introduce a cross-lingual consistency loss that encourages similarity between embeddings of the same sample across languages. For each pair of languages (l_i, l_j) as shown in equation 4. This loss aligns embeddings across languages, promoting language-invariant features.

$$L_{\text{cross-}l} = \frac{1}{|\mathcal{L}|(|\mathcal{L}|-1)} \sum_{i \neq j} \|\hat{y}^{(l_i)}_{lang} - \hat{y}^{(l_j)}_{lang}\|^2 \quad (4)$$

The notation $|\mathcal{L}|$ denotes the total number of languages in this set.

3.5 Embedding Extraction with mBERT

Each text x from the "text" column, we pass it through mBERT, which produces a sequence of hidden states for each token in the text. The embedding corresponding to the $[CLS]$ token from the final hidden layer is then extracted as the representation for input text as shown in equation 5.

$$\mathbf{h}^e_{\text{CLS}} = \text{RoBERTa}(x)[\text{CLS}] \quad (5)$$

where, $\mathbf{h}^e_{\text{CLS}} \in \mathbb{R}^e$ is the CLS token embedding, and e is the embedding size of the model's output.

3.6 Model Generalization for MGT Detection

After obtaining the embedding $\mathbf{h}^e_{\text{CLS}}$, we pass it through the Model Prediction Network, which predicts the specific model responsible for generating the text. The output of this network is the predicted model label $\hat{y}_m$ as shown in equation 6.

$$\hat{y}_m = f_{\text{model}}(\mathbf{h}^e_{\text{CLS}}) \quad (6)$$

Given that the training and testing set includes 43 and 20 different models respectively, we introduce a model generalization loss to reduce reliance on specific training models.

The Cross-Model Pairwise Loss promote model-invariant features by minimizing the divergence between embeddings from different models, as in equation 7. Noise Augmentation adds Gaussian noise $\epsilon \sim \mathcal{N}(0, \sigma^2)$ during training to simulate unseen models as $\hat{y}^{\text{aug}}_m = \hat{y}_m + \epsilon$.

$$L_{\text{model-gen}} = \frac{1}{|\mathcal{M}|(|\mathcal{M}|-1)} \sum_{m \neq m'} \|\hat{y}_m - \hat{y}_{m'}\|^2 \quad (7)$$

$|\mathcal{M}|$ denotes the total number of generated model.

3.7 AI vs. Human Classification Network

The CLS token embedding $\mathbf{h}^e_{\text{CLS}}$ is passed to the AI vs. Human Classification Network. This network is a fully connected layer that outputs the probability of whether the text is human-written or machine-generated. The binary cross-entropy loss is used to compute the classification output as in equation 8.

$$L_{\text{label}} = -\frac{1}{N} \sum_{i=1}^{N} (y_i \log(\hat{y}_i) + (1-y_i)\log(1-\hat{y}_i)) \quad (8)$$

Where, $\hat{y}_i$ is the predicted probability for the i-th sample, y_i is the true label, N is the total number of samples.

3.8 Total Loss Function

Our model is optimized with a combination of label classification, cross-lingual, and model generalization losses. The total loss function is given by equation 9.

$$L_{\text{total}} = \alpha L_{\text{label}} + \beta L_{\text{cross-}l} + \gamma L_{\text{model-gen}} \quad (9)$$

where α, β, and γ are hyperparameters controlling the contributions of each component.

3.9 Training and Evaluation

We train the model by minimizing L_{total} with gradient descent using the AdamW optimizer. The CLS token embedding, which is 768 dimensions for mBERT serves as the input to fully connected hidden layers across the task-specific networks, each configured with 512 and 256 neurons and ReLU activations. The Macro F1 score used for evaluation to ensure balanced performance across classes. Further details of experimental setup in presented in section A.1.

During development phase, we consider different models with varied training strategies, detailed in Table 3. This includes direct fine-tuning of pre-trained language models (PLMs) such as *XLM-RoBERTa* (Wiciaputra et al., 2021) and *mBERT* (Wu and Dredze, 2020) as the initial model. Furthermore, the *mBERT + CM* model utilizes cross-model adaptation (Section 3.6), while the *mBERT + CL* model applies Cross-Lingual Fusion (Section 3.3). The ***MLDet*** model incorporates Cross-Lingual Adaptation and Model Generalization strategies, as described in Section 3.

4 Results

The comprehensive analysis of the performance of various models on MGT detection based on micro F1, macro F1 score and accuracy are presented in Table 3. Final model, **MTDet** achieves macro F1 (classwise) score of 0.7739, outperforming other models.

Model	Macro F1	Micro F1	Accu.
XLM-RoBERTa	0.4133	0.4631	0.4631
mBERT	0.5203	0.8352	0.8352
mBERT + CM	0.5832	0.8523	0.8521
mBERT + CL	0.6044	0.8264	0.8264
MTDet (Final)	0.7739	0.7938	0.7938

Table 3: Performance scores of different models on Dev Dataset.

The result of evaluating on the test dataset is tabulated in Table 4. Final model, **MLDet**, demonstrates a balanced performance on both macro and micro F1 scores, achieving 0.7067 and 0.7187 respectively. Although it does not reach the highest micro F1 score, its macro F1 performance suggests a more balanced generalization across different languages and domains, reflecting its robustness in multilingual MGT detection.

Test Model	Macro F1	Micro F1
XLM-RoBERTa	0.3876	0.6798
mBERT	0.4307	0.7135
mBERT + CM	0.5678	0.8123
mBERT + CL	0.4897	0.8650
MLDet (Final)	0.7067	0.7187

Table 4: Performance comparison of various test models on Macro and Micro F1 scores.

5 Analysis

The performance of our **MLDet** model, as presented in Tables 3 and 4, highlights its strengths in achieving a balanced Macro and Micro F1 score. While direct PLM (mBERT) models may perform better in terms of accuracy and Micro F1, their low Class-wise (Macro) F1 scores indicate a bias toward majority classes in the dataset (as discussed in Table 1). These models also struggle to handle diverse languages and text generated by different AI models. In comparison, the mBERT + CM model slightly outperforms the mBERT + CL model in accuracy and micro F1 but falls short in macro F1, highlighting the importance of adaptation to unseen language pairs and model generalization. Our final **MTDet** model (mBERT + CM + CL) successfully balances macro and micro F1 scores, showcasing the effectiveness of integrating advanced cross-lingual adaptation and model generalization strategies.

However, the final model performs better on the development dataset compared to the test dataset. As noted in Section 2, the languages and generation models in the training and development datasets are similar, whereas the test dataset introduces different languages and generation models. Despite this increased challenge, the model still outperforms others in this scenario.

6 Conclusions

In conclusion, the robust performance of **MLDet** on diverse multilingual datasets underscores the importance of incorporating cross-lingual adaptation and model generalization strategies. A robust performance on the test dataset with a macro F1 score of 0.7067. By capturing a wide range of linguistic and contextual information, these strategies allow the model to generalize effectively across languages and domains, positioning **MLDet** as a versatile and efficient solution for MGT detection in multilingual settings.

References

Wissam Antoun, Fady Baly, and Hazem Hajj. 2020. Arabert: Transformer-based model for arabic language understanding. *arXiv preprint arXiv:2003.00104*.

Wissam Antoun, Virginie Mouilleron, Benoît Sagot, and Djamé Seddah. 2023. Towards a robust detection of language model-generated text: Is chatgpt that easy to detect? In *Actes de CORIA-TALN 2023. Actes de la 30e Conférence sur le Traitement Automatique des Langues Naturelles (TALN), volume 1: travaux de recherche originaux–articles longs*, pages 14–27.

Sankalp Bahad, Yash Bhaskar, and Parameswari Krishnamurthy. 2024. Fine-tuning language models for ai vs human generated text detection. In *Proceedings of the 18th International Workshop on Semantic Evaluation (SemEval-2024)*, pages 918–921.

Sebastian Gehrmann, Hendrik Strobelt, and Alexander M Rush. 2019. Gltr: Statistical detection and visualization of generated text. *arXiv preprint arXiv:1906.04043*.

A Hans, A Schwarzschild, V Cherepanova, H Kazemi, A Saha, M Goldblum, J Geiping, and T Goldstein. Spotting llms with binoculars: Zero-shot detection of machine-generated text, 2024. *URL: https://arxiv.org/abs/2401.12070*.

Ehtesham Hashmi, Sule Yildirim Yayilgan, Ibrahim A Hameed, Muhammad Mudassar Yamin, Mohib Ullah, and Mohamed Abomhara. 2024. Enhancing multilingual hate speech detection: From language-specific insights to cross-linguistic integration. *IEEE Access*.

Daphne Ippolito, Daniel Duckworth, Chris Callison-Burch, and Douglas Eck. 2019. Automatic detection of generated text is easiest when humans are fooled. *arXiv preprint arXiv:1911.00650*.

Kalpesh Krishna, Yixiao Song, Marzena Karpinska, John Wieting, and Mohit Iyyer. 2024. Paraphrasing evades detectors of ai-generated text, but retrieval is an effective defense. *Advances in Neural Information Processing Systems*, 36.

Weixin Liang, Mert Yuksekgonul, Yining Mao, Eric Wu, and James Zou. 2023. Gpt detectors are biased against non-native english writers. *Patterns*, 4(7).

S Matthew Liao. 2020. *Ethics of artificial intelligence*. Oxford University Press.

Xiaoming Liu, Zhaohan Zhang, Yichen Wang, Hang Pu, Yu Lan, and Chao Shen. 2022. Coco: Coherence-enhanced machine-generated text detection under data limitation with contrastive learning. *arXiv preprint arXiv:2212.10341*.

Yikang Liu, Ziyin Zhang, Wanyang Zhang, Shisen Yue, Xiaojing Zhao, Xinyuan Cheng, Yiwen Zhang, and Hai Hu. 2023. Argugpt: evaluating, understanding and identifying argumentative essays generated by gpt models. *arXiv preprint arXiv:2304.07666*.

Dominik Macko, Jakub Kopal, Robert Moro, and Ivan Srba. 2024. Multisocial: Multilingual benchmark of machine-generated text detection of social-media texts. *arXiv preprint arXiv:2406.12549*.

Dominik Macko, Robert Moro, Adaku Uchendu, Jason Samuel Lucas, Michiharu Yamashita, Matúš Pikuliak, Ivan Srba, Thai Le, Dongwon Lee, Jakub Simko, et al. 2023. Multitude: Large-scale multilingual machine-generated text detection benchmark. *arXiv preprint arXiv:2310.13606*.

Eric Mitchell, Yoonho Lee, Alexander Khazatsky, Christopher D Manning, and Chelsea Finn. 2023. Detectgpt: Zero-shot machine-generated text detection using probability curvature. In *International Conference on Machine Learning*, pages 24950–24962. PMLR.

Rexhep Shijaku and Ercan Canhasi. 2023. Chatgpt generated text detection. *Publisher: Unpublished*.

Irene Solaiman, Miles Brundage, Jack Clark, Amanda Askell, Ariel Herbert-Voss, Jeff Wu, Alec Radford, Gretchen Krueger, Jong Wook Kim, Sarah Kreps, et al. 2019. Release strategies and the social impacts of language models. *arXiv preprint arXiv:1908.09203*.

Jinyan Su, Terry Yue Zhuo, Di Wang, and Preslav Nakov. 2023. Detectllm: Leveraging log rank information for zero-shot detection of machine-generated text. *arXiv preprint arXiv:2306.05540*.

Zijun Sun, Xiaoya Li, Xiaofei Sun, Yuxian Meng, Xiang Ao, Qing He, Fei Wu, and Jiwei Li. 2021. Chinesebert: Chinese pretraining enhanced by glyph and pinyin information. *arXiv preprint arXiv:2106.16038*.

Teo Susnjak and Timothy R McIntosh. 2024. Chatgpt: The end of online exam integrity? *Education Sciences*, 14(6):656.

Adaku Uchendu, Zeyu Ma, Thai Le, Rui Zhang, and Dongwon Lee. 2021. Turingbench: A benchmark environment for turing test in the age of neural text generation. *arXiv preprint arXiv:2109.13296*.

Yuxia Wang, Artem Shelmanov, Jonibek Mansurov, Akim Tsvigun, Vladislav Mikhailov, Rui Xing, Zhuohan Xie, Jiahui Geng, Giovanni Puccetti, Ekaterina Artemova, Jinyan Su, Minh Ngoc Ta, Mervat Abassy, Kareem Elozeiri, Saad El Dine Ahmed, Maiya Goloburda, Tarek Mahmoud, Raj Vardhan Tomar, Alexander Aziz, Nurkhan Laiyk, Osama Mohammed Afzal, Ryuto Koike, Masahiro Kaneko, Alham Fikri Aji, Nizar Habash, Iryna Gurevych, and Preslav Nakov. 2025. Genai content detection task 1: English and multilingual machine-generated text detection: Ai vs. human. In *Proceedings of the 1st Workshop on GenAI Content Detection*, Abu Dhabi, UAE. International Conference on Computational Linguistics.

Zecong Wang, Jiaxi Cheng, Chen Cui, and Chenhao Yu. 2023. Implementing bert and fine-tuned roberta to detect ai generated news by chatgpt. *ArXiv*, abs/2306.07401.

Yakobus Keenan Wiciaputra, Julio Christian Young, and Andre Rusli. 2021. Bilingual text classification in english and indonesian via transfer learning using xlm-roberta. *International Journal of Advances in Soft Computing & Its Applications*, 13(3).

Shijie Wu and Mark Dredze. 2020. Are all languages created equal in multilingual bert? *arXiv preprint arXiv:2005.09093*.

Rowan Zellers, Ari Holtzman, Hannah Rashkin, Yonatan Bisk, Ali Farhadi, Franziska Roesner, and Yejin Choi. 2019. Defending against neural fake news. *Advances in neural information processing systems*, 32.

Wanjun Zhong, Duyu Tang, Zenan Xu, Ruize Wang, Nan Duan, Ming Zhou, Jiahai Wang, and Jian Yin. 2020. Neural deepfake detection with factual structure of text. *arXiv preprint arXiv:2010.07475*.

A Example Appendix

A.1 Details of Experimental Setups

The experimental setup for this study includes a comprehensive range of hyperparameters, multilingual datasets, and model embeddings tailored to effectively detect machine-generated text across diverse languages and domains.

Key hyperparameters, mention in Table 4 such as learning rate, batch size, and dropout rate, were carefully tuned to optimize model performance. Additionally, weights for classification, domain, and cross-lingual loss were experimentally adjusted to ensure the model's adaptability to varied linguistic structures. The optimizer used was Adam, with specific parameters for Beta values and epsilon, while learning rate scheduling was customized based on experimental results. The setup is designed to capture fine-grained cross-lingual features, thereby enabling robust language-specific and language-agnostic pattern recognition.

A.2 Details of Dataset and Used Model

The table 2 summarizes the diversity in datasets: Train/Dev (9 lang, 43 models, 36 domains) and Test (16 lang, 20 models, 27 domains), highlighting broader testing scope.

A.2.1 Training Dataset detail

Traning dataset with 7 columns id,source, sub_source, language, model, label and text

Hyperparameter	**Typical Values**
Learning Rate (η)	$1e-5$ to $1e-3$
Batch Size	16, 32, 64
Number of Epochs	100 to 500
Weight for Classification Loss (λ)	Tuned based on experiment
Weight for Domain Loss (γ)	Tuned based on experiment
Weight for Cross-Lingual Loss (δ)	Tuned based on experiment
Dropout Rate	0.1 to 0.5
Gradient Reversal Layer Parameter	Tuned based on experiment
Hidden Layer Dimensions	Tuned based on experiment
Optimizer (Adam Parameters)	Beta1: 0.9, Beta2: 0.999, Epsilon: $1e-8$
Learning Rate Scheduler Parameters	Tuned based on experiment

Table 5: List of Hyper parameters for the Experiment during Training

The dataset includes diverse **languages** Table 6 with English (229,209 human, 381,467 AI) dominating, followed by Chinese (19,315 human, 15,969 AI). Bulgarian (4,205 human, 3,886 AI) and German (231 human, 4,462 AI) emphasize AI. Indonesian, Urdu, and Russian show balanced distributions, while Italian contains only AI samples (4,174).

The experimental setup includes diverse **generation models**: OpenAI's GPT series (`GPT-3.5-Turbo`, `Davinci`, `GPT4`), BLOOM models (`Bloomz`, `bloom_7b`), Meta's `Llama3`, `OPT`, and `Llama2-fine-tuned`, along with `Flan_T5`, `T0`, and specialized models (`Gemma`, `Jais-30b`). These cover multilingual and task-specific applications, emphasizing robust, fine-tuned, and scalable AI capabilities.

A.3 Testing Dataset details

The testing dataset expands the linguistic range, incorporating additional languages such as Kazakh, Norwegian, and Hindi as mention Table 8, thus testing the model's capacity to generalize to unseen linguistic contexts. A broad array of generative models, including recent releases like GPT-4, Llama, and Baichuan, are represented, allowing a thorough evaluation of the model's effectiveness

Language (Code)	Human	AI
Arabic (ar)	344	1770
Bulgarian (bg)	4205	3886
German (de)	231	4462
English (en)	229209	381467
Indonesian (id)	1895	2081
Italian (it)	0	4174
Russian (ru)	684	630
Urdu (ur)	2085	1676
Chinese (zh)	19315	15969

Table 6: Counts of Human and AI instances across languages in Training Dataset.

Language	Embedding
English	*RoBERTa*
Chinese	*Chinese-BERT*
Bulgarian	*XLM-RoBERTa*
German	*GottBERT*
Italian	*AlBERTo*
Indonesian	*IndoBERT*
Urdu	*UrduBERT*
Arabic	*AraBERT*
Russian	*RuBERT*

Table 7: Languages and their corresponding embeddings during Training.

Language	Human	AI
Arabic	4350	6320
Chinese	29947	33062
Dutch	600	600
German	1865	0
Hebrew	1182	0
Hindi	599	600
Indonesian	600	600
Italian	2496	2800
Japanese	300	300
Kazakh	1171	1300
Norwegian	1544	0
Russian	13039	13094
Spanish	600	600
Urdu	13190	17315
Vietnamese	1126	1200
Russian	1025	0

Table 8: Counts of Human and AI instances across various languages in Testing Dataset.

across diverse AI text generation systems. This experimental design facilitates a detailed assessment of the model's cross-lingual performance and robustness against various language models, ensuring comprehensive validation of the approach.

Model	Count
Human	73634
GPT-4o	28538
GPT-4o-mini	6845
gpt4o	6591
Vikhrmodels	6503
gpt-4o-2024-05-13	5998
Baichuan2-13B-Chat	5521
ChatGLM3-6B	5359
Llama 3.1 405B instruct	4000
gpt-4o	2400
gpt-4	1545
GPT-4-turbo	1400
glm-4-9b-chat	778
claude-3-5-sonnet	773
GPT4	299
Qwen	297
GPT3.5	297
ChatGLM	295
Baichuan	283
qwen2.5 72b	69

Table 9: Counts of instances for different models in Testing Dataset.

Table 9:The model distribution includes 73,634 human samples and a variety of AI models: `GPT-4o` (28,538), `GPT-4o-mini` (6,845), `Vikhrmodels` (6,503), and `gpt-4o-2024-05-13` (5,998). Other models include `Baichuan2-13B-Chat` (5,521), `ChatGLM3-6B` (5,359), `Llama 3.1 405B instruct` (4,000), and smaller counts for models like `GPT-4-turbo` (1,400), `glm-4-9b-chat` (778), and `GPT4` (299). The dataset highlights diverse AI capabilities across various architectures and scales.

A.3.1 Detail of Language-Specific Embedding Used

The dataset is organized by language, embedding models, and instance counts for human and AI content 6. Training spans nine languages with language-specific models (e.g., RoBERTa for English, Chinese-BERT for Chinese, AraBERT for Arabic) as mention Table 7, enabling nuanced feature extraction. It ensures a balanced multilingual setup, with English and Chinese dominating, and sufficient representation for Bulgarian, Indonesian, and Urdu.

Nota AI at GenAI Detection Task 1: Unseen Language-Aware Detection System for Multilingual Machine-Generated Text

Hancheol Park **Jaeyeon Kim** **Geonmin Kim** **Tae-Ho Kim**
Nota Inc.
{hancheol.park,jaeyeon.kim,geonmin.kim,thkim}@nota.ai

Abstract

Recently, large language models (LLMs) have demonstrated unprecedented capabilities in language generation, yet they still often produce incorrect information. Therefore, determining whether a text was generated by an LLM has become one of the factors that must be considered when evaluating its reliability. In this paper, we discuss methods to determine whether texts written in various languages were authored by humans or generated by LLMs. We have discovered that the classification accuracy significantly decreases for texts written in languages not observed during the training process, and we aim to address this issue. We propose a method to improve performance for unseen languages by using token-level predictive distributions extracted from various LLMs and text embeddings from a multilingual pre-trained language model. With the proposed method, we achieved third place out of 25 teams in Subtask B (binary multilingual machine-generated text detection) of Shared Task 1, with an F1 macro score of 0.7532.[1]

1 Introduction

Recently proposed large language models (LLMs) have demonstrated the ability to generate natural language with a level of fluency akin to that of humans, but they can still produce content that includes incorrect information (Azaria and Mitchell, 2023; Ji et al., 2023). Due to this fluency, people may not realize that the generated text contains inaccuracies, making it easier for false information to spread as if it were true. This can lead to various negative consequences. As a result, detecting text generated by LLMs has become increasingly important. In particular, with numerous language models now supporting multilingual text generation, identifying LLM-generated text across different languages has also become a significant research topic.

In this paper, we discuss methods to determine whether texts written in various languages are authored by humans or generated by LLMs. More specifically, we describe the system we developed for Subtask B of Shared Task 1 (i.e., binary multilingual machine-generated text (MGT) detection) (Wang et al., 2025) at the COLING 2025 Workshop on Detecting AI Generated Content (DAIGenC). The goal of this task is to develop a high-performance binary classification system. To create the dataset used in this task, a variety of LLMs, ranging from closed models such as GPT-4 to open-source models such as the LLaMA series (Dubey et al., 2024), were utilized. One of the main challenges in this shared task is that a significant number of samples in the evaluation set are written in languages that the models did not observe during the training phase.

It is known that when pretrained language models (PLMs)[2], which have been pre-trained on multilingual raw corpora, are fine-tuned with large-scale natural language understanding task datasets in specific languages, these models can effectively perform those tasks even on samples written in languages not observed during training (Gaim et al., 2023). This is referred to as zero-shot cross-lingual transfer learning (Artetxe et al., 2020). In this work, we conducted a preliminary study to examine the effectiveness of zero-shot cross-lingual transfer learning in multilingual MGT detection. We trained the *multilingual E5-large* (Wang et al., 2024) model on two different datasets. One dataset consisted of the entire training data provided for Subtask B of Shared Task 1, and the other was composed only

[1] Our code is available at https://github.com/nota-github/NotaAI_Multilingual_MGT_Detection

[2] Since LLMs are also pre-trained language models, there could be confusion regarding the terminology. In this paper, we will refer to encoder-based language models, such as *BERT* (Devlin et al., 2019) and *RoBERTa* (Liu et al., 2019), which have been used for natural language understanding tasks, as PLMs.

Proceedings of the 1st Workshop on GenAI Content Detection (GenAIDetect), pages 191–196
January 19, 2025.

of samples written in English from that dataset. Evaluation was conducted on 27,045 samples from the development set, excluding English samples. The model trained on the entire dataset showed a very high F1 score (0.9806), as there were no samples written in unseen languages. However, when the model was trained only on English samples, although there was some evidence of zero-shot cross-lingual transfer learning, a significant drop in performance was observed (F1 score: 0.7965).

In this work, samples written in seen languages are inferred using a multilingual PLM trained through a standard supervised fine-tuning approach. To more accurately distinguish the source of texts written in seen languages, we investigate various multilingual PLMs. However, for texts written in unseen languages, inference is performed differently from the traditional approach. To determine whether samples written in unseen languages are MGTs, we explore features that can be commonly used for the multilingual MGT detection task, regardless of the language.

In monolingual MGT detection, LLMs are known to assign high probability value to each generated token of the MGT (Sarvazyan et al., 2024). However, it is unclear whether this will be useful in multilingual MGT detection. This is because many unseen languages are likely low-resource languages with insufficient training data, meaning LLMs may not have learned many tokens for these languages. Therefore, it is uncertain whether LLMs will assign high probabilities to all tokens in texts written in such unseen languages. In this study, we examine the effectiveness of a model that uses token-level predictive distributions extracted from various LLMs as features for multilingual MGT detection. The previous study (Sarvazyan et al., 2024) used only the LLaMA-2 models, but we utilized various models to reflect the characteristics of different LLMs. To address the issue of differing tokenization results across models, we also propose a novel network architecture. Additionally, we found that using meaning representations extracted from a multilingual PLM that had not been fine-tuned further improved performance. Previously, such meaning representations were not utilized together.

The experimental results showed that token-level predictive distributions extracted from various LLMs and embeddings from a multilingual PLM are useful in multilingual MGT detection. The system we proposed achieved third place out of 25 teams in the Shared Task 1, with an F1 macro score of 0.7532.

2 System Overview

Our MGT detection system first identifies the language in which the given text is written. We use LangID[3] as the language identification tool. If the given text is written in a language observed during training, it is inferred using a model fine-tuned with supervised learning on a multilingual PLM (§2.1). Otherwise, it is inferred using a model that utilizes token-level predictive distributions extracted from various LLMs as features, along with a meaning representation from a multilingual PLM (§2.2).

2.1 Fine-Tuning a Multilingual PLM on a Labeled MGT Detection Dataset

If the given text is in a language present in the training data, inference is performed using a supervised fine-tuned multilingual PLM. The PLM is trained to solve the binary classification problem by minimizing the cross-entropy loss. After fine-tuning, we evaluated the performance of various multilingual PLMs using a development set composed solely of samples written in seen languages. We use the PLM that performed the best among them.

2.2 Multilingual MGT Detector for Unseen Languages

As features that can be commonly used in the multilingual MGT detection task regardless of the language, we utilize information from the predictive distributions of each token when a text is fed into LLMs. We extract three features, which are known to be useful in monolingual MGT detection (Sarvazyan et al., 2024), from the predictive distributions of each token.

- **Log probabilty of the predicted token (F1):** This feature represents the log probability of the next token predicted with the highest probability for a given token input from an LLM.
- **Log probabilty of the generated token (F2):** This feature is the log probability of the token actually generated for a given token input in the LLM.
- **Entropy of the predictive distribution (F3):** It represents the entropy value of the probability distribution of the predicted next tokens.

[3]https://github.com/saffsd/langid.py

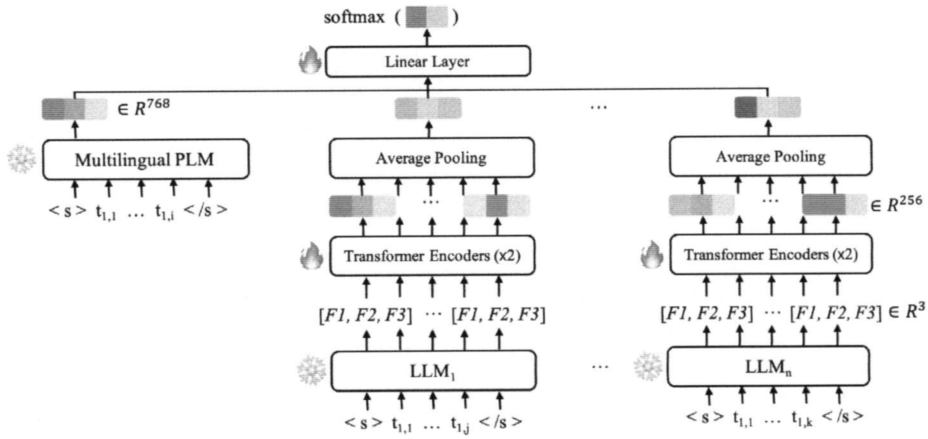

Figure 1: A description of the proposed model for classifying whether a text written in an unseen language is MGT or not. The ice symbol represents a module whose parameters are not updated during training, while the flame symbol indicates a module whose parameters are updated.

As shown in Figure 1, tokenized sample texts are fed into N different LLMs. Since each LLM has a different tokenization method, the given input text may be split into a different number of tokens. The three features extracted from the predictive distributions for each token are then used as inputs to the transformer encoder, producing 256 dimensional hidden states. These features are combined into a single feature vector for all input tokens through average pooling. The feature vectors extracted from the LLMs are concatenated and serve as input to the classifier (i.e., linear layer). In this study, we use three different LLMs.

We also utilize the meaning representation extracted from a multilingual PLM. As a preliminary study, we translated 20 random English texts into all the languages used in the training and devtest sets provided for this shared task, and then extracted text embeddings from *XLM-RoBERTa-base* (Conneau et al., 2020). We considered the hidden state of the <s> token in the last layer as the text embedding, and visualized these embeddings in 2D using t-SNE. As a result, texts sharing similar meanings were positioned close to each other, regardless of the language, while texts with different meanings were positioned farther apart. This phenomenon has been widely discussed in previous research (Ding et al., 2022). Although this feature is language-agnostic and its relation to multilingual MGT is still uncertain, empirically, we observed that this feature improves the MGT detection performance. Before applying this feature, the F1 score on the development set was 0.7114, but it improved significantly to 0.7370. As a result, our system utilizes this feature as well.

One plausible reason why the meaning representation could be useful is the following: LLMs often generate texts that deviate from common sense. Unless multilingual PLMs are intentionally trained to learn noise, these texts are likely to differ significantly from the common-sense knowledge learned by the PLMs. In other words, texts containing such incorrect information may be out-of-distribution samples and could be represented far from samples containing accurate knowledge in the embedding space. We will examine this hypothesis further in future work.

We trained this detector using the features described so far, optimizing it to minimize the cross-entropy loss. The specific language models we used are described in more detail in Section 3.2.

3 Implementation Details

3.1 Datasets

The datasets provided in Shared Task 1 is as follows: For model training, 674,083 training samples and 288,894 samples from the development set are used. Both of these datasets consist of samples written in the same nine languages. For leaderboard evaluation, the devtest dataset and the test set contain 74,081 and 151,425 samples, respectively, with samples written in 11 and 16 different languages.

	F1
XLM-R_{Base}	0.9426
XLM-R_{Large}	0.9648
mE5$_{Base}$	0.9653
mE5$_{Large}$	**0.9728**

Table 1: Performance of fine-tuned multilingual PLMs on the development set

Rank	Team	F1 Macro	F1 Micro
1	Grape	0.7916	0.7962
2	rockstart	0.7557	0.7564
3	**Nota AI (Ours)**	**0.7532**	**0.7591**
4	LuxVeri	0.7513	0.7527
5	TechExperts(IPN)	0.7463	0.7474
6	azlearning	0.7436	0.7449
7	nampfiev1995	0.7427	0.7440
	Baseline	0.7416	0.7426

Table 2: Top 7 leaderboard for Shared Task1

3.2 Models

The models used in our proposed system are as follows: For samples written in seen languages, we used the fine-tuned *multilingual e5-large* model because this model showed the best performance on the development set among various mutlingual PLMs (see Table 1). For samples written in unseen languages, we used *XLM-RoBERTa-base* as the multilingual PLM. Additionally, since our method uses various LLMs, we aimed to reduce computational costs for inference by employing the following smaller LLMs (sLLMs): *Llama-3.2-1B-Instruct* (Dubey et al., 2024), *Qwen2.5-1.5B-Instruct* (Team, 2024), and *Phi-3-mini-128k-instruct* (Abdin et al., 2024). We have confirmed that these three sLLMs have already learned all the languages used in the training, development, and devtest sets.

3.3 Hyperparameters

All PLMs used in this experiment were trained with the same hyperparameters. The learning rate was set to 5e-5 with a linear decay. We trained for 3 epochs, with a warmup ratio of 0.01, and selected the models that showed the best performance on the development set. The AdamW optimizer (Loshchilov and Hutter, 2019) was used for parameter updates, and the weight decay was set to 0.1. The model that uses predictive distribution information was trained with the following hyperparameters: it was trained for 50 epochs with a learning rate of 2e-4 and linear decay. Both the weight decay and warmup ratio were set to 0.01.

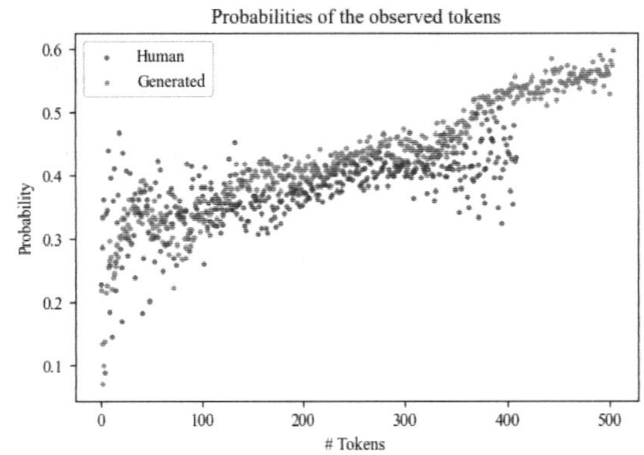

Figure 2: The average probability assigned by the LLM to the generated tokens, based on the token length of the text. The measurements were taken using samples of unseen languages from the devtest set, and the probabilities of the generated tokens were calculated using *Llama-3.2-1B-Instruct*.

4 Results and Discussion

4.1 Leaderboard

As described in Table 2, we achieved third place out of 25 teams in Subtask B (binary multilingual MGT detection) of Shared Task 1, with an F1 macro score of 0.7532.

4.2 Discussion

As mentioned in Section 2.2, it is uncertain whether token-level predictive distributions are helpful for samples written in unseen languages in multilingual MGT detection. To investigate this, we examined the average probabilities of generated tokens for samples from unseen languages in the devtest set, categorized by token length. As shown in Figure 2, we observed that higher probabilities are assigned to generated text compared to human-written text. In other words, this can be considered a discriminative feature for determining whether the text is MGT.

Furthermore, we investigated whether the proposed method is actually effective for samples in unseen languages. We trained the model on English data only and then evaluated the MGT detection performance on samples written in unseen languages from the devtest set. When compared to the *multilingual E5-large* model (F1: 0.9030), which performed zero-shot cross-lingual transfer learning, our method showed better performance with an F1 score of 0.9175.

5 Conclusion

In this work, we proposed a system for determining whether samples written in unseen languages are MGTs or not, and our approach achieved third place in Subtask B of Shared Task 1. However, while we obtained a relatively high F1 score compared to the baseline, it was not significantly higher. For future work, we should focus more on investigating features that can better distinguish samples in unseen languages.

Limitations

We achieved a high rank of third place in this shared task, but there are some limitations in our methods. First, our approach relies on distinguishing between languages, which means that misidentifying the language type increases the likelihood of making an incorrect classification for that sample. Additionally, while we utilize sLLMs, extracting token-level predictive distributions involves significant computational costs.

Acknowledgments

This work was supported by Artificial intelligence industrial convergence cluster development project funded by the Ministry of Science and ICT (MSIT, Korea) & Gwangju Metropolitan City.

References

Marah Abdin, Jyoti Aneja, Hany Awadalla, Ahmed Awadallah, Ammar Ahmad Awan, Nguyen Bach, Amit Bahree, Arash Bakhtiari, Jianmin Bao, Harkirat Behl, et al. 2024. Phi-3 technical report: A highly capable language model locally on your phone. *arXiv preprint arXiv:2404.14219*.

Mikel Artetxe, Sebastian Ruder, and Dani Yogatama. 2020. On the cross-lingual transferability of monolingual representations. In *Proceedings of the 58th Annual Meeting of the Association for Computational Linguistics*, pages 4623–4637, Online. Association for Computational Linguistics.

Amos Azaria and Tom Mitchell. 2023. The internal state of an LLM knows when it's lying. In *Findings of the Association for Computational Linguistics: EMNLP 2023*, pages 967–976, Singapore. Association for Computational Linguistics.

Alexis Conneau, Kartikay Khandelwal, Naman Goyal, Vishrav Chaudhary, Guillaume Wenzek, Francisco Guzmán, Edouard Grave, Myle Ott, Luke Zettlemoyer, and Veselin Stoyanov. 2020. Unsupervised cross-lingual representation learning at scale. In *Proceedings of the 58th Annual Meeting of the Association for Computational Linguistics*, pages 8440–8451, Online. Association for Computational Linguistics.

Jacob Devlin, Ming-Wei Chang, Kenton Lee, and Kristina Toutanova. 2019. BERT: Pre-training of deep bidirectional transformers for language understanding. In *Proceedings of the 2019 Conference of the North American Chapter of the Association for Computational Linguistics: Human Language Technologies, Volume 1 (Long and Short Papers)*, pages 4171–4186, Minneapolis, Minnesota. Association for Computational Linguistics.

Kunbo Ding, Weijie Liu, Yuejian Fang, Weiquan Mao, Zhe Zhao, Tao Zhu, Haoyan Liu, Rong Tian, and Yiren Chen. 2022. A simple and effective method to improve zero-shot cross-lingual transfer learning. In *Proceedings of the 29th International Conference on Computational Linguistics*, pages 4372–4380, Gyeongju, Republic of Korea. International Committee on Computational Linguistics.

Abhimanyu Dubey, Abhinav Jauhri, Abhinav Pandey, Abhishek Kadian, Ahmad Al-Dahle, Aiesha Letman, Akhil Mathur, Alan Schelten, Amy Yang, Angela Fan, et al. 2024. The llama 3 herd of models. *arXiv preprint arXiv:2407.21783*.

Fitsum Gaim, Wonsuk Yang, Hancheol Park, and Jong Park. 2023. Question-answering in a low-resourced language: Benchmark dataset and models for Tigrinya. In *Proceedings of the 61st Annual Meeting of the Association for Computational Linguistics (Volume 1: Long Papers)*, pages 11857–11870, Toronto, Canada. Association for Computational Linguistics.

Ziwei Ji, Nayeon Lee, Rita Frieske, Tiezheng Yu, Dan Su, Yan Xu, Etsuko Ishii, Ye Jin Bang, Adrea Madotto, and Pascale Fung. 2023. Survey of hallucination in natural language generation. *ACM Computing Surveys*, 55:1–38.

Yinhan Liu, Myle Ott, Naman Goyal, Jingfei Du, Mandar Joshi, Danqi Chen, Omer Levy, Mike Lewis, Luke Zettlemoyer, and Veselin Stoyanov. 2019. Roberta: A robustly optimized bert pretraining approach. *arXiv preprint arXiv:1907.11692*.

Ilya Loshchilov and Frank Hutter. 2019. Decoupled weight decay regularization. In *International Conference on Learning Representations*.

Areg Mikael Sarvazyan, José Ángel González, and Marc Franco-salvador. 2024. Genaios at SemEval-2024 task 8: Detecting machine-generated text by mixing language model probabilistic features. In *Proceedings of the 18th International Workshop on Semantic Evaluation (SemEval-2024)*, pages 101–107, Mexico City, Mexico. Association for Computational Linguistics.

Qwen Team. 2024. Qwen2.5: A party of foundation models.

Liang Wang, Nan Yang, Xiaolong Huang, Linjun Yang, Rangan Majumder, and Furu Wei. 2024. The llama 3 herd of models. *arXiv preprint arXiv:2402.05672*.

Yuxia Wang, Artem Shelmanov, Jonibek Mansurov, Akim Tsvigun, Vladislav Mikhailov, Rui Xing, Zhuohan Xie, Jiahui Geng, Giovanni Puccetti, Ekaterina Artemova, Jinyan Su, Minh Ngoc Ta, Mervat Abassy, Kareem Elozeiri, Saad El Dine Ahmed, Maiya Goloburda, Tarek Mahmoud, Raj Vardhan Tomar, Alexander Aziz, Nurkhan Laiyk, Osama Mohammed Afzal, Ryuto Koike, Masahiro Kaneko, Alham Fikri Aji, Nizar Habash, Iryna Gurevych, and Preslav Nakov. 2025. GenAI content detection task 1: English and multilingual machine-generated text detection: AI vs. human. In *Proceedings of the 1st Workshop on GenAI Content Detection (GenAIDetect)*, Abu Dhabi, UAE. International Conference on Computational Linguistics.

CNLP-NITS-PP at GenAI Detection Task 1: AI-Generated Text Using Transformer-Based Approaches

Annepaka Yadagiri, Reddi Mohana Krishna, L D M S Sai Teja, M Srikar Vardhan and Partha Pakray
Department of Computer Science & Engineering
National Institute of Technology Silchar, Assam, India, 788010
{annepaka22_rs, redd_pg_23, lekkalad_ug, mangadoddis_ug, partha}@cse.nits.ac.in

Abstract

In the current digital landscape, distinguishing between text generated by humans and that created by large language models has become increasingly complex. This challenge is exacerbated by advanced LLMs such as the Gemini, ChatGPT, GPT-4, and LLaMa, which can produce highly sophisticated, human-like text. This indistinguishability introduces a range of challenges across different sectors. Cybersecurity increases the risk of social engineering and misinformation, while social media aids the spread of biased or false content. The educational sector faces issues of academic integrity, and within large, multi-team environments, these models add complexity to managing interactions between human and AI agents. To address these challenges, we approached the problem as a binary classification task using an English-language benchmark COLING dataset. We employed transformer-based neural network models, including *BERT*, *DistilBERT*, and *RoBERTa*, fine-tuning each model with optimized hyperparameters to maximize classification accuracy. Our team, *CNLP-NITS-PP* has achieved the 23rd rank in subtask 1 at Coling-2025 for machine-generated text detection in English with a Main Score (*F1 Macro*) of 0.6502 and *micro-F1* score of 0.6876.

1 Introduction

Large Language Models (*LLMs*) represent a significant advancement in Natural Language Processing (*NLP*), advancing development in applications such as machine translation, text analysis, text generation, and question answering (Bommasani et al., 2021; Chowdhery et al., 2023). In academic, industrial, and everyday contexts, the increasing deployment of LLM-powered applications, such as ChatGPT[1], highlights their transformative potential. However, this rapid integration also underscores the importance of understanding their capabilities and limitations to manage expectations and address ethical, societal, and technical challenges effectively (Bender et al., 2021).

Detecting AI-Generated Text (*AGT*) focuses on leveraging Artificial Intelligence (*AI*) to identify and distinguish content produced by AI from Human-Written Text (*HWT*). This area has gained significant importance due to the rapid advancements in Deep Learning (*DL*), which have enabled widespread applications of AGT in content creation, virtual assistants, and more. However, these developments also introduce challenges, including the propagation of misinformation, potential privacy violations, and ethical risks (Al-kfairy et al., 2024). Consequently, AGT detection has emerged as a critical domain in AI research, aimed at mitigating these challenges and ensuring accountability in using generative AI technologies (Bender et al., 2021).

AGT detection research has emerged as a critical area within NLP, driven by advancements in DL. The introduction of robust models, such as Recurrent Neural Networks (*RNN*) (Lipton, 2015), Long Short-Term Memory Networks (*LSTM*) (Hochreiter, 1997), and Transformers (Vaswani, 2017), has significantly enhanced AI capabilities in text generation. These models now produce high-quality content, including articles, dialogues, and news reports. However, their misuse poses substantial risks, such as disseminating misinformation, deception of readers, and propagation of harmful content.

DL plays a pivotal role in generating AGT. DL models can produce realistic and coherent text by analyzing linguistic patterns and structures through training on extensive datasets. Pre-Trained Language Models (PLMs) based on the Transformer architecture (*e.g., GPT-3, BERT*) have demonstrated exceptional performance across various NLP tasks, contributing significantly to AGT development (Vaswani, 2017; Brown, 2020).

However, the widespread adoption of DL tech-

[1] https://chatgpt.com/

Proceedings of the 1st Workshop on GenAI Content Detection (GenAIDetect), pages 197–202
January 19, 2025. ©2025 International Conference on Computational Linguistics

niques for AGT generation has raised several challenges. These include the potential for spreading misinformation, such as AI-generated fake news and deceptive advertisements that could influence public opinion (Al-kfairy et al., 2024). Additionally, personal data may be exploited to generate misleading or targeted fraudulent content (Bender et al., 2021). Furthermore, DL-powered AI can be misused to create inappropriate material, including violent, pornographic, or hate speech content, which may be widely disseminated (Zellers et al., 2019).

Numerous researchers are developing strategies to detect and identify problematic content to address the challenges associated with AGT. These strategies include rule-based and statistical approaches, as well as ML techniques like Support Vector Machines (*SVM*) and Random Forests (*RF*), which are commonly used for building detection models (Aristantia et al., 2024). Additionally, combining these techniques with DL models, such as those based on the Transformer architecture, is being explored to improve detection accuracy. This paper introduces a tool designed to detect LLM-generated AI text using Transformer-based models to improve detection accuracy and provide insights for future research.

2 Related Work

Various commercial and open-source tools, such as GPTZero, ZeroGPT[2], AI Content Detector, and GPT-2 Output Detector (Mitchell et al., 2023), have emerged to detect AI-generated content effectively. Additionally, active research focuses on curating specialized datasets and determining which features and classifiers can enhance classification performance. For example, (Yu et al., 2023) compiled a dataset of human and AI-generated abstracts to assess commercial and non-commercial detection systems, though the dataset is currently limited to English.

Recent studies have experimented with different detection methodologies, such as using *XGBoost classifiers* (Shijaku and Canhasi, 2023), decision tree algorithms (Zaitsu and Jin, 2023), and transformer-based models (Guo et al., 2023). Notably, analyzed text from English customer reviews, developing a transformer-based classifier that achieved a classification accuracy of 79%. These efforts demonstrate a trend toward optimizing detection systems, enhancing reliability, and expanding detection capabilities across various languages and text types.

[2]https://www.zerogpt.com/

3 Proposed Methodology

3.1 Problem Statement

Given the rapid advancements and adoption of LLMs, it is increasingly challenging to differentiate between HWT and AGT. Identifying AGT can be defined as a classification problem: determining whether a given sequence of words $S = \{w_1, w_2, \ldots, w_n\}$ was generated by an AI model or by a human.

Formally, let S represent a text sample of n words. The problem can then be framed as:

- **Input:** A text sample S where $S = \{w_1, w_2, \ldots, w_n\}$.
- **Output:** A binary label $y \in \{0, 1\}$, where:
  - $y = 0$ *denotes HWT,*
  - $y = 1$ *denotes AGT.*

3.2 Dataset Description

In the COLING Workshop on MGT Detection Task 1, a binary classification approach is employed to distinguish whether a given text is generated by an AI or authored by a human (Wang et al., 2025). A diverse dataset is compiled by initially gathering English-language datasets, including HC3 (Guo et al., 2023), MAGE (Li et al., 2024), and M4GT (Wang et al., 2024). These datasets are subsequently merged and refined into a final consolidated dataset for further analysis. The statistical properties of the refined dataset are presented in Table 1. In contrast, Figure 1 visually compares the training and development datasets.

Label	English	
	Train Count	**Dev Count**
Human	228,922	98,328
AI	381,845	163,430
Total	610,767	261,758

Table 1: Dataset Label Counts for English Train and English Dev

3.3 System Description

This paper presents our methodology and results for the MGT Detection Task 1, which focuses on identifying AGT. The primary objective of this task

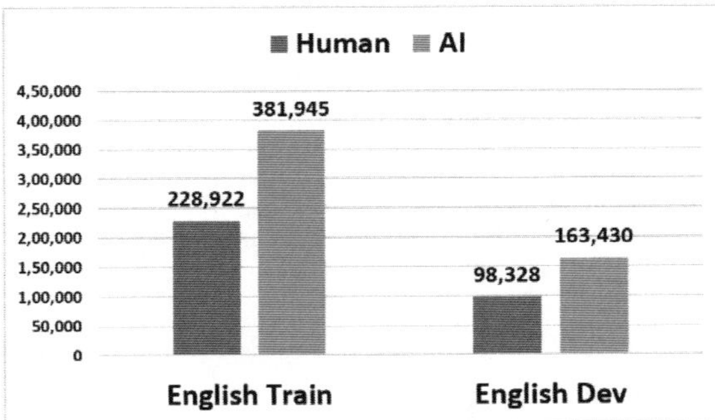

Figure 1: Visually compared to Train and Dev dataset

Parameter	Value
Activation Function	Sigmoid
Optimizer	AdamW
Loss Function	binary_crossentropy
Learning Rate	2×10^{-5}
Batch Size	16
Number of Epochs	03
Dropout	0.2
ModelCheckpoint	Yes
EarlyStopping	Yes
Patience	5

Table 2: Hyperparameters utilized across all experiments

is to classify whether a given text segment has been produced by a machine or authored by a human. Our participation was specifically in Subtask A, which deals exclusively with English texts.

We employed a two-pronged approach combining the fine-tuned **DistilBERT** model (Sanh, 2019), optimized for capturing semantic nuances, and a rule-based feature extraction strategy. Key **hyperparameters** were adjusted to enhance performance for the task as shown in Table 2.

In parallel, we implemented a rule-based approach to extract a set of **linguistic and statistical features** that could complement the semantic insights of the model. These features included measures such as **Average Line Length, Vocabulary richness, Word Density, and Part-Of-Speech (POS) tag distributions**, computed for each text sample. Such features were chosen based on their potential to highlight subtle stylistic and structural differences between HWT and AGT. The following sample text is from the COLING dataset.

Sample text = *"Hitler's plans for the succession and power structure after his death are shrouded in mystery, as he never explicitly wrote down his intentions. However, it is known that he designated several potential successors, including Heinrich Himmler, Hermann Göring, and Joseph Goebbels, each with their own strengths and weaknesses."*

Average Line Lenght: In NLP, the average line length refers to the mean number of words per line in a given text dataset (Guo et al., 2023).

$$\text{Average line length} = \frac{\text{Total word count}}{\text{Total line count}} \quad (1)$$

For example, consider the above sample text: Total word count = 63, Total line count = 2. Thus, the average line length is 31.5 words per line.

Vocabulary Richness: It quantifies the uniqueness of words within a given text (Guo et al., 2023).

$$\text{Vocabulary Richness} = \frac{\text{Total Number of Words}}{\text{Number of Unique Words}} \quad (2)$$

For the above sample text, the number of unique words is 43, and the total number of words is 63, so we got the vocabulary richness as 0.746.

Word Density: In NLP, word density measures the concentration of unique words in a given text (Guo et al., 2023).

$$\text{Word Density} = \frac{100 \cdot \text{Vocabulary Size}}{\text{No of Lines} \cdot \text{Average Line Len}} \quad (3)$$

For the above sample text, the unique word count is 43, the average line length is 31.5, and the number of lines is 2, so we got the word density as 74.6.

Part-Of-Speech tag: POS tags are labels assigned to each word in a text to indicate its grammatical category, such as noun, verb, adjective, etc (Guo et al., 2023).

The above sample text contains various POS distributed as follows: Nouns (*NN, NNS, NNP, NNPS*) appear 13 times, with words like "plans", "succession", "power", and proper nouns like "Himmler", "Goebbels", and "Göring." Verbs (*VB, VBD, VBG, VBN, VBP, VBZ*) are used 7 times, including "are," "shrouded," "wrote," and "designated." Punctuation marks (*., „ :, (,), ", ", "" ', !, ?, ;,* -) occur 7 times, such as in "mystery", "death", and "intentions". Determiners (*DT, PDT, WDT*) appear 6 times, including words like "the" and "his". Pronouns (*PRP*) are used 6 times, such as "his," "he," and "it". Proper nouns (*NNP, NNPS*) also occur 7 times, such as "Hitler's", "Heinrich", and "Himmler". Adjectives (*JJ, JJR, JJS*) appear 2 times with words like "potential" and "own". Auxiliary verbs (*MD*) do not appear in the text. Adverbs (*RB, RBR, RBS*) are used 3 times, including "never" and "explicitly". Particles (*RP*) appear once with "down",

Subordinating conjunctions (*IN*) are used 6 times, including "for," "after," and "that". Numbers (*CD*) are absent in this text. Foreign words (*FW*) and interjections (*UH*) do not appear. Prepositions (*IN*) like "for" and "with" are used 6 times. Symbols (*SYM*) and spaces (*SP*) are not present, and coordinating conjunctions (*CC*) such as "and" appear 3 times.

The extracted linguistic features were subsequently integrated with the DistilBERT-based embeddings, creating a hybrid feature set that combines text-based and numerical characteristics. This integration aimed to enhance the system's ability to distinguish between the two types of content by leveraging deep semantic understanding and surface-level textual patterns. Below is the architecture description.

Architecture Description: The custom model architecture described in Figure 2 combines a pre-trained DistilBERT model with additional feature processing for sequence classification. The model uses the **DistilBERTForSequenceClassification** module, which includes the **DistilBERTModel** for generating contextual embeddings. The model leverages a transformer-based architecture, comprising six layers of TransformerBlocks, each consisting of MultiHeadSelfAttention and a **Feed-Forward Network (FFN)** with *GELU* activation. These blocks enable the model to capture complex relationships within input sequences. The model further incorporates a pre-classifier layer that refines the BERT output by projecting it to a 768-dimensional space, followed by a final classifier layer that reduces the dimensionality to two output nodes for classification. A dropout layer with a 0.2 rate is also used to prevent overfitting. Beyond the BERT layers, the model also integrates a fully connected layer **(feature_fc)** that processes additional input features, followed by a **ReLU** activation and another dropout layer (*0.3 rate*). It is important to note that the additional features are not separately normalized, and the activation function (*ReLU*) is applied directly within the neural network layers, which ensures that normalization is not exclusively used on the features. Finally, the outputs from the BERT model (*768*) and the additional features from the neural network layer with ReLU activation (*64*) are concatenated and passed through a final classifier layer (*832 input features*) and subjected to a **sigmoid** activation function, which outputs probabilities for each of the two classes. This design combines the robust contextual understanding of DistilBERT with additional feature-based inputs for enhanced predictive performance in sequence classification tasks.

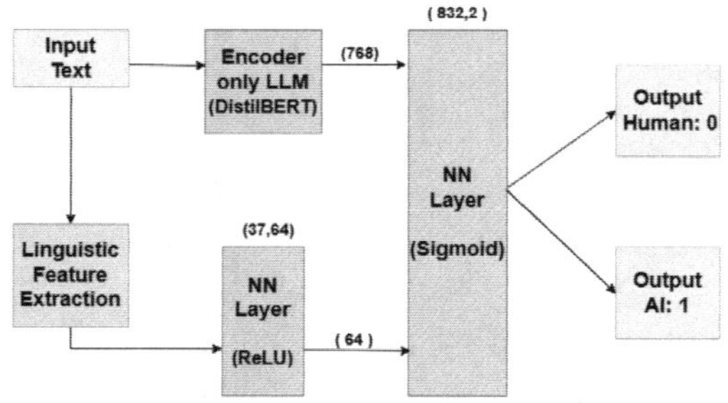

Figure 2: Training Architecture for AGT Detection

Our final system demonstrated strong performance, achieving an **F1 score** of **0.6513** on the test set for Subtask A. This placed us **23rd** out of 36 participating teams, reflecting the competitiveness of our approach. While there is room for further improvement, our results underscore the **effectiveness of combining transformer-based embeddings with handcrafted linguistic features**, showcasing the potential of hybrid models in AI text detection tasks.

3.4 Results Analysis

The comparison between the baseline results in Table 3 and the results obtained using linguistic features in Table 4 underscores the significant benefits of incorporating linguistic features. Training accuracy increased notably from **84.28** to **92.32**, accompanied by a substantial reduction in training loss from **0.355** to **0.193**. Validation metrics also showed measurable improvements, with accuracy rising from **79.25** to **81.62** and the F1-score increasing from **0.773** to **0.818**. These results highlight linguistic feature's efficacy in enhancing training and validation performance, indicating their value in improving model robustness and generalization.

The results from the leaderboard are displayed in Table 5, showcasing our team's achievements. These results were achieved using the DistilBERT model enhanced with linguistic features, with hyperparameters tuned as illustrated in Table 2.

4 Conclusion

Our approach to the MGT Detection Task 1 effectively combined DistilBERT's semantic embeddings with rule-based linguistic features and hyperparameters. This hybrid strategy enhanced

Epoch	Dataset	Accuracy	Loss	F1 Score
1	Train	0.842	0.355	0.835
	Val	0.792	0.631	0.773
2	Train	0.878	0.286	0.872
	Val	0.799	0.343	0.801
3	Train	0.890	0.225	0.895
	Val	0.801	0.372	0.804

Table 3: Baseline Results for Training and Validation Metrics

Epoch	Dataset	Accuracy	Loss	F1 Score
1	Train	0.858	0.323	0.863
	Val	0.808	0.428	0.812
2	Train	0.894	0.253	0.897
	Val	0.815	0.433	0.816
3	Train	0.923	0.193	0.925
	Val	0.816	0.486	0.818

Table 4: Training and Validation Metrics Using Linguistic Features

the model's ability to distinguish between human-written and AI-generated text. The model showed steady improvement during training, with training accuracy rising from 85.83 to 92.32 and the F1 score increasing from 0.863 to 0.925. On the test set, our system achieved a **Main F1 Macro score of 0.6502** and an **Auxiliary F1 Micro score of 0.6876**, ranking 23rd out of 36 teams. These results demonstrate the effectiveness of our feature integration approach, though future work should focus on improving generalization through better feature selection and regularization.

Task	Main (F1 Macro)	Auxiliary (F1 Micro)
English	0.6502	0.6876

Table 5: Test Results by Leaderboard

References

Mousa Al-kfairy, Dheya Mustafa, Nir Kshetri, Mazen Insiew, and Omar Alfandi. 2024. Ethical challenges and solutions of generative ai: an interdisciplinary perspective. In *Informatics*, volume 11, page 58. MDPI.

Dita Wahyuni Aristantia, Muhammad Baharuddin, Nur Mazidah, and Zaenab Tri Lestari. 2024. Learning model of arabic in indonesia?: A study of the curriculum system at bahrul ulum tambakberas islamic boarding school, jombang and an-nuqayah, madura. *Edumaspul: Jurnal Pendidikan*, 8(1):485–499.

Emily M Bender, Timnit Gebru, Angelina McMillan-Major, and Shmargaret Shmitchell. 2021. On the dangers of stochastic parrots: Can language models be too big? In *Proceedings of the 2021 ACM conference on fairness, accountability, and transparency*, pages 610–623.

Rishi Bommasani, Drew A Hudson, Ehsan Adeli, Russ Altman, Simran Arora, Sydney von Arx, Michael S Bernstein, Jeannette Bohg, Antoine Bosselut, Emma Brunskill, et al. 2021. On the opportunities and risks of foundation models. *arXiv preprint arXiv:2108.07258*.

Tom B Brown. 2020. Language models are few-shot learners. *arXiv preprint arXiv:2005.14165*.

Aakanksha Chowdhery, Sharan Narang, Jacob Devlin, Maarten Bosma, Gaurav Mishra, Adam Roberts, Paul Barham, Hyung Won Chung, Charles Sutton, Sebastian Gehrmann, et al. 2023. Palm: Scaling language modeling with pathways. *Journal of Machine Learning Research*, 24(240):1–113.

Biyang Guo, Xin Zhang, Ziyuan Wang, Minqi Jiang, Jinran Nie, Yuxuan Ding, Jianwei Yue, and Yupeng Wu. 2023. How close is chatgpt to human experts? comparison corpus, evaluation, and detection. *arXiv preprint arXiv:2301.07597*.

S Hochreiter. 1997. Long short-term memory. *Neural Computation MIT-Press*.

Yafu Li, Qintong Li, Leyang Cui, Wei Bi, Zhilin Wang, Longyue Wang, Linyi Yang, Shuming Shi, and Yue Zhang. 2024. MAGE: Machine-generated text detection in the wild. In *Proceedings of the 62nd Annual Meeting of the Association for Computational Linguistics (Volume 1: Long Papers)*, pages 36–53, Bangkok, Thailand. Association for Computational Linguistics.

Zachary Chase Lipton. 2015. A critical review of recurrent neural networks for sequence learning. *arXiv Preprint, CoRR, abs/1506.00019*.

Eric Mitchell, Yoonho Lee, Alexander Khazatsky, Christopher D Manning, and Chelsea Finn. 2023. Detectgpt: Zero-shot machine-generated text detection using probability curvature. In *International Conference on Machine Learning*, pages 24950–24962. PMLR.

V Sanh. 2019. Distilbert, a distilled version of bert: smaller, faster, cheaper and lighter. *arXiv preprint arXiv:1910.01108*.

Rexhep Shijaku and Ercan Canhasi. 2023. Chatgpt generated text detection. *Publisher: Unpublished*.

A Vaswani. 2017. Attention is all you need. *Advances in Neural Information Processing Systems*.

Yuxia Wang, Jonibek Mansurov, Petar Ivanov, Jinyan Su, Artem Shelmanov, Akim Tsvigun, Osama Mohammed Afzal, Tarek Mahmoud, Giovanni Puccetti, Thomas Arnold, Alham Aji, Nizar Habash, Iryna Gurevych, and Preslav Nakov. 2024. M4GT-bench: Evaluation benchmark for black-box machine-generated text detection. In *Proceedings of the 62nd*

Annual Meeting of the Association for Computational Linguistics (Volume 1: Long Papers), pages 3964–3992, Bangkok, Thailand. Association for Computational Linguistics.

Yuxia Wang, Artem Shelmanov, Jonibek Mansurov, Akim Tsvigun, Vladislav Mikhailov, Rui Xing, Zhuohan Xie, Jiahui Geng, Giovanni Puccetti, Ekaterina Artemova, Jinyan Su, Minh Ngoc Ta, Mervat Abassy, Kareem Elozeiri, Saad El Dine Ahmed, Maiya Goloburda, Tarek Mahmoud, Raj Vardhan Tomar, Alexander Aziz, Nurkhan Laiyk, Osama Mohammed Afzal, Ryuto Koike, Masahiro Kaneko, Alham Fikri Aji, Nizar Habash, Iryna Gurevych, and Preslav Nakov. 2025. GenAI content detection task 1: English and multilingual machine-generated text detection: AI vs. human. In *Proceedings of the 1st Workshop on GenAI Content Detection (GenAIDetect)*, Abu Dhabi, UAE. International Conference on Computational Linguistics.

Peipeng Yu, Jiahan Chen, Xuan Feng, and Zhihua Xia. 2023. Cheat: A large-scale dataset for detecting chatgpt-written abstracts. *arXiv preprint arXiv:2304.12008*.

Wataru Zaitsu and Mingzhe Jin. 2023. Distinguishing chatgpt (-3.5,-4)-generated and human-written papers through japanese stylometric analysis. *PLoS One*, 18(8):e0288453.

Rowan Zellers, Ari Holtzman, Hannah Rashkin, Yonatan Bisk, Ali Farhadi, Franziska Roesner, and Yejin Choi. 2019. Defending against neural fake news. *Advances in neural information processing systems*, 32.

LuxVeri at GenAI Detection Task 1: Inverse Perplexity Weighted Ensemble for Robust Detection of AI-Generated Text across English and Multilingual Contexts

Md Kamrujjaman Mobin[1], Md Saiful Islam[1, 2]
[1]Computer Science and Engineering, Shahjalal University of Science and Technology, Sylhet, Bangladesh
[2]Computing Science, University of Alberta, Edmonton, Alberta, Canada

Abstract

This paper presents a system developed for Task 1 of the COLING 2025 Workshop on Detecting AI-Generated Content, focusing on the binary classification of machine-generated versus human-written text. Our approach utilizes an ensemble of models, with weights assigned according to each model's inverse perplexity, to enhance classification accuracy. For the English text detection task, we combined RoBERTa-base, RoBERTa-base with the OpenAI detector, and BERT-base-cased, achieving a Macro F1-score of 0.7458, which ranked us 12th out of 35 teams. We ensembled RemBERT, XLM-RoBERTa-base, and BERT-base-multilingual-case for the multilingual text detection task, employing the same inverse perplexity weighting technique. This resulted in a Macro F1-score of 0.7513, positioning us 4th out of 25 teams. Our results demonstrate the effectiveness of inverse perplexity weighting in improving the robustness of machine-generated text detection across both monolingual and multilingual settings, highlighting the potential of ensemble methods for this challenging task.

1 Introduction

The rapid advancement of language models such as GPT (Radford et al., 2019) and BERT (Devlin et al., 2019) has increased machine-generated content, raising significant concerns about misinformation and academic integrity. Identifying AI-generated text becomes more challenging in multilingual contexts, where linguistic diversity adds further complexity to model generalization. While existing approaches perform well in English, their effectiveness decreases when applied to languages with diverse syntactic and semantic structures.

In Task 1 of the COLING 2025 Workshop on Detecting AI-Generated Content (Wang et al., 2025), we propose an ensemble-based solution to address these issues. For English detection, we combine RoBERTa-base (Liu et al., 2019), OpenAI's AI text detector (Solaiman et al., 2019), and BERT-base-cased (Devlin et al., 2019). For multilingual detection, we integrate RemBERT (Chung et al., 2021), XLM-RoBERTa-base (Conneau et al., 2019), and BERT-base-multilingual-cased (Devlin et al., 2019). To further improve performance, we incorporate inverse perplexity weighting to give greater priority to models that produce lower perplexity scores. Our ensemble approach achieved a Macro F1-score of 0.7458 (Micro F1: 0.7568) in English, placing us 12th out of 35 teams, and a Macro F1-score of 0.7513 (Micro F1: 0.7527) for the multilingual tasks, ranking 4th out of 25 teams.

We encountered several challenges during this work. One major issue was data imbalance, as human-written content vastly outnumbered AI-generated samples. To address this, we employed data augmentation and optimized our sampling strategies. Another challenge involved ensuring the models' generalization across different languages and writing styles, often with limited training data. This highlights the importance of additional fine-tuning and the need to explore alternative architectures that can better handle diverse linguistic inputs.

This paper presents a robust ensemble approach for detecting AI-generated content, with strong performance across both English and multilingual tasks. However, significant opportunities remain for improving model generalization and addressing data imbalance, which will be crucial for future advancements in this field. The following sections will discuss the dataset, methodology, results, a detailed analysis of the findings, and conclusions drawn from this study.

2 Background

2.1 Dataset

The provided dataset includes training and validation sets for two subtasks: Subtask A (English-only

Proceedings of the 1st Workshop on GenAI Content Detection (GenAIDetect), pages 203–208
January 19, 2025.

Dataset	en	zh	bg	de	it	id	ur	ar	ru
Training	610,676	35,284	8,091	4,693	4,174	3,976	3,761	2,114	1,314
Validation	261,849	14,772	3,489	2,059	1,843	1,803	1,573	906	600

Table 1: Data distribution for multilingual training and validation datasets, including the number of entries per language. The English dataset is consistent across both English-only and multilingual contexts, so it is omitted from the table for clarity.

Machine-Generated Text Detection) and Subtask B (Multilingual Machine-Generated Text Detection). Subtask A consists of over 610,000 English-only entries in the training set and around 261,000 in the validation set, each labeled as machine-generated or human-generated. These texts are sourced from various platforms, with information on their origin and creation model (e.g., GPT-4, human). Subtask B extends the dataset to include over 674,000 training entries and approximately 288,000 validation entries across nine languages, including English, Chinese, and Bulgarian. Each entry contains details on the source, sub-source, language, model, label, and text. Data distribution details are shown in Table 1.

2.2 Related Work

The detection of AI-generated text has garnered significant attention with the advent of large language models (LLMs) such as GPT (Radford et al., 2019) and BERT (Devlin et al., 2019). Fine-tuning Transformer-based models for binary classification has shown efficacy; however, challenges persist, particularly in multilingual settings where data biases impede generalization (Zellers et al., 2019; Solaiman et al., 2019).

Ensemble methods combining BERT, RoBERTa, and GPT variants have enhanced robustness across domains and languages (Schick and Schütze, 2020). Perplexity-based weighting strategies further optimize individual model contributions (Clark et al., 2019). Multilingual models like XLM-RoBERTa (Conneau et al., 2019) and RemBERT (Chung et al., 2021) improve cross-lingual performance, though low-resource languages remain challenging (Hu et al., 2020).

Recent advancements in shared tasks, such as those introduced by SemEval (Fetahu et al., 2023; Wang et al., 2024), have refined methodologies through task-specific fine-tuning and the integration of multilingual pre-trained models (Eger et al., 2023; Siino, 2024).

Building upon these foundations, our work employs an inverse perplexity-weighted ensemble approach to optimize model contributions, enhancing robustness in both monolingual and multilingual detection scenarios.

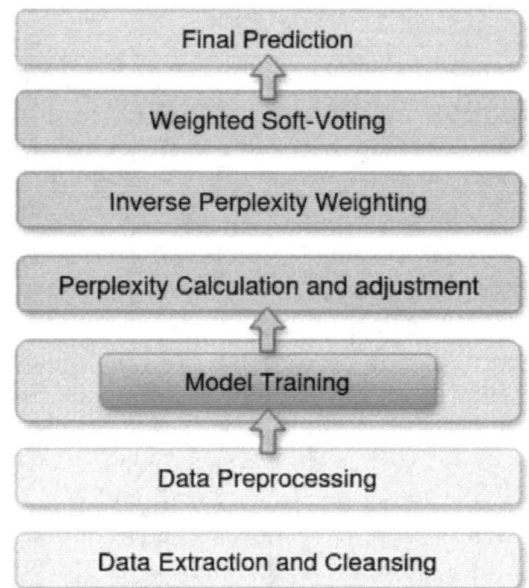

Figure 1: Overall Framework of our Proposed System.

3 System Overview

We developed an ensemble approach for AI-generated text detection across English and multilingual contexts, using Transformer models with a weighted voting strategy based on inverse perplexity for improved accuracy. The system overview is shown in Figure 1.

3.1 Ensemble Model Selection and Justification

We selected six Transformer-based models for our ensemble: three for English and three for multilingual contexts, chosen for their ability to capture linguistic and syntactic patterns.

- **English Models**: The models utilized in our work include **RoBERTa-base**, renowned for its robust performance in natural language understanding, effectively capturing deep syntactic and semantic patterns (Liu et al., 2019). Additionally, the **RoBERTa-base OpenAI detector** is fine-tuned to detect

Dataset	en	zh	bg	de	it	id	ur	ar	ru
Training	40,000	20,000	8,091	4,693	4,174	3,976	3,761	2,114	1,314
Validation	26,000	10,000	3,489	2,059	1,843	1,803	1,573	906	600

Table 2: Reduced data distribution for the multilingual task after balancing by scaling down English and Chinese samples to improve performance in underrepresented languages.

AI-generated content by identifying subtle machine-generated patterns (Solaiman et al., 2019). Lastly, **BERT-base-cased** is incorporated for its capability to handle case-sensitive distinctions, which are critical for nuanced classification tasks (Devlin et al., 2019).

- **Multilingual Models**: For Multilingual, we employed **RemBERT**, a model optimized for multilingual tasks, demonstrating exceptional performance in syntactic and semantic understanding across languages (Chung et al., 2021). Furthermore, **XLM-RoBERTa-base** is employed for its strength in cross-lingual applications, adeptly handling diverse language structures (Conneau et al., 2019). Additionally, **BERT-base-multilingual-cased** is used as it is specifically designed to capture linguistic diversity and perform effectively in multilingual tasks (Devlin et al., 2019).

We trained these models on the dataset provided as part of the shared task 1 (Wang et al., 2025), including human-authored and AI-generated content. This enabled the ensemble to generalize effectively across both English and multilingual contexts.

3.2 Data Pre-processing

The multilingual task presented a significant data imbalance across languages, as shown in Table 1, which details the original distribution of training and validation samples. For instance, the dataset included 610,676 English (en) samples and 35,284 Chinese (zh) samples, whereas underrepresented languages like Urdu (ur), Arabic (ar), and Russian (ru) had far fewer samples (3,761, 2,114, and 1,314, respectively). This imbalance hindered the model's ability to predict outputs for these underrepresented languages accurately.

To mitigate this issue, we implemented a dataset balancing strategy by reducing the number of English and Chinese samples to a proportionate scale. This adjustment enabled the model to better focus on learning patterns in the underrepresented languages, thereby enhancing overall performance and reducing biases in predictions. The detailed data distribution after applying this balancing strategy is presented in Table 2.

Following this, text data was processed using model-specific tokenizers, with truncation and padding applied as needed. To optimize memory usage and training efficiency, text length was calculated and sorted by word count, minimizing unnecessary padding. A fixed random seed was used throughout to ensure reproducibility.

Hyperparameter	Value
Number of Epochs	$2 \sim 3$
Learning Rate	$1 \times 10^{-5} \sim 2 \times 10^{-5}$
Training Batch Size	4
Validation Batch Size	16
Early Stopping Patience	5 validation steps
Early Stopping Threshold	0.001
Weight Decay	0.01
Optimizer	AdamW
Loss Function	Binary Cross-Entropy
Evaluation Strategy	Every ¼ epoch
Checkpointing Strategy	Validation loss

Table 3: Training Configuration

3.3 Training Procedure

The model was fine-tuned using the Hugging Face Transformers library[1] for both English and multilingual text classification tasks. Datasets were processed into Hugging Face Dataset objects, with tokenization performed using AutoTokenizer for models like RemBERT and RoBERTa-base. The architecture was adapted for classification tasks with appropriate label mappings.

Key hyperparameters, including learning rate, batch size, and weight decay, were optimized through empirical experiments to balance performance and efficiency. Learning rates between 1×10^{-5} and 2×10^{-5} were tested, with lower rates promoting smoother convergence. A batch size of 4 for training and 16 for validation balanced memory and efficiency.

[1]Hugging Face Transformers: `https://huggingface.co/transformers/`

English-only Task				Multilingual Task			
Model	Micro F1-Score	Macro F1-Score	Rank	Model	Micro F1-Score	Macro F1-Score	Rank
RoBERTa + RoBERTa OpenAI + BERT cased	0.7568	0.7458	12/35	RemBERT + XLM-R + BERT multilingual	0.7527	0.7513	4/25
RoBERTa + RoBERTa OpenAI	0.7495	0.7380	–	RemBERT	0.7507	0.7489	–
Baseline(RoBERTa)*	0.7381	0.7342	–	RemBERT + XLM-R	0.7473	0.7435	–
RoBERTa + BERT cased	0.7275	0.7229	–	Baseline(XLM-R)*	0.7426	0.7416	–

Table 4: Performance of various experimented models on English-only and multilingual tasks compared with baseline results.

Hyperparameter tuning reduced overfitting and improved generalization, leading to faster convergence and better validation performance. Early stopping (patience of 5 steps, threshold of 0.001) prevented overfitting and enhanced robustness.

Checkpoints were saved for each epoch, and the best model was retained for testing. Further details of the final configurations are in Table 3, ensuring effective fine-tuning across both datasets.

3.4 Ensemble Voting Strategy

Our ensemble employs a weighted soft-voting strategy, combining predictions from three different models for each subtask. The weights are determined based on inverse perplexity, with lower perplexity values reflecting higher confidence.

3.4.1 Perplexity Calculation

For each model, we compute the perplexity based on its predictions. The perplexity P is computed using the Negative Log Likelihood formula:

$$P = \exp\left(-\frac{1}{N}\sum_{i=1}^{N}\log(p(y_i \mid x_i))\right)$$

where $p(y_i \mid x_i)$ is the predicted probability for the true label y_i, and N is the number of test samples. Lower perplexity values indicate higher confidence.

To compute perplexity, we use each model's logits, apply softmax to obtain probabilities, and then calculate perplexity based on the true labels and these probabilities.

3.4.2 Perplexity-Based Weighting Adjustment

To calculate model weights, each model's perplexity is adjusted by subtracting 1, creating an effective weighting scale. The weight w_i for model i is then computed as the inverse of this adjusted perplexity and normalized across models, giving higher confidence models greater influence.

$$w_i = \frac{1/(P_i - 1)}{\sum_{j=1}^{M}(1/(P_j - 1))}$$

where M represents the total number of models, and P_i is the original perplexity of model i.

3.4.3 Weighted Soft-Voting

Each model's predicted probabilities are scaled by its weight and summed to form the final ensemble prediction. This weighted voting prioritizes models with higher confidence (lower perplexity), giving them greater influence on the final decision. The ensemble's final prediction for each class c is:

$$p_{\text{ensemble}}(c) = \sum_{i=1}^{M} w_i \cdot p_i(c)$$

where $p_i(c)$ is the predicted probability for class c by model i, and w_i is its weight.

This method enhances ensemble accuracy by prioritizing predictions from more confident models, improving overall performance.

4 Results

This section presents the performance of our ensemble approach for Task 1 at the COLING 2025 Workshop on Detecting AI-Generated Content, evaluated using the Macro F1-score. Detailed results are shown in Table 5.

The baseline scores provided by the task organizers (Wang et al., 2025) used RoBERTa-base (Liu et al., 2019) for the English track and XLM-RoBERTa-base (Conneau et al., 2019) for the multilingual track. These scores serve as benchmarks for our ensemble method.

During testing, models in the ensemble were weighted based on perplexity, with lower-perplexity models given greater influence. This approach, along with sorting test data by text length, reduced inference time by 40% while generating predictions using softmax and weighted averaging.

For the English-only task, our ensemble of RoBERTa-base, RoBERTa-base OpenAI detector, and BERT-base-cased achieved a Macro F1-score of 0.7458, outperforming the baseline (0.7342) and ranking 12th out of 35 teams. Similarly, for the multilingual task, our ensemble of RemBERT, XLM-RoBERTa-base, and BERT-base-multilingual-cased achieved a Macro F1-score of 0.7513, surpassing the baseline (0.7416) and ranking 4th out of 25 teams. The combination of these models effectively enhanced both language-specific and cross-lingual accuracy.

Table 5 highlights the effectiveness of Inverse Perplexity Weighting, which achieved the highest Macro F1-scores for both tasks (0.7458 for English and 0.7513 for multilingual). This method dynamically prioritizes models with lower uncertainty in their predictions, outperforming other techniques such as accuracy-based weighting, mean ensembling, and majority voting.

Our ensemble also outperformed individual models, such as RoBERTa-base (0.7342) for the English track and the dual combination of RemBERT + XLM-R (0.7435) for the multilingual track. This demonstrates the effectiveness of combining diverse models to achieve better performance.

Ensemble Technique	English Task (Macro F1)	Multilingual Task (Macro F1)
Inverse Perplexity Weighting	**0.7458**	**0.7513**
Accuracy Based Weighting	0.7251	0.7393
Mean Ensemble	0.7153	0.7211
Majority Voting	0.6850	0.7005

Table 5: Comparison of ensemble techniques for English-only and multilingual tasks, highlighting the effectiveness of Inverse Perplexity Weighting.

5 Discussion and Conclusion

In this work, we presented an ensemble approach to detect AI-generated content across English and multilingual datasets. By combining multiple pre-trained models, including RoBERTa-base, OpenAI detector, BERT-base-cased for English, and RemBERT, XLM-RoBERTa-base, BERT-base-multilingual-cased for multilingual tasks, and applying inverse perplexity weighting, our ensemble demonstrated strong performance. It achieved a Macro F1-score of 0.7458 (Micro F1: 0.7568) for English, ranking 12th, and 0.7513 (Micro F1: 0.7527) for multilingual tasks, ranking 4th.

Compared to individual models, our ensemble consistently outperformed or matched their performance. For example, in the English task, the ensemble scored 0.7568, surpassing RoBERTa + OpenAI detector (0.7381) and BERT (0.7275). Similarly, the multilingual task achieved 0.7527, exceeding RemBERT + XLM-R (0.7473) and RemBERT (0.7507). Notably, our ensemble also outperformed baseline models, with a Macro F1-score of 0.7458 for English (baseline: 0.7342 achieved by RoBERTa) and 0.7513 for multilingual (baseline: 0.7416 achieved by XLM-RoBERTa). These results highlight the effectiveness of combining model strengths to improve detection accuracy.

A key challenge faced during the multilingual task was the data imbalance between well-represented languages like English and Chinese and underrepresented ones such as Urdu, Arabic, and Russian. This disparity hindered the model's accuracy for underrepresented languages. To address this, we scale down samples from overrepresented languages to balance the dataset. This adjustment improved performance across languages, validating the effectiveness of our approach.

Despite these successes, challenges persist. Detecting AI-generated content in multilingual contexts remains complex and demands further refinement in model architectures and data processing techniques. Future work could explore advanced methods for mitigating data imbalance, such as data augmentation or active learning, to enhance the model's generalization ability across diverse languages. Additionally, more sophisticated ensemble strategies or domain-specific models could improve detection accuracy.

In conclusion, this study demonstrates the effectiveness of an ensemble approach for detecting AI-generated content across English and multilingual datasets. Addressing data imbalance and using inverse perplexity weighting improved performance, though ongoing challenges highlight the need for continuous innovation in AI detection systems.

References

Hyung Won Chung, Thibault Févry, Henry Tsai, Melvin Johnson, and Sebastian Ruder. 2021. Rethinking embedding coupling in pre-trained language models. In *9th International Conference on Learning Representations, ICLR 2021, Virtual Event, Austria, May 3-7, 2021*. OpenReview.net.

Christopher Clark, Kevin Gimpel, and Noah A Smith. 2019. Ensemble methods for detection of machine-generated text. In *Proceedings of ACL 2019*, pages 47–56.

Alexis Conneau, Kartikay Khandelwal, Naman Goyal, Vishrav Chaudhary, Guillaume Wenzek, Francisco Guzmán, Edouard Grave, Myle Ott, Luke Zettlemoyer, and Veselin Stoyanov. 2019. Unsupervised cross-lingual representation learning at scale. *CoRR*, abs/1911.02116.

Jacob Devlin, Ming-Wei Chang, Kenton Lee, et al. 2019. Bert: Pre-training of deep bidirectional transformers for language understanding. In *Proceedings of NAACL-HLT 2019*, pages 4171–4186.

S. Eger et al. 2023. Semeval-2023: Ai-generated text detection task. In *Proceedings of SemEval 2023*.

Besnik Fetahu, Sudipta Kar, Zhiyu Chen, Oleg Rokhlenko, and Shervin Malmasi. 2023. SemEval-2023 task 2: Fine-grained multilingual named entity recognition (MultiCoNER 2). In *Proceedings of the 17th International Workshop on Semantic Evaluation (SemEval-2023)*, pages 2247–2265, Toronto, Canada. Association for Computational Linguistics.

Jing Hu, Yizhe Li, and Zhiyuan Zhang. 2020. Multilingual pretraining for cross-lingual natural language understanding. In *Proceedings of NAACL 2020*, pages 1–10.

Y. Liu et al. 2019. Roberta: A robustly optimized bert pretraining approach. *arXiv preprint arXiv:1907.11692*.

Alec Radford, Karthik Narasimhan, Tim Salimans, et al. 2019. Language models are unsupervised multitask learners.

Timo Schick and Hinrich Schütze. 2020. Exploiting cloze questions for few-shot text classification. In *Proceedings of ACL 2020*, pages 255–265.

Marco Siino. 2024. BadRock at SemEval-2024 task 8: DistilBERT to detect multigenerator, multidomain and multilingual black-box machine-generated text. In *Proceedings of the 18th International Workshop on Semantic Evaluation (SemEval-2024)*, pages 239–245, Mexico City, Mexico.

Irene Solaiman, Miles Brundage, Jack Clark, Amanda Askell, Ariel Herbert-Voss, Jeff Wu, Alec Radford, Gretchen Krueger, Jong Wook Kim, Sarah Kreps, et al. 2019. Release strategies and the social impacts of language models. *arXiv preprint arXiv:1908.09203*.

Yuxia Wang, Jonibek Mansurov, Petar Ivanov, Jinyan Su, Artem Shelmanov, Akim Tsvigun, Osama Mohammed Afzal, Tarek Mahmoud, Giovanni Puccetti, Thomas Arnold, Chenxi Whitehouse, Alham Fikri Aji, Nizar Habash, Iryna Gurevych, and Preslav Nakov. 2024. Semeval-2024 task 8: Multidomain, multimodel and multilingual machine-generated text detection. *Preprint*, arXiv:2404.14183.

Yuxia Wang, Artem Shelmanov, Jonibek Mansurov, Akim Tsvigun, Vladislav Mikhailov, Rui Xing, Zhuohan Xie, Jiahui Geng, Giovanni Puccetti, Ekaterina Artemova, Jinyan Su, Minh Ngoc Ta, Mervat Abassy, Kareem Elozeiri, Saad El Dine Ahmed, Maiya Goloburda, Tarek Mahmoud, Raj Vardhan Tomar, Alexander Aziz, Nurkhan Laiyk, Osama Mohammed Afzal, Ryuto Koike, Masahiro Kaneko, Alham Fikri Aji, Nizar Habash, Iryna Gurevych, and Preslav Nakov. 2025. GenAI content detection task 1: English and multilingual machine-generated text detection: AI vs. human. In *Proceedings of the 1st Workshop on GenAI Content Detection (GenAIDetect)*, Abu Dhabi, UAE. International Conference on Computational Linguistics.

Rowan Zellers, Aidan Holtzman, Anna Yu, et al. 2019. Defending against neural fake news. In *Proceedings of NeurIPS 2019*, pages 10089–10101.

A Appendix

Tools & Libraries	Version
Python	3.10.14
Pandas	2.2.2
NumPy	1.26.4
PyTorch	2.4.0
Transformers	4.44.2
Evaluate	0.4.3
WandB	0.16.6

Table 6: Main tools and libraries used in our system

Table 6 provide the details about the corresponding libraries, which are beneficial to help replicate our experiments.

Grape at GenAI Detection Task 1: Leveraging Compact Models and Linguistic Features for Robust Machine-Generated Text Detection

Nhi Hoai Doan and **Kentaro Inui**
Mohamed bin Zayed University of Artificial Intelligence (MBZUAI)
{nhi.doan, kentaro.inui}@mbzuai.ac.ae

Abstract

In this project, we aim to solve two Subtasks of Task 1: Binary Multilingual Machine-Generated Text(MGT) Detection (Human vs. Machine) as part of the COLING 2025 Workshop on MGT Detection(Wang et al., 2025) by different approaches. The first method is separate fine-tuned small language models on the specific subtask. The second approach enhances this methodology by incorporating linguistic, syntactic, and semantic features, using ensemble learning to combine these features with model predictions for a more robust classification. By evaluating and comparing these approaches, we want to identify the most effective techniques for detecting machine-generated content across languages, offering insights into improving automated verification tools amid the rapid growth of LLM-generated text in digital spaces. The code of this project is available at here.

1 Introduction

The rapid development of large language models (LLMs) such as GPT-4o, Claude3.5, and Gemini1.5-pro has led to an explosion of machine-generated text across various channels, including news, social media, and academic publications. Khalifa and Albadawy (2024), based on 24 studies of academic domains, points out that using artificial intelligence enhances the productivity of researchers. While this advancement is promising, it has raised significant concerns about misuse, including spreading misinformation and potential disruptions in educational contexts due to the unpredictable nuance of these language models. To address these issues, it is crucial to develop effective systems for distinguishing between human-written and machine-generated content. There are two subtasks in the Task 1:

- Subtask A: English-only machine-generated text(MGT) detection.
- Subtask B: Multilingual MGT detection with nine languages.

The primary goal of this project is to develop an automatic detection system capable of distinguishing machine-generated text from human-written text using small-sized language models. By integrating models with fewer parameters—thus lower computational demands—we aim to demonstrate that effective detection does not require large, resource-intensive models. Specifically, our objectives are to:

- Explore important linguistic, syntactic, and semantic features for human and machine text-generated differentiation.
- Implement and evaluate **newly released language models** in small sizes for text classification.
- Assess model performance and provide insights on machine-generated content detection effectiveness.

2 Related Work

Recent research has focused on detecting machine-generated text using various techniques. For the traditional methodologies, GLTR uses statistical methods to detect generated text with an improvement in human detection of fake text from 54% to 72%(Gehrmann et al., 2019). With the explosive growth of Transformers and Large Language Models(LLMs), Uchendu et al. (2021) shows that FAIR_wmt20 and GPT-3 excel at generating human-like text. Recently, in the *SemEval-2024 Task 8: Multidomain, Multimodel and Multilingual Machine-Generated Text Detection*(Wang et al., 2024), many researchers have tried to apply different approaches, such as statistical, language models, and LLMs to solve the *Subtask A: Human vs. Machine Classification*. Sarvazyan et al. (2024)

Proceedings of the 1st Workshop on GenAI Content Detection (GenAIDetect), pages 209–217
January 19, 2025.

study mixing Llama-2 features, achieved top accuracy. Their performance relies on multiple LLMs and features, focusing on the last tokens. Other teams also attempt to use language models, such as RoBERTa or XLM-RoBERTa(Sarvazyan et al., 2024; Petukhova et al., 2024; Tran et al., 2024).

Regarding our hardware limitations, we want to try to evaluate newly released language models in small sizes. In addition, all previous works on the SemEval-2024 Task 8 mostly work with LLMs. Based on the success of Sarvazyan et al. (2024) with Llama-2, we consider using Llama3(Dubey et al., 2024). While Spiegel and Macko (2024) proposed combined fine-tuned LLMs with zero-shot statistical methods, employing a two-step majority voting system for predictions, Petukhova et al. (2024) utilized a fine-tuned baseline - RoBERTa augmented with diverse linguistic features. All these methods surpass the baseline and achieve good results, supporting our approach, which is a potential way to mix LLMs with traditional linguistic features.

3 Proposed Approach

Recent released large language models, such as Llama 3 (Dubey et al., 2024) or Gemma 2 (Team et al., 2024), are now available in smaller configurations. These smaller models still perform well on popular benchmarks while being more compatible with hardware constraints. Therefore, we decided to fine-tune these models for our task, utilizing their smaller versions to match our hardware limitations.

3.1 Subtask A: Monolingual - English

This subtask focuses on detecting machine-generated text in English generated by *hc3, m4gt, and mage*. We want to use fine-tuned language models and traditional linguistic features as their potential performance from previous research on the same task (Spiegel and Macko, 2024; Tran et al., 2024). The methodology integrates neural network-based approaches with gradient boosting and combines the outputs through a majority voting mechanism. The strategy is outlined in Figure 1:

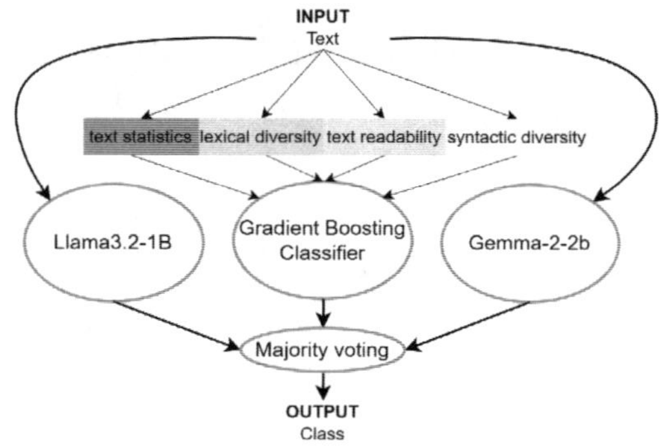

Figure 1: Approach for monolingual task

Fine-Tuning of Small Language Models: The recent availability of smaller, efficient language models, such as Llama3.2-1B and Gemma-2-2B, makes them suitable candidates for fine-tuning on this task. Despite their compact size, these models maintain competitive performance, comparable to larger counterparts like Mixtral 8x7B and GPT-3.5. Fine-tuning these models on the task-specific dataset enables them to capture intricate patterns indicative of machine-generated content. Their efficient architecture ensures compatibility with hardware constraints, allowing faster training and inference.

Gradient Boosting Classifier with Linguistic Features: In addition to fine-tuning Llama3.2-1b and Gemma-2-2B, a gradient-boosting classifier will be trained using a comprehensive set of linguistic features extracted from the text. These metrics can provide helpful information when the input to language models is limited. Therefore, adding other linguistic features will allow them to gain information from the truncation part. As desired from the work of (Petukhova et al., 2024), we use four metrics with updated features as follows:

- *Syntactic Complexity*: Metrics obtained from *spaCy*[1] such as average sentence length, average number of noun phrases per sentence, and average number of verbs per sentence capture syntactic patterns and variations within the text.

- *Readability Metrics*: include Flesch Reading Ease, Flesch-Kincaid Grade Level, Gunning Fog Index, SMOG Index, and others assess the ease or difficulty of reading the text. We get these metrics by using the *textstat* package[2].

- *Lexical Diversity*: Metrics such as Type-Token Ratio (TTR), Maas TTR, Hypergeometric Distribution Diversity (HDD), and Mean Length of Textual Diversity (MLTD)[3] provide

[1] https://pypi.org/project/spacy/
[2] https://pypi.org/project/textstat/
[3] https://pypi.org/project/lexical-diversity/

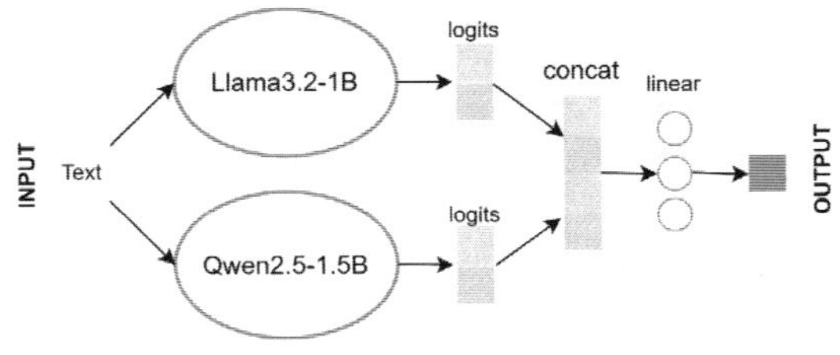

Figure 2: Ensemble model for multilingual task

insights into the lexical richness of the text. Machine-generated texts may exhibit unusual lexical patterns, making these metrics valuable.

- *Text Statistics*: Basic statistics such as the number of difficult words, unique word count, and sentence count offer additional context about the text structure. These can reveal inconsistencies or unnatural pasts often present in machine-generated content.

By combining these diverse features, the gradient-boosting classifier can capture non-linear relationships between linguistic characteristics and the target variable, complementing the capabilities of the fine-tuned language models.

Majority Voting Ensemble: To enhance the robustness and accuracy of the system, a majority voting mechanism will be employed to combine the outputs of the three models: fine-tuned versions of Llama3.2-1b and Gemma-2-2B and the gradient boosting classifier. Each model will provide its prediction, and the final decision will be determined by the majority vote among the three. This ensemble approach leverages each component's strengths, balancing the fine-tuned models' deep contextual understanding with the interpretability and feature-driven analysis of the gradient-boosting classifier.

3.2 Subtask B: Multilingual

This subtask extends the detection of machine-generated text to a multilingual setting. Given the time constraints and resource limitations, the approach will leverage two fine-tuned multilingual models, Llama-3 1B and Qwen-2.5 1.5B (Hui et al., 2024). These models have been selected for their efficient architectures and ability to handle multiple languages effectively. The methodology for Subtask B follows a similar ensemble-based strategy as outlined in Subtask A, with modifications to accommodate multilingual data.

As we see in Figure 2, an ensemble architecture has been developed to combine the strengths of Llama-3 and Qwen-2.5. Each model is fine-tuned separately on the training dataset, and their outputs are then combined through learnable weights. We do not use text linguistic features here because of inconsistent and unavailable support tools for non-English languages. Therefore, we choose to create ensemble models based on fine-tuned multilingual models.

4 General settings

4.1 Experiments

For each subtask, we fine-tune and measure the results of each small model individually before applying majority and ensemble learning methods. The hyperparameters of Llama3.2-1b, Gemma-2-2B, and Qwen2.5-1.5B are learning rate = 2e-5, batch size = 16, max token length = 256, lora = 16, and epoch = 5. Our hardware computation resource is 1× NVIDIA GeForce RTX4090 24GB and is limited to 24 hours.

4.2 Evaluation metrics and baselines

The official evaluation metric is the macro f1-score. Another metric is micro-F1. The task also provided a baseline result for the English track using RoBERTa, which is 81.63. The result for the multilingual track using XLM-R is 65.46.

5 Results

5.1 Subtask A: English-only MGT detection

Overall, the results of the methods for Subtask A, as shown in Table 1, confirm our intuition. The *2SLMs* is a combination of 2 small language models by averaging logits of them. While *2SLMs* combination

Model	Macro F1	Micro F1
Linguistic Features	0.7094	0.7148
Llama3.2-1b	0.8798	0.8843
Gemma-2-2B	0.9070	0.9100
2SLMs	0.9088	0.9117
Majority Voting	**0.9225**	**0.9248**

Table 1: Performance of models on Subtask A dev_test set

improves slightly, adding linguistic features generally increases both metrics. This can be explained by the fact that we had to limit the maximum token length with the two small language models due to hardware constraints. It allowed the model to consider information from the truncated part of the text. For example, one case when *Majority Voting* successfully recognizes the text generated by *human* but *2SLMs* fails:

`<260 tokens>. . . Fill the bowl with enough cool tap water to cover the rice by an inch or two. Use your hand to gently stir the rice, then lift the strainer from the bowl. The water in the bowl will be cloudy from the rice starch. Empty the water, set the strainer in the bowl again, and repeat the process until the water is, more or less, clear. You'll probably have to change the water two or three times. Drain the rice. Pour enough wate . . . < 400 tokens>`

We can see that this text has more than 700 tokens which exceeds our max token length = 256. Previous part of the text describe step by step to prepare a dish but only after the considered context, we see the colloquial phrases like *"you'll probably have to change the water two or three times"* which align with human authorship. In addition, in the rest 400 tokens, it also contains natural and diversity words. Therefore, *Linguistic Features* could have the decision making power in such these cases.

5.2 Subtask B: Multilingual MGT detection

We employ two small language models for multilingual machine-generated text detection in this subtask, as illustrated in Table 2. The ensemble model achieved the best Macro F1 score at 0.7388, indicating its effectiveness in balancing the accuracy across different classes. Combining both models, the ensemble approach enhances generalization across multiple languages, which is beneficial in multilingual settings. However, the Micro F1 score (0.8829) slightly declined compared to Qwen2.5-1.5B, suggesting that while the ensemble model captures class balance well, it may sacrifice a bit of precision on individual sample classifications.

Model	Macro F1	Micro F1
Llama3.2-1b	0.6878	0.8619
Qwen2.5-1.5B	0.7292	**0.8869**
Ensemble	**0.7388**	0.8829

Table 2: Performance of models on Subtask B dev_test set

5.3 Results on the test set

Based on the results of the development dataset, we selected the Majority model and the Ensemble model to submit as the final results in Table 3. Since the golden labels are not publicly available, we cannot definitively conclude which approach is the most effective. However, for Subtask A, our result was 0.8188 — approximately a 0.09-point improvement over the baseline and 0.05-point improvement in Subtask B — indicating that these are promising approaches.

Subtask	Model	Macro F1	Rank
A	Baseline	0.7342	4/35
	Majority Voting	**0.8188**	
B	Baseline	0.7416	1/25
	Ensemble	**0.7916**	

Table 3: Our performance on the test set with **Score** is as *Macro F1*

Generally, ensemble learning is a potential approach, especially when each component has its own strength. In our study, small language models can solve our hardware limitation while maintaining good performance; their disadvantage is that they do not fully capture all information of the text. These models, even when combined, usually give similar results. Our intuition is that in the case of conflicts, the result of the model with more parameters is favored. However, additional linguistic features can handle these cases by looking for the whole text. Although this paper does not evaluate the individual contribution of each feature, we believe that further exploration could yield improvements in model performance.

The organization describes more details about other team methods in subtask A in Table 4. The top-ranking team, Advacheck, utilized a multi-task system with a shared Transformer encoder (DeBERTa-v3-base) and multiple classification heads, leveraging multi-task learning to optimize performance. Unibuc-NLP ranked 2nd with a combination of masked (XLM-RoBERTa) and causal (Qwen 2.5-0.5B) language models, enhanced by LoRA fine-tuning. At the same time, Fraunhofer SIT used adapters for task-specific optimization on RoBERTa-base. While more complex than the top teams' methods, our ensemble-based strategy demonstrates the value of integrating diverse model outputs to achieve competitive performance. Future enhancements could include incorporating multi-task learning or adapter-based approaches for further gains.

Team Name	Ranking	Small PLM	LLM	Feature Combination	Ensemble
Advacheck	1	✓			
Unibuc-NLP	2		✓		
FraunhoferSIT	3	✓			
Our team	4	✓	✓		✓
TechExperts(IPN)	5		✓		

Table 4: English subtask participants overview

Regarding the multilingual test set, we have the result analysis from the organization (Wang et al., 2025) as in Table 5 and Table 6.

When comparing our proposed approach with other teams as described in Table 5 (Wang et al., 2025), our method demonstrates a clear focus on efficiency and robustness by leveraging Small PLMs and ensemble techniques, achieving the top ranking. Unlike teams such as Nota AI and Lux Veri, who utilized broader combinations of techniques, including LLMs and feature engineering, our streamlined approach highlights the effectiveness of simplicity combined with targeted ensemble learning.

Team Name	Ranking	Small PLM	LLM	Feature Combination	Ensemble
Our team	1	✓			✓
Nota AI	3	✓	✓	✓	✓
Lux Veri	4	✓			✓
TechExperts (IPN)	5		✓		

Table 5: Multilingual subtask participants overview.

From Table 6, we could see that our team result for Subtask B Multilingual surpassed the baseline by around 5 percent, and our gap with the second team is 4 percent overall. In the test set, six hidden languages were not present in the training set of this task: Kazakh (KK), Vietnamese(VI), Hindi(HI), Hebrew(HE), Norwegian(NO), and Japanese(JA). Because models are not exposed to many linguistic patterns, structures, and features during training, it is difficult for them to generalize to unknown languages. For example, we achieved only 51.8 on Hindi.

6 Conclusion

We successfully addressed both subtasks using majority voting and ensemble methods. Our approach comprised fine-tuned small language models and linguistic features, contributing to robust task performance. Specifically, fine-tuning small language models allowed us to capture critical nuances in the data while maintaining computational efficiency. Meanwhile, incorporating linguistic features, such as syntactic complexity, readability metrics, and lexical diversity, added a complementary layer of information that enhanced the ensemble's overall effectiveness.

Limitations

Although the result in Section 5.1 shows that using linguistic features improves the model's performance, we have not investigated each feature. Furthermore, no additional linguistic features specific to each language are analyzed regarding the multilingual track. Future work could be research such features, including syntax-specific markers, morphological distinctions, and domain-specific language idiosyncrasies for each language to provide valuable insights and boost classification accuracy.

References

Abhimanyu Dubey, Abhinav Jauhri, Abhinav Pandey, Abhishek Kadian, Ahmad Al-Dahle, Aiesha Letman, Akhil Mathur, Alan Schelten, Amy Yang, Angela Fan, Anirudh Goyal, Anthony Hartshorn, Aobo Yang, Archi Mitra, Archie Sravankumar, Artem Korenev, Arthur Hinsvark, Arun Rao, Aston Zhang, Aurelien Rodriguez, Austen Gregerson, Ava Spataru, Baptiste Roziere, Bethany Biron, Binh Tang, Bobbie Chern, Charlotte Caucheteux, Chaya Nayak, Chloe Bi, Chris Marra, Chris McConnell, Christian Keller, Christophe Touret, Chunyang Wu, Corinne Wong, Cristian Canton Ferrer, Cyrus Nikolaidis, Damien Allonsius, Daniel Song, Danielle Pintz, Danny Livshits, David Esiobu, Dhruv Choudhary, Dhruv Mahajan, Diego Garcia-Olano, Diego Perino, Dieuwke Hupkes, Egor Lakomkin, Ehab AlBadawy, Elina Lobanova, Emily Dinan, Eric Michael Smith, Filip Radenovic, Frank Zhang, Gabriel Synnaeve, Gabrielle Lee, Georgia Lewis Anderson, Graeme Nail, Gregoire Mialon, Guan Pang, Guillem Cucurell, Hailey Nguyen, Hannah Korevaar, Hu Xu, Hugo Touvron, Iliyan Zarov, Imanol Arrieta Ibarra, Isabel Kloumann, Ishan Misra, Ivan Evtimov, Jade Copet, Jaewon Lee, Jan Geffert, Jana Vranes, Jason Park, Jay Mahadeokar,

Table 6: Multilingual subtask detection accuracy across 15 languages. *Underlined languages were not present in the training data.*

Rank	**All**	**ZH**	**UR**	**RU**	**AR**	**IT**	**KK**	**VI**	**DE**	**NO**	**ID**	**NL**	**ES**	**HI**	**HE**	**JA**
Size	151,425	63,009	30,505	27,158	10,670	5,296	2,471	2,326	1,865	1,544	1,200	1,200	1,200	1,199	1,182	600
Our team	79.6	94.2	68.7	67.1	71.2	52.9	55.5	90.5	88.3	80.3	89.6	82.2	89.5	51.8	86.7	77.0
2	75.6	84.7	64.6	74.2	57.9	52.9	83.8	83.5	96.4	76.0	51.7	90.6	91.2	69.6	96.8	95.3
3	75.9	90.2	67.2	58.9	66.8	52.9	92.5	74.7	88.8	72.2	87.4	68.9	47.1	70.6	96.4	72.2
4	75.3	87.6	64.6	63.9	61.3	52.9	75.8	83.4	94.9	88.5	53.5	92.2	90.4	73.0	97.3	92.2
BL	74.8	87.3	68.4	55.3	68.4	52.9	82.8	85.3	85.2	69.8	68.2	92.5	90.5	71.3	89.3	90.0
5	74.7	90.1	64.1	56.0	69.1	52.9	62.9	87.6	59.6	69.8	93.8	81.0	90.4	69.1	96.5	95.0
6	74.5	84.2	65.0	67.9	66.8	52.9	47.5	81.8	93.5	83.2	83.9	85.9	88.9	69.1	89.8	78.2

Jeet Shah, Jelmer van der Linde, Jennifer Billock, Jenny Hong, Jenya Lee, Jeremy Fu, Jianfeng Chi, Jianyu Huang, Jiawen Liu, Jie Wang, Jiecao Yu, Joanna Bitton, Joe Spisak, Jongsoo Park, Joseph Rocca, Joshua Johnstun, Joshua Saxe, Junteng Jia, Kalyan Vasuden Alwala, Kartikeya Upasani, Kate Plawiak, Ke Li, Kenneth Heafield, Kevin Stone, Khalid El-Arini, Krithika Iyer, Kshitiz Malik, Kuenley Chiu, Kunal Bhalla, Lauren Rantala-Yeary, Laurens van der Maaten, Lawrence Chen, Liang Tan, Liz Jenkins, Louis Martin, Lovish Madaan, Lubo Malo, Lukas Blecher, Lukas Landzaat, Luke de Oliveira, Madeline Muzzi, Mahesh Pasupuleti, Mannat Singh, Manohar Paluri, Marcin Kardas, Mathew Oldham, Mathieu Rita, Maya Pavlova, Melanie Kambadur, Mike Lewis, Min Si, Mitesh Kumar Singh, Mona Hassan, Naman Goyal, Narjes Torabi, Nikolay Bashlykov, Nikolay Bogoychev, Niladri Chatterji, Olivier Duchenne, Onur Çelebi, Patrick Alrassy, Pengchuan Zhang, Pengwei Li, Petar Vasic, Peter Weng, Prajjwal Bhargava, Pratik Dubal, Praveen Krishnan, Punit Singh Koura, Puxin Xu, Qing He, Qingxiao Dong, Ragavan Srinivasan, Raj Ganapathy, Ramon Calderer, Ricardo Silveira Cabral, Robert Stojnic, Roberta Raileanu, Rohit Girdhar, Rohit Patel, Romain Sauvestre, Ronnie Polidoro, Roshan Sumbaly, Ross Taylor, Ruan Silva, Rui Hou, Rui Wang, Saghar Hosseini, Sahana Chennabasappa, Sanjay Singh, Sean Bell, Seohyun Sonia Kim, Sergey Edunov, Shaoliang Nie, Sharan Narang, Sharath Raparthy, Sheng Shen, Shengye Wan, Shruti Bhosale, Shun Zhang, Simon Vandenhende, Soumya Batra, Spencer Whitman, Sten Sootla, Stephane Collot, Suchin Gururangan, Sydney Borodinsky, Tamar Herman, Tara Fowler, Tarek Sheasha, Thomas Georgiou, Thomas Scialom, Tobias Speckbacher, Todor Mihaylov, Tong Xiao, Ujjwal Karn, Vedanuj Goswami, Vibhor Gupta, Vignesh Ramanathan, Viktor Kerkez, Vincent Gonguet, Virginie Do, Vish Vogeti, Vladan Petrovic, Weiwei Chu, Wenhan Xiong, Wenyin Fu, Whitney Meers, Xavier Martinet, Xiaodong Wang, Xiaoqing Ellen Tan, Xinfeng Xie, Xuchao Jia, Xuewei Wang, Yaelle Goldschlag, Yashesh Gaur, Yasmine Babaei, Yi Wen, Yiwen Song, Yuchen Zhang, Yue Li, Yuning Mao, Zacharie Delpierre Coudert, Zheng Yan, Zhengxing Chen, Zoe Papakipos, Aaditya Singh, Aaron Grattafiori, Abha Jain, Adam Kelsey, Adam Shajnfeld, Adithya Gangidi, Adolfo Victoria, Ahuva Goldstand, Ajay Menon, Ajay Sharma, Alex Boesenberg, Alex Vaughan, Alexei Baevski, Allie Feinstein, Amanda Kallet, Amit Sangani, Anam Yunus, Andrei Lupu, Andres Alvarado, Andrew Caples, Andrew Gu, Andrew Ho, Andrew Poulton, Andrew Ryan, Ankit Ramchandani, Annie Franco, Aparajita Saraf, Arkabandhu Chowdhury, Ashley Gabriel, Ashwin Bharambe, Assaf Eisenman, Azadeh Yazdan, Beau James, Ben Maurer, Benjamin Leonhardi, Bernie Huang, Beth Loyd, Beto De Paola, Bhargavi Paranjape, Bing Liu, Bo Wu, Boyu Ni, Braden Hancock, Bram Wasti, Brandon Spence, Brani Stojkovic, Brian Gamido, Britt Montalvo, Carl Parker, Carly Burton, Catalina Mejia, Changhan Wang, Changkyu Kim, Chao Zhou, Chester Hu, Ching-Hsiang Chu, Chris Cai, Chris Tindal, Christoph Feichtenhofer, Damon Civin, Dana Beaty, Daniel Kreymer, Daniel Li, Danny Wyatt, David Adkins, David Xu, Davide Testuggine, Delia David, Devi Parikh, Diana Liskovich, Didem Foss, Dingkang Wang, Duc Le, Dustin Holland, Edward Dowling, Eissa Jamil, Elaine Montgomery, Eleonora Presani, Emily Hahn, Emily Wood, Erik Brinkman, Esteban Arcaute, Evan Dunbar, Evan Smothers, Fei Sun, Felix Kreuk, Feng Tian, Firat Ozgenel, Francesco Caggioni, Francisco Guzmán, Frank Kanayet, Frank Seide, Gabriela Medina Florez, Gabriella Schwarz, Gada Badeer, Georgia Swee, Gil Halpern, Govind Thattai, Grant Herman, Grigory Sizov, Guangyi, Zhang, Guna Lakshminarayanan, Hamid Shojanazeri, Han Zou, Hannah Wang, Hanwen Zha, Haroun Habeeb, Harrison Rudolph, Helen Suk, Henry Aspegren, Hunter Goldman, Ibrahim Damlaj, Igor Molybog, Igor Tufanov, Irina-Elena Veliche, Itai Gat, Jake Weissman, James Geboski, James Kohli, Japhet Asher, Jean-Baptiste Gaya, Jeff Marcus, Jeff Tang, Jennifer Chan, Jenny Zhen, Jeremy Reizenstein, Jeremy Teboul, Jessica Zhong, Jian Jin, Jingyi Yang, Joe Cummings, Jon Carvill, Jon Shepard, Jonathan McPhie, Jonathan Torres, Josh Ginsburg, Junjie Wang, Kai Wu, Kam Hou U, Karan Saxena, Karthik Prasad, Kartikay Khandelwal, Katayoun Zand, Kathy Matosich, Kaushik Veeraraghavan, Kelly Michelena, Keqian Li, Kun Huang, Kunal Chawla, Kushal Lakhotia, Kyle Huang, Lailin Chen, Lakshya Garg, Lavender A, Leandro Silva, Lee Bell, Lei Zhang, Liangpeng Guo, Licheng Yu, Liron Moshkovich, Luca Wehrstedt, Madian Khabsa, Manav Avalani, Manish Bhatt, Maria Tsimpoukelli, Martynas Mankus, Matan Hasson, Matthew Lennie, Matthias Reso, Maxim Groshev, Maxim Naumov, Maya Lathi, Meghan Keneally, Michael L. Seltzer, Michal Valko, Michelle Restrepo, Mihir Patel, Mik Vyatskov, Mikayel Samvelyan, Mike Clark, Mike Macey, Mike Wang, Miquel Jubert Hermoso, Mo Metanat, Mohammad Rastegari, Munish Bansal, Nandhini Santhanam, Natascha Parks,

Natasha White, Navyata Bawa, Nayan Singhal, Nick Egebo, Nicolas Usunier, Nikolay Pavlovich Laptev, Ning Dong, Ning Zhang, Norman Cheng, Oleg Chernoguz, Olivia Hart, Omkar Salpekar, Ozlem Kalinli, Parkin Kent, Parth Parekh, Paul Saab, Pavan Balaji, Pedro Rittner, Philip Bontrager, Pierre Roux, Piotr Dollar, Polina Zvyagina, Prashant Ratanchandani, Pritish Yuvraj, Qian Liang, Rachad Alao, Rachel Rodriguez, Rafi Ayub, Raghotham Murthy, Raghu Nayani, Rahul Mitra, Raymond Li, Rebekkah Hogan, Robin Battey, Rocky Wang, Rohan Maheswari, Russ Howes, Ruty Rinott, Sai Jayesh Bondu, Samyak Datta, Sara Chugh, Sara Hunt, Sargun Dhillon, Sasha Sidorov, Satadru Pan, Saurabh Verma, Seiji Yamamoto, Sharadh Ramaswamy, Shaun Lindsay, Shaun Lindsay, Sheng Feng, Shenghao Lin, Shengxin Cindy Zha, Shiva Shankar, Shuqiang Zhang, Shuqiang Zhang, Sinong Wang, Sneha Agarwal, Soji Sajuyigbe, Soumith Chintala, Stephanie Max, Stephen Chen, Steve Kehoe, Steve Satterfield, Sudarshan Govindaprasad, Sumit Gupta, Sungmin Cho, Sunny Virk, Suraj Subramanian, Sy Choudhury, Sydney Goldman, Tal Remez, Tamar Glaser, Tamara Best, Thilo Kohler, Thomas Robinson, Tianhe Li, Tianjun Zhang, Tim Matthews, Timothy Chou, Tzook Shaked, Varun Vontimitta, Victoria Ajayi, Victoria Montanez, Vijai Mohan, Vinay Satish Kumar, Vishal Mangla, Vítor Albiero, Vlad Ionescu, Vlad Poenaru, Vlad Tiberiu Mihailescu, Vladimir Ivanov, Wei Li, Wenchen Wang, Wenwen Jiang, Wes Bouaziz, Will Constable, Xiaocheng Tang, Xiaofang Wang, Xiaojian Wu, Xiaolan Wang, Xide Xia, Xilun Wu, Xinbo Gao, Yanjun Chen, Ye Hu, Ye Jia, Ye Qi, Yenda Li, Yilin Zhang, Ying Zhang, Yossi Adi, Youngjin Nam, Yu, Wang, Yuchen Hao, Yundi Qian, Yuzi He, Zach Rait, Zachary DeVito, Zef Rosnbrick, Zhaoduo Wen, Zhenyu Yang, and Zhiwei Zhao. 2024. The llama 3 herd of models. *Preprint*, arXiv:2407.21783.

Sebastian Gehrmann, Hendrik Strobelt, and Alexander Rush. 2019. GLTR: Statistical detection and visualization of generated text. In *Proceedings of the 57th Annual Meeting of the Association for Computational Linguistics: System Demonstrations*, pages 111–116, Florence, Italy. Association for Computational Linguistics.

Binyuan Hui, Jian Yang, Zeyu Cui, Jiaxi Yang, Dayiheng Liu, Lei Zhang, Tianyu Liu, Jiajun Zhang, Bowen Yu, Kai Dang, An Yang, Rui Men, Fei Huang, Xingzhang Ren, Xuancheng Ren, Jingren Zhou, and Junyang Lin. 2024. Qwen2.5-coder technical report. *Preprint*, arXiv:2409.12186.

Mohamed Khalifa and Mona Albadawy. 2024. Using artificial intelligence in academic writing and research: An essential productivity tool. *Computer Methods and Programs in Biomedicine Update*, 5:100145.

Kseniia Petukhova, Roman Kazakov, and Ekaterina Kochmar. 2024. PetKaz at SemEval-2024 task 8: Can linguistics capture the specifics of LLM-generated text? In *Proceedings of the 18th International Workshop on Semantic Evaluation (SemEval-2024)*, pages 1140–1147, Mexico City, Mexico. Association for Computational Linguistics.

Areg Mikael Sarvazyan, José Ángel González, and Marc Franco-salvador. 2024. Genaios at SemEval-2024 task 8: Detecting machine-generated text by mixing language model probabilistic features. In *Proceedings of the 18th International Workshop on Semantic Evaluation (SemEval-2024)*, pages 101–107, Mexico City, Mexico. Association for Computational Linguistics.

Michal Spiegel and Dominik Macko. 2024. KInIT at SemEval-2024 task 8: Fine-tuned LLMs for multilingual machine-generated text detection. In *Proceedings of the 18th International Workshop on Semantic Evaluation (SemEval-2024)*, pages 558–564, Mexico City, Mexico. Association for Computational Linguistics.

Gemma Team, Morgane Riviere, Shreya Pathak, Pier Giuseppe Sessa, Cassidy Hardin, Surya Bhupatiraju, Léonard Hussenot, Thomas Mesnard, Bobak Shahriari, Alexandre Ramé, Johan Ferret, Peter Liu, Pouya Tafti, Abe Friesen, Michelle Casbon, Sabela Ramos, Ravin Kumar, Charline Le Lan, Sammy Jerome, Anton Tsitsulin, Nino Vieillard, Piotr Stanczyk, Sertan Girgin, Nikola Momchev, Matt Hoffman, Shantanu Thakoor, Jean-Bastien Grill, Behnam Neyshabur, Olivier Bachem, Alanna Walton, Aliaksei Severyn, Alicia Parrish, Aliya Ahmad, Allen Hutchison, Alvin Abdagic, Amanda Carl, Amy Shen, Andy Brock, Andy Coenen, Anthony Laforge, Antonia Paterson, Ben Bastian, Bilal Piot, Bo Wu, Brandon Royal, Charlie Chen, Chintu Kumar, Chris Perry, Chris Welty, Christopher A. Choquette-Choo, Danila Sinopalnikov, David Weinberger, Dimple Vijaykumar, Dominika Rogozińska, Dustin Herbison, Elisa Bandy, Emma Wang, Eric Noland, Erica Moreira, Evan Senter, Evgenii Eltyshev, Francesco Visin, Gabriel Rasskin, Gary Wei, Glenn Cameron, Gus Martins, Hadi Hashemi, Hanna Klimczak-Plucińska, Harleen Batra, Harsh Dhand, Ivan Nardini, Jacinda Mein, Jack Zhou, James Svensson, Jeff Stanway, Jetha Chan, Jin Peng Zhou, Joana Carrasqueira, Joana Iljazi, Jocelyn Becker, Joe Fernandez, Joost van Amersfoort, Josh Gordon, Josh Lipschultz, Josh Newlan, Ju yeong Ji, Kareem Mohamed, Kartikeya Badola, Kat Black, Katie Millican, Keelin McDonell, Kelvin Nguyen, Kiranbir Sodhia, Kish Greene, Lars Lowe Sjoesund, Lauren Usui, Laurent Sifre, Lena Heuermann, Leticia Lago, Lilly McNealus, Livio Baldini Soares, Logan Kilpatrick, Lucas Dixon, Luciano Martins, Machel Reid, Manvinder Singh, Mark Iverson, Martin Görner, Mat Velloso, Mateo Wirth, Matt Davidow, Matt Miller, Matthew Rahtz, Matthew Watson, Meg Risdal, Mehran Kazemi, Michael Moynihan, Ming Zhang, Minsuk Kahng, Minwoo Park, Mofi Rahman, Mohit Khatwani, Natalie Dao, Nenshad Bardoliwalla, Nesh Devanathan, Neta Dumai, Nilay Chauhan, Oscar Wahltinez, Pankil Botarda, Parker Barnes, Paul Barham, Paul Michel, Pengchong Jin, Petko Georgiev, Phil Culliton, Pradeep Kuppala, Ramona Comanescu, Ramona Merhej, Reena

Jana, Reza Ardeshir Rokni, Rishabh Agarwal, Ryan Mullins, Samaneh Saadat, Sara Mc Carthy, Sarah Cogan, Sarah Perrin, Sébastien M. R. Arnold, Sebastian Krause, Shengyang Dai, Shruti Garg, Shruti Sheth, Sue Ronstrom, Susan Chan, Timothy Jordan, Ting Yu, Tom Eccles, Tom Hennigan, Tomas Kocisky, Tulsee Doshi, Vihan Jain, Vikas Yadav, Vilobh Meshram, Vishal Dharmadhikari, Warren Barkley, Wei Wei, Wenming Ye, Woohyun Han, Woosuk Kwon, Xiang Xu, Zhe Shen, Zhitao Gong, Zichuan Wei, Victor Cotruta, Phoebe Kirk, Anand Rao, Minh Giang, Ludovic Peran, Tris Warkentin, Eli Collins, Joelle Barral, Zoubin Ghahramani, Raia Hadsell, D. Sculley, Jeanine Banks, Anca Dragan, Slav Petrov, Oriol Vinyals, Jeff Dean, Demis Hassabis, Koray Kavukcuoglu, Clement Farabet, Elena Buchatskaya, Sebastian Borgeaud, Noah Fiedel, Armand Joulin, Kathleen Kenealy, Robert Dadashi, and Alek Andreev. 2024. Gemma 2: Improving open language models at a practical size. *Preprint*, arXiv:2408.00118.

Hanh Thi Hong Tran, Tien Nam Nguyen, Antoine Doucet, and Senja Pollak. 2024. L3i++ at SemEval-2024 task 8: Can fine-tuned large language model detect multigenerator, multidomain, and multilingual black-box machine-generated text? In *Proceedings of the 18th International Workshop on Semantic Evaluation (SemEval-2024)*, pages 13–21, Mexico City, Mexico. Association for Computational Linguistics.

Adaku Uchendu, Zeyu Ma, Thai Le, Rui Zhang, and Dongwon Lee. 2021. TURINGBENCH: A benchmark environment for Turing test in the age of neural text generation. In *Findings of the Association for Computational Linguistics: EMNLP 2021*, pages 2001–2016, Punta Cana, Dominican Republic. Association for Computational Linguistics.

Yuxia Wang, Jonibek Mansurov, Petar Ivanov, Jinyan Su, Artem Shelmanov, Akim Tsvigun, Osama Mohammed Afzal, Tarek Mahmoud, Giovanni Puccetti, and Thomas Arnold. 2024. SemEval-2024 task 8: Multidomain, multimodel and multilingual machine-generated text detection. In *Proceedings of the 18th International Workshop on Semantic Evaluation (SemEval-2024)*, pages 2057–2079, Mexico City, Mexico. Association for Computational Linguistics.

Yuxia Wang, Artem Shelmanov, Jonibek Mansurov, Akim Tsvigun, Vladislav Mikhailov, Rui Xing, Zhuohan Xie, Jiahui Geng, Giovanni Puccetti, Ekaterina Artemova, Jinyan Su, Minh Ngoc Ta, Mervat Abassy, Kareem Elozeiri, Saad El Dine Ahmed, Maiya Goloburda, Tarek Mahmoud, Raj Vardhan Tomar, Alexander Aziz, Nurkhan Laiyk, Osama Mohammed Afzal, Ryuto Koike, Masahiro Kaneko, Alham Fikri Aji, Nizar Habash, Iryna Gurevych, and Preslav Nakov. 2025. GenAI content detection task 1: English and multilingual machine-generated text detection: AI vs. human. In *Proceedings of the 1st Workshop on GenAI Content Detection (GenAIDetect)*, Abu Dhabi, UAE. International Conference on Computational Linguistics.

Table 7: Summary of monolingual training dataset for subtask A

Src	*Train*		*Dev*	
	Human	Machine	Human	Machine
hc3	39140	18091	16855	7917
m4gt	86782	181081	37220	71197
mage	103000	182673	44253	84316
total	228922	381845	98328	163430

Table 8: Summary of multilingual training dataset for subtask B

Lan	*Train*		*Dev*	
	Human	Machine	Human	Machine
ar	344	1770	150	756
bg	4205	3886	1795	1694
en	223911	386877	98041	163808
de	231	4462	102	1957
id	1895	2081	886	917
it	0	4174	0	1843
ru	684	630	316	284
ur	2085	1676	853	720
zh	19315	15969	8023	6749
total	257968	416115	110166	178728

A. Data Analysis

The task provides datasets in multiple domains and multi-model and multilingual text. The organizer extends this dataset from the one provided in *SemEval-2024 Task 8*. Details of the English-only subtask are in Table 7. The ratio of text for each class *human* or *machine* is consistent in both the train and dev set, around 37 %. Table 8 illustrates the distribution of the number of each class per language in two datasets. We see an imbalance across languages that more than 90 % of the text in the training dataset is English. This could cause the model to find it hard to identify each language because using an external dataset is not allowed by the organizer.

Regarding text's length, as we see in Figure 3, while around 70% of the text has a length of 250, the rest are in a range from there to more than 20000 words per text. Using linguistic features can gain valuable information from the truncated part, which small language models ignore.

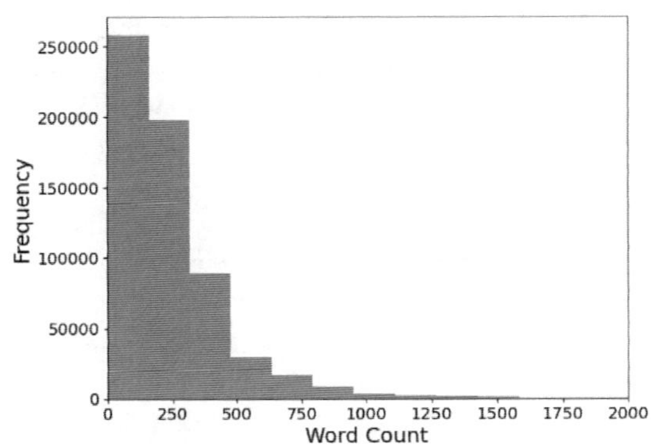

(a) Train Dataset

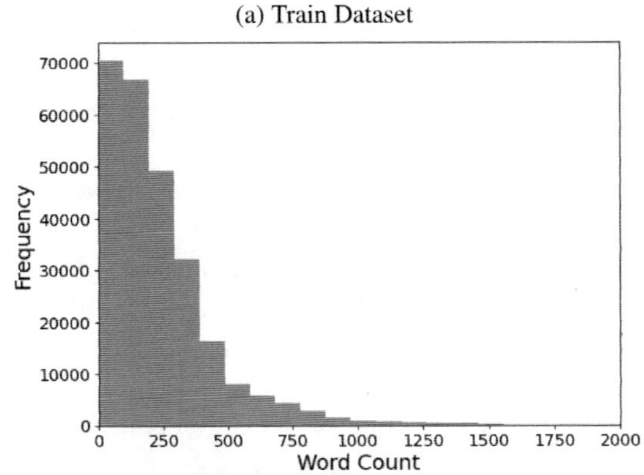

(b) Dev Dataset

Figure 3: Distribution of number of words per text in English datasets

AAIG at GenAI Detection Task 1: Exploring Syntactically-Aware, Resource-Efficient Small Autoregressive Decoders for AI Content Detection

Avanti Bhandarkar, Ronald Wilson and Damon Woodard
Florida Institute for National Security
University of Florida, Gainesville, FL, USA
{avantibhandarkar, ronaldwilson, dwoodard}@ufl.edu

Abstract

This paper presents a lightweight and efficient approach to AI-generated content detection using small autoregressive fine-tuned decoders (AFDs) for secure, on-device deployment. Motivated by resource-efficiency, syntactic awareness, and bias mitigation, our model employs small language models (SLMs) with autoregressive pre-training and loss fusion to accurately distinguish between human and AI-generated content while significantly reducing computational demands. The system achieved highest macro-F1 score of 0.8186, with the submitted model scoring 0.7874–both significantly outperforming the task baseline while reducing model parameters by $\approx$60%. Notably, our approach mitigates biases, improving recall for human-authored text by over 60%. Ranking 8th out of 36 participants, these results confirm the feasibility and competitiveness of small AFDs in challenging, adversarial settings, making them ideal for privacy-preserving, on-device deployment suitable for real-world applications.

1 Introduction

Advancements in Generative AI (GenAI) powered by large language models (LLMs) have significantly improved natural language generation (NLG) capabilities. AI-generated text, often indistinguishable from human writing, presents risks to information integrity, trust, and security (Gehrmann et al., 2019; Ippolito et al., 2020; Wu et al., 2024). The widespread availability of open-source, user-friendly LLMs enables individuals with minimal expertise to conduct misinformation, disinformation, and phishing campaigns, highlighting the need for accurate AI content detection. However, most research rallies behind sophisticated, resource-intensive solutions, often overlooking the security and privacy aspect of AI content detection. Most solutions require cloud connectivity or extensive computational resources, making them impractical for secure, on-device deployment.

Many existing approaches depend on complex architectures, including large pre-trained models (PLMs) like RoBERTa-large and Longformer (Li et al., 2024), or leverage larger LLMs like LLaMA (Hans et al., 2024) through techniques such as instruction-tuning (Wang et al., 2024a). Others employ ensemble methods that combine multiple LLMs (Sheykhlan et al., 2024; Abburi et al., 2023; Lai et al., 2024; El-Sayed and Nasr, 2023; Sarvazyan et al., 2024), that can significantly increase latency. In contrast, we focus on lightweight models that are optimized for secure, on-device deployment. On-device processing supports real-time analysis, essential for fast-paced environments, while also enhancing privacy by retaining sensitive data locally and reducing risks associated with transmitting information to external servers (Xu et al., 2024). This is particularly important for security-sensitive fields such as defense, healthcare, finance, and personal communications, where protecting data from unauthorized access is critical. This study evaluates the feasibility of small autoregressive fine-tuned decoders (AFDs) for efficient and secure AI-generated content detection.

Our approach is guided by three motivations: First, using SLMs ($\leq$135M parameters) suitable for on-device deployment, enabling privacy, real-time processing, and accessibility; Second, leveraging an autoregressive pre-training objective that mirrors the sequential nature of language production, enhancing syntactic awareness essential for detecting structural nuances to differentiate human and machine language; and third, employing a loss fusion strategy to learn from difficult examples and encourage class separation for bias mitigation.

The proposed system, using SmolLM, achieved the highest macro-F1 score of 0.8186 on the test set, significantly outperforming the task baseline (macro-F1 of 0.7568) under similar settings, while also reducing the number of parameters by $\approx$60%. Our submitted model (selected based on validation

Proceedings of the 1st Workshop on GenAI Content Detection (GenAIDetect), pages 218–224
January 19, 2025.

performance) attained a macro-F1 score of 0.7874, ranking 8th among 36 participants. These results underscore the potential of small AFDs for effective on-device AI-content detection.

2 Task Description

In the COLING Workshop on Detection AI Generated Content, Task 1 posed a binary classification problem: determining whether a given text is machine- or human-authored (Wang et al., 2025). Our investigation focused on Subtask A, which targets English-only MGT detection and extends the SemEval Shared Task 8 (Subtask A)(Wang et al., 2024b). Table 1 shows summary statistics for the provided datasets. From our analysis, this task presented three key challenges to test the model generalizability involving unfamiliar data sources, unknown LLMs as well as adversarially modified texts from Mixset (Zhang et al., 2024), LLM-DetectAIve (Abassy et al., 2024), and CU-DRT (Tao et al., 2024).

Table 1: Summary statistics of shared task subsets

Property		Train	Val	Dev	Test
#Sources		3	3	2	6
#LLMs		40	40	5	14
Human	#Samples	228,922	98,328	13,371	34,675
	Avg Len	302	303	339	270
Machine	#Samples	381,845	163,430	19,186	39,266
	Avg Len	273	272	417	411

3 System Overview

Our approach centers on fine-tuning small autoregressive decoders combined with a loss fusion strategy to enhance classification performance. Anticipating the presence of surprise domains and LLMs in the test set, we experimented with two distinct loss functions to optimize performance, particularly on challenging examples.

3.1 Model Selection

The selection of AFDs is driven by two core reasons: bias mitigation and syntactic awareness.

Related research indicates that models like RoBERTa, though powerful, tend to display a bias toward synthetic text, resulting in a high rate of false negatives when classifying human-generated text (Ciccarelli et al., 2024). This suggests that machine-generated content has an identifiable structural pattern that models such as RoBERTa -which are not specifically optimized for language generation- might misinterpret as "non-human". In contrast, autoregressive language models are trained with a next-token prediction objective, which naturally aligns with human language composition, making them more attuned to syntactic patterns typical of human writing. This syntactic awareness is particularly valuable for distinguishing subtle linguistic cues that differentiate human from machine-generated text. Additionally, the "LLM race" has led to the development of increasingly compact SLMs, such as MobileLLM, SmolLM, and GPT-Neo, that achieve high performance on various text generation and reasoning tasks with fewer parameters, enabling efficient, on-device deployment (Xu et al., 2024). These qualities make small AFDs effective and practical for real-world AI-content detection.

3.2 Loss Fusion

As an additional measure for bias mitigation, we employ a loss fusion strategy. We experiment with two primary loss functions: **Cross-Entropy** (Mao et al., 2023), which minimizes classification errors by measuring the divergence between predicted probabilities and true labels, and **Focal Loss** (Mukhoti et al., 2020), which addresses class imbalance by penalizing misclassifications on harder-to-classify examples or ambiguous cases. Additionally, following Ai et al. (2022), we incorporate **Contrastive Loss** as an auxiliary loss that structures the embedding space by pulling similar samples closer and pushing dissimilar ones apart (Dipta and Shahriar, 2024). The final loss is a linear combination of the primary and auxiliary losses.

To evaluate the impact of the auxiliary loss, we also conduct ablation-like experiments using primary loss alone. Thus, our experiments include four different loss configurations: two primary losses (cross-entropy and focal) applied alone and also combined with contrastive loss.

4 Experimental Setup

We evaluate five different SLMs ($\leq$135M parameters), selected for their suitability for on-device deployment (Lu et al., 2024). These include SmolLM (Allal et al., 2024), GPT2 (Radford et al., 2019), GPT-Neo (Black et al., 2021), OPT (Zhang et al., 2022) and MobileLLM (Liu et al., 2024). Since the task baseline (RoBERTa-Large) has significantly more parameters than our selected models, we also include RoBERTa-Base as a baseline for fair per-

Table 2: Summary of results: Best-performing systems per phase are **highlighted**, and second-best <u>underlined</u>.

	System Details			Macro-F1				Test-Recall	
	Model	#Param.	Loss	Val	Dev	Test	%Gain	Human	LLM
Task Baseline	Roberta-L[3]	406M	CE[1]	0.9489	0.8017	0.7139	2.20↑	0.4951	0.9465
			CE + Con[2]	0.9473	0.7823	0.7475	5.57↑	0.5437	0.9581
			Focal	<u>0.9699</u>	0.8677	0.7568	4.94↑	0.5863	0.9293
			Focal + Con	0.9611	0.8122	0.7516	1.59↑	0.5697	0.9371
Our Baseline	Roberta-B[4]	125M	CE	0.9362	0.7898	0.6919	0.00	0.4507	0.9558
			CE + Con	0.9324	0.7653	0.6918	0.00	0.4540	0.9514
			Focal	0.9408	0.7795	0.7074	0.00	0.4675	0.9670
			Focal + Con	0.9489	0.8166	0.7358	0.00	0.5455	0.9323
Proposed System	SmolLM	135M	CE	0.9683	0.8642	0.8104	11.58↑	0.7218	0.8953
			CE + Con	**0.9793**	<u>0.8679</u>	0.7874*	9.56↑	0.6669	0.9051
			Focal	0.9627	0.8678	**0.8186**	11.12↑	0.7509	0.8830
			Focal + Con	0.9690	**0.8777**	<u>0.8135</u>	7.78↑	0.7281	0.8953
System Alternatives	GPT2	117M	CE	0.9354	0.7904	0.7085	1.67↑	0.4765	0.9581
			CE + Con	0.9361	0.7889	0.6670	2.48↓	0.4092	0.9574
			Focal	0.9235	0.7754	0.6867	2.07↓	0.4369	0.9626
			Focal + Con	0.9580	0.8210	0.7314	0.43↓	0.5420	0.9274
	GPT-Neo	125M	CE	0.9665	0.8062	0.7886	9.68↑	0.7603	0.8160
			CE + Con	0.9461	0.8240	0.7464	5.46↑	0.6832	0.8079
			Focal	0.9583	0.8166	0.7812	7.38↑	0.7401	0.8207
			Focal + Con	0.9656	0.8277	0.8070	7.13↑	0.7935	0.8204
	OPT	125M	CE	0.9647	0.8121	0.7024	1.05↑	0.5252	0.8872
			CE + Con	0.9622	0.7946	0.7115	1.97↑	0.5906	0.8332
			Focal	0.9588	0.8346	0.7243	1.69↑	0.5262	0.9311
			Focal + Con	0.9649	0.8400	0.7041	3.17↓	0.5614	0.8498
	MobileLLM	125M	CE	0.9608	0.8187	0.7225	3.06↑	0.6007	0.8446
			CE + Con	0.9593	0.8131	0.7164	2.46↑	0.6002	0.8328
			Focal	0.9620	0.8187	0.7276	2.02↑	0.6067	0.8485
			Focal + Con	0.9622	0.8246	0.7078	2.80↓	0.6121	0.8030

Abbrev: [1] Cross-Entropy Loss; [2] Contrastive Loss; [3] Roberta-Large; [4] Roberta-Base. Note: %Gain represents the performance improvement over our baseline (RoBERTa-base), with arrows (↑/↓) indicating increase or decrease. Test performance of the submitted system is marked with (*).

formance comparison. To align with our objective of testing the feasibility of small AFDs, we adopt a simple architecture: a single linear layer added on top of the frozen AFDs for classification, with a dropout layer (dropout rate = 0.3) applied before classification. Each text sample is represented using mean pooling of all token embeddings. Maximum length is set to 512 tokens, with shorter samples padded and longer samples truncated to max length.

We use a 50:50 split of the provided validation dataset for validation and testing. Training employs early stopping (with patience = 2), retaining the model with the lowest validation loss. Optimization is performed using the AdamW optimizer with a linear warmup scheduler (10% warmup steps). The learning rate is set to 2×10^{-5}, with a batch size of 32. Although the maximum training epochs are set to 15, early stopping is usually triggered within 4 epochs in practice. Mixed-precision training with gradient scaling is used to speed-up training. No further hyperparameter tuning is performed. We release our data and source code for reproducibility[1].

5 Results

Table 2 presents the results from our comprehensive evaluation of five recent AFDs. Three key insights emerge: First, most of the AFDs outperform baseline models by a significant margin, confirming our hypothesis. Second, the best-performing system demonstrates effective bias mitigation. Finally, contrastive learning appears unnecessary, as AFDs demonstrate inherent class separability.

We evaluated 20 models across four loss configurations and five AFDs, with *15 achieving a positive gain over the baseline—a **75%** success rate*, validating our hypothesis and highlighting the effectiveness of small AFDs for AI-generated content detection. The highest performance was achieved with the SmolLM model, likely due to its training on the high-quality SmolLM-Corpus (Ben Allal et al., 2024), which includes a mix of

[1] https://github.com/AvantiB/AAIG-at-GenAI-Detection-Task-1

human and synthetically generated text.

To analyze performance imbalance between the human and LLM classes, we examined their Recall scores on the test set. While baseline models achieve high recall for the LLM class, they perform poorly on the human class - confirming the bias reported in previous studies. In contrast, AFD models show a slight decrease in LLM recall but deliver a substantial improvement in recall for the human class - effectively mitigating bias. *Our best model increases human recall by 60% and 28% over our and task baselines, with minor LLM recall reductions of 9% and 5%, respectively.*

Focal loss consistently outperforms cross-entropy, but the addition of contrastive loss does not always lead to performance improvements. While contrastive loss occasionally enhances the performance of PLMs, AFDs generally show a decline when it is applied. This can be attributed to the already well-separated nature of AFD embeddings where further enforcing separation may over-penalize instances near class boundaries. This observation reinforces the suitability of AFDs, as their inherent syntactic awareness provides strong separability, making additional loss optimization redundant and reducing computational overhead.

Can ensembling AFDs improve performance? Although the primary goal of this paper is to demonstrate that small LMs are as capable, if not superior, to LLMs, the variability in performance between models raises the question of whether ensembling them could improve results. For instance, GPT-2 performs better than SmolLM in detecting the LLM class, while SmolLM outperforms GPT-2 for the Human class. This suggests that if the models leverage different aspects of the text for detecting AI-generated content, ensembling them might lead to performance gains.

We test this hypothesis by experimenting with all combinations (N=1,2,3,4,5) of AFDs using majority voting on the test set. Figure 1 presents a box-and-whisker plot of performance across different ensemble configurations, where a wider spread reflects greater variability based on the combination of AFDs in the ensemble. Although no significant improvement over the proposed single AFD system is observed, some performance gains are evident, particularly in the Focal+Contrastive loss setup, which achieves the highest macro-F1 score of 0.8295– 9.37 %Gain over the baseline.

Two main findings from the ensemble testing arise: First, performance tends to degrade as the number of models in the ensemble increases, with the best performance achieved at N=2, and second, the combination of SmolLM and GPT-2 consistently delivers strong results. As previously noted, their complementary strengths make this ensemble particularly robust, with each model enhancing the other's performance. Additionally, some improvements are observed when SmolLM is combined with GPT-Neo or OPT.

This suggests that *the success of the ensemble relies heavily on the proposed system using SmolLM, whose complementary strengths enhance other models, highlighting its potential for refinement in low-resource setups.*

6 Discussion

Given the test set's significant differences from the training set, namely, unfamiliar data sources, adversarially modified text, and unknown LLMs, it is imperative to analyze their impact on model performance.

Figure 2 presents a box-and-whisker plot of model performance by data source, with greater spread indicating variability. Overall, the *Human class shows lower performance compared to the LLM class*, with variations across sources. Mixset and CUDRT have the highest misclassification rate for the LLM class, likely due to the inclusion of adversarially perturbed text samples. For the Human class, Mixset, DetectAIve, and ieltsduck show the lowest performance. DetectAIve and ieltsduck contain IELTS test takers' data, likely written by non-native English speakers, contributing to misclassifications. In Mixset, LLM-modified samples labeled as human may also lead to errors.

The perturbation operations performed on each dataset are described in Table 3 with the performance per operation depicted in Figure 3. Overall, *adversarial perturbations increase susceptibility to misclassifications*. Notably, the "summary" operation from the CUDRT dataset results in highest misclassification rate, likely due to concise nature of text, providing insufficient information for accurate classification. Similarly, the "polish" and "complete" operations also degrade performance. However, recent studies suggest that incorporating small amounts of adversarial examples in training can improve detectors' ability to handle perturbed AI-generated content (Zhang et al., 2024).

Detection accuracy for each LLM in the test set is depicted in Figure 4. Variations of the Chat-

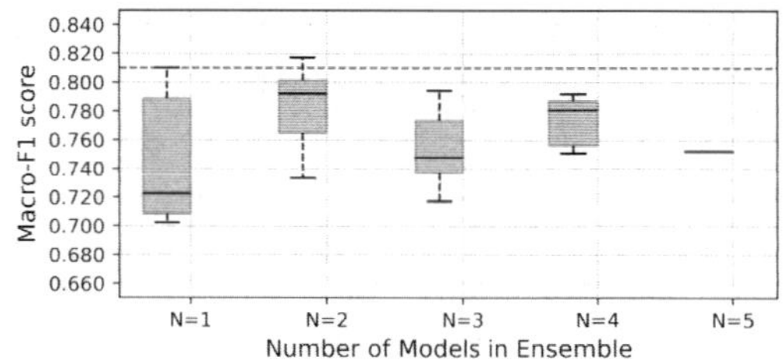

(a) Loss: Cross-Entropy

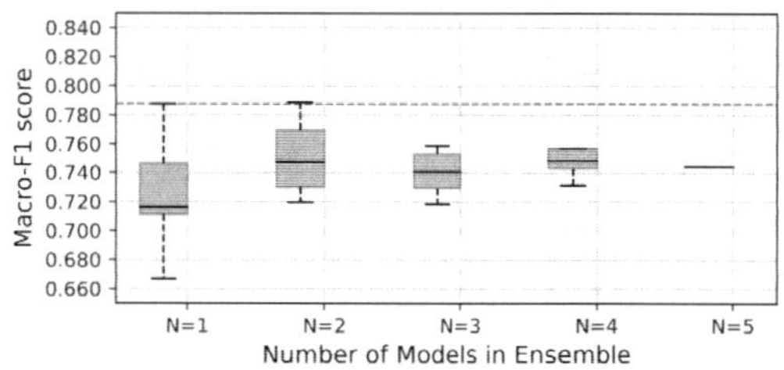

(b) Loss: Cross-Entropy+Contrastive

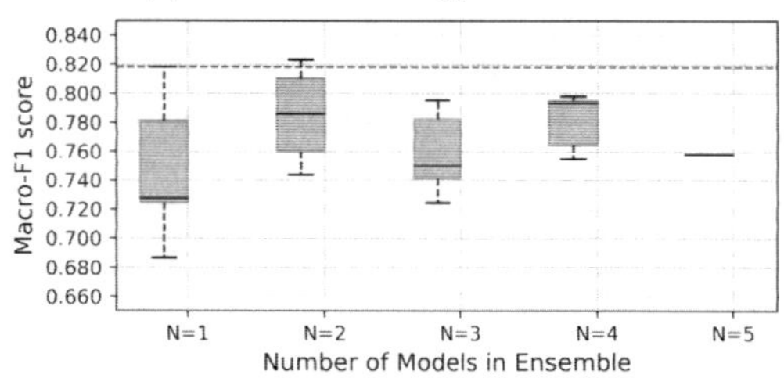

(c) Loss: Focal

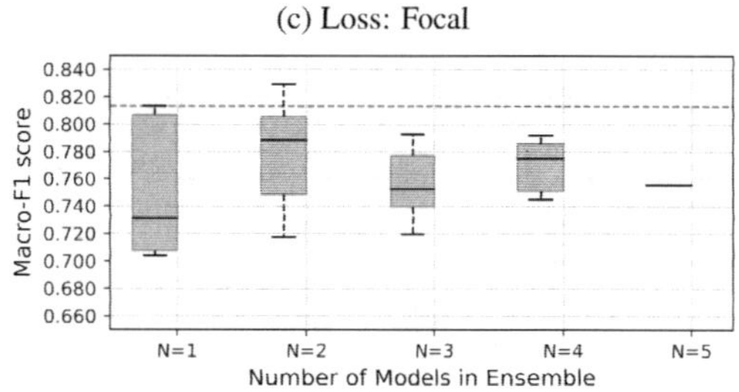

(d) Loss: Focal+Contrastive

Figure 1: Ensemble of AFDs using majority voting across different loss function configurations. Red dashed line represents the performance of proposed (single AFD) system. Spread of boxes represents performance variability due to choice of AFDs in ensemble.

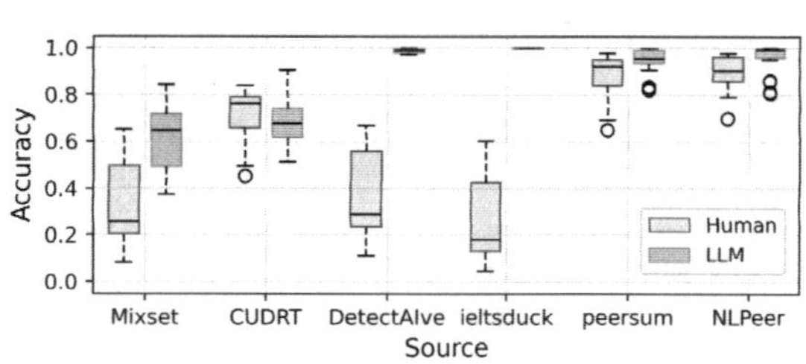

Figure 2: Model performance by source of data

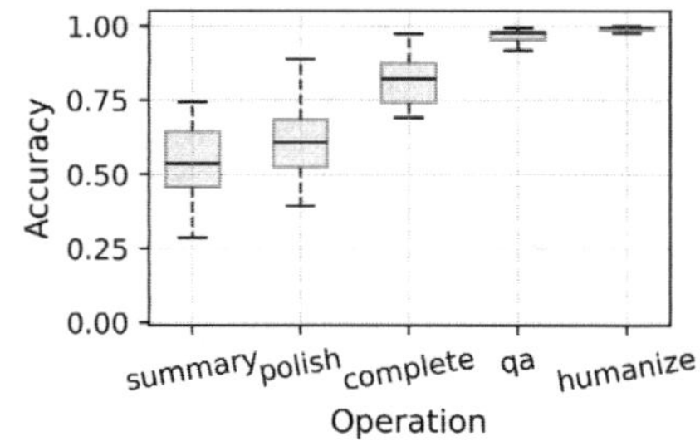

Figure 3: Performance across adversarial perturbations

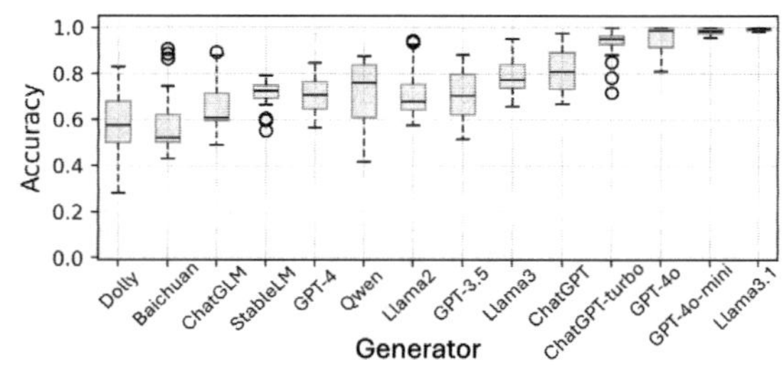

Figure 4: Model performance per LLM in test set

GPT family demonstrate stronger detection, likely due to the inclusion of related models from the same family in the training set. Nevertheless, the generalization of performance across data sources underscores our model's effectiveness. Moreover, ChatGPT's detectability aligns with existing research (Bhandarkar et al., 2024), ensuring safety against misuse of most widely used chatbot. In contrast, lesser-known models like Dolly and Baichuan show lower detection rates, highlighting areas for improvement.

7 Conclusion

This paper addresses the challenge of secure on-device AI content detection by proposing a simple yet effective solution leveraging small AFDs. With their resource-efficient design and syntactic alignment enabled by autoregressive pre-training, the proposed approach-combining AFDs with loss fusion, particularly focal loss-outperforms larger, resource-intensive models by a large margin while reducing model size. Our proposed approach mitigates bias, maintains generalization, and handles challenging data, including unknown domains, unseen LLMs, and adversarially modified text. These results highlight the potential of small AFDs as efficient backbones or ensemble components, especially in scenarios requiring data privacy and faster AI-content detection.

References

Mervat Abassy, Kareem Elozeiri, Alexander Aziz, Minh Ta, Raj Tomar, Bimarsha Adhikari, Saad Ahmed, Yuxia Wang, Osama Mohammed Afzal, Zhuohan Xie, et al. 2024. Llm-detectaive: a tool for fine-grained machine-generated text detection. In *Proceedings of the 2024 Conference on Empirical Methods in Natural Language Processing: System Demonstrations*, pages 336–343.

Harika Abburi, Michael Suesserman, Nirmala Pudota, Balaji Veeramani, Edward Bowen, and Sanmitra Bhattacharya. 2023. Generative ai text classification using ensemble llm approaches. *arXiv preprint arXiv:2309.07755*.

Bo Ai, Yuchen Wang, Yugin Tan, and Samson Tan. 2022. Whodunit? learning to contrast for authorship attribution. In *Proceedings of the 2nd Conference of the Asia-Pacific Chapter of the Association for Computational Linguistics and the 12th International Joint Conference on Natural Language Processing (Volume 1: Long Papers)*, pages 1142–1157, Online only. Association for Computational Linguistics.

Loubna Ben Allal, Anton Lozhkov, Elie Bakouch, Leandro von Werra, and Thomas Wolf. 2024. Smollm - blazingly fast and remarkably powerful.

Loubna Ben Allal, Anton Lozhkov, Guilherme Penedo, Thomas Wolf, and Leandro von Werra. 2024. Smollm-corpus.

Avanti Bhandarkar, Ronald Wilson, Anushka Swarup, Mengdi Zhu, and Damon Woodard. 2024. Is the digital forensics and incident response pipeline ready for text-based threats in llm era? *Preprint*, arXiv:2407.17870.

Sid Black, Gao Leo, Phil Wang, Connor Leahy, and Stella Biderman. 2021. GPT-Neo: Large Scale Autoregressive Language Modeling with Mesh-Tensorflow. If you use this software, please cite it using these metadata.

Vittorio Ciccarelli, Cornelia Genz, Nele Mastracchio, Wiebke Petersen, Anna Stein, and Hanxin Xia. 2024. Team art-nat-hhu at semeval-2024 task 8: Stylistically informed fusion model for mgt-detection. In *Proceedings of the 18th International Workshop on Semantic Evaluation (SemEval-2024)*, pages 1690–1697.

Shubhashis Roy Dipta and Sadat Shahriar. 2024. Hu at semeval-2024 task 8a: Can contrastive learning learn embeddings to detect machine-generated text? *arXiv preprint arXiv:2402.11815*.

Ahmed El-Sayed and Omar Nasr. 2023. An ensemble based approach to detecting LLM-generated texts. In *Proceedings of the 21st Annual Workshop of the Australasian Language Technology Association*, pages 164–168, Melbourne, Australia. Association for Computational Linguistics.

Sebastian Gehrmann, Hendrik Strobelt, and Alexander M Rush. 2019. Gltr: Statistical detection and visualization of generated text. In *Proceedings of the 57th Annual Meeting of the Association for Computational Linguistics: System Demonstrations*, pages 111–116.

Abhimanyu Hans, Avi Schwarzschild, Valeriia Cherepanova, Hamid Kazemi, Aniruddha Saha, Micah Goldblum, Jonas Geiping, and Tom Goldstein. 2024. Spotting llms with binoculars: Zero-shot detection of machine-generated text. *arXiv preprint arXiv:2401.12070*.

Daphne Ippolito, Daniel Duckworth, Chris Callison-Burch, and Douglas Eck. 2020. Automatic detection of generated text is easiest when humans are fooled. In *Proceedings of the 58th Annual Meeting of the Association for Computational Linguistics*, pages 1808–1822.

Zhixin Lai, Xuesheng Zhang, and Suiyao Chen. 2024. Adaptive ensembles of fine-tuned transformers for llm-generated text detection. *arXiv preprint arXiv:2403.13335*.

Yafu Li, Qintong Li, Leyang Cui, Wei Bi, Zhilin Wang, Longyue Wang, Linyi Yang, Shuming Shi, and Yue Zhang. 2024. MAGE: Machine-generated text detection in the wild. In *Proceedings of the 62nd Annual Meeting of the Association for Computational Linguistics (Volume 1: Long Papers)*, pages 36–53, Bangkok, Thailand. Association for Computational Linguistics.

Zechun Liu, Changsheng Zhao, Forrest Iandola, Chen Lai, Yuandong Tian, Igor Fedorov, Yunyang Xiong, Ernie Chang, Yangyang Shi, Raghuraman Krishnamoorthi, et al. 2024. Mobilellm: Optimizing sub-billion parameter language models for on-device use cases. In *Forty-first International Conference on Machine Learning*.

Zhenyan Lu, Xiang Li, Dongqi Cai, Rongjie Yi, Fangming Liu, Xiwen Zhang, Nicholas D Lane, and Mengwei Xu. 2024. Small language models: Survey, measurements, and insights. *arXiv preprint arXiv:2409.15790*.

Anqi Mao, Mehryar Mohri, and Yutao Zhong. 2023. Cross-entropy loss functions: Theoretical analysis and applications. In *International conference on Machine learning*, pages 23803–23828. PMLR.

Jishnu Mukhoti, Viveka Kulharia, Amartya Sanyal, Stuart Golodetz, Philip Torr, and Puneet Dokania. 2020. Calibrating deep neural networks using focal loss. *Advances in Neural Information Processing Systems*, 33:15288–15299.

Alec Radford, Jeffrey Wu, Rewon Child, David Luan, Dario Amodei, Ilya Sutskever, et al. 2019. Language models are unsupervised multitask learners.

Areg Mikael Sarvazyan, José Ángel González, and Marc Franco-salvador. 2024. Genaios at SemEval-2024 task 8: Detecting machine-generated text by mixing language model probabilistic features. In *Proceedings of the 18th International Workshop on Semantic Evaluation (SemEval-2024)*, pages 101–107, Mexico City, Mexico. Association for Computational Linguistics.

M Sheykhlan, S Abdoljabbar, and M Mahmoudabad. 2024. Team karami-kheiri at pan: enhancing machine-generated text detection with ensemble learning based on transformer models. *Working Notes of CLEF*.

Zhen Tao, Zhiyu Li, Dinghao Xi, and Wei Xu. 2024. Cudrt: Benchmarking the detection of human vs. large language models generated texts. *arXiv preprint arXiv:2406.09056*.

Rongsheng Wang, Haoming Chen, Ruizhe Zhou, Han Ma, Yaofei Duan, Yanlan Kang, Songhua Yang, Baoyu Fan, and Tao Tan. 2024a. Llm-detector: Improving ai-generated chinese text detection with open-source llm instruction tuning. *arXiv preprint arXiv:2402.01158*.

Yuxia Wang, Jonibek Mansurov, Petar Ivanov, Jinyan Su, Artem Shelmanov, Akim Tsvigun, Osama Mohammed Afzal, Tarek Mahmoud, Giovanni Puccetti, and Thomas Arnold. 2024b. SemEval-2024 task 8: Multidomain, multimodel and multilingual machine-generated text detection. In *Proceedings of the 18th International Workshop on Semantic Evaluation (SemEval-2024)*, pages 2057–2079, Mexico City, Mexico. Association for Computational Linguistics.

Yuxia Wang, Artem Shelmanov, Jonibek Mansurov, Akim Tsvigun, Vladislav Mikhailov, Rui Xing, Zhuohan Xie, Jiahui Geng, Giovanni Puccetti, Ekaterina Artemova, Jinyan Su, Minh Ngoc Ta, Mervat Abassy, Kareem Elozeiri, Saad El Dine Ahmed, Maiya Goloburda, Tarek Mahmoud, Raj Vardhan Tomar, Alexander Aziz, Nurkhan Laiyk, Osama Mohammed Afzal, Ryuto Koike, Masahiro Kaneko, Alham Fikri Aji, Nizar Habash, Iryna Gurevych, and Preslav Nakov. 2025. GenAI content detection task 1: English and multilingual machine-generated text detection: AI vs. human. In *Proceedings of the 1st Workshop on GenAI Content Detection (GenAIDetect)*, Abu Dhabi, UAE. International Conference on Computational Linguistics.

Junchao Wu, Shu Yang, Runzhe Zhan, Yulin Yuan, Derek F. Wong, and Lidia S. Chao. 2024. A survey on llm-generated text detection: Necessity, methods, and future directions. *Preprint*, arXiv:2310.14724.

Jiajun Xu, Zhiyuan Li, Wei Chen, Qun Wang, Xin Gao, Qi Cai, and Ziyuan Ling. 2024. On-device language models: A comprehensive review. *Preprint*, arXiv:2409.00088.

Qihui Zhang, Chujie Gao, Dongping Chen, Yue Huang, Yixin Huang, Zhenyang Sun, Shilin Zhang, Weiye Li, Zhengyan Fu, Yao Wan, et al. 2024. Llm-as-a-coauthor: Can mixed human-written and machine-generated text be detected? In *Findings of the Association for Computational Linguistics: NAACL 2024*, pages 409–436.

Susan Zhang, Stephen Roller, Naman Goyal, Mikel Artetxe, Moya Chen, Shuohui Chen, Christopher Dewan, Mona Diab, Xian Li, Xi Victoria Lin, et al. 2022. Opt: Open pre-trained transformer language models. *arXiv preprint arXiv:2205.01068*.

A Appendix

Table 3: Perturbation Operations from Various Datasets. (*) denotes LLM-generated text labeled as human

Operation	Description	Source		
		Mixset	DetectAIve	CUDRT
Polish	Improve quality, fluency, accuracy; includes refine, rewrite, paraphrase, etc.	✓	✓	✓
Complete	Generate part LLM, part human text by completing a given text portion	✓		✓
Q/A	LLMs act as expert to provide detailed answers to questions.			✓
Summary	Generate concise summary, highlighting main points and key information.			✓
Humanize	Add human-like noise (e.g., typos, grammatical errors, tags).	✓*	✓	

TurQUaz at GenAI Detection Task 1: Dr. Perplexity or: How I Learned to Stop Worrying and Love the Finetuning

Kaan Efe Keleş
TOBB University of Economics and Technology
kaanefekeles@etu.edu.tr

Mucahid Kutlu
Qatar University
mucahidkutlu@qu.edu.qa

Abstract

This paper details our methods for addressing Task 1 of the GenAI Content Detection shared tasks, which focus on distinguishing AI-generated text from human-written content. The task comprises two subtasks: Subtask A, centered on English-only datasets, and Subtask B, which extends the challenge to multilingual data. Our approach uses a fine-tuned XLM-RoBERTa model for classification, complemented by features including perplexity and TF-IDF. While perplexity is commonly regarded as a useful indicator for identifying machine-generated text, our findings suggest its limitations in multi-model and multilingual contexts. Our approach ranked 6th in Subtask A, but a submission issue left our Subtask B unranked, where it would have placed 23rd.

1 Introduction

The rapid proliferation of large language models (LLMs) has brought both remarkable advancements and significant challenges to the field of natural language processing (NLP). While these models enable unprecedented levels of fluency and coherence in generated text, their potential for misuse—ranging from generating misleading information to creating plagiarized content—necessitates robust detection methods. Distinguishing between human-written and machine-generated text has thus become a critical area of research, especially in multilingual and multi-model contexts.

Task 1 of the GenAI Content Detection shared tasks (Wang et al., 2025), addresses these challenges by focusing on the development of robust classifiers capable of identifying AI-generated text. This task is divided into two subtasks: Subtask A, which deals with English-only datasets, and Subtask B, which extends detection to multilingual datasets.

In this paper, we present our approaches for Subtask A and Subtask B. For Subtask A, we relied on a fine-tuned version of the XLM-RoBERTa model, achieving competitive performance. For Subtask B, we explored the integration of additional features such as perplexity and term frequency-inverse document frequency (TF-IDF). While perplexity has traditionally been considered a valuable metric for identifying machine-generated text (Varshney et al., 2020), we found its effectiveness limited in complex, multilingual scenarios.

Our approaches were ranked 6th place out of 35 participants in Subtask A. Unfortunately, due to a submission-related issue, our entry for Subtask B was not officially ranked. However, it would have placed 23rd out of 26 participants.

2 Related Work

The advance of LLMs has necessitated the development of robust methods for detecting machine-generated text. This has become a critical research area due to the potential misuse of LLMs for generating misleading or plagiarized content (Adelani et al., 2019; Pan et al., 2023). Early zero-shot detection methods, relying on statistical features like log probability and rank (Solaiman et al., 2019; Gehrmann et al., 2019; Ippolito et al., 2020), are computationally efficient but often lack robustness as models improve in generating text that closely resembles human writing (He et al., 2024).

More sophisticated zero-shot approaches have been proposed to address these shortcomings. DetectGPT (Mitchell et al., 2023) use the concept of probability curvature, comparing the log probability of a text with perturbed versions to identify machine-generated content.

Supervised detection, training classifiers on labeled data, has also been investigated (Uchendu et al., 2020; Guo et al., 2023). However, these methods suffer from limitations related to data requirements and generalization across domains and LLMs. Similarly, watermarking techniques

Proceedings of the 1st Workshop on GenAI Content Detection (GenAIDetect), pages 225–229
January 19, 2025.

(Kirchenbauer et al., 2023; Keleş et al., 2023), while promising, have shown vulnerability to paraphrasing attacks (Krishna et al., 2024; Sadasivan et al., 2023).

3 Proposed Approach

For both Subtask A and Subtask B, we fine-tuned the Facebook XLM-RoBERTa base model[1 2 3] (Conneau et al., 2020).

In Subtask A, we submitted the labels from the bare fine-tuned classifier, as we were unable to improve its performance using additional features including perplexity. For Subtask B, we aimed to enhance the classifier's performance by incorporating additional features including TF-IDF, the source language as a one-hot encoded feature, and perplexity values derived from the Llama 3.2 1B model (Dubey et al., 2024). These combined features were fed into an XGBoost classifier to improve overall performance. While our goal was to evaluate the effectiveness of perplexity as a predictive metric, we found it to be a suboptimal measure in this multi-source, multi-language context.

3.1 Perplexity

Perplexity (PPL) is a key metric used to evaluate how well a language model predicts a sequence of text, making it particularly useful for detecting machine-generated content. For a tokenized sequence $X = (x_1, x_2, \ldots, x_N)$, perplexity is calculated as:

$$\text{PPL}(X) = \exp\left(-\frac{1}{N}\sum_{i=1}^{N}\log P_\theta(x_i \mid x_{<i})\right)$$

where:

- N is the total number of tokens in the sequence.
- $P_\theta(x_i \mid x_{<i})$ is the model's predicted probability of token x_i given all preceding tokens $x_{<i}$.

Lower perplexity scores indicate that the text is more predictable according to the model. In the context of machine-generated text, since the generation process often samples tokens based on higher probability from the model's vocabulary, the output tends to include more likely tokens. This results in lower perplexity scores, which can suggest machine generation. On the other hand human-generated text often exhibits higher perplexity because humans do not always use the most statistically probable words; instead, they may choose words that are less predictable, adding creativity and nuance to the text. This higher perplexity reflects the diversity and unpredictability inherent in human language. Figure 1 shows the distribution of perplexity scores for AI-generated and human-written texts on the shared-task data.

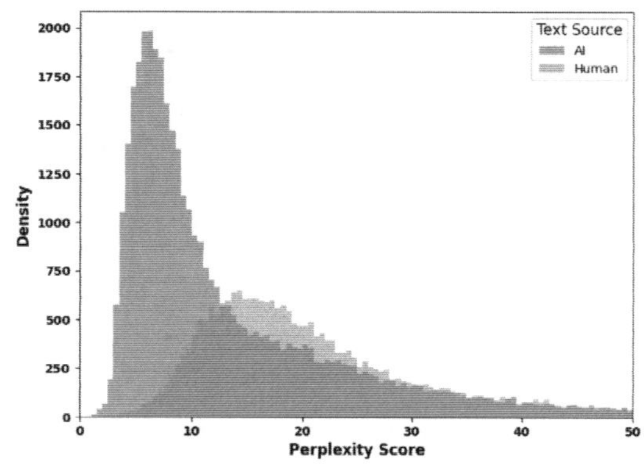

Figure 1: Distribution of perplexity scores for AI-generated (orange) and human-written (blue) texts for Subtask B's validation and test set combined.

Perplexity scores are influenced by various factors, including the specific language model, tokenization methods, and the language of the text. Models may assign higher perplexity to less common languages due to their under-representation in training data. While perplexity offers insights into text predictability, it has limitations as a sole indicator of text quality. Research indicates that perplexity is unreliable for evaluating text quality, as it can be affected by text length, repetition, and punctuation (Wang et al., 2022). These limitations also apply when using perplexity to detect machine-generated text.

4 Experiments

4.1 Perplexity as a Predictive Metric

As shown in Figure 1, Table 1, and Table 2, AI-generated texts generally exhibit lower perplexity scores compared to human-written texts. However, this trend varies significantly depending on

[1] https://huggingface.co/FacebookAI/xlm-roberta-base

[2] https://huggingface.co/keles/fine_tuned_xlm_roberta_for_en

[3] https://huggingface.co/keles/fine_tuned_xlm_roberta_for_mgtd2

the language and the source model. Although the distributions differ, there is no clear distinction or clustering between the two types of texts.

Lang	Type	Min	Max	Median	Mean
en	AI	1.20	31589.12	9.71	17.39
	Human	2.35	2235.15	19.29	28.17
zh	AI	1.35	1e5	11.74	240.60
	Human	3.69	1.4e6	57.74	1622.03
it	AI	4.39	53.35	9.56	12.54
	Human	-	-	-	-
de	AI	4.47	50.41	11.43	13.15
	Human	4.05	17.68	11.14	11.36
ur	AI	1.60	6.93	3.51	3.67
	Human	3.63	23.06	9.17	9.44
bg	AI	4.71	25.12	10.09	10.66
	Human	4.43	65.97	14.40	15.58
id	AI	4.46	17.07	7.07	7.39
	Human	5.58	41.96	13.04	13.80
ar	AI	7.23	53.82	15.29	18.04
	Human	14.05	46.83	21.08	23.27
ru	AI	4.44	42.49	11.39	12.89
	Human	4.00	31.47	8.27	9.73

Table 1: Perplexity statistics from the Llama-3.2-1B model across various languages, comparing AI-generated and human-written texts. Notably, Italian (it) lacks human-written text statistics due to the absence of such instances in the training set. Overall, AI-generated texts generally exhibit lower mean perplexity scores than human-written texts in most languages, with Russian (ru) and German (de) being notable exceptions.

Model	Min	Max	Median	Mean
human	2.35	1.4e6	19.79	148.00
gpt-3.5-turbo	1.60	132.66	7.35	9.27
gpt-35	2.15	1e5	6.03	132.77
davinci	1.35	4671.52	9.77	13.76
cohere	1.61	32.47	5.58	6.14
bloomz	1.52	140.70	12.06	13.05
text-davinci-003	2.36	348.87	8.42	10.90
mixtral-8x7b	2.37	12074.41	6.14	17.99
text-davinci-002	2.70	320.81	8.31	12.65
llama3-70b	2.56	102.10	6.63	9.40
gemma-7b-it	4.02	115.08	11.03	13.68
llama3-8b	1.99	55.92	7.01	9.93
gpt4o	2.68	21.80	7.33	7.52
gpt4	2.95	18.88	5.96	6.31

Table 2: Perplexity statistics from the Llama-3.2-1B model across different text generation models and human writing.

Due to space constraints, we have not detailed all the models tested for perplexity calculations, but our experiments revealed surprising findings about model size. Larger models, including those with up to 9 billion parameters, did not demonstrate any meaningful improvement in discrimination ability. These results suggest that model size may not be a critical factor in the effectiveness of perplexity-based detection methods.

4.2 Implementation Details

4.2.1 Subtask A

As can be inferred from Table 3, perplexity as an additional did not measurably improve the overall performance.

Methodology	F1 Score
XGBoost (FTC + TF-IDF + Perplexity)	0.974
XGBoost (FTC + TF-IDF)	0.973
FTC	0.969

Table 3: F1 Scores for Various Feature Combinations on the Validation Set for Subtask A. FTC refers to the labels produced by the fine-tuned classifier. When used with XGBoost, the probability assigned by the fine-tuned classifier to the positive label is included as a feature.

4.2.2 Subtask B

As can be inferred from Table 4, perplexity as an additional feature did not measurably improve the overall performance.

Methodology	F1 Score
XGBoost (FTC + TF-IDF + Perplexity)	0.972
XGBoost (FTC + TF-IDF)	0.972
FTC	0.966

Table 4: F1 Scores for Various Feature Combinations on the Validation Set for Subtask B. FTC refers to the labels produced by the fine-tuned classifier. When used with XGBoost, the probability assigned by the fine-tuned classifier to the positive label is included as a feature.

4.3 Dataset

4.3.1 Subtask A

This subtask focuses solely on English data sourced from various origins. Of this data, 62.5% is labeled as AI-generated, while 37.5% is labeled as human-written. The datapoints were randomly shuffled and then divided into 90% for training, 8% for testing, and 2% for validation.

The given train set was randomly shuffled and then divided into 90% for training, 8% for testing, and 2% for validation. We observed that the number of positive cases in the test-development set is much less than the one in the trainset. So we set the decision boundary to 0.97.

4.3.2 Subtask B

The train and the leaderboard test datasets for subtask B, as shown in Figures 2 and 3 respectively, both exhibit significant language imbalances, albeit with notably different distributions. While the training set is dominated by English texts, the leaderboard test set presents an entirely different skew. We determined the language distribution of the test dataset using the langdetect library (Shuyo, 2010), which employs Naive Bayesian filtering for automatic language identification. The detection revealed Chinese (zh) as the dominant language with approximately 60,000 samples (39.8% of the dataset), followed by Urdu (ur) with 30,504 samples (20.1%) and Russian (ru) with 29,036 samples (19.2%). This substantial shift in language distribution between train and test sets, particularly the pivot from Indo-European languages in training to a test set dominated by Asian languages, presents an interesting challenge for fairly evaluating the model's cross-lingual generalization capabilities and robustness to language distribution shifts.

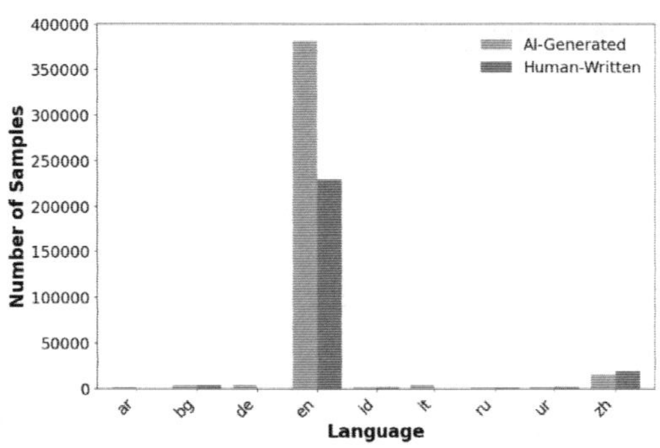

Figure 2: Distribution of AI-generated and human-written texts across different languages in the train dataset. The plot shows a clear imbalance in the dataset, with English (en) having the highest number of samples.

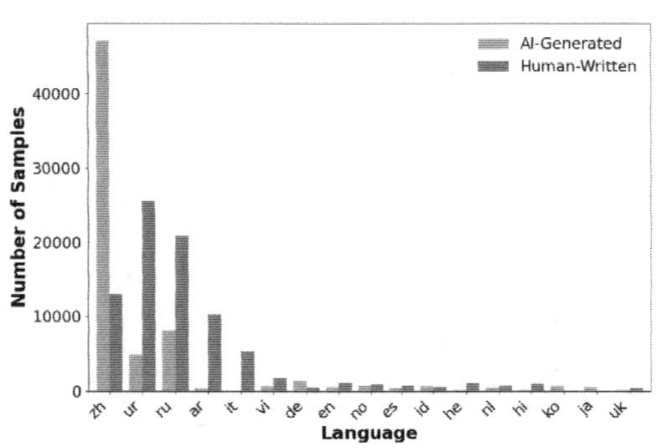

Figure 3: Distribution of AI-generated and human-written texts across different languages in the test dataset. The plot shows a clear imbalance in the dataset, with Chinese (zh) having the highest number of samples.

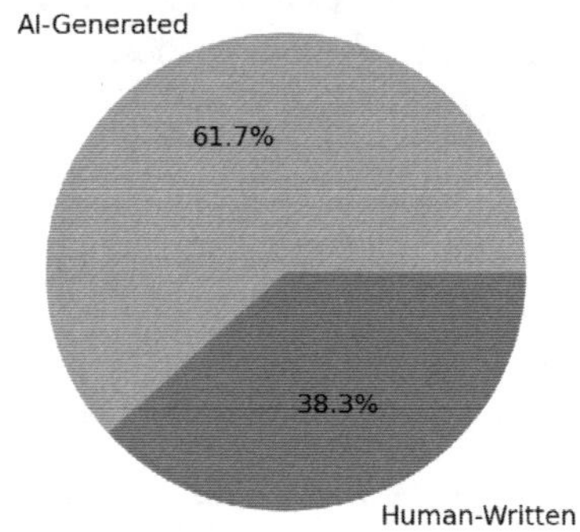

Figure 4: Distribution of AI-Generated vs Human-Written Samples for Subtask B

4.4 Results

The results of our submissions are summarized in Table 5. For Subtask A, which focuses on English-only datasets, our approach achieved an F1 score of 0.85 on the development set and 0.80 on the test set, reflecting a competitive performance. For Subtask B, encompassing multilingual data, the F1 scores were 0.65 and 0.64 on the development and test sets, respectively.

Subtask	Development (F1)	Test (F1)
Subtask A	0.85	0.80
Subtask B	0.65	0.64

Table 5: F1 scores for Subtask A and Subtask B on the development and test datasets, demonstrating the model's performance in detecting AI-generated versus human-written text.

5 Conclusions

In this paper, we presented our approach to the GenAI Content Detection shared tasks, focusing on distinguishing AI-generated from human-written text in both monolingual and multilingual contexts. Our primary findings indicate that while fine-tuned XLM-RoBERTa models can achieve competitive performance, the incorporation of additional features such as perplexity scores did not yield significant improvements in detection accuracy. This was particularly evident in the multilingual context, where perplexity's effectiveness varied considerably across different languages and source models.

References

David Ifeoluwa Adelani, Haotian Mai, Fuming Fang, Huy H. Nguyen, Junichi Yamagishi, and Isao

Echizen. 2019. Generating sentiment-preserving fake online reviews using neural language models and their human- and machine-based detection. *Preprint*, arXiv:1907.09177.

Alexis Conneau, Kartikay Khandelwal, Naman Goyal, Vishrav Chaudhary, Guillaume Wenzek, Francisco Guzmán, Edouard Grave, Myle Ott, Luke Zettlemoyer, and Veselin Stoyanov. 2020. Unsupervised cross-lingual representation learning at scale. *Preprint*, arXiv:1911.02116.

Abhimanyu Dubey, Abhinav Jauhri, Abhinav Pandey, Abhishek Kadian, Ahmad Al-Dahle, Aiesha Letman, Akhil Mathur, Alan Schelten, Amy Yang, Angela Fan, et al. 2024. The llama 3 herd of models. *arXiv preprint arXiv:2407.21783*.

Sebastian Gehrmann, Hendrik Strobelt, and Alexander M. Rush. 2019. GLTR: statistical detection and visualization of generated text. *CoRR*, abs/1906.04043.

Biyang Guo, Xin Zhang, Ziyuan Wang, Minqi Jiang, Jinran Nie, Yuxuan Ding, Jianwei Yue, and Yupeng Wu. 2023. How close is chatgpt to human experts? comparison corpus, evaluation, and detection. *arXiv preprint arXiv:2301.07597*.

Xinlei He, Xinyue Shen, Zeyuan Chen, Michael Backes, and Yang Zhang. 2024. Mgtbench: Benchmarking machine-generated text detection. *Preprint*, arXiv:2303.14822.

Daphne Ippolito, Daniel Duckworth, Chris Callison-Burch, and Douglas Eck. 2020. Automatic detection of generated text is easiest when humans are fooled. In *Proceedings of the 58th Annual Meeting of the Association for Computational Linguistics*, pages 1808–1822, Online. Association for Computational Linguistics.

Kaan Efe Keleş, Ömer Kaan Gürbüz, and Mucahid Kutlu. 2023. I know you did not write that! a sampling based watermarking method for identifying machine generated text. *Preprint*, arXiv:2311.18054.

John Kirchenbauer, Jonas Geiping, Yuxin Wen, Jonathan Katz, Ian Miers, and Tom Goldstein. 2023. A watermark for large language models. In *International Conference on Machine Learning*, pages 17061–17084. PMLR.

Kalpesh Krishna, Yixiao Song, Marzena Karpinska, John Wieting, and Mohit Iyyer. 2024. Paraphrasing evades detectors of ai-generated text, but retrieval is an effective defense. *Advances in Neural Information Processing Systems*, 36.

Eric Mitchell, Yoonho Lee, Alexander Khazatsky, Christopher D. Manning, and Chelsea Finn. 2023. Detectgpt: Zero-shot machine-generated text detection using probability curvature. *arXiv preprint*

Yikang Pan, Liangming Pan, Wenhu Chen, Preslav Nakov, Min-Yen Kan, and William Yang Wang. 2023. On the risk of misinformation pollution with large language models. *Preprint*, arXiv:2305.13661.

Vinu Sankar Sadasivan, Aounon Kumar, Sriram Balasubramanian, Wenxiao Wang, and Soheil Feizi. 2023. Can ai-generated text be reliably detected? *arXiv preprint arXiv:2303.11156*.

Nakatani Shuyo. 2010. Language detection library for java.

Irene Solaiman, Miles Brundage, Jack Clark, Amanda Askell, Ariel Herbert-Voss, Jeff Wu, Alec Radford, Gretchen Krueger, Jong Wook Kim, Sarah Kreps, Miles McCain, Alex Newhouse, Jason Blazakis, Kris McGuffie, and Jasmine Wang. 2019. Release strategies and the social impacts of language models. *Preprint*, arXiv:1908.09203.

Adaku Uchendu, Thai Le, Kai Shu, and Dongwon Lee. 2020. Authorship attribution for neural text generation. In *Proceedings of the 2020 Conference on Empirical Methods in Natural Language Processing (EMNLP)*, pages 8384–8395, Online. Association for Computational Linguistics.

Lav R Varshney, Nitish Shirish Keskar, and Richard Socher. 2020. Limits of detecting text generated by large-scale language models. In *2020 Information Theory and Applications Workshop (ITA)*, pages 1–5. IEEE.

Yequan Wang, Jiawen Deng, Aixin Sun, and Xuying Meng. 2022. Perplexity from plm is unreliable for evaluating text quality. *arXiv preprint arXiv:2210.05892*.

Yuxia Wang, Artem Shelmanov, Jonibek Mansurov, Akim Tsvigun, Vladislav Mikhailov, Rui Xing, Zhuohan Xie, Jiahui Geng, Giovanni Puccetti, Ekaterina Artemova, Jinyan Su, Minh Ngoc Ta, Mervat Abassy, Kareem Elozeiri, Saad El Dine Ahmed, Maiya Goloburda, Tarek Mahmoud, Raj Vardhan Tomar, Alexander Aziz, Nurkhan Laiyk, Osama Mohammed Afzal, Ryuto Koike, Masahiro Kaneko, Alham Fikri Aji, Nizar Habash, Iryna Gurevych, and Preslav Nakov. 2025. GenAI content detection task 1: English and multilingual machine-generated text detection: AI vs. human. In *Proceedings of the 1st Workshop on GenAI Content Detection (GenAIDetect)*, Abu Dhabi, UAE. International Conference on Computational Linguistics.

AI-Monitors at GenAI Detection Task 1: Fast and Scalable Machine Generated Text Detection

Azad Singh[1], Vishnu Tripathi[1], Ravindra Kumar Pandey[1], Pragyanand Saho[1], Prakhar Joshi[1], Neel Mani[1], Richa Alagh[2], Pallaw Mishra[3], Piyush Arora[4]
Dev Sanskriti Vishwavidyalaya Haridwar[1], Graphic Era University [2],
Safexpress Private Limited[3], American Express AI Labs[4]
{azad.singh|vishnu.tripathi|ravindra.pandey}@aicentre.org
{pragyanand.saho|prakhar.joshi}@aicentre.org |neel.mani@dsvv.ac.in
richaalagh@gmail.com|pallaw.mishra@safexpress.com|piyush.arora1@aexp.com

Abstract

We describe the work carried out by our team, *AI-Monitors*, on the Binary Multilingual Machine-Generated Text Detection (Human vs. Machine) task at COLING 2025. This task aims to determine whether a given text is generated by a machine or authored by a human. We propose a lightweight, simple, and scalable approach using encoder models such as RoBERTa and XLM-R We provide an in-depth analysis based on our experiments. Our study found that carefully exploring fine-tuned parameters such as i) no. of training epochs, ii) maximum input size, iii) handling class imbalance etc., plays an important role in building an effective system to achieve good results and can significantly impact the underlying tasks. We found the optimum setting of these parameters can lead to a difference of about 5-6% in absolute terms for measure such as accuracy and F1 measure. The paper presents crucial insights into optimal parameter selection for fine-tuning RoBERTa and XLM-R based models to detect whether a given text is generated by a machine or a human.

1 Introduction

Large language models (LLMs) like GPT-4, Claude 3.5, and Gemini 1.5-pro have rapidly become mainstream tools, offering highly fluent and articulate text generation across a wide range of applications, from social media and news to academic and educational content. These models are capable of producing human-like responses to various queries, making them increasingly attractive for replacing human labor in tasks such as content creation, customer support, and even academic writing.

This challenge (Wang et al., 2025) underscores the need for automated systems designed to detect machine-generated content. As LLMs become more sophisticated and pervasive, developing robust detection methods is critical to preventing misuse. These systems could help mitigate the risks of misinformation, ensure academic integrity, and provide safeguards against the over-reliance on machine-generated material in sensitive contexts.

This work is part of a larger project where we are building solutions for emerging plagiarism detection, LLM-based response generation detection for academic studies, and assignments. One major issue is the difficulty humans face in distinguishing machine-generated text from human-written content. This has posed significant challenges when analyzing and evaluating student assignments and open-book answers, where there are potential issues with using LLM-generated answers and challenges in accurately detecting them. This problem calls for the development of effective automated systems for grading, assessment, and identifying whether a text is generated by a human or a machine. Additionally, it is important to identify instances where machine-generated content has been post-edited by humans to avoid detection by automatic systems.

In this paper we describe the work carried out by our team *AI-Monitors* on the Binary Multilingual Machine-Generated Text Detection (Human vs. Machine) task at COLING 2025 (Wang et al., 2025). Towards building a fast scalable system which can auto-train and learn with more data, we focused on exploring RoBERTa and XLM-R models as they have shown to perform well for this task (Wang et al., 2024).

Main Contributions:

- In our study, we explore different fine-tuning parameters, such as *training epochs, base model, maximum input size, and how to handle data imbalance*.
- The paper presents crucial insights into optimal parameter selection for fine-tuning RoBERTa and XLM-R based models to detect whether a given text is generated by a machine or a human.

Proceedings of the 1st Workshop on GenAI Content Detection (GenAIDetect), pages 230–235
January 19, 2025.

- We are releasing our code on GitHub [1] so that this work can be expanded and used by other teams to develop more effective solutions

The paper is organized as follows: Section 2 presents related work on automatic detection of machine generated text. Section 3 provides an overview of the architectures that we explore in this work. Section 4 presents the data and tools details, Section 5 showcases our results. Section 6 talks about our lessons learned and Section 7 presents conclusion and future work.

2 Related Work

Automatic detection of machine-generated text is typically framed as a binary classification task, where, for a given input, we must classify whether it is generated by a machine or a human (Wang et al., 2024, 2025). Two main approaches are commonly used: one relies on supervised techniques, which require large training datasets, while the other relies on unsupervised approaches using common detection models such as RoBERTa (Liu et al., 2019), XLM-R (Conneau et al., 2020; Goyal et al., 2021), or stylistic features. Jawahar et al. (2020) provides a critical survey of the pros and cons of various alternatives for detecting machine-generated text.

Given sufficient training data, some prior works (Solaiman et al., 2019; Fagni et al., 2021) have experimented with fine-tuning the RoBERTa language model for the detection task. Solaiman et al. (2019) found that RoBERTa established state-of-the-art performance in identifying web pages generated by the largest GPT-2 model, achieving an accuracy of approximately 95%. Fagni et al. (2021) demonstrated that the RoBERTa detector also set the state-of-the-art in accurately distinguishing machine-generated tweets from human-written tweets, outperforming both traditional machine learning models (e.g., bag-of-words) and complex neural network models (e.g., RNN, CNN) by a large margin. This promising result suggests that the RoBERTa detector can generalize well to previously unseen publication sources, such as Twitter.

The automatic detection systems comprise approaches that are used to detect domains including the one that USTC-BUPT has developed for SemEval-2024 Task 8 with the help

[1] https://github.com/aimonitors25/machine-generated-text-detection

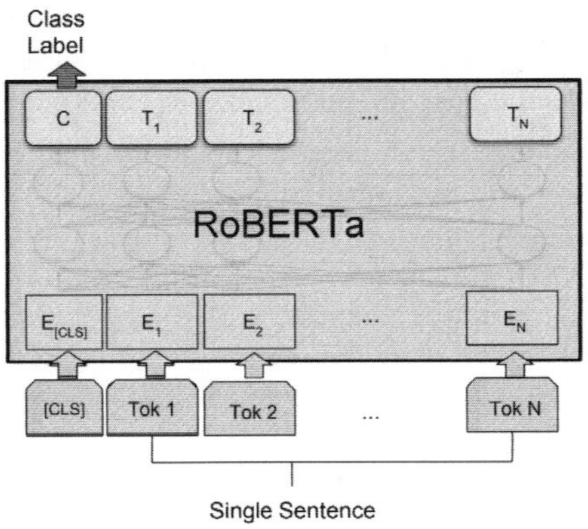

Figure 1: RoBERTa model

of DATeD, LLAM, TLE, and AuDM for monolingual as well as multilingual detection targets (Guo et al., 2024). Further, black-box machine-generated text detection where LLMs are fine-tuned with parameter-efficient smaller LLMs and per-language classification-threshold calibration was proposed and was proved to perform well in SemEval-2024 Task 8 (Spiegel and Macko, 2024). Another valuable contribution is Genaios' LLM IXTIC system in which several LLaMA-2 models operate within a Transformer Encoder framework; this system performed extremely well in the monolingual track and underlines the role of token-level probabilistic features for text classification (Sarvazyan et al., 2024).

3 Methodology

In the task of distinguishing between human-written and machine-generated text, we are performing finetuning of RoBERTa and XLM-R. RoBERTa (Liu et al., 2019), is a robust transformer-based language model, adapted to better capture the nuances in writing style and language patterns that differentiate human and machine-generated content. The model is trained on a labeled dataset consisting of both machine-generated and human-written articles to learn these distinctions. Figure 1 shows an illustration of the RoBERTa model.

To build effective and efficient solution we explore different parameters as shown in Table 1. We conduct following experiments to determine the optimum settings in terms of i) no. of training epochs, ii) maximum input size, iii) handling class imbalance, and iv) selection of base model.

Parameter type	Parameter Values
Base Model	[RoBERTa, XLM-R]
Fine-tuning Epochs	[1 to 5]
Max Input Token Size	[128, 256]
Weighting parameters (human: machine)	[1:1, 2:1, 3:2]

Table 1: Investigative parameters - experimental setup

4 Dataset and Tools Used

The dataset is divided into three primary subsets: Training Data, Development (Dev) Data, and Test Data. Each of these subsets contains different amounts of data, categorized into two main classes: *Machine* and *Human* as shown in Table 2

Stats	Train Data	Dev Data	Test Data
Total	610,765	261,758	73,941
Machine	381,843	163,430	39,266
Human	228,922	98,328	34,675

Table 2: Data Statistics

There is a noticeable class imbalance in the training and development sets, with the Machine class significantly outnumbering the Human class. This could lead to challenges in model training, where the model might become biased toward the majority class (Machine). Hence in our experiments we explored weighing the minority class more as compared to equal weights for both the classes. The test set is relatively more balanced between the two classes, which is important for evaluating the model's ability to generalize to both Machine and Human instances.

Table 3 provide details on the length of the input text across train, dev and test set, where we report common metrics such as count, mean, std, min, max and percentile based no. of input tokens. As the mean length is around 250 and 50% no. of tokens are less than 300, hence we select two values for our investigation for max input tokens size 128 and 256.

5 Results

We performed multiple parameters explorations as described in Table 1, Below we discuss the results of our investigations and learning from same.

RoBERTA vs XLM-R: We tested two models—Roberta and XLM-R—and evaluated their performance over different epochs the results are summarized in the table 4.

Length stats	Train set	Dev set	Test set
count	610,765	261,758	73,941
mean	244.53	244.87	295.43
std	235.08	235.31	185.98
min	1	1	1
25%	91	91	171
50%	186	187	296
75%	320	320	396
max	4,752	2,916	10,743

Table 3: Input text length for train, dev and test set

Models	Epoch	Dev Set	Test Set
Roberta	1	86.61	**73.78**
XLM-R	1	92.68	71.79
Roberta	3	96.05	71.79
XLM-R	3	94.16	72.40
Roberta	5	**97.82**	72.64
XLM-R	5	95.18	72.50

Table 4: Accuracy results on the dev and test set using max input tokens=128

The XLM-R model performed better in the dev set, achieving an accuracy of 92.68% after 1 epoch, compared to 86.61% for RoBERTa. However, the RoBERTa model saw greater improvements with more training, reaching 96.05% and then 97.82% accuracy on the dev set after 3 and 5 epochs, respectively. Thus, we used RoBERTa for further explorations of optimum parameters. This best solution was also the submission of the official leader board for the shared task. More details to follow in the later section.

RoBERTa finetuning - max input size explorations: Table 5 presents the results in the dev and test data set to determine the optimum no. of the maximum input size. As described in Section 4, we explored max input size=128, 256. We found the results are quite better with max input size =256, accuracy results on dev set are quite similar, but we see quite some boost in the test set while using no. of tokens as 256. We used these settings for further explorations.

RoBERTa finetuning - no. of epochs: Table 6 represents the results of the fine-tuning of RoBERTa with the maximum input token size of 256, across different epochs. We find that model

RoBERTa	Input Size	Dev Set	Test Set
Epoch-1	128	86.61	73.78
Epoch-2	128	95.97	71.80
Epoch-3	128	96.05	71.79
Epoch-1	256	94.40	72.40
Epoch-2	256	95.97	74.21
Epoch-3	**256**	**96.72**	**74.91**

Table 5: Accuracy results on the dev and test set

learning is becoming saturated and loss becoming static. Thus, results are coming similar post Epoch-3. The model is trained with a batch size of 32. We used Adam optimized with learning rate as $2e-5$, and weight_decay as 0.01.

Epoch	Dev Set	Test Set
Epoch-1	94.40	72.40
Epoch-2	95.97	74.21
Epoch-3	**96.72**	**74.91**
Epoch-4	**96.72**	**74.91**

Table 6: RoBERTa max input size=256, accuracy results on the dev and test set

RoBERTa finetuning - handling class imbalance: As discussed in Section 4, train dataset is quite imbalanced, thus to effectively learn signals we tried exploring weighing the minority class more. Table 7 presents the results of different weighing scores to handle class imbalance. The results across the dev and test sets are quite close and vary. We see the best test set performance on model with weights (2.0:1.0) w.r.t, (human:machine). However for dev set best performance is obtained without weighing the classes differently.

	Weight 1:1		Weight 2:1		Weight 3:2	
Epoch	Dev	Test	Dev	Test	Dev	Test
1	94.40	72.40	94.23	72.1	95.16	69.98
2	95.97	74.21	95.92	**74.99**	95.46	71.13
3	**96.72**	74.91	95.76	73.13	95.88	72.06

Table 7: RoBERTa max input size=256, accuracy results on the dev and test set, handling class imbalance

Official Solution on the benchmarking leaderboard: Table 8 presents the results of our official submission to the shared task. This submission is based on a finetuned RoBERTa model, using maximum input size as 128 tokens and no. separate weights for class imbalance. This combination gave the best results on the dev set as shown in Table 4. These settings seems to be not the optimum as reviewed with other experiments that we performed post the task deadline.

Models	F1-Macro	F1-Micro
Best System	**83.07**	**83.11**
Baseline	73.42	73.81
Our Submission	70.57	72.64

Table 8: Results on the blind test set, F1-Micro represents Accuracy

6 Lessons Learned

1. Our initial experiments were over-fitted on the majority class, and hence, our understanding of whether the solution is generic was limited due to insufficient testing of different parameter settings and configurations, as discussed in Table 1
2. There is a need for carefully examining the choice of base models, parameters and settings.
3. Overall, the analysis and investigation after the official submission, using the test and development sets, indicate that a better understanding of various factors, such as training epochs, base model, maximum input size, and how to handle data imbalance, can lead to an improvement of about 5-6% in the metric scores, as shown in this paper.
4. We plan to continue these explorations as part of a larger project where we are working towards a general solution for handling plagiarism detection and LLM-generated text detection in academic settings.

7 Conclusion & Future Work

A critical survey on automatic text detection (Jawahar et al., 2020) provides a summary of key error categories made by these automated models, namely: *fluency, brevity, factuality, spurious entries, contradictions, repetitions, common sense reasoning, typos, grammatical errors etc,.* We plan to perform a similar error analysis on this task dataset and work towards building a hybrid pipeline that leverages techniques like those in (Sarvazyan et al., 2024). A summary of this pipeline on leveraging transformer encoder that incorporates token-level probabilistic features extracted from the Llama models is shown in Figure 2 and discussed in Appendix A. In future, we aim to explore ensemble-based solutions, comprising a simple fine-tuned RoBERTa pipeline alongside a richer pipeline as described in Appendix A, that leverages multiple LLMs to better capture patterns and data distributions for detecting machine generated text.

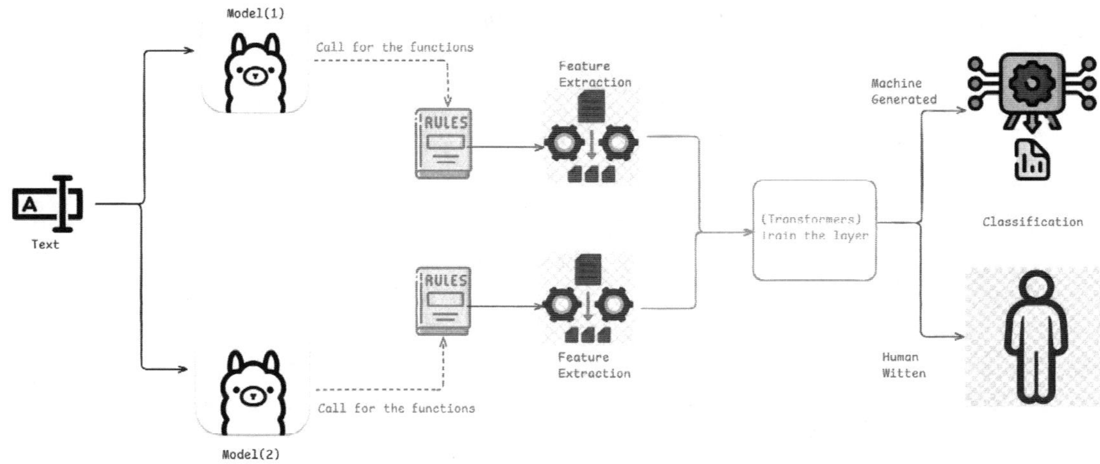

Figure 2: Transformer Encoder Architecture with Llama Model for Extracting Statistical Features from Text

Acknowledgments

We would like to thank the Task Organizers for organizing such an interesting and relevant benchmarking task.

References

Alexis Conneau, Kartikay Khandelwal, Naman Goyal, Vishrav Chaudhary, Guillaume Wenzek, Francisco Guzmán, Edouard Grave, Myle Ott, Luke Zettlemoyer, and Veselin Stoyanov. 2020. Unsupervised cross-lingual representation learning at scale. *Preprint*, arXiv:1911.02116.

Tiziano Fagni, Fabrizio Falchi, Margherita Gambini, Antonio Martella, and Maurizio Tesconi. 2021. Tweepfake: About detecting deepfake tweets. *Plos one*, 16(5):e0251415.

Naman Goyal, Jingfei Du, Myle Ott, Giri Anantharaman, and Alexis Conneau. 2021. Larger-scale transformers for multilingual masked language modeling. *arXiv preprint arXiv:2105.00572*.

Zikang Guo, Kaijie Jiao, Xingyu Yao, Yuning Wan, Haoran Li, Benfeng Xu, Licheng Zhang, Quan Wang, Yongdong Zhang, and Zhendong Mao. 2024. Ustcbupt at semeval-2024 task 8: Enhancing machine-generated text detection via domain adversarial neural networks and llm embeddings. In *Proceedings of the 18th International Workshop on Semantic Evaluation (SemEval-2024)*, pages 1511–1522.

Ganesh Jawahar, Muhammad Abdul-Mageed, and Laks VS Lakshmanan. 2020. Automatic detection of machine generated text: A critical survey. *arXiv preprint arXiv:2011.01314*.

Yinhan Liu, Myle Ott, Naman Goyal, Jingfei Du, Mandar Joshi, Danqi Chen, Omer Levy, Mike Lewis, Luke Zettlemoyer, and Veselin Stoyanov. 2019. Roberta: A robustly optimized BERT pretraining approach. *CoRR*, abs/1907.11692.

Areg Mikael Sarvazyan, José-Ángel González, and Marc Franco-Salvador. 2024. Genaios at semeval-2024 task 8: Detecting machine-generated text by mixing language model probabilistic features. In *Proceedings of the 18th International Workshop on Semantic Evaluation (SemEval-2024)*, pages 101–107.

Irene Solaiman, Miles Brundage, Jack Clark, Amanda Askell, Ariel Herbert-Voss, Jeff Wu, Alec Radford, Gretchen Krueger, Jong Wook Kim, Sarah Kreps, et al. 2019. Release strategies and the social impacts of language models. *arXiv preprint arXiv:1908.09203*.

Michal Spiegel and Dominik Macko. 2024. Kinit at semeval-2024 task 8: Fine-tuned llms for multilingual machine-generated text detection. *arXiv preprint arXiv:2402.13671*.

Yuxia Wang, Jonibek Mansurov, Petar Ivanov, Jinyan Su, Artem Shelmanov, Akim Tsvigun, Osama Mohammed Afzal, Tarek Mahmoud, Giovanni Puccetti, Thomas Arnold, et al. 2024. Semeval-2024 task 8: Multidomain, multimodel and multilingual machine-generated text detection. *arXiv preprint arXiv:2404.14183*.

Yuxia Wang, Artem Shelmanov, Jonibek Mansurov, Akim Tsvigun, Vladislav Mikhailov, Rui Xing, Zhuohan Xie, Jiahui Geng, Giovanni Puccetti, Ekaterina Artemova, Jinyan Su, Minh Ngoc Ta, Mervat Abassy, Kareem Elozeiri, Saad El Dine Ahmed, Maiya Goloburda, Tarek Mahmoud, Raj Vardhan Tomar, Alexander Aziz, Nurkhan Laiyk, Osama Mohammed Afzal, Ryuto Koike, Masahiro Kaneko, Alham Fikri Aji, Nizar Habash, Iryna Gurevych, and Preslav Nakov. 2025. GenAI content detection task 1: English and multilingual machine-generated text detection: AI vs. human. In *Proceedings of the 1st*

Workshop on GenAI Content Detection (GenAIDetect), Abu Dhabi, UAE. International Conference on Computational Linguistics.

Appendix A

Transformer Encoder with Llama to extract statistical Features: Motivated by (Sarvazyan et al., 2024) we explored alternative approach that leverages a transformer encoder and incorporates token-level probabilistic features extracted from the Llama models as shown in Figure 2. The features used for each token in a given text are: i) the log probability of the observed token, ii) the log probability of the predicted token, iii) the entropy of the token distribution, iv) the rank of the observed token, v) the log rank and vi) the LLM-Deviation.

These features are designed to capture the statistical "style" of machine-generated text (MGT) in a precise manner. The log probabilities provide insight into how confidently the model predicts each token. At the same time, the entropy captures the unpredictability or randomness in the generation process, and the Rank and Log Rank are also noted by the model in terms of tokens where the lower Rank represents higher confidence in the correct token. LLM-Deviation assesses the variance of the model outputs from a uniform distribution reflecting higher structure in the MGT model's outputs. These probabilistic measures are particularly useful for distinguishing between human writing, which tends to be more diverse and unpredictable, and machine-generated text, which often follows more structured patterns.

Advacheck at GenAI Detection Task 1: AI Detection Powered by Domain-Aware Multi-Tasking

German Gritsai[1,2], **Anastasia Voznyuk**[1], **Ildar Khabutdinov**[1,2], **Andrey Grabovoy**[1]
[1]Advacheck OÜ, Estonia
[2]Université Grenoble Alpes, France
{gritsai, voznyuk, khabutdinov, grabovoy}@advacheck.com

Abstract

The paper describes a system designed by Advacheck team to recognise machine-generated and human-written texts in the monolingual subtask of GenAI Detection Task 1 competition. Our developed system is a multi-task architecture with shared Transformer Encoder between several classification heads. One head is responsible for binary classification between human-written and machine-generated texts, while the other heads are auxiliary multiclass classifiers for texts of different domains from particular datasets. As multiclass heads were trained to distinguish the domains presented in the data, they provide a better understanding of the samples. This approach led us to achieve the first place in the official ranking with 83.07% macro F_1-score on the test set and bypass the baseline by 10%. We further study obtained system through ablation, error and representation analyses, finding that multi-task learning outperforms single-task mode and simultaneous tasks form a cluster structure in embeddings space. We release our code and model[1].

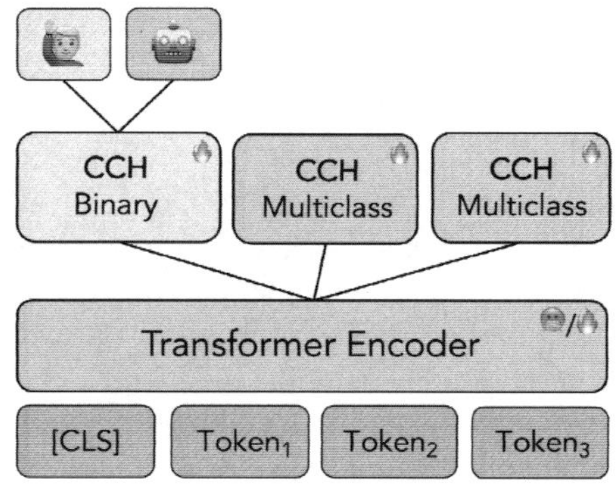

Figure 1: Overview of the proposed multi-task architecture. Modules marked only with 🔥 are trainable at all stages. The weights of the Transformer Encoder are frozen 🥶 at the first stage of training and trainable 🔥 at the second one. The Custom Classification Head (CCH) described in Appendix A is used for predictions.

1 Introduction

With the continuous improvement of Large Language Models (LLMs), the task of detection machine-generated texts demands more and more attention from the community. The potential cases of misuse include malicious usage by students (Zeng et al., 2023; Koike et al., 2023) and scientists (Ma et al., 2023; Gritsay et al., 2023a). Furthermore, this is often the cause of plagiarism (Avetisyan et al., 2023) and spam (Labonne and Moran, 2023). The mentioned things are encouraging researchers to improve methods for detecting artificial text simultaneously with enhancing generation methods.

The task of detecting machine-generated texts is usually formulated as a binary text classification task (Jawahar et al., 2020). The most common solutions are to fine-tune the Transformer-based model (Gritsay et al., 2023b) or to use zero-shot approaches with intrinsic statistics of the text (Mitchell et al., 2023; Hans et al., 2024). While these methods perform well on in-domain tasks (Uchendu et al., 2021), they are not robust to change of the domain, generator model, or language of the texts (Wang et al., 2024a; Tulchinskii et al., 2023; Kuznetsov et al., 2024). Meanwhile, for the detection of AI-content in the wild such a change is, on the contrary, a more realistic setup (Dugan et al., 2024). Beyond this, the data presented for the detection task may be of poor quality, which also complicates the challenge of the detection task (Gritsai et al., 2024). Therefore, the goal is to obtain a model that is robust to the presence of data of poor quality and with a lot of noise, and, in addition, to make this model capable to adapt to new domains.

[1]https://github.com/Advacheck-OU/ai-detector-coling2025

Proceedings of the 1st Workshop on GenAI Content Detection (GenAIDetect), pages 236–243
January 19, 2025. ©2025 International Conference on Computational Linguistics

The high coherence and quality of writing achieved by modern LLMs makes it difficult to find a specific sample-counted qualitative feature by which it would be possible to create a hyperplane in the space of texts and separate generated from human-generated ones. One of the possible refinements of the representations from the single-task learning architecture is the multi-task learning (MTL) (Crawshaw, 2020; Gritsay et al., 2022). It was also noted that systems with MTL architecture had achieved high results in the previous competitions (Guo et al., 2024), therefore we decided to utilize this approach in our work. In this paper we discuss our solution as the Advacheck team at GenAI Content Detection Task 1: English and Multilingual Machine-generated Text Detection: AI vs. Human (Wang et al., 2025). Our method shows that with additional internal data analysis and embedding alignment using MTL, it is still possible to achieve high performance in detecting fragments in cross-domain and cross-generator setups on texts from the advanced LLMs. As we forced model to focus on various domains, it allowed us to form a cluster domain-wise structure for the text representations in the vector space. In our research, we show that (1) multi-task learning outperforms the default single-task, (2) cluster structure is formed at the shared encoder (3) compare different configurations of the system and (4) analyse the errors of the system.

2 Task Definition

The monolingual subtask of *Task 1: Binary Multilingual Machine-Generated Text Detection* focuses on identifying whether the English text was entirely authored by a human or generated by a language model. The competition is the continuation and improvement of the *SemEval Shared Task 8 (subtask A)* (Wang et al., 2024b) and combines refreshed training and testing samples from different domains and novel LLMs. The statistics of the dataset are summarised in Appendix C. The official evaluation metric for the monolingual subtask is Macro F_1-score and the additional metric is Micro F_1-score.

3 System Overview

Why multi-task learning? In the current task formulation we have more than 600k texts in the training set with dozens of domains and generation models. Such an amount is very noisy for a binary classification task, because it can be challenging for a model to distinguish between relevant and irrelevant features. Multi-task learning may help the model focus on those features that actually matter as other tasks will update representation of samples with inner information. Our aim is to obtain fine-grained representations of the data that ideally ignores data-dependent noise and generalises well. Since different tasks involve distinct noises, a model trained on multiple tasks simultaneously is able to learn a more general representation. Furthermore, it reduces the risk of overfitting.

Model. We propose an MTL architecture with hard parameter sharing (HPS), it is depicted in Figure 1. In HPS, a common Transformer-based encoder is used for multiple tasks. After several variations of set of parallel heads, we focused on three custom classification heads (CCH) for simultaneous training:

- Binary CCH head for solving the initial monolingual subtask [2 classes]
- Multiclass CCH to define a sub-source within the HC3 (Su et al., 2024) source [5 classes]
- Multiclass CCH for sub-source detection within the M4GT (Wang et al., 2024a) source [6 classes]

The model was trained in two phases: fine-tuning chosen classifiers with frozen 🥶 shared encoder weights and fine-tuning the complete model with all weights unfrozen 🔥. These learning stages help to shift the distribution of the encoder weights in the right direction and avoid overfitting (Xie et al., 2021). At the inference stage, only binary CCH predictions used for final classification.

4 Experiments

We focused on the monolingual subtask, carrying out comparisons among models and ablations of the best system. For these we employed the original training and development splits provided by the organizers. Our objective here was to reveal the quality improvement in multi-task training compared to single-task training.

4.1 Model Comparison

Baselines. As models for comparison we chose Logistic Regression classifier (Chao-Ying Joanne Peng and Ingersoll, 2002) with TF-IDF

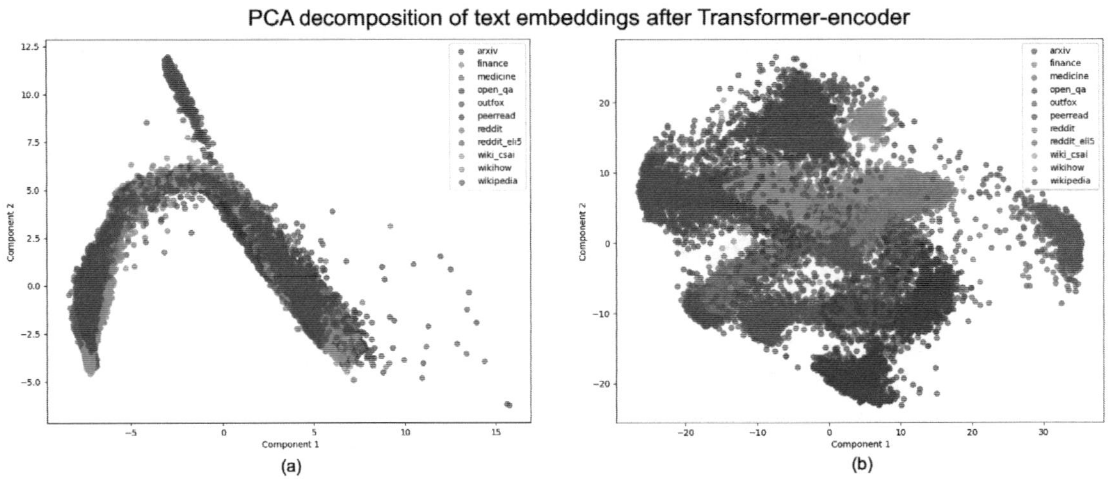

Figure 2: Two principal component decomposition of PCA for texts from the development subsample. In (a) the vector space structure for the `deberta-v3-base` fine-tuned in single-task mode is shown, while figure (b) shows the same model but fine-tuned in MTL mode with two additional custom classification heads.

Model	Development	Test
TF-IDF with LogReg	63.53	60.93
DeBERTaV3 base	82.56	78.52
MTL: 1 stage	80.51	78.67
MTL: 2 stage	87.33	81.55
MTL: 2 stage + threshold	**87.96**	**83.07**

Table 1: Results of model comparison on the test and development set. The highlighted metric is macro F_1-score (%).

Rank	System	F_1-score (%)
1	**Advacheck (germgr)**	**83.07**
2	tmatchitan	83.01
3	karla	82.80
15	*baseline*	73.42
36	nitstejasrikar	44.89

Table 2: Final results on the official ranking. Bold denotes our team's placement.

features on word n-grams, and DeBERTa-v3 fine-tuned in two-stage mode described earlier, but in single-task setting. In the MTL approach, we compared checkpoints from different stages, and also explored the effect of adding thresholds on the output of the final classifier. We chose DeBERTa-v3 base for the baseline and the backbone in our system, as it is currently state-of-the-art model for supervised fine-tuning for binary classification (Macko et al., 2023).

The results are presented in Table 1. It can be seen that there is a weak correlation between the gap within the predictions on the dev and test subsamples. For example, the presence of a threshold after the final layer affected the dev result only slightly, but at the same time allowed us to achieve a winning result on the test set. The hyperparameters of the final model are given in Appendix B.

5 Results

Table 2 reports the leaderboard results on the test set, where our system, Advacheck, achieves a macro F_1-score of 83.07%, outperforming approaches of the other participants and ranking first. Our solution surpassed the claimed baseline by 10%.

6 Analysis

6.1 Embeddings after MTL

We made a comparison of text embeddings after fine-tuning stages. Samples from development part of data were forwarded to the Transformer-encoder and `[CLS]` vectors were extracted as outputs. We visualised these vectors using PCA in Figure 2. We observe that the alignment of the representations, which was mentioned above, introduces a cluster domain-wise structure. Although the clusters are not perfectly separable, a meaningful difference between the standard BERT-like model and MTL

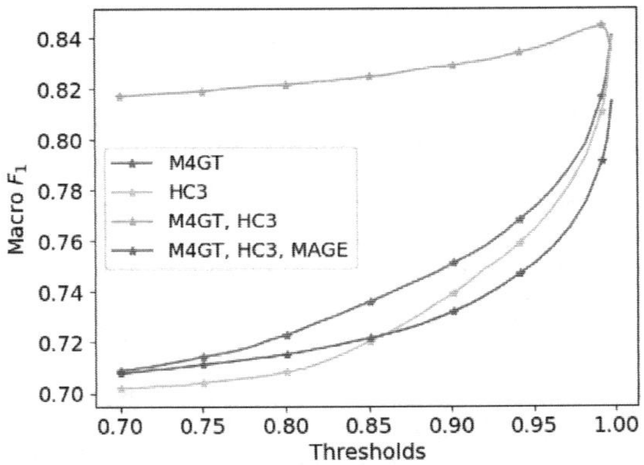

Figure 3: Macro F_1-score on the test set of different configuration of the systems depending on the threshold.

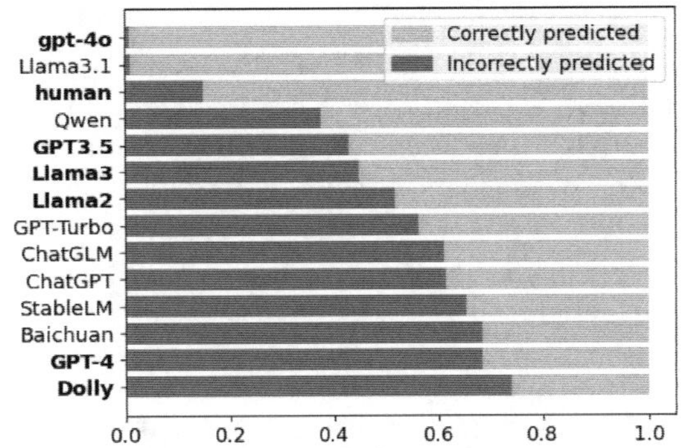

Figure 4: Proportion of predictions for different generators from test set. Labels in **bold** are generators texts from which are present in the train set.

Task Head	Development	Test
HC3	92.27	82.70
M4GT	91.70	81.07
MTL (HC3 + M4GT)	87.96	83.07
HC3 + M4GT + MAGE	91.43	79.23

Table 3: Comparison of different configurations of heads and tasks trained simultaneously in MTL architecture. The highlighted metric is macro F_1-score (%).

fine-tuning pipelines can be seen. Additional decompositions are presented in Appendix E.

6.2 Ablations

To provide further analysis on the multi-task setup we experimented with configurations of our systems, changing the number of multiclass CCH. The system on the leaderboard has 2 Multiclass CCH, and we ran ablation experiments with 1 CCH and 3 CCH. The results are in the Table 3. Setups with 1 and 3 CCH showed better performance on the development set, but marginally dropped in performance on the test set compared to setup with 2 CCH. What is also interesting is that the results obtained on HC3-trained CCH are similar to the results obtained in M4GT-trained CCH, although M4GT has 10 times more training data than HC3. Additionaly, we experimented with the threshold values on all our configurations. The figures are shown in the Figure 3 and reaffirm the choice of the final system and threshold for it.

6.3 Error Analysis

Answers on different datasets. The two datasets with the highest percentage of incorrect predictions are Mixset (Zhang et al., 2024) and CUDRT (Tao et al., 2024), while the texts in the other datasets are detected with very high precision. We attribute this to the additional manipulations with these texts, such as rewriting, "humanizing" and other editing, done by the authors of the initial datasets. Other texts in the test set and in train set, on the other hand, are the raw output of generation models, without post-processing them, or otherwise not stated. See more details in Appendix D. In future iterations, it may be worth trying to address these challenges with the post-processing addition for some samples in the training data.

Answers on different generators. The proportions of correct and incorrect predictions on test set with respect to different generators are shown in Figure 4. The majority of texts in the test set are either human-written or generated with `gpt-4o` and our system predicted labels for them very accurately, therefore compensating the poorer performance on other generators. Still, our system is not yet robust enough to the change of generators, such as texts from some of the unseen detectors, and we will focus future research on addressing generalisation gaps and refining the approach for unseen generators.

7 Conclusion

In this paper we described the system by the Advacheck team in the monolingual subtask at GenAI Detection Task 1 competition. We proposed solution with multi-task learning architecture that consists of shared Transformer Encoder and composition of one binary and two multiclass Custom Classification Heads. Our system obtained the best results in the official ranking bypassing the baseline by 10%. Adding tasks for training in parallel reveal the formation of a cluster structure in the space of embeddings, helping to achieve high results despite the presence of a large amount of noisy data. Also, it has been demonstrated that training a similar model but in single-task mode loses to the proposed approach, and configurations with one or three multiclass heads also perform worse than our final system.

References

K. Avetisyan, G. Gritsay, and A. Grabovoy. 2023. Cross-lingual plagiarism detection: Two are better than one. *Program. Comput. Softw.*, 49(4):346–354.

Kuk Lida Lee Chao-Ying Joanne Peng and Gary M. Ingersoll. 2002. An introduction to logistic regression analysis and reporting. *The Journal of Educational Research*, 96(1):3–14.

Michael Crawshaw. 2020. Multi-task learning with deep neural networks: A survey. *Preprint*, arXiv:2009.09796.

Liam Dugan, Alyssa Hwang, Filip Trhlik, Josh Magnus Ludan, Andrew Zhu, Hainiu Xu, Daphne Ippolito, and Chris Callison-Burch. 2024. Raid: A shared benchmark for robust evaluation of machine-generated text detectors. *Preprint*, arXiv:2405.07940.

German Gritsai, Anastasia Voznyuk, Andrey Grabovoy, and Yury Chekhovich. 2024. Are ai detectors good enough? a survey on quality of datasets with machine-generated texts. *Preprint*, arXiv:2410.14677.

German Gritsay, Andrey Grabovoy, and Yury Chekhovich. 2022. Automatic detection of machine generated texts: Need more tokens. In *2022 Ivannikov Memorial Workshop (IVMEM)*, pages 20–26.

German Gritsay, Andrey Grabovoy, Aleksandr Kildyakov, and Yury Chekhovich. 2023a. Artificially generated text fragments search in academic documents. In *Doklady Mathematics*, volume 108, pages S434–S442. Springer.

German Gritsay, Andrey Grabovoy, Aleksandr Kildyakov, and Yury Chekhovich. 2023b. Automated text identification: Multilingual transformer-based models approach. In *IberLEF@ SEPLN*.

Zikang Guo, Kaijie Jiao, Xingyu Yao, Yuning Wan, Haoran Li, Benfeng Xu, Licheng Zhang, Quan Wang, Yongdong Zhang, and Zhendong Mao. 2024. USTC-BUPT at SemEval-2024 task 8: Enhancing machine-generated text detection via domain adversarial neural networks and LLM embeddings. In *Proceedings of the 18th International Workshop on Semantic Evaluation (SemEval-2024)*, pages 1511–1522, Mexico City, Mexico. Association for Computational Linguistics.

Abhimanyu Hans, Avi Schwarzschild, Valeriia Cherepanova, Hamid Kazemi, Aniruddha Saha, Micah Goldblum, Jonas Geiping, and Tom Goldstein. 2024. Spotting llms with binoculars: Zero-shot detection of machine-generated text. *Preprint*, arXiv:2401.12070.

Dan Hendrycks and Kevin Gimpel. 2023. Gaussian error linear units (gelus). *Preprint*, arXiv:1606.08415.

Ganesh Jawahar, Muhammad Abdul-Mageed, and Laks Lakshmanan, V.S. 2020. Automatic detection of machine generated text: A critical survey. In *Proceedings of the 28th International Conference on Computational Linguistics*, pages 2296–2309, Barcelona, Spain (Online). International Committee on Computational Linguistics.

Ryuto Koike, Masahiro Kaneko, and Naoaki Okazaki. 2023. Outfox: Llm-generated essay detection through in-context learning with adversarially generated examples. In *AAAI Conference on Artificial Intelligence*.

Kristian Kuznetsov, Eduard Tulchinskii, Laida Kushnareva, German Magai, Serguei Barannikov, Sergey Nikolenko, and Irina Piontkovskaya. 2024. Robust ai-generated text detection by restricted embeddings. *Preprint*, arXiv:2410.08113.

Maxime Labonne and Sean Moran. 2023. Spam-t5: Benchmarking large language models for few-shot email spam detection. *Preprint*, arXiv:2304.01238.

Yongqiang Ma, Jiawei Liu, Fan Yi, Qikai Cheng, Yong Huang, Wei Lu, and Xiaozhong Liu. 2023. Ai vs. human – differentiation analysis of scientific content generation. *Preprint*, arXiv:2301.10416.

Dominik Macko, Robert Moro, Adaku Uchendu, Jason Lucas, Michiharu Yamashita, Matúš Pikuliak, Ivan Srba, Thai Le, Dongwon Lee, Jakub Simko, and Maria Bielikova. 2023. Multitude: Large-scale multilingual machine-generated text detection benchmark. In *Proceedings of the 2023 Conference on Empirical Methods in Natural Language Processing*, page 9960–9987. Association for Computational Linguistics.

Eric Mitchell, Yoonho Lee, Alexander Khazatsky, Christopher D. Manning, and Chelsea Finn. 2023. Detectgpt: Zero-shot machine-generated text detection using probability curvature. *Preprint*, arXiv:2301.11305.

Zhenpeng Su, Xing Wu, Wei Zhou, Guangyuan Ma, and Songlin Hu. 2024. Hc3 plus: A semantic-invariant human chatgpt comparison corpus. *Preprint*, arXiv:2309.02731.

Zhen Tao, Yanfang Chen, Dinghao Xi, Zhiyu Li, and Wei Xu. 2024. Cudrt: Benchmarking the detection models of human vs. large language models generated texts. *Preprint*, arXiv:2406.09056.

Eduard Tulchinskii, Kristian Kuznetsov, Laida Kushnareva, Daniil Cherniavskii, Sergey Nikolenko, Evgeny Burnaev, Serguei Barannikov, and Irina Piontkovskaya. 2023. Intrinsic dimension estimation for robust detection of ai-generated texts. In *Proceedings of the 37th International Conference on Neural Information Processing Systems*, NIPS '23, Red Hook, NY, USA. Curran Associates Inc.

Adaku Uchendu, Zeyu Ma, Thai Le, Rui Zhang, and Dongwon Lee. 2021. TURINGBENCH: A benchmark environment for Turing test in the age of neural text generation. In *Findings of the Association for Computational Linguistics: EMNLP 2021*, pages 2001–2016, Punta Cana, Dominican Republic. Association for Computational Linguistics.

Yuxia Wang, Jonibek Mansurov, Petar Ivanov, Jinyan Su, Artem Shelmanov, Akim Tsvigun, Osama Mohammed Afzal, Tarek Mahmoud, Giovanni Puccetti, Thomas Arnold, Alham Aji, Nizar Habash, Iryna Gurevych, and Preslav Nakov. 2024a. M4GT-bench: Evaluation benchmark for black-box machine-generated text detection. In *Proceedings of the 62nd Annual Meeting of the Association for Computational Linguistics (Volume 1: Long Papers)*, pages 3964–3992, Bangkok, Thailand. Association for Computational Linguistics.

Yuxia Wang, Jonibek Mansurov, Petar Ivanov, Jinyan Su, Artem Shelmanov, Akim Tsvigun, Chenxi Whitehouse, Osama Mohammed Afzal, Tarek Mahmoud, Giovanni Puccetti, Thomas Arnold, Alham Fikri Aji, Nizar Habash, Iryna Gurevych, and Preslav Nakov. 2024b. Semeval-2024 task 8: Multigenerator, multidomain, and multilingual black-box machine-generated text detection. In *Proceedings of the 18th International Workshop on Semantic Evaluation*, SemEval 2024, Mexico, Mexico.

Yuxia Wang, Artem Shelmanov, Jonibek Mansurov, Akim Tsvigun, Vladislav Mikhailov, Rui Xing, Zhuohan Xie, Jiahui Geng, Giovanni Puccetti, Ekaterina Artemova, Jinyan Su, Minh Ngoc Ta, Mervat Abassy, Kareem Elozeiri, Saad El Dine Ahmed, Maiya Goloburda, Tarek Mahmoud, Raj Vardhan Tomar, Alexander Aziz, Nurkhan Laiyk, Osama Mohammed Afzal, Ryuto Koike, Masahiro Kaneko, Alham Fikri Aji, Nizar Habash, Iryna Gurevych, and Preslav Nakov. 2025. GenAI content detection task 1: English and multilingual machine-generated text detection: AI vs. human. In *Proceedings of the 1st Workshop on GenAI Content Detection (GenAIDetect)*, Abu Dhabi, UAE. International Conference on Computational Linguistics.

Sang Michael Xie, Tengyu Ma, and Percy Liang. 2021. Composed fine-tuning: Freezing pre-trained denoising autoencoders for improved generalization. In *Proceedings of the 38th International Conference on Machine Learning*, volume 139 of *Proceedings of Machine Learning Research*, pages 11424–11435. PMLR

Zijie Zeng, Lele Sha, Yuheng Li, Kaixun Yang, Dragan Gašević, and Guanliang Chen. 2023. Towards automatic boundary detection for human-ai collaborative hybrid essay in education. *Preprint*, arXiv:2307.12267.

Qihui Zhang, Chujie Gao, Dongping Chen, Yue Huang, Yixin Huang, Zhenyang Sun, Shilin Zhang, Weiye Li, Zhengyan Fu, Yao Wan, and Lichao Sun. 2024. Llm-as-a-coauthor: Can mixed human-written and machine-generated text be detected? *Preprint*, arXiv:2401.05952.

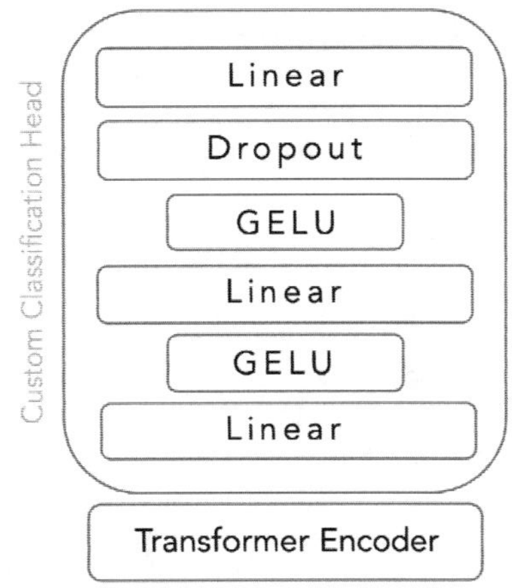

Figure 5: The architecture of the custom classification head used in the described approach. Value of `dropout` is equal to 0.5.

A Custom Classification Head

In our approach, we replaced the default one-layer linear classifier with a more extended version by adding multiple layers, the final structure of Custom Classification Head (CCH) is shown in Figure 5. We chose GELU (Hendrycks and Gimpel, 2023) as the activation feature and added dropout. In earlier experiments, when compared with the base head, this adaptation gives a higher quality therefore we used it in all subsequent experiments.

B Final System Hyperparameters

Our final system is MTL architecture with shared `deberta-v3-base` encoder and 3 CCH. The training of main system was conducted on NVIDIA GeForce RTX 3090 and the training of other configurations on NVIDIA A100. See hyperparameters in Table 4.

C Provided Data

The organizers of the competition provided data for the train and development stages of the evolving

Hyperparameters	1st stage	2nd stage
Epochs	1	1
Learning rate (LR)	3e-4	3e-6
Warmup steps	50	75
Weight decay	0.01	0.01
Batch size	32	16
Classifier threshold	-	0.92

Table 4: Hyperparameters for fine-tuning MTL architecture. We trained for 1 epoch in both stages with possibility of early exit.

solutions. This is the continuation and improvement of the SemEval Shared Task 8 samples. New domains and generation models were added to the data; details of train and dev sets are shown in Table 7. In addition, a separate development dataset was available on the CodaBench[2] platform where the competition was held; its statistics are shown in Table 5.

Source	Development Set	
	Human	Machine
RAID	13371	0
LLM-DetectAIve	0	19186
Total		32557

Table 5: Statistics on development data from CodaBench platform for monolingual subtask of the GenAI Detection Task 1.

Source	Test Set	
	Human	Machine
CUDRT	12287	10691
IELTS Duck	9747	12418
PeerSum	5080	6995
LLM-DetectAIve	1635	900
Mixset	0	1086
NLPeer	5326	5376
Total	34075	37466

Table 6: Statistics on test data for monolingual subtask of the GenAI Detection Task 1.

[2]https://www.codabench.org/competitions/3734/

D Percentage of Failures

See Figure 6 for detailed proportions of incorrectly predicted texts from CUDRT and Mixset.

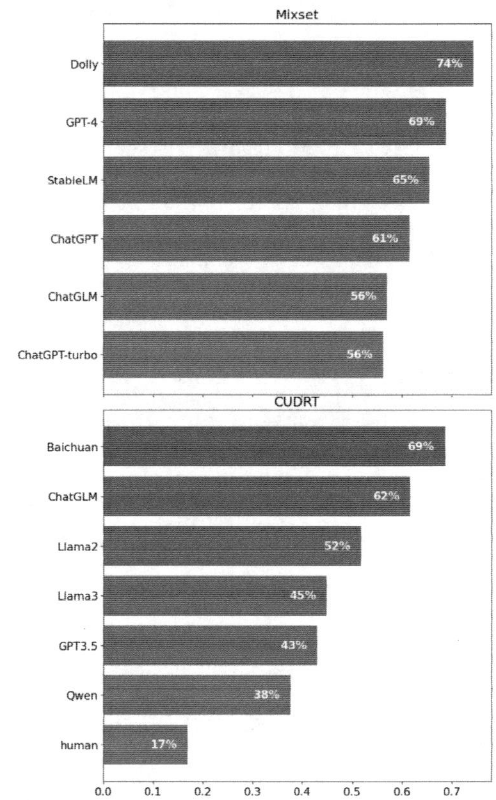

Figure 6: The percentage of falsely labelled texts from two subdatasets in test set.

E Decomposition Study

In addition to the PCA decomposition of text embeddings after passes on our system, we mapped the logit decomposition of two multiclass heads – CCH on HC3 and CCH on M4GT. We sampled the texts from the dev set, passed them through the encoder and the corresponding classifiers, and then decomposed the logits. From Figure 7, we can observe that the data after the classifiers passes remain in the expected cluster structure intended by shared encoder. On the dataset HC3 this can be seen more clearly. With these plots we can also understand how well the multiclass classification heads were trained directly, as they were not used for the inference.

Source	Sub-sources	Training Set		Dev Set	
		Human	**Machine**	**Human**	**Machine**
HC3	Finance, Medicine, OpenQA, Reddit_ELI5, Wiki_CSAI	39140	17671	16501	7917
M4GT	Arxiv, Outfox, PeerRead, Reddit, WikiHow, Wikipedia	86682	180381	36420	74167
MAGE	CMV, CNN, DialogSum, ELI5, HellaSwag, IMDB, PubMed, Roct, SciGen, SQUAD, TLDR, WP, XSum, Yelp	103100	183793	45407	81462
	Total	228922	381845	98328	163430

Table 7: Statistics on training and development data from monolingual subtask of the GenAI Detection Task 1.

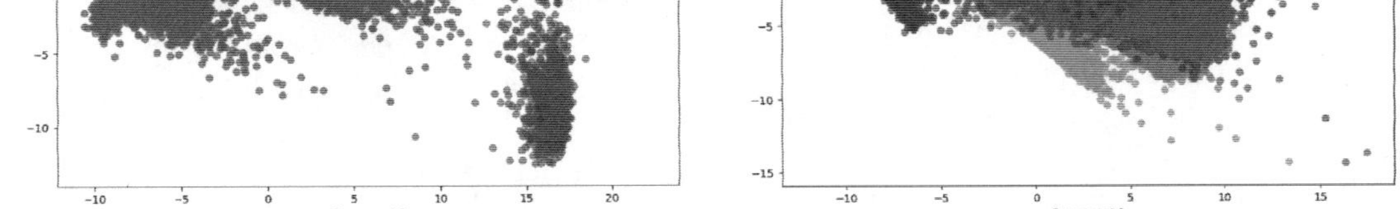

Figure 7: Two principal component decomposition of PCA for texts from development sub-sample. We decomposed here by PCA the logits of the texts after the corresponding multiclass classifiers, namely HC3 and M4GT.

GenAI Content Detection Task 1: English and Multilingual Machine-Generated Text Detection: AI vs. Human

Yuxia Wang[1], Artem Shelmanov[1], Jonibek Mansurov[1], Akim Tsvigun[2,3], Vladislav Mikhailov[4], Rui Xing[1], Zhuohan Xie[1], Jiahui Geng[1], Giovanni Puccetti[5], Ekaterina Artemova[6], Jinyan Su[1,10], Minh Ngoc Ta[9], Mervat Abassy[13], Kareem Elozeiri[11], Saad El Dine Ahmed[13], Maiya Goloburda[1], Tarek Mahmoud[1], Raj Vardhan Tomar[14], Alexander Aziz[15], Nurkhan Laiyk[1], Osama Mohammed Afzal[1], Ryuto Koike[7], Masahiro Kaneko[1,7], Alham Fikri Aji[1], Nizar Habash[1,8], Iryna Gurevych[1,12], Preslav Nakov[1]

[1]MBZUAI [2]Nebius AI [3]KU Leuven [4]University of Oslo [5]ISTI-CNR [6]Toloka AI
[7]Institute of Science Tokyo [8]New York University Abu Dhabi
[9]BKAI Research Center, Hanoi University of Science and Technology [10]Cornell University
[11]Zewail City of Science and Technology [12]TU Darmstadt [13]Alexandria University
[14]Cluster Innovation Center, University of Delhi [15]University of Florida
{yuxia.wang, artem.shelmanov, preslav.nakov}@mbzuai.ac.ae

Abstract

We present the GenAI Content Detection Task 1 – a shared task on binary machine generated text detection, conducted as a part of the GenAI workshop at COLING 2025. The task consists of two subtasks: Monolingual (English) and Multilingual. The shared task attracted many participants: 36 teams made official submissions to the Monolingual subtask during the test phase and 27 teams – to the Multilingual. We provide a comprehensive overview of the data, a summary of the results – including system rankings and performance scores – detailed descriptions of the participating systems, and an in-depth analysis of submissions.[1]

1 Introduction

The success and popularity of Large Language Models (LLMs) have led to the proliferation of generative artificial intelligence (GenAI) content, which is now widely applied across numerous aspects of daily life. However, this widespread adoption has brought several concerns to light, including challenges to the integrity of student assignments and the potential for fabricated content to mislead individuals (Wang et al., 2024d). As generative LLMs continue to advance rapidly, it is becoming increasingly difficult for humans to distinguish machine-generated content from authentic human-authored text. Consequently, developing effective methods to address these challenges is crucial. To this end, we propose a GenAI content detection task, with Task 1 focusing specifically on the detection of machine-generated text in both English and multilingual contexts. This task is the continuation of SemEval Shared Task 8 (Wang et al., 2024b). The new task introduces a broader range of languages and domains while incorporating updated generators that leverage the latest LLMs.

The task consists of two subtasks: **Monolingual (English) subtask A** and **Multilingual subtask B**. The data for the shared task covers various domains and LLM generators. The data for English subtask covers diverse domains, including peer reviews, student essays, scientific papers, news articles, social media, emails, speech content and so on, similar for multilingual subtask data, with the test set involving more than 8 domains. To construct the data for the shared task, we produced machine-generated texts (MGTs), using state-of-the-art LLMs, including GPT-4/4o, Mistral (Jiang et al., 2023), Llama-3.1 (Dubey et al., 2024), Vikhr-Nemo (Nikolich et al., 2024), Qwen-2 (Yang et al., 2024), etc. Multilingual subtask data encompasses 21 unique languages.

The task attracted 36 participants who made official submissions during the test phase for the monolingual subtask A and 27 participants who made official submissions to the multilingual subtask B.

2 Related Work

This section discusses prior work about machine-generated text detection methods, datasets and shared tasks.

2.1 Detection Methods

There are mainly two commonly used approaches for detecting machine-generated text, training-free and training-based. Training-free detection

[1]https://github.com/mbzuai-nlp/COLING-2025-Workshop-on-MGT-Detection-Task1

Proceedings of the 1st Workshop on GenAI Content Detection (GenAIDetect), pages 244–261
January 19, 2025.

methods leverage statistical characteristics of texts for identifying MGTs (Solaiman et al., 2019; Gehrmann et al., 2019). Various features have been explored, such as perplexity (Vasilatos et al., 2023), perplexity curvature (Mitchell et al., 2023), log rank (Su et al., 2023), intrinsic dimensionality (Tulchinskii et al., 2024) and N-gram analysis (Yang et al., 2023). Revise-Detect hypothesizes that machine-generated texts would be edited less by LLMs than human-written texts (Zhu et al., 2023). Binoculars (Hans et al., 2024) employs two LLMs to calculate the ratio of perplexity to cross-perplexity, assessing how one LLM responds to the next token predictions of another. Training based detectors typically fine-tune a pre-trained model for binary classification (Yu et al., 2023; Zhan et al., 2023), utilizing techniques such as adversarial training (Hu et al., 2023) and abstention (Tian et al., 2023). Verma et al. (2023) fine-tune a linear classifier on top of the learned representations.

2.2 Datasets

There are many efforts in detecting machine-generated text benchmarks. HC3 (Guo et al., 2023a) contains both Chinese and English text from ChatGPT. Other datasets such as MGTBench (He et al., 2023), ArguGPT (Liu et al., 2023) and DeepfakeTextDetect (Li et al., 2023) consider texts generated by various LLMs. M4 and M4GT-Bench(Wang et al., 2024d,a) are two comprehensive datasets covering multiple domains, languages and generators. MULTITuDE (Macko et al., 2023) includes texts in 11 languages, while the MAiDE-up dataset (Ignat et al., 2024) focuses on hotel reviews generated in 10 languages by GPT-4. MultiSocial (Macko et al., 2024) benchmarks MGT detection in the social media domain for 22 languages and 5 social media platforms.

2.3 Shared Tasks

Several shared tasks have been organized to address the problem of detecting machine-generated texts. *2023 ALTA shared task* (Molla et al., 2023) focuses specifically on identifying GPT-generated texts. *DAGPap22 shared task* (Chamezopoulos et al., 2024) targets the detection of machine-generated scientific papers. *SemEval 2024 shared task 8* (Wang et al., 2024b) introduced four subtasks: monolingual and multilingual binary classification (whether the text is generated by machine or written by human), multi-way classification distinguishing different generators, and human-machine text boundary detection, attracting participation from hundreds of teams.

There has been growing interest in detecting machine-generated text in non-English languages, such as Russian in *RuATD Shared task 2022* (Shamardina et al., 2022, 2024), Spanish in *IberLEF 2023* (Sarvazyan et al., 2023), and Dutch in *CLIN33* (Fivez et al., 2024). The multilingual detection task on SemEval-2024 Task 8 (Wang et al., 2024b) covers 9 languages, utilizing the M4GT-Bench dataset (Wang et al., 2024c).

3 Shared Task Description

3.1 Overview

The shared task was conducted in two phases: the development phase August 27, 2024 – October 29, 2024 and the test phase October 30 – November 4, 2024. During the training phase, the participants were given access to the texts and labels of the training and validation subsets, as well as to the texts of the dev-test subset. The dev-test set was made available to participants to evaluate the generalization capabilities of their detectors on distinct data during the development phase.

After the start of the test phase, we opened the labels of the dev-test and provided access to the texts of the test subset with a limited number of submission attempts to prevent leakage. After the finish of the test phase, we have released the labels of the test set, so the participants could perform some ablation studies.

As per the rules of the Task, participants were required to use only the data provided by the organizers to develop their models and were prohibited from utilizing any additional training data.

3.2 Datasets

The data for the Task is split into four subsets: training, development, dev-test, and test. Texts and labels for all subsets are publicly available at Github repository. Tables 1 and 2 present the descriptive statistics of the data.

3.2.1 Training and Development Sets

The training data for both English and multilingual subtasks was constructed using three large-scale multilingual machine-generated text datasets — HC3 (Guo et al., 2023b), M4GT-Bench (Wang et al., 2024c), and MAGE (Li et al., 2024). We merged all collected data, removed repeated texts,

Split	Source	Data License	#Generators	#Domains	Human	MGT	H+M	Total
Train	HC3	CC BY-SA-4.0	1	5	39,140	18,671	57,811	610,767
	M4GT	CC BY-SA-4.0	14	6	86,782	181,081	267,863	
	MAGE	Apache-2.0	27	14	103,000	182,093	285,093	
Dev	HC3	CC BY-SA-4.0	1	5	16,855	7,917	24,772	261,758
	M4GT	CC BY-SA-4.0	14	6	37,220	77,267	114,487	
	MAGE	Apache-2.0	27	14	44,253	78,246	122,499	
Dev-test	RAID	MIT	0	–	13,371	0	13,371	32,557
	LLM-DetectAIve	CC BY-SA-4.0	5	–	0	19,186	19,186	
Test	CUDRT	CC BY-SA-4.0	6	6	12,287	10,691	22,978	73,941
	IELTS	Apache-2.0	2	1	11,382	13,318	24,700	
	NLPeer	Apache-2.0	1	1	5,326	5,376	10,702	
	PeerSum	Apache-2.0	2	1	5,080	6,995	12,075	
	MixSet	CC BY-SA-4.0	7	9	600	2,886	3,486	
Total					375,296	603,727	979,023	**979,023**

Table 1: **English subtask** statistical information of training, development, dev-test, and test sets.

Split	Source	Data License	Lang	#Generators	#Domains	Human	MGT	H+M	Total
Train	HC3	CC BY-SA-4.0	zh, en	1	9	54,655	30,670	85,325	674,083
	M4GT	CC BY-SA-4.0	9	16	13	100,359	203,525	303,884	
	MAGE	Apache-2.0	en	27	14	102,954	181,920	284,874	
Dev	HC3	CC BY-SA-4.0	zh, en	1	9	22,981	12,718	35,699	288,894
	M4GT	CC BY-SA-4.0	9	16	13	42,886	87,591	130,477	
	MAGE	Apache-2.0	en	27	14	44,299	78,419	122,718	
Dev-test	MULTITuDE	GPL-3.0	11	8	–	7,992	66,089	74,081	74,081
Test	29 sources	–	15	19	–	73,634	77,791	151,425	151,425
Total						449,760	738,723	1,188,483	**1,188,483**

Table 2: **Multilingual subtask** statistics of training, development, dev-test, and test sets. M4GT includes 9 languages: en, de, id, it, zh, bg, ar, ur, ru. MULTITuDE includes 11 languages: de, en, uk, es, nl, ca, ru, pt, ar, zh, cs.

and randomly split into train and development sets by the ratio of 7:3. See detailed distribution over different languages, domains and generators in Appendix A.1.

3.2.2 Dev-Test Set

English Subtask A: we utilized 13,371 human-written texts from RAID (Dugan et al., 2024) and sampled 19,186 MGTs from LLM-DetectAIve (Abassy et al., 2024). The latter contains MGTs of three types: (i) fully MGTs, (ii) human-written and then machine-polished texts, and (iii) machine-generated and then machine-humanized texts.

Multilingual Subtask B: we sampled data from MULTITuDE (Macko et al., 2023) as the multilingual dev-test set.

3.2.3 Test Set

For the test set, in addition to leveraging MixSet (Zhang et al., 2024) and CUDRT (Tao et al., 2024), the majority of test sets is collected by our team, particularly multilingual subtask. Note that the dataset of CUDRT has not been released to the public before we used it as a subset of the test set.

English Subtask A uses Mixset and a subset of CUDRT. Based on the IELTS essays, we collected generations from *Llama3.1-70B-versatile* and *GPT-4o-mini*. We further generated academic paper peer reviews based on NLPeer and PeerSum, using *GPT-4o* and *GPT-4o-mini*.

Multilingual Subtask B: in addition to two datasets — we used Urdu fake news detection datasets generated by Ali et al. (2024), and sampled data from the CUDRT Chinese subset, the rest of multilingual test set was all newly collected, involving 27 different corpus and spanning 15 languages, with six of them are not seen in training, dev and dev-test sets. It covers Arabic, Chinese, Dutch, German, **Hebrew**, **Hindi**, Indonesian, Italian, **Japanese**, **Kazakh**, **Norwegian**, Russian, Spanish, Urdu, and **Vietnamese** (languages highlighted with the bold font were not seen in the training data).[2] See detailed distribution over sources,

[2]We included 15 languages in the training, dev and dev-test

Task	Set	Accuracy	F1
Subtask A	Dev	96.2	95.9 / 96.2
	Dev-Test	83.1	81.6 / 82.6
	Test	74.9	73.4 / 73.8
Subtask B	Dev	95.2	94.8 / 95.2
	Dev-Test	84.7	65.5 / 85.7
	Test	74.7	74.2 / 74.3

Table 3: Baseline performance on the Dev, Dev-Test, and Test sets for according to accuracy and macro F1.

domains, and models in Appendix A.2.

3.3 Baselines

Detector We fine-tuned pre-trained transformer-based models on the training sets as baselines. For *subtask A*, we fine-tuned RoBERTa, and XLM-R for *subtask B* to handle with multilingual data.

Fine-tuning was performed using the Hugging Face `Trainer` API with the following configuration: learning rate of 2×10^{-5}, batch size of 16 for both training and evaluation, weight decay of 0.1, and a total of 3 training epochs. Models were evaluated at the end of each epoch, and we keep the best model determined by development set performance, for the subsequent testing.

Results on Dev, Dev-test, and Test Sets Baseline results on the dev, dev-test, and test sets for both subtask A and B are demonstrated in Table 3. The baseline models showed strong performance on the development (dev) sets, particularly for subtask A, achieving high accuracy and F1-scores. However, performance declined on the dev-test and test sets, indicating potential overfitting or challenges in adapting to unseen data distributions.

For subtask B, the multilingual setting introduced additional complexity, as reflected in the relatively lower macro-average metrics, which emphasizes the difficulty of generalizing across multiple languages. These baseline results provide a reference point for participants and highlight the challenges of detecting machine-generated text, especially in multilingual contexts.

4 Participants' Submissions

In this section, we first describe ranking, macro-F1 and accuracy of participants, followed by a brief description of all submitted systems. We classify

Rank	Team	Macro-F1	Accuracy
1	Advacheck	83.07	83.11
2	Unibuc-NLP	83.01	83.33
3	Fraunhofer SIT	82.80	82.89
4	Grape	81.88	82.23
5	TechExperts(IPN)	81.53	81.81
6	TurQUaz	80.68	80.74
7	SzegedAI	79.10	79.29
8	AAIG	78.74	79.34
9	DCBU	77.13	78.01
10	Alfa	75.37	76.42
11	L3i++	74.63	75.54
12	LuxVeri	74.58	75.68
13	azlearning	74.14	75.17
14	honghanhh	73.94	75.14
–	**Baseline**	73.42	74.89
15	VX1291	72.93	74.83
–	cuettransform	72.32	73.16
16	rockstart	72.24	73.89
17	batirsdu	71.01	71.42
18	IPN-CIC	70.68	72.42
19	Ai-Monitors	70.57	72.65
20	semanticcuet	70.05	71.96
21	hmcgovern	68.48	69.51
22	abhirak0603	68.02	70.50
23	cnlpnitspp	65.02	68.76
24	mail6djj	64.66	68.46
25	bennben	63.32	67.48
26	saehyunma	62.80	67.25
27	yuwert777	62.14	66.69
28	seven	59.09	63.20
29	fangsifan	58.48	62.68
30	yaoxy	57.28	64.20
31	jojoc	54.16	60.37
32	dominikmacko	49.94	50.78
33	tropaleum	49.57	50.60
34	starlight1	47.57	56.65
35	nitstejasrikar	44.89	57.24

Table 4: **English subtask** leaderboard results. The main performance metric is macro-F1. Accuracy is used as an auxiliary performance metric.

methods into (1) above vs. below the baseline, (2) black-box vs. white-box, (3) zero-shot vs. fine-tuning, (4) fine-tuning based on small models vs. large models, and (5) ensemble or not.

To describe systems participating in the English and Multilingual subtasks separately, in the text we add the subscript **English:rank** to participants in the English subtask and the subscript **Multi:rank** to participants in the multilingual subtask. For example the team **Fraunhofer SIT** is ranked 3rd in the English subtask and referred to as **Fraunhofer SIT**$_{\textbf{English:3}}$ while it is ranked 10th in the Multilingual subtask and thus referred to as **Fraunhofer SIT**$_{\textbf{Multi:10}}$.

sets — Arabic, **Bulgarian**, **Catalan**, Chinese, Czech, Dutch, **English**, **German**, Indonesian, Italian, **Portuguese**, Russian, Spanish, **Ukrainian**, and Urdu.

Team Name	Ranking	Small PLM	LLM	Feature Combination	Ensemble
Advacheck	1	✓			
Unibuc-NLP	2		✓		
Fraunhofer SIT	3	✓			
Grape	4	✓	✓		✓
TechExperts(IPN)	5		✓		
TurQUaz	6	✓	✓	✓	✓
SzegedAI	7	✓			✓
AAIG	8	✓			
DCBU	9	✓	✓	✓	✓
L3i++	11		✓		
LuxVeri	12	✓		✓	
IPN-CIC	18	✓			
Ai-Monitors	19	✓			

Table 5: **English subtask** participants overview.

4.1 English Subtask

4.1.1 Results and Rank

The English subtask attracted 36 submissions in total. Table 4 presents the complete rankings. The competition saw a remarkably tight race among the top performers with only 0.27 macro-F1 points separating the top three teams: **Advacheck**$_{\textbf{English:1}}$ (83.07), **Unibuc-NLP**$_{\textbf{English:2}}$ (83.01), and **Fraunhofer SIT**$_{\textbf{English:3}}$ (82.8). Interestingly, while the team **Advacheck**$_{\textbf{English:1}}$ secured the first place by the main metric, **Unibuc-NLP**$_{\textbf{English:2}}$ achieved a slightly higher accuracy (83.33 vs. 83.11), highlighting the razor-thin margins between top performers.

Fourteen teams outperformed the baseline (73.42 macro-F1) according to the main metric with scores varying from 83.07 to 44.89. The inability of most submissions to surpass the baseline underscores the complexity of the task.

4.1.2 System Description

Table 5 presents an overview of the English subtask participants' systems.[3]

Team Advacheck$_{\textbf{English:1}}$ (Gritsai et al., 2025) develops a multi-task system with a shared Transformer Encoder (DeBERTa-v3-base) between several classification heads. This system includes a primary binary classification head and additional multiclass heads for text domain classification. The ablation studies show that multi-task learning outperforms single-task modes, with simultaneous tasks forming cluster structures in the embeddings space.

Team Unibuc-NLP$_{\textbf{English:2}}$ (Teodor-George Marchitan, 2025) utilized both masked (XLM-RoBERTa-base) and causal language models (Qwen2.5-0.5B; Yang et al. (2024)),[4] with the Qwen-based classifier performing on par with Gritsai et al.. The authors report that LORA fine-tuning XLM-RoBERTa promotes a strong performance.

Team Fraunhofer SIT$_{\textbf{English:3}}$ (Schäfer and Steinebach, 2025) combined an MGT detection adapter with a multi-genre natural language inference adapter over RoBERTa-base.

Team Grape$_{\textbf{English:4}}$ (Doan and Inui, 2025), first, finetuned Llama-3.2-1B (Dubey et al., 2024) and gemma-2-2b (Team et al., 2024) for the MGT detection task. Second, they combined linguistic features with the model predictions by leveraging ensemble learning for more robust classification.

Team TechExperts(IPN)$_{\textbf{English:5}}$ similar to Doan and Inui fine-tuned gemma-2b for the MGT detection task, which confirms the effectiveness of the small model in identifying the generated content.

Other teams ranked in top-20 developed the MGT detectors by (i) fine-tuning a model (**Team TurQUaz**$_{\textbf{English:6}}$; Keleş and Kutlu, 2025; **Team AAIG**$_{\textbf{English:8}}$; Bhandarkar et al., 2025; **Team IPN-CIC**$_{\textbf{English:18}}$; Abiola et al., 2025; **Team Ai-Monitors**$_{\textbf{English:19}}$; Singh et al., 2025); (ii) ensembling models and features (**Team SzegedAI**$_{\textbf{English:7}}$; Kiss and Berend, 2025; **Team DCBU**$_{\textbf{English:9}}$; Zhang et al., 2025; **Team Lux Veri**$_{\textbf{English:12}}$; Mobin and Islam, 2025); and (ii) utilizing label supervision (**Team L3i++**$_{\textbf{English:11}}$; Tran and Nguyen, 2025).

4.2 Multilingual Subtask

4.2.1 Results and Ranks

The multilingual subtask received 27 submissions with complete rankings demonstrated in Table 6.

The most notable feature of this subtask was the exceptional performance of the team "Grape", achieving macro-F1 score of 79.16, significantly outperforming other competitors. A substantial gap of 3.59 macro-F1 points between the winner and the second place "rockstart" (75.57) underscores the effectiveness of the "Grape" team approach to multilingual MGT detection.

In this subtask, only seven teams managed to surpass the baseline score of 74.16 with scores

[3]Top ranking teams that lack a system description do so because the authors did not submit a manuscripts and did not provide a short description of their system.

[4]https://qwenlm.github.io/blog/qwen2.5/

Rank	Team	Macro-F1	Accuray
1	Grape	79.16	79.62
–	jykim*	75.96	76.56
2	rockstart	75.57	75.64
3	Nota AI	75.32	75.91
4	LuxVeri	75.13	75.27
5	TechExperts(IPN)	74.63	74.74
6	azlearning	74.36	74.49
7	nampfiev1995	74.27	74.40
–	**Baseline**	74.16	74.74
8	starlight1	73.78	73.92
9	abit7431	72.65	73.48
10	Fraunhofer SIT	72.58	73.61
11	mail6djj	72.24	73.34
12	saehyunma	72.20	73.52
13	seven	71.40	72.00
14	jojoc	70.72	70.99
15	OSINT	70.67	71.87
16	yaoxy	69.54	71.51
17	VX1291	69.47	70.50
18	bennben	69.13	69.63
19	fangsifan	68.60	69.57
20	yuwert777	68.45	70.65
21	honghanhh	67.61	67.91
22	tmarchitan	66.29	67.11
–	keles	64.24	64.41
23	batirsdu	62.59	63.05
24	sohailwaleed2	52.53	52.59
25	dominikmacko	51.03	51.05

Table 6: **Multilingual subtask** leaderboard results. Submissions marked with "*" use additional training data and, therefore, are not incorporated in the ranking.

Team Name	Ranking	Small PLM	LLM	Feature Combination	Ensemble
Grape	1	✓	✓		✓
Nota AI	3	✓	✓	✓	✓
LuxVeri	4	✓			✓
TechExperts(IPN)	5		✓		
Fraunhofer SIT	10	✓			
OSINT	15	✓			

Table 7: **Multilingual subtask** participants overview.

ranging from 79.16 to 51.03. This indicates the increased difficulty of detecting MGT text among multiple languages simultaneously.

The overall lower scores in this subtask compared to the English subtask (top score 79.16 vs. 83.07) highlight the additional complexity introduced by multilingual detection and room for improvement.

4.2.2 System Description

Table 7 presents an overview of the multilingual subtask participants' systems.

Team Grape$_{Multi:1}$ (Doan and Inui, 2025), ranked 1 in the multilingual leaderboard, adopted two approaches in the task. They first separately fine-tuned small language models tailored to the specific subtask and then trained an ensemble model on top of them. Through evaluating and comparing these approaches, the team identified the most effective techniques for detecting machine-generated content across languages.

Team NotaAI$_{Multi:3}$ (Park et al., 2025) secured the third place in the task. They developed the system that addresses the challenge of detecting MGT in languages not observed during training, where model accuracy tends to decline significantly. The proposed multilingual MGT detection system employs a two-step approach: first, a language identification tool determines the language of the input text. If the language has been observed during training, the text is processed using a model fine-tuned on a multilingual PLM. For languages not seen during training, the system utilizes a model that combines token-level predictive distributions extracted from various LLMs with a meaning representation derived from a multilingual PLM.

Team LuxVeri$_{Multi:4}$ (Mobin and Islam, 2025) earned the 4th place. They utilized an ensemble of models, where weights are assigned based on each model's inverse perplexity to improve classification accuracy. The system combined RemBERT, XLM-RoBERTa-base, and BERT-base-multilingual-cased using the same weighted ensemble strategy. The results highlight the effectiveness of inverse perplexity-based weighting for robust detection of machine-generated text in both monolingual and multilingual settings.

Team TecExperts(IPN)$_{Multi:5}$ (Mehak et al., 2025) leveraged the gemma-2b model, fine-tuned specifically for the Shared Task 1 datasets to achieve strong performance.

Team L3i++$_{Multi:7}$ (Tran and Nguyen, 2025) studied a label-supervised adaptation configuration for LLaMA-as-a-judge for the task. In detail, they explore the feasibility of fine-tuning LLaMA with label supervision in masked and unmasked, unidirectional and bidirectional settings, to discriminate the texts generated by machines and humans in monolingual and multilingual corpora.

Other Systems The other systems explored various approaches, including exploring the integration of additional features such as perplexity and Tf-IDF (**Team TurQUaz$_{Multi:22}$**; Keleş and

Rank	All	MixSet	CUDRT	IELTS	PeerReview
1	83.1	48.0	67.1	89.9	97.2
2	83.3	66.7	75.9	82.6	94.1
3	82.9	58.9	71.0	88.8	92.1
4	82.2	64.7	73.2	79.1	97.4
5	81.8	59.2	72.7	80.8	95.5
6	80.7	47.2	72.6	78.1	96.9
7	75.7	54.9	71.0	63.1	97.2
8	79.3	62.3	75.4	69.0	97.2
9	78.0	60.0	74.6	66.3	96.9
10	76.4	59.8	75.5	64.2	93.2
11	75.5	60.9	70.3	66.9	92.5
12	75.7	56.6	74.0	61.9	95.2
13	75.2	62.8	70.8	65.3	92.2
14	75.1	66.6	72.8	62.7	92.2
BL	74.9	62.0	72.1	63.4	92.2
15	74.8	73.2	71.9	63.0	90.8
-	73.2	53.5	71.3	62.8	89.3
16	73.9	64.3	71.2	62.6	90.3
17	71.4	53.9	69.6	70.8	76.6
18	72.4	65.4	70.6	62.2	86.5
19	72.7	72.6	70.4	63.6	84.8
20	72.0	69.8	70.4	66.5	79.8
21	69.5	50.7	64.0	65.7	82.0
22	70.5	70.6	66.7	65.3	80.0
23	68.8	73.7	66.9	61.7	77.6
24	68.5	65.7	67.3	57.4	82.0
25	67.5	67.6	67.7	58.0	77.5
26	67.2	68.2	67.2	57.3	78.0
27	66.7	67.4	67.1	57.1	76.5
28	63.2	68.3	67.8	57.1	64.4
29	63.5	67.7	68.6	57.6	64.0
30	64.2	77.7	64.5	58.6	67.9
31	60.4	77.7	64.6	58.3	55.6
32	50.8	56.0	49.7	51.1	50.7
33	50.6	56.7	49.1	50.7	51.0
34	56.6	80.8	60.6	54.9	50.9
35	57.2	82.3	56.4	54.0	57.8

Table 8: **English subtask detection accuracy** across four domains.

Kutlu, 2025), finetuning models such as XLM-RoBERTa on the training set for the final evaluation, as incorporating adapter fusion led to worse results (**Team Fraunhofer SIT$_{\textbf{Multi:10}}$**; Schäfer and Steinebach, 2025), XML-R and mBERT models (**Team IPN$_{\textbf{Multi:9}}$**; Abiola et al., 2025 and QWen and RoBERTa models (**Team Unibuc-NLP$_{\textbf{Multi:22}}$**; Teodor-George Marchitan, 2025); and combining language-specific embeddings with fusion techniques to create a unified, language-agnostic feature representation (**Team OSINT$_{\textbf{Multi:15}}$**; Agrahari and Sanasam, 2025).

5 Analysis

Based on the test set, we analyze submitted systems by comparing the detection accuracy on (1) in-domain vs. out-of-domain, (2) seen vs. unseen languages, and (3) generations produced using normal prompts vs. prompts attempting to fill the gap between human and machine based on observations in manual annotations.

5.1 English In-domain vs. Out-of-domain

Results in Table 8 show the accuracy of 36 submitted systems across four component datasets in the English test set. Significant variance across domains reveals different generalization and robustness across detection systems.

Performance for in-domain datasets, such as IELTS and PeerReview, is generally higher than out-of-domain datasets MixSet and CUDRT. Top systems ranking 1-5 achieve scores around 80% on in-domain datasets. For example, top1 Team "Advacheck" scored 83.1% on IELTS essays and 89.9% on PeerReview. Moreover, accuracies are $\geq$90% for all teams above the baseline on PeerReview including the baseline itself. The consistently-high performance suggests that peer reviews (PeerRead) in the M4GT-Bench training set have effectively facilitated detectors in capturing domain-specific patterns during training, and thus generalizing well to similar-content PeerReview in the test set. For IELTS essays, the performance trend differs slightly from PeerReview. Despite student essays presented in the training set M4GT-Bench, only the first five teams managed to achieve scores $\geq$80%. This lies in the fact that essays sampled from OUTFOX in M4GT-Bench were written by English native speakers, while English is the second language for authors who attended the IELTS test. Subtle differences between essays in the training and test result in accuracy declines on the test set, which to some extent reveals the vulnerability of detectors against tiny distribution perturbations.

Out-of-domain dataset MixSet is the most challenging subset due to its varied and unseen content genres including game reviews, email, blog, and speech content. Top-ranked teams (ranks 1–5) experienced a substantial performance drop on MixSet — accuracy in the range of 48–66.7%. This may also attribute to the humanization and adaption of machine-generated text in MixSet. The former refers to modifying MGT to more closely mimic the natural noise that human writing always brings, introducing typo, grammatical mistakes, links, and tags. The latter refers to modifying MGT to ensure its alignment to fluency and naturalness to human linguistic habits without introducing any error expression. Detection systems struggle with highly heterogeneous and less structured data, which is exacerbated by the humanization and adaption operations of MGT in MixSet.

A surprising observation on MixSet is that all

Rank Size	All 151,425	News 57,590	Wiki 11,687	Essay 2,201	QA 24,854	Summary 13,600	Tweet 1,325	GovR 19,736	Other 4,214
1	79.6	65.1	80.2	99.3	98.9	70.0	94.5	87.0	84.2
2	75.6	64.0	87.1	81.0	91.9	79.1	100.0	69.1	48.2
3	75.9	60.7	81.0	97.7	96.2	65.2	72.0	81.7	91.1
4	75.3	60.7	87.9	91.0	93.2	71.7	98.9	75.2	58.6
BL	74.8	61.6	85.2	97.7	94.1	58.6	94.4	76.2	83.2
5	74.7	60.2	74.7	97.7	98.9	59.7	65.3	75.0	96.2
6	74.5	59.8	79.6	90.9	95.1	82.8	95.5	62.6	82.7
7	74.4	59.8	79.7	90.7	95.2	82.1	93.8	62.9	79.4
8	73.9	58.1	81.2	98.5	92.9	73.5	29.1	81.2	70.7
9	73.5	61.1	85.0	94.7	94.5	64.8	87.8	78.7	60.3
10	73.6	60.8	77.3	94.2	95.4	61.3	91.9	80.5	86.8
11	73.3	60.2	83.9	96.7	94.9	60.0	56.0	82.4	61.8
12	73.5	62.2	81.4	93.3	95.9	64.8	41.0	83.5	68.2
13	72.0	56.3	42.3	99.2	99.2	70.9	33.7	89.0	67.3
14	71.0	56.0	55.2	97.0	92.4	76.3	0.1	81.1	85.6
15	50.3	51.0	42.4	60.0	51.2	49.7	33.9	61.9	62.1
16	71.5	59.6	44.0	97.0	99.2	59.5	57.7	89.3	58.1
17	50.2	50.8	43.2	57.7	50.7	49.9	36.6	59.8	60.8
18	69.6	55.0	45.8	97.7	92.2	71.5	2.3	82.7	85.2
19	70.5	54.5	33.5	99.1	99.1	73.1	6.4	88.7	77.6
20	70.7	60.9	41.7	93.5	99.1	63.5	45.3	86.8	61.3
21	67.9	61.7	69.9	63.6	78.1	78.0	49.4	71.8	60.7
22	67.1	57.4	51.8	83.4	94.7	61.5	100.0	80.7	20.9
23	49.7	49.1	57.0	45.5	49.1	50.3	64.5	40.1	39.4
24	52.6	45.3	35.0	83.0	72.4	67.3	99.3	46.6	17.8
25	51.0	50.4	53.0	51.0	51.8	52.0	56.1	48.4	48.9

Table 9: **Multilingual subtask detection accuracy** across eight domains (Wiki: Wikipedia, GovR: GovReport).

teams above the baseline struggled to improve $\leq 5\%$ compared to the baseline 62%, while 15 teams below the baseline achieved improvements $\geq 5\%$, with remarkable scores achieved by the last two teams — 80.8% and 82.3%, showing a stark contrast to their performance on other datasets.

Domains involved in CUDRT partially overlapped with the training data domains (e.g., news), while thesis is out of the training data though similar to academic papers, leading to the accuracy between Mixset and PeerReview. Most teams including the baseline scored between 65–75%, demonstrating moderate adaptability to this dataset.

5.2 Multilingual Subtask

We analyze submissions from three perspectives.

5.2.1 In-domain vs. Out-of-domain

We divided 29 sources across 15 languages into 8 domains: News, Wikipedia, Essay, question answering (QA), Summary, Tweet, government reports (GovReport), and others (e.g., poetry).

Table 9 presents the multilingual Subtask accuracy across 8 domains. In-domain datasets (News, Wikipedia, QA and Summary) consistently achieve higher accuracies due to their structured and training-aligned nature. Baseline accuracies for these domains are relatively strong, with significant improvements by the top-performing teams. Notably, the top-ranked team achieved peak performance of over 98% in QA, while the second-ranked team attained over 87% in Wikipedia. Though the genre of summary presented in the training data, they are English text. Summaries in the test set are Russian and Arabic, so summary domain posed notable challenges for detector, performing poorly across both baselines and team submissions. This underscores the difficulty of distinguishing machine-generated summaries from human-written ones in this domain.

Conversely, out-of-domain datasets (Essay, Tweet, GovReport, and Other) presented greater challenges, reflecting the systems' struggles to generalize to unseen styles or informal text. While structured datasets like essays and GovReport performed moderately well, with top-team accuracies exceeding 85%, informal and noisy domains such as tweets exhibited the lowest performance, with accuracies peaking at just 69.99%. This stark contrast highlights the need for more effective generalization strategies. Interestingly, we observed an anomaly in the tweet domain: two teams (ranked second and 22nd) achieved perfect accuracy (100%). This suggests that specialized

Rank Size	All 151,425	Fill-gap 32,487	Original 17,017	Others 101,921
1	79.6	91.1	94.2	73.5
2	75.6	75.9	84.0	74.1
3	75.9	89.7	92.2	68.8
4	75.3	81.5	86.9	71.4
BL	74.8	87.6	89.0	68.3
5	74.7	84.6	96.6	67.9
6	74.5	75.6	90.1	71.5
7	74.4	75.4	90.3	71.4
8	73.9	88.5	87.1	67.0
9	73.5	86.7	93.1	66.0
10	73.6	92.9	93.0	64.2
11	73.3	88.3	91.6	65.5
12	73.5	91.6	94.3	64.3
13	72.0	93.7	95.7	61.1
14	71.0	90.4	86.3	62.3
15	50.3	66.7	64.8	42.7
16	71.5	93.2	96.4	60.4
17	50.2	64.7	62.9	43.5
18	69.6	91.6	86.5	59.8
19	70.5	94.9	95.1	58.6
20	70.7	93.8	96.1	59.0
21	67.9	79.9	71.5	63.5
22	67.1	84.6	94.4	57.0
23	49.7	36.1	37.4	56.1
24	52.6	66.4	60.3	46.9
25	51.0	48.2	48.5	52.4

Table 10: **Multilingual subtask detection accuracy** between generations using original prompts vs. prompts aiming to fill the gap between human and machine, corresponding to columns of *Original* vs. *Fill-gap*. All is the whole multilingual test set.

approaches tailored to this domain can yield exceptional results, though these may involve overfitting to specific dataset patterns.

Overall, the results reveal a persistent gap between in-domain and out-of-domain performance, emphasizing the importance of domain adaptation and robust methods for handling unstructured or unseen data. At the same time, the findings demonstrate the potential for domain-specific optimizations in challenging contexts.

5.2.2 General Prompts vs. Improved Prompts

We compare system's accuracy results on text generated by ordinary prompts and the well-designed prompts that are used to fill the human and machine generations gap. MGTs using the improved prompts appear to make detection tasks more challenging. Our improved prompts aim to make machine-generated text more similar to human-written text by instructing LLMs how to generate human-like text and to avoid presenting distinguishable signals in formats, where these features were summarized from our observations in manual annotations in distinguishing human and machine text.

As shown in Table 10, in scenarios where detectors are tasked with identifying machine-generated text created using our improved prompts (Fill-gap in the Table 10), there is a noticeable decrease in accuracy compared to detecting machine-generated text created with the original prompts. This decline is particularly evident in higher ranks, with team 2 experiencing an 8% drop, team 5 a 12% drop, and teams 6 and 7 around a 15% drop. This decrease in performance suggests that the improved prompts, which were designed to narrow the gap between machine-generated and human-generated texts, may have inadvertently made the machine output too similar to human-like text, complicating the detector's ability to distinguish between the two. However, there are exceptions to this trend. Notably, team 8 (rank 8) and team 14 (rank 14) show improved results when using Fill-gap prompts, with accuracy increasing from 87.08% to 88.55% for team 8 and from 86.30% to 90.39% for team 14. This improvement may be due to a misalignment of features between their detector design and our improved machine-generated prompt design.

This suggests that we can learn from machine-generated examples to design better prompts that make the machine-generated text more natural and less detectable. However, it also exposes the vulnerability of detectors — they can be easily fooled when we adjust the prompts.

5.2.3 Seen Languages vs. Unseen Languages

Table 11 presents the detection accuracy on the multilingual subtask across 15 languages, including seen and unseen languages during the training process. The top-performing languages in terms of detection accuracy are generally those seen during training, with the highest accuracy observed on Chinese (94.2), followed by Russian (89.6) and Spanish (89.5). For Arabic (AR), Italian (IT), and Dutch (NL), the performance is slightly lower but still competitive, demonstrating the model's steady generalization to seen languages.

For unseen languages, such as Hindi (HI) and Hebrew (HE), there is a noticeable drop in performance compared to seen languages. For example, the top-performing team achieved only 51.8 on Hindi. It is challenging for models to generalize to unseen languages, due to the limited exposure to linguistic patterns, structures, and features during training. It is worth noting that some unseen

Rank Size	**All** 151,425	**ZH** 63,009	**UR** 30,505	**RU** 27,158	**AR** 10,670	**IT** 5,296	**KK** 2,471	**VI** 2,326	**DE** 1,865	**NO** 1,544	**ID** 1,200	**NL** 1,200	**ES** 1,200	**HI** 1,199	**HE** 1,182	**JA** 600
1	79.6	94.2	68.7	67.1	71.2	52.9	55.5	90.5	88.3	80.3	89.6	82.2	89.5	51.8	86.7	77.0
2	75.6	84.7	64.6	74.2	57.9	52.9	83.8	83.5	96.4	76.0	51.7	90.6	91.2	69.6	96.8	95.3
3	75.9	90.2	67.2	58.9	66.8	52.9	92.5	74.7	88.8	72.2	87.4	68.9	47.1	70.6	96.4	72.2
4	75.3	87.6	64.6	63.9	61.3	52.9	75.8	83.4	94.9	88.5	53.5	92.2	90.4	73.0	97.3	92.2
BL	74.8	87.3	68.4	55.3	68.4	52.9	82.8	85.3	85.2	69.8	68.2	92.5	90.5	71.3	89.3	90.0
5	74.7	90.1	64.1	56.0	69.1	52.9	62.9	87.6	59.6	69.8	93.8	81.0	90.4	69.1	96.5	95.0
6	74.5	84.2	65.0	67.9	66.8	52.9	47.5	81.8	93.5	83.2	83.9	85.9	88.9	69.1	89.8	78.2
7	74.4	84.4	64.9	67.7	65.4	52.9	47.5	82.0	92.2	85.8	83.4	85.4	89.2	68.8	90.1	75.2
8	73.9	88.3	58.7	67.0	58.4	52.9	93.0	65.9	89.6	61.6	50.5	80.7	88.0	61.4	82.7	61.2
9	73.5	85.1	67.0	59.8	60.8	52.9	90.6	87.2	82.8	78.2	48.7	78.0	83.1	54.5	89.6	74.3
10	73.6	86.0	67.6	56.0	69.1	52.9	86.8	80.4	65.0	52.8	73.8	87.4	85.4	63.5	85.7	86.0
11	73.3	87.4	63.4	58.2	55.6	52.9	89.4	79.7	87.0	66.6	73.9	82.1	87.4	70.5	93.3	79.5
12	73.5	85.3	68.0	61.5	54.3	52.9	92.7	62.0	87.8	63.7	80.3	85.3	86.3	63.0	86.2	59.5
13	72.0	93.2	55.4	63.3	55.4	52.9	93.0	65.9	5.2	25.8	71.2	50.2	50.0	61.4	1.7	61.2
14	71.0	87.0	54.3	68.7	61.2	52.8	54.7	63.8	77.1	54.7	49.7	57.1	64.9	53.5	0.0	52.0
15	50.3	50.9	52.0	49.0	53.0	50.4	52.1	49.7	33.9	33.2	49.7	50.3	50.7	50.4	32.1	50.0
16	71.5	91.3	62.4	55.5	53.7	52.9	89.4	79.7	5.3	28.9	79.9	50.2	50.0	70.3	1.9	79.5
17	50.2	50.6	51.4	49.3	52.8	50.1	52.2	50.1	35.9	34.5	49.3	50.3	50.2	50.6	34.2	53.3
18	69.6	87.4	54.5	63.8	61.1	52.9	55.7	57.0	58.2	23.1	50.3	55.2	59.3	53.7	0.0	54.3
19	70.5	92.2	51.6	65.5	56.5	52.8	54.7	63.8	4.2	23.8	70.6	50.1	50.0	53.5	0.0	52.0
20	70.7	87.6	65.6	58.3	52.0	52.9	92.7	62.0	5.0	28.2	81.7	50.2	50.0	63.0	1.9	59.5
21	67.9	71.9	51.7	80.1	55.3	78.3	48.1	63.8	93.8	82.1	72.4	83.5	84.7	52.3	31.7	63.8
22	67.1	82.5	61.5	55.3	45.8	52.9	94.2	71.6	12.0	27.9	57.5	63.3	73.6	53.5	20.3	57.2
23	49.7	49.2	48.4	50.7	47.4	49.0	50.3	49.7	65.5	63.5	50.4	51.1	49.2	51.9	64.5	52.0
24	52.6	60.7	45.7	58.9	28.8	52.9	47.5	48.1	5.8	39.8	47.7	49.5	51.2	46.0	5.8	27.0
25	51.0	51.1	49.9	51.5	50.8	50.1	50.1	52.3	55.9	54.5	52.5	54.0	49.9	52.4	53.7	52.0

Table 11: **Multilingual subtask detection accuracy** across 15 languages. Underlined languages were not present in the training data.

languages perform relatively well, such as Kazakh (KK) and Vietnamese (VI), achieving relatively high scores. This may result from knowledge transfer from similar languages to the unseen, like Russian to Kazakh, and Chinese to Vietnamese.

Overall, the models perform well on seen languages, and scores decline significantly on unseen languages.The dataset size and the nature of a language (e.g., script, structure, and linguistic features) play an important role in the model's ability to generalize.

6 Conclusion

In this work, we presented the dataset, baseline, participating systems and a detailed analysis across various detection methods for GenAI shared task 1: binary machine generated text detection. We explored both English and multilingual settings with diverse domains, LLM generators, and languages. All submitted systems show good performance on domains and languages that are seen during training, while witness the significant declines on unseen domains and languages. Moreover, detectors show remarkable vulnerability when machine-generated text is adapted to mimic humans, either by introducing typo, link, and tags, or by using fill-human-machine gap prompts. We expect our task can attract more researchers to develop robust and generalized detection models, and our analysis insights can provide a direction for future work, advancing research in machine-generated content detection.

Limitations

Despite providing a comprehensive dataset that spans multiple generators and domains and testing both English and Multilingual settings our study encounters several limitations that pave the way for future research.

Firstly, all the text samples (human and machine generated) used in this work come from existing open-source datasets and resources. While the sources of the test set have not been released prior to the conclusion of the challenge there is a limited possibility of data leakage. Participants were not allowed to use any external data and we trust they did not, however, pre-trained models could have seen part of the test set during their training and it would be impossible to know it.

Secondly, we don't have a detailed analysis of the differences between the datasets we joined together so that it is hard to understand if they have replicated or near-replicated samples and more in general how similar or not they are. In the future we will try to measure the performance of MGT detectors trained on the train set of one of these datasets when tested on each of the others to measure how close are the distributions of each pair of datasets among those we used.

Finally, we only look at binary classification

tasks (human vs. machine) while it would be relevant to understand the performance of detectors in a multiclass classification scenario (human vs. machine1 vs. machine2 vs. ...), this would have been difficult to arrange correctly using the different datasets we have collected since isolating the specific versions of each model becomes harder over time (specifically with closed source ones) and therefore we avoided doing it. Future work should account for this scenario too.

Ethics and Broader Impact

This section outlines potential ethical considerations related to our work.

Data Collection and Licenses A primary ethical consideration is the data license. We reused pre-existing dataset, such as HC3, M4GT-Bench, MAGE, RAID, OUTFOX and LLM-DetectAIve, which have been publicly released for research purposes under clear licensing agreements. We adhere to the intended usage of all these dataset licenses.

Security Implications The dataset underpinning our shared task aims to foster the development of robust MGT detection systems, which are vital in addressing security and ethical concerns. These systems play a crucial role in identifying and mitigating misuse cases, such as preventing the spread of automated misinformation campaigns, which can undermine public discourse, and protecting individuals and organizations from potential financial losses through deceptive machine-generated content. In sensitive domains like journalism, academia, and legal proceedings, where the authenticity and accuracy of information are incredibly important, MGT detection is vital to maintaining content integrity and public trust. Beyond these fields, robust detection mechanisms contribute to the broader goal of promoting digital literacy by raising public awareness of the strengths and limitations of LLMs. This fosters a healthy skepticism towards digital content, encouraging users to critically evaluate the information they encounter.

Moreover, in multilingual contexts, detecting MGT becomes significantly more challenging due to the diversity of linguistic and cultural nuances. Advanced detection systems should address these complexities to prevent vulnerabilities, such as exploitation of less-resourced languages for disinformation. By ensuring the reliability of multilingual machine-generated content, these systems enhance global trust in AI technologies and protect against the security risks that arise from their misuse.

References

Mervat Abassy, Kareem Elozeiri, Alexander Aziz, Minh Ngoc Ta, Raj Vardhan Tomar, Bimarsha Adhikari, Saad El Dine Ahmed, Yuxia Wang, Osama Mohammed Afzal, Zhuohan Xie, Jonibek Mansurov, Ekaterina Artemova, Vladislav Mikhailov, Rui Xing, Jiahui Geng, Hasan Iqbal, Zain Muhammad Mujahid, Tarek Mahmoud, Akim Tsvigun, Alham Fikri Aji, Artem Shelmanov, Nizar Habash, Iryna Gurevych, and Preslav Nakov. 2024. LLM-DetectAIve: a tool for fine-grained machine-generated text detection. In *Proceedings of the 2024 Conference on Empirical Methods in Natural Language Processing: System Demonstrations*, pages 336–343, Miami, Florida, USA. Association for Computational Linguistics.

Tolulope O. Abiola, Tewodros A. Bizuneh, Fatima Uroosa, Nida Hafeez, Grigori Sidorov, Olga Kolesnikova, and Olumide E. Ojo. 2025. Advancing multilingual machine-generated text detection: Insights from the coling workshop task. In *Proceedings of the 1st Workshop on GenAI Content Detection (GenAIDetect)*, Abu Dhabi, UAE. International Conference on Computational Linguistics.

Shifali Agrahari and Ranbir Sanasam. 2025. Team osint at genai detection task 1: Multilingual mgt detection:leveraging cross-lingual adaptation for robust llms text identification. In *Proceedings of the 1st Workshop on GenAI Content Detection (GenAIDetect)*, Abu Dhabi, UAE. International Conference on Computational Linguistics.

Muhammad Zain Ali, Yuxia Wang, Bernhard Pfahringer, and Tony Smith. 2024. Detection of human and machine-authored fake news in urdu. *arXiv preprint arXiv:2410.19517*.

Avanti Bhandarkar, Ronald Wilson, and Damon Woodard. 2025. Aaig at genai content detection task 1: Exploring syntactically-aware, resource-efficient small autoregressive decoders for ai content detection. In *Proceedings of the 1st Workshop on GenAI Content Detection (GenAIDetect)*, Abu Dhabi, UAE. International Conference on Computational Linguistics.

Savvas Chamezopoulos, Drahomira Herrmannova, Anita De Waard, Domenic Rosati, and Yury Kashnitsky. 2024. Overview of the dagpap24 shared task on detecting automatically generated scientific paper. In *Proceedings of the Fourth Workshop on Scholarly Document Processing (SDP 2024)*, pages 7–11.

Nhi Doan and Kentaro Inui. 2025. Grape at genai content detection task 1: Llm agents in multilingual machine-generated text detection. In *Proceedings of the 1st Workshop on GenAI Content Detection (GenAIDetect)*, Abu Dhabi, UAE. International Conference on Computational Linguistics.

Abhimanyu Dubey, Abhinav Jauhri, Abhinav Pandey, Abhishek Kadian, Ahmad Al-Dahle, Aiesha Letman, Akhil Mathur, Alan Schelten, Amy Yang, Angela Fan, et al. 2024. The Llama 3 Herd of Models. *arXiv preprint arXiv:2407.21783*.

Liam Dugan, Alyssa Hwang, Filip Trhlík, Andrew Zhu, Josh Magnus Ludan, Hainiu Xu, Daphne Ippolito, and Chris Callison-Burch. 2024. RAID: A shared benchmark for robust evaluation of machine-generated text detectors. In *Proceedings of the 62nd Annual Meeting of the Association for Computational Linguistics (Volume 1: Long Papers)*, pages 12463–12492, Bangkok, Thailand. Association for Computational Linguistics.

Pieter Fivez, Walter Daelemans, Tim Van de Cruys, Yury Kashnitsky, Savvas Chamezopoulos, Hadi Mohammadi, Anastasia Giachanou, Ayoub Bagheri, Wessel Poelman, Juraj Vladika, et al. 2024. The clin33 shared task on the detection of text generated by large language models. *Computational Linguistics in the Netherlands Journal*, 13:233–259.

Sebastian Gehrmann, Hendrik Strobelt, and Alexander M Rush. 2019. Gltr: Statistical detection and visualization of generated text. *arXiv preprint arXiv:1906.04043*.

German Gritsai, Anastasia Voznyuk, Ildar Khabutdinov, and Andrey Grabovoy. 2025. Advacheck at genai detection task 1: Ai detection powered by domain-aware multi-tasking. In *Proceedings of the 1st Workshop on GenAI Content Detection (GenAIDetect)*, Abu Dhabi, UAE. International Conference on Computational Linguistics.

Biyang Guo, Xin Zhang, Ziyuan Wang, Minqi Jiang, Jinran Nie, Yuxuan Ding, Jianwei Yue, and Yupeng Wu. 2023a. How close is chatgpt to human experts? comparison corpus, evaluation, and detection. *arXiv preprint arXiv:2301.07597*.

Biyang Guo, Xin Zhang, Ziyuan Wang, Minqi Jiang, Jinran Nie, Yuxuan Ding, Jianwei Yue, and Yupeng Wu. 2023b. How close is chatgpt to human experts? comparison corpus, evaluation, and detection. *arXiv preprint arxiv:2301.07597*.

Abhimanyu Hans, Avi Schwarzschild, Valeriia Cherepanova, Hamid Kazemi, Aniruddha Saha, Micah Goldblum, Jonas Geiping, and Tom Goldstein. 2024. Spotting llms with binoculars: Zero-shot detection of machine-generated text. *arXiv preprint arXiv:2401.12070*.

Xinlei He, Xinyue Shen, Zeyuan Chen, Michael Backes, and Yang Zhang. 2023. Mgtbench: Benchmarking machine-generated text detection. *arXiv preprint arXiv:2303.14822*.

Xiaomeng Hu, Pin-Yu Chen, and Tsung-Yi Ho. 2023. Radar: Robust ai-text detection via adversarial learning. *Advances in Neural Information Processing Systems*, 36:15077–15095.

Oana Ignat, Xiaomeng Xu, and Rada Mihalcea. 2024. Maide-up: Multilingual deception detection of gpt-generated hotel reviews. *arXiv preprint arXiv:2404.12938*.

Albert Q Jiang, Alexandre Sablayrolles, Arthur Mensch, Chris Bamford, Devendra Singh Chaplot, Diego de las Casas, Florian Bressand, Gianna Lengyel, Guillaume Lample, Lucile Saulnier, et al. 2023. Mistral 7b. *arXiv preprint arXiv:2310.06825*.

Kaan Efe Keleş and Mucahid Kutlu. 2025. Turquaz at genai detection task 1: Dr. perplexity or: How i learned to stop worrying and love the finetuning. In *Proceedings of the 1st Workshop on GenAI Content Detection (GenAIDetect)*, Abu Dhabi, UAE. International Conference on Computational Linguistics.

Mihály Kiss and Gábor Berend. 2025. Beyond binary: Soft-voting multi-class classification for binary machine-generated text detection across diverse language models. In *International Conference on Computational Linguistics*, Abu Dhabi, UAE. Association for Computational Linguistics.

Yafu Li, Qintong Li, Leyang Cui, Wei Bi, Longyue Wang, Linyi Yang, Shuming Shi, and Yue Zhang. 2023. Deepfake text detection in the wild. *arXiv preprint arXiv:2305.13242*.

Yafu Li, Qintong Li, Leyang Cui, Wei Bi, Zhilin Wang, Longyue Wang, Linyi Yang, Shuming Shi, and Yue Zhang. 2024. MAGE: Machine-generated text detection in the wild. In *Proceedings of the 62nd Annual Meeting of the Association for Computational Linguistics (Volume 1: Long Papers)*, pages 36–53, Bangkok, Thailand. Association for Computational Linguistics.

Yikang Liu, Ziyin Zhang, Wanyang Zhang, Shisen Yue, Xiaojing Zhao, Xinyuan Cheng, Yiwen Zhang, and Hai Hu. 2023. Argugpt: evaluating, understanding and identifying argumentative essays generated by gpt models. *arXiv preprint arXiv:2304.07666*.

Dominik Macko, Jakub Kopal, Robert Moro, and Ivan Srba. 2024. Multisocial: Multilingual benchmark of machine-generated text detection of social-media texts. *arXiv preprint arXiv:2406.12549*.

Dominik Macko, Robert Moro, Adaku Uchendu, Jason Lucas, Michiharu Yamashita, Matúš Pikuliak, Ivan Srba, Thai Le, Dongwon Lee, Jakub Simko, and Maria Bielikova. 2023. MULTITuDE: Large-scale multilingual machine-generated text detection benchmark. In *Proceedings of the 2023 Conference on Empirical Methods in Natural Language Processing*, pages 9960–9987, Singapore. Association for Computational Linguistics.

Gull Mehak, Amna Qasim, Abdul Gafar Manuel Meque, Nisar Hussain, Grigori Sidorov, and Alexander Gelbuk. 2025. Tecexperts(ipn) at genai detection task 1: Ensuring content authenticity: Detecting ai-generated text in english and multilingual contexts.

In *Proceedings of the 1st Workshop on GenAI Content Detection (GenAIDetect)*, Abu Dhabi, UAE. International Conference on Computational Linguistics.

Eric Mitchell, Yoonho Lee, Alexander Khazatsky, Christopher D Manning, and Chelsea Finn. 2023. Detectgpt: Zero-shot machine-generated text detection using probability curvature. In *International Conference on Machine Learning*, pages 24950–24962. PMLR.

Md Kamrujjaman Mobin and Md Saiful Islam. 2025. Luxveri at genai detection task 1: Inverse perplexity weighted ensemble for robust detection of ai-generated text across english and multilingual contexts. In *Proceedings of the 1st Workshop on GenAI Content Detection (GenAIDetect)*, Abu Dhabi, UAE. International Conference on Computational Linguistics.

Diego Molla, Haolan Zhan, Xuanli He, and Qiongkai Xu. 2023. Overview of the 2023 alta shared task: Discriminate between human-written and machine-generated text. In *Proceedings of the 21st Annual Workshop of the Australasian Language Technology Association*, pages 148–152.

Aleksandr Nikolich, Konstantin Korolev, Sergei Bratchikov, Igor Kiselev, and Artem Shelmanov. 2024. Vikhr: Constructing a state-of-the-art bilingual open-source instruction-following large language model for Russian. In *Proceedings of the Fourth Workshop on Multilingual Representation Learning (MRL 2024)*, pages 189–199, Miami, Florida, USA. Association for Computational Linguistics.

Hancheol Park, Jaeyeon Kim, Geonmin Kim, and Tae-Ho Kim. 2025. Nota ai at genai detection task 1: Unseen language-aware detection system for multilingual machine-generated text. In *Proceedings of the 1st Workshop on GenAI Content Detection (GenAIDetect)*, Abu Dhabi, UAE. International Conference on Computational Linguistics.

Areg Mikael Sarvazyan, José Ángel González, Marc Franco-Salvador, Francisco Rangel, Berta Chulvi, and Paolo Rosso. 2023. Overview of autextification at iberlef 2023: Detection and attribution of machine-generated text in multiple domains. *arXiv preprint arXiv:2309.11285*.

Karla Schäfer and Martin Steinebach. 2025. Fraunhofer sit at genai content detection task 1: Adapter fusion for ai-generated text detection. In *Proceedings of the 1st Workshop on GenAI Content Detection (GenAIDetect)*, Abu Dhabi, UAE. International Conference on Computational Linguistics.

Tatiana Shamardina, Vladislav Mikhailov, Daniil Cherniankskii, Alena Fenogenova, Marat Saidov, Anastasiya Valeeva, Tatiana Shavrina, Ivan Smurov, Elena Tutubalina, and Ekaterina Artemova. 2022. Findings of the the ruatd shared task 2022 on artificial text detection in russian. *arXiv preprint arXiv:2206.01583*.

Tatiana Shamardina, Marat Saidov, Alena Fenogenova, Aleksandr Tumanov, Alina Zemlyakova, Anna Lebedeva, Ekaterina Gryaznova, Tatiana Shavrina, Vladislav Mikhailov, and Ekaterina Artemova. 2024. Coat: Corpus of artificial texts. *Natural Language Processing*, pages 1–26.

Azad Singh, Vishnu Tripathi, Ravindra Kumar Pandey, Pragyanand Saho, Prakhar Joshi, Neel Mani, Richa Alagh, Pallaw Mishra, and Piyush Arora. 2025. Ai-monitors at genai detection task 1: Fast and scalable machine generated text detection. In *Proceedings of the 1st Workshop on GenAI Content Detection (GenAIDetect)*, Abu Dhabi, UAE. International Conference on Computational Linguistics.

Irene Solaiman, Miles Brundage, Jack Clark, Amanda Askell, Ariel Herbert-Voss, Jeff Wu, Alec Radford, Gretchen Krueger, Jong Wook Kim, Sarah Kreps, et al. 2019. Release strategies and the social impacts of language models. *arXiv preprint arXiv:1908.09203*.

Jinyan Su, Terry Zhuo, Di Wang, and Preslav Nakov. 2023. Detectllm: Leveraging log rank information for zero-shot detection of machine-generated text. In *Findings of the Association for Computational Linguistics: EMNLP 2023*, pages 12395–12412.

Zhen Tao, Zhiyu Li, Dinghao Xi, and Wei Xu. 2024. CUDRT: benchmarking the detection of human vs. large language models generated texts. *CoRR*, abs/2406.09056.

Gemma Team, Morgane Riviere, Shreya Pathak, Pier Giuseppe Sessa, Cassidy Hardin, Surya Bhupatiraju, Léonard Hussenot, Thomas Mesnard, Bobak Shahriari, Alexandre Ramé, et al. 2024. Gemma 2: Improving Open Language Models at a Practical Size. *arXiv preprint arXiv:2408.00118*.

Liviu P. Dinu Teodor-George Marchitan, Claudiu Creanga. 2025. Team unibuc - nlp at coling-2025 task 1: Qwen it detect machine-generated text. In *Proceedings of the 1st Workshop on GenAI Content Detection (GenAIDetect)*, Abu Dhabi, UAE. International Conference on Computational Linguistics.

Yuchuan Tian, Hanting Chen, Xutao Wang, Zheyuan Bai, Qinghua Zhang, Ruifeng Li, Chao Xu, and Yunhe Wang. 2023. Multiscale positive-unlabeled detection of ai-generated texts. *arXiv preprint arXiv:2305.18149*.

Hanh Thi Hong Tran and Nam Tien Nguyen. 2025. L3i++ at genai detection task 1: Can label-supervised llama detect machine-generated text? In *Proceedings of the 1st Workshop on GenAI Content Detection (GenAIDetect)*, Abu Dhabi, UAE. International Conference on Computational Linguistics.

Eduard Tulchinskii, Kristian Kuznetsov, Laida Kushnareva, Daniil Cherniavskii, Sergey Nikolenko, Evgeny Burnaev, Serguei Barannikov, and Irina Piontkovskaya. 2024. Intrinsic dimension estimation for robust detection of ai-generated texts. *Advances in Neural Information Processing Systems*, 36.

Christoforos Vasilatos, Manaar Alam, Talal Rahwan, Yasir Zaki, and Michail Maniatakos. 2023. Howkgpt: Investigating the detection of chatgpt-generated university student homework through context-aware perplexity analysis. *arXiv preprint arXiv:2305.18226*.

Vivek Verma, Eve Fleisig, Nicholas Tomlin, and Dan Klein. 2023. Ghostbuster: Detecting text ghostwritten by large language models. *arXiv preprint arXiv:2305.15047*.

Yuxia Wang, Jonibek Mansurov, Petar Ivanov, Jinyan Su, Artem Shelmanov, Akim Tsvigun, Osama Mohanned Afzal, Tarek Mahmoud, Giovanni Puccetti, Thomas Arnold, Alham Fikri Aji, Nizar Habash, Iryna Gurevych, and Preslav Nakov. 2024a. M4gt-bench: Evaluation benchmark for black-box machine-generated text detection. *CoRR*, abs/2402.11175.

Yuxia Wang, Jonibek Mansurov, Petar Ivanov, Jinyan Su, Artem Shelmanov, Akim Tsvigun, Osama Mohammed Afzal, Tarek Mahmoud, Giovanni Puccetti, and Thomas Arnold. 2024b. SemEval-2024 task 8: Multidomain, multimodel and multilingual machine-generated text detection. In *Proceedings of the 18th International Workshop on Semantic Evaluation (SemEval-2024)*, pages 2057–2079, Mexico City, Mexico. Association for Computational Linguistics.

Yuxia Wang, Jonibek Mansurov, Petar Ivanov, Jinyan Su, Artem Shelmanov, Akim Tsvigun, Osama Mohammed Afzal, Tarek Mahmoud, Giovanni Puccetti, Thomas Arnold, Alham Aji, Nizar Habash, Iryna Gurevych, and Preslav Nakov. 2024c. M4GT-bench: Evaluation benchmark for black-box machine-generated text detection. In *Proceedings of the 62nd Annual Meeting of the Association for Computational Linguistics (Volume 1: Long Papers)*, pages 3964–3992, Bangkok, Thailand. Association for Computational Linguistics.

Yuxia Wang, Jonibek Mansurov, Petar Ivanov, Jinyan Su, Artem Shelmanov, Akim Tsvigun, Chenxi Whitehouse, Osama Mohammed Afzal, Tarek Mahmoud, Toru Sasaki, Thomas Arnold, Alham Aji, Nizar Habash, Iryna Gurevych, and Preslav Nakov. 2024d. M4: Multi-generator, multi-domain, and multilingual black-box machine-generated text detection. In *Proceedings of the 18th Conference of the European Chapter of the Association for Computational Linguistics (Volume 1: Long Papers)*, pages 1369–1407, St. Julian's, Malta. Association for Computational Linguistics.

An Yang, Baosong Yang, Binyuan Hui, Bo Zheng, Bowen Yu, Chang Zhou, Chengpeng Li, Chengyuan Li, Dayiheng Liu, Fei Huang, et al. 2024. Qwen2 technical report. *arXiv preprint arXiv:2407.10671*.

Xianjun Yang, Wei Cheng, Yue Wu, Linda Petzold, William Yang Wang, and Haifeng Chen. 2023. Dna-gpt: Divergent n-gram analysis for training-free detection of gpt-generated text. *arXiv preprint arXiv:2305.17359*.

Xiao Yu, Yuang Qi, Kejiang Chen, Guoqiang Chen, Xi Yang, Pengyuan Zhu, Weiming Zhang, and Nenghai Yu. 2023. Gpt paternity test: Gpt generated text detection with gpt genetic inheritance. *CoRR*.

Haolan Zhan, Xuanli He, Qiongkai Xu, Yuxiang Wu, and Pontus Stenetorp. 2023. G3detector: General gpt-generated text detector. *arXiv preprint arXiv:2305.12680*.

Qihui Zhang, Chujie Gao, Dongping Chen, Yue Huang, Yixin Huang, Zhenyang Sun, Shilin Zhang, Weiye Li, Zhengyan Fu, Yao Wan, and Lichao Sun. 2024. LLM-as-a-coauthor: Can mixed human-written and machine-generated text be detected? In *Findings of the Association for Computational Linguistics: NAACL 2024*, pages 409–436, Mexico City, Mexico. Association for Computational Linguistics.

Zhaowen Zhang, Songhao Chen, and Bingquan Liu. 2025. Dcbu at genai detection task 1: Enhancing machine-generated text detection with semantic and probabilistic features. In *Proceedings of the 1st Workshop on GenAI Content Detection (GenAIDetect)*, Abu Dhabi, UAE. International Conference on Computational Linguistics.

Biru Zhu, Lifan Yuan, Ganqu Cui, Yangyi Chen, Chong Fu, Bingxiang He, Yangdong Deng, Zhiyuan Liu, Maosong Sun, and Ming Gu. 2023. Beat llms at their own game: Zero-shot llm-generated text detection via querying chatgpt. In *Proceedings of the 2023 Conference on Empirical Methods in Natural Language Processing*, pages 7470–7483.

Appendix

A Dataset Distributions

A.1 Training and Development Sets

Tables 12 and 13 respectively demonstrate the statistical information of training and development sets across different sources of English and multilingual subtasls, and Table 14 shows the distribution over generators for datasets of HC3, M4GT-Bench and MAGE — the three component datasets of training and development sets for both English and multilingual subtasks.

Source	Sub-source	Training Set			Development Set		
		Human	Machine	Total	Human	Machine	Total
HC3	finance	2579	3189	5768	1113	1301	2414
	medicine	886	883	1769	352	380	732
	open_g	823	2339	3162	364	1015	1379
	reddit_tl5	34329	11680	46009	14781	4959	19740
	wiki_sai	523	580	1103	245	262	507
M4GT-Bench	arxiv	22484	30684	53168	9487	13003	22490
	outfox	2162	40973	43135	995	17390	18385
	peerread	3300	16169	19469	1398	6749	8147
	reddit	20353	32609	52962	8663	14076	22739
	wikihow	19454	35305	54759	8532	15168	23700
	wikipedia	19029	25341	44370	8145	10881	19026
MAGE	cmv	6020	16592	22612	2618	7026	9644
	cnn	265	0	265	131	0	131
	dialogsum	210	0	210	98	0	98
	eli5	15347	21849	37196	6451	9340	15791
	hswag	6806	19169	25975	2903	8085	10988
	imdb	269	0	269	107	0	107
	pubmed	273	0	273	105	0	105
	roct	6916	20008	26924	2930	8439	11369
	sci_en	6613	14390	21003	2891	6145	9036
	squad	14519	14875	29394	6333	6330	12663
	tldr	5558	15808	21366	2329	6930	9259
	wp	7919	21215	29134	3393	9390	12783
	xsum	6992	22129	29121	2925	9621	12546
	yelp	25293	16058	41351	11039	6940	17979
Grand Total		228922	381845	610767	98328	163430	261758

Table 12: **Monolingual subtask**: statistical information of training and development sets across different sources.

Source	Sub-source	Lang	Training Set			Development Set		
			Human	Machine	Total	Human	Machine	Total
HC3	baike	zh	2996	3211	6207	1247	1378	2625
	finance	en	2638	3135	5773	1054	1355	2409
		zh	1103	1393	2496	438	560	998
	law	zh	494	353	847	196	145	341
	medicine	en	874	901	1775	364	362	726
		zh	741	739	1480	317	327	644
	nlpcc_dbqa	zh	1155	2718	3873	543	1094	1637
	open_qa	en	840	2394	3234	347	960	1307
		zh	5212	2683	7895	2148	1117	3265
	psychology	zh	3546	773	4319	1505	309	1814
	reddit_eli5	en	34510	11776	46286	14600	4863	19463
	wiki_csai	en	546	594	1140	222	248	470
M4GT-Bench	Baike/Web QA	zh	4068	4099	8167	1629	1819	3448
	CHANGE-it NEWS	it	0	4174	4174	0	1843	1843
	News/Wikipedia	ar	344	1770	2114	150	756	906
		de	231	4462	4693	102	1957	2059
	RuATD	ru	684	630	1314	316	284	600
	True & Fake News	bg	4205	3886	8091	1795	1694	3489
	Urdu-news	ur	2085	1676	3761	853	720	1573
	arxiv	en	22508	30649	53157	9463	13038	22501
	id_newspaper_2018	id	1895	2081	3976	886	917	1803
	outfox	en	2196	40878	43074	961	17485	18446
	peerread	en	3291	16174	19465	1407	6744	8151
	reddit	en	20385	32535	52920	8631	14150	22781
	wikihow	en	19492	35187	54679	8494	15286	23780
	wikipedia	en	18975	25324	44299	8199	10898	19097
MAGE	cmv	en	6009	16476	22485	2629	7142	9771
	cnn	en	275	0	275	121	0	121
	dialogsum	en	197	0	197	111	0	111
	eli5	en	15214	21714	36928	6584	9475	16059
	hswag	en	6780	19163	25943	2929	8091	11020
	imdb	en	260	0	260	116	0	116
	pubmed	en	262	0	262	116	0	116
	roct	en	6820	19875	26695	3026	8572	11598
	sci-gen	en	6682	14308	20990	2822	6227	9049
	squad	en	14495	14914	29409	6357	6291	12648
	tldr	en	5526	15858	21384	2361	6880	9241
	wp	en	7941	21406	29347	3371	9199	12570
	xsum	en	6991	22202	29193	2926	9548	12474
	yelp	en	25502	16004	41506	10830	6994	17824
Grand Total			257968	416115	674083	110166	178728	288894

Table 13: **Multilingual subtask**: statistical information of training and development sets across different sources and languages.

Source	Model	Training Set		Development Set	
		Human	Machine	Human	Machine
HC3	gpt-35	0	18671	0	7917
	human	39140	0	16855	0
	bloomz	0	21061	0	8991
	cohere	0	20808	0	8896
	davinci	0	19345	0	8210
	dolly	0	8932	0	3931
	dolly-v2-12b	0	1938	0	831
	gemma-7b-it	0	12162	0	5240
	gemma2-9b-it	0	8366	0	3629
M4GT-Bench	gpt-3.5-turbo	0	25856	0	11005
	gpt4	0	9956	0	4300
	gpt4o	0	10374	0	4247
	human	86782	0	37220	0
	llama3-70b	0	12333	0	5181
	llama3-8b	0	12057	0	5290
	mixtral-8x7b	0	15865	0	6623
	text-davinci-003	0	2028	0	893
MAGE	13B	0	5385	0	2367
	30B	0	5769	0	2380
	65B	0	5815	0	2404
	7B	0	5083	0	2166
	GLM130B	0	4398	0	1842
	bloom_{7b}	0	5151	0	2201
	$\text{flan}_{5,\text{base}}$	0	6566	0	2887
	$\text{flan}_{5,\text{large}}$	0	6500	0	2893
	$\text{flan}_{5,\text{small}}$	0	6570	0	2811
	$\text{flan}_{5,\text{xl}}$	0	6429	0	2739
	$\text{flan}_{5,\text{xxl}}$	0	6532	0	2777
	gpt-3.5-turbo	0	15991	0	6682
	gpt_j	0	3468	0	1480
	gpt_{neox}	0	4734	0	2021
	human	103000	0	44253	0
	$\text{opt}_{1.3b}$	0	5553	0	2351
	opt_{125m}	0	5735	0	2469
	opt_{3b}	0	4988	0	2296
	$\text{opt}_{2.7b}$	0	5736	0	2586
	opt_{30b}	0	5637	0	2376
	opt_{350m}	0	5128	0	2252
	$\text{opt}_{6.7b}$	0	5642	0	2378
	$\text{opt}_{\text{iml}30b}$	0	6008	0	2619
	$\text{opt}_{\text{iml,max}1.3b}$	0	6176	0	2660
	t0_{1b}	0	6309	0	2620
	t0_{3b}	0	6602	0	2849
	text-davinci-002	0	14884	0	6359
	text-davinci-003	0	15304	0	6781
Grand Total		228922	381845	98328	163430

Table 14: Generator distribution over three component of training and development sets.

A.2 Test Sets

Table 15 shows the statistical distribution of English test sets in different domains and generators. Tables 16 and 16 present the distribution of the multilingual test set over different languages, domains and generators (see details).

Source / Domain	License	# Human	# MGT	LLM Generator List
CUDRT-en subset	CC BY-SA 4.0	12939	10800	GPT-3.5-turbo, Llama2, Llama3, ChatGLM, Baichuan, Qwen (1800 samples each)
Mixset	CC BY-SA 4.0	600	3000	-
LLM-DetectAIve-IELTS	huggingface	1635	900	llama-3.1-70B-versatile (900 samples)
IELTSDuck	Apache-2.0	10932	12418	GPT-4o-mini-2024-07-18, (10932), llama-3.1-70B-versatile (1486)
NLPeer	Apache-2.0	5376	5376	GPT-4o-2024-05-13 (5376)
Peersum	Github	5157	6997	GPT-4o-2024-08-06 (3501), GPT-4o-mini-2024-07-18 (3496)
Total	-	36639	39491	-
After deduplication	-	35393	39363	-
After removing short text	-	34675	39266	-

Table 15: Statistics of the English test set

Source / Domain	Language	# Human	# MGT	LLM Generator List
Cudrt-Subset	Chinese	12565	1500	GPT-3.5 (300), Qwen (300), GPT-4 (300), ChatGLM (300), Baichuan (300)
High School Student Essay	Chinese	3502	1556	GLM-4-9b-chat (778), Claude-3.5-sonnet (778)
Zhihu-Qa	Chinese	12524	10269	GPT-4o-2024-08-06 (3423), GPT-4o-mini-2024-07-18 (6846)
Mnbvc-Qa-Zhihu	Chinese	3000	3000	GPT-4o-2024-05-13 (3000)
Govreport	Chinese	2975	17695	GPT-4o-2024-05-13 (5932), ChatGLM3-6B (5821)
Easc (Summary)	Arabic	153	306	GPT-4o-2024-08-06 (306)
Tweets	Arabic	1400	3400	GPT-4 (1700), GPT-4o-2024-08-06 (1400), Qwen-2.5 72B (300)
Kalimat Youm 7 News	Arabic	1000	2000	GPT-4o-2024-05-13 (1000), Ace-GPT (1000)
Sanad (News)	Arabic	3000	3000	GPT-4o-2024-05-13 (3000)
Summaries	Russian	6562	6582	GPT-4o-2024-08-06 (3300), Vikhrmodels/Vikhr-Nemo-12B-Instruct-R-21-09-24 (3282)
News	Russian	6494	6539	GPT-4o-2024-08-06 (3295), Vikhrmodels/Vikhr-Nemo-12B-Instruct-R-21-09-24 (3244)
Wikipedia	Russian	1025	3049	GPT-4-0613 (999), Vikhrmodels/it-5.4-fp16-orpo-v2 (1025), AnatoliiPotapov/T-lite-instruct-0.1 (1025)

Table 16: Statistics of the multilingual test sets, part 1

Source / Domain	Language	# Human	# MGT	LLM Generator List
Wikipedia	Hebrew	1182	2173	GPT-4-0613 (991), dicta-il/dictalm2.0-instruct (1182)
Wikipedia	German	1865	2529	GPT-4-0613 (957), LeoLM/leo-hessianai-13b-chat (1572)
Wikipedia	Norwegian	1544	2543	GPT-4-0613 (999), norallm/normistral-7b-warm-instruct (1544)
Wikipedia	Spanish	600	600	Llama 3.1 405B instruct (600)
Wikipedia	Dutch	600	600	Llama 3.1 405B instruct (600)
Wikipedia	kaz	1300	1300	GPT-4o-2024-08-06 (1300)
Dice (News)	Italian	2800	2800	Llama 3.1 405B instruct (2800)
News	Urdu	13497	17472	GPT-4o-2024-08-06 (17472)
News	Hindi	600	600	GPT-4o-2024-08-06 (600)
News	Japanese	300	300	GPT-4o-2024-08-06 (300)
News	Vietnamese	600	600	GPT-4o-2024-08-06 (600)
Wikipedia	Vietnamese	600	600	GPT-4o-2024-08-06 (600)
Poetry	Indonesian	600	600	GPT-4o-2024-08-06 (600)
Total	-	80288	91613	-
Non-duplicated	-	78424	79305	-
Remove Short Text	-	73634	77791	-

Table 17: Statistics of the multilingual test sets, part 2

CIC-NLP at GenAI Detection Task 1: Advancing Multilingual Machine-Generated Text Detection

Abiola T. O[1], Tewodros A. B[1], Fatima Uroosa[1], Nida Hafeez[1], Ojo O. E.[1], Sidorov G.[1], Kolesnikova O.[1]

[1]Instituto Politécnico Nacional, Centro de Investigación en Computación, CDMX, Mexico.

kolesnikova@cic.ipn.mx

Abstract

Machine-written texts are gradually becoming indistinguishable from human-generated texts, leading to the need to use sophisticated methods to detect them. Team CIC-NLP presents work in the Gen-AI Content Detection Task 1 at COLING 2025 Workshop: the focus of our work is on Subtask B of Task 1, which is the classification of text written by machines and human authors, with particular attention paid to identifying multilingual binary classification problem. Usng mBERT, we addressed the binary classification task using the dataset provided by the GenAI Detection Task team. mBERT acchieved a macro-average F1-score of 0.72 as well as an accuracy score of 0.73.

1 Introduction

Several researchers have worked on various binary classification tasks using ML models and LLMs in NLP, focusing on different areas such as hate speech detection (Zamir et al., 2024a; Ahani et al., 2024; Tonja et al., 2022; Ojo et al., 2022), sentiment analysis (Zhang et al., 2023; Hadi et al., 2024), fake news detection (Zamir et al., 2024b; Kanta and Sidorov, 2023), and hope speech identification (Tash et al., 2024a). These efforts aim to discern the nuanced aspects of human communication. Some of these classification tasks have been conducted on non-English and multilingual texts (Kanta and Sidorov, 2023; Ojo et al., 2023; Kolesnikova et al., 2024).

With the advancements in Large Language Models (LLMs), machine-generated content across various platforms, including news outlets, social media, educational, and academic publications (He et al., 2023) has reached an outstanding quality. Recent models like ChatGPT, GPT-4 (OpenAI, 2023), LLaMA 2 (Touvron et al., 2023), and Jais (Sengupta et al., 2023) generated remarkable coherence in responding to diverse user queries. This rapid advancement has raised concerns about the potential misuse of machine-generated text in different fields such as journalism, education, and academia (Uchendu et al., 2023; Crothers et al., 2023b), in addition to the influence on operations (Goldstein et al., 2023), disinformation (Buchanan et al., 2021), spam, or unethical authorship (Crothers et al., 2023a). Moreover, it poses challenges to maintain information integrity and ensure the accuracy of shared information. Consequently, the ability to effectively distinguish between human-generated and machine-generated content has become crucial for detecting possible instances of misuse (Jawahar et al., 2020; Stiff and Johansson, 2022; Macko et al., 2023). While significant progress has been made in detecting machine-generated text in English, we still need to improve it in multilingual settings.

In response to this gap, COLING Workshop organizers launched Gen-AI Content Detection Task 1: This shared Gen-AI Content Detection Task 1 introduces a new Binary Multilingual MGT Detection challenge to accelerate research in this area and improve cross-lingual detection capabilities (Wang et al., 2025) (Chowdhury et al., 2025) (Dugan et al., 2025). Being a shared task, it brings together researchers and practitioners interested in detecting machine-generated content reliably in many languages, reflecting the collaborative spirit and multidisciplinary innovation of shared tasks. At the broader level, the Gen-AI Content Detection Task 1 also highlights the importance of machine-generated text (MGT) detection. Also, it addresses the problem of keeping content authentic, fighting misinformation, and driving ethical use cases of AI in the multilingual realm. As CIC-NLP team, we used mBERT to detect and classify MGT as distinguished from human-generated text (HWT), the method used and results obtained are extensively highlighted in other sections of this report.

Proceedings of the 1st Workshop on GenAI Content Detection (GenAIDetect), pages 262–270

2 Literature Review

Over the last few years there has been a great focus in the use of language models which in turn has created the need for keen classification of authentic and fake texts; this was historically stated mostly as a binary problem. The GenAI Detection Task 1 includes distinguishing between text written by a human and text written by a computer. There are two key approaches that have been broadly applied to text classification : classification with supervised methods (Kolesnikova and Gelbukh, 2019; Gelbukh and Kolesnikova, 2010; Kolesnikova and Gelbukh, 2010; Adebanji et al., 2022; Ojo et al., 2020; Gutiérrez-Hinojosa et al., 2023) and unsupervised (zero-shot) methods (Ojo et al., 2024a,b; Calvo and Gelbukh, 2004). Supervised methods normally do better in terms of accuracy but are more likely to overfit, particularly when new language structures are used (Su et al., 2023). On the other hand, unsupervised methods offer flexibility due to the absence of label information, however, they might call for impractical white-box access to the generating model.

Huge advancements in LLMs are currently driven by various platforms such as ChatGPT powered by GPT-3.5, GPT-4 (OpenAI, 2023), OPT (Zhang et al., 2022), LLaMA (Touvron et al., 2023), PaLM (Chowdhery et al., 2023), LaMDA (y Arcas, 2022), and BLOOM, and emergent models like Vicuna (Zheng et al., 2023) and Alpaca (Taori et al., 2023). These models containing millions to billions of parameters are trained on huge amounts of data, have shown extraordinary results across multiple fields including finance, customer support, and the educational sector. Some of their most impressive features include their ability to write text that references human-generated text so closely that most people will initially find it hard to distinguish between the two. Also, it is possible to note that their multilingual skills enable them to generate clear and high-quality text in more than fifty languages (Workshop et al., 2022), thus making them more and more appropriate in the global business environment, but at the same time posing even higher problems to MGT detection.

To the best of our knowledge, several benchmarks have been proposed to assess multilingual MGT detection models in different languages (Wang et al., 2024). For example, the Human ChatGPT Comparison Corpus (HC3) (Guo et al., 2023) compares ChatGPT-generated text and human-written text, with authentications of English and Chinese languages using logistic regression models and RoBERTa-based classifiers built from features of Giant Language Model Test Room (GLTR). Others have replicated such approaches by testing other detectors including RoBERTa, XLM-R (Conneau, 2019), logistic regression based on features from NELA and other stylometric classifiers (Li et al., 2014; Horne et al., 2019). MULTITuDE has also been introduced by researchers within the news domain for 11 languages that offers a strong test bed for multilingual detection baselines (Macko et al., 2023). To detect MGT, researchers released benchmark environment (Uchendu et al., 2021) (Jawahar et al., 2020) to compare machine-generated text detection across multiple languages using monolingual and multilingual BERT models, which is consistent. As a result of comparison, it was found that multilingual-specific models tend to perform better than others. (Ruder et al., 2021) discussed challenges in multilingual NLP tasks and strategies for model adaptation across languages. While their work on sentiment analysis is almost exclusively concerned with model adaptation, their observations about the problem of improving machine-generated sentences are relevant for our work. Also, according to current literature, transformer models, such as LoRA-RoBERTa and XLM-RoBERTa, are found to be more accurate compared to classical machine learning techniques in multilingual MGT detection tasks, see for example (Xiong et al., 2024).

To summarize, researchers have been able to refine their methods of distinguishing human writing from computer scripts by integrating statistical analysis with other language models. The further development of these approaches proves that there are still challenges to differentiating between the advanced results produced by LLMs and works created by humans. Prior work has mainly considered the classification of synthetic text in few languages, certain LLMs, or certain domains like news (Zellers et al., 2019). Our work extends this scope to multiple languages and include a range of diverse and popular LLMs across different domains. To sum up, the previous methods and works provided useful information regarding the efficiency of various approaches to identifying AI vs. human written text, but more works required.

3 Methodology

We deployed multiple NLP techniques for data preprocessing, detection, and sorting to assess the performance of our approach to the Binary Multilingual Machine-Generated Text Detection task in the context of transformer-based models. Next, we loaded and preprocessed a broad multilingual dataset to normalize input formats and then applied language detection to guarantee certain types of processing on specific languages. We tokenized text into language-appropriate segments, translated text between language pairs, and sorted operations adjusted to that language's unique characteristics in this Gen-AI Content Detection Task 1. Using the mBert language model, which we pretrained and fine-tuned on the provided training datasets, we enhanced the model output by carefully approaching various linguistic constructs. Focusing on efficient management of code-mixed and pure multilingual data, our methodology determined the tokenization method by polyglot such that each input is associated with a particular language.

3.1 Dataset Analysis

The dataset provided for the Binary Multilingual Machine-Generated Text Detection task includes text data across nine diverse languages. This linguistic diversity adds complexity to Gen-AI Content Detection Task 1 (binary multilingual classification problem), requiring models that can handle varying scripts, grammatical structures, and cultural nuances in text patterns. The diversity of the training dataset used in this Gen-AI Content Detection Task 1 is further highlighted in (Wang et al., 2025) (Chowdhury et al., 2025) (Dugan et al., 2025) .

3.1.1 Language Distribution

The dataset is balanced concerning languages so that models trained on it can generalize to multilingual text. Each language presents unique challenges: Arabic and Urdu are right-to-left languages, their grammar is more than complex in script; German and Russian have more intricate grammar and syntactical structure.

3.1.2 Content Sources

The dataset contains text samples that are extracted from online sources such as social media posts, articles from web pages, and other digital content. This variety corresponds to the broad range of text that models may encounter in actual deployment, from informal posts to more structured forms of article-style content.

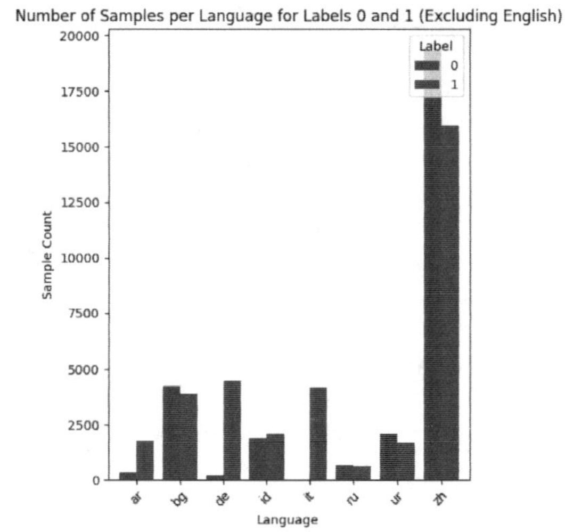

Figure 1: Languages in the training dataset (English excluded)

3.1.3 Class Labels

The dataset is labeled with each entry as human-generated (1) or machine-generated (0). Due to these binary labels, this is a simple classification task for models to learn to distinguish fine-grained features associated with machine generation (such as repetitive phrasing and lower variation in tone).

3.1.4 Tokenization and Script Variability

The dataset is multilingual; we adopted a polyglot multilingual tokenizer to segment the texts. This tokenizer was found reliable even with Chinese texts that have no spacing and also with some Cyrillic systems. Arabic and Urdu are abjad-based scripts, meaning they provide mostly consonants and have fewer vowels, and all these disparities in the multilingual text data were accounted for to enhance the model in classification.

3.1.5 Potential Language-Specific Features

Machine-generated text may have different features that show the distinct characteristics of each language. For example, Arabic and Urdu have complex morphology, which can show up in stylistic differences in machine-generated text compared to English and German, so detecting human vs. machine-generated text for these languages would be subtler.

3.1.6 Text Length and Complexity

The text lengths and simplicity levels of the dataset are probably very different from those of the online sources. Short, informal texts (e.g., social media snippets) and longer, structured articles offer diverse linguistic challenges. The variety supports the ability to train models that can process variations of text lengths and learn the stylistic characteristics inherent to machine generation for each language.

3.1.7 Class Imbalance

One of the main factors of the dataset's design is the balance among languages and classes. When evaluating the model, a macro-average F1-score will handle minor imbalances and ensure the model's robust performance in all languages involved.

The dataset has a multilingual, balanced structure to capture languages and to train a model for working well with many linguistic backgrounds. Our analysis of languages and classes in this section serves as a basis for understanding the diversity within the dataset and for building preprocessing pipelines and model architectures suited for varied language patterns and scripts.

3.2 Shared Task Description

The Binary Multilingual Machine-Generated Text Detection Task, part of Gen-AI Content Detection Task 1, gave the participants a rich multilingual dataset for distinguishing human- and machine-generated text. The dataset contains content from various languages across domains, including social media, news articles, and educational materials. We had machine-generated or human-authored labels for each text entry; we carefully labeled them in the binary classification tasks.

Finally, we participated in developing models to reliably detect machine-generated text across different languages, evidence of the need for cross-lingual detection abilities. The macro-average F1-score was evaluated as a metric based on precision and recall while covering multiple languages and text types. The purpose of the shared Gen-AI Content Detection Task 1 was to develop multilingual capabilities for machine-generated text detection with the growing demand for authenticity in multilingual digital content and for innovations in reliably detecting AI-generated content within different linguistic contexts.

3.3 Model Architecture

Our model architecture is built on fine-tuning mBERT for multilingual GenAI Detection Task 1, with a focus on the binary classification of MGT and HWT with the challenge of making it robust to efficiently classify different languages. For this purpose we chose the mBERT-cased version, a choice for dealing with more than one language, including less-resourced ones. This architecture integrates three primary modules: language detection and tokenization with polyglot, and training and prediction with mBERT which we optimized to capture different languages in the datasets and unseen ones that surfaced in the test dataset.

We trained the model with a few meticulously chosen hyperparameters for optimizing the training process with the ADAM optimizer and adjusting the learning rate to best suite the classification. The metrics we used are exclusively listed in the appendix section of this paper. The categorical cross-entropy was used as a loss function, and the batch size was well adjusted to maximize the computing resources available as well as prevent overfitting. We also adopted early stopping to prevent overfitting using validation performance-enabled training across the three epochs. Three epochs were used as a time factor and computational resources at our disposal were considered. The model was engineered to be computationally fast and memory efficient overall. Its design makes it scalable to the large datasets provided and maintains high performance.

3.4 Experimental Setup

Our experiments employed a training validation split on the multilingual set, configured language-specific preprocessing rules, and set up the model in a high-performance computing environment. The translation and detection models were initialized and then fine-tuned using the training dataset to capture multilingual patterns using weights from pre-trained models. We built a complete evaluation pipeline to monitor model performance in each language and used accuracy and F1-score as critical metrics. Unseen test data were used for model evaluation and generalization. Additionally, the model was evaluated in language-agnostic embeddings, using multiple languages and contexts to show robustness. The model hyper-parameters have also been experimentally optimized to trade precision with increased computational efficiency.

Epoch	Training Loss	Validation Loss	F1-score
1	0.200	0.241	0.916
2	0.093	0.286	0.925
3	0.046	0.155	0.953

Table 1: Metrics generated by the model during training

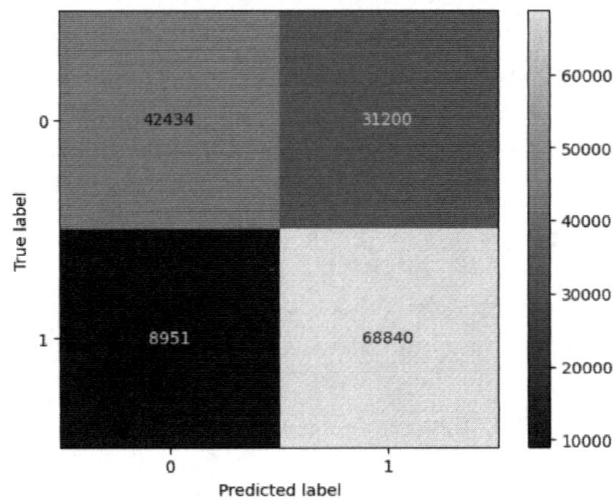

Figure 2: Confusion matrix

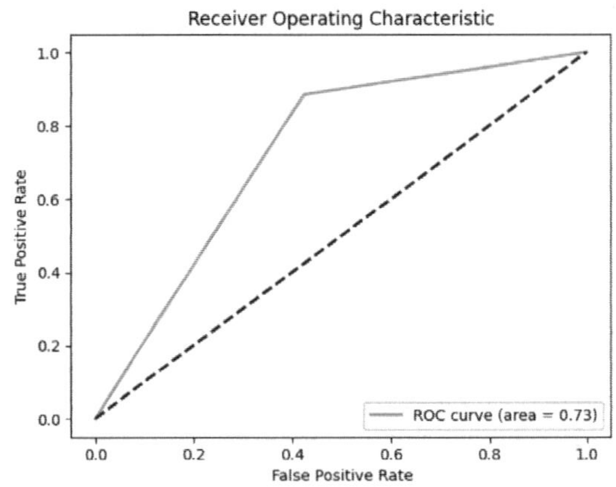

Figure 3: ROC curve

Model	Micro_F1	Macro_F1
mBERT	0.734	0.726

Table 2: Result obtained from the test set

3.5 Predictions on Unseen Data

We evaluated the model's generalizability on unseen data with text entries in multiple languages. The model generated predictions to see how it translated, sorted and identified machine-generated text. The model's output for translation with linguistic accuracy, language-specific sorting correctness, and detection precision were analyzed. We showed that the multilingual model preserves language nuances, sorts accurately, and identifies machine-generated text reliably on a diverse set of language pairs. We found that language performance differed slightly in low-resource languages, but the model met the multilingual detection benchmarks of the shared Gen-AI Content Detection Task 1.

4 Results

On the test set, the model predicted the classes with an accuracy of 0.7348 and a macro-average F1-score of 0.7265, which indicates balanced test performance across the languages. Our results also demonstrate that the model is capable of handling multiple languages without much performance degradation. We present figure 2 showing the confusion matrix for better analysis of the model predictions as it revealed the model strength towards accurately predicting MGT with accuracy of 0.88 and the model got weak results by confusing some HWT for MGT with accuracy of 0.58.

5 Conclusion

This paper shows how a multilingual transformer-based model detects machine-generated text in various languages. Our results confirm the model's adaptability and scalability and evidence to its promising performance in high-resource languages and its potential for improvement in low-resource scenarios. We show that with appropriate data preprocessing, machine-generated text detection can be successfully extended to multilingual applications using fine-tuning and balanced datasets. This work will be continued to improve the performance for low-resource languages and deploy the model to handle more complex linguistic features such as code-switching and mixed scripts.

Ethics Statement

This paper is fully committed to transparency and ethical AI utilization, especially in multilingual digital content authentication. Ethical responsibility must be first prioritized for machine-generated text detection, as wrong classifications may impact individuals and organizations. However, we take the responsible use of our model seriously and want feedback on minimizing any negative impacts. A primary goal is to add value to online digital content verification, combatting misinformation while paying due respect to the plurality of the linguistic scopes in online media.

Acknowledgments

The work was done with partial support from the Mexican Government through the grant A1-S-47854 of CONACYT, Mexico, grants 20241816, 20241819, and 20240951 of the Secretaría de Investigación y Posgrado of the Instituto Politécnico Nacional, Mexico. The authors thank the CONACYT for the computing resources brought to them through the Plataforma de Aprendizaje Profundo para Tecnologías del Lenguaje of the Laboratorio de Supercómputo of the INAOE, Mexico and acknowledge the support of Microsoft through the Microsoft Latin America PhD Award.

References

O.O. Adebanji, I. Gelbukh, H. Calvo, and O.E. Ojo. 2022. Sequential models for sentiment analysis: A comparative study. In O. Pichardo Lagunas, J. Martínez-Miranda, and B. Martínez Seis, editors, *Advances in Computational Intelligence. MICAI 2022. Lecture Notes in Computer Science*, volume 13613, pages 220–231. Springer, Cham.

Z. Ahani, M. Tash, M. Zamir, and I. Gelbukh. 2024. Zavira@ dravidianlangtech 2024: Telugu hate speech detection using lstm. In *Proceedings of the Fourth Workshop on Speech, Vision, and Language Technologies for Dravidian Languages*, pages 107–112.

NiCole T. Buchanan, Marisol Perez, Mitchell J. Prinstein, and Idia B. Thurston. 2021. Upending racism in psychological science: Strategies to change how science is conducted, reported, reviewed, and disseminated. *American Psychologist*, 76(7):1097–1112.

Hiram Calvo and Alexander Gelbukh. 2004. Unsupervised learning of ontology-linked selectional preferences. In *Progress in Pattern Recognition, Image Analysis and Applications: 9th Iberoamerican Congress on Pattern Recognition, CIARP 2004, Puebla, Mexico, October 26-29, 2004. Proceedings 9*, pages 418–424. Springer.

Aakanksha Chowdhery, Sharan Narang, Jacob Devlin, Maarten Bosma, Gaurav Mishra, Adam Roberts, Paul Barham, Hyung Won Chung, Charles Sutton, Sebastian Gehrmann, et al. 2023. Palm: Scaling language modeling with pathways. *Journal of Machine Learning Research*, 24(240):1–113.

Shammur Absar Chowdhury, Hind Al-Merekhi, Mucahid Kutlu, Kaan Efe Keleş, Fatema Ahmad, Tasnim Mohiuddin, Georgios Mikros, and Firoj Alam. 2025. GenAI content detection task 2: AI vs. human – academic essay authenticity challenge. In *Proceedings of the 1st Workshop on GenAI Content Detection (GenAIDetect)*, Abu Dhabi, UAE. International Conference on Computational Linguistics.

A. Conneau. 2019. Unsupervised cross-lingual representation learning at scale. *arXiv preprint arXiv:1911.02116*.

E. Crothers, N. Japkowicz, and H. Viktor. 2023a. Machine-generated text: A comprehensive survey of threat models and detection methods. *arXiv preprint arXiv:2210.07321*.

Evan Crothers, Nathalie Japkowicz, and Herna L. Viktor. 2023b. Machine-generated text: A comprehensive survey of threat models and detection methods. *IEEE Access*.

Liam Dugan, Andrew Zhu, Firoj Alam, Preslav Nakov, Marianna Apidianaki, and Callison-Burch Chris. 2025. Genai content detection task 3: Cross-domain machine generated text detection challenge. In *Proceedings of the 1st Workshop on GenAI Content Detection (GenAIDetect)*, Abu Dhabi, UAE. International Conference on Computational Linguistics.

Alexander Gelbukh and Olga Kolesnikova. 2010. Supervised learning for semantic classification of spanish collocations. In J.F. Martínez-Trinidad, J.A. Carrasco-Ochoa, and J. Kittler, editors, *Advances in Pattern Recognition. MCPR 2010. Lecture Notes in Computer Science*, volume 6256, pages 311–320. Springer, Berlin, Heidelberg.

J. A. Goldstein, G. Sastry, M. Musser, R. DiResta, M. Gentzel, and K. Sedova. 2023. Generative language models and automated influence operations: Emerging threats and potential mitigations. *arXiv preprint arXiv:2301.04246*.

Biyang Guo, Xin Zhang, Ziyuan Wang, Minqi Jiang, Jinran Nie, Yuxuan Ding, Jianwei Yue, and Yupeng Wu. 2023. How close is chatgpt to human experts? comparison corpus, evaluation, and detection. *arXiv preprint arXiv:2301.07597*.

Sandra J. Gutiérrez-Hinojosa, Hiram Calvo, and Marco A. Moreno-Armendáriz. 2023. Automatic extractive summaries using supervised learning approach. *Open Review Journal*.

Muhammad Usman Hadi, Qasem Al Tashi, Abbas Shah, Rizwan Qureshi, Amgad Muneer, Muhammad Irfan, Anas Zafar, Muhammad Bilal Shaikh, Naveed Akhtar, Jia Wu, et al. 2024. Large language models: a comprehensive survey of its applications, challenges, limitations, and future prospects. *Authorea Preprints*.

Xinlei He, Xinyue Shen, Zeyuan Chen, Michael Backes, and Yang Zhang. 2023. Mgtbench: Benchmarking machine-generated text detection. *arXiv preprint arXiv:2303.14822*.

Benjamin D. Horne, Jeppe Nørregaard, and Sibel Adali. 2019. Robust fake news detection over time and attack. *ACM Transactions on Intelligent Systems and Technology (TIST)*, 11(1):1–23.

Ganesh Jawahar, Muhammad Abdul-Mageed, and Laks Lakshmanan, V.S. 2020. Automatic detection of machine generated text: A critical survey. In *Proceedings of the 28th International Conference on Computational Linguistics*, pages 2296–2309, Barcelona, Spain (Online). International Committee on Computational Linguistics.

Selam Kanta and Grigori Sidorov. 2023. Selam@ dravidianlangtech: Sentiment analysis of code-mixed dravidian texts using svm classification. In *Proceedings of the Third Workshop on Speech and Language Technologies for Dravidian Languages*, pages 176–179.

Olga Kolesnikova and Alexander Gelbukh. 2010. Supervised machine learning for predicting the meaning of verb-noun combinations in spanish. In G. Sidorov, A. Hernández Aguirre, and C.A. Reyes García, editors, *Advances in Soft Computing. MICAI 2010. Lecture Notes in Computer Science*, volume 6438, pages 260–269. Springer, Berlin, Heidelberg.

Olga Kolesnikova and Alexander Gelbukh. 2019. A study of lexical function detection with word2vec and supervised machine learning. *Special Section: Selected Papers of LKE 2019*.

Olga Kolesnikova, Mesay Gemeda Yigezu, Alexander Gelbukh, Selam Abitte, and Grigori Sidorov. 2024. Detecting multilingual hate speech targeting immigrants and women on twitter. *Journal of Intelligent and Fuzzy Systems*, 10.3233(IFS-219350).

Jenny S. Li, John V. Monaco, Li-Chiou Chen, and Charles C. Tappert. 2014. Authorship authentication using short messages from social networking sites. In *Proceedings of the 2014 IEEE 11th International Conference on e-Business Engineering*, pages 314–319. IEEE.

Dominik Macko, Robert Moro, Adaku Uchendu, Jason Samuel Lucas, Michiharu Yamashita, Matúš Pikuliak, Ivan Srba, et al. 2023. MULTITuDE: Large-scale multilingual machine-generated text detection benchmark. *arXiv preprint arXiv:2310.13606*.

O. E. Ojo, T.-H. Ta, A. Gelbukh, H. Calvo, G. Sidorov, and O. O. Adebanji. 2022. Automatic hate speech detection using deep neural networks and word embedding. *Computación y Sistemas*, 26(2):1007–1013.

O.E. Ojo, A. Gelbukh, H. Calvo, O.O. Adebanji, and G. Sidorov. 2020. Sentiment detection in economics texts. In L. Martínez-Villaseñor, O. Herrera-Alcántara, H. Ponce, and F.A. Castro-Espinoza, editors, *Advances in Computational Intelligence. MICAI 2020. Lecture Notes in Computer Science*, volume 12469, pages 318–329. Springer, Cham.

Olumide E. Ojo, Olaronke O. Adebanji, Hiram Calvo, Damian O. Dieke, Olumuyiwa E. Ojo, Seye E. Akinsanya, Tolulope O. Abiola, and Anna Feldman. 2023. Legend at araieval shared task: Persuasion technique detection using a language-agnostic text representation model. In *Proceedings of the First Arabic Natural Language Processing Conference (ArabicNLP 2023)*. Association for Computational Linguistics.

Olumide E. Ojo, Olaronke O. Adebanji, Alexander Gelbukh, Hiram Calvo, and Anna Feldman. 2024a. Medai dialog corpus (medic): Zero-shot classification of doctor and ai responses in health consultations. *Preprint*, arXiv:2310.12489.

Olumide Ebenezer Ojo, Olaronke Oluwayemisi Adebanji, Alexander Gelbukh, Hiram Calvo, and Anna Feldman. 2024b. Evaluating embeddings for one-shot classification of doctor-ai consultations. *Preprint*, arXiv:2402.04442.

R. OpenAI. 2023. Gpt-4 technical report. *arXiv preprint arXiv:2303.08774*.

Sebastian Ruder, Noah Constant, Jan Botha, Aditya Siddhant, Orhan Firat, Jinlan Fu, Pengfei Liu, Junjie Hu, Dan Garrette, Graham Neubig, and Melvin Johnson. 2021. XTREME-R: Towards more challenging and nuanced multilingual evaluation. In *Proceedings of the 2021 Conference on Empirical Methods in Natural Language Processing*, pages 10215–10245, Online and Punta Cana, Dominican Republic. Association for Computational Linguistics.

Neha Sengupta, Sunil Kumar Sahu, Bokang Jia, Satheesh Katipomu, Haonan Li, Fajri Koto, William Marshall, Gurpreet Gosal, Cynthia Liu, Zhiming Chen, Osama Mohammed Afzal, Samta Kamboj, Onkar Pandit, Rahul Pal, Lalit Pradhan, Zain Muhammad Mujahid, Massa Baali, Xudong Han, Sondos Mahmoud Bsharat, Alham Fikri Aji, Zhiqiang Shen, Zhengzhong Liu, Natalia Vassilieva, Joel Hestness, Andy Hock, Andrew Feldman, Jonathan Lee, Andrew Jackson, Hector Xuguang Ren, Preslav Nakov, Timothy Baldwin, and Eric Xing. 2023. Jais and jais-chat: Arabic-centric foundation and instruction-tuned open generative large language models. *arXiv preprint arXiv:2308.16149*.

H. Stiff and F. Johansson. 2022. Detecting computer-generated disinformation. *International Journal of Data Science and Analytics*, 13(4):363–383.

Jinyan Su, Terry Yue Zhuo, Di Wang, and Preslav Nakov. 2023. Detectllm: Leveraging log rank information for zero-shot detection of machine-generated text. *arXiv preprint arXiv:2306.05540*.

Rohan Taori, Ishaan Gulrajani, Tianyi Zhang, Yann Dubois, Xuechen Li, Carlos Guestrin, Percy Liang, and Tatsunori B. Hashimoto. 2023. Stanford alpaca: An instruction-following llama model.

M. Tash, Z. Ahani, M. Zamir, O. Kolesnikova, and G. Sidorov. 2024a. Lidoma@ lt-edi 2024: Tamil hate speech detection in migration discourse. In *Proceedings of the Fourth Workshop on Language Technology for Equality, Diversity, Inclusion*, pages 184–189.

A. L. Tonja, M. Arif, O. Kolesnikova, A. Gelbukh, and G. Sidorov. 2022. Detection of aggressive and violent incidents from social media in spanish using pre-trained language model. In *Proceedings of the Iberian Languages Evaluation Forum (IberLEF 2022), CEUR Workshop Proceedings*. CEUR-WS.org.

Hugo Touvron, Thibaut Lavril, Gautier Izacard, Xavier Martinet, Marie-Anne Lachaux, Timothée Lacroix, Baptiste Rozière, et al. 2023. Llama: Open and efficient foundation language models. *arXiv preprint arXiv:2302.13971*.

Adaku Uchendu, Thai Le, and Dongwon Lee. 2023. Attribution and obfuscation of neural text authorship: A data mining perspective. *ACM SIGKDD Explorations Newsletter*, 25(1):1–18.

Adaku Uchendu, Zeyu Ma, Thai Le, Rui Zhang, and Dongwon Lee. 2021. Turingbench: A benchmark environment for turing test in the age of neural text generation. *arXiv preprint arXiv:2109.13296*.

Yuxia Wang, Jonibek Mansurov, Petar Ivanov, Jinyan Su, Artem Shelmanov, Akim Tsvigun, Osama Mohammed Afzal, et al. 2024. SemEval-2024 Task 8: Multidomain, multimodel and multilingual machine-generated text detection. *arXiv preprint arXiv:2404.14183*.

Yuxia Wang, Artem Shelmanov, Jonibek Mansurov, Akim Tsvigun, Vladislav Mikhailov, Rui Xing, Zhuohan Xie, Jiahui Geng, Giovanni Puccetti, Ekaterina Artemova, Jinyan Su, Minh Ngoc Ta, Mervat Abassy, Kareem Elozeiri, Saad El Dine Ahmed, Maiya Goloburda, Tarek Mahmoud, Raj Vardhan Tomar, Alexander Aziz, Nurkhan Laiyk, Osama Mohammed Afzal, Ryuto Koike, Masahiro Kaneko, Alham Fikri Aji, Nizar Habash, Iryna Gurevych, and Preslav Nakov. 2025. GenAI content detection task 1: English and multilingual machine-generated text detection: AI vs. human. In *Proceedings of the 1st Workshop on GenAI Content Detection (GenAIDetect)*, Abu Dhabi, UAE. International Conference on Computational Linguistics.

BigScience Workshop, Teven Le Scao, Angela Fan, Christopher Akiki, Ellie Pavlick, Suzana Ilić, Daniel Hesslow, et al. 2022. BLOOM: A 176b-parameter open-access multilingual language model. *arXiv preprint arXiv:2211.05100*.

Feng Xiong, Thanet Markchom, Ziwei Zheng, Subin Jung, Varun Ojha, and Huizhi Liang. 2024. NCL-UoR at SemEval-2024 Task 8: Fine-tuning large language models for multigenerator, multidomain, and multilingual machine-generated text detection. In *Proceedings of the 18th International Workshop on Semantic Evaluation (SemEval-2024)*, pages 163–169.

Blaise Agüera y Arcas. 2022. Do large language models understand us? *Daedalus*, 151(2):183–197.

M. Zamir, M. Tash, Z. Ahani, A. Gelbukh, and G. Sidorov. 2024a. Lidoma@ dravidianlangtech 2024: Identifying hate speech in telugu code-mixed: A bert multilingual. In *Proceedings of the Fourth Workshop on Speech, Vision, and Language Technologies for Dravidian Languages*, pages 101–106.

M. Zamir, M. Tash, Z. Ahani, A. Gelbukh, and G. Sidorov. 2024b. Tayyab@ dravidianlangtech 2024: Detecting fake news in malayalam lstm approach and challenges. In *Proceedings of the Fourth Workshop on Speech, Vision, and Language Technologies for Dravidian Languages*, pages 113–118.

Rowan Zellers, Ari Holtzman, Hannah Rashkin, Yonatan Bisk, Ali Farhadi, Franziska Roesner, and Yejin Choi. 2019. Defending against neural fake news. *Advances in Neural Information Processing Systems*, 32.

Susan Zhang, Stephen Roller, Naman Goyal, Mikel Artetxe, Moya Chen, Shuohui Chen, Christopher Dewan, et al. 2022. OPT: Open pre-trained transformer language models. *arXiv preprint arXiv:2205.01068*.

Wenxuan Zhang, Yue Deng, Bing Liu, Sinno Jialin Pan, and Lidong Bing. 2023. Sentiment analysis in the era of large language models: A reality check. *arXiv preprint arXiv:2305.15005*.

Lianmin Zheng, Wei-Lin Chiang, Ying Sheng, Tianle Li, Siyuan Zhuang, Zhanghao Wu, Yonghao Zhuang, et al. 2023. LMSYS-Chat-1M: A large-scale real-world LLM conversation dataset. *arXiv preprint arXiv:2309.11998*.

A Appendix

Training Arguments

training_args = TrainingArguments(
output_dir=output_dir,
evaluation_strategy="epoch",
save_strategy='epoch',
load_best_model_at_end=True,
learning_rate=2e-5,
per_device_train_batch_size=128,
per_device_eval_batch_size=128,
num_train_epochs=3,
weight_decay=0.01,
logging_dir='./logs',
logging_steps=10,
fp16=True, Enable mixed precision
gradient_accumulation_steps=2,
)

Tokenizer

tokenizer = AutoTokenizer.from_pretrained('bert-base-multilingual-cased')

```
def tokenize_function(examples):
encoding = tokenizer(
examples["tokens"],
padding="max_length",
truncation=True,
is_split_into_words=True,
max_length=512
)
encoding["labels"] = examples["label"]
encoding["id"] = examples["id"]
return encoding
tokenized_train ñew_ds['train'].map(tokenize_function,
batched=True, num_proc=8)
tokenized_dev ñew_ds['dev'].map(tokenize_function,
batched=True, num_proc=8)
tokenized_test t̄okenized_test.remove_columns(["tokens"])
```

CIC-NLP at GenAI Detection Task 1: Leveraging DistilBERT for Detecting Machine-Generated Text in English

Abiola T. O.[1], Ojo O. E.[1], Tewodros A. B.[1], Abiola J. O. [2], Oladepo T. O.[2], Adebanji O. O. [1], Sidorov G.[1], Kolesnikova O.[1]

[1]Instituto Politécnico Nacional, Centro de Investigación en Computación, CDMX, Mexico.
[2]Federal University Oye-Ekiti, Nigeria.
kolesnikova@cic.ipn.mx

Abstract

As machine-generated texts (MGT) become increasingly similar to human writing, these distinctions are harder to identify. In this paper, we as the CIC-NLP team present our submission to the Gen-AI Content Detection Workshop at COLING 2025 for Task 1 Subtask A, which involves distinguishing between text generated by LLMs and text authored by humans, with an emphasis on detecting English-only MGT. We applied the DistilBERT model to this binary classification task using the dataset provided by the organizers. Fine-tuning the model effectively differentiated between the classes, resulting in a micro-average F1-score of 0.70 on the evaluation test set. We provide a detailed explanation of the fine-tuning parameters and steps involved in our analysis.

1 Introduction

The rapid advancement of large language models (LLMs) has revolutionized NLP across all fields (Yigezu et al., 2023; Kolesnikova et al., 2023; Adebanji et al., 2024; García-Vázquez et al., 2023; Laureano and Calvo, 2024; Aguilar-Canto et al., 2023; Ojo et al., 2024). Machine-generated text (MGT) refers to text produced using AI algorithms with little or no human intervention. On the other hand, human-written text (HWT) relies on natural language and contextual understanding in its approach to construction. AI models are able to generate new content by being trained on large text datasets. However, it can be challenging for AI models to replicate the attributes of HWT accurately. In this work, we leverage the intricacies between MGT and HWT to develop a model that can successfully distinguish between the two.

AI models can generate grammatically correct and contextually relevant text, but they often lack true cohesion between the sentences they produce (Zheng, 2024). HWT conveys personal experience, emotions, and cultural understanding in its content, while MGT can only mimic surface-level emotional cues without grasping the underlying sentiment or context, leading to misrepresentation. Detecting MGT means identifying and carefully analyzing misleading or inappropriate content (Garib and Coffelt, 2024). This detection has also become crucial for addressing ethical issues arising from using AI (Ansarullah et al., 2024). LLMs often reflect biases and limitations inherent in the data on which they were trained(Gallegos et al., 2024). MGT may lean toward certain linguistic patterns, expressions, or topics that are common in the training dataset, which can differ from the more varied and dynamic expressions found in HWT. These biases can also help distinguish between MGT and HWT.

To address some of these highlighted issues, the organizers of COLING Workshop 2025 introduced a large novel dataset (Wang et al., 2025), (Chowdhury et al., 2025), (Dugan et al., 2025). The uniqueness of this dataset is the fact that it broadly covers different text types from several human and AI sources, thus making it a valuable dataset to test several proposed models in exploring the attributes of MGT and HWT.

2 Related Work

Early efforts in detecting MGT focused on identifying telltale signs of machine output, such as lack of coherence, repetitive patterns, or unnatural phrasing (Maimone and Jolley, 2023). However, as generative models continue to improve significantly in terms of fluency, the challenge of detecting MGT has become increasingly difficult. Traditional rule-based approaches and ML classifiers have been largely insufficient to keep pace with the increasingly sophisticated text classification capabilities of deep learning (DL) models (Kierner et al., 2023). Recent approaches have thus turned to DL, particularly transformer-based models, which offer state-of-the-art performance

Proceedings of the 1st Workshop on GenAI Content Detection (GenAIDetect), pages 271–277
January 19, 2025.

in various NLP tasks (Hoang; Damián et al., 2024; Ojo et al., 2023b,a; Soto et al., 2024).

The introduction of transformer models marked a significant breakthrough in NLP. Research by various authors has shown that transformer-based models are effective in performing a range of NLP tasks (Balouchzahi et al., 2021; Ojo et al., 2023c). DistilBERT has recently been explored for various text classification tasks, including sentiment analysis (Sidorov et al., 2023; Eyob et al., 2024; Ojo et al., 2023b) and text summarization (Alshanqiti et al., 2021). Its efficiency and robustness make it a promising candidate for distinguishing between MGT and HWT. The key advantage of using DistilBERT for this task lies in its ability to effectively capture semantic and syntactic patterns in text, which are often subtle yet critical for differentiating between the two types of text.

The authors in (Li et al., 2024) explored the challenges and feasibility of detecting AI-generated text across various domains and LLMs. They highlighted the growing ability of LLMs to generate human-like text, emphasizing the need for effective detection methods to mitigate risks such as misinformation and plagiarism. They argued that previous research had been limited to specific domains or language models, while real-world detectors needed to handle diverse inputs without prior knowledge of their source. To address this gap, they created a testbed containing a variety of human-written and machine-generated texts from multiple LLMs. Their results revealed significant challenges in distinguishing between human-authored and machine-generated texts, especially with out-of-distribution data. The authors also investigated linguistic patterns that could aid in differentiation, using tools like Stanza to analyze named entities, part-of-speech tags, and other features. Their analysis showed that including texts from diverse domains and LLMs reduced the linguistic differences between human and machine-generated texts, making detection more difficult.

The approach described in (Fernández-Hernández et al., 2023) focused on the participation of the Turing-Testers team in the AuTexTification shared task at IberLEF 2023, which aimed at automated text identification. The task consisted of two subtasks: the first involved distinguishing between human-written and machine-generated texts, while the second focused on attributing texts to specific large language models (LLMs). The authors addressed subtask 1 in both English and Spanish, testing a combination of traditional machine learning and deep learning methods, along with integrating additional metadata related to readability, complexity, sentiment, emotion, and toxicity of the texts. The experiments demonstrated the effectiveness of fine-tuning a multilingual BERT uncased model for detecting AI-generated texts. However, the inclusion of additional features, such as metadata, led to a decrease in performance, even compared to traditional machine learning models, suggesting that BERT's architecture alone was sufficient for classifying text. The authors concluded that, while their experiments provided valuable insights into the effectiveness of different models for detecting AI-generated text, further research was needed.

3 AI vs Human Text Detection

3.1 Dataset Analysis

Datasets for training, development, and testing were provided by the organizers through Hugging Face and Google Drive. The datasets consist of the ID, Text, Source, and Label columns, the label columns consist of two numerical values 0 and 1, where 1 marks the text generated by humans and 0 for the text generated by AI. The task involves binary classification of the test texts into human or AI-written categories after running and fine-tuning the model through the training and development stages. The dataset comprises 610,767 training samples with 381,845 samples being machine-generated and 228,822 human-generated text, furthermore, the development dataset consists of 261,758 samples with 163,430 samples being machine-generated texts and 98,328 human texts. Figures 1 and 2 give a view of the sources of the training dataset and the LLM models used to generate texts.

3.2 Application of DistilBERT

Using the Transformers Library from Hugging Face, we took some steps into data engineering by preparing and formatting it to be a suitable input for the model, then employed them in training and evaluation. The methodology adopted in these steps is outlined in Section 4, where we explain how we designed the DistilBERT base model architecture and proceeded to encode and load the dataset for further processing.

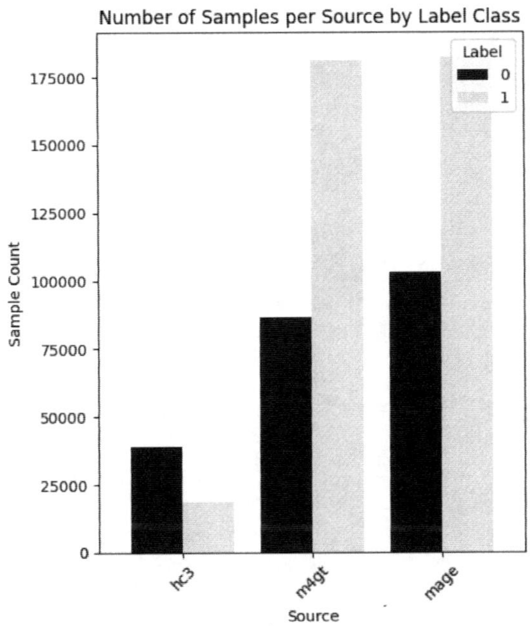

Figure 1: Number of samples by source

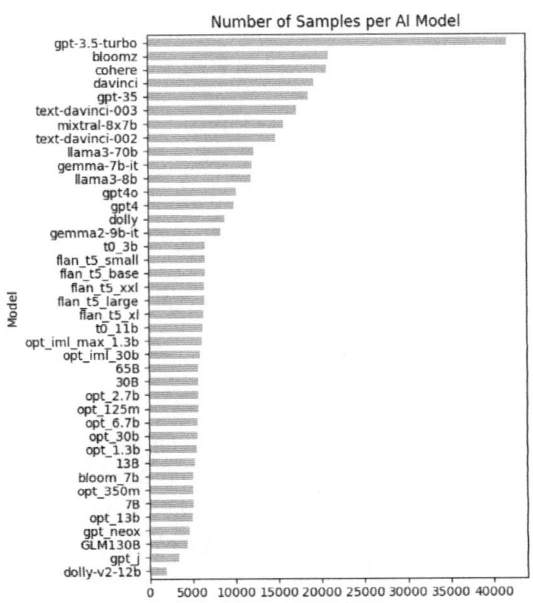

Figure 2: Number of samples generated by different LLM models

4 System Setup and Experiments

4.1 System Setup

We fine-tuned the model by adding a classification layer on the pre-trained DistilBERT architecture to enable it to perform binary classification.

We applied an amount of regularization to the model to prevent overfitting and biases. This was done to address the class imbalance in the dataset and ensure balanced learning across the classes by minimizing potential biases that may arise due to uneven class distributions.

With the adaptation of early stopping and model checkpointing, the best-performing model (based on the F1-score) was saved during training, which helped to prevent overfitting and ensured that the model selected for evaluation had the highest validation performance. This also ensured saving model checkpoints at the end of every epoch.

We used a cosine-annealing learning rate schedule, which gradually reduces the learning rate over time. This scheduling strategy helped stabilize training by lowering the learning rate as the model converged, often resulting in better final model performance.

4.2 Experiments

We adopted the training strategy to focus on fine-tuning the DistilBERT model, specifically the distilbert-base-uncased version; this allowed the model to accommodate the unique characteristics that define the classes in our dataset. This was done by carefully selecting some key hyperparameters and configurations to enhance the models's performance.

The model was trained over 3 epochs, and we leverage available GPU memory, and gradient accumulation steps of 2 to balance memory usage. Mixed precision was utilized to accelerate training by enabling mixed precision training, with early stopping enabled based on F1-score improvements. Additionally, a cosine learning rate scheduler was applied to modulate the learning rate as we optimized batch size for memory and computational efficiency. We used warm-up steps to enable a short warm-up period where the learning rate gradually increases, helping the model to avoid instability at the start of training and smoothing the convergence. Also, we accumulate gradients over two batches before performing an update and using DataCollatorWithPadding to ensure that the input sequences were dynamically padded to the maximum length within each batch, minimizing wasted computation on padding tokens to improve training speed and efficiency. The results of the training and validation stages of the model are displayed in Table 1, and the loss plot and F1-score plot of the training and validation stages are shown in Figures 3 and 4,

Epoch	Training Loss	Validation Loss	Accuracy	F1-score
1	0.1975	0.1759	0.9270	0.9263
2	0.1038	0.1509	0.9439	0.9434
3	0.0541	0.1807	0.9466	0.9461

Table 1: Metrics for each epoch including training and validation losses, accuracy, and F1-score.

Model	Micro-average_F1	Macro-average_F1
DistilBERT	0.7068	0.7242

Table 2: Result obtained from the test dataset

respectively.

We evaluated each epoch, allowing us to monitor the model's progress closely. This helped to ensure that our model's training and validation performance was aligned and aided in identifying overfitting or underfitting early.

Evaluation of the model was done using the micro-average F1-score, which is the default metric for this subtask. The evaluation on the development dataset was performed after each training epoch to track how well the model was doing on the task and closely monitor its progress.

5 Results

In this section, we present the results of the test dataset provided by the organizers of the COLING 2025 conference as predicted by the pre-trained DistilBERT model on the English test supplied through Google Drive. The prediction of the model was uploaded to the Codabench platform featured by the organizers of the conference for submission, and the micro- and macro-average F1 scores were computed accordingly. The results proved the model's ability to distinguish between human-written text and AI-generated text. The details of the results are presented in Table 2.

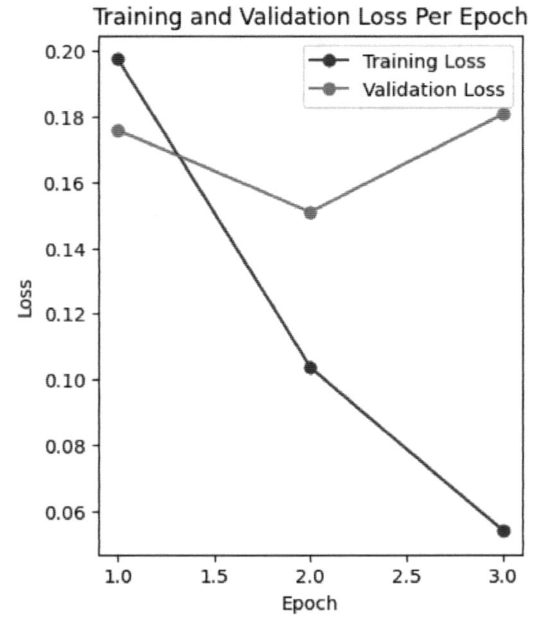

Figure 3: Training and development data loss plot per epoch

6 Conclusions

The application of DistilBERT, a compact and efficient transformer model for the detection of AI-generated text illustrates the advancement in the potential of transformer-based models to distinguish nuances in language style and origin. This task addresses specific challenges concerning the size of the dataset and the fact that LLM AI-generated text often mimics human-like patterns, thereby requiring the model to capture subtle stylistic and structural differences. Our approach leverages DistilBERT's efficient architecture and tokenizer capabilities to effectively identify these distinctions with a micro-average F1-score of 0.70. This result highlights DistilBERT's ability to generalize and perform well on the intricate task of text detection and classification, showing that smaller models can yield robust outcomes even in sophisticated NLP tasks.

The performance obtained in our experiments emphasizes both the viability of DistilBERT in this domain and the promise of continued exploration with other transformer-based models. Future work will focus on expanding the dataset to cover a broader array of AI-generated text from various models and fine-tuning DistilBERT and similar models to achieve even more refined detection capabilities.

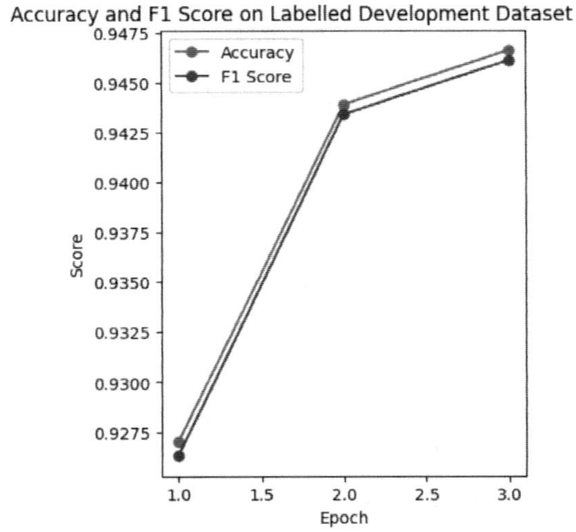

Figure 4: F1-score plot on labeled development dataset

Acknowledgments

The work was done with partial support from the Mexican Government through the grant A1-S-47854 of CONACYT, Mexico, grants 20241816, 20241819, and 20240951 of the Secretaría de Investigación y Posgrado of the Instituto Politécnico Nacional, Mexico. The authors thank the CONACYT for the computing resources brought to them through the Plataforma de Aprendizaje Profundo para Tecnologías del Lenguaje of the Laboratorio de Supercómputo of the INAOE, Mexico and acknowledge the support of Microsoft through the Microsoft Latin America PhD Award.

References

Olaronke Oluwayemisi Adebanji, Olumide Ebenezer Ojo, Hiram Calvo, Irina Gelbukh, and Grigori Sidorov. 2024. Adaptation of transformer-based models for depression detection. *Computación y Sistemas*, 28(1).

Fernando Aguilar-Canto, Marco A Cardoso-Moreno, Diana Jiménez, and Hiram Calvo. 2023. Gpt-2 versus gpt-3 and bloom: Llms for llms generative text detection. In *IberLEF@ SEPLN*.

Abdullah Alshanqiti, Abdallah Namoun, Aeshah Alsughayyir, Aisha Mousa Mashraqi, Abdul Rehman Gilal, and Sami Saad Albouq. 2021. Leveraging distilbert for summarizing arabic text: an extractive dual-stage approach. *IEEE Access*, 9:135594–135607.

Syed Immamul Ansarullah, Mudasir Manzoor Kirmani, Sami Alshmrany, and Arfat Firdous. 2024. Ethical issues around artificial intelligence. In *A Biologist s Guide to Artificial Intelligence*, pages 301–314. Elsevier.

Fazlourrahman Balouchzahi, Hosahalli Lakshmaiah Shashirekha, and Grigori Sidorov. 2021. Mucic at checkthat! 2021: Fado-fake news detection and domain identification using transformers ensembling. In *CLEF (Working Notes)*, pages 455–464.

Shammur Absar Chowdhury, Hind Al-Merekhi, Mucahid Kutlu, Kaan Efe Keleş, Fatema Ahmad, Tasnim Mohiuddin, Georgios Mikros, and Firoj Alam. 2025. GenAI content detection task 2: AI vs. human – academic essay authenticity challenge. In *Proceedings of the 1st Workshop on GenAI Content Detection (GenAIDetect)*, Abu Dhabi, UAE. International Conference on Computational Linguistics.

Sergio Damián, Brian Herrera, David Vázquez, Hiram Calvo, Edgardo Felipe-Riverón, and Cornelio Yáñez-Márquez. 2024. Dsvs at pan 2024: Ensemble approach of transformer-based language models for analyzing conspiracy theories against critical thinking narratives.

Liam Dugan, Andrew Zhu, Firoj Alam, Preslav Nakov, Marianna Apidianaki, and Callison-Burch Chris. 2025. Genai content detection task 3: Cross-domain machine generated text detection challenge. In *Proceedings of the 1st Workshop on GenAI Content Detection (GenAIDetect)*, Abu Dhabi, UAE. International Conference on Computational Linguistics.

Lemlem Eyob, Tsadkan Yitbarek, Amna Naseeb, Grigori Sidorov, and Ildar Batyrshin. 2024. Enhancing hope speech detection on twitter using machine learning and transformer models.

Alberto Fernández-Hernández, Juan Luis Arboledas-Márquez, Julián Ariza-Merino, and Salud María Jiménez Zafra. 2023. Taming the turing test: Exploring machine learning approaches to discriminate human vs. ai-generated texts. In *IberLEF@ SEPLN*.

Isabel O Gallegos, Ryan A Rossi, Joe Barrow, Md Mehrab Tanjim, Sungchul Kim, Franck Dernoncourt, Tong Yu, Ruiyi Zhang, and Nesreen K Ahmed. 2024. Bias and fairness in large language models: A survey. *Computational Linguistics*, pages 1–79.

Omar García-Vázquez, Tania Alcántara, Hiram Calvo, and Grigori Sidorov. 2023. Llm's for spanish song text analysis and classification using language variants. In *Mexican International Conference on Artificial Intelligence*, pages 118–127. Springer.

Ali Garib and Tina A Coffelt. 2024. Detecting the anomalies: Exploring implications of qualitative research in identifying ai-generated text for ai-assisted composition instruction. *Computers and Composition*, 73:102869.

Thang Ta Hoang. The combination of bert and data oversampling for answer type prediction.

Slawomir Kierner, Jacek Kucharski, and Zofia Kierner. 2023. Taxonomy of hybrid architectures involving rule-based reasoning and machine learning in clinical decision systems: A scoping review. *Journal of Biomedical Informatics*, 144:104428.

Olga Kolesnikova, Mesay Gemeda Yigezu, Atnafu Lambebo Tonja, Michael Meles Woldeyohannis, Grigori Sidorov, and Alexander Gelbukh. 2023. Ginger disease detection using a computer vision pre-trained model. In *Innovations in Machine and Deep Learning: Case Studies and Applications*, pages 419–432. Springer.

Mayte H Laureano and Hiram Calvo. 2024. Computational study of dream interpretations: Psychoanalytic human vs artificial analyses. In *2024 IEEE Congress on Evolutionary Computation (CEC)*, pages 1–9. IEEE.

Yafu Li, Qintong Li, Leyang Cui, Wei Bi, Zhilin Wang, Longyue Wang, Linyi Yang, Shuming Shi, and Yue Zhang. 2024. MAGE: Machine-generated text detection in the wild. In *Proceedings of the 62nd Annual Meeting of the Association for Computational Linguistics (Volume 1: Long Papers)*, pages 36–53, Bangkok, Thailand. Association for Computational Linguistics.

Luciane Maimone and Jason Jolley. 2023. Looks like google to me: Instructor ability to detect machine translation in l2 spanish writing. *Foreign Language Annals*, 56(3):627–644.

Olumide E Ojo, Olaronke O Adebanji, Hiram Calvo, Damian O Dieke, Olumuyiwa E Ojo, Seye E Akinsanya, Tolulope O Abiola, and Anna Feldman. 2023a. Legend at araieval shared task: Persuasion technique detection using a language-agnostic text representation model. In *1st Arabic Natural Language Processing Conference, ArabicNLP 2023*, pages 594–599. Association for Computational Linguistics (ACL).

Olumide E Ojo, Olaronke O Adebanji, Hiram Calvo, Alexander Gelbukh, Anna Feldman, and Ofir Ben Shoham. 2024. Doctor or ai? efficient neural network for response classification in health consultations. *IEEE Access*.

Olumide Ebenezer Ojo, Olaronke Oluwayemisi Adebanji, Hiram Calvo, Alexander Gelbukh, Anna Feldman, and Grigori Sidorov. 2023b. Hate and offensive content identification in indo-aryan languages using transformer-based models.

Olumide Ebenezer Ojo, Hoang Thang Ta, Alexander Gelbukh, Hiram Calvo, Olaronke Oluwayemisi Adebanji, and Grigori Sidorov. 2023c. Transformer-based approaches to sentiment detection. In *Recent Developments and the New Directions of Research, Foundations, and Applications: Selected Papers of the 8th World Conference on Soft Computing, February 03–05, 2022, Baku, Azerbaijan, Vol. II*, pages 101–110. Springer.

Grigori Sidorov, Fazlourrahman Balouchzahi, Sabur Butt, and Alexander Gelbukh. 2023. Regret and hope on transformers: An analysis of transformers on regret and hope speech detection datasets. *Applied Sciences*, 13(6):3983.

Miguel Soto, Cesar Macias, Marco Cardoso-Moreno, Tania Alcántara, Omar García, and Hiram Calvo. 2024. Cognicic at emospeech-iberlef2024: Exploring multimodal emotion recognition in spanish: Deep learning approaches for speech-text analysis.

Yuxia Wang, Artem Shelmanov, Jonibek Mansurov, Akim Tsvigun, Vladislav Mikhailov, Rui Xing, Zhuohan Xie, Jiahui Geng, Giovanni Puccetti, Ekaterina Artemova, Jinyan Su, Minh Ngoc Ta, Mervat Abassy, Kareem Elozeiri, Saad El Dine Ahmed, Maiya Goloburda, Tarek Mahmoud, Raj Vardhan Tomar, Alexander Aziz, Nurkhan Laiyk, Osama Mohammed Afzal, Ryuto Koike, Masahiro Kaneko, Alham Fikri Aji, Nizar Habash, Iryna Gurevych, and Preslav Nakov. 2025. GenAI content detection task 1: English and multilingual machine-generated text detection: AI vs. human. In *Proceedings of the 1st Workshop on GenAI Content Detection (GenAIDetect)*, Abu Dhabi, UAE. International Conference on Computational Linguistics.

Mesay Gemeda Yigezu, Tadesse Kebede, Olga Kolesnikova, Grigori Sidorov, and Alexander Gelbukh. 2023. Habesha@ dravidianlangtech: Utilizing deep and transfer learning approaches for sentiment analysis. In *Proceedings of the Third Workshop on Speech and Language Technologies for Dravidian Languages*, pages 239–243.

Wenxin Zheng. 2024. Ai vs. human: A comparative study of cohesion and coherence in academic texts between human-written and chatgpt-generated texts.

A Appendix

Initialize data collator for padding
data_collator = DataCollatorWithPadding(tokenizer=tokenizer) Use the initialized tokenizer

Define the Trainer without early stopping
trainer = Trainer(
model=model,
args=training_args,
train_dataset=train_dataset,
eval_dataset=dev_dataset,
compute_metrics=compute_metrics, Add custom metrics
data_collator=data_collator Use data collator for dynamic padding
)

training_args = TrainingArguments(
output_dir='./results',

eval_strategy='epoch', Evaluate at the end of each epoch
per_device_train_batch_size=256, Larger batch size if memory allows
per_device_eval_batch_size=256,
gradient_accumulation_steps=2, Adjust for GPU memory usage
num_train_epochs=3, Adjust as needed
weight_decay=0.02,
logging_dir='./logs',
logging_steps=10,
fp16=True, Enable mixed precision
bf16=False, Use bfloat16 if supported (set to True for supported hardware)
dataloader_num_workers=8, Increase CPU utilization for data loading
save_strategy="epoch",
load_best_model_at_end=True,
metric_for_best_model="f1", Use F1 score for model selection
save_total_limit=2, Limit saved checkpoints to avoid large storage use
lr_scheduler_type="cosine", Add learning rate scheduling
warmup_steps=500, Warmup to prevent early overfitting
save_steps=1000, Save model periodically
)

Initialize data collator for padding
data_collator = DataCollatorWithPadding(tokenizer=tokenizer) Use the initialized tokenizer

Define the Trainer without early stopping
trainer = Trainer(
model=model,
args=training_args,
train_dataset=train_dataset,
eval_dataset=dev_dataset,
compute_metrics=compute_metrics, Add custom metrics
data_collator=data_collator Use data collator for dynamic padding
)

from transformers import DistilBertTokenizer
from torch.utils.data import Dataset
tokenizer = DistilBertTokenizer.from_pretrained('distilbert-base-uncased')
class CustomDatasett(Dataset):
def __init__(self, examples):
self.examples = examples
def __len__(self):
return len(self.examples)
def __getitem__(self, idx):
example = self.examples[idx]
Tokenize the cleaned text
encoding = tokenizer(
example['cleaned_text'],
truncation=True,
padding='max_length',
max_length=512,
return_tensors='pt'
)
return
'input_ids': encoding['input_ids'].flatten(),
'attention_mask': encoding['attention_mask'].flatten(),
'id': example['id']

test_dataset = CustomDatasett(tokenized_testset)

nits_teja_srikar at GenAI Detection Task 2: Distinguishing Human and AI-Generated Essays Using Machine Learning and Transformer Models

L D M S Sai Teja, Annepaka Yadagiri, M Srikar Vardhan and Partha Pakray
Department of Computer Science & Engineering
National Institute of Technology Silchar, Assam, India, 788010
{lekkalad_ug, annepaka22_rs, mangadoddis_ug, partha}@cse.nits.ac.in

Abstract

This paper presents models to differentiate between human-written and AI-generated essays, addressing challenges posed by advanced AI models like ChatGPT and Claude. Using a structured dataset, we fine-tune multiple machine learning models, including XGBoost and Logistic Regression, along with ensemble learning and k-fold cross-validation. The dataset is processed through text cleaning, lemmatization, stemming, and part-of-speech tagging, followed by TF-IDF vectorization before training. Our team nits_teja_srikar achieves high accuracy, with DistilBERT performing at 77.3% accuracy, standing at 20th position for English, and XLM-RoBERTa excelling in Arabic at 92.2%, standing at 14th position in the official leaderboard, demonstrating the model's potential for real-world applications.

1 Introduction

Generative Artificial Intelligence (AI) tools (Tkachov, 2024) are revolutionizing the creation of text, images, and videos, reshaping how society consumes and produces online content. As these technologies advance, distinguishing between AI-generated and human-generated content has become increasingly challenging. AI-Generated Content (*AIGC*) (Staff, 2024) spans a broad range of media, including text, code, images, and music, with rapidly expanding applications in areas such as news reports, blog posts, scriptwriting, and marketing copy.

A study published in *The Public Library of Science (PLOS)* found that readers were more likely to agree with arguments in AI-generated essays than those in human-written ones (Bal and Veltkamp, 2013). These findings underscore the increasing need for models reliably differentiating between AI-generated and human-authored content. In this paper, we employ a fine-tuning approach utilizing multiple Machine Learning (*ML*) models, including XGBoost and Logistic Regression (Google-Research), along with their k-fold cross-validation variants (Ismail et al., 2023), and an ensemble learning method. A hybrid model integrating all models and their k-fold variants was developed using ensemble learning (Xiong et al., 2024) and transformer models using DistilBERT (Sanh et al., 2019) and XLM-RoBERTa (Conneau et al., 2019) to further improve detection accuracy in distinguishing between human and AI-generated essays.

2 Related Work

Liao et al. (Liao et al., 2023) proposed an ethical framework for Artificial Intelligence Generated Content (*AIGC*) within the healthcare sector. This study investigated the differences between medical texts authored by ChatGPT and those written by healthcare professionals. Additionally, the authors developed machine learning workflows aimed at identifying and distinguishing medical texts generated by ChatGPT. To achieve this, they curated datasets, with one dataset consisting of ChatGPT-generated medical texts and the other containing texts authored by human experts. Subsequently, they implemented ML methods to determine the source of the medical text content.

Alamleh et al. (Alamleh et al., 2023) assessed the effectiveness of various ML methods in differentiating AI-generated text from text authored by humans. To carry out this analysis, they collected responses from computer science students to both essay and programming assignments. Using this dataset, they trained and evaluated multiple machine learning models, including Support Vector Machines (*SVM*), Logistic Regression (*LR*), Neural Networks (*NN*), Random Forest (*RF*), and Decision Trees (*DT*).

Chen et al. (Chen et al., 2023) proposed a novel approach to distinguish between texts written

Proceedings of the 1st Workshop on GenAI Content Detection (GenAIDetect), pages 278–283
January 19, 2025.

by humans and those generated by ChatGPT using language-based techniques. The researchers collected and released a curated dataset named OpenGPTText, comprising rephrased content created through ChatGPT.

2.1 Problem Statement

The primary objective of this task is to classify the provided essays as either **Human-generated** or **AI-generated** in two languages: **English** and **Arabic**. This classification problem aims to assess the *authenticity* of the text, ensuring a reliable distinction between human-authored and AI-generated content. The ability to detect AI-generated text effectively is crucial for applications such as content moderation, academic integrity, and automated scoring systems (Genai-content-detection / Genai-content-detection-coling-2025 · GitLab, n.d.).

2.2 Dataset Description

We used data from the shared task dataset provided by the Linguistic Data Consortium (LDC) (ETS Corpus of Non-Native Written English, n.d.) by COLING 2025 (Chowdhury et al., 2025). The ETS Corpus of Non-Native Written English includes 12,100 TOEFL essays from speakers of 11 non-English languages. Additionally, AI-generated essays from models like GPT-3.5-Turbo (Mrbullwinkle, 2024), GPT-4o (Stryker, 2024), Gemini-1.5 (Google AI for Developers, n.d.), and others were incorporated. This combination of human and AI-generated content facilitates a thorough comparative analysis, which significantly contributes to research in authorship detection, automatic scoring, and understanding the distinctions between human and AI writing.

2.3 Dataset Visualization

This visualization highlights the key differences between AI-generated and human-authored essays [1] [2], focusing on several critical aspects. It presents the variations in essay length distribution (1b), (2b), and a comparative analysis of essay lengths by source. Additionally, it offers insights into key textual metrics, including word count, sentence count, and unique word count (1a), (2a), shedding light on the structural and stylistic differences between the two types of content. This analysis highlights the distinct features of human and AI writing, contributing to a deeper understanding of their unique characteristics.

3 Methodology

We leverage both traditional machine-learning models and advanced transformer-based models. Below, we provide a detailed technical description of our methodology for both datasets.

3.1 Preprocessing Techniques

We employed preprocessing techniques like Cleaning, lowercasing, lemmatization and stemming, POS tagging, removing stop words to enhance data quality: 1) Text Cleaning: Removal of punctuation, special characters, and redundant spaces. 2) Lowercasing: Uniform formatting of all text entries. 3) Lemmatization and Stemming: Standardization of word forms for better vectorization. 4) POS Tagging: Advanced feature extraction by identifying grammatical roles using spacy library. 5) Stopword Removal: Elimination of common words with minimal semantic contribution.

```
input_text = "The quick brown foxes were jumping
     joyfully, over the lazy dogs!"

After preprocessing:

pos = "quick/ADJ brown/ADJ foxes/NOUN jumping/
    VERB joyfully/ADV lazy/ADJ dogs/NOUN"

result = "quick brown foxes jumping joyfully
    lazy dogs"
```

3.2 TF-IDF Vectorization

To effectively analyze text data, we convert documents into numerical representations using **Term Frequency-Inverse Document Frequency (*TF-IDF*)** vectorization. This method assigns importance to words based on their occurrence within individual documents and across the entire corpus. TF-IDF helps emphasize significant terms while downplaying those that are common but carry little meaning.

Term Frequency-Inverse Document Frequency (*TF-IDF*):

$$\text{TF}(t, d_i) = \frac{f_{t,d_i}}{\sum_{t' \in d_i} f_{t',d_i}} \quad (1)$$

$$\text{IDF}(t, D) = \log \left(\frac{N}{|\{d_j \in D : t \in d_j\}| + 1} \right) \quad (2)$$

TF-IDF Calculation and Matrix Construction: The TF-IDF score for a term t in document d_i is computed as the product of its Term Frequency (TF) and Inverse Document Frequency (IDF):

$$\text{TF-IDF}(t, d_i, D) = \text{TF}(t, d_i) \times \text{IDF}(t, D) \quad (3)$$

Each document is represented as a vector of TF-IDF values, with $x_i = (\text{TF-IDF}(t_1, d_i, D), \ldots, \text{TF-IDF}(t_m, d_i, D))$, where m is the vocabulary size. Stacking these vectors for all N documents forms a TF-IDF matrix $X \in \mathbb{R}^{N \times m}$, where each row corresponds to a document, and each column corresponds to a term.

To ensure uniformity, we apply Euclidean (L2) normalization:

$$x_i^{\text{norm}} = \frac{x_i}{\|x_i\|_2} = \frac{x_i}{\sqrt{\sum_{j=1}^{m} x_{ij}^2}} \quad (4)$$

where x_{ij} is the TF-IDF value of the jth term in the ith document.

3.3 HyperParameters

In this training, SparseCategoricalCrossentropy was used as the loss function for multi-class classification (Mao et al., 2023). Optimizers Adam and AdamW (Jakartamitul, 2024) were applied with learning rates of 5e-4 and 2e-5, respectively. Key metrics included SparseCategoricalAccuracy, ROC AUC (Bowers and Zhou, 2019), Accuracy, Precision, Recall, F1 Score, and MCC (Chicco and Jurman, 2020). The training was performed over 3 epochs with batch size 16 and 5-fold cross-validation, preserving class distribution. TF-IDF vectorization used 5000 max_features to optimize efficiency, and soft voting was applied in the ensemble model for enhanced accuracy. Overall hyperparameters can be seen in Table 1

3.4 Models for English Dataset

For the English dataset D_{eng}, we employ the following models:

Logistic Regression with K-fold Cross-Validation We split the dataset into k folds and train the logistic regression model iteratively. The logistic regression function is defined as:

$$\hat{y}_i = \sigma(w^\top x_i + b) = \frac{1}{1 + e^{-(w^\top x_i + b)}}$$

where $\sigma(\cdot)$ is the sigmoid function, and w, b are learned parameters.

Parameter	Value
Loss Function	SSCE
Optimizer	Adam, AdamW
Learning Rate	5e-4, 2e-5
Metrics	Accu, Prec, Recall, F1
Batch Size	16
Number of Epochs	3 (Transformer models)
Early Stopping	No
n_splits	5
max_features	5000
Voting	soft

Table 1: Model Hyperparameters

XGBoost with K-fold Cross-Validation XGBoost minimizes the following objective function:

$$\mathcal{L} = \sum_{i=1}^{n} \ell(\hat{y}_i, y_i) + \sum_{k=1}^{K} \Omega(f_k)$$

where $\ell(\hat{y}_i, y_i)$ is the loss function, and $\Omega(f_k)$ is the regularization term.

Ensemble Learning We combine predictions from logistic regression, XGBoost, and CatBoost using a weighted majority voting scheme:

$$\hat{y} = \arg\max_c \sum_{m=1}^{M} w_m \cdot \mathbb{I}(\hat{y}_m = c)$$

where M is the number of models, w_m is the weight of the mth model, and $\mathbb{I}(\cdot)$ is the indicator function.

DistilBERT Transformer We use the DistilBERT pretrained transformer as a binary classifier to distinguish between human-written and AI-generated essays. DistilBERT, a lighter version of BERT, retains its ability to capture subtle linguistic and contextual patterns while being computationally efficient. The classifier processes input text to generate hidden representations h_i, and the final prediction is made with:

$$\hat{y}_i = \text{softmax}(W h_i + b)$$

where W and b are trainable parameters, and $\hat{y}_i$ is the probability distribution over the two classes. The output class is determined by the highest probability score.

3.5 Model for Arabic Dataset

Given that our dataset is in Arabic, XLM-RoBERTa ensures better performance by leveraging its pre-trained embeddings specific to the language. The model produces rich contextual embeddings for each input sequence, which are fed into a classification layer. For Arabic, the pre-trained embeddings are particularly significant, as they capture complex morphological and syntactic patterns that are challenging to model through linguistic features alone. The final prediction is computed as:

$$\hat{y}_i = \text{softmax}(Wh_i + b)$$

where h_i is the contextual representation of the input, and W and b are trainable parameters. The softmax layer outputs a probability distribution over the target classes, allowing the model to classify the text accurately within the given context.

Model	ROC	Acc	Pre	Rec	F1
LR	1.00	0.99	0.99	1.00	0.99
XGB	0.99	0.98	0.98	0.99	0.99
CatB	0.92	0.89	0.92	0.92	0.92
En	0.99	0.99	0.99	0.99	0.99

Table 2: Performance Metrics of Machine Learning Models on English Dataset

Model	Acc	Pre	Rec	F1
DistilBERT-En	0.99	0.95	1.00	0.97
XLM-R-Ar	0.94	1.00	0.91	0.95
DistilBERT-Ar	0.91	0.93	0.91	0.91

Table 3: Performance Metrics of Transformer Models

4 Results

The DistilBERT model excels in the English dataset, while XLM-RoBERTa performs well in Arabic. The confusion matrix highlights their accuracy and offers insights into their classification performance.

For English, DistilBERT-English achieves a perfect recall of 1.0 and an F1-score of 0.97. The ensemble model, combining Logistic Regression, XGBoost, and CatBoost, reaches an accuracy of 0.996 and an F1-score of 0.997. Overall results can be seen in Table 2. In contrast, Arabic models show lower performance, with XLM-RoBERTa Arabic leading in precision at 1.0 and an F1-score of 0.95, while DistilBERT-Arabic has an F1-score of 0.91. This highlights the challenges faced by Arabic models. The transformer-based models results can be seen in the Table 3

4.1 Ablation Studies

To evaluate the impact of preprocessing, feature extraction, and ensemble components, we conducted systematic experiments:

- **Preprocessing:** Removing *stemming and lemmatization* improved transformer models' performance by 1.43 on English datasets. Removing *POS tagging* reduced traditional model accuracy by 1.8, indicating its importance for feature engineering.
- **Feature Extraction:** Traditional models saw a 6% accuracy improvement using TF-IDF, while transformers performed better with raw text due to their pre-trained embeddings.

Preprocessing steps such as lemmatization and part-of-speech tagging play a vital role in feature extraction for traditional models. However, minimal preprocessing often yields better performance for transformer-based models by effectively utilizing raw textual features.

Model	Acc	Pre	Rec	F1
English	0.773	0.875	0.649	0.658
Arabic	0.922	0.943	0.882	0.904

Table 4: Final Test Results in Leaderboard

We got 77% accuracy on English essays, and performance on Arabic essays was significantly higher. Several linguistic and dataset-specific factors contribute to this gap. Firstly, Arabic's morphological complexity, including intricate word forms and inflections, presents challenges for tokenization and embedding generation. Unlike English, where words have simpler inflections, Arabic requires handling more complex word transformations, which can be harder for DistilBERT to capture. Additionally, Arabic's right-to-left writing and unique orthographic conventions further complicate processing.

Moreover, Arabic requires more sophisticated preprocessing steps, such as handling diacritics and lemmatization, which might not have been as effectively implemented as for English. Finally, cultural and stylistic differences between English and Arabic writing may also contribute to the difficulty in detecting AI-generated content in Arabic.

5 Conclusion

Our study demonstrates the efficacy of various ML and transformer-based models in distinguishing between human-generated and AI-generated essays in both English and Arabic. Utilizing models like DistilBERT and XLM-RoBERTa, we achieved superior detection precisions of 0.875 for English and a strong performance of 0.943 for Arabic, as shown in Table 4, highlighting their adaptability to diverse linguistic contexts. The ensemble methods further enhanced classification accuracy, emphasizing the importance of robust detection systems as AI-generated content becomes increasingly prevalent. Future work could explore additional linguistic features and cross-domain applications to improve detection capabilities and address challenges in Arabic model performance.

Label	Count	Word	Sentence	Unique
Human	629	300.24	15.57	173.48
AI	1467	284.07	14.51	155.24

(a) Comparison of Metrics in Number Counts English

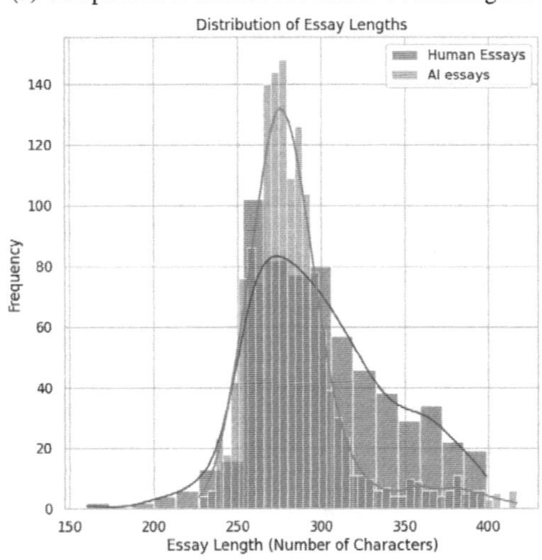

(b) Train Data Essay Length Distribution

Figure 1: Train Data Visualization for Language English

Label	Count	Word	Sentence	Unique
Human	1145	241.51	8.71	169.54
AI	925	200.96	14.33	137.57

(a) Comparison of Textual Metrics in Number Counts

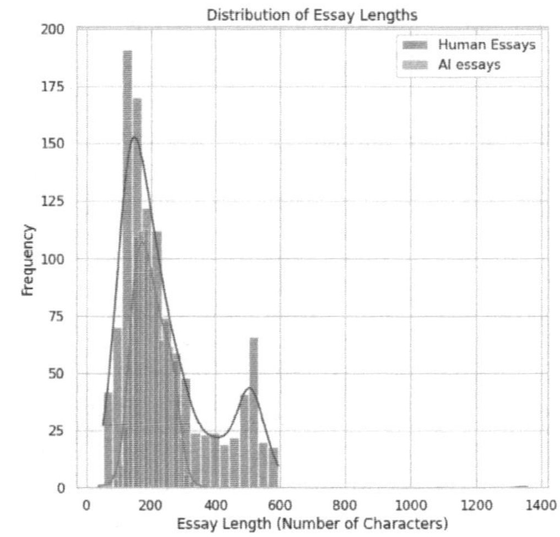

(b) Train Data Essay Length Distribution

Figure 2: Train Data Visualization for Arabic

References

Hosam Alamleh, Ali Abdullah S AlQahtani, and AbdElRahman ElSaid. 2023. Distinguishing human-written and chatgpt-generated text using machine learning. In *2023 Systems and Information Engineering Design Symposium (SIEDS)*, pages 154–158. IEEE.

P. M. Bal and M. Veltkamp. 2013. How does fiction reading influence empathy? an experimental investigation on the role of emotional transportation. *PLoS ONE*, 8(1):e55341.

A. J. Bowers and X. Zhou. 2019. Receiver operating characteristic (roc) area under the curve (auc): A diagnostic measure for evaluating the accuracy of predictors of education outcomes. *Journal of Education for Students Placed at Risk (JESPAR)*, 24(1):20–46.

Yutian Chen, Hao Kang, Vivian Zhai, Liangze Li, Rita Singh, and Bhiksha Raj. 2023. Gpt-sentinel: Distinguishing human and chatgpt generated content. *arXiv preprint arXiv:2305.07969*.

D. Chicco and G. Jurman. 2020. The advantages of the matthews correlation coefficient (mcc) over f1 score and accuracy in binary classification evaluation. *BMC Genomics*, 21(1).

Shammur Absar Chowdhury, Hind Al-Merekhi, Mucahid Kutlu, Kaan Efe Keleş, Fatema Ahmad, Tasnim Mohiuddin, Georgios Mikros, and Firoj Alam. 2025. GenAI content detection task 2: AI vs. human – academic essay authenticity challenge. In *Proceedings of the 1st Workshop on GenAI Content Detection (GenAIDetect)*, Abu Dhabi, UAE. International Conference on Computational Linguistics.

A. Conneau, K. Khandelwal, N. Goyal, V. Chaudhary, G. Wenzek, F. Guzmán, E. Grave, M. Ott, L. Zettlemoyer, and V. Stoyanov. 2019. Unsupervised cross-lingual representation learning at scale. *arXiv.org*.

ETS Corpus of Non-Native Written English. n.d. Ets corpus of non-native written english - linguistic data consortium. https://catalog.ldc.upenn.edu/LDC2014T06. Accessed: 2024-10-28.

Genai-content-detection / Genai-content-detection-coling-2025 · GitLab. n.d. Genai content detection / genai content detection coling-2025. GitLab. Accessed: October 29, 2024.

Google AI for Developers. n.d. Gemini models.

Google-Research. Github - google-research/tuning_playbook: A playbook for systematically maximizing the performance of deep learning models. https://github.com/google-research/tuning_playbook. N.d., Accessed: 2024-10-27.

W. N. Ismail, H. A. Alsalamah, and E. A. Mohamed. 2023. Genetic-efficient fine-tuning with layer pruning on multimodal covid-19 medical imaging. *Neural Computing and Applications*, 36(6):3215–3237.

Jakartamitul. 2024. Exploring the adamw pytorch optimizer - scriptoverflow. https://scriptoverflow.com/exploring-the-adamw-pytorch-optimizer/. Accessed: October 30, 2024.

Wenxiong Liao, Zhengliang Liu, Haixing Dai, Shaochen Xu, Zihao Wu, Yiyang Zhang, Xiaoke Huang, Dajiang Zhu, Hongmin Cai, Quanzheng Li, et al. 2023. Differentiating chatgpt-generated and human-written medical texts: quantitative study. *JMIR Medical Education*, 9(1):e48904.

A. Mao, M. Mohri, and Y. Zhong. 2023. Cross-entropy loss functions: Theoretical analysis and applications. https://arxiv.org/abs/2304.07288.

Mrbullwinkle. 2024. Work with the gpt-35-turbo and gpt-4 models - azure openai service.

V. Sanh, L. Debut, J. Chaumond, and T. Wolf. 2019. Distilbert, a distilled version of bert: smaller, faster, cheaper and lighter. *arXiv.org*.

C. Staff. 2024. What is generative ai? definition, applications, and impact. https://www.coursera.org/articles/what-is-generative-ai.

C. Stryker. 2024. Gpt-4o. what is gpt-4o?

N. Tkachov. 2024. Chatgpt and other ai assistants: An ultimate comparison | beetroot. Accessed: 2024-10-27.

F. Xiong, T. Markchom, Z. Zheng, S. Jung, V. Ojha, and H. Liang. 2024. Fine-tuning large language models for multigenerator, multidomain, and multilingual machine-generated text detection. Ensemble Methods: Foundations and Algorithms.

IntegrityAI at GenAI Detection Task 2: Detecting Machine-Generated Academic Essays in English and Arabic Using ELECTRA and Stylometry

Mohammad AL-Smadi
Digital Learning and Online Education Office
Qatar University, Doha, Qatar
malsmadi@qu.edu.qa

Abstract

Recent research has investigated the problem of detecting machine-generated essays for academic purposes. To address this challenge, this research utilizes pre-trained, transformer-based models fine-tuned on Arabic and English academic essays with stylometric features. Custom models based on ELECTRA for English and AraELECTRA for Arabic were trained and evaluated using a benchmark dataset. Proposed models achieved excellent results with an F1-score of 99.7%, ranking 2nd among of 26 teams in the English subtask, and 98.4%, finishing 1st out of 23 teams in the Arabic one.

1 Introduction

Since the launch of ChatGPT in November 2022, research on developing models for artificial intelligence (AI)-generated text detection has increased. This increase reflects growing concerns about maintaining academic integrity in the face of advanced generative AI (GenAI) tools capable of producing human-like text (Al-Smadi, 2023). Guo et al. (2023) were among the first working on this topic by developing a dataset named the "Human ChatGPT Comparison Corpus (HC3)" out of nearly 40,000 questions from different datasets along with their answers provided by humans. They also generated responses to these questions by ChatGPT and used the combined dataset to train detectors in both English and Chinese. The developed models included machine and deep learning based models like RoBERTa (Liu, 2019) and demonstrated decent performance across different scenarios.

Another paper focused on detecting ChatGPT-generated text written in English and French (Antoun et al., 2023a). The English model was trained using the HC3 dataset. The authors also translated some of its English content to French and included additional small French out-of-domain dataset of 113 French responses from ChatGPT and 116 from BingGPT. They fine-tuned two pre-trained models, CamemBERT (Martin et al., 2019) and CamemBERTa (Antoun et al., 2023b), using the French dataset, and RoBERTa (Liu, 2019) and ELECTRA (Clark, 2020) models using the English one. They also used XLM-R (Conneau, 2019) as multi-language model for the combined datasets of both languages. Research results showed that all models demonstrated good performance in identifying machine-generated content within the same domain, but when tested on out-of-domain content, their results dropped.

Alshammari et al. (2024) used transformer-based models, namely AraELECTRA (Antoun et al., 2020) and XML-R (Conneau, 2019) to solve the challenges of machine-generated Arabic text identification. The authors focused on the influence of diacritics on detection model performance. Their method showed great accuracy on the AIRABIC benchmark dataset. Other research utilized stylometric features to detect machine-generated content. For instance, Kutbi et al. (2024) introduced a machine learning model with stylometry for identifying "Contract cheating", the act of students depending on others to complete academic assignments on their behalf, by detecting deviations from a learner's distinctive writing style, which achieved excellent accuracy in their research. Opara (2024) developed a data-driven model named "StyloAI" trained with 31 stylometric features to detect machine-generated content. "StyloAI" performance outperformed other models on the same dataset.

Wee and Reimer (2023) discovered that AI identification technologies classified human-written writings translated from non-English languages as AI-generated, which raised worries among non-native English speakers (Liang et al., 2023). Moreover, Weber-Wulff et al. (2023) tested many AI text identification systems and found that they were neither accurate nor dependable, especially when

Proceedings of the 1st Workshop on GenAI Content Detection (GenAIDetect), pages 284–289

Language	Train Size	Dev. Size	Eval. Size	Test Size
Arabic	2070 (AI: 925, Human: 1145)	481 (AI: 299, Human: 182)	886	293
English	2096 (AI: 1467, Human: 629)	1626 (AI: 391, Human: 1235)	869	1130

Table 1: Summary of Arabic and English Datasets by subtask and type (Train, Development, Evaluation, and Test)

content masking techniques were used.

This research aims at addressing the challenge of AI-generated text. The rest of this paper is organized as follows: Section 2 discusses the research methodology, Section 3 presents the findings, and Section 4 concludes the study and highlights future directions.

2 Research Methodology

2.1 Task

This research is based on our participation in the shared task "GenAI Content Detection Task 2: AI vs. Human – Academic Essay Authenticity Challenge" (Chowdhury et al., 2025), which is organized as part of the "Workshop on Detecting AI Generated Content at the 31st International Conference on Computational Linguistics (COLING 2025)". The task aims at encouraging researchers to submit their research for detecting AI-generated academic essays. The task is designed to have three phases: (a) Models training and validation, (b) First evaluation phase, also referred as development phase, and (c) Models testing phase. Participated teams were ranked based on the results achieved in the final phase, i.e. models testing phase. The task covers content generated in two languages, Arabic and English. The next section explains in more detail the datasets provided for model training, validation, and testing.

2.2 Dataset

The datasets for this task consist of essays generated by generative AI models and human written ones. The essays authored by humans were curated from the "ETS Corpus of Non-Native Written English"[1], whereas the AI-generated ones were generated using seven different models including, GPT-3.5-Turbo, GPT-4o, GPT-4o-mini, Gemini-1.5, Llama-3.1 (8B), Phi-3.5-mini and Claude-3.5.

The datasets are designed to cover the three-phase task as discussed in the previous section. Each dataset consists of, (a) a train dataset for models training, (b) a validation dataset to fin-tune models parameters and evaluate model's performance during training phase, (c) an evaluation dataset, which is used to evaluate the model performance in a controlled environment before the final testing phase, and (d) a test dataset for the final testing phase, which is designed to assess the model's generalization and performance on completely unseen data.

Table 1 describes the sizes of the task's datasets by type and language. As described in the table, the Arabic dataset contains a balanced training set of 2,070 essays, which include 925 AI-generated essays, and 1,145 human-authored essays. This balance establishes an equitable foundation for training models to detect stylistic distinctions between AI and human text. In contrast, the English dataset has an imbalance in its training data, with 2,096 essays dominated by AI-generated texts (1,467 AI generated against 629 Human written). This skewed distribution may lead to model bias problem.

2.3 Baseline Model

The task organizers have implemented the following baseline model (Chowdhury et al., 2025). For each language, a baseline model is trained using an n-gram approach, specifically unigrams. The textual content of the essays is transformed into a Term Frequency-Inverse Document Frequency (TF-IDF) representation, with the features limited to a maximum of 10,000. Finally, the performance is evaluated by training a Support Vector Machine (SVM) classifier on this feature representation.

2.4 IntegrityAI Model

The proposed model is based on ELECTRA (Clark, 2020) and its implementation named AraELECTRA (Antoun et al., 2020), which is a model specifically tuned for the Arabic language. ELECTRA is an encoder only transformer that is designed to enhance the efficiency of implementing models for NLP tasks. Instead of implementing a masked language model (MLM), ELECTRA utilizes a unique training strategy known as "replaced token detection". While other encoder only transformers (such as BERT (Kenton and Toutanova, 2019)) implement MLM training strategy by predicting masked

[1] https://catalog.ldc.upenn.edu/LDC2014T06

Feature	ELECTRA-Small	ELECTRA-Base	ELECTRA-Large
Hidden Size	256	768	1024
Number of Layers	12	12	24
Number of Attention Heads	4	12	16
Total Parameters	14 million	110 million	335 million

Table 2: Comparison of ELECTRA-Small, ELECTRA-Base, and ELECTRA-Large models. AraELECTRA has the same features on ELECTRA-Base

Feature	Description
Word Count	Total number of words in the text.
Sentence Count	Total number of sentences in the text.
Average Sentence Length (words)	Average number of words per sentence.
Vocabulary Richness (Type-Token Ratio)	Ratio of unique words to total words, indicating vocabulary diversity.
Average Word Length (characters)	Average number of characters per word.
Commas	Number of comma punctuation marks in the text.
Periods	Number of period punctuation marks in the text.

Table 3: Description of stylometric features extracted from the dataset.

words in a sentence, ELECTRA relies on its generator component to generate plausible alternatives to replace some tokens in the input text. Then, uses the discriminator component to detect whether the token is replaced or original. The "replaced token detection" training strategy, requires the model to evaluate and learn all the input text tokens instead of the masked ones - as in BERT - which increases the model efficiency and minimizes the number of training epochs required to train the model. ELECTRA has three different pre-trained models that were used in this research, see Table 2 for differences between them[2].

As depicted in Figure 1, the same model architecture was used for both the Arabic and English text classification. The ELECTRA model was trained on the English dataset, whereas its tuned version on Arabic, i.e., AraELECTRA was trained on the Arabic dataset. Both datasets went into a standard preprocessing phase, then stylometirc features were extracted and used with the text embeddings to train the pretrained models (see Table 3 for more information about extracted features). The following layers were added to enhance the models' performance:

1. Dropout Layer: is a regularization technique where, during training, random neurons are temporarily ignored ("dropped out") to prevent overfitting and improve the model's generalization (Srivastava et al., 2014).

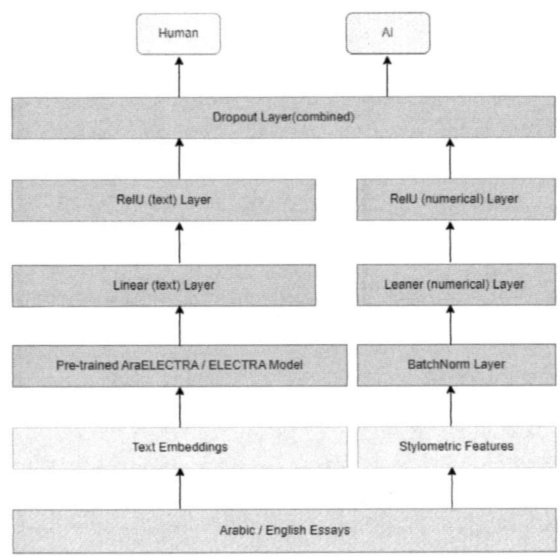

Figure 1: The architecture of the ELECTRA-based models with stylometric features.

2. Batch Normalization ("BatchNorm1d"): normalizes the features of the input vector, stabilizing learning, and aiding in faster and more stable training (Ioffe and Szegedy, 2015).

3. Fully Connected (Linear) Layers: these layers are basic neural network layers where every input is connected to every output by a learned weight. These layers include: (a) "numerical": takes the batch-normalized numerical features and projects them onto a new space to learn a higher-level rep-

[2]https://github.com/google-research/electra

Model	Eval. Phase F1 (%)	Testing Phase F1 (%)
AraELECTRA_base_discriminator	99.8	**98.4**
AraELECTRA_base_discriminator without features	-	96.9
Baseline-Arabic Model	57.5	46.1
ELECTRA_small_discriminator	100.0	98.5
ELECTRA_small_discriminator without features	-	96.1
ELECTRA_large_discriminator	100.0	**99.7**
Baseline-English Model	29.8	47.8

Table 4: Evaluation (i.e. models' development phase) and testing results for Arabic and English developed models in comparison to the baseline model.

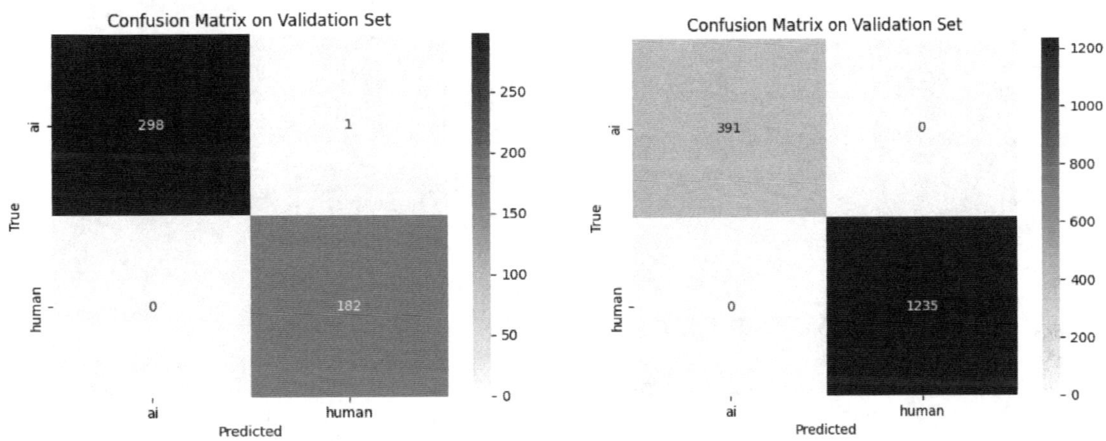

Figure 2: Confusion matrices on the validation sets (Arabic dataset on the left).

resentation of these features. (b) "text": processes the [CLS] token embedding from the ELECTRA model output, allowing the model to further tailor this representation for the task at hand.

4. Rectified Linear Unit (ReLU) activation Function: is a non-linear operation used after linear layers to introduce non-linear properties to the model, making it capable of learning more complex patterns (Glorot et al., 2011). This layer is used after each of the fully connected layers (numerical and text) to add non-linearity to the model, which helps in learning complex patterns in the data.

5. Output Layer (Fully Connected (Linear)): after processing through their respective pathways, both text and numerical data features are combined (concatenated) to form a unified feature vector. This combined feature vector is then passed to a final fully connected layer (combined), which outputs the logits for the classification categories.

The models were trained for 10 epochs with the option of (early_stopping_patience=2) implemented to avoid model overfitting during training. Models participating in this task were evaluated and ranked based on their achieved F1-score.

3 Results and Findings

Table 4 presents the developed models results for Arabic and English datasets. Results show that models achieved high F1 scores of 99.8% for the Arabic dataset and 100% for the English dataset in the evaluation phase and maintained that high performance in the testing phase with (98.4% and 98.5%, for Arabic and English datasets respectively). This achievement demonstrates that the models are not only well-tuned to the training data but also maintain their discriminative power on new and unseen data. This finding is also represented by the confusion matrices on the validation datasets. The trained model on the English dataset classified all 'ai' and 'human' labels accurately. Whereas, The trained model on the Arabic dataset had a near-perfect classification with only one instance of 'ai' being misclassified as 'human' (see Figure 2).

To evaluate the impact of the stylometric features on the model performance, we trained the models without features. The results demonstrate that ex-

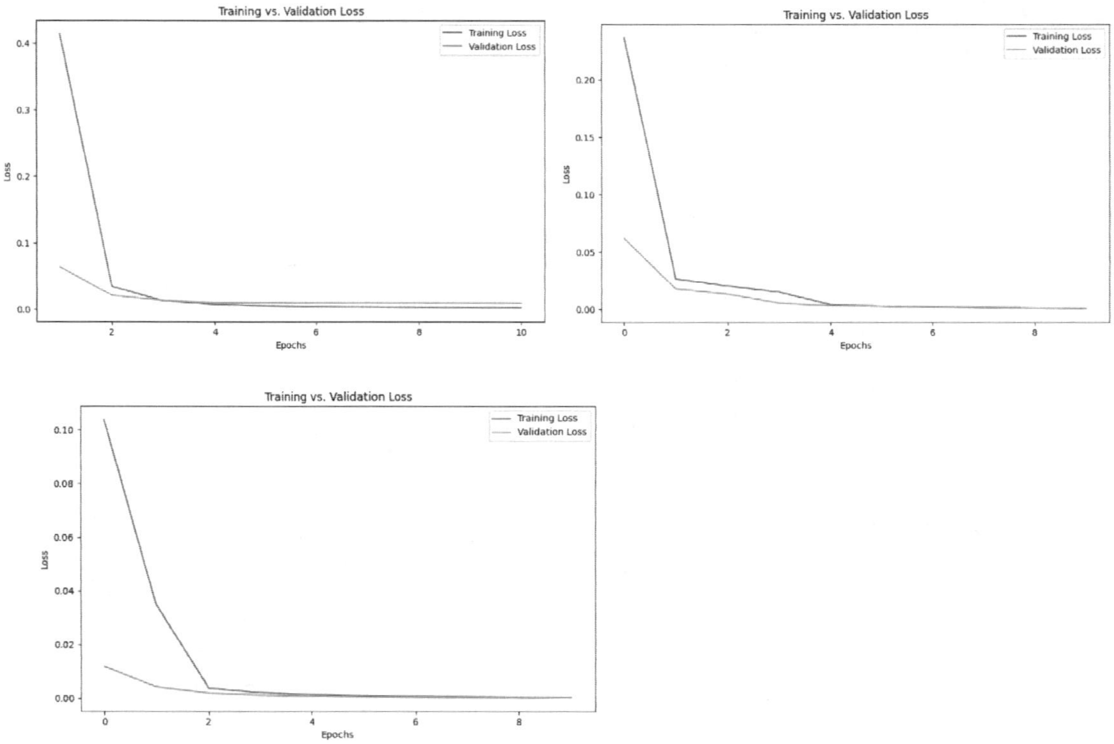

Figure 3: Training vs. validation loss values after each epoch of models training (AraELECTRA the upper left corner, ELECTRA_small on the right upper corner, and ELECTRA_large on the left lower corner)

cluding these features leads to a decrease in model performance, with a 1.5% and 2.4% drop in F1 score for AraELECTRA and ELECTRA models, respectively. This indicates that extracted features enhanced model predictions. Despite the modest decline, the impact underscores the importance of these features for better generalization.

The results of training vs. validation Loss values after each epoch of models training in Figure 3, show that the training loss rapidly declined from the first epoch and then quickly stabilized to run in parallel with the validation loss. Both values of training and validation loss kept decreasing smoothly until the end of models training epoch without any sign of overfitting, as the validation loss remains close to the training loss throughout the training process. This was also maintained by enabling the option of early_stopping during the models training. Moreover, this also indicates that both models generalizes very well when confronted by new unseen data.

The rapid stabilization of loss values may indicate that more complex model architectures might achieve even better results. Therefore, we trained the ELECTRA_large instead of the ELECTRA_small model for the english subtask for 10 epochs as well. As, expected the ELECTRA_large achieved better results with F1 score of 99.7%.

For more information on the results of other participating teams in the task, the reader is redirected to (Chowdhury et al., 2025).

4 Conclusion and Future Work

This study demonstrates the efficacy of transformer-based models for identifying machine-generated academic articles. Using ELECTRA-Small for English and AraELECTRA-Base for Arabic, paired with stylometric characteristics, our models produced remarkable F1-scores of 98.5% and 98.4%, respectively. Experiments using ELECTRA-Large for English revealed the possibility of even better F1-score, reaching 99.7%, but at a larger computing cost.

Our proposed models offer an adaptable solution that balances performance and efficiency and is appropriate for a variety of hardware setups. To improve robustness, future study might focus on real-time detection, expanding to new academic areas, and extending language coverage.

References

Mohammad Al-Smadi. 2023. Chatgpt and beyond: The generative ai revolution in education. *arXiv preprint arXiv:2311.15198*.

Hamed Alshammari, Ahmed El-Sayed, and Khaled Elleithy. 2024. Ai-generated text detector for arabic language using encoder-based transformer architecture. *Big Data and Cognitive Computing*, 8(3):32.

Wissam Antoun, Fady Baly, and Hazem Hajj. 2020. Araelectra: Pre-training text discriminators for arabic language understanding. *arXiv preprint arXiv:2012.15516*.

Wissam Antoun, Virginie Mouilleron, Benoît Sagot, and Djamé Seddah. 2023a. Towards a robust detection of language model generated text: Is chatgpt that easy to detect? *arXiv preprint arXiv:2306.05871*.

Wissam Antoun, Benoît Sagot, and Djamé Seddah. 2023b. Data-efficient french language modeling with camemberta. *arXiv preprint arXiv:2306.01497*.

Shammur Absar Chowdhury, Hind Al-Merekhi, Mucahid Kutlu, Kaan Efe Keleş, Fatema Ahmad, Tasnim Mohiuddin, Georgios Mikros, and Firoj Alam. 2025. GenAI content detection task 2: AI vs. human – academic essay authenticity challenge. In *Proceedings of the 1st Workshop on GenAI Content Detection (GenAIDetect)*, Abu Dhabi, UAE. International Conference on Computational Linguistics.

K Clark. 2020. Electra: Pre-training text encoders as discriminators rather than generators. *arXiv preprint arXiv:2003.10555*.

A Conneau. 2019. Unsupervised cross-lingual representation learning at scale. *arXiv preprint arXiv:1911.02116*.

Xavier Glorot, Antoine Bordes, and Yoshua Bengio. 2011. Deep sparse rectifier neural networks. In *Proceedings of the fourteenth international conference on artificial intelligence and statistics*, pages 315–323. JMLR Workshop and Conference Proceedings.

Biyang Guo, Xin Zhang, Ziyuan Wang, Minqi Jiang, Jinran Nie, Yuxuan Ding, Jianwei Yue, and Yupeng Wu. 2023. How close is chatgpt to human experts? comparison corpus, evaluation, and detection. *arXiv preprint arXiv:2301.07597*.

Sergey Ioffe and Christian Szegedy. 2015. Batch normalization: Accelerating deep network training by reducing internal covariate shift. *arXiv preprint arXiv:1502.03167*.

Jacob Devlin Ming-Wei Chang Kenton and Lee Kristina Toutanova. 2019. Bert: Pre-training of deep bidirectional transformers for language understanding. In *Proceedings of naacL-HLT*, volume 1, page 2. Minneapolis, Minnesota.

Mohammed Kutbi, Ali H. Al-Hoorie, and Abbas H. Al-Shammari. 2024. Detecting contract cheating through linguistic fingerprint. *Humanities and Social Sciences Communications*, 11:1–9.

Weixin Liang, Mert Yuksekgonul, Yining Mao, Eric Wu, and James Y. Zou. 2023. Gpt detectors are biased against non-native english writers. *Patterns*, 4.

Yinhan Liu. 2019. Roberta: A robustly optimized bert pretraining approach. *arXiv preprint arXiv:1907.11692*, 364.

Louis Martin, Benjamin Muller, Pedro Javier Ortiz Suárez, Yoann Dupont, Laurent Romary, Éric Villemonte de La Clergerie, Djamé Seddah, and Benoît Sagot. 2019. Camembert: a tasty french language model. *arXiv preprint arXiv:1911.03894*.

Chidimma Opara. 2024. Styloai: Distinguishing ai-generated content with stylometric analysis. In *Artificial Intelligence in Education. Posters and Late Breaking Results, Workshops and Tutorials, Industry and Innovation Tracks, Practitioners, Doctoral Consortium and Blue Sky*, pages 105–114, Cham. Springer Nature Switzerland.

Nitish Srivastava, Geoffrey Hinton, Alex Krizhevsky, Ilya Sutskever, and Ruslan Salakhutdinov. 2014. Dropout: a simple way to prevent neural networks from overfitting. *The journal of machine learning research*, 15(1):1929–1958.

Debora Weber-Wulff, Alla Anohina-Naumeca, Sonja Bjelobaba, Tomáš Foltýnek, Jean Guerrero-Dib, Olumide Popoola, Petr Šigut, and Lorna Waddington. 2023. Testing of detection tools for ai-generated text. *International Journal for Educational Integrity*, 19(1):26.

Hin Boo Wee and James D Reimer. 2023. Non-english academics face inequality via ai-generated essays and countermeasure tools. *BioScience*, 73(7):476–478.

CMI-AIGCX at GenAI Detection Task 2: Leveraging Multilingual Proxy LLMs for Machine-Generated Text Detection in Academic Essays

Kaijie Jiao[1], **Xingyu Yao**[2], **Shixuan Ma**[2], **Sifan Fang**[2], **Zikang Guo**[1], **Benfeng Xu**[1]
Licheng Zhang[1], **Quan Wang**[2], **Yongdong Zhang**[1] and **Zhendong Mao**[1*]
[1]University of Science and Technology of China, Hefei, China
[2]MOE Key Laboratory of Trustworthy Distributed Computing and Service,
Beijing University of Posts and Telecommunications, Beijing, China
zdmao@ustc.edu.cn

Abstract

This paper presents the approach we proposed for GenAI Detection Task 2, which aims to classify a given text as either machine-generated or human-written, with a particular emphasis on academic essays. We participated in subtasks A and B, which focus on detecting English and Arabic essays, respectively. We propose a simple and efficient method for detecting machine-generated essays, where we use the Llama-3.1-8B as a proxy to capture the essence of each token in the text. These essences are processed and classified using a refined feature classification network. Our approach does not require fine-tuning the LLM. Instead, we leverage its extensive multilingual knowledge acquired during pretraining to significantly enhance detection performance. The results validate the effectiveness of our approach and demonstrate that leveraging a proxy model with diverse multilingual knowledge can significantly enhance the detection of machine-generated text across multiple languages, regardless of model size. In Subtask A, we achieved an F1 score of **99.9%**, ranking **first** out of 26 teams. In Subtask B, we achieved an F1 score of 96.5%, placing fourth out of 22 teams, with the same score as the third-place team.

1 Introduction

The capabilities of large language models (LLMs) are advancing rapidly, with models like, ChatGPT (OpenAI, 2022), GPT-4 (OpenAI et al., 2024), Google Gemini (Team et al., 2024), and Llama3.1 (Dubey et al., 2024) generating increasingly fluent and human-like text. Students can easily leverage these models to produce coherent, logical texts for assignments or essays, which profoundly impacts traditional educational methods of learning and evaluation, leading to issues in academic integrity and a weakening of critical thinking skills. However, humans perform only slightly better than random chance in distinguishing between machine-generated and human-written text (Mitchell et al., 2023), underscoring the urgent need for an automated system to identify machine-generated content. To address this, (Chowdhury et al., 2025) organized the GenAI Detection Task 2, a challenge focused on detecting machine-generated academic essays in English and Arabic to uphold academic authenticity and prevent the misuse of LLMs in educational contexts.

Most current methods for detecting machine-generated text can be generally categorized into two approaches (Taguchi et al., 2024): zero-shot detection and supervised detection. The former is time-consuming and suffers from performance degradation when the generation model is unknown, while the latter like RoBERTa-based detection (Guo et al., 2023) requires fine-tuning large models, which is resource-intensive and often lacks multilingual capabilities. In contrast, we employed a multilingual model, such as Llama-3.1-8B (Dubey et al., 2024), as a proxy. By extracting high-dimensional token essences and classifying them with a convolutional neural network, our model achieves high accuracy even without knowledge of the generation model. Furthermore, it does not require fine-tuning and effectively utilizes the multilingual knowledge embedded in the LLM's pretraining, making it a simple, efficient solution for detecting machine-generated text in both English and Arabic.

In Subtask A, our model achieved an F1 score of **0.999**, ranking **first** among 26 teams. In Subtask B, we obtained an F1 score of 0.965, securing fourth place among 22 teams. **In short, our contributions are as follows**: (1) Utilizing the last-layer essences of proxy LLMs as features enhances detection performance. (2) The scale of the proxy LLMs does not significantly improve detection accuracy. (3) Proxy LLMs with broader multilingual knowledge exhibit higher detection accuracy.

*Corresponding author: Zhendong Mao.

Proceedings of the 1st Workshop on GenAI Content Detection (GenAIDetect), pages 290–298
January 19, 2025.

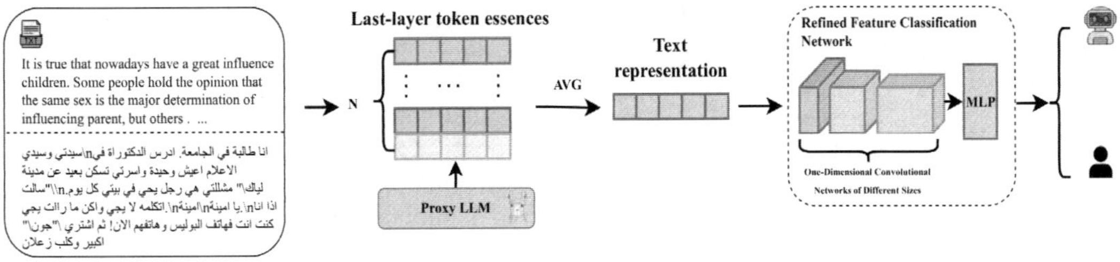

Figure 1: System Architecture

2 Related Work

Machine-generated text detection methods can generally be divided into two categories. The first category is zero-shot detection, where the simplest approach involves calculating the average log-likelihood of a text (Solaiman et al., 2019b), establishing a strong baseline for many zero-shot detection methods. More advanced techniques, such as DetectGPT (Mitchell et al., 2023) and its improved version Fast-DetectGPT (Bao et al., 2023), have shown that machine-generated text tends to fall within regions of negative probability curvature, effectively enabling machine-generated text detection. However, these approaches are often time-intensive and experience a significant performance drop when the generation model is unknown. The second category involves supervised detection methods. For instance, (Zhan et al., 2023) employed a fine-tuned RoBERTa-large (Liu et al., 2019) as a detector, but found it challenging to generalize effectively across different generation models. The T5-sentinel (Chen et al., 2023) addresses text detection by leveraging the next-token prediction capability of T5 (Raffel et al., 2023). Additionally, (Hu et al., 2023) introduced an iterative training process involving both a paraphraser and a detector, aiming to enhance robustness against paraphrasing attacks.

(Bhattacharjee and Liu, 2024) integrated the text to be detected into the prompt and directly asked ChatGPT whether the text is machine-generated or human-written, which is similar to our method, as both approaches leverage LLMs. However, our method does not directly inquire whether a text is machine-generated using LLM, nor does it require fine-tuning the LLM. Instead, it harnesses the high-dimensional multilingual representation capabilities of Llama-3.1-8B and the text is simply input into Llama-3.1-8B to extract token essences (refer to the last layer hidden states) as features, which are then fed into a classifier for final classification.

3 System Overview

To obtain a meaningful representation for the input text, we feed it into a proxy LLM, Llama-3.1-8B (Dubey et al., 2024), to extract essences from the last layer of the proxy LLM and subsequently pass the average of the essences through the Refined Feature Classification Network (RFCN), the overall model structure is shown in Figure 1.

The original text to be detected is first tokenized, with shorter sequences padded and longer ones truncated to a maximum length of 1024 tokens, resulting in the tokenized sequence $\boldsymbol{x} = \{x_1, x_2, \ldots, x_n\}$, the procedure is as follows:

Token essences from the Proxy LLM The tokenized sequence $\boldsymbol{x}$ is input into the Llama-3.1-8B model, which supports text across multiple languages. As $\boldsymbol{x}$ passes through the proxy LLM, it generates hidden states for each token at each layer. We specifically focus on the last-layer token essences (hidden states) of the proxy LLM, which serve as the high-level representations of each token. These token essences encapsulate both their individual meanings and the broader context within the text. Here, the representation quality across different languages is consistent. Supplementary details can be found in the Appendix B. To derive a single representation $\boldsymbol{h}$ of the input text, we take the average of the essences across all n tokens.

Refined Feature Classification Network The averaged representation $\boldsymbol{h}$ is then input into the RFCN for classification. In the first stage, the CNN extracts relevant features from the input through three convolutional and pooling layers, progressively capturing more complex patterns information. In the second stage, the refined features are passed through three fully connected layers, where each layer fine-tunes the representations by learning complex relationships and interactions between

Team	F1
starlight	0.997
saehyunMa	0.993
Fsf	0.993
Team_1-800-SHARED-TASKS	0.990
tesla	0.986
Baseline	0.478
CMI-AIGCX (ours)	**0.999**
w/o LLM	0.673
w/o RFCN	0.982

Table 1: Top: performance on English track. Bottom: ablation study about LLM and RFCN.

Team	F1
msmadi	**0.984**
Team_USTC-BUPT	0.972
starlight	0.965
apricity	0.960
Team_AAST-NLP	0.957
Team_1-800-SHARED-TASKS	0.952
Baseline	0.461
CMI-AIGCX (ours)	0.965
w/o LLM	0.606
w/o RFCN	0.934

Table 2: Top: performance on Arabic track. Bottom: ablation study about LLM and RFCN.

features, ultimately outputting the class probabilities p. The detailed design concept can be found in the Appendix C. The model is trained by minimizing the cross-entropy loss.

4 Experimental setup

4.1 Datesets and Evaluation Metrics

Datasets The dataset consists of essays written by humans and generated by AI, with a specific example shown in Appendix A. The human-written essays were curated from the ETS Corpus of Non-Native Written English (Blanchard et al., 2014). For the AI-generated essays, the organizers used seven models, including GPT-3.5-Turbo (OpenAI, 2022), GPT-4o (OpenAI et al., 2024), GPT-4o-mini (OpenAI et al., 2024), Gemini-1.5 (Team et al., 2024), Llama-3.1 (Dubey et al., 2024), Phi-3.5-mini (Abdin et al., 2024), and Claude-3.5 (Anthropic, 2024), to generate academic essays. The detailed data distribution is provided in Tables 5 and 6 in Appendix E.

Evaluation Metrics For both Subtask A and Subtask B, the primary evaluation metric is macro-F1, calculated as the harmonic mean of precision and recall.

4.2 Training

We utilize Llama as the proxy LLM for obtaining token essences, with the maximum length set to 1024. For the CNN, the input channel is set to 1, where three convolutional layers are employed, with the number of kernels being 32, 64, and 96 respectively. The sizes of their corresponding kernels are 24, 16, and 8. More details are provided in Appendix D.

5 Results

In this section, we present the results of our final submission to demonstrate the effectiveness of our approach, comparing our system's performance with that of several top-performing teams, and highlight key insights from our analysis.

5.1 Subtask A: English track

A total of 26 teams participated in the English track. Due to space constraints, this paper compares and analyzes the systems of several notable teams, including starlight, saehyunMa, Fsf, Team_1-800-SHARED-TASKS, and tesla. The official results are presented in Table 1. Our system achieved an accuracy, recall, and F1 score of 99.9%, securing first place in the official rankings. This outstanding performance underscores the significant superiority and effectiveness of our approach in the detection of machine-generated English texts.

5.2 Subtask B: Arabic track

A total of 22 teams participated in the Arabic track of the competition. This paper only compares and analyzes the systems of selected teams, including msmadi, Team_USTC-BUPT, starlight, CMI-AIGCX (ours), apricity, Team_AAST-NLP, and Team_1-800-SHARED-TASKS. According to the official results (as shown in Table 2), Our system achieved an F1 score of 96.5%, ranking fourth. This result highlights that our approach excels not only in detecting machine-generated English texts but also proves highly effective for Arabic texts, underscoring its robust cross-lingual applicability and efficiency.

5.3 Ablation Study

We conducted a comprehensive ablation experiment to separately assess the effectiveness of LLM token essences and RFCN components within our model. The experimental outcomes, presented in Tables 1 and 2, reveal significant insights. When LLM token essences were excluded and tokens from the XLM-RoBERTa (Solaiman et al., 2019a) were directly input into the RFCN, the F1 scores for Subtasks A and B declined to 67.3% and 60.6%, respectively. This suggests that the multilingual knowledge encoded in LLM token essences during pretraining provides superior feature representations for detecting machine-generated text. Additionally, substituting the RFCN with an MLP resulted in F1 scores of 98.2% and 93.4% for Subtasks A and B, respectively. This underscores the capability of CNNs to capture local dependencies and recognize repetitive patterns across different positions in the text—essential features that enable the RFCN to effectively integrate token essences across entire text sequences. These findings substantiate both the effectiveness and necessity of the components within our proposed approach.

5.4 Scale and Multilingual Knowledge of Proxy Model

We conducted extensive experiments using LLM of varying scales, including 8 billion and 70 billion parameters, and models with different levels of multilingual knowledge, such as Llama-2 and Llama-3.1, as proxy models for subtasks A and B.

The experimental results are presented in Tables 3 and 4. Notably, the Llama-3-8B model, despite being approximately one-tenth the size of Llama-2-70B, achieved F1 scores of 99.2% and 93.8% for Subtasks A and B, respectively, outperforming Llama-2-70B by 7.1% and 1.9%. When comparing Llama-3-8B to Llama-3-70B, despite the latter's larger scale, the performance improvement was marginal, with increases of only 0.2% and 1.4% for Subtasks A and B, respectively. These results suggest that the scale of the proxy model is not the primary determinant of performance in detecting machine-generated text.

Furthermore, when the proxy model was Llama-3.1-8B, the F1 score for subtask A was 99.9%, which was 7.8% higher than Llama-2-70B and 0.5% higher than Llama-3-70B. For subtask B, the F1 score was 96.5%, which was 4.6% more than Llama-2-70B and 1.3% more than Llama-3-70B.

Proxy Model	F1
Llama-2-70B	0.921
Llama-3-8B	0.992
Llama-3-70B	0.994
Llama-3.1-8B (ours)	**0.999**

Table 3: Performance on English track using different scale and multilingual knowledge of proxy model.

Proxy Model	F1
Llama-2-70B	0.919
Llama-3-8B	0.938
Llama-3-70B	0.952
Llama-3.1-8B (ours)	**0.965**

Table 4: Performance on Arabic track using different scale and multilingual knowledge of proxy model.

This indicates that the performance of multilingual machine-generated text detection is not solely dependent on the scale of the model but is significantly influenced by the richness of multilingual knowledge within the LLMs.

Upon further analysis, we found that Llama-2-70B's training data was primarily in English, which limits its multilingual capabilities. While Llama-3-8B and 70B were pre-trained on multilingual data, they were initially intended for English use. In contrast, the Llama-3.1 series was pre-trained on a corpus of 15 trillion multilingual tokens, making it a more effective proxy model for detecting machine-generated essays in both English and Arabic. More details are in Appendices F.1 and F.2.

6 Conclusion

This paper presents our approach and results for the GenAI Detection Task 2, where our system ranked first in the English track and tied for third in the Arabic subtask. We adopted an efficient strategy, using proxy LLM to generate fused token essences, which were then classified via a refined feature classification network. This method capitalizes on the multilingual representational capacity of LLMs without fine-tuning, enhancing performance in detecting machine-generated text. Our findings further underscore that proxy models with extensive multilingual knowledge markedly improve detection in multilingual contexts. Future work will explore the broader application of multilingual LLMs in language generation detection and investigate optimized strategies to leverage LLM token essences.

Acknowledgements

This work is supported by the National Natural Science Foundation of China (No.62222212, 62121002).

Limitations

Given the limited number of languages in the dataset, we validated the effectiveness of our model only on machine-generated texts in English and Arabic. Future experiments will extend this validation to a broader range of languages. Our model has demonstrated outstanding performance on Llama-3.1-8B. Furthermore, an analysis of the results from Llama-3-8B and Llama-3-70B indicates that increasing the model size does not significantly improve performance, which is why we did not conduct experiments on Llama-3.1-70B. Moving forward, we plan to experiment with additional LLMs on more diverse datasets to determine which proxy LLM is most effective for detecting machine-generated texts. Since the official has not released the true labels of the test data, it is impossible to analyze the specific error cases. We will further optimize our results after the true labels of the test dataset are released.

References

Marah I Abdin, Sam Ade Jacobs, Ammar Ahmad Awan, Jyoti Aneja, Ahmed Awadallah, Hany Hassan Awadalla, Nguyen Bach, Amit Bahree, Arash Bakhtiari, Harkirat Behl, Alon Benhaim, Misha Bilenko, Johan Bjorck, Sébastien Bubeck, Martin Cai, Caio César Teodoro Mendes, Weizhu Chen, Vishrav Chaudhary, Parul Chopra, Allie Del Giorno, Gustavo de Rosa, Matthew Dixon, Ronen Eldan, Dan Iter, Abhishek Goswami, Suriya Gunasekar, Emman Haider, Junheng Hao, Russell J. Hewett, Jamie Huynh, Mojan Javaheripi, Xin Jin, Piero Kauffmann, Nikos Karampatziakis, Dongwoo Kim, Mahmoud Khademi, Lev Kurilenko, James R. Lee, Yin Tat Lee, Yuanzhi Li, Chen Liang, Weishung Liu, Xihui (Eric) Lin, Zeqi Lin, Piyush Madan, Arindam Mitra, Hardik Modi, Anh Nguyen, Brandon Norick, Barun Patra, Daniel Perez-Becker, Thomas Portet, Reid Pryzant, Heyang Qin, Marko Radmilac, Corby Rosset, Sambudha Roy, Olli Saarikivi, Amin Saied, Adil Salim, Michael Santacroce, Shital Shah, Ning Shang, Hiteshi Sharma, Xia Song, Olatunji Ruwase, Xin Wang, Rachel Ward, Guanhua Wang, Philipp Witte, Michael Wyatt, Can Xu, Jiahang Xu, Weijian Xu, Sonali Yadav, Fan Yang, Ziyi Yang, Donghan Yu, Chengruidong Zhang, Cyril Zhang, Jianwen Zhang, Li Lyna Zhang, Yi Zhang, Yunan Zhang, and Xiren Zhou. 2024. Phi-3 technical report: A highly capable language model locally on your phone. Technical Report MSR-TR-2024-12, Microsoft.

Anthropic. 2024. Claude 3.5 sonnet.

Guangsheng Bao, Yanbin Zhao, Zhiyang Teng, Linyi Yang, and Yue Zhang. 2023. Fast-detectgpt: Efficient zero-shot detection of machine-generated text via conditional probability curvature. *arXiv preprint arXiv:2310.05130*.

Amrita Bhattacharjee and Huan Liu. 2024. Fighting fire with fire: can chatgpt detect ai-generated text? *ACM SIGKDD Explorations Newsletter*, 25(2):14–21.

Daniel Blanchard, Joel Tetreault, Derrick Higgins, Aoife Cahill, and Martin Chodorow. 2014. Ets corpus of non-native written english.

Yutian Chen, Hao Kang, Vivian Zhai, Liangze Li, Rita Singh, and Bhiksha Raj. 2023. Token prediction as implicit classification to identify LLM-generated text. In *Proceedings of the 2023 Conference on Empirical Methods in Natural Language Processing*, pages 13112–13120, Singapore. Association for Computational Linguistics.

Shammur Absar Chowdhury, Hind Al-Merekhi, Mucahid Kutlu, Kaan Efe Keleş, Fatema Ahmad, Tasnim Mohiuddin, Georgios Mikros, and Firoj Alam. 2025. GenAI content detection task 2: AI vs. human – academic essay authenticity challenge. In *Proceedings of the 1st Workshop on GenAI Content Detection (GenAIDetect)*, Abu Dhabi, UAE. International Conference on Computational Linguistics.

Abhimanyu Dubey, Abhinav Jauhri, Abhinav Pandey, Abhishek Kadian, Ahmad Al-Dahle, Aiesha Letman, Akhil Mathur, Alan Schelten, Amy Yang, Angela Fan, Anirudh Goyal, Anthony Hartshorn, Aobo Yang, Archi Mitra, Archie Sravankumar, Artem Korenev, Arthur Hinsvark, Arun Rao, Aston Zhang, Aurelien Rodriguez, Austen Gregerson, Ava Spataru, Baptiste Roziere, Bethany Biron, Binh Tang, Bobbie Chern, Charlotte Caucheteux, Chaya Nayak, Chloe Bi, Chris Marra, Chris McConnell, Christian Keller, Christophe Touret, Chunyang Wu, Corinne Wong, Cristian Canton Ferrer, Cyrus Nikolaidis, Damien Allonsius, Daniel Song, Danielle Pintz, Danny Livshits, David Esiobu, Dhruv Choudhary, Dhruv Mahajan, Diego Garcia-Olano, Diego Perino, Dieuwke Hupkes, Egor Lakomkin, Ehab AlBadawy, Elina Lobanova, Emily Dinan, Eric Michael Smith, Filip Radenovic, Frank Zhang, Gabriel Synnaeve, Gabrielle Lee, Georgia Lewis Anderson, Graeme Nail, Gregoire Mialon, Guan Pang, Guillem Cucurell, Hailey Nguyen, Hannah Korevaar, Hu Xu, Hugo Touvron, Iliyan Zarov, Imanol Arrieta Ibarra, Isabel Kloumann, Ishan Misra, Ivan Evtimov, Jade Copet, Jaewon Lee, Jan Geffert, Jana Vranes, Jason Park, Jay Mahadeokar, Jeet Shah, Jelmer van der Linde, Jennifer Billock, Jenny Hong, Jenya Lee, Jeremy Fu, Jianfeng Chi, Jianyu Huang, Jiawen Liu, Jie Wang, Jiecao Yu, Joanna Bitton, Joe Spisak, Jongsoo Park, Joseph Rocca, Joshua Johnstun, Joshua Saxe, Junteng Jia,

Kalyan Vasuden Alwala, Kartikeya Upasani, Kate Plawiak, Ke Li, Kenneth Heafield, Kevin Stone, Khalid El-Arini, Krithika Iyer, Kshitiz Malik, Kuenley Chiu, Kunal Bhalla, Lauren Rantala-Yeary, Laurens van der Maaten, Lawrence Chen, Liang Tan, Liz Jenkins, Louis Martin, Lovish Madaan, Lubo Malo, Lukas Blecher, Lukas Landzaat, Luke de Oliveira, Madeline Muzzi, Mahesh Pasupuleti, Mannat Singh, Manohar Paluri, Marcin Kardas, Mathew Oldham, Mathieu Rita, Maya Pavlova, Melanie Kambadur, Mike Lewis, Min Si, Mitesh Kumar Singh, Mona Hassan, Naman Goyal, Narjes Torabi, Nikolay Bashlykov, Nikolay Bogoychev, Niladri Chatterji, Olivier Duchenne, Onur Çelebi, Patrick Alrassy, Pengchuan Zhang, Pengwei Li, Petar Vasic, Peter Weng, Prajjwal Bhargava, Pratik Dubal, Praveen Krishnan, Punit Singh Koura, Puxin Xu, Qing He, Qingxiao Dong, Ragavan Srinivasan, Raj Ganapathy, Ramon Calderer, Ricardo Silveira Cabral, Robert Stojnic, Roberta Raileanu, Rohit Girdhar, Rohit Patel, Romain Sauvestre, Ronnie Polidoro, Roshan Sumbaly, Ross Taylor, Ruan Silva, Rui Hou, Rui Wang, Saghar Hosseini, Sahana Chennabasappa, Sanjay Singh, Sean Bell, Seohyun Sonia Kim, Sergey Edunov, Shaoliang Nie, Sharan Narang, Sharath Raparthy, Sheng Shen, Shengye Wan, Shruti Bhosale, Shun Zhang, Simon Vandenhende, Soumya Batra, Spencer Whitman, Sten Sootla, Stephane Collot, Suchin Gururangan, Sydney Borodinsky, Tamar Herman, Tara Fowler, Tarek Sheasha, Thomas Georgiou, Thomas Scialom, Tobias Speckbacher, Todor Mihaylov, Tong Xiao, Ujjwal Karn, Vedanuj Goswami, Vibhor Gupta, Vignesh Ramanathan, Viktor Kerkez, Vincent Gonguet, Virginie Do, Vish Vogeti, Vladan Petrovic, Weiwei Chu, Wenhan Xiong, Wenyin Fu, Whitney Meers, Xavier Martinet, Xiaodong Wang, Xiaoqing Ellen Tan, Xinfeng Xie, Xuchao Jia, Xuewei Wang, Yaelle Goldschlag, Yashesh Gaur, Yasmine Babaei, Yi Wen, Yiwen Song, Yuchen Zhang, Yue Li, Yuning Mao, Zacharie Delpierre Coudert, Zheng Yan, Zhengxing Chen, Zoe Papakipos, Aaditya Singh, Aaron Grattafiori, Abha Jain, Adam Kelsey, Adam Shajnfeld, Adithya Gangidi, Adolfo Victoria, Ahuva Goldstand, Ajay Menon, Ajay Sharma, Alex Boesenberg, Alex Vaughan, Alexei Baevski, Allie Feinstein, Amanda Kallet, Amit Sangani, Anam Yunus, Andrei Lupu, Andres Alvarado, Andrew Caples, Andrew Gu, Andrew Ho, Andrew Poulton, Andrew Ryan, Ankit Ramchandani, Annie Franco, Aparajita Saraf, Arkabandhu Chowdhury, Ashley Gabriel, Ashwin Bharambe, Assaf Eisenman, Azadeh Yazdan, Beau James, Ben Maurer, Benjamin Leonhardi, Bernie Huang, Beth Loyd, Beto De Paola, Bhargavi Paranjape, Bing Liu, Bo Wu, Boyu Ni, Braden Hancock, Bram Wasti, Brandon Spence, Brani Stojkovic, Brian Gamido, Britt Montalvo, Carl Parker, Carly Burton, Catalina Mejia, Changhan Wang, Changkyu Kim, Chao Zhou, Chester Hu, Ching-Hsiang Chu, Chris Cai, Chris Tindal, Christoph Feichtenhofer, Damon Civin, Dana Beaty, Daniel Kreymer, Daniel Li, Danny Wyatt, David Adkins, David Xu, Davide Testuggine, Delia David, Devi Parikh, Diana Liskovich, Didem Foss, Dingkang Wang, Duc Le, Dustin Holland, Edward Dowling, Eissa Jamil, Elaine Montgomery, Eleonora Presani, Emily Hahn, Emily Wood, Erik Brinkman, Esteban Arcaute, Evan Dunbar, Evan Smothers, Fei Sun, Felix Kreuk, Feng Tian, Firat Ozgenel, Francesco Caggioni, Francisco Guzmán, Frank Kanayet, Frank Seide, Gabriela Medina Florez, Gabriella Schwarz, Gada Badeer, Georgia Swee, Gil Halpern, Govind Thattai, Grant Herman, Grigory Sizov, Guangyi, Zhang, Guna Lakshminarayanan, Hamid Shojanazeri, Han Zou, Hannah Wang, Hanwen Zha, Haroun Habeeb, Harrison Rudolph, Helen Suk, Henry Aspegren, Hunter Goldman, Ibrahim Damlaj, Igor Molybog, Igor Tufanov, Irina-Elena Veliche, Itai Gat, Jake Weissman, James Geboski, James Kohli, Japhet Asher, Jean-Baptiste Gaya, Jeff Marcus, Jeff Tang, Jennifer Chan, Jenny Zhen, Jeremy Reizenstein, Jeremy Teboul, Jessica Zhong, Jian Jin, Jingyi Yang, Joe Cummings, Jon Carvill, Jon Shepard, Jonathan McPhie, Jonathan Torres, Josh Ginsburg, Junjie Wang, Kai Wu, Kam Hou U, Karan Saxena, Karthik Prasad, Kartikay Khandelwal, Katayoun Zand, Kathy Matosich, Kaushik Veeraraghavan, Kelly Michelena, Keqian Li, Kun Huang, Kunal Chawla, Kushal Lakhotia, Kyle Huang, Lailin Chen, Lakshya Garg, Lavender A, Leandro Silva, Lee Bell, Lei Zhang, Liangpeng Guo, Licheng Yu, Liron Moshkovich, Luca Wehrstedt, Madian Khabsa, Manav Avalani, Manish Bhatt, Maria Tsimpoukelli, Martynas Mankus, Matan Hasson, Matthew Lennie, Matthias Reso, Maxim Groshev, Maxim Naumov, Maya Lathi, Meghan Keneally, Michael L. Seltzer, Michal Valko, Michelle Restrepo, Mihir Patel, Mik Vyatskov, Mikayel Samvelyan, Mike Clark, Mike Macey, Mike Wang, Miquel Jubert Hermoso, Mo Metanat, Mohammad Rastegari, Munish Bansal, Nandhini Santhanam, Natascha Parks, Natasha White, Navyata Bawa, Nayan Singhal, Nick Egebo, Nicolas Usunier, Nikolay Pavlovich Laptev, Ning Dong, Ning Zhang, Norman Cheng, Oleg Chernoguz, Olivia Hart, Omkar Salpekar, Ozlem Kalinli, Parkin Kent, Parth Parekh, Paul Saab, Pavan Balaji, Pedro Rittner, Philip Bontrager, Pierre Roux, Piotr Dollar, Polina Zvyagina, Prashant Ratanchandani, Pritish Yuvraj, Qian Liang, Rachad Alao, Rachel Rodriguez, Rafi Ayub, Raghotham Murthy, Raghu Nayani, Rahul Mitra, Raymond Li, Rebekkah Hogan, Robin Battey, Rocky Wang, Rohan Maheswari, Russ Howes, Ruty Rinott, Sai Jayesh Bondu, Samyak Datta, Sara Chugh, Sara Hunt, Sargun Dhillon, Sasha Sidorov, Satadru Pan, Saurabh Verma, Seiji Yamamoto, Sharadh Ramaswamy, Shaun Lindsay, Shaun Lindsay, Sheng Feng, Shenghao Lin, Shengxin Cindy Zha, Shiva Shankar, Shuqiang Zhang, Shuqiang Zhang, Sinong Wang, Sneha Agarwal, Soji Sajuyigbe, Soumith Chintala, Stephanie Max, Stephen Chen, Steve Kehoe, Steve Satterfield, Sudarshan Govindaprasad, Sumit Gupta, Sungmin Cho, Sunny Virk, Suraj Subramanian, Sy Choudhury, Sydney Goldman, Tal Remez, Tamar Glaser, Tamara Best, Thilo Kohler, Thomas Robinson, Tianhe Li, Tianjun Zhang, Tim Matthews, Timothy Chou, Tzook Shaked, Varun Vontimitta, Victoria Ajayi, Victoria Montanez, Vijai Mohan, Vinay Satish Kumar, Vishal Mangla, Vítor Albiero, Vlad Ionescu, Vlad Poenaru, Vlad Tiberiu Mihailescu, Vladimir Ivanov, Wei Li,

Wenchen Wang, Wenwen Jiang, Wes Bouaziz, Will Constable, Xiaocheng Tang, Xiaofang Wang, Xiaojian Wu, Xiaolan Wang, Xide Xia, Xilun Wu, Xinbo Gao, Yanjun Chen, Ye Hu, Ye Jia, Ye Qi, Yenda Li, Yilin Zhang, Ying Zhang, Yossi Adi, Youngjin Nam, Yu, Wang, Yuchen Hao, Yundi Qian, Yuzi He, Zach Rait, Zachary DeVito, Zef Rosnbrick, Zhaoduo Wen, Zhenyu Yang, and Zhiwei Zhao. 2024. The llama 3 herd of models. *Preprint*, arXiv:2407.21783.

Biyang Guo, Xin Zhang, Ziyuan Wang, Minqi Jiang, Jinran Nie, Yuxuan Ding, Jianwei Yue, and Yupeng Wu. 2023. How close is chatgpt to human experts? comparison corpus, evaluation, and detection. *arXiv preprint arXiv:2301.07597*.

Xiaomeng Hu, Pin-Yu Chen, and Tsung-Yi Ho. 2023. Radar: Robust ai-text detection via adversarial learning. *Advances in Neural Information Processing Systems*, 36:15077–15095.

Yinhan Liu, Myle Ott, Naman Goyal, Jingfei Du, Mandar Joshi, Danqi Chen, Omer Levy, Mike Lewis, Luke Zettlemoyer, and Veselin Stoyanov. 2019. Roberta: A robustly optimized bert pretraining approach. *Preprint*, arXiv:1907.11692.

Eric Mitchell, Yoonho Lee, Alexander Khazatsky, Christopher D Manning, and Chelsea Finn. 2023. Detectgpt: Zero-shot machine-generated text detection using probability curvature. In *International Conference on Machine Learning*, pages 24950–24962. PMLR.

OpenAI. 2022. Chatgpt: Optimizing language models for dialogue.

OpenAI, Josh Achiam, Steven Adler, Sandhini Agarwal, Lama Ahmad, Ilge Akkaya, Florencia Leoni Aleman, Diogo Almeida, Janko Altenschmidt, Sam Altman, Shyamal Anadkat, Red Avila, Igor Babuschkin, Suchir Balaji, Valerie Balcom, Paul Baltescu, Haiming Bao, Mohammad Bavarian, Jeff Belgum, Irwan Bello, Jake Berdine, Gabriel Bernadett-Shapiro, Christopher Berner, Lenny Bogdonoff, Oleg Boiko, Madelaine Boyd, Anna-Luisa Brakman, Greg Brockman, Tim Brooks, Miles Brundage, Kevin Button, Trevor Cai, Rosie Campbell, Andrew Cann, Brittany Carey, Chelsea Carlson, Rory Carmichael, Brooke Chan, Che Chang, Fotis Chantzis, Derek Chen, Sully Chen, Ruby Chen, Jason Chen, Mark Chen, Ben Chess, Chester Cho, Casey Chu, Hyung Won Chung, Dave Cummings, Jeremiah Currier, Yunxing Dai, Cory Decareaux, Thomas Degry, Noah Deutsch, Damien Deville, Arka Dhar, David Dohan, Steve Dowling, Sheila Dunning, Adrien Ecoffet, Atty Eleti, Tyna Eloundou, David Farhi, Liam Fedus, Niko Felix, Simón Posada Fishman, Juston Forte, Isabella Fulford, Leo Gao, Elie Georges, Christian Gibson, Vik Goel, Tarun Gogineni, Gabriel Goh, Rapha Gontijo-Lopes, Jonathan Gordon, Morgan Grafstein, Scott Gray, Ryan Greene, Joshua Gross, Shixiang Shane Gu, Yufei Guo, Chris Hallacy, Jesse Han, Jeff Harris, Yuchen He, Mike Heaton, Johannes Heidecke, Chris Hesse, Alan Hickey, Wade Hickey, Peter Hoeschele, Brandon Houghton, Kenny Hsu, Shengli Hu, Xin Hu, Joost Huizinga, Shantanu Jain, Shawn Jain, Joanne Jang, Angela Jiang, Roger Jiang, Haozhun Jin, Denny Jin, Shino Jomoto, Billie Jonn, Heewoo Jun, Tomer Kaftan, Łukasz Kaiser, Ali Kamali, Ingmar Kanitscheider, Nitish Shirish Keskar, Tabarak Khan, Logan Kilpatrick, Jong Wook Kim, Christina Kim, Yongjik Kim, Jan Hendrik Kirchner, Jamie Kiros, Matt Knight, Daniel Kokotajlo, Łukasz Kondraciuk, Andrew Kondrich, Aris Konstantinidis, Kyle Kosic, Gretchen Krueger, Vishal Kuo, Michael Lampe, Ikai Lan, Teddy Lee, Jan Leike, Jade Leung, Daniel Levy, Chak Ming Li, Rachel Lim, Molly Lin, Stephanie Lin, Mateusz Litwin, Theresa Lopez, Ryan Lowe, Patricia Lue, Anna Makanju, Kim Malfacini, Sam Manning, Todor Markov, Yaniv Markovski, Bianca Martin, Katie Mayer, Andrew Mayne, Bob McGrew, Scott Mayer McKinney, Christine McLeavey, Paul McMillan, Jake McNeil, David Medina, Aalok Mehta, Jacob Menick, Luke Metz, Andrey Mishchenko, Pamela Mishkin, Vinnie Monaco, Evan Morikawa, Daniel Mossing, Tong Mu, Mira Murati, Oleg Murk, David Mély, Ashvin Nair, Reiichiro Nakano, Rajeev Nayak, Arvind Neelakantan, Richard Ngo, Hyeonwoo Noh, Long Ouyang, Cullen O'Keefe, Jakub Pachocki, Alex Paino, Joe Palermo, Ashley Pantuliano, Giambattista Parascandolo, Joel Parish, Emy Parparita, Alex Passos, Mikhail Pavlov, Andrew Peng, Adam Perelman, Filipe de Avila Belbute Peres, Michael Petrov, Henrique Ponde de Oliveira Pinto, Michael, Pokorny, Michelle Pokrass, Vitchyr H. Pong, Tolly Powell, Alethea Power, Boris Power, Elizabeth Proehl, Raul Puri, Alec Radford, Jack Rae, Aditya Ramesh, Cameron Raymond, Francis Real, Kendra Rimbach, Carl Ross, Bob Rotsted, Henri Roussez, Nick Ryder, Mario Saltarelli, Ted Sanders, Shibani Santurkar, Girish Sastry, Heather Schmidt, David Schnurr, John Schulman, Daniel Selsam, Kyla Sheppard, Toki Sherbakov, Jessica Shieh, Sarah Shoker, Pranav Shyam, Szymon Sidor, Eric Sigler, Maddie Simens, Jordan Sitkin, Katarina Slama, Ian Sohl, Benjamin Sokolowsky, Yang Song, Natalie Staudacher, Felipe Petroski Such, Natalie Summers, Ilya Sutskever, Jie Tang, Nikolas Tezak, Madeleine B. Thompson, Phil Tillet, Amin Tootoonchian, Elizabeth Tseng, Preston Tuggle, Nick Turley, Jerry Tworek, Juan Felipe Cerón Uribe, Andrea Vallone, Arun Vijayvergiya, Chelsea Voss, Carroll Wainwright, Justin Jay Wang, Alvin Wang, Ben Wang, Jonathan Ward, Jason Wei, CJ Weinmann, Akila Welihinda, Peter Welinder, Jiayi Weng, Lilian Weng, Matt Wiethoff, Dave Willner, Clemens Winter, Samuel Wolrich, Hannah Wong, Lauren Workman, Sherwin Wu, Jeff Wu, Michael Wu, Kai Xiao, Tao Xu, Sarah Yoo, Kevin Yu, Qiming Yuan, Wojciech Zaremba, Rowan Zellers, Chong Zhang, Marvin Zhang, Shengjia Zhao, Tianhao Zheng, Juntang Zhuang, William Zhuk, and Barret Zoph. 2024. Gpt-4 technical report. *Preprint*, arXiv:2303.08774.

Colin Raffel, Noam Shazeer, Adam Roberts, Katherine Lee, Sharan Narang, Michael Matena, Yanqi Zhou, Wei Li, and Peter J. Liu. 2023. Exploring the limits of transfer learning with a unified text-to-text transformer. *Preprint*, arXiv:1910.10683.

Irene Solaiman, Miles Brundage, Jack Clark, Amanda Askell, Ariel Herbert-Voss, Jeff Wu, Alec Radford, Gretchen Krueger, Jong Wook Kim, Sarah Kreps, Miles McCain, Alex Newhouse, Jason Blazakis, Kris McGuffie, and Jasmine Wang. 2019a. Release strategies and the social impacts of language models. *Preprint*, arXiv:1908.09203.

Irene Solaiman, Miles Brundage, Jack Clark, Amanda Askell, Ariel Herbert-Voss, Jeff Wu, Alec Radford, Gretchen Krueger, Jong Wook Kim, Sarah Kreps, et al. 2019b. Release strategies and the social impacts of language models. *arXiv preprint arXiv:1908.09203*.

Kaito Taguchi, Yujie Gu, and Kouichi Sakurai. 2024. The impact of prompts on zero-shot detection of ai-generated text. *arXiv preprint arXiv:2403.20127*.

Gemini Team, Rohan Anil, Sebastian Borgeaud, Jean-Baptiste Alayrac, Jiahui Yu, Radu Soricut, Johan Schalkwyk, Andrew M. Dai, Anja Hauth, Katie Millican, David Silver, Melvin Johnson, Ioannis Antonoglou, Julian Schrittwieser, Amelia Glaese, Jilin Chen, Emily Pitler, Timothy Lillicrap, Angeliki Lazaridou, Orhan Firat, and James Molloy. 2024. Gemini: A family of highly capable multimodal models. *Preprint*, arXiv:2312.11805.

Hugo Touvron, Louis Martin, Kevin Stone, Peter Albert, Amjad Almahairi, Yasmine Babaei, Nikolay Bashlykov, Soumya Batra, Prajjwal Bhargava, Shruti Bhosale, Dan Bikel, Lukas Blecher, Cristian Canton Ferrer, Moya Chen, Guillem Cucurull, David Esiobu, Jude Fernandes, Jeremy Fu, Wenyin Fu, Brian Fuller, Cynthia Gao, Vedanuj Goswami, Naman Goyal, Anthony Hartshorn, Saghar Hosseini, Rui Hou, Hakan Inan, Marcin Kardas, Viktor Kerkez, Madian Khabsa, Isabel Kloumann, Artem Korenev, Punit Singh Koura, Marie-Anne Lachaux, Thibaut Lavril, Jenya Lee, Diana Liskovich, Yinghai Lu, Yuning Mao, Xavier Martinet, Todor Mihaylov, Pushkar Mishra, Igor Molybog, Yixin Nie, Andrew Poulton, Jeremy Reizenstein, Rashi Rungta, Kalyan Saladi, Alan Schelten, Ruan Silva, Eric Michael Smith, Ranjan Subramanian, Xiaoqing Ellen Tan, Binh Tang, Ross Taylor, Adina Williams, Jian Xiang Kuan, Puxin Xu, Zheng Yan, Iliyan Zarov, Yuchen Zhang, Angela Fan, Melanie Kambadur, Sharan Narang, Aurelien Rodriguez, Robert Stojnic, Sergey Edunov, and Thomas Scialom. 2023. Llama 2: Open foundation and fine-tuned chat models. *Preprint*, arXiv:2307.09288.

Haolan Zhan, Xuanli He, Qiongkai Xu, Yuxiang Wu, and Pontus Stenetorp. 2023. G3detector: General gpt-generated text detector. *Preprint*, arXiv:2305.12680.

A Example of English and Arabic essays

We randomly select an essay from the English and Arabic datasets, as shown in Figures 2 and 3.

I disagree with the statement that the development of artificial intelligence will create more jobs than it will eliminate. While it is true that AI has the potential to automate certain tasks and improve efficiency, I believe that its development will ultimately lead to more job losses than gains.\n\nOne of the main reasons for this is that many jobs that are currently done by humans can be easily automated with the help of AI. For example, self-service kiosks have already replaced many cashiers in retail stores, and AI-powered customer service chatbots are becoming increasingly common. Additionally, many manufacturing jobs are being replaced by robots and other machines that can perform tasks faster and more accurately than humans. These job losses will not be offset by the creation of new jobs, as the demand for human workers in these areas will decrease.\n\nFurthermore, while AI may create some new jobs in fields such as AI development and deployment, these jobs will likely require highly specialized skills and education. Many people may not have the necessary skills to compete for these jobs, and therefore will not benefit from the development of AI. This could lead to a widening of the gap between the rich and the poor, as those who have the skills and education to work with AI will be better off than those who do not.\n\nIn conclusion, while AI has the potential to bring many benefits, I believe that its development will ultimately lead to more job losses than gains. As AI becomes more widespread, it is likely to automate many jobs that are currently done by humans, leading to significant unemployment. Therefore, policymakers and educators must take steps to prepare workers for the changing job market and to ensure that the benefits of AI are shared by all.

Figure 2: English machine-generated essay

قبل .حمله مع واشتركنا التصريح واخذنا وذهبنا النظام تخالف لا لكي تصريح يتطلب والحج الحرام البيت في الحج الى ذهبن
طويلا انتزرنا الحمله حافلة الى وصلنا ما نوعاً متعبا الاغراض تجهيز فكان واجهناها التي الصعوبات بعض هناك كان الذهاب
لانتظاره فنضطر المحدده بالمواعيد لاياتي البعض كان تأخرنا في الرئيسي السبب كان وهذا متأخرين وصل البعض وكان
كانت سفوريه والاخر القران يقرأ البعض وكان جداً طويلا الطريق كان مكه الى وانطلقنا لتاخر أعذار لديه يكون والبعض
نفسي في كبيرة هذه الأجواء أثر كان الممتعه والفعاليات المسابقات بعض الطريق منتصف في وكان جميله ايمانية اجواء
فقط الحج من افضل بانها قال وسلم عليه الله صلى والرسول العمرة الحجو كانت لان طواف فأخذنا محرمين مكه الى وصلنا
الى توجهنا ثم الغروب حتى فيها ومكثنا عرفه الى التاسع اليوم في ذهبنا ثم ومن الثامن اليوم حتى مكه في ومكثنا .فعله ما وهو
والمغرب العشاء وصلينا مزدلفه

Figure 3: Human-written Arabic essay

B Ensure consistent representation quality across different languages

The Llama-3.1-8B model is pretrained on a large-scale multilingual corpus, which enables it to learn the structures, syntactic patterns, and semantic relationships across a variety of languages. This multilingual training allows the model to generate token embeddings that capture both language-specific and language-independent features. Even though the model encounters tokens from different languages, it maps them into a shared embedding space, ensuring that semantically similar words are represented in a comparable way. This approach ensures consistent representation quality across different languages.

C The detailed design concept of the RFCN

The motivation behind designing the RFCN is to better leverage the local features of the text for classification, which are essential for distinguishing between human and machine-generated text. For the task of AI-generated text detection, the choice of three convolutional layers and specific kernel sizes (24, 16, 8) is aimed at effectively extracting text features. Using three convolutional layers allows for the extraction of progressively complex features from the text. In AI-generated text detection, this is crucial for capturing both simple language patterns and more complex syntactic structures and semantic information. Each layer's features enhance the model's ability to detect subtle differences in AI-generated text. The first kernel (24-sized) has a smaller receptive field, primarily capturing smaller local text patterns. The second kernel (16-sized) provides a medium receptive field, targeting phrase-level structural patterns. The last kernel (8-sized) features the largest receptive field, integrating more contextual information to focus on long-range dependencies. These specific kernel sizes and their corresponding receptive fields enable the model to extract features at multiple levels of granularity.

D Detailed Experimental Setup

We use the AdamW optimizer with a linear warmup decay learning schedule and a dropout of 0.1. The batch size and learning rate are set to 128 and 3e-4, and the model is trained for 20 epochs. During the training of our model, the training and validation datasets for Subtasks A and B were merged at a ratio of 19:1 to form new training and validation sets. We monitored the accuracy on the validation set to select the checkpoint with the best performance. The final training dataset consisted of the complete training and validation sets for each subtask, with the entire validation set evaluated after each training epoch. We selected the model that performed best on the validation set as the final model.

E Datasets

Datasets The detailed distribution of data categories in the dataset is as follows. The proportion of human and AI categories in the test set has not yet been disclosed, and as such, the table only presents the total number of samples in the test set. For a comprehensive breakdown of the data distribution, please refer to (Chowdhury et al., 2025).

	Train	Dev	Test
human	629	1235	
AI	1467	391	
Total	2096	1626	1129

Table 5: Dataset division of subtask A.

	Train	Dev	Test
human	1145	182	
AI	925	299	
Total	2070	481	293

Table 6: Dataset division of subtask B.

F Llama

In this section, we provide an overview of the pre-training corpora of Llama-2, Llama-3, and Llama-3.1, along with their intended purposes, which helps to explain the differences in their performance on multilingual tasks.

F.1 Llama-2

Llama-2 (Touvron et al., 2023), released by Meta in 2023, is an open-source suite of LLMs available in configurations of 7 billion (7B), 13 billion (13B), and 70 billion (70B) parameters. The model's pre-training involved approximately 2 trillion tokens, marking a 40% increase in data volume compared to Llama-1. These tokens were drawn from publicly accessible online sources, explicitly excluding data from the products or services of Meta. In addition to an expanded context window, increasing from 2,048 to 4,096 tokens, the 70B model also implemented Grouped-Query Attention (GQA) to enhance inference capabilities and computational efficiency. However, the pre-training corpus of Llama-2-70B is primarily in English, making it unsuitable for multilingual tasks.

F.2 Llama-3 and Llama-3.1

Llama-3 (Dubey et al., 2024) represents Meta's most recent advancement in LLM technology, launched in 2024 with parameter configurations of 8 billion (8B), 70 billion (70B), and later extended to 405 billion (405B) parameters in the Llama-3.1 series. Although Llama-3-8B and 70B were pre-trained on multilingual data, they were intended for commercial and research use in English, which made them more optimized for English-language tasks. In contrast, the Llama-3.1 series was pre-trained on a significantly larger corpus comprising approximately 15 trillion tokens (Dubey et al., 2024), far exceeding the corpus size of Llama-2. This expanded corpus includes data across a diverse set of over 30 languages, such as English, German, French, Italian, Portuguese, Hindi, Spanish, and Thai. Llama 3.1 is intended for commercial and research use in multiple languages, which we believe significantly enhances its adaptability to multilingual tasks when employed as a proxy model.

EssayDetect at GenAI Detection Task 2: Guardians of Academic Integrity: Multilingual Detection of AI-Generated Essays

Shifali Agrahari, Subhashi Jayant,
Saurabh Kumar, and Sanasam Ranbir Singh
Department of Computer Science and Engineering
Indian Institute of Technology Guwahati
{a.shifali, j.subhashi, saurabh1003, ranbir}@iitg.ac.in

Abstract

Detecting AI-generated text in the field of academia is becoming very prominent. This paper presents a solution for Task 2: AI vs. Human – Academic Essay Authenticity Challenge in the COLING 2025 DAIGenC Workshop [1]. The rise of Large Language models (LLMs) like ChatGPT has posed significant challenges to academic integrity, particularly in detecting AI-generated essays. To address this, we propose a fusion model that combines pre-trained language model embeddings with stylometric and linguistic features. Our approach, tested on both English and Arabic, utilizes adaptive training and attention mechanisms to enhance F1 scores, address class imbalance, and capture linguistic nuances across languages. This work advances multilingual solutions for detecting AI-generated text in academia.

1 Introduction

The exponential growth of Large Language Models (LLMs) has led to widespread applications, including language translation, question answering, text generation, and beyond. However, their unauthorized use by students to complete homework, write essays, and write content-specific questions compromises academic integrity, highlighting the need for AI-driven LLM text detection. Using AI-generated content in academic contexts also poses challenges related to plagiarism (Liao, 2020).

The existing literature proposes various methods for AI-generated text detection, including feature-based models, supervised, zero-shot, and adversarial approaches. All of these models are designed to improve the result of detection in different languages and styles. Despite achieving decent overall accuracy, these methods still suffer from high false positives, where human-generated text is misclassified as AI-generated. Furthermore, class-wise accuracy remains a challenge, indicating room for improvement in distinguishing between human-generated text and AI-generated text.

To address these issues, The COLING 2025 Workshop on DAIGenC (Chowdhury et al., 2025) Task 2, *"AI vs. Human – Academic Essay Authenticity Challenge"* aims to identify machine-generated essays to safeguard academic integrity and prevent misuse of LLMs in education.

The task, framed as—*"Given an essay, identify whether it is generated by a machine or authored by a human"*—is a binary classification challenge divided into two sub-tasks: Subtask A for English essays and Subtask B for Arabic.

Our final model is a fusion of feature-based models and PLM embeddings. Initially, the PLM showed poor performance with a bias toward the majority class. By integrating linguistic and stylistic features, we improved the overall Macro F1 score. Our focus addressed three key challenges: capturing feature dependencies, handling class imbalance, and optimizing training to preserve linguistic representations in lower layers while enabling higher layers to capture task-specific (Essay) stylistic differences.

2 Related Work

Over the last few years, numerous approaches have been proposed to tackle the task of AI-generated text detection. Detecting machine-generated text is formulated primarily as a binary classification task (Zellers et al., 2019; Gehrmann et al., 2019; Ippolito et al., 2019), naively distinguishing between human-written and machine-generated text. In general, there are three main approaches: the supervised methods (Wang et al., 2023; Uchendu et al., 2021; Zellers et al., 2019; Zhong et al., 2020; Liu et al., 2023, 2022), the unsupervised ones, such as zero-shot methods (Solaiman et al., 2019; Ippolito et al., 2019; Mitchell et al., 2023; Su et al.,

[1] https://gitlab.com/genai-content-detection/genai-content-detection-coling-2025

Proceedings of the 1st Workshop on GenAI Content Detection (GenAIDetect), pages 299–306
January 19, 2025.

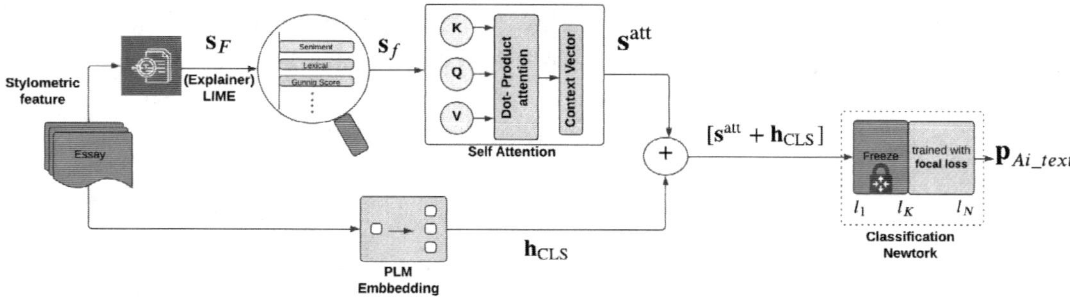

Figure 1: Proposed detector model architecture: fusion stylometric features with a PLM embedding.

2023; Hans et al.; Shijaku and Canhasi, 2023) and adversarial measures on detection accuracy (Susnjak and McIntosh, 2024; Liang et al., 2023), especially within the education domain. For example, (Antoun et al., 2023) evaluates the robustness of the detectors against character-level perturbations or misspelled words, focusing on French as a case study. (Krishna et al., 2024) train a generative model (DIPPER) to paraphrase paragraphs to evade detection. Although supervised approaches yield relatively better results, they are susceptible to overfitting (Mitchell et al., 2023; Su et al., 2023).

There are some techniques like feature-based, fusion, and ensemble methods, such as word count, vocabulary richness, and readability concatenated ML, Neural based or finetuned (Solaiman et al., 2019; Kumarage et al., 2023; Shah et al., 2023; Nguyen-Son et al., 2017; Mindner et al., 2023; Kumarage and Liu, 2023).

3 Proposed Model

We use a fusion model that combines stylometric features with PLM embeddings, fine-tuned together for binary classification of AI vs. human text.

3.1 Stylometric Features

The stylometric features aim to capture different stylistic signals within a given text. As mentioned in Table 1, the stylometric features capture stylistic signals in three categories: Phraseology (how the author organizes words and phrases), Lexical Diversity (measures how varied the author's vocabulary), and Syntactic Diversity (author structured sentences and conveying emotions), definition of these features mentioned in Section A.2.1

3.2 Model

For each text input instance, we first extract the stylometric features as vector $\mathbf{s}_F \in \mathbb{R}^F$ where F is the number of stylometric features as mentioned in Table 1 then apply *LIME* (Local Interpretable model-agnostic Explanations) to select the most distinguishing feature as a vector $\mathbf{s}_f \in \mathbb{R}^f$, where f is the number of important features. These features help distinguish between human and AI-texts.

To capture the dependencies within the stylometric features, we apply a *self-attention* mechanism over the stylometric features, producing an attention-weighted vector $\mathbf{s}^{\text{att}} = \text{Attention}(\mathbf{s}_f)$. This attention function assigns weights to each stylometric feature based on its relevance to the dependency between the features.

In parallel, we obtain the CLS token embedding from the final hidden layer of the PLM, denoted as $\mathbf{h}_{\text{CLS}}$. This embedding captures the semantic meaning of the entire input text.

Next, we concatenate the attention-weighted stylometric vector $\mathbf{s}^{\text{att}}$ with the CLS token embedding $\mathbf{h}_{\text{CLS}}$ to create a combined feature vector $\mathbf{f}_{\text{concat}}$, defined equation 1. This vector is then passed through the classification network which is layer-wise freezing during fine-tuning. Let the PLM layers be represented as $l_1, l_2, \ldots, l_n$, where l_1 is the lowest layer and l_n is the highest. We freeze the parameters $\theta_{l_1}, \ldots, \theta_{l_k}$ of the lower layer, which are initialized with pre-trained weights that preserve general linguistic representations, and update $\theta_{l_{k+1}}, \ldots, \theta_{l_n}$ for higher layers, as in equation 2, Here, k is a hyperparameter that determines how many of the lower layers of the pre-trained model remain frozen, retaining their general linguistic representations while the higher layers are fine-tuned.

$$\mathbf{f}_{\text{concat}} = [\mathbf{s}^{\text{att}}; \mathbf{h}_{\text{CLS}}] \quad (1)$$

$$L_{\text{fine-tune}} = \sum_{i=k+1}^{n} L(\theta_{l_i}) \quad (2)$$

The parameters $\theta_{l_{k+1}}, \ldots, \theta_{l_n}$ transform $\mathbf{f}_{\text{concat}}$

Stylometry Analysis	Feature Sets
Phraseology	Word count, Sentence count, Paragraph count, Mean, Standard deviation of word count per sentence, Word count per paragraph, Total punctuation count, Exclamation count and Sentence count per paragraph
Lexical Diversity	Syllables count, Comma count, Stopwords count, Unique words count, Lexical Diversity, Type token ratio, Flesch reading ease, Flesch Kincaid grade and Gunning fog
Syntactic Diversity	Sentiment polarity, Sentiment subjectivity, Proportion of nouns, Proportion of verbs, Proportion of adjectives and Proportion of adverbs

Table 1: Different stylometric feature categories and corresponding feature sets (Mindner et al., 2023) (defined in A.2.1 and for detail result A.3)

into r, which is then passed through the final layer l_n for classification.

The final layer l_n generates the output representation $\mathbf{r}$, which is then passed through a softmax activation function to compute the class probabilities $p_\theta(y|\mathbf{r})$, where $y \in 0, 1$ indicates the class of the text (0 for "human-written" and 1 for "AI-generated"). The softmax function is defined as:

$$p_\theta(y|\mathbf{r}) = \frac{\exp(\mathbf{W}_y^T \mathbf{r} + b_y)}{\sum_{y'} \exp(\mathbf{W}_{y'}^T \mathbf{r} + b_{y'})} \quad (3)$$

To address class imbalance, we apply focal loss, which modifies the cross-entropy loss by focusing more on difficult-to-classify examples. The focal loss for an input $\mathbf{r}$ and label y is given by:

$$\mathcal{L}_{\text{focal}} = -\alpha(1 - p_\theta(y|\mathbf{r}))^\gamma \log(p_\theta(y|\mathbf{r})) \quad (4)$$

Here, α is a balancing factor for class importance, and γ is a focusing parameter that down-weights easy examples. The focusing parameter γ is typically set between 0 and 5, with higher values making the model focus more on hard-to-classify instances. Specifically, γ controls the rate at which the modulating factor $(1 - p_\theta(y|\mathbf{r}))^\gamma$ reduces the loss for well-classified examples. The model is trained using focal loss and optimized through backpropagation.

In the testing phase, each text input instance is passed to the the trained model and the output $\mathbf{r}$ is processed by the softmax function to predict the class $\hat{y} = \arg\max_y p_\theta(y|\mathbf{r})$.

Model performance is evaluated using accuracy, Macro precision, Macro recall, and Macro F1-score which are discussed in Results section.

4 Experiments

4.1 Dataset

For each task, there are three datasets provided by (Chowdhury et al., 2025): Train, Dev and Test. Training and development data with labels (AI or human) for the development phase and for the evaluation phase, testing data without labels for both tasks. All descriptions with respect to the size of data set is mentioned in Table 2.

Data	Train		Dev		w/o label	
	#AI	#Human	#AI	#Human	#Dev	#Test
English	1467	629	391	1235	567	1130
Arabic	925	1145	299	182	293	886

Table 2: Dataset count distribution across training, development, and testing set.

4.2 Experimental Setup

For both Subtasks, the hyperparameters include an epoch size ranging from 50 to 250, while the batch size is fixed at 32, determined by the available GPU resources. Further details of the experimental setup are presented in Section A.1.

4.3 Feature and Model Selection

To improve model interpretability, we use **LIME** as mentioned (Ribeiro et al., 2016) for feature selection, helping identify the most influential features for detecting AI-generated text. Feature details of LIME are presented in Appendix A.2.1.

For subtask A (English essays), calculate the linguistic and stylometric characteristics mentioned in Table 1. LIME highlights such as average sentence length, number of stop words, type token ration,

model	Feature	F1
Baseline (n-gram)	-	0.478
RoBERTa-base	-	0.462
BERT-base-uncased	-	0.567
DeBERTa-base	-	0.617
BERT-base-uncased	Yes	0.818
RoBERTa-base	Yes	0.796
DistilBERT-base-uncased	Yes	0.931
DeBERTa-base	**Yes**	**0.978**

Table 3: model Performance of Macro F1 on test Data with and without Features for Subtask A English

etc., are the top 12 most discriminative characteristics. For subtask B (Arabic essays), 11 features such as Sentiments and Flesch reading ease are highly discriminative features after applying LIME. However, certain features, such as part-of-speech (POS) tags are less straightforward in Arabic due to its rich morphology, lack of strict word order, and complex inflectional system compared to languages like English.. Details of features are given in Section A.3.

For this experiment, we consider pretrained language models such as *RoBERTa* (Liu, 2019), *BERT* (Devlin, 2018), *DeBERTa* (He et al., 2020), and *DistilBERT* (Sanh, 2019) for Subtask A, which focuses on English essays. For Subtask B, we use multilingual pretrained language models, including *XLM-RoBERTa* (Wiciaputra et al., 2021) and *AraBERT* (Antoun et al., 2020), both of which are transformer-based models designed for understanding the Arabic language.

5 Results and Analysis

Table 3 (for English) and Table 4 (for Arabic) show the results of the test dataset. The baseline results were provided by the organizer, while all other results are based on our experimental findings. For Subtask A, our proposed model, the fusion of *DeBERTa-base* and the symmetry characteristics, achieves the highest score of 0.978 on testing dataset. For Subtask B, our proposed model, Fusion of *AraBERT* and Stylometry features, achieves the best performance with an F1 score of 0.9429. Notably, in Subtask A, other models also show competitive performance when combined with features. In Subtask B, *AraBERT* without features achieves an impressive F1 score of 0.9214, leveraging its design tailored to the Arabic language to effectively capture its unique linguistic features. Such Arabic-specific models are optimized for the language's morphology and syntax, often providing slight performance advantages in specialized tasks. Figure 2 illustrates the confusion matrix for the development dataset using our proposed models for both subtasks. It can be observed that Arabic data tend to be misclassified more frequently compared to English data.

Table 5 highlights the strong performance of our final models, which secured 10th position in Subtask A (English) and 13th position in Subtask B (Arabic) in the official task rankings.

model	Feature	F1
Baseline (n-gram)	-	0.4605
XLM-RoBERTa-base	-	0.9188
AraBERT v02	-	0.9214
XLM-RoBERTa-base	Yes	0.9414
AraBERT v02	**Yes**	**0.9429**

Table 4: model performance of Macro F1 on Test Data with and without Features for Subtask B Arabic

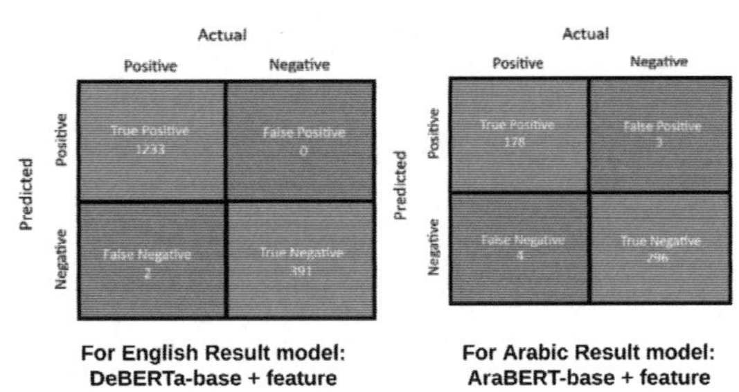

Figure 2: Performance Metrics on development Dataset

Task	Acc.	P	R	F1	Rank
A-English	0.978	0.968	0.984	0.975	10
B-Arabic	0.942	0.949	0.919	0.932	13

Table 5: Leadboard Score of Our Final model

6 Conclusion

The unethical misuse of LLMs in academic contexts poses challenges to integrity, highlighting the need for effective AI-generated text detection. Our fusion model, combining stylometric features with PLM embeddings, addresses 3 key challenges identifying highly discriminative ones using LIME, focal loss for addressing class imbalance and apply layer-wise freezing during fine tuning to capture task-specific stylistic differences in essays. These strategies have significantly improved model performance. For Subtask A (English), our DeBERTa + features model achieved a Macro F1 score of 0.978, while for Subtask B (Arabic), the AraBERT + features model scored 0.9429. Future work may refine these techniques to further enhance model's classwise F1 and generalization.

References

Wissam Antoun, Fady Baly, and Hazem Hajj. 2020. Arabert: Transformer-based model for arabic language understanding. *arXiv preprint arXiv:2003.00104*.

Wissam Antoun, Virginie Mouilleron, Benoît Sagot, and Djamé Seddah. 2023. Towards a robust detection of language model-generated text: Is chatgpt that easy to detect? In *Actes de CORIA-TALN 2023. Actes de la 30e Conférence sur le Traitement Automatique des Langues Naturelles (TALN), volume 1: travaux de recherche originaux–articles longs*, pages 14–27.

Shammur Absar Chowdhury, Hind Al-Merekhi, Mucahid Kutlu, Kaan Efe Keleş, Fatema Ahmad, Tasnim Mohiuddin, Georgios Mikros, and Firoj Alam. 2025. GenAI content detection task 2: AI vs. human – academic essay authenticity challenge. In *Proceedings of the 1st Workshop on GenAI Content Detection (GenAIDetect)*, Abu Dhabi, UAE. International Conference on Computational Linguistics.

Jacob Devlin. 2018. Bert: Pre-training of deep bidirectional transformers for language understanding. *arXiv preprint arXiv:1810.04805*.

Sebastian Gehrmann, Hendrik Strobelt, and Alexander M Rush. 2019. Gltr: Statistical detection and visualization of generated text. *arXiv preprint arXiv:1906.04043*.

A Hans, A Schwarzschild, V Cherepanova, H Kazemi, A Saha, M Goldblum, J Geiping, and T Goldstein. Spotting llms with binoculars: Zero-shot detection of machine-generated text, 2024. *URL: https://arxiv.org/abs/2401.12070*.

Pengcheng He, Xiaodong Liu, Jianfeng Gao, and Weizhu Chen. 2020. Deberta: Decoding-enhanced bert with disentangled attention. *arXiv preprint arXiv:2006.03654*.

Daphne Ippolito, Daniel Duckworth, Chris Callison-Burch, and Douglas Eck. 2019. Automatic detection of generated text is easiest when humans are fooled. *arXiv preprint arXiv:1911.00650*.

Kalpesh Krishna, Yixiao Song, Marzena Karpinska, John Wieting, and Mohit Iyyer. 2024. Paraphrasing evades detectors of ai-generated text, but retrieval is an effective defense. *Advances in Neural Information Processing Systems*, 36.

Tharindu Kumarage, Joshua Garland, Amrita Bhattacharjee, Kirill Trapeznikov, Scott Ruston, and Huan Liu. 2023. Stylometric detection of ai-generated text in twitter timelines. *arXiv preprint arXiv:2303.03697*.

Tharindu Kumarage and Huan Liu. 2023. Neural authorship attribution: Stylometric analysis on large language models. In *2023 International Conference on Cyber-Enabled Distributed Computing and Knowledge Discovery (CyberC)*, pages 51–54. IEEE Computer Society.

Weixin Liang, Mert Yuksekgonul, Yining Mao, Eric Wu, and James Zou. 2023. Gpt detectors are biased against non-native english writers. *Patterns*, 4(7).

S Matthew Liao. 2020. *Ethics of artificial intelligence*. Oxford University Press.

Xiaoming Liu, Zhaohan Zhang, Yichen Wang, Hang Pu, Yu Lan, and Chao Shen. 2022. Coco: Coherence-enhanced machine-generated text detection under data limitation with contrastive learning. *arXiv preprint arXiv:2212.10341*.

Yikang Liu, Ziyin Zhang, Wanyang Zhang, Shisen Yue, Xiaojing Zhao, Xinyuan Cheng, Yiwen Zhang, and Hai Hu. 2023. Argugpt: evaluating, understanding and identifying argumentative essays generated by gpt models. *arXiv preprint arXiv:2304.07666*.

Yinhan Liu. 2019. Roberta: A robustly optimized bert pretraining approach. *arXiv preprint arXiv:1907.11692*, 364.

Lorenz Mindner, Tim Schlippe, and Kristina Schaaff. 2023. Classification of human-and ai-generated texts: Investigating features for chatgpt. In *International Conference on Artificial Intelligence in Education Technology*, pages 152–170. Springer.

Eric Mitchell, Yoonho Lee, Alexander Khazatsky, Christopher D Manning, and Chelsea Finn. 2023. Detectgpt: Zero-shot machine-generated text detection using probability curvature. In *International Conference on Machine Learning*, pages 24950–24962. PMLR.

Hoang-Quoc Nguyen-Son, Ngoc-Dung T Tieu, Huy H Nguyen, Junichi Yamagishi, and Isao Echi Zen. 2017. Identifying computer-generated text using statistical analysis. In *2017 Asia-Pacific Signal and Information Processing Association Annual Summit and Conference (APSIPA ASC)*, pages 1504–1511. IEEE.

Adam Paszke, Sam Gross, Francisco Massa, Adam Lerer, James Bradbury, Gregory Chanan, Trevor Killeen, Zeming Lin, Natalia Gimelshein, Luca Antiga, et al. 2019. Pytorch: An imperative style, high-performance deep learning library. *Advances in neural information processing systems*, 32.

Marco Tulio Ribeiro, Sameer Singh, and Carlos Guestrin. 2016. " why should i trust you?" explaining the predictions of any classifier. In *Proceedings of* the 22nd ACM SIGKDD international conference on knowledge discovery and data mining, pages 1135–1144.

V Sanh. 2019. Distilbert, a distilled version of bert: smaller, faster, cheaper and lighter. *arXiv preprint arXiv:1910.01108.*

Aditya Shah, Prateek Ranka, Urmi Dedhia, Shruti Prasad, Siddhi Muni, and Kiran Bhowmick. 2023. Detecting and unmasking ai-generated texts through explainable artificial intelligence using stylistic features. *International Journal of Advanced Computer Science and Applications*, 14(10).

Rexhep Shijaku and Ercan Canhasi. 2023. Chatgpt generated text detection. *Publisher: Unpublished.*

Irene Solaiman, Miles Brundage, Jack Clark, Amanda Askell, Ariel Herbert-Voss, Jeff Wu, Alec Radford, Gretchen Krueger, Jong Wook Kim, Sarah Kreps, et al. 2019. Release strategies and the social impacts of language models. *arXiv preprint arXiv:1908.09203.*

Jinyan Su, Terry Yue Zhuo, Di Wang, and Preslav Nakov. 2023. Detectllm: Leveraging log rank information for zero-shot detection of machine-generated text. *arXiv preprint arXiv:2306.05540.*

Teo Susnjak and Timothy R McIntosh. 2024. Chatgpt: The end of online exam integrity? *Education Sciences*, 14(6):656.

Adaku Uchendu, Zeyu Ma, Thai Le, Rui Zhang, and Dongwon Lee. 2021. Turingbench: A benchmark environment for turing test in the age of neural text generation. *arXiv preprint arXiv:2109.13296.*

Zecong Wang, Jiaxi Cheng, Chen Cui, and Chenhao Yu. 2023. Implementing bert and fine-tuned roberta to detect ai generated news by chatgpt. *ArXiv*, abs/2306.07401.

Yakobus Keenan Wiciaputra, Julio Christian Young, and Andre Rusli. 2021. Bilingual text classification in english and indonesian via transfer learning using xlm-roberta. *International Journal of Advances in Soft Computing & Its Applications*, 13(3).

Rowan Zellers, Ari Holtzman, Hannah Rashkin, Yonatan Bisk, Ali Farhadi, Franziska Roesner, and Yejin Choi. 2019. Defending against neural fake news. *Advances in neural information processing systems*, 32.

Wanjun Zhong, Duyu Tang, Zenan Xu, Ruize Wang, Nan Duan, Ming Zhou, Jiahai Wang, and Jian Yin. 2020. Neural deepfake detection with factual structure of text. *arXiv preprint arXiv:2010.07475.*

A Example Appendix

A.1 Details of Experimental Setups

As mention in Table 6, We employ two experimental setups. In the first, we fine-tune the Pre-Trained Language model (PLM) independently for each subtask over 50 epochs, using the Adam optimizer with a learning rate of 2×10^{-5} and L2 regularization (weight decay 0.01). The second setup uses the PLM for training with batch normalization, and 0.5 dropout. The model is trained with a 2×10^{-5} learning rate, L2 regularization of 0.01, and early stopping after 25 epochs. Focal loss addresses class imbalance, emphasizing hard-to-classify examples. All experiments are implemented in PyTorch (Paszke et al., 2019), for efficient training and handling of large datasets.

Hyperparameter	**Setup: Fine-tuning PLM**
Epochs	10-250
Batch Size	5
k	6 layer
Learning Rate	2×10^{-5}
Optimizer	Adam
L2 Regularization	Weight decay: 0.01
Loss Function	Focal Loss

Table 6: Hyperparameter settings for Setup 1: Fine-tuning PLM.

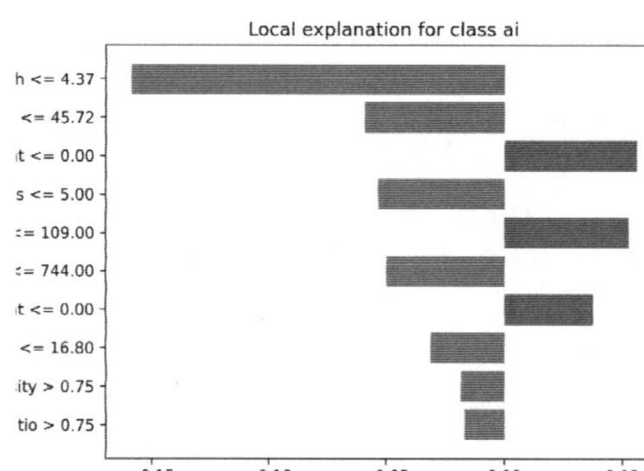

Figure 3: LIME Explanation for Subtask B as mentioned in (Ribeiro et al., 2016)

A.2 Stylometry Analysis Feature Sets

A.2.1 Phraseology

The phraseology features analyze the structure of the text, such as word, sentence, and paragraph counts, along with punctuation-related features like exclamation counts. These features help in understanding how the text is organized and how frequently punctuation marks are used.

A.2.2 Lexical Diversity

- **Type-Token Ratio (TTR):** A measure of lexical variety, ratio of UWC and WC, where UWC is the number of unique words and WC is the total word count.
- **Flesch Reading Ease (FRE):** A readability test:

$$\text{FRE} = 206.835 - 1.015 \times \left(\frac{WC}{SC}\right) - 84.6 \times \left(\frac{SC}{\text{Syllables}}\right)$$

- **Flesch-Kincaid Grade (FKG):** A readability metric indicating the U.S. school grade level required to understand the text:

$$\text{FKG} = 0.39 \times \left(\frac{WC}{SC}\right) + 11.8 \times \left(\frac{\text{Syllables}}{WC}\right) - 15.59$$

- **Gunning Fog Index (GFI):** A readability test estimating the years of formal education required to understand the text:

$$\text{GFI} = 0.4 \times \left(\frac{WC}{SC} + 100 \times \frac{\text{Complex Words}}{WC}\right)$$

  where complex words are those with three or more syllables.

A.2.3 Syntactic Diversity

Sentiment Polarity measure of the emotional tone of the text, ranging from -1 (-ve) to 1 (+ve).Sentiment Subjectivity measure of how subjective or opinion-based the text is, usually ranging from 0 (objective) to 1 (subjective).

A.3 Features Analysis of English & Arabic

Table 8 and Table 7 compare linguistic and stylometric features between AI-generated and human-written essays in English and Arabic. For instance, in English essays, AI texts exhibit higher average word counts (321.37 vs. 254.0) and sentence counts (13.22 vs. 9.0). Similarly, in Arabic essays, AI texts display longer average word counts (215.11 vs. 251.17) but fewer unique words (136.84 vs. 169.37). Other features, such as readability scores (e.g., Flesch Reading Ease), sentiment metrics, and part-of-speech proportions, indicate stylistic differences, highlighting AI's more mechanical and less nuanced language use compared to humans.

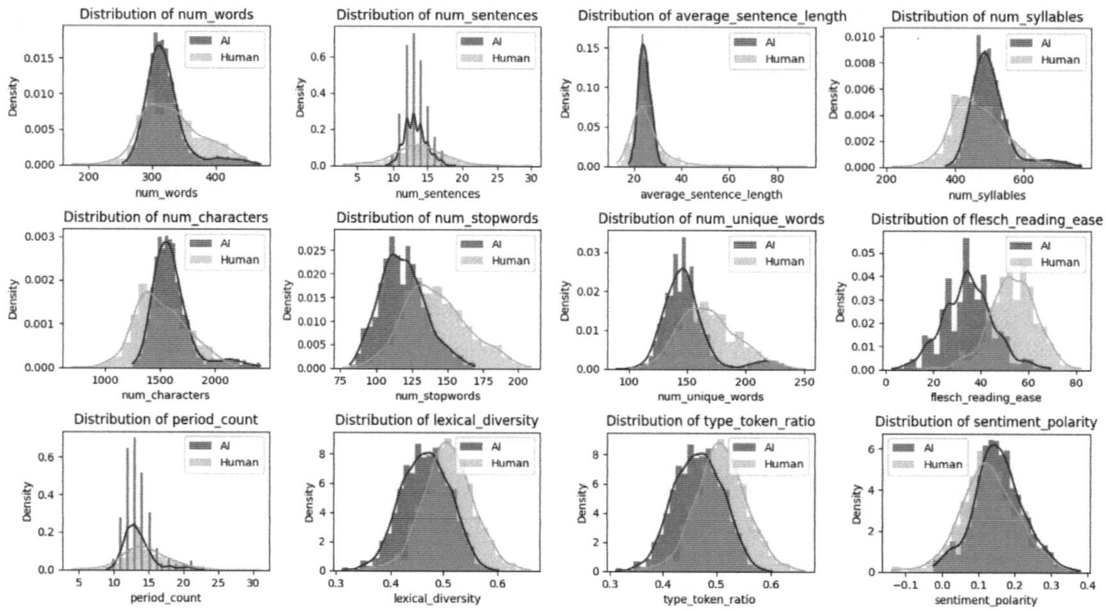

Figure 4: Distribution of features for AI and Human labels.

#	Feature	Max		Min		Avg	
		AI	**Human**	**AI**	**Human**	**AI**	**Human**
1	num_words	1555	664	45	54	215.11	251.17
2	num_sentences	223	38	2	1	13.34	7.13
3	avg_sentence_length	453	524	5.94	5.60	17.39	73.09
4	num_syllables	1356	592	54	51	202.34	239.95
5	num_characters	6759	2996	164	199	1042.74	1130.41
6	num_stopwords	444	196	0	9	44.75	61.10
7	num_unique_words	254	442	8	42	136.84	169.37
8	flesch_reading_ease	117.26	116.45	-336.55	-382.23	105.15	53.02
9	flesch_kincaid_grade	172.50	190.00	-2.00	-1.70	2.64	22.80
10	avg_word_length	8.23	6.77	3.64	3.22	4.87	4.42
11	type_token_ratio	0.92	0.91	0.01	0.44	0.66	0.70
12	comma_count	23	57	0	0	0.14	0.73
13	period_count	222	97	2	0	13.33	7.72
14	exclamation_count	1	14	0	0	0.00	0.18
15	lexical_diversity	0.92	0.91	0.01	0.44	0.66	0.70

Table 7: Feature Statistics for AI and Human Texts for Arabic Essay (Subtask B).

#	Feature	Max		Min		Avg	
		AI	**Human**	**AI**	**Human**	**AI**	**Human**
1	#words	471.0	254.0	321.37	449.0	174.0	332.21
2	#sentences	19.0	9.0	13.22	30.0	3.0	13.68
3	avg. sentence length	33.22	17.78	24.48	92.0	12.74	26.16
4	#syllables	770.0	372.0	504.96	680.0	218.0	467.32
5	#characters	2412.0	1254.0	1609.69	2212.0	703.0	1518.70
6	#stopwords	169.0	82.0	118.84	209.0	77.0	141.71
7	#unique words	243.0	89.0	149.73	251.0	101.0	168.19
8	flesch reading ease	69.31	2.85	34.67	81.93	13.35	53.25
9	flesch kincaid grade	17.8	8.3	13.71	25.6	5.5	11.17
10	gunning fog	18.68	9.72	13.89	26.74	6.72	12.52
11	#comma	42.0	10.0	22.42	38.0	1.0	15.72
12	#period	23.0	9.0	13.52	31.0	4.0	14.58
13	#exclamation	0.0	0.0	0.0	3.0	0.0	0.03
14	type token ratio	0.602	0.312	0.466	0.663	0.352	0.508
15	lexical diversity	0.602	0.312	0.466	0.663	0.352	0.508
16	sentiment polarity	0.380	-0.023	0.155	0.355	-0.138	0.130
17	sentiment subjectivity	0.709	0.208	0.445	0.722	0.284	0.472
18	pos proportion noun	0.330	0.171	0.255	0.322	0.144	0.230
19	pos proportion verb	0.180	0.064	0.113	0.193	0.067	0.119
20	pos proportion adj	0.179	0.049	0.112	0.176	0.038	0.089
21	pos proportion adv	0.088	0.006	0.040	0.098	0.011	0.048

Table 8: Linguistic and Stylometric Features Comparison in English Essays.

CNLP-NITS-PP at GenAI Detection Task 2: Leveraging DistilBERT and XLM-RoBERTa for Multilingual AI-Generated Text Detection

Annepaka Yadagiri, Reddi Mohana Krishna and Partha Pakray
Department of Computer Science & Engineering
National Institute of Technology Silchar, Assam, India, 788010
{annepaka22_rs, reddi_pg_23, partha}@cse.nits.ac.in

Abstract

In today's digital landscape, distinguishing between human-authored essays and content generated by advanced Large Language Models such as ChatGPT, GPT-4, Gemini, and LLaMa has become increasingly complex. This differentiation is essential across sectors like academia, cybersecurity, social media, and education, where the authenticity of written material is often crucial. Addressing this challenge, the COLING 2025 competition introduced Task 2, a binary classification task to separate AI-generated text from human-authored content. Using a benchmark dataset for English and Arabic, developing a methodology that fine-tuned various transformer-based neural networks, including CNN-LSTM, RNN, Bi-GRU, BERT, DistilBERT, GPT-2, and RoBERTa. Our Team_CNLP-NITS-PP achieved competitive performance through meticulous hyperparameter optimization, reaching a Recall score of 0.825. Specifically, we ranked 18th in the English sub-task A with an accuracy of 0.77 and 20th in the Arabic sub-task B with an accuracy of 0.59. These results underscore the potential of transformer-based models in academic settings to detect AI-generated content effectively, laying a foundation for more advanced methods in essay authenticity verification.

1 Introduction

Large Language Models (*LLMs*), such as ChatGPT [1] have made remarkable advances in generating human-like text responses, leading to diverse and sophisticated outputs tailored to specific prompts. While these advancements open up extensive practical applications, they also present challenges, including concerns over academic integrity and questions surrounding actual authorship. Considerable research has been devoted to distinguishing Machine-Generated Texts (*MGT*) from Human-Written Texts (*HWT*). This has primarily involved model-based techniques (Wang et al., 2023; Bhattacharjee et al., 2023) and statistical analysis methods to examine distinct text characteristics (Hans et al., 2024). Several platforms like GPTZero (Touvron et al., 2023) and Sapling have effectively differentiated MGT from HWT.

Detection of MGT has commonly employed a binary classification approach to distinguish between MGT and HWT. However, advancements in LLMs have blurred these distinctions, challenging the efficacy of straightforward classification techniques. For instance, in statistical detection, the linguistic features of an MGT might closely resemble those typically found in HWT, leading to potential misclassification. Similarly, model-based approaches often need help to generalize effectively; they are typically trained on specific datasets or models and may not perform as accurately as newer models emerge with distinct characteristics. Additionally, many detection systems need more transparency. Although some detection tools attempt to integrate explanatory elements, they often fail to deliver insightful interpretations, as observed in evaluations of models like GPTZero (Touvron et al., 2023).

2 Related Work

Zero-shot detection methods leverage statistical attributes to differentiate MGT from HWT. Research in this area has explored various Language Model (*LM*) driven features such as entropy (He et al., 2023), average log probability scores (Solaiman et al., 2019), and perplexity (Wu et al., 2023) as indicators. As LMs advance, generating increasingly sophisticated text, recent zero-shot detection methods (Mitchell et al., 2023) have evolved to capture high-level characteristics in generated content.

One notable zero-shot detection model, Binoculars (Hans et al., 2024), uses LMs to make next-token predictions across text positions. By analyzing the log perplexity ratio relative to baseline text,

[1] https://chatgpt.com/

Proceedings of the 1st Workshop on GenAI Content Detection (GenAIDetect), pages 307–311
January 19, 2025.

Binoculars identifies nuanced discrepancies that help distinguish MGT from HWT effectively. This technique represents an essential advancement in zero-shot detection, adapting to the sophisticated language features characteristic of current LLM outputs.

3 Methodology

3.1 Problem Statement

This research aims to develop a classification system that can identify machine-generated essays, uphold academic integrity, and mitigate the misuse of LLMs in educational contexts. The system receives as input a set of essays authored by both human writers (*including native and non-native speakers*) and by LLMs in both English and Arabic languages.

This task is defined as a binary classification problem, aiming to classify each essay as machine-generated or human-authored. The problem can be formally stated as follows:

- **Input:** A text sample E consisting of n tokens, where $E = \{w_1, w_2, \ldots, w_n\}$.
- **Output:** A binary label $y \in \{0, 1\}$, where:
  - $y = 0$ denotes a human-authored essay,
  - $y = 1$ denotes a machine-generated essay.

To approach this classification task, features $F(E) = \{f_1, f_2, \ldots, f_m\}$ are extracted from each essay E, capturing various linguistic, syntactic, and semantic characteristics. These features may include lexical patterns, syntactic structures, token frequency distributions, and transformer-based embeddings tailored to English and Arabic text properties.

The classification model $f : E \rightarrow y$ seeks to assign a probability $P(y = 1|E)$ that represents the likelihood of the text E being machine-generated. The model's performance is evaluated on a large corpus of annotated text samples, aiming to achieve robust classification across different linguistic profiles and LLM-generated writing styles.

3.2 Dataset Description

The dataset comprises essays authored by humans alongside texts generated by various AI models (Chowdhury et al., 2025). Human-written essays were sourced from the ETS Corpus of Non-Native Written English [2]. For AI-generated content, we utilized outputs from seven distinct open and closed LMs, including GPT-3.5-Turbo, GPT-4o, GPT-4o-mini, Gemini-1.5, Llama-3.1 (*8B*), Phi-3.5-mini, and Claude-3.5. Tables 1,2 present the dataset statistics for English and Arabic. Additionally, Figures 1 and 2 provide a visual comparison between human and AI-generated essays for English and Arabic datasets, respectively.

Label	English	
	Train Count	Dev Count
Human	629	1235
AI	1467	391
Total	2096	1626

Table 1: Dataset Label Counts for English Train and Development

Label	Arabic	
	Train Count	Dev Count
Human	1145	182
AI	925	299
Total	2070	481

Table 2: Dataset Label Counts for Arabic Train and Development

3.3 System Description

This paper presents our approach to the MGT Detection Task 2, aimed at detecting AI-generated content. The task involves classifying whether a given text is machine-generated or human-written, with our solution applied to both Subtask A (*English texts*) and Subtask B (*Arabic academic essays*). For Subtask A, we used the DistilBERT model, while for Subtask B, we employed the XLM-RoBERTa model. In addition, we used a rule-based method to extract semantic features like *average line length, vocabulary richness, word density, POS tags, and stop word frequency* to enhance the model's ability to detect AI-generated text. The DistilBERT model generates contextual embeddings and is followed by a pre-classifier layer to refine the output. We added a fully connected layer to incorporate additional features, using ReLU activation and dropout layers to prevent overfitting. The final output is obtained by concatenating the features and passing them through a classification

[2] https://catalog.ldc.upenn.edu/LDC2014T06

layer with a sigmoid activation to generate probabilities. Our model was trained and used on a system with an Intel Xeon CPU, 64GB RAM, and an NVIDIA Quadro GPU. Finally, we achieved an accuracy of 0.771 in Subtask A and Subtask B with an accuracy of 0.59. This result demonstrates the effectiveness of combining transformer-based models with additional feature-based enhancements in identifying AI-generated content.

Parameter	Value
Activation Function	Sigmoid
Optimizer	AdamW
Loss Function	binary_crossentropy
Learning Rate	2×10^{-5}
Batch Size	16
Number of Epochs	05
Dropout	0.3
ModelCheckpoint	Yes
EarlyStopping	Yes
Patience	2

Table 3: Hyperparameters utilized across all experiments

Model for English Language

To classify human-written versus AI-generated essays, we utilize the DistilBERT transformer model for Sub Task A. DistilBERT is a streamlined version of the original BERT model, designed for computational efficiency without compromising the core interpretative capabilities of BERT. This optimized model is well-suited for tasks requiring nuanced linguistic analysis and rapid processing. DistilBERT's architecture enables the capture of complex linguistic patterns and contextual information, essential for distinguishing subtle differences between human-authored and AI-generated content.

The classifier processes the input text to produce hidden representations h_i for each token. However, in this model, the final prediction is based on the hidden representation of the [CLS] token, designed to capture the aggregated semantic and syntactic information from the entire sequence. The prediction is computed by applying the softmax function to the [CLS] token's hidden state, as shown below:

$$\hat{y}_i = \text{softmax}(W h_{[\text{CLS}]} + b) \quad (1)$$

Here, $h_{[\text{CLS}]}$ represents the hidden representation of the [CLS] token. The parameters W and b are trainable components of the model. The softmax function generates a probability distribution across the two classes: Human-written and AI-generated. The final classification decision is based on the class with the highest probability ($\hat{y}_i$)

Model for Arabic Language

To classify human-written versus AI-generated essays in Arabic (Sub Task B), we adopted the XLM-RoBERTa model. XLM-RoBERTa is chosen for its pre-trained language-specific embeddings, which enhance its performance across multiple languages. This model generates detailed contextual embeddings for each input sequence and passes them through a classification layer for predictions. To improve classification accuracy, we incorporated additional semantic features, such as vocabulary richness, average sentence length, and stop word frequency, which helped capture the distinctions between AI-generated and human-authored essays.

The final prediction is derived from a weighted combination of the model's contextual embeddings and the extracted semantic features. This allows for a robust and accurate classification outcome.

Error Analysis: We utilized the XLM-Roberta model, which was trained on data from 100 languages, including Arabic. However, this model was not explicitly fine-tuned for the Arabic language, which may limit its performance on tasks that require a deep understanding of Arabic syntax and semantics.

3.4 Results Analysis

Among state-of-the-art transformer-based models, DistilBERT demonstrated strong performance on the English dataset, while XLM-RoBERTa proved effective for the Arabic dataset. The DistilBERT model achieved high results on English text classification, with a recall of 0.82, an F1-score of 0.77, and an accuracy of 0.77, highlighting the improved performance achieved through ensemble techniques. In comparison, models for the Arabic dataset showed relatively lower performance, with XLM-RoBERTa emerging as the best performer. XLM-RoBERTa achieved a precision of 0.55, an F1-score of 0.55, and an accuracy of 0.59. These results underscore the challenges in achieving comparable performance with Arabic models and indicate areas for further optimization in multilingual transformer-based text classification.

Model	Acc	Pre	Rec	F1
DistilBERT-En	0.77	0.784	0.82	0.77
XLM-RoBERTa-Ar	0.59	0.55	0.56	0.55

Table 4: Test Results given by Leaderboard

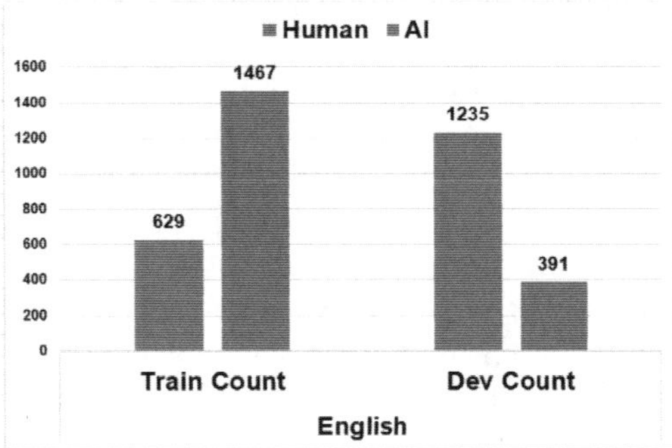

Figure 1: Visual Comparison of English Training and Development Datasets

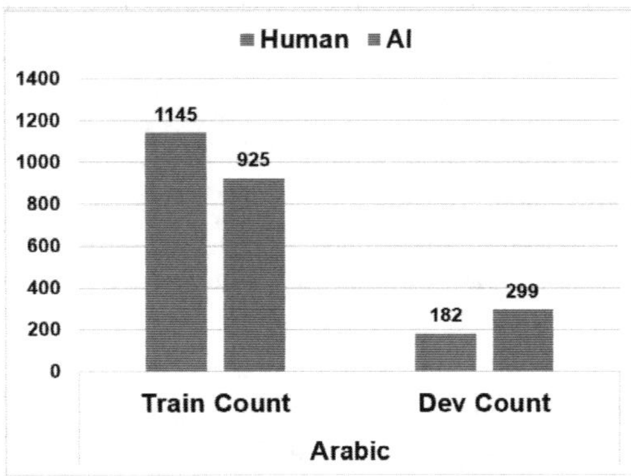

Figure 2: Visual Comparison of Arabic Training and Development Datasets

4 Conclusion

This study demonstrates the effectiveness of transformer-based models, such as DistilBERT and XLM-RoBERTa, distinguishing between human-written and AI-generated essays across English and Arabic. Our Team CNLP-NITS-PP achieved a high detection recall of 0.825 for English and an accuracy of 0.590 for Arabic, indicating these models' adaptability to diverse linguistic contexts. Ensemble methods further improved classification accuracy, underscoring the importance of robust detection systems as AI-generated content continues to proliferate. Future research could investigate additional linguistic features and cross-domain applications to enhance detection performance and address the specific challenges observed with Arabic models.

5 Future Work

We utilized the XLM-Roberta model, which was trained on data from 100 languages, including Arabic. However, this model was not explicitly fine-tuned for the Arabic language, which may limit its performance on tasks that require a deep understanding of Arabic syntax and semantics. We plan to explore models specifically fine-tuned on Arabic datasets for future work. These specialized models are expected better to understand the nuances and complexities of the Arabic language, potentially leading to improved accuracy in detecting AI-generated content in Arabic texts. By focusing on optimized models for Arabic, we aim to enhance the overall performance of our approach in this specific context.

References

Amrita Bhattacharjee, Tharindu Kumarage, Raha Moraffah, and Huan Liu. 2023. Conda: Contrastive domain adaptation for ai-generated text detection. *arXiv preprint arXiv:2309.03992*.

Shammur Absar Chowdhury, Hind Al-Merekhi, Mucahid Kutlu, Kaan Efe Keleş, Fatema Ahmad, Tasnim Mohiuddin, Georgios Mikros, and Firoj Alam. 2025. GenAI content detection task 2: AI vs. human – academic essay authenticity challenge. In *Proceedings of the 1st Workshop on GenAI Content Detection (GenAIDetect)*, Abu Dhabi, UAE. International Conference on Computational Linguistics.

Abhimanyu Hans, Avi Schwarzschild, Valeriia Cherepanova, Hamid Kazemi, Aniruddha Saha, Micah Goldblum, Jonas Geiping, and Tom Goldstein. 2024. Spotting llms with binoculars: Zero-shot detection of machine-generated text. *arXiv preprint arXiv:2401.12070*.

Xinlei He, Xinyue Shen, Zeyuan Chen, Michael Backes, and Yang Zhang. 2023. Mgtbench: Benchmarking machine-generated text detection. *arXiv preprint arXiv:2303.14822*.

Eric Mitchell, Yoonho Lee, Alexander Khazatsky, Christopher D Manning, and Chelsea Finn. 2023. Detectgpt: Zero-shot machine-generated text detection using probability curvature. In *International Conference on Machine Learning*, pages 24950–24962. PMLR.

Irene Solaiman, Miles Brundage, Jack Clark, Amanda Askell, Ariel Herbert-Voss, Jeff Wu, Alec Radford, Gretchen Krueger, Jong Wook Kim, Sarah Kreps, et al. 2019. Release strategies and the social impacts of language models. *arXiv preprint arXiv:1908.09203*.

Hugo Touvron, Thibaut Lavril, Gautier Izacard, Xavier Martinet, Marie-Anne Lachaux, Timothée Lacroix, Baptiste Rozière, Naman Goyal, Eric Hambro, Faisal Azhar, et al. 2023. Llama: Open and efficient foundation language models. *arXiv preprint arXiv:2302.13971*.

Pengyu Wang, Linyang Li, Ke Ren, Botian Jiang, Dong Zhang, and Xipeng Qiu. 2023. Seqxgpt: Sentence-level ai-generated text detection. *arXiv preprint arXiv:2310.08903*.

Kangxi Wu, Liang Pang, Huawei Shen, Xueqi Cheng, and Tat-Seng Chua. 2023. Llmdet: A third party large language models generated text detection tool. *arXiv preprint arXiv:2305.15004*.

RA at GenAI Detection Task 2: Fine-tuned Language Models For Detection of Academic Authenticity, Results and Thoughts

Rana Gharib
Arab Academy For Science and Technology
ranagharib044@gmail.com

Ahmed Elgendy
Queen's Universty
ahmed.elgendy@queensu.ca

Abstract

This paper assesses the performance of "RA" in the Academic Essay Authenticity Challenge, which saw nearly 30 teams participating in each subtask. We employed cutting-edge transformer-based models to achieve our results. Our models consistently exceeded both the mean and median scores across the tasks. Notably, we achieved an F1-score of 0.969 in classifying AI-generated essays in English and an F1-score of 0.957 for classifying AI-generated essays in Arabic. Additionally, this paper offers insights into the current state of AI-generated models and argues that the benchmarking methods currently in use do not accurately reflect real-world scenarios.

1 Introduction

Large Language Models (LLMs), as advanced artificial intelligence (AI) systems, have been trained on vast amounts of text data and can generate, summarize and comprehend human languages with impressive fluency (Naveed et al., 2024). As these models are based on deep learning architectures, primarily transformer, they can learn complex language patterns and respond end-to-end with impressions very similar to human interaction. Recently, models such as GPT-4, Mistral (Jiang et al., 2023), LLaMA (Touvron et al., 2023), etc have enabled significant advances in AI language processing for natural language understanding and generation tasks.

Their promise, however, raises serious ethical and social concerns about honesty, transparency, and misuse (Abdurahman et al., 2024). A major area where AI could create change is education. AI offers personalized learning, providing students with tailored resources that enhance effectiveness. However, the accessibility of writing tools questions academic integrity, as students may bypass essential learning processes that promote critical thinking, creativity, and problem-solving skills.

Addressing these challenges is crucial for maximizing AI's benefits while minimizing its risks. The Academic Essay Authenticity 2024 Shared Task (Chowdhury et al., 2025) focuses on creating systems to distinguish human-written text from AI-generated content and provides a validation dataset. Our model builds on recent efforts by fine-tuning multiple language models using an ensemble approach. This paper covers data analysis, pipeline, results, related work, and future directions, highlighting real-world improvements.

2 Related Work

This section examines recent advancements in detecting content generated by large language models (LLMs). With the rapid adoption of LLMs and associated challenges, researchers have increasingly focused on this area. Numerous studies have introduced systems employing both deep learning and traditional machine learning to address the authenticity and reliability concerns of AI-generated content across various fields. The widespread use of AI-generative models has fueled the development of methods to detect text generated by these models, especially to safeguard integrity in domains such as education. Broadly, classification methods fall into two categories: white-box and black-box approaches. White-box methods require direct model access and include techniques like word-level probability analysis, perturbations (Mitchell et al., 2023), and local rank perturbations. In contrast, black-box methods work without model access and include supervised learning with linguistic features (Prova, 2024), supervised learning with pretrained LMs (Wang et al., 2023), and regeneration techniques. Recent years have also seen the creation of various datasets aimed at advancing AI-generated text detection (Fraser et al., 2024), alongside shared tasks dedicated to developing novel, robust approaches (Sarvazyan et al., 2023; Fivez et al.,

Proceedings of the 1st Workshop on GenAI Content Detection (GenAIDetect), pages 312–316
January 19, 2025.

2024; Molla et al., 2023). However, a research gap persists in detecting AI-generated text in Arabic. The datasets for Arabic are often sourced from various resources, lacking cohesion and presenting limited challenge. Notably, a specialized dataset for Arabic was created to aid model development but contains only 1,000 examples (Alshammari and El-Sayed, 2023).

3 Dataset & Task Description

The shared task on Academic Essay Authenticity Challenge[1] consists of two main subtasks. Each subtask will be discussed in details in the following subsections. The provided dataset primarily comprises essays created either by a human or through promopting a generative language model. The subsequent subsections will present an overview of the distribution for each dataset, emphasizing the challenges posed by imbalances and a complete description of each dataset.

3.1 Subtask A: English Academic Essay Authenticity

The first subtask is a binary classification problem where essays given are classified into two distinct classes: "Human-Generated", and "AI-Generated". Table 1 illustrates the data distribution for the different classes within the dataset. The dataset comprises essays written by both human authors and AI systems. The human-authored essays have been curated from the ETS Corpus of Non-Native Written English. For the AI-generated content, we utilized seven diverse models, both open-source and proprietary, including GPT-3.5-Turbo, GPT-4o, GPT-4o-mini, Gemini-1.5, Llama-3.1 (8B), Phi-3.5-mini, and Claude-3.5.

	Training	Validation
Human	629	1235
AI	1467	391
Overall	2096	1626

Table 1: Subtask A's Dataset Distribution.

3.2 Subtask B: Arabic Academic Essay Authenticity

The second subtask is a binary classification problem where essays given are classified into two classes: "Human-Generated", and "AI-Generated". Table 2 illustrates the data distribution for the different classes within the dataset.

	Training	Validation
Human	1145	182
AI	925	299
Overall	2070	481

Table 2: Subtask B's Dataset Distribution.

3.3 Data Preprocessing

For both subtasks, no additional data preprocessing steps were applied beyond those inherent to the models themselves. This decision was based on the rationale that AI models, unlike humans, exhibit distinctive patterns in their writing, such as the frequency of punctuation marks and spelling accuracy, among other aspects, which can serve as discriminative features for our models.

4 Methodology

4.1 Language Models

Several language models were experimented with through the process of fine-tuning, driven by their remarkable performance in the context of our specific topic, We finetuned RoBERTa (Liu et al., 2019), XLM-RoBERTa (Conneau et al., 2020), mBERT and DeBERTa (He et al., 2021) for subtask A. All of the models showed similar performance on the validation set but for mBERT which has a slightly less performance. As for subtask B, we fine-tuned AraBERT (Antoun et al., 2020), ArBERT and MarBERT (Abdul-Mageed et al., 2021). AraBERT showed superior performance in terms of F1-score on all of the subtask as will be shown in the results section.

4.2 Loss Function

In the experimentation with various loss functions to optimize model performance, several options were tested, including Cross-Entropy Loss, Focal Loss, Tversky Loss, and Dice Loss. Each of these loss functions was evaluated based on their ability to handle class imbalance and improve the model's predictive accuracy. It was found that Focal Tversky Loss (Abraham and Khan, 2018) and Dice Loss (Li et al., 2020) produced the best results in terms of balancing sensitivity and specificity. However, Dice Loss was ultimately chosen for its superior performance, as it consistently outperformed the

[1] https://codalab.lisn.upsaclay.fr/competitions/20118

others in handling overlapping classes and achieving higher overall performance during the validation phase. Therefore, Dice Loss was selected as the final loss function for the model.

$$\text{Dice Loss} = 1 - \frac{2 \cdot \sum y_{\text{true}} \cdot y_{\text{pred}} + \epsilon}{\sum y_{\text{pred}}^2 + \sum y_{\text{true}}^2 + \epsilon} \quad (1)$$

4.3 Majority Voting

Majority voting is an ensemble technique where multiple classifiers make predictions, and the final prediction is based on the most frequent class label. This method helps mitigate issues like overfitting and bias by combining the strengths of different models, leading to improved accuracy and robustness. It reduces the impact of errors from individual classifiers, providing a more reliable and generalized prediction. Equation 2 illustrates majority voting.

$$\hat{y} = \arg \max_{c \in \{c_1, c_2, \ldots, c_k\}} \sum_{i=1}^{n} \delta(y_i = c) \quad (2)$$

4.4 Experiment Settings

The training procedure was conducted using Kaggle's [2] free-to-use platform, which provides 29 GB of RAM, a 16 GB NVIDIA P100 GPU, and Python. The autofit functionality from ktrain (Maiya, 2022) was utilized, incorporating a triangular learning rate policy (Smith, 2017).

Hyperparameter	**Task 3**	**Task 6**
Epochs	5	5
Learning Rate	2e-5	1e-5, 2e-5
Batch Size	8	8, 4
Max length	350	350
Optimizer	Adam	Adam
Early Stopping Patience	3	3
Reduce On Plateau	2	2
Loss Function	Dice Loss	Dice Loss

Table 3: Training Hyperparameters. Parameters shown for RoBERTa, DeBERTa and XLM-RoBERTa for tasks A and AraBERT for task B, respectively.

5 Results

5.1 Subtask A

Table 4 illustrates our ensemble-based model's performance on the test set . The Ensemble-based model used a majority voting scheme for DeBERTa, Roberta and XLM-RoBERTa. Our approach ranked 12th in the overall rankings leaderboard.

Model	**Precision**	**Recall**	**F1-Score**
Top-3 Ensemble	0.975	0.964	0.969

Table 4: Results For Subtask A.

This straightforward, quick-to-train, and easy-to-implement online learning upon approach secured 12th place in Subtask A. We opted for a relatively simple model to demonstrate that current basic methods can effectively handle datasets, though they may encounter challenges in real-world applications.

5.2 Subtask B

Table 5 illustrates our ensemble-based model's performance on the test set . The Ensemble-based model used a majority voting scheme for different fine-tuned version of AraBERT. Our approach ranked 6th in the overall rankings leaderboard. This straightforward, quick-to-train, and easy-to-implement online learning upon approach secured 6th place in Subtask B. We opted for a relatively simple model to demonstrate that current basic methods can effectively handle datasets, though they may encounter challenges in real-world applications.

Model	**Precision**	**Recall**	**F1-Score**
Top-3 Ensemble	0.956	0.959	0.957

Table 5: Results For Subtask A.

6 Discussion and Future Work

The relative success of our model highlights the potential for language models to serve as effective tools for detecting AI-generated text. However, we believe that the current benchmarking and fine-tuning approaches have certain limitations, particularly because they overlook the complexities present in real-life scenarios. Unlike controlled experimental settings, practical applications of AI detection face a range of unpredictable variables that make straightforward classification difficult.

In recent years, various tactics have emerged among internet users to bypass AI detectors. Some

[2] https://www.kaggle.com/

of these strategies involve adding "human" features to the text, such as intentional spelling mistakes, varied linguistic complexity, shifts between active and passive voice, or even missed punctuation marks. Other methods aim to modify the generated text from the model's perspective, employing techniques like repetitive paraphrasing, contextual word substitutions, random alterations (including word swaps or deletions), and sentence-level rearrangements. More advanced strategies include combining outputs from multiple models or utilizing auto-completion to produce hybrid texts, adding further layers of complexity.

This phenomenon has been explored extensively in the literature concerning English essays (Perkins et al., 2024). Yet, to our knowledge, it remains largely unexplored in the context of Arabic language detection. Given the linguistic richness and structural complexity of Arabic, this language poses unique challenges for models fine-tuned on existing datasets, potentially requiring new and specialized approaches for effective detection.

Developing a comprehensive dataset that encompasses all these approaches and beyond is an exciting direction for us. Additionally, we believe that multilingual language models, despite their impressive capabilities, exhibit a distinct linguistic signature. This opens up opportunities for research into the multilingual aspect, where data from various sources—such as generative models and multiple languages—can be utilized to train our detectors, allowing us to observe the effects of multilingual data.

7 Conclusion

This paper introduces an approach for detecting academic authenticity using an ensemble of language models. Despite its simplicity, the method achieves high performance after only a few epochs. While this is advantageous, it also has drawbacks. The straightforward nature of the approach, when trained on benchmark datasets, may not accurately represent its performance in real-world scenarios. We discuss several factors that could challenge the model's effectiveness and call on researchers to address these challenges in future work.

Acknowledgments

This research is supported by the Vector Scholarship in Artificial Intelligence, provided through the Vector Institute as the second author is a receipt of the Vector Scholarship for the year 2024-2025.

References

Muhammad Abdul-Mageed, AbdelRahim Elmadany, and El Moatez Billah Nagoudi. 2021. Arbert marbert: Deep bidirectional transformers for arabic. *Preprint*, arXiv:2101.01785.

Suhaib Abdurahman, Mohammad Atari, Farzan Karimi-Malekabadi, Mona J Xue, Jackson Trager, Peter S Park, Preni Golazizian, Ali Omrani, and Morteza Dehghani. 2024. Perils and opportunities in using large language models in psychological research. *PNAS Nexus*, 3(7).

Nabila Abraham and Naimul Mefraz Khan. 2018. A novel focal tversky loss function with improved attention u-net for lesion segmentation. *Preprint*, arXiv:1810.07842.

Hamed Alshammari and Ahmed El-Sayed. 2023. Airabic: Arabic dataset for performance evaluation of ai detectors. *2023 International Conference on Machine Learning and Applications (ICMLA)*, pages 864–870.

Wissam Antoun, Fady Baly, and Hazem Hajj. 2020. AraBERT: Transformer-based model for Arabic language understanding. In *Proceedings of the 4th Workshop on Open-Source Arabic Corpora and Processing Tools, with a Shared Task on Offensive Language Detection*, pages 9–15, Marseille, France. European Language Resource Association.

Shammur Absar Chowdhury, Hind Al-Merekhi, Mucahid Kutlu, Kaan Efe Keleş, Fatema Ahmad, Tasnim Mohiuddin, Georgios Mikros, and Firoj Alam. 2025. GenAI content detection task 2: AI vs. human – academic essay authenticity challenge. In *Proceedings of the 1st Workshop on GenAI Content Detection (GenAIDetect)*, Abu Dhabi, UAE. International Conference on Computational Linguistics.

Alexis Conneau, Kartikay Khandelwal, Naman Goyal, Vishrav Chaudhary, Guillaume Wenzek, Francisco Guzmán, Edouard Grave, Myle Ott, Luke Zettlemoyer, and Veselin Stoyanov. 2020. Unsupervised cross-lingual representation learning at scale. *Preprint*, arXiv:1911.02116.

Pieter Fivez, Walter Daelemans, Tim Van de Cruys, Yury Kashnitsky, Savvas Chamezopoulos, Hadi Mohammadi, Anastasia Giachanou, Ayoub Bagheri, Wessel Poelman, Juraj Vladika, Esther Ploeger, Johannes Bjerva, Florian Matthes, and Hans van Halteren. 2024. The clin33 shared task on the detection of text generated by large language models. *Computational Linguistics in the Netherlands Journal*, 13:233–259.

Kathleen C. Fraser, Hillary Dawkins, and Svetlana Kiritchenko. 2024. Detecting ai-generated text: Factors influencing detectability with current methods. *Preprint*, arXiv:2406.15583.

Pengcheng He, Xiaodong Liu, Jianfeng Gao, and Weizhu Chen. 2021. Deberta: Decoding-enhanced bert with disentangled attention. *Preprint*, arXiv:2006.03654.

Albert Q. Jiang, Alexandre Sablayrolles, Arthur Mensch, Chris Bamford, Devendra Singh Chaplot, Diego de las Casas, Florian Bressand, Gianna Lengyel, Guillaume Lample, Lucile Saulnier, Lélio Renard Lavaud, Marie-Anne Lachaux, Pierre Stock, Teven Le Scao, Thibaut Lavril, Thomas Wang, Timothée Lacroix, and William El Sayed. 2023. Mistral 7b. *Preprint*, arXiv:2310.06825.

Xiaoya Li, Xiaofei Sun, Yuxian Meng, Junjun Liang, Fei Wu, and Jiwei Li. 2020. Dice loss for data-imbalanced NLP tasks. In *Proceedings of the 58th Annual Meeting of the Association for Computational Linguistics*, pages 465–476, Online. Association for Computational Linguistics.

Yinhan Liu, Myle Ott, Naman Goyal, Jingfei Du, Mandar Joshi, Danqi Chen, Omer Levy, Mike Lewis, Luke Zettlemoyer, and Veselin Stoyanov. 2019. Roberta: A robustly optimized bert pretraining approach. *Preprint*, arXiv:1907.11692.

Arun S. Maiya. 2022. ktrain: A low-code library for augmented machine learning. *Preprint*, arXiv:2004.10703.

Eric Mitchell, Yoonho Lee, Alexander Khazatsky, Christopher D. Manning, and Chelsea Finn. 2023. Detectgpt: Zero-shot machine-generated text detection using probability curvature. *Preprint*, arXiv:2301.11305.

Diego Molla, Haolan Zhan, Xuanli He, and Qiongkai Xu. 2023. Overview of the 2023 ALTA shared task: Discriminate between human-written and machine-generated text. In *Proceedings of the 21st Annual Workshop of the Australasian Language Technology Association*, pages 148–152, Melbourne, Australia. Association for Computational Linguistics.

Humza Naveed, Asad Ullah Khan, Shi Qiu, Muhammad Saqib, Saeed Anwar, Muhammad Usman, Naveed Akhtar, Nick Barnes, and Ajmal Mian. 2024. A comprehensive overview of large language models. *Preprint*, arXiv:2307.06435.

Mike Perkins, Jasper Roe, Binh H. Vu, Darius Postma, Don Hickerson, James McGaughran, and Huy Q. Khuat. 2024. Simple techniques to bypass GenAI text detectors: implications for inclusive education. *International Journal of Educational Technology in Higher Education*, 21(1).

Nuzhat Prova. 2024. Detecting ai generated text based on nlp and machine learning approaches. *Preprint*, arXiv:2404.10032.

Areg Mikael Sarvazyan, José Ángel González, Marc Franco-Salvador, Francisco Rangel, Berta Chulvi, and Paolo Rosso. 2023. Overview of autextification at iberlef 2023: Detection and attribution of machine-generated text in multiple domains. *Preprint*, arXiv:2309.11285.

Leslie N. Smith. 2017. Cyclical learning rates for training neural networks. *Preprint*, arXiv:1506.01186.

Hugo Touvron, Thibaut Lavril, Gautier Izacard, Xavier Martinet, Marie-Anne Lachaux, Timothée Lacroix, Baptiste Rozière, Naman Goyal, Eric Hambro, Faisal Azhar, Aurelien Rodriguez, Armand Joulin, Edouard Grave, and Guillaume Lample. 2023. Llama: Open and efficient foundation language models. *Preprint*, arXiv:2302.13971.

Zecong Wang, Jiaxi Cheng, Chen Cui, and Chenhao Yu. 2023. Implementing bert and fine-tuned roberta to detect ai generated news by chatgpt. *Preprint*, arXiv:2306.07401.

Tesla at GenAI Detection Task 2: Fast and Scalable Method for Detection of Academic Essay Authenticity

Vijayasaradhi Indurthi
IIIT Hyderabad
vijayasaradhi.i@research.iiit.ac.in

Vasudeva Varma
IIIT Hyderabad
vv@iiit.ac.in

Abstract

This paper describes a simple yet effective method to identify if academic essays have been written by students or generated through the language models in English language. We extract a set of style, language complexity, bias and subjectivity, and emotion-based features that can be used to distinguish human-written essays from machine-generated essays. Our methods rank 6th on the leaderboard, achieving an impressive F1-score of 0.986.

1 Introduction

The emergence of large language models (LLMs) such as ChatGPT, GPT-4, Claude, and other similar applications has revolutionized text generation, creating highly coherent and human-like essays. While these advancements hold promise for educational tools and creative writing, they also pose significant challenges to academic integrity. Specifically, misusing machine-generated essays in educational settings threatens to undermine genuine learning and assessment. To address this issue, the task of distinguishing between human-authored and machine-generated essays has gained critical importance. This binary classification task focuses on identifying English-language essays as machine-generated or human-written. The task's details are outlined in the task overview paper (Chowdhury et al., 2025).

An ideal text detector should be accurate, easy to train and should be robust to any adversarial attacks. It should be easy to train, inference should be fast and probably is agnostic to the machine learning model that is used to generate the text.

Our approach involves identifying key textual features based on style and statistical counts of specific words, words involving complexity, bias, affect, and moral features. By transforming the text into various feature spaces and using the transformed vectors to train simple classical ML algorithms.

Participation in this task revealed several key insights. Our system achieved 6th position on the leaderboard. However, challenges persist in distinguishing highly sophisticated machine-generated texts from essays written by proficient human authors, particularly in cases where LLMs simulate idiosyncratic human writing styles. This highlights the need for further exploration of subtle linguistic markers and the inclusion of diverse training data. Quantitatively, our system achieved an F1 score of 0.986 on the test set, achieving 6th position on the leaderboard. We have made our codebase publicly available [1] to facilitate future research in this area. We hope this encourages further innovation and collaboration in safeguarding academic integrity through advancements in machine-generated text detection.

2 Related Work

Ever since Large Language Models have started to generate coherent, human like text, the task of identifying machine generated task has gained significant attention. As the complete list of works for detecting machine generated text is exhaustive, we list some of the key works that attempt to identify machine generated text.

Primarily, the methods can be broadly categorized into 3 categories: Methods involving language specific features with simple ML models. These models usually use a simple Bag of Words or extract specific linguistic features and train traditional classification models like Logistic Regression, SVM, Random Forests or a simple neural network on the extracted feature values. The advantages with these kind of models is that they are quick to train and evaluate.

Methods involving fine-tuning a transformer (encoder or decoder only) models. These models usually use a transformer encoder architecture like

[1] https://github.com/saradhix/COLING25_DAIGen_Task2

Proceedings of the 1st Workshop on GenAI Content Detection (GenAIDetect), pages 317–322

BERT, RoBERTa or a decoder only architecture like GPT to learn a classifier. This involves fine-tuning the model on both the classes of data. As the models are originally pretrained on large quantities of text, these models can understand the structure of the text.

Methods that have the text generation model available. These methods use a language model and compute per-token probability and per-token ranks in the predicted next token distribution. These methods use these probabilities to train a simple classifier that are used to train classifier models. The primary disadvantage of these methods is that they require the text generation model to compute the token probabilities. In the real-world, access to the model that is used to generate the text may not be possible.

The creators of GPT model Solaiman et al. (2019) develop a simple model that uses tf-idf features on unigrams and bigrams fed to a logistic regression model for identifying text generated from GPT-2 models with an accuracy of 88%.

Uchendu et al. (2020) train simple models on psychological features with simple neural network architectures to determine if an article is written by a human or a language model.

Zellers et al. (2019) develop a model on top of GROVER model that can identify fake news articles written by GPT-2. Solaiman et al. (2019) fine-tune RoBERTa model for the task to identify the texts generated by the largest variant of the GPT-2 model with an accuracy of 95%.

Fagni et al. (2021) show that a fine-tuned RoBERTa model can spot machine generated tweets from human tweets with over 90% accuracy.

Gehrmann et al. (2019) develop a tool GLTR [2] that uses the per-token probability and per-token rank in the predicted next token distribution and the entropy of the predicted next token to determine if the text is human written or machine-generated.

Mitchell et al. (2023) introduced DetectGPT, a zero-shot detection method that leverages the curvature of a language model's probability function to identify machine-generated text without requiring any training data. This approach demonstrated effectiveness across various LLMs and datasets.

Yang et al. (2023) introduced DNA-GPT, a training-free detection technique that utilizes divergent n-gram analysis. By comparing regenerated text segments with original ones, this method effectively identified discrepancies indicative of machine generation, offering a promising direction for explainable detection.

Wang et al. (2023) developed M4, a benchmark dataset with texts generated from various generators, domains, and languages. Their empirical study revealed that existing detectors often misclassify machine-generated text as human-written, particularly when encountering unseen generators or domains, indicating significant room for improvement.

Bao et al. (2023) presented Fast-DetectGPT, an efficient zero-shot detection method that reduces computational costs associated with previous approaches like DetectGPT. By introducing conditional probability curvature, this method offers a scalable solution for real-time detection applications.

Li et al. (2024) presented MAGE, a comprehensive testbed evaluating detection methods across diverse domains and LLMs. They fine-tune a Longformer Beltagy et al. (2020) that can detect machine generated content with 86.61% on unseen models.

Dugan et al. (2024) propose RAID, a benchmark designed to evaluate the robustness of machine-generated text detectors against adversarial attacks and unseen models. Their study demonstrated that many detectors can easily be circumvented, setting a new standard for evaluating and improving detection methodologies.

3 System Overview

We formulate the problem of identifying the given essay in English as human-written vs. machine-generated as a binary text classification problem. We identify a comprehensive set of linguistically motivated and statistical features for text analysis. We transform the essay into this feature space and use the feature matrix to train classical machine learning algorithms.

We use a set of style, language complexity, bias and subjectivity, and emotion-based features of the text to train machine learning models on these features. These features capture the style, syntax, fluency and other psycholinguistic characteristics of the text. The features have been used to identify fake news (Horne et al., 2019). The code to extract these features has been packaged into a Python package that is easy and fast. [3]

[2] http://gltr.io/

[3] https://github.com/BenjaminDHorne/NELAFeatures

These features fall broadly into these categories:

1. **Style**: These include the fraction of quote characters, exclamation, number of words that are all capitalized, number of stop words, and counts of various parts of speech tags and counts of special characters. 50 features are identified in this category.

2. **Complexity**: Type token Ratio, average word length, word count, Flesch Kincaid Grade level, smog index, Coleman Liau Index and Lix scores. There are 7 features in this category.

3. **Bias**: Fraction of bias words, assertatives, factives, hedges, report verbs, positive opinion words, negative opinion words. There are 8 features in this category.

4. **Affect**: These include a fraction of positive opinion words, neutral opinion words, negative opinion words, Valence Arousal Dominance (VAD) scores of positive, negative, and neutral words, word level and sentence level sentiment scores. There are 9 features in this category.

5. **Moral**: These features include counts of words that indicate Harm Virtue and Vice, Fairness Virtue and Vice, Authority Virtue and Vice, Purity Virtue and Vice, and General Morality. There are 11 features in this category.

We deliberately avoided methods involving finetuning transformer-based models because we wanted to develop a lightweight, fast, and scalable model for detecting machine-generated texts.

4 Experimental Setup

The task organizers have shared a dataset that can be used to train the various machine-learning models. The dataset contained a predefined split to be used for training and evaluation.

The organizers shared the unlabeled test set for making predictions with the trained models. As the test set labels are not publicly released, we do not know the exact number of essays that were machine-generated vs written by Human in the test set.

Table 1 mentions the number of samples present in each of the splits provided by the organizers.

	Human	**Machine**	**Total**
Train	629	1467	2096
Dev	1235	391	1626
Test	Unknown	Unknown	1130

Table 1: Samples in various splits of the dataset

We used the same split as provided by the organizers. We trained multiple ML algorithms after transforming the text through feature extraction. We used the NELA-features python package to extract features from the text.

We experimented with 4 different machine learning algorithms: Logistic Regression, Random Forest, Randomized Decision Trees(Extra Trees), and XGBoost. We used scikit-learn for training our models. We have used the default hyperparameters provided by the scikit-learn while training our models.

The official metric for this task is the macro F1 score.

5 Results

The official *test* set results scored on CodaLab have been presented below in Table 3.

Features	**Model**	**F1 (macro)**
All	Logistic Regression	*0.9949*
All	Random Forest	0.9729
All	Extra Trees	**0.9859**
All	XGBoost	0.9355

Table 3: Results on the official test set

Since only 1 submission is considered for the final evaluation, we used the model that gave the best F1-score on the development set.

Table 2 shows the results of different models with different feature combinations on the development set.

From the results of the development set, we observe that the **complexity** features were most helpful for this task. Using just the **complexity** features alone gave very good results, with an F1 score of 0.9916 using Logistic Regression model. Style features gave an F1-score of 0.9442 using XGBoost. **Complexity** features again gave high performance of F1-score of 0.9916 with Logistic Regression model. **Moral** and **Affect** features did not perform as much as the other feature group.

We can observe that models trained with all concatenated features gave higher accuracy and F1

Model →	LR		RF		ExtraTrees		XGB	
Feature Group ↓	Acc.	F1	Acc.	F1	Acc.	F1	Acc.	F1
Style	0.8204	0.7970	0.9699	**0.9603**	0.9668	0.9565	0.9569	0.9442
Complexity	0.9938	**0.9916**	0.9477	0.9247	0.9520	0.9315	0.9428	0.9184
Bias	0.2405	0.1939	0.6470	0.6250	0.6648	0.6486	0.7165	**0.6846**
Affect	0.2970	0.2724	0.7841	0.7533	0.7608	0.7322	0.8272	**0.7883**
Moral	0.2405	0.1939	0.5480	0.4967	0.5467	0.4944	0.5806	**0.5294**
All	0.9932	0.9908	0.9938	0.9916	**0.9969**	**0.9958**	0.9711	0.9614

Table 2: *Dev* Set Accuracy and Macro-F1 scores

metric than using any one of the feature groups.

Motivated by the high performance of 'All features' with Extra Trees model, we trained a model using all the training and development data. We used this model to make inferences on the test data.

However, after the shared task deadline has passed, the organizers have allowed for submitting the predictions of other models on the official test set for comparison. Table 3 show that Logistic Regression model with all the features has performed the best on the test set with an F1-score of 0.9949 that might have placed us in 3rd position.

The official test set results place us in the 6th position of the leaderboard with an accuracy of 0.9876 and a macro F1 score of 0.9859.

6 Discussion

From the trained models, we found the most important features that are useful for discriminating between machine-generated essays and human-written essays. Table 4 lists the top discriminatory features. We visualize the distribution of the feature values in the human-written and ai-generated classes as histograms to understand them in greater detail. Here are some of the observations:

- Human essays use more stop words than machine-generated essays.
- Human essays have less average word length compared to the essays generated by AI.
- Machine-generated essays have lower readability scores like the Coleman Liau Index, Lix Readability Index, Smog Index, and the Flesch Kincaid Grade level. This is because humans tend to write shorter sentences and use fewer words per sentence.
- Compared to machine-generated essays, the usage of coordinating conjunctions is slightly more in human-written essays.

Rank	Feature
1	Fraction of stop words
2	Average Word Length
3	Fraction of punctuations
4	Coleman Liau Index
5	Lix Readability Index
6	Fraction of Existential there
7	Smog Index
8	Fraction of Coordinating Conjunctions
9	Flesch Kincaid Grade Level
10	Type Token Ratio

Table 4: Top 10 most important features

- Human essays have more occurrences of existential 'there' usage than AI-generated essays.

Section A, shows the histogram of the top 10 features among both the classes. We can observe the differences in the distribution of the top 10 features.

7 Conclusion

We conclude that the NELA features can be used to identify machine-generated text with high accuracy, as shown through the evaluation of the test set.

We feel that our model is robust to adversarial inputs through perturbations. As a future work, we plan to evaluate our model by adversely perturbing the input. We plan to explore the robustness of our methods to domain shifts.

References

Guangsheng Bao, Yanbin Zhao, Zhiyang Teng, Linyi Yang, and Yue Zhang. 2023. Fast-detectgpt: Efficient zero-shot detection of machine-generated text via conditional probability curvature. *arXiv preprint arXiv:2310.05130*.

Iz Beltagy, Matthew E Peters, and Arman Cohan. 2020.

Longformer: The long-document transformer. *arXiv preprint arXiv:2004.05150*.

Shammur Absar Chowdhury, Hind AL-Merekhi, Mucahid Kutlu, Kaan Efe Keleş, Fatema Ahmad, Tasnim Mohiuddin, Georgios Mikros, and Firoj Alam. 2025. GenAI content detection task 2: AI vs. human – academic essay authenticity challenge. In *Proceedings of the 1st Workshop on GenAI Content Detection (GenAIDetect)*, Abu Dhabi, UAE. International Conference on Computational Linguistics.

Liam Dugan, Alyssa Hwang, Filip Trhlik, Josh Magnus Ludan, Andrew Zhu, Hainiu Xu, Daphne Ippolito, and Chris Callison-Burch. 2024. Raid: A shared benchmark for robust evaluation of machine-generated text detectors. *arXiv preprint arXiv:2405.07940*.

Tiziano Fagni, Fabrizio Falchi, Margherita Gambini, Antonio Martella, and Maurizio Tesconi. 2021. Tweepfake: About detecting deepfake tweets. *Plos one*, 16(5):e0251415.

Sebastian Gehrmann, Hendrik Strobelt, and Alexander M Rush. 2019. Gltr: Statistical detection and visualization of generated text. *arXiv preprint arXiv:1906.04043*.

Benjamin D Horne, Jeppe Nørregaard, and Sibel Adali. 2019. Robust fake news detection over time and attack. *ACM Transactions on Intelligent Systems and Technology (TIST)*, 11(1):1–23.

Yafu Li, Qintong Li, Leyang Cui, Wei Bi, Zhilin Wang, Longyue Wang, Linyi Yang, Shuming Shi, and Yue Zhang. 2024. Mage: Machine-generated text detection in the wild. In *Proceedings of the 62nd Annual Meeting of the Association for Computational Linguistics (Volume 1: Long Papers)*, pages 36–53.

Eric Mitchell, Yoonho Lee, Alexander Khazatsky, Christopher D Manning, and Chelsea Finn. 2023. Detectgpt: Zero-shot machine-generated text detection using probability curvature. In *International Conference on Machine Learning*, pages 24950–24962. PMLR.

Irene Solaiman, Miles Brundage, Jack Clark, Amanda Askell, Ariel Herbert-Voss, Jeff Wu, Alec Radford, Gretchen Krueger, Jong Wook Kim, Sarah Kreps, et al. 2019. Release strategies and the social impacts of language models. *arXiv preprint arXiv:1908.09203*.

Adaku Uchendu, Thai Le, Kai Shu, and Dongwon Lee. 2020. Authorship attribution for neural text generation. In *Proceedings of the 2020 conference on empirical methods in natural language processing (EMNLP)*, pages 8384–8395.

Yuxia Wang, Jonibek Mansurov, Petar Ivanov, Jinyan Su, Artem Shelmanov, Akim Tsvigun, Chenxi Whitehouse, Osama Mohammed Afzal, Tarek Mahmoud, Toru Sasaki, et al. 2023. M4: Multi-generator, multi-domain, and multi-lingual black-box machine-generated text detection. *arXiv preprint arXiv:2305.14902*.

Xianjun Yang, Wei Cheng, Yue Wu, Linda Petzold, William Yang Wang, and Haifeng Chen. 2023. Dna-gpt: Divergent n-gram analysis for training-free detection of gpt-generated text. *arXiv preprint arXiv:2305.17359*.

Rowan Zellers, Ari Holtzman, Hannah Rashkin, Yonatan Bisk, Ali Farhadi, Franziska Roesner, and Yejin Choi. 2019. Defending against neural fake news. *Advances in neural information processing systems*, 32.

A Appendix

Figures 1 to 10 show the histograms of the top features across the two classes of the essays.

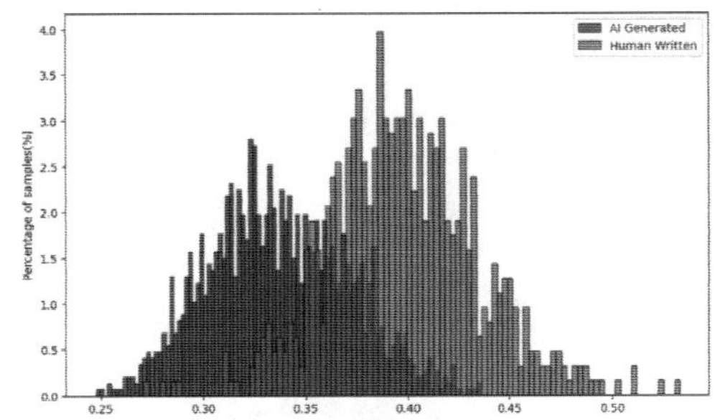

Figure 1: Histogram of the fraction of stopwords

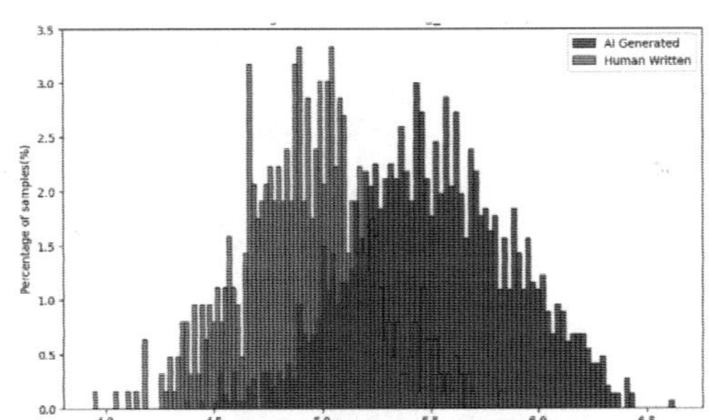

Figure 2: Histogram of Average Word Length

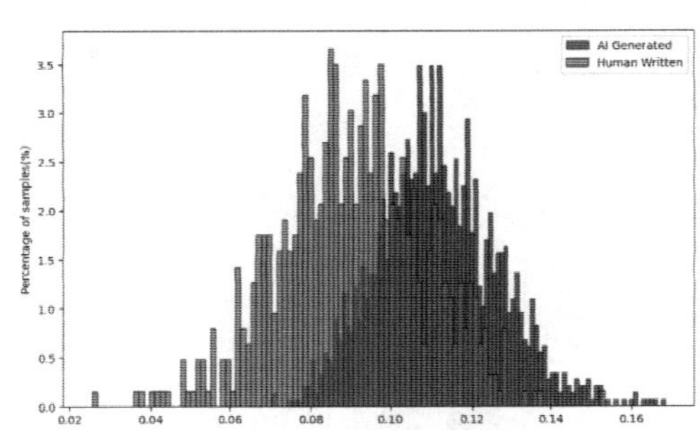

Figure 3: Histogram of the fraction of all punctuation words

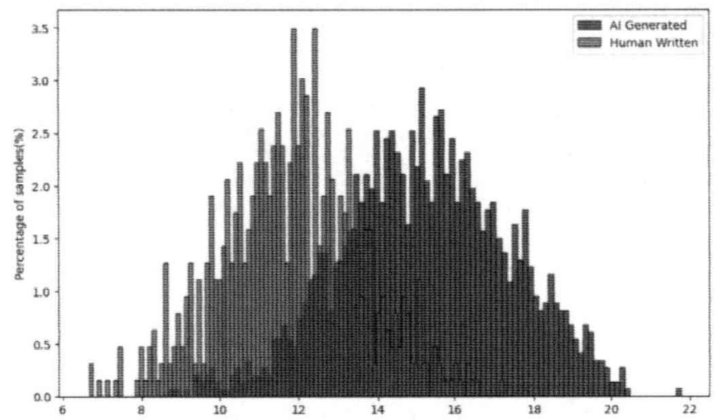

Figure 4: Histogram of Coleman Liau Index

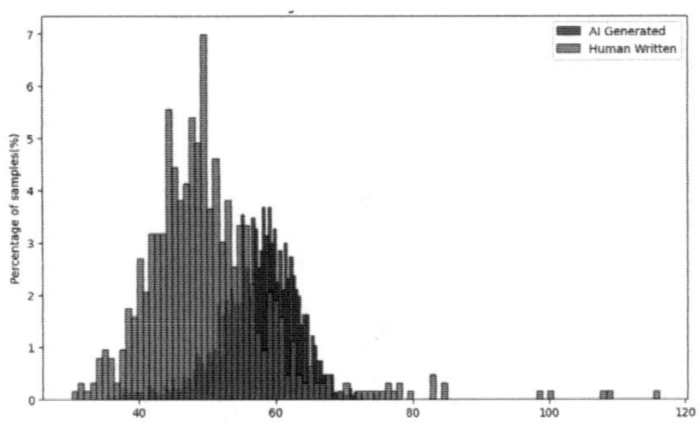

Figure 5: Histogram of Lix Readability Index

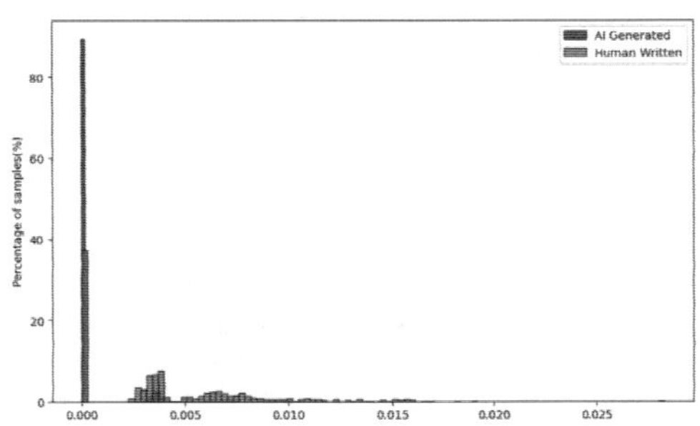

Figure 6: Histogram of Fraction of Existential 'there'

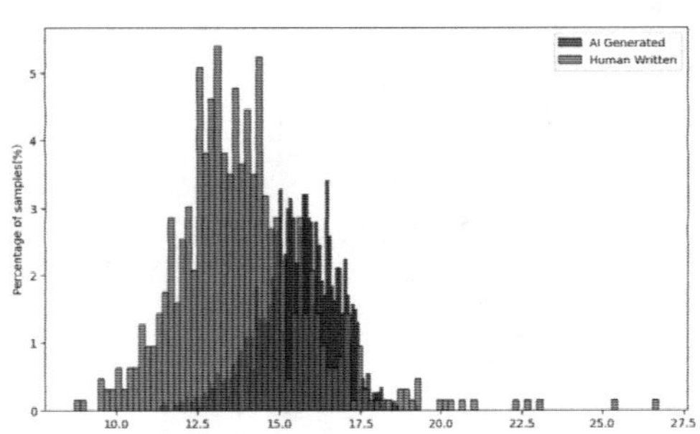

Figure 7: Histogram of Smog Index

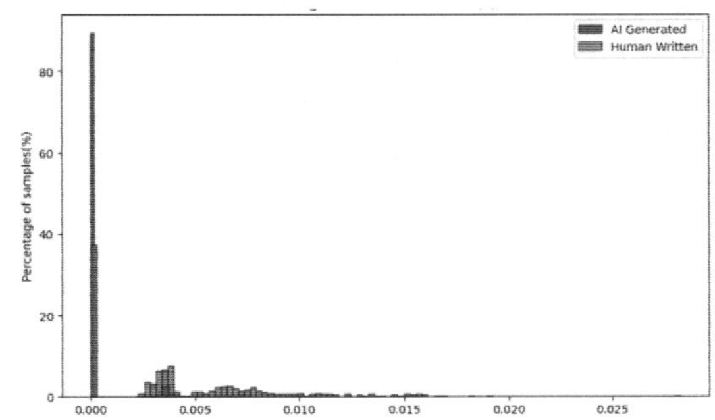

Figure 8: Histogram of Fraction of Coordinating Conjunctions

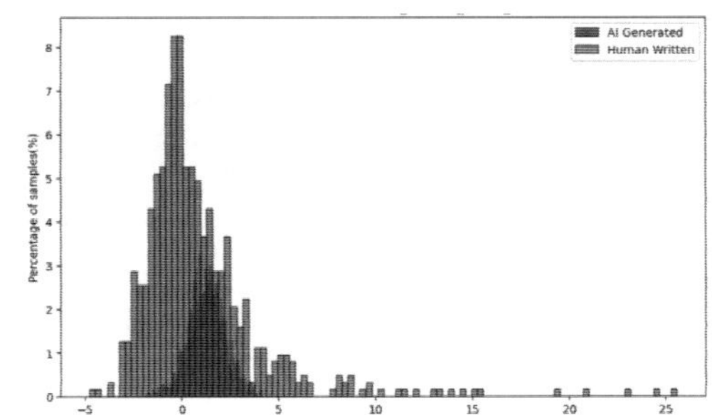

Figure 9: Histogram of Flesch Kincaid Grade Level

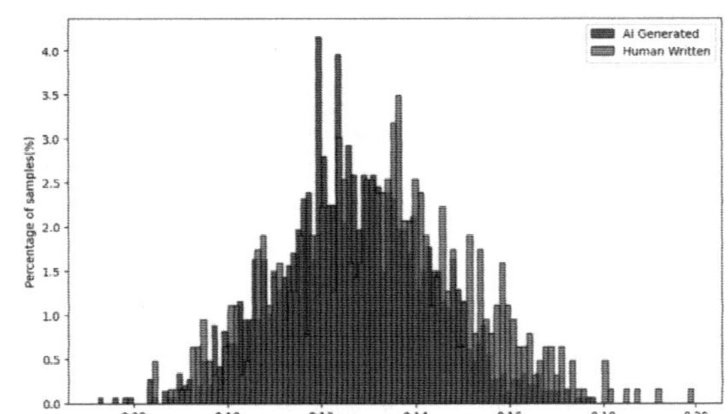

Figure 10: Histogram of Type Token Ratio

GenAI Content Detection Task 2: AI vs. Human – Academic Essay Authenticity Challenge

Shammur Absar Chowdhury[1], **Hind Almerekhi**[1], **Mucahid Kutlu**[2], **Kaan Efe Keleş**[3], **Fatema Ahmad**[1], **Tasnim Mohiuddin**[1], **George Mikros**[4], **Firoj Alam**[1]
[1]Qatar Computing Research Institute, HBKU, Qatar, [2]Qatar University, Qatar
[3]TOBB ETU, Türkiye, [4]Hamad Bin Khalifa University, Qatar
{shchowdhury, halmerekhi, fakter, mmohiuddin, gmikros, fialam}@hbku.edu.qa
mucahidkutlu@qu.edu.qa, kaanefekeles@etu.edu.tr

Abstract

This paper presents a comprehensive overview of the first edition of the *Academic Essay Authenticity Challenge*, organized as part of the GenAI Content Detection shared tasks collocated with COLING 2025. This challenge focuses on detecting machine-generated *vs* human-authored essays for academic purposes. The task is defined as follows: *"Given an essay, identify whether it is generated by a machine or authored by a human."* The challenge involves two languages: English and Arabic. During the evaluation phase, 25 teams submitted systems for English and 21 teams for Arabic, reflecting substantial interest in the task. Finally, five teams submitted system description papers. The majority of submissions utilized fine-tuned transformer-based models, with one team employing Large Language Models (LLMs) such as Llama 2 and Llama 3. This paper outlines the task formulation, details the dataset construction process, and explains the evaluation framework. Additionally, we present a summary of the approaches adopted by participating teams. Nearly all submitted systems outperformed the n-gram-based baseline, with the top-performing systems achieving F1 scores exceeding 0.98 for both languages, indicating significant progress in the detection of machine-generated text.

1 Introduction

The rapid progress in Artificial Intelligence (AI) and the proliferation of generative content produced by LLMs have introduced transformative opportunities across various domains — yet they also pose profound challenges (Wu et al., 2023). One such challenge lies in the detection and prevention of misuse of LLMs in contexts such as fake news, misinformation, disinformation, and academic dishonesty (Tang et al., 2024). For instance, the volume of AI-generated news on misinformation-prone websites surged by 457% between January 1, 2022, and May 1, 2023, with a corresponding increase of 57.3% on mainstream platforms (Hanley and Durumeric, 2024). These issues pose substantial barriers to the broader adoption of LLMs, thereby limiting their potential across various applications. Effectively detecting LLM-generated content is crucial for leveraging the capabilities of these models while mitigating associated risks.

Researchers have responded to these challenges through a variety of approaches. Previous methods include classification algorithms designed to distinguish between AI-generated and human-authored text (Guo et al., 2023), as well as watermarking techniques (Szyller et al., 2021; He et al., 2022; Kirchenbauer et al., 2023). These watermarking approaches strategically embed imperceptible signatures within generated texts, enabling model-specific identification while maintaining human-indistinguishable quality. Other recent efforts have focused on the creation of question-answering datasets such as M4 (Wang et al., 2024b), generated by humans and ChatGPT in both English and Chinese and the associated shared task (Wang et al., 2024a).

Within academic settings, concerns surrounding the potential misuse of LLMs have intensified, particularly regarding academic dishonesty involving AI-assisted essay writing and problem-solving. Recent research has made considerable progress in the development of datasets and benchmarking efforts to address these issues. For instance, Yu et al. (2023) introduced the CHEAT dataset, which focuses on abstracts from IEEE Xplore, while Wang et al. (2024b) developed a comprehensive multilingual dataset. Additionally, Dugan et al. (2024) presented a robust dataset designed to address the challenge of detecting machine-generated text.

Despite these efforts, large-scale initiatives in academic contexts remain limited. Hence, this shared task aims to bridge this gap by tackling the task of distinguishing AI-generated essays from

Proceedings of the 1st Workshop on GenAI Content Detection (GenAIDetect), pages 323–333
January 19, 2025.

human-authored ones. The challenge attracted substantial interest, with 99 teams registered to access the dataset and 56 teams actively participating in the development and evaluation phases. In the evaluation phase, 25 teams submitted systems for English, and 21 teams participated for Arabic. Furthermore, five teams submitted system description papers. The majority of participating systems employed transformer-based models, while one team utilized state-of-the-art LLMs such as Llama 2 and Llama 3. Notably, most submissions outperformed the traditional n-gram-based baseline, signaling substantial progress in AI-generated content detection methodologies.

The subsequent sections of this paper are structured as follows: Section 2 provides a comprehensive review of related work. Section 3 presents the task formulation and dataset setup. Section 4 presents empirical results and offers a comprehensive overview of participating systems. Finally, Section 5 concludes with a summary of findings and future directions.

2 Related Work

The detection of AI-generated text relies on analyzing statistical patterns and linguistic features that distinguish human and machine writing styles. Zaitsu and Jin (2023) highlight that AI-generated text tends to use repetitive sentence patterns and a limited vocabulary, prioritizing clarity over the nuanced variations of human writing. Similarly, Weber-Wulff et al. (2023) report that such texts often exhibit lower syntactic complexity and reduced lexical diversity, making them identifiable through these markers. Additionally, Gallé et al. (2021) report that higher predictability in word n-gram is a key indicator of machine generated text.

Machine learning approaches have become central to AI-generated text detection. Darda et al. (2023) explored traditional classification algorithms such as Support Vector Machines (SVM) and Random Forest. Vora et al. (2023) propose a multimodal approach that uses BERT to analyze syntactic and semantic features of text and CNN architectures for image. Mikros et al. (2023) investigated using stylometric features and transformer-based models. Their findings showed that ensemble techniques, particularly those employing majority voting, outperformed individual classifiers.

There has also been effort to combine different machine learning approaches. For instance, deep learning architectures can extract features from text, while traditional classifiers make predictions based on these features, leveraging the strengths of both techniques (Bhattacharjee et al., 2023). Incorporating user feedback further enhances hybrid models, enabling them to adapt to real-world usage patterns (Rashidi et al., 2023).

Despite advancements in detection methodologies, significant limitations persist. Weber-Wulff et al. (2023) reveal that many detection tools struggle with high rates of false positives and false negatives, indicating a need for further refinement. According to Perkins et al. (2024), humans naturally incorporate varying sentence lengths and structures in their writing, creating what researchers call "burstiness"—a key feature that distinguishes human-authored content from AI-generated text. This variation in writing style, along with occasional grammatical inconsistencies and stylistic irregularities, represents the natural "imperfections" that make human writing unique. Interestingly, Liang et al. (2023) found that texts with lower levels of perplexity and coherence—characteristics often found in writing by non-native English speakers—are more likely to be flagged as human-authored.

Another challenge in AI-generated content detection is the lack of transparency in models' predictions, reducing their applicability in real-life scenarios, particularly in high-stakes contexts such as academia and forensic applications. Thus, a number of researchers worked on developing explainable AI (XAI) methods for AI generated text detection. For instance, Shah et al. (2023) develop an XAI model using stylistic features. Wu and Flanagan (2023) proposes a hybrid approach that combine statistical analysis with machine learning techniques. Additionally, the integration of user feedback into hybrid models may facilitate the development of more adaptive systems that can learn from usage patterns (Rashidi et al., 2023).

3 Task and Dataset

3.1 Task Definition

The main objective of the task is to detect whether the given candidate essay is AI-generated or human-written. Given the input essay $\mathbf{e}$, the task is to design a text detector $\mathcal{D}(\mathbf{e})$, such that the model outputs label indicating AI-generated or Human-authored content. For this edition, we designed the task as binary classification problem.

System Prompt	You are a **{study_level}** student from **{country}**, preparing for the TOEFL exam. Your English proficiency level is **{proficiency_level}**. Your task is to write a well-structured TOEFL essay in response to the given prompt. Ensure your essay is clear and coherent, following the standard essay format: an introduction, body paragraphs, and a conclusion. Focus on presenting your ideas logically, using appropriate language, and providing relevant examples to support your arguments. Aim to demonstrate your proficiency in English through organized thought and effective communication.
User Prompt	Do you agree or disagree with the following statement: **"{statement}"** Write a well-structured essay expressing your opinion. Be sure to use specific reasons and examples to support your viewpoint. The essay should be between **{min_length}** and **{max_length}** words in length. Please provide only an essay and in a JSON object. No additional text or explanation. **{"essay": "your essay"}**

Table 1: Example of *System* and *User Prompts* for training and validation in English essay generation. Similar prompts were used for Arabic essays. Variables include study_level ={'pre-university','university'}, proficiency_levels={'low','medium','high'}, country_list={'Arabic', 'German', 'French', 'Hindi', 'Italian', 'Japanese', 'Korean', 'Spanish', 'Telugu', 'Turkish', 'Chinese'}. For Arabic prompts, an additional variable, nativity={'native','non-native'} is used.

3.2 Datasets

The task aims to develop a system specifically designed for detecting AI generated text in academic essays. The dataset comprises essays authored by both native and non-native speakers, alongside AI-generated content. A significant challenge in this task was collecting authentic human-authored academic essays while addressing the following considerations:

- Ensuring author privacy, obtaining informed consent, and ethically sourcing the content.
- Verifying that the collected essays were genuinely authored by humans, free from any AI interference or plagiarism.
- Acquiring a diverse set of essays representing different academic levels and cultural backgrounds to ensure inclusivity in the dataset.

For the task, we focused on two languages: English and Arabic. For each language, we provided training, validation, dev-test, and the final test sets, which included human-authored and AI-generated texts. We released these data splits in two phases – *(i) Development phase* – we released the training, validation, and mock test data (dev-test); *(ii) Evaluation phase* – we released the final test set which is used to rank the submitted system. Below, we discuss the dataset design for the development and final evaluation phases, respectively.

3.3 Development Phase

During the development phase we have released training, validation, and dev-test. For this phase, we first collected human-authored essays and essay topics. To create the data splits, we carefully designed each set to ensure unique essay topics, avoiding overlap between training, validation, and dev-test datasets.

Furthermore, within each split, we manually categorized the essay topics based on their thematic similarity. This classification is used to assign topics for generating essays using LLMs, and the rest is reserved exclusively for selecting human-authored essays from various existing datasets mentioned below. The final statistics of the dataset released in this phases are presented in Table 5.

Human-authored Essay The human-authored data was sourced from different language assessment datasets, including examinations like IELTS, and TOEFL among others. To ensure the authenticity of human-authored content, we selected essays that were either handwritten or composed in a supervised classroom setting, explicitly to make

sure that none of the texts were created with the assistance of generative technologies or online articles. This approach was designed to maintain the integrity of the datasets and accurately represent human academic writing.
For the English, we collected essay statements (essay prompt) and essays from:

- **IELTS Writing Scored Essays** Dataset[1] contains 1200 academic essays for varieties of prompts. Each essays are accompanied by the examiners' feedback along with scores

- **ETS Corpus of Non-Native Written English** corpus[2] contains 12,100 academic essays, written addressing eight different prompts, by non-native speakers from 11 different countries, as part TOEFL English proficiency exam. The dataset includes the speaker's native language along with scores they obtained for the corresponding essays. While the dataset was originally designed for native language identification tasks, its rich collection of academic essays, makes it highly suitable for supporting our AI-generated text detection efforts.

As for the Arabic subtask, the datasets we use are the following:

- **Arabic Learner Corpus (ALC)**[3] (Alfaifi and Atwell, 2013) includes 1,197 essays written by both native and non-native Arabic pre-university/university speakers from 67 nationalities. The dataset includes speakers' nationality along with the information if the essay was written in class or as homework. For the task, we only selected in-class essays, manually excluded off-topic essays, and reviewed the essays for any corrections.

- **Qatari Corpus of Argumentative Writing (QCAW) dataset**[4] (Zaghouani et al., 2024) is a collection of 195 argumentative essays written by native Arabic undergraduate students. The prompts given to the student were inspired by TOEFL writing exercises (Ahmed et al., 2023).

- **The CERCLL corpus**[5] includes ≈ 270 essays written by non-native (L2) and heritage Arabic speakers.[6] The dataset includes information about the speakers' proficiency, along with the type – L2 *vs* heritage speakers. The dataset covers a wide range of topics and multiple genres, including description, narration, and instruction essays.

AI-generated Essay The generated essays, for both languages, utilized seven state-of-the art LLMs including: GPT-3.5-Turbo (2023-03-15-preview), GPT-4o (2024-08-06), GPT-4o-mini (2024-07-18) (OpenAI, 2024), Gemini-1.5 (Team, 2024), phi3.5,[7] Llama-3.1 (8B) (Abdin et al., 2024), and Claude-3.5.[8] To produce these essays, we designed the prompts by utilizing a selected subset of essay statements from the aforementioned datasets. The designed prompts included detailed instructions to emulate human writing styles, specify essay length requirements, and incorporate predefined personas reflecting various factors such as nativity and/or language proficiency, following the metadata and statistics obtained from the human-authored essay collections. This approach ensured the generation of essays that closely resemble real-world human writing in both style and content. An example of such a prompt is shown in Table 1.

3.4 Evaluation Phase

For the evaluation, we designed and developed a novel dataset, the **G**enerated and **R**eal **A**cademic **C**orpus for **E**valuation (GRACE), which includes both human-authored and AI-generated essays in English and Arabic.

3.4.1 Data Collection

For designing the human-authored portion of the dataset, we began by carefully designing test set essay statements aligned with those used in development phase topics. We selected five different essay types, and under each type, we created several essay statements (see Table 4 for examples). The topics include social influence & technology, lifestyle choices & preferences, cultural & global perspective, environmental & societal responsibility, and personal growth & experience.

[1] https://www.kaggle.com/datasets/mazlumi/ielts-writing-scored-essays-dataset
[2] https://catalog.ldc.upenn.edu/LDC2014T06
[3] https://www.arabiclearnercorpus.com
[4] https://catalog.ldc.upenn.edu/LDC2022T04
[5] https://cercll.arizona.edu/arabic-corpus/
[6] The original dataset is available in pdf format.
[7] https://huggingface.co/microsoft/Phi-3.5-mini-instruct
[8] https://www.anthropic.com/news/claude-3-5-sonnet

```
You are tasked with generating creative and rigorous academic essays.
Here's how:
1) Topics Selection: You are provided with a set of topics: «<20 random topics»>. First, choose one topic at random from this list.
2) Generate Related Topics: Based on the chosen topic, create 10 new topic ideas. These should be different from the chosen topic but related in a way that someone interested in the initial topic might also find these new ideas engaging.
3) Select Final Topic: From the 10 new topics, pick one at random to focus on.
4) Choose a Profession: List 10 random professions that are entirely unrelated to the final topic, ensuring that they come from different fields or disciplines. These professions should be distinct enough that their practitioners would not typically engage with or have knowledge about the topic. Then, select one profession at random from this list.
5) Choose a Writing Style: List 10 distinct writing styles (e.g., persuasive, narrative, descriptive) and choose one at random.
6) Essay Writing: Write an academic and creative essay on the chosen topic. This essay should be written from the perspective of someone in the chosen profession and in the selected writing style. Do not ever mention the chosen profession or writing style in the essay itself. Do not include any personal opinions or experiences with regarding to the profession in the essay. Do not mention anything about the chosen profession whatsoever.
Your output should be in JSON format, structured as follows:
{ "selected_topic": "<randomly selected topic from the given topics>", "generated_topics": [ "<generated topic 1>", "<generated topic 2>", "...", "<generated topic 10>" ], "final_topic": "<randomly selected topic from generated_topics>", "professions": [ "<profession 1>", "<profession 2>", "...", "<profession 10>" ], "selected_profession": "<randomly selected profession from professions>", "writing_styles": [ "<style 1>", "<style 2>", "...", "<style 10>" ], "selected_writing_style": "<randomly selected style from writing_styles>", "essay": "<generated essay>" }
Please proceed with this format to generate a fully structured JSON output. Remember to keep the content diverse and creative throughout the process. The essay should be comprehensive, detailed, and reflective of rigorous academic standards. The essay must be multiple paragraphs long (at least 1 page's worth). Return only the valid JSON output and nothing else. Good luck!
```

Table 2: **Freehand prompt** used to generate AI generated essays for the final test set.

Essay Writing by Recruited Participants: We then recruited[9] university students, both monolingual and bilingual, contribute to the essay writing. The participants were provided with a list of essay statements in their respective languages (either English or Arabic) and were asked to complete each essay within 30 minutes. They were instructed to limit the essays to 350–500 words and ensure they included an introduction, main arguments, and a conclusion. The essays must be written in Modern Standard Arabic (MSA) for Arabic, or in formal English for the English essays.

Collected Essay Assignments: Additionally, we collected previously submitted English *essay assignments* from university students to enrich the dataset.

Anonymization of Personal Information In the collected *essay assignments* we noticed that there were some information containing mentions of entities. Therefore, we anonymized them to ensure the removal of any information that could directly or indirectly identify the author or reveal any private information about an entity that is not publicly known. This process was essential to uphold privacy standards and ethical considerations.

To achieve this, we followed these guidelines:

- *Author Identification Removal*: Any mention of names, addresses, affiliations, or specific details that could identify the essay's author was redacted.
- *Private Entity Information*: Any references to non-public entities, such as organizations, businesses, or private individuals mentioned in the essays, were removed or replaced with generic terms.
- *Sensitive Content*: Sensitive information, such as health conditions, financial details, or other personal data, was also removed to ensure privacy.
- *Consistency*: Replacement terms were standardized (e.g., "[NAME]", "[ADDRESS]", "[ORGANIZATION]") to maintain consistency throughout the dataset.

A team of five trained annotators was recruited

[9]We use a third-party company for the reward money. The amount was decided based on the standard local rate for data annotation

```
Thoroughly rewrite the provided academic essay to enhance clarity, diversity in sentence structure,
and vocabulary richness, all while maintaining the original meaning and intent. Your goal is to
produce a refined and nuanced version of the text.
Aim to increase the essay's length by adding substantial elaborations, exploring various perspectives,
and providing comprehensive explanations that will offer a deeply layered and extensive output.
Deliver the output exclusively in JSON format with a single key "text" as shown below, ensuring that
no additional information or comments are included:
{{ "text": "<rewritten_and_greatly_expanded_academic_essay>" }}
Here is the passage to rewrite and extensively expand:
«<original_passage_start»> {the passage to be paraphrased} «<original_passage_end»>
```

Table 3: **Paraphrasing prompt** used to generate AI generated essays for the final test set.

Question Type	Example Statements
Agree or Disagree	Do you agree or disagree with the following statement? People should be encouraged to take risks, even if there is a chance of failure. Use specific reasons and examples to support your answer.
Preference	Some people prefer to spend their money on experiences, such as travel or concerts, while others prefer to save for physical possessions, such as a car or a home. Which approach do you prefer, and why? Use specific reasons and examples to support your choice.
If/Imaginary Situations	If you could have any superpower, such as the ability to fly or become invisible, which one would you choose, and why? Use specific reasons and examples to explain your answer.
Advan. and Disadvan.	What are the advantages and disadvantages of living in a large city? Use specific reasons and examples to support your answer.
Descriptive	Describe a memorable trip you have taken and explain what made it special. Use specific details to support your response.

Table 4: Examples of different question types and corresponding essay statements (prompts).

Label	Train	Valid	Dev-Test	Total
		English		
AI	925	299	712	1,936
Human	1,145	182	174	1,501
Total	2,070	481	886	3,437
		Arabic		
AI	1,467	391	369	2,227
Human	629	1,235	500	2,364
Total	2096	1,626	869	4,591

Table 5: Development phase: dataset and label distribution

to carry out this task. Each annotator was provided with clear anonymization guidelines and examples to ensure consistency and accuracy. Such anonymization steps ensure that the dataset meets ethical standards for research.

3.4.2 Data Generation

For the AI-generated essays, we followed two distinct methodologies:

- *Freehand Generation:* An instruct-tuned LLM, namely gpt-4o, independently generated essays using the *Freehand Generation Prompt* shown in Table 2. The prompt was designed to ensure diverse outputs. We were inspired by the prompting techniques proposed by Chen et al. (2024).
- *Paraphrasing Human-Written Text:* Using the *Paraphrasing Prompt* shown in Table 3, human-authored essays were rephrased by an instruct-tuned LLM, namely claude-3.5 to generate stylistically varied yet semantically equivalent AI-written versions. The resulting text comprises a mix of human-written and AI-generated content, designed to challenge the effectiveness of detection methods.

Category	English	Arabic	Total
AI (Free)	400	100	500
AI (Para)	365	98	463
Human	365	95	460
Total	1,130	293	1,423

Table 6: Distribution of essays by *category* and *language* across the test set. Free - freehand generation, Para - paraphrasing-based generation.

The final GRACE dataset comprises a balanced distribution of human-written and AI-generated essays. Table 6 provides a detailed breakdown across languages and generation methods.

3.5 Baseline and Evaluation Setup

3.5.1 Baseline

For all languages, we train an n-gram (unigram, $n = 1$) based baseline model. We transformed the texual content of the essays into a TF-IDF (Term Frequency-Inverse Document Frequency) representation with a maximum of 10k features. A Support Vector Machine (SVM) classifier is then trained on this feature representation to evaluate its performance.

3.5.2 Evaluation Setup

The task was organized into two phases, corresponding to the previously described dataset development process:

- **Development phase**: We released the train and validation subsets, and participants submitted runs on the dev-test set through a competition on Codalab.[10]
- **Evaluation phase**: We released the official test subset – GRACE, and the participants were given four days to submit their final predictions through the same Codalab competition URL. Only the latest submission from each team was considered official and was used for the final team ranking.

3.5.3 Evaluation Measure:

We measure the performance of the participating systems using accuracy, macro- precision, recall and F1 measure. However, official ranking was based on macro-F1.

4 Results and Overview of the Systems

In Table 7, we present the results of participants' systems for both Arabic and English including baseline. For Arabic, all systems outperformed the n-gram baseline, whereas, for English, three teams performed below the baseline. The task generated significant interest, with 56 teams registering to participate. However, the number of system submissions was nearly halved, and ultimately, only five teams submitted system description papers. In Table 8, we provide an overview of the participating systems for which a description paper was submitted. For Arabic top team, **IntegrityAI** (AL-Smadi, 2025), fine-tuned Electra model. For English top team, **CMI-AIGCX** (Kaijie et al., 2025), used LLMs (Llama 2 and 3) and also fine-tuned XLM-roberta model.

[10]https://codalab.lisn.upsaclay.fr/competitions/20118

Team **IntegrityAI** (AL-Smadi, 2025) fine-tuned ELECTRA-small for English and AraELECTRA-base for Arabic to balance high performance with computational efficiency. Stylometric features, including word count, sentence length, and vocabulary richness, were incorporated to enhance detection capabilities. The lightweight models achieved F1-scores of 0.985 for English and 0.984 for Arabic, demonstrating the effectiveness of combining transformer-based architectures with stylometric analysis. The system was further optimized for deployment on GPUs with moderate memory capacity, ensuring both efficiency and accessibility. Larger models, such as ELECTRA-large, were also tested, achieving an F1-score of 0.997 for English, demonstrating the potential for even greater accuracy with additional computational resources.

Team **CMI-AIGCX** (Kaijie et al., 2025) proposed a method leveraging the Llama-3.1-8B model as a proxy to capture the semantic feature of each token in the text. These token representations were subsequently used to train a model. Instead of fine-tuning an LLM, they leveraged multilingual knowledge and trained a model to enhance detection performance. Their approach demonstrated that using a proxy model with diverse multilingual knowledge can effectively detect machine-generated text across multiple languages, regardless of model size. For English, an F1 score of 0.999 was achieved, securing first place out of 25 teams. For Arabic, an F1 score of 0.965 was obtained, which ranked fourth among 21 teams.

Team **Tesla** (Indurthi and Varma, 2025) extracted a comprehensive set of features encompassing style, language complexity, bias, subjectivity, and emotion. These features were used to train four machine learning algorithms: Logistic Regression, Random Forest, Randomized Decision Trees (Extra Trees), and XGBoost, leveraging diverse approaches to optimize detection performance. Their methods ranked 6th on the leaderboard for the English subtask, achieving an F1-score of 0.986.

Team **EssayDetect** (Agrahari et al., 2025) proposed a fusion model by integrating pre-trained language model embeddings with stylometric and linguistic features to improve classification accuracy. The contributions were threefold: *(i)* LIME was utilized to identify and highlight highly discriminative features, *(ii)* focal loss was employed to address class imbalance, and *(iii)* layer-wise freezing was implemented during fine-tuning to preserve core linguistic representations in the lower layers while

Arabic						English					
Team	Acc	P	R	F1	Rank	Team	Acc	P	R	F1	Rank
IntegrityAI	0.986	0.990	0.979	0.984	1	CMI-AIGCX	0.999	0.999	0.999	0.999	1
USTC-BUPT	0.976	0.983	0.963	0.972	2	starlight	0.997	0.998	0.996	0.997	2
starlight	0.969	0.964	0.966	0.965	3	saehyunMa	0.994	0.995	0.990	0.993	3
CMI-AIGCX	0.969	0.966	0.964	0.965	4	Fsf	0.994	0.995	0.990	0.993	4
apricity	0.966	0.969	0.953	0.960	5	1-800	0.991	0.987	0.993	0.990	5
RA	0.962	0.956	0.959	0.957	6	Tesla	0.988	0.983	0.989	0.986	6
1-800	0.959	0.961	0.945	0.952	7	apricity	0.988	0.983	0.989	0.986	7
Lkminnow	0.956	0.943	0.959	0.950	8	small	0.984	0.981	0.983	0.982	8
alpaca0000001	0.949	0.937	0.948	0.942	9	jojoc	0.982	0.975	0.985	0.980	9
jojoc	0.949	0.939	0.946	0.942	10	EssayDetect	0.978	0.968	0.984	0.975	10
small	0.945	0.938	0.938	0.938	11	ShixuanMa	0.976	0.968	0.979	0.973	11
jebish7	0.945	0.945	0.929	0.937	12	RA	0.973	0.975	0.964	0.969	12
EssayDetect	0.942	0.949	0.919	0.932	13	alpaca0000001	0.956	0.940	0.967	0.951	13
nits_teja_srikar	0.922	0.943	0.882	0.904	14	Lkminnow	0.932	0.913	0.943	0.925	14
Mashixuan	0.898	0.877	0.911	0.889	15	IntegrityAI	0.880	0.864	0.911	0.873	15
Sinai	0.829	0.821	0.866	0.822	16	USTC-BUPT	0.878	0.922	0.812	0.842	16
Vasudha	0.816	0.796	0.831	0.804	17	jebish7	0.847	0.908	0.763	0.794	17
ShixuanMa	0.758	0.783	0.818	0.754	18	CNLP-NITS-PP	0.777	0.784	0.825	0.771	18
gaoyf	0.608	0.720	0.707	0.607	19	Mashixuan	0.742	0.778	0.809	0.739	19
CNLP-NITS-PP	0.590	0.557	0.563	0.557	20	nits_teja_srikar	0.773	0.875	0.649	0.658	20
halcyonized	0.495	0.488	0.487	0.475	21	Vasudha	0.517	0.700	0.643	0.509	21
Baseline	0.474	0.480	0.477	0.461	-	Mahavir_IIITA	0.512	0.683	0.634	0.504	22
						Baseline	0.495	0.494	0.494	0.478	-
						halcyonized	0.493	0.494	0.493	0.477	23
						gaoyf	0.391	0.523	0.514	0.374	24
						Sinai	0.354	0.602	0.519	0.298	25

Table 7: The official results for Arabic and English are ranked based on the official metric: macro-F1. Teams that submitted a system description paper are highlighted in skyblue.

Team	Lang.		Models										Misc	
	Arabic	English	LLama2	LLama3	BERT	RoBERTa	XLM-r	ALBERT	DistilBERT	DeBERTa	Electra	AraBERT	Prep.	Info.
IntegrityAI	1	15									☑		☑	☑
CMI-AIGCX	4	1	☑	☑			☑						☑	
Tesla		6												
EssayDetect	13	10			☑	☑	☑	☑	☑					
RA	6	12				☑				☑		☑		

Table 8: Overview of the approaches. The numbers in the language box refer to the position of the team in the official ranking. Prep.: Preprocessing. Info.: Info. Extraction.

enabling the higher layers to capture task-specific stylistic differences in essays.

Team **RA** (Gharib and Elgendy, 2025) fine-tuned several models for English, including RoBERTa, XLM-RoBERTa, mBERT, and DeBERTa. Similar performance was observed across all models on the validation set, except for mBERT, which exhibited slightly lower performance. For Arabic, AraBERT, ArBERT, and MarBERT were fine-tuned on the full dataset. AraBERT consistently demonstrated superior performance in terms of F1-score across both languages. The models consistently exceeded both the mean and median scores across tasks, achieving an F1-score of 0.969 in classifying AI-generated essays in English and 0.957 in Arabic.

5 Conclusion and Future Work

We presented an overview of the shared task on the *Academic Essay Challenge*. The task attracted significant attention, with a total of 56 teams registering to participate in the development and evaluation phases. Of these, 21 teams submitted official results on the test set for Arabic, and 25 teams did so for English. Finally, five teams submitted task description papers. Most systems fine-tuned transformer-based language models; however, several teams also incorporated additional features, such as style, language complexity, bias, subjectivity, and emotion. For both languages, the top-performing teams achieved F1 scores above 0.98.

Limitations

A major limitation of the dataset is its small size, particularly for Arabic, which restricts the development of more robust models. The challenging nature of academic essay collection is reflected in the limited dataset size. Future studies could focus on curating larger datasets to enable the creation of more challenging tasks and the development of more robust models.

Ethical Considerations

The datasets used in the shared task may reflect subjective biases or perspectives of the essay authors, even though they followed the provided instructions. Importantly, the datasets do not include any personal information, and no such information was collected during the data curation process. Therefore, we do not anticipate any ethical concerns related to privacy. Furthermore, the dataset was shared only with participants who signed an agreement, ensuring responsible use of the dataset.

Acknowledgments

The work of F. Alam and G. Mikrosis partially supported by HBKU signature grant (HBKU-OVPR-SRG-02-2). The findings achieved herein are solely the responsibility of the authors.

References

Marah Abdin, Sam Ade Jacobs, Ammar Ahmad Awan, Jyoti Aneja, Ahmed Awadallah, Hany Awadalla, Nguyen Bach, Amit Bahree, Arash Bakhtiari, Harkirat Behl, et al. 2024. Phi-3 technical report: A highly capable language model locally on your phone. *arXiv preprint arXiv:2404.14219*.

Shifali Agrahari, Subhashi Jayant, Saurabh Kumar, and Ranbir Sanasam. 2025. Team EssayDetect at GenAI Detection Task 2: Guardians of Academic Integrity: Multilingual Detection of AI-Generated Essays. In *Proceedings of the 1st Workshop on GenAI Content Detection (GenAIDetect)*, Abu Dhabi, UAE. International Conference on Computational Linguistics.

Abdelhamid M. Ahmed, Xiao Zhang, Lameya M. Rezk, and Wajdi Zaghouani. 2023. Building an annotated l1 arabic/l2 english bilingual writer corpus: The qatari corpus of argumentative writing (qcaw). *Corpus-based Studies across Humanities*, 1(1):183–215.

Mohammad AL-Smadi. 2025. IntegrityAI at GenAI Detection Task 2: Detecting Machine-Generated Academic Essays in English and Arabic Using ELECTRA and Stylometry. In *Proceedings of the 1st Workshop on GenAI Content Detection (GenAIDetect)*, Abu Dhabi, UAE. International Conference on Computational Linguistics.

AYG Alfaifi and ES Atwell. 2013. Arabic learner corpus v1: A new resource for arabic language research. In *Second Workshop on Arabic Corpus Linguistics*.

Amrita Bhattacharjee, Tharindu Kumarage, Raha Moraffah, and Huan Liu. 2023. ConDA: Contrastive domain adaptation for AI-generated text detection. In *Proceedings of the 13th International Joint Conference on Natural Language Processing and the 3rd Conference of the Asia-Pacific Chapter of the Association for Computational Linguistics (Volume 1: Long Papers)*, pages 598–610, Nusa Dua, Bali. Association for Computational Linguistics.

Jiuhai Chen, Rifaa Qadri, Yuxin Wen, Neel Jain, John Kirchenbauer, Tianyi Zhou, and Tom Goldstein. 2024. Genqa: Generating millions of instructions from a handful of prompts. *Preprint*, arXiv:2406.10323.

Kohinoor Monish Darda, Marion Carre, and Emily S. Cross. 2023. Value attributed to text-based archives generated by artificial intelligence. *Royal Society Open Science*, 10(2):220915.

Liam Dugan, Alyssa Hwang, Filip Trhlík, Andrew Zhu, Josh Magnus Ludan, Hainiu Xu, Daphne Ippolito, and Chris Callison-Burch. 2024. RAID: A shared benchmark for robust evaluation of machine-generated text detectors. In *Proceedings of the 62nd Annual Meeting of the Association for Computational Linguistics (Volume 1: Long Papers)*, pages 12463–12492, Bangkok, Thailand. Association for Computational Linguistics.

Matthias Gallé, Jos Rozen, Germán Kruszewski, and Hady Elsahar. 2021. Unsupervised and distributional detection of machine-generated text. *arXiv preprint arXiv:2111.02878*.

Rana Gharib and Ahmed Elgendy. 2025. RA at GenAI Detection Task 2: Fine-tuned Language Models For Detection of Academic Authenticity, Results and Thoughts. In *Proceedings of the 1st Workshop on GenAI Content Detection (GenAIDetect)*, Abu Dhabi, UAE. International Conference on Computational Linguistics.

Biyang Guo, Xin Zhang, Ziyuan Wang, Minqi Jiang, Jinran Nie, Yuxuan Ding, Jianwei Yue, and Yupeng Wu. 2023. How close is chatgpt to human experts? comparison corpus, evaluation, and detection. *arXiv preprint arXiv:2301.07597*.

Hans WA Hanley and Zakir Durumeric. 2024. Machine-made media: Monitoring the mobilization of machine-generated articles on misinformation and mainstream news websites. In *Proceedings of the International AAAI Conference on Web and Social Media*, volume 18, pages 542–556.

Xuanli He, Qiongkai Xu, Lingjuan Lyu, Fangzhao Wu, and Chenguang Wang. 2022. Protecting intellectual property of language generation apis with lexical watermark. *Proceedings of the AAAI Conference on Artificial Intelligence*, 36(10):10758–10766.

Vijayasaradhi Indurthi and Vasudeva Varma. 2025. Tesla at GenAI Content Detection Task 1: LLM Agents in Multilingual Machine-Generated Text Detection. In *Proceedings of the 1st Workshop on GenAI Content Detection (GenAIDetect)*, Abu Dhabi, UAE. International Conference on Computational Linguistics.

Jiao Kaijie, Yao Xingyu, Ma Shixuan, Fang Sifan, Guo Zikang, Xu Benfeng, Zhang Licheng, Wang Quan, Zhang Yongdong, and Mao Zhendong. 2025. CMI-AIGCX at GenAI Detection Task 2: Leveraging Multilingual Proxy LLMs for Machine-Generated Text Detection in Academic Essays. In *Proceedings of the 1st Workshop on GenAI Content Detection (GenAIDetect)*, Abu Dhabi, UAE. International Conference on Computational Linguistics.

John Kirchenbauer, Jonas Geiping, Yuxin Wen, Jonathan Katz, Ian Miers, and Tom Goldstein. 2023. A watermark for large language models. In *International Conference on Machine Learning*, pages 17061–17084. PMLR.

Weixin Liang, Mert Yuksekgonul, Yining Mao, Eric Wu, and James Zou. 2023. GPT detectors are biased against non-native english writers. *Patterns*, 4(7):100779.

George Mikros, Athanasios Koursaris, Dimitrios Bilianos, and George Markopoulos. 2023. AI-writing detection using an ensemble of transformers and stylometric features. In *Proceedings of the Iberian Languages Evaluation Forum (IberLEF 2023) co-located with the Conference of the Spanish Society for Natural Language Processing (SEPLN 2023)*, volume 3496 of *CEUR Workshop Proceedings*, pages 1–14, Jaén, Spain.

OpenAI. 2024. Gpt-4o mini: Advancing cost-efficient intelligence. *OpenAI Blog*.

Mike Perkins, Jasper Roe, Binh H. Vu, Darius Postma, Don Hickerson, James McGaughran, and Huy Q. Khuat. 2024. Simple techniques to bypass GenAI text detectors: Implications for inclusive education. *International Journal of Educational Technology in Higher Education*, 21(1):53.

Hooman H. Rashidi, Brandon D. Fennell, Samer Albahra, Bo Hu, and Tom Gorbett. 2023. The chatgpt conundrum: Human-generated scientific manuscripts misidentified as ai creations by ai text detection tool. *Journal of Pathology Informatics*, 14:100342.

Aditya Shah, Prateek Ranka, Urmi Dedhia, Shruti Prasad, Siddhi Muni, and Kiran Bhowmick. 2023. Detecting and unmasking AI-generated texts through explainable artificial intelligence using stylistic features. *International Journal of Advanced Computer Science and Applications*, 14(10):1–10.

Sebastian Szyller, Buse Gul Atli, Samuel Marchal, and N. Asokan. 2021. Dawn: Dynamic adversarial watermarking of neural networks. In *Proceedings of the 29th ACM International Conference on Multimedia*, MM '21, page 4417–4425, New York, NY, USA. Association for Computing Machinery.

Ruixiang Tang, Yu-Neng Chuang, and Xia Hu. 2024. The science of detecting llm-generated text. *Communications of the ACM*, 67(4):50–59.

Gemini Team. 2024. Gemini 1.5: Unlocking multimodal understanding across millions of tokens of context. *arXiv preprint arXiv:2403.05530*.

Vismay Vora, Jenil Savla, Deevya Mehta, and Aruna Gawade. 2023. A multimodal approach for detecting AI generated content using BERT and CNN. *International Journal on Recent and Innovation Trends in Computing and Communication*, 11(9):691–701.

Yuxia Wang, Jonibek Mansurov, Petar Ivanov, Jinyan Su, Artem Shelmanov, Akim Tsvigun, Osama Mohammed Afzal, Tarek Mahmoud, Giovanni Puccetti, Thomas Arnold, Thomas Arnold, Chenxi Whitehouse, Alham Fikri Aji, Nizar Habash, Iryna Gurevych, and Preslav Nakov. 2024a. SemEval-2024 Task 8: Multidomain, multimodel and multilingual machine-generated text detection. In *Proceedings of the 18th International Workshop on Semantic Evaluation (SemEval-2024)*, pages 2057–2079, Mexico City, Mexico. Association for Computational Linguistics.

Yuxia Wang, Jonibek Mansurov, Petar Ivanov, Jinyan Su, Artem Shelmanov, Akim Tsvigun, Chenxi Whitehouse, Osama Mohammed Afzal, Tarek Mahmoud, Toru Sasaki, Thomas Arnold, Alham Aji, Nizar Habash, Iryna Gurevych, and Preslav Nakov. 2024b. M4: Multi-generator, multi-domain, and multilingual black-box machine-generated text detection. In *Proceedings of the 18th Conference of the European Chapter of the Association for Computational Linguistics (Volume 1: Long Papers)*, pages 1369–1407, St. Julian's, Malta. Association for Computational Linguistics.

Debora Weber-Wulff, Alla Anohina-Naumeca, Sonja Bjelobaba, Tomáš Foltýnek, Jean Guerrero-Dib, Olumide Popoola, Petr Šigut, and Lorna Waddington. 2023. Testing of detection tools for AI-generated text. *International Journal for Educational Integrity*, 19(1):1–39.

Hongyu Wu and Tom Flanagan. 2023. The limits of AI content detectors. *Journal of Student Research*, 12(3):1–7.

Junchao Wu, Shu Yang, Runzhe Zhan, Yulin Yuan, Derek F Wong, and Lidia S Chao. 2023. A survey on llm-gernerated text detection: Necessity, methods, and future directions. *arXiv preprint arXiv:2310.14724*.

Peipeng Yu, Jiahan Chen, Xuan Feng, and Zhihua Xia. 2023. Cheat: A large-scale dataset for detecting chatgpt-written abstracts. *arXiv preprint arXiv:2304.12008*.

Wajdi Zaghouani, Abdelhamid Ahmed, Xiao Zhang, and Lameya Rezk. 2024. QCAW 1.0: Building a qatari corpus of student argumentative writing. In *Proceedings of the 2024 Joint International Conference on Computational Linguistics, Language Resources and Evaluation (LREC-COLING 2024)*, pages 13382–13394, Torino, Italia. ELRA and ICCL.

Wataru Zaitsu and Mingzhe Jin. 2023. Distinguishing chatgpt(-3.5, -4)-generated and human-written papers through japanese stylometric analysis. *PLOS ONE*, 18(8):1–12.

CNLP-NITS-PP at GenAI Detection Task 3: Cross-Domain Machine-Generated Text Detection Using DistilBERT Techniques

L D M S Sai Teja, Annepaka Yadagiri, M Srikar Vardhan and Partha Pakray
Department of Computer Science & Engineering
National Institute of Technology Silchar, Assam, India, 788010
{lekkalad_ug, annepaka22_rs, mangadoddis_ug, partha}@cse.nits.ac.in

Abstract

This paper presents a Cross-domain Machine-Generated Text Detection model developed for the COLING 2025 Workshop on Detecting AI-generated Content (DAIGenC). As large language models evolve, detecting machine-generated text becomes increasingly challenging, particularly in contexts like misinformation and academic integrity. While current detectors perform well on unseen data, they remain vulnerable to adversarial strategies, including paraphrasing, homoglyphs, misspellings, synonyms, whitespace manipulations, etc. We introduce a framework to address these adversarial tactics designed to bypass detection systems by adversarial training. Our team DistilBERT-NITS detector placed 7th in the Non-Adversarial Attacks category, and Adversarial-submission-3 achieved 17th in the Adversarial Attacks category.

1 Introduction

Large Language Models (*LLMs*) (Touvron et al., 2023; Anil et al., 2023) have quickly established themselves as transformative tools in Natural Language Processing (*NLP*). These models gain substantial internal knowledge by undergoing extensive pre-training on massive datasets in a self-supervised manner, enabling them to excel in various tasks, from answering factual queries and generating coherent text to handling intricate reasoning processes. This versatility has brought substantial advancements across various NLP application areas.

Despite these advancements, ethical concerns have surfaced regarding inherent risks (McKenna et al., 2023; Bian et al., 2023; Ferrara, 2023), such as the potential for misinformation, hallucinations in generated outputs, and even biases against certain groups. Growing awareness of these issues has spurred research into detecting AI-generated text. However, AI-text detectors may carry similar vulnerabilities as neural network models (Szegedy, 2013), inspiring related studies (Sadasivan et al., 2023; Krishna et al., 2024) that explore paraphrasing attacks designed to deceive detector predictions. It is contended that examining potential adversarial attacks on text detectors is crucial, as weaknesses in AI detection systems can be identified before deployment in practical settings, such as academic plagiarism detection, thereby supporting the development of effective countermeasures.

Current detection methods are generally classified into three main categories: statistical approaches (Mitchell et al., 2023) that use metrics like entropy, perplexity, and log-likelihood; neural classifiers (Guo et al., 2023) trained on supervised datasets labeled as human or AI-generated; and watermarking techniques (Kirchenbauer et al., 2023) that embed subtle patterns into AI-generated text. However, research on adversarial perturbations specifically targeting AI-text detectors still needs to be completed. For example, (Sadasivan et al., 2023) investigated paraphrasing to alter Machine-Generated Text (MGT) in adversarial attacks, while (Shi et al., 2024) employed LLMs to create adversarial word candidates through a search-based approach. Although these studies have shown that AI detectors can be vulnerable to adversarial modifications, the impact of such attacks on detector performance in complex, real-world conditions is still largely unexamined.

2 Related Work

Most research on adversarial attacks has focused on image detection (Kong et al., 2021; Akhtar et al., 2021; Xu et al., 2020), as text data presents unique challenges due to its discrete structure, making it harder to create imperceptible modifications compared to image data, where subtle pixel changes can go largely unnoticed (Peng et al., 2023). Some general text classification adversarial attacks, such

Proceedings of the 1st Workshop on GenAI Content Detection (GenAIDetect), pages 334–339
January 19, 2025.

as those by (Damodaran, 2021; Gao et al., 2018), have demonstrated this. Recently, studies have turned toward adversarial attacks on neural text detectors: (Xu et al., 2020) found that introducing minor spelling errors and homoglyph replacements can significantly lower detection rates for GPT-2-generated text. Similarly, (Liang et al., 2023a) showed that character-level perturbations also affect RoBERTa-based detectors (Liang et al., 2023b) further revealed that existing detectors are vulnerable to simple rephrasing and may even mistakenly label texts written by non-native speakers as AI-generated.

Due to the susceptibility of current methods to adversarial attacks, several researchers have proposed approaches to enhance their robustness, including work by (Liang et al., 2023b; Shi et al., 2024). Although watermarking techniques have also been explored for identifying AI-generated text, they are generally considered vulnerable to adversarial tactics, particularly those based on mutation and paraphrasing (Sadasivan et al., 2023; Kirchenbauer et al., 2023).

3 Methodology

3.1 Dataset Description

As shown in Table 1, the RAID dataset contains over 10 million generated samples across diverse models, content domains, decoding strategies, and adversarial attacks. Models include ChatGPT, GPT-4, GPT-3, Llama 2, Cohere, MPT-30B, and Mistral 7B, covering content from Reddit, IMDb, Wikipedia, and news articles. Decoding strategies such as Greedy, Sampling, Greedy+Repetition Penalty, and Sampling+Repetition Penalty are used alongside adversarial techniques like paraphrasing, homoglyph, perplexity misspelling, synonyms, whitespace, upperlower, number, insert_paragraphs, article_deletion, alternative_spelling, and zero_width_space. This dataset supports research on model performance, generation diversity, and robustness against adversarial attacks.

Task	Label	Train	Dev
Non-Adversarial	Human (0)	13,371	4,855
	Machine (1)	454,614	165,070
Adversarial	Human (0)	160,452	58,260
	Machine (1)	5,455,368	1,980,840

Table 1: Statistics of Train and Development Data for Non-Adversarial and Adversarial Tasks.

3.2 System Description

This paper presents our approach to Task 3 in the COLING Workshop on MGT Detection, which emphasizes cross-domain robustness in AI-generated content detection (Dugan et al., 2025). The primary objective of this task is to classify whether a given text is machine-generated or human-authored, even when the content spans multiple domains. We participated in both Subtask A *(Non-Adversarial Cross-Domain MGT Detection)* and Subtask B (*Adversarial Cross-Domain MGT Detection*), which involve handling text from eight diverse domains, produced by eleven generative models and four decoding strategies. We first classify whether the text has been adversarially attacked to detect adversarial attacks in text. If an attack is detected, the text undergoes preprocessing to mitigate the attack, after which the preprocessed text proceeds to our model for further MGT detection. Our approach to finetuning the DistilBERT model uses hyperparameters to extract semantic features.

3.2.1 Experimental Setup and Data Sampling

The experiment was conducted in a Jupyter Notebook on a machine powered by an ***Intel® Xeon® W-2155 CPU @ 3.30GHz with 20 cores and an NVIDIA Quadro P2000 GPU*** for handling LLM tasks. The system was also equipped with 64 GB of RAM. Python served as the programming language, utilizing the libraries `Numpy`, `Pandas`, `SKlearn`, and `TensorFlow`.

To reduce the computational load, only 40% of the adversarial data is sampled based on the unique `adv_source_id`. This is done by selecting a random sample of rows corresponding to 40% of the unique IDs in the training set. This sampled data is then prepared for further processing, ensuring the dataset remains manageable while representing a substantial portion of the original data. The sampled data is reset for indexing and is ready for the pipeline's next steps.

3.2.2 Preprocessing:

As evidenced by the analysis, all attacks target plain text, and the dataset maintains a balance, with an equal number of rows for each attack type, as reflected in the supporting figure. Next, the code implements a preprocessing pipeline to clean and standardize text (*Every text attacked and non-attacked*). The attacks, such *as paraphrasing, homoglyph, perplexity misspelling, synonyms, whitespace, upperlower, number, insert paragraphs, article deletion, alternative_spelling, and zero_width_space* can confuse NLP systems. The preprocessing steps address these issues by applying several transformations. Homoglyphs, which are visually similar but distinct characters (*e.g., numbers or symbols resembling letters*), are replaced using a predefined mapping. Additionally, alternative spellings (*like British versus American English*) are normalized, ensuring consistency in spelling. Numbers are converted to their word equivalents, and extra spaces or zero-width spaces are removed. The text is also converted to lowercase, and punctuation is stripped for uniformity. By implementing these techniques, the pipeline cleans up adversarially manipulated text, making it more suitable for analysis while maintaining its original meaning. This process ensures that NLP models can better understand and process the input text without being misled by adversarial perturbations.

```
input_text = "Th!s 1s @n ex@mple txt w1th
    h0m0glyphs, zerowidth\u200bspaces, and
    incorr3ct spelling."

After preprocessing:

output_text = "this is an example text with
    homoglyphs, zerowidthspaces, and incorrect
    spelling."
```

3.2.3 Adversarial Detection:

After preprocessing, we obtained both the Raw Text and the Preprocessed Text for each input. We employed several factors like the combination of **Cosine Similarity** and **Edit Distance**, **Word Overlap ratio**, and **Homoglyph Substitution Count** to analyze surface-level changes (*e.g., homoglyph substitutions, misspellings*) on text embeddings generated by the `distilbert-base-uncased` model.

Cosine similarity: A widely used metric for its simplicity, interpretability, and computational efficiency for capturing semantic meaning. Its values range from -1 (*completely dissimilar*) to 1 (*identical*), providing an intuitive similarity measure. This will focus solely on the directional alignment of embeddings. Furthermore, its low computational complexity ensures scalability, making it ideal for processing large datasets efficiently.

$$\text{Cosine Similarity: } \cos(\theta) = \frac{\vec{A} \cdot \vec{B}}{\|\vec{A}\| \|\vec{B}\|} \quad (1)$$

Here, $\vec{A}$ and $\vec{B}$ represent the embedding vectors, $\vec{A} \cdot \vec{B}$ denotes their dot product, and $\|\vec{A}\|$ and $\|\vec{B}\|$ represent their magnitudes (*L2 norms*). The resulting similarity score ranges between -1 and 1. Where: **1** indicates perfect similarity (*identical direction*), **0** indicates orthogonality (*no similarity*), and **-1** indicates complete opposition (*opposite direction*).

Edit Distance: Specifically, Levenshtein Distance calculates the minimum number of edits required to transform one string into another. This detects small, surface-level changes.

$$\text{Levenshtein Distance}(s_1, s_2) = \min \left\{ \begin{matrix} \text{Insert,} \\ \text{Delete,} \\ \text{Substitute} \end{matrix} \right\}$$

To combine these two measures, we can apply a hybrid approach that leverages the strengths of both metrics. The combined similarity score, S_{new}, can be represented as:

$$S_{new} = \alpha \cdot \text{CS} + (1 - \alpha) \cdot \beta \quad (2)$$

$$CS = \text{Cosine Similarity}(A, B) \quad (3)$$

$$\beta = (1 - \frac{\text{Levenshtein Distance}(A, B)}{\max(\text{len}(A), \text{len}(B))}) \quad (4)$$

Where: - A and B are the two texts being compared. - α is a weight parameter that controls the contribution of each metric. - $\text{len}(A)$ and $\text{len}(B)$ are the lengths of the two texts. - β normalizes the Levenshtein distance to a range between 0 and 1.

Word Overlap Ratio: is a metric used to quantify the similarity between two text sequences by comparing the number of common words to the total number of unique words across both sequences.

Let W_1 and W_2 represent the sets of words in two text sequences.

$$\text{Word Overlap Ratio} = \frac{|W_1 \cap W_2|}{|W_1 \cup W_2|} \quad (5)$$

Let x represent a text that is not attacked. Upon preprocessing, x remains unchanged, denoted as x'. Computing the cosine similarity between x and x', we obtain a value of 1, as x and x' are identical:

$$\text{CosineSimilarity}(x, x') = 1, \quad \text{when } x = x'.$$

Conversely, if x is an attacked text, preprocessing yields a modified version x'. The cosine similarity between x and x' will deviate from 1, reflecting the difference introduced by the attack:

$$\text{CosineSimilarity}(x, x') \neq 1, \quad \text{when } x \neq x'.$$

This approach effectively captures adversarial manipulations, enabling robust detection based on the interplay between cosine similarity and edit distance metrics.

3.2.4 Classification Model Architecture:

After calculating the adversarial detecting factors, the text embeddings and the factors combined undergo classification using a fine-tuned `DistilBERT` model as shown in Figure 1 for distinguishing human-generated and machine-generated text. The detailed architecture of the DistilBERT model is depicted in Figure 2. The Figure 2 illustrates the internal workings of the model, particularly highlighting the implementation process obtained from the code `model.to(device)`. The model is trained with a batch size of 16 for 3 epochs using the `AdamW` optimizer and `CrossEntropyLoss`, all the hyperparameters are shown in the Table 2. During training, the model's performance is evaluated on key metrics like accuracy, precision, recall, and F1 score, ensuring robustness against adversarial attacks. By fine-tuning the model with this approach, it can better classify text accurately in real-world scenarios, even when it contains adversarial modifications.

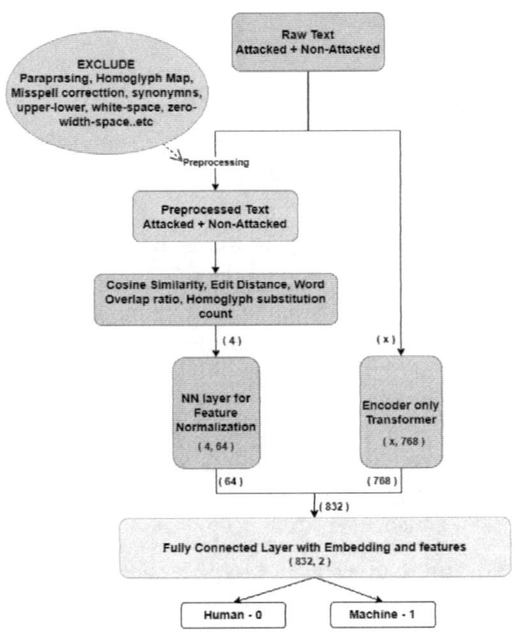

Figure 1: Architecture workflow

3.3 Results Analysis

Due to computational constraints and limited space as per the requirements, we sampled only 40% of the dataset. The table 4 presents the training epochs for the non-adversarial data, the table 5 presents the training epochs for the adversarial data, where the evaluation metrics Accuracy, Precision, Recall, F1 Score, and Loss were used. Additionally, Table

Parameter	Value
Max Seq Leng	128
Batch Size	16, 32
Learning Rate	2e-5,5e-4
Epochs	3, 5
Patience	2
Minimum Delta	0.001
Loss	CrossEntropyLoss
Optimizer	AdamW

Table 2: Model Hyperparameters

3 shows the test results in final leaderboard performance for both adversarial and non-adversarial data. Although this model may not yet be equipped to handle more advanced semantic and synthetic adversarial attacks, we will consider these and strive to improve our work in the future by incorporating new techniques.

4 Conclusion

In this study, we developed a robust framework using a fine-tuned DistilBERT-NITS model to detect MGT across diverse domains, focusing on adversarial scenarios. Our approach ranked 7th in non-adversarial detection and 17th in adversarial detection at the COLING Workshop, involves preprocessing text to mitigate detected adversarial manipulations, enhancing detection accuracy. These findings support the potential of lightweight models to handle adversarial and cross-domain MGT detection effectively. Future work will be focused on refining this method to improve robustness and adaptability against evolving adversarial tactics.

References

Naveed Akhtar, Ajmal Mian, Navid Kardan, and Mubarak Shah. 2021. Advances in adversarial attacks and defenses in computer vision: A survey. *IEEE Access*, 9:155161–155196.

Rohan Anil, Andrew M Dai, Orhan Firat, Melvin Johnson, Dmitry Lepikhin, Alexandre Passos, Siamak Shakeri, Emanuel Taropa, Paige Bailey, Zhifeng Chen, et al. 2023. Palm 2 technical report. *arXiv preprint arXiv:2305.10403*.

Ning Bian, Peilin Liu, Xianpei Han, Hongyu Lin, Yaojie Lu, Ben He, and Le Sun. 2023. A drop of ink may make a million think: The spread of false information in large language models. *arXiv preprint arXiv:2305.04812*.

Detector	Aggregate	chatgpt	gpt4	gpt3	gpt2	mistral	mistral-chat	cohere	cohere-chat	llama-chat	mpt	mpt-chat
DistilBERT-NITS (Non-Adv)	0.905	0.989	0.967	0.835	0.880	0.846	0.976	0.639	0.835	0.987	0.884	0.985
Adversarial-submission-3	0.467	0.553	0.533	0.306	0.375	0.543	0.514	0.244	0.341	0.591	0.445	0.516

Table 3: Performance Metrics for chatgpt, gpt, mistral, cohere, llama, and mpt Models

Epoch	Dataset	Loss	Acc	F1
1	Train	0.059	0.978	0.975
	Dev	0.132	0.971	0.957
2	Train	0.029	0.988	0.988
	Dev	0.173	0.969	0.956
3	Train	0.013	0.995	0.995
	Dev	0.232	0.956	0.950

Table 4: Training and Development Metrics Across Epochs on Non-Adversarial Data

Epoch	Dataset	Loss	Acc	F1
1	Train	0.080	0.977	0.972
	Dev	0.262	0.919	0.931
2	Train	0.037	0.989	0.988
	Dev	0.261	0.946	0.944
3	Train	0.027	0.992	0.992
	Dev	0.360	0.926	0.934

Table 5: Training and Development Metrics Across Epochs on Adversarial Data

Prithiviraj Damodaran. 2021. Parrot: Paraphrase generation for nlu. *Parrot: Paraphrase generation for nlu.*

Liam Dugan, Andrew Zhu, Firoj Alam, Preslav Nakov, Marianna Apidianaki, and Callison-Burch Chris. 2025. Genai content detection task 3: Cross-domain machine generated text detection challenge. In *Proceedings of the 1st Workshop on GenAI Content Detection (GenAIDetect)*, Abu Dhabi, UAE. International Conference on Computational Linguistics.

Emilio Ferrara. 2023. Should chatgpt be biased? challenges and risks of bias in large language models. *arXiv preprint arXiv:2304.03738.*

Ji Gao, Jack Lanchantin, Mary Lou Soffa, and Yanjun Qi. 2018. Black-box generation of adversarial text sequences to evade deep learning classifiers. In *2018 IEEE Security and Privacy Workshops (SPW)*, pages 50–56. IEEE.

Biyang Guo, Xin Zhang, Ziyuan Wang, Minqi Jiang, Jinran Nie, Yuxuan Ding, Jianwei Yue, and Yupeng Wu. 2023. How close is chatgpt to human experts? comparison corpus, evaluation, and detection. *arXiv preprint arXiv:2301.07597.*

John Kirchenbauer, Jonas Geiping, Yuxin Wen, Jonathan Katz, Ian Miers, and Tom Goldstein. 2023. A watermark for large language models. In *International Conference on Machine Learning*, pages 17061–17084. PMLR.

Zixiao Kong, Jingfeng Xue, Yong Wang, Lu Huang, Zequn Niu, and Feng Li. 2021. A survey on adversarial attack in the age of artificial intelligence. *Wireless Communications and Mobile Computing*, 2021(1):4907754.

Kalpesh Krishna, Yixiao Song, Marzena Karpinska, John Wieting, and Mohit Iyyer. 2024. Paraphrasing evades detectors of ai-generated text, but retrieval is an effective defense. *Advances in Neural Information Processing Systems*, 36.

Gongbo Liang, Jesus Guerrero, and Izzat Alsmadi. 2023a. Mutation-based adversarial attacks on neural text detectors. *arXiv preprint arXiv:2302.05794.*

Weixin Liang, Mert Yuksekgonul, Yining Mao, Eric Wu, and James Zou. 2023b. Gpt detectors are biased against non-native english writers. *Patterns*, 4(7).

Nick McKenna, Tianyi Li, Liang Cheng, Mohammad Javad Hosseini, Mark Johnson, and Mark Steedman. 2023. Sources of hallucination by large language models on inference tasks. *arXiv preprint arXiv:2305.14552.*

Eric Mitchell, Yoonho Lee, Alexander Khazatsky, Christopher D Manning, and Chelsea Finn. 2023. Detectgpt: Zero-shot machine-generated text detection using probability curvature. In *International Conference on Machine Learning*, pages 24950–24962. PMLR.

Hao Peng, Zhe Wang, Dandan Zhao, Yiming Wu, Jianming Han, Shixin Guo, Shouling Ji, and Ming Zhong. 2023. Efficient text-based evolution algorithm to hard-label adversarial attacks on text. *Journal of King Saud University-Computer and Information Sciences*, 35(5):101539.

Vinu Sankar Sadasivan, Aounon Kumar, Sriram Balasubramanian, Wenxiao Wang, and Soheil Feizi. 2023. Can ai-generated text be reliably detected? *arXiv preprint arXiv:2303.11156.*

Zhouxing Shi, Yihan Wang, Fan Yin, Xiangning Chen, Kai-Wei Chang, and Cho-Jui Hsieh. 2024. Red teaming language model detectors with language models. *Transactions of the Association for Computational Linguistics*, 12:174–189.

C Szegedy. 2013. Intriguing properties of neural networks. *arXiv preprint arXiv:1312.6199*.

Hugo Touvron, Louis Martin, Kevin Stone, Peter Albert, Amjad Almahairi, Yasmine Babaei, Nikolay Bashlykov, Soumya Batra, Prajjwal Bhargava, Shruti Bhosale, et al. 2023. Llama 2: Open foundation and fine-tuned chat models. *arXiv preprint arXiv:2307.09288*.

Han Xu, Yao Ma, Hao-Chen Liu, Debayan Deb, Hui Liu, Ji-Liang Tang, and Anil K Jain. 2020. Adversarial attacks and defenses in images, graphs and text: A review. *International journal of automation and computing*, 17:151–178.

A Appendix

```
model.to(device)

CustomModel(
  (bert): DistilBertForSequenceClassification(
    (distilbert): DistilBertModel(
      (embeddings): Embeddings(
        (word_embeddings): Embedding(30522, 768, padding_idx=0)
        (position_embeddings): Embedding(512, 768)
        (LayerNorm): LayerNorm((768,), eps=1e-12, elementwise_affine=True)
        (dropout): Dropout(p=0.1, inplace=False)
      )
      (transformer): Transformer(
        (layer): ModuleList(
          (0-5): 6 x TransformerBlock(
            (attention): MultiHeadSelfAttention(
              (dropout): Dropout(p=0.1, inplace=False)
              (q_lin): Linear(in_features=768, out_features=768, bias=True)
              (k_lin): Linear(in_features=768, out_features=768, bias=True)
              (v_lin): Linear(in_features=768, out_features=768, bias=True)
              (out_lin): Linear(in_features=768, out_features=768, bias=True)
            )
            (sa_layer_norm): LayerNorm((768,), eps=1e-12, elementwise_affine=True)
            (ffn): FFN(
              (dropout): Dropout(p=0.1, inplace=False)
              (lin1): Linear(in_features=768, out_features=3072, bias=True)
              (lin2): Linear(in_features=3072, out_features=768, bias=True)
              (activation): GELUActivation()
            )
            (output_layer_norm): LayerNorm((768,), eps=1e-12, elementwise_affine=True)
          )
        )
      )
    )
    (pre_classifier): Linear(in_features=768, out_features=768, bias=True)
    (classifier): Linear(in_features=768, out_features=2, bias=True)
    (dropout): Dropout(p=0.2, inplace=False)
  )
  (feature_fc): Linear(in_features=4, out_features=64, bias=True)
  (relu): ReLU()
  (dropout): Dropout(p=0.3, inplace=False)
  (classifier): Linear(in_features=832, out_features=2, bias=True)
  (sigmoid): Sigmoid()
)
```

Figure 2: DistilBERT Model Architecture

Leidos at GenAI Detection Task 3: A Weight-Balanced Transformer Approach for AI Generated Text Detection Across Domains

Abishek R Edikala† and **Gregorios A Katsios**† and **Noelie V Creaghe** and **Ning Yu**
Leidos
{abishek.r.edikala, gregorios.a.katsios, noelie.v.creaghe, ning.yu}@leidos.com
† Authors contributed equally to this work.

Abstract

Advancements in Large Language Models (LLMs) blur the distinction between human and machine-generated text (MGT), raising concerns about misinformation and academic dishonesty. Existing MGT detection methods often fail to generalize across domains and generator models. We address this by framing MGT detection as a text classification task using transformer-based models. Utilizing Distil-RoBERTa-Base, we train four classifiers (binary and multi-class, with and without class weighting) on the RAID dataset (Dugan et al., 2024). Our systems placed first to fourth in the COLING 2025 MGT Detection Challenge Task 3 (Dugan et al., 2025). Internal in-domain and zero-shot evaluations reveal that applying class weighting improves detector performance, especially with multi-class classification training. Our best model effectively generalizes to unseen domains and generators, demonstrating that transformer-based models are robust detectors of machine-generated text.

1 Introduction

The rapid advancement of Large Language Models (LLMs) has made it increasingly difficult to distinguish between human-written and machine-generated text. This challenge poses significant risks in areas such as misinformation dissemination, academic dishonesty, and the breach of trust in online communications. Existing detection methods often rely on small datasets and struggle to generalize across different domains and generator models.

We formulate the detection task as both binary and multi-class classification, and examine the use of class weighting to investigate the impact of class imbalance on detection performance. We build and evaluate four Distil-RoBERTa-Base[1] based models trained with RAID dataset (Dugan et al., 2024), which contains over 6 million text samples from 11 generator models across 8 domains. To assess generalizability, we conduct additional cross-domain evaluations using the MGT Detection Task 1 dataset (Wang et al., 2025), which includes texts from 41 models not seen during training. Our results demonstrate that incorporating class weighting improves detection accuracy and that our models perform effectively across both familiar and unfamiliar domains and generator models. According to the COLING 2025 MGT Detection Challenge Task 3 (Dugan et al., 2025) official evaluation, our models surpass commercial MGT detection tools and achieved top rankings.

2 Related Work

Authorship attribution has a long history, and machine authorship is a recent focus. For example, IARPA's recent HIATUS program (Human Interpretable Attribution of Text using Underlying Structure)[2] takes both human and machine authorship into consideration. According to Leidos' experience in HIATUS, we found that with sufficient training data, transformer-based encoder models can effectively learn features that discriminate authorship and consistently outperformed feature-based approaches.

There are more efforts treating MGT detection as a classification problem. For example, Xiong et al. 2024 addressed multilingual MGT detection in SemEval-2024 Task 8, which includes binary classification (human vs. machine) and model attribution. Their study found that fine-tuned transformer-based models significantly outperformed traditional machine learning methods, demonstrating superior effectiveness in accurately detecting and at-

Approved for public release under eTrace approval ID# 24-leidos-1113-28544

[1] https://huggingface.co/distilroberta-base
[2] https://www.iarpa.gov/research-programs/hiatus

Proceedings of the 1st Workshop on GenAI Content Detection (GenAIDetect), pages 340–346
January 19, 2025.

tributing machine-generated content across various contexts. LLM-DetectAIve (Abassy et al., 2024) categorizes machine-generated texts into four types: purely human-written, entirely machine-generated, machine-generated then humanized, and human-written then machine-polished. This nuanced approach is impactful in educational and academic settings where subtle LLM edits may hide machine involvement. However, its reliance on the narrows scope of the M4GT-Bench (Wang et al., 2024) dataset may cause LLM-DetectAIve to perform accurately within familiar domains but struggle with unfamiliar ones, leading to high false positive rates and reduced accuracy in diverse real-world scenarios.

Dugan et al. 2024 introduced RAID, a comprehensive benchmark with over 6 million text samples from 11 models across 8 domains, incorporating adversarial attacks and diverse decoding strategies. Evaluating 12 detectors under a fixed 5% false positive rate revealed that open-source detectors often misclassified human-written texts and lacked robustness against minor text modifications and adversarial attacks. The study highlighted that while detectors perform well on familiar data, they struggle to generalize to unseen domains and models, underscoring the need for more resilient MGT detection methods.

3 Method

We approach MGT detection as a classification task using Transformer-based models. Our base model, Distil-RoBERTa-Base[3] (Sanh et al., 2019), is a parameter-efficient, distilled variant of RoBERTa (Liu, 2019) that enables robust detection with limited resources. We train four MGT detectors to evaluate both binary and multi-class classification, exploring the effects of class weighting to address dataset imbalance, to distinguish human-written from machine-generated text.

1. **Binary Classifier without Class Weighting (BC)**: Human vs. Machine, trained without applying class weights.

2. **Binary Classifier with Class Weighting (BW)**: Similar to the BC model but trained with class weights to address class imbalance.

3. **Multi-class Classifier without Class Weighting (MC)**: A multi-class classifier that predicts which generator model produced the text or if it was human-written, trained without class weights.

4. **Multi-class Classifier with Class Weighting (MW)**: The same as the MC model but trained with class weights to mitigate class imbalance.

For the BW and MW models, we compute balanced class weights using the following formula:

$$w_i = \frac{N}{C \times n_i}$$

Where N is the total number of samples in the dataset, C is the total number of classes and n_i is the number of samples in class i. This formula distributes weights evenly across classes by normalizing with the total number of classes, which helps prevent extreme weighting in cases of high imbalance.

We select this method to balance the loss contributions across classes due to its simplicity and effectiveness in enhancing the model's generalizability. Alternative strategies, such as oversampling underrepresented classes or using synthetic data augmentation techniques, can address class imbalance but add complexity and pose the risk of overfitting (Hassanat et al., 2022). Another alternative is Focal Loss (Lin, 2017) that dynamically adjusts the loss based on sample difficulty. This approach can be effective, but demands extensive hyper-parameter tuning, which is impractical given our resource constraints. Our class weighting scheme, though static and less adaptable to extreme imbalance, is resource-efficient and easy to implement.

Baseline (OD) As a baseline, we apply the RoBERTa-Large-OpenAI-Detector[4], an open-source model that is also featured as a baseline on the shared task, directly to our test sets in a zero-shot manner. This enables us to gauge the models performance on our unofficial test sets.

3.1 Data

Randomly sampling from the main training split of RAID (Dugan et al., 2024), we reserve 50K examples for validation and 400K examples for testing, with the remaining examples forming our training set.

To further assess the robustness of our MGT detectors, we also leverage Task 1 dataset (Wang et al.,

[3] https://huggingface.co/distilroberta-base

[4] https://huggingface.co/openai-community/roberta-large-openai-detector

2025) for cross-domain evaluation. Although there is minimal overlap between the generator models in RAID and those in Task 1, the datasets differ in domains and generation techniques, effectively rendering Task 1 out-of-domain (OOD) relative to a model trained solely on RAID. Additional details on the Task 1 dataset composition can be found on their official GitHub page[5]. For our evaluation, we merge the Task 1 training and development sets, excluding models with fewer than 10K examples. From the remaining models, we sample 10K examples each, ensuring equal representation across different sources. Table 2 details model and source distributions in our cross-domain evaluation.

4 Results

This section presents two sets of results: 1) performances of our four MGT detectors against RAID-derived test set, and 2) performances of the best-performing model according to 1) against out-of-domain task 1 dataset to further demonstrate model's robustness.

For each input example, a machine-likelihood score is calculated as $S = 1 - p(\text{"human"}|x)$, representing the probability that the input sample x is machine-generated. The share task adopts the same evaluation metric in RAID (Dugan et al., 2024) to measure how well each detector identifies machine-generated text while only misclassifying 5% of human-written text. Specifically, it is the true positive rate (TPR) after calibrating the decision thresholds to ensure a false positive rate (FPR) of 5%. If the FPR can be optimized to less than 5%, the evaluation script will attempt to do so.

4.1 In-Domain

Table 1 shows the overall performance of our four submissions across all domains and generator models, for both subtask A and B. Among the approaches, the Multi-class Classifier with Class Weighting (MW) detector outperforms the best when detecting MGT with adversarial attacks, more than 84% improvement over the baseline model in our self-evaluation. This suggests that training detectors with large multi-domain and multi-generator data is necessary for achieving robust performance on challenging benchmark like RAID. All four detectors achieve excellent performance when detecting MGT without adversarial attacks, exceeding 0.99 TPR at 5% FPR in the official evaluation. In all results, class-weighted detectors demonstrate a slight performance advantage over their non-weighted counterparts.

Detector	Adversarial		Non-Adversarial	
	Self	Official	Self	Official
BC(1.0.1)	0.986	0.957	0.997	0.991
BW(1.0.3)	0.989	0.972	**0.998**	**0.994**
MC(1.0.4)	0.986	0.976	0.997	0.992
MW(1.0.2)	**0.992**	**0.977**	0.997	0.993
OD	0.539	N/A	0.582	N/A

Table 1: Overall TPR at 5% FPR in our internal and the share task official evaluation, for Subtask A (Non-adversarial cross-domain MGT detection) ans Sub task B (Adversarial). Note: The detector version in '( )' corresponds to our submission 'Leidos Detector v1.0.x'.

In a heatmap, Figure 1 illustrates the performance of our best model (MW) for Subtask B. The model generally maintains high performance cross domains and generators, except for the Cohere generator model with Reviews domain text. As evidenced by the leaderboard, most submissions see performance drop on this subset, highlights a challenging aspect of Cohere generated review text and necessitates further analysis.

Figures 2 and 3 depict the impact of generator decoding strategies and specific adversarial attacks on the performance of the MW detector. While random sampling, a common technique to increase the diversity of generated text, marginally hinders detection compared to greedy decoding; a repetition penalty, another diversity-enhancing method, shows no significant impact on our detector. Overall, our model remains robust against different forms of text manipulation: most types of adversarial attack did not impact MGT detection, except for paraphrase (2.5% drop) and zero-width space (0.5% drop) attacks. In the RAID data, LLM paraphrased human-written text remains label as "human", which we argue is a gray area and may potentially contributes to our detector's decreased performance for this attack.

4.2 Cross-Domain

Figure 4 illustrates the aggregate performance of our best-performing model (MW) on the cross-domain dataset derived from Task 1 (Wang et al., 2025). We observe that our detector maintains high performance across both new domains and never-before-seen generator models. The results suggest that our detector effectively generalize to different application domains and generator models

[5] https://github.com/mbzuai-nlp/COLING-2025-Workshop-on-MGT-Detection-Task1/

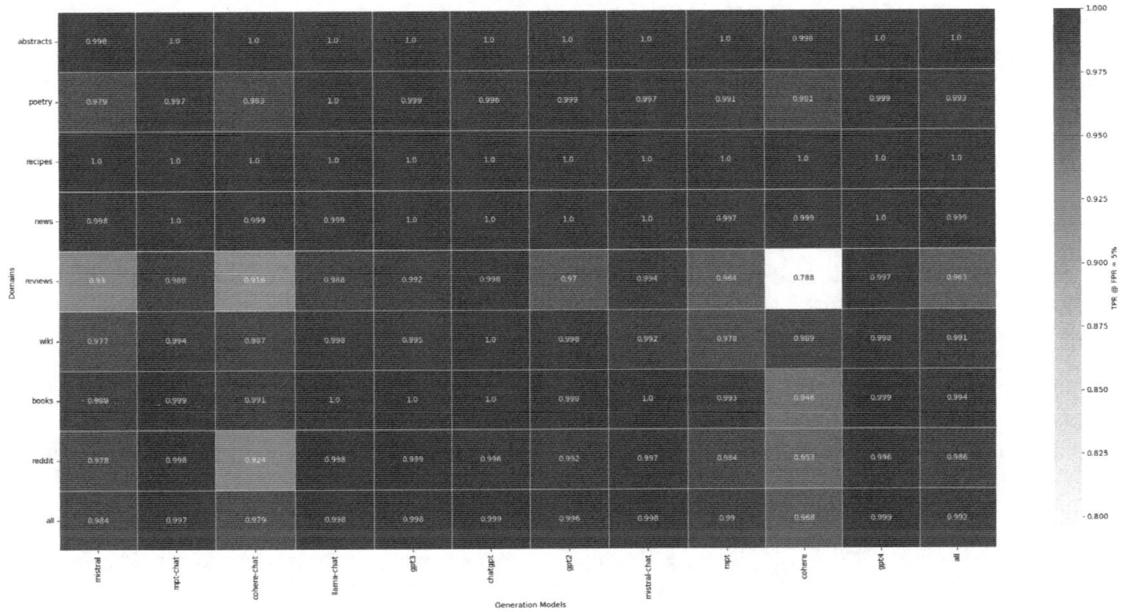

Figure 1: Heatmap measuring TPR at 5% FPR of our Multiclass Weighted (MW) detector across generators and domains, using our RAID-derived test set.

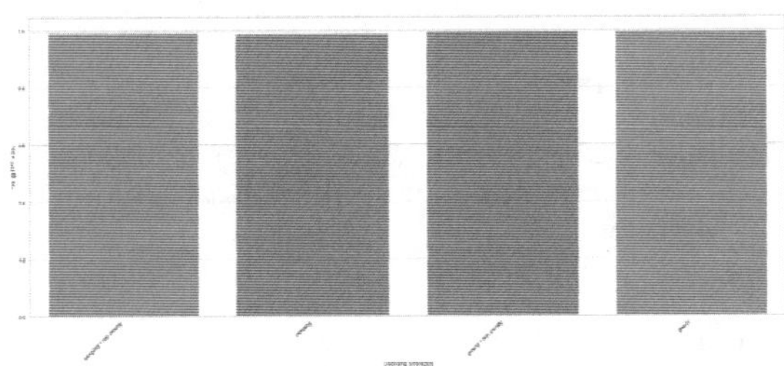

Figure 2: Impact of decoding strategy (x-axis) on MW detector performance (y-axis).

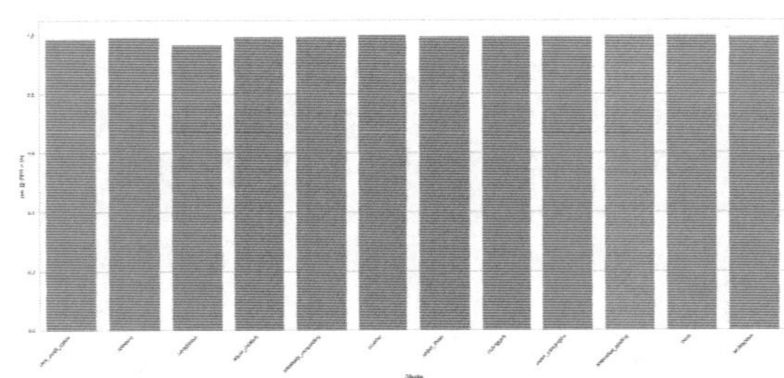

Figure 3: Impact of adversarial attack strategy on MW detector performance.

not encountered during training.

Our detector's strong performance may result not only from its generalization capabilities but also from training data overlap among generator models. LLMs are trained on massive datasets, that often overlap, causing them to generate similar outputs by drawing from the same underlying data (a phenomenon known as memorization or data leakage). This similarity might lead our detector to recognize common patterns across different generators.

5 Conclusion

In this paper, we address the challenges of detecting machine-generated text (MGT) from multiple domains and different generators. Four variants of the DistilRoBERTa-Base model are trained on large and diverse RAID dataset, all achieving highly promising results. Specifically, the multi-class classifier with class weighting (MW) performs the best in both multi-domain and cross-domain evaluations despite of adversarial attacks. This suggests that our approach generalizes well across multiple different domains, unseen generator models, and text manipulations.

Our study demonstrates that transformer-based models with class weighting are effective for MGT detection, representing a significant step toward robust and generalizable detection techniques. However, the strong performance may be influenced by factors limiting true generalizability. Specifically, shared training data among LLM generators might lead detectors to recognize common patterns rather than genuinely generalize across different generators. Additionally, the current evaluation method sets decision thresholds based on a 5% FPR during testing, whereas in practice, thresholds are learned and fixed during training. These aspects require further investigation to ensure detection reliability. In future work, we aim to address these limitations and extend experiments to quantify the impact of training data size.

6 Ethical Considerations and Limitations

Our models may inherit biases present in the training data, which could result in unfair performance across various demographics or content types. This bias poses an ethical concern, as it may lead to higher rates of misclassification of human-written text, especially for underrepresented groups. To mitigate these issues, it is important that datasets are high-quality and diverse. Evaluating model performance across various subgroups and implementing techniques to detect and reduce bias in both models and datasets are essential for model development.

MGT detectors could be misused to infringe on privacy or suppress free speech. Broad adoption may also discourage creative or assistive uses of language models if content is misclassified as machine-generated. While misclassifications may be rare with highly accurate detectors, bias can persist if the majority of the training data isn't written by professional authors. To prevent misuse and protect individual rights, establishing ethical guidelines and usage policies is crucial. Clear policies are needed to differentiate between unethical practices and acceptable uses, governing the ethical deployment of MGT detectors.

The complexity of transformer-based models poses challenges for transparency and explainability. Incorporating explainable AI techniques can help users understand and trust the detector's decisions. These methods can make model decisions more interpretable and are important as they enable accountability and encourage human-machine collaboration.

Although our models performed well on the evaluation datasets, they may not generalize to all future models or domains due to the quick evolution of language models. Data overlap among language models may contribute to the detectors recognizing patterns rather than truly generalizing, potentially inflating performance metrics. Continuous updates and retraining are necessary to maintain performance. Minimizing data overlap is important to better assess true generalization capabilities.

Our goal is to responsibly contribute to the development of MGT detection technologies that are fair, transparent, and beneficial to society.

References

Mervat Abassy, Kareem Elozeiri, Alexander Aziz, Minh Ngoc Ta, Raj Vardhan Tomar, Bimarsha Adhikari, Saad El Dine Ahmed, Yuxia Wang, Osama Mohammed Afzal, Zhuohan Xie, et al. 2024. Llm-detectaive: a tool for fine-grained machine-generated text detection. *arXiv preprint arXiv:2408.04284*.

Liam Dugan, Alyssa Hwang, Filip Trhlik, Josh Magnus Ludan, Andrew Zhu, Hainiu Xu, Daphne Ippolito, and Chris Callison-Burch. 2024. Raid: A shared benchmark for robust evaluation of machine-generated text detectors. *arXiv preprint arXiv:2405.07940*.

Liam Dugan, Andrew Zhu, Firoj Alam, Preslav Nakov, Marianna Apidianaki, and Callison-Burch Chris. 2025. Genai content detection task 3: Cross-domain machine generated text detection challenge. In *Proceedings of the 1st Workshop on GenAI Content Detection (GenAIDetect)*, Abu Dhabi, UAE. International Conference on Computational Linguistics.

Ahmad B Hassanat, Ahmad S Tarawneh, Ghada A Altarawneh, and Abdullah Almuhaimeed. 2022. Stop oversampling for class imbalance learning: A critical review. *arXiv preprint arXiv:2202.03579*.

T Lin. 2017. Focal loss for dense object detection. *arXiv preprint arXiv:1708.02002*.

Yinhan Liu. 2019. Roberta: A robustly optimized bert pretraining approach. *arXiv preprint arXiv:1907.11692*, 364.

Victor Sanh, Lysandre Debut, Julien Chaumond, and Thomas Wolf. 2019. Distilbert, a distilled version of bert: smaller, faster, cheaper and lighter. *ArXiv*, abs/1910.01108.

Yuxia Wang, Jonibek Mansurov, Petar Ivanov, Jinyan Su, Artem Shelmanov, Akim Tsvigun, Osama Mohanned Afzal, Tarek Mahmoud, Giovanni Puccetti, Thomas Arnold, et al. 2024. M4gt-bench: Evaluation benchmark for black-box machine-generated text detection. *arXiv preprint arXiv:2402.11175*.

Yuxia Wang, Artem Shelmanov, Jonibek Mansurov, Akim Tsvigun, Vladislav Mikhailov, Rui Xing, Zhuohan Xie, Jiahui Geng, Giovanni Puccetti, Ekaterina Artemova, Jinyan Su, Minh Ngoc Ta, Mervat Abassy, Kareem Elozeiri, Saad El Dine Ahmed, Maiya Goloburda, Tarek Mahmoud, Raj Vardhan Tomar, Alexander Aziz, Nurkhan Laiyk, Osama Mohammed Afzal, Ryuto Koike, Masahiro Kaneko, Alham Fikri Aji, Nizar Habash, Iryna Gurevych, and Preslav Nakov. 2025. Genai content detection task

1: English and multilingual machine-generated text detection: Ai vs. human. In *Proceedings of the 31st International Conference on Computational Linguistics (COLING)*, Abu Dhabi, UAE. Association for Computational Linguistics.

Feng Xiong, Thanet Markchom, Ziwei Zheng, Subin Jung, Varun Ojha, and Huizhi Liang. 2024. Fine-tuning large language models for multigenerator, multidomain, and multilingual machine-generated text detection. *arXiv preprint arXiv:2401.12326*.

A Appendix

A.1 Cross-Domain Evaluation Composition

Table 2 provides the exact number of examples per model and source used in our corss-domain evaluation.

Model	Source	# Examples
Bloomz	M4GT	10000
Cohere	M4GT	10000
Davinci	M4GT	10000
Dolly	M4GT	10000
Gemma-2-9B-it	M4GT	10000
Gemma-7B-it	M4GT	10000
GPT-3.5	HC3	10000
GPT-3.5-Turbo	M4GT	5000
	Mage	5000
GPT-4	M4GT	10000
GPT-4o	M4GT	10000
Human	HC3	3333
	M4GT	3333
	Mage	3333
LLaMa-3-70B	M4GT	10000
LLaMa-3-8B	M4GT	10000
Mixtral-8x7B	M4GT	10000
Text-Davinci-002	Mage	10000

Table 2: Number of examples per model and source in our Task-1-derived test set.

A.2 Cross-Domain Evaluation Results

Figure 4 illustrates the aggregate performance of our best-performing model (MW) on the cross-domain dataset derived from Task 1.

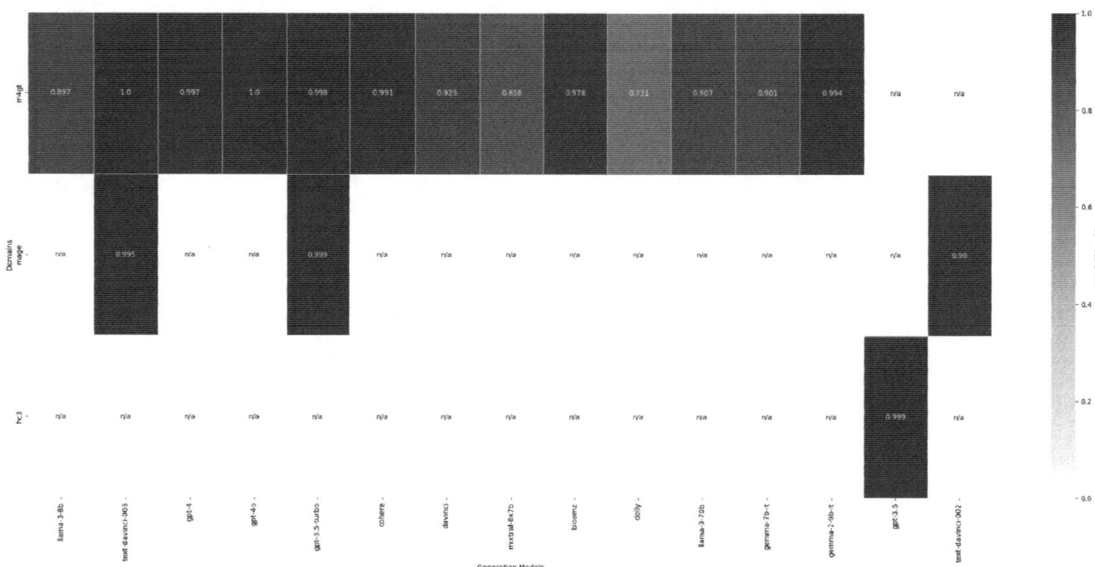

Figure 4: Heatmap measuring Accuracy at FPR 5% of our Multiclass Weighted (MW) detector across generators and domains using our Task-1-derived test set. Empty cells of the heatmap ("n/a") correspond to model and source combinations that are not present in the COLING 2025 MGT Detection Challenge Task 1 dataset.

Pangram at GenAI Detection Task 3: An Active Learning Approach to Machine-Generated Text Detection

Bradley Emi and **Max Spero** and **Elyas Masrour**
Pangram Labs, Inc.
Correspondence: info@pangram.com

Abstract

Deep learning approaches to machine-generated text detection typically suffer from chronic undertraining due to premature convergence. In our submission to the COLING Shared Task 3, we employ a two-stage training procedure to mitigate undertraining. First, we train an LLM-based classifier on a large multilingual dataset comprised of a wide variety of domains, languages, prompts, and LLMs. Then, we run offline inference on the AI-labeled side of the RAID train split, selecting the examples with the highest error and their human counterpart examples to continue training the model. We employ several preprocessing strategies to improve the robustness of the model. As a result, we achieve the highest score on the adversarial attack portion of the RAID leaderboard.

1 Introduction

We employ the same approach to the COLING Machine-Generated Text Detection task (Dugan et al., 2025) as we describe for our main production model at Pangram Labs (Emi and Spero, 2024). As we describe in our technical report, classifier accuracy when training deep learning models to detect AI-generated text does not naturally obey scaling laws. Classifier performance scales sublinearly as the size of the dataset used to train AI-generated text classifiers increases, ultimately even converging to a regime in which adding more data to the classifier no longer helps performance at all (e.g., validation loss stops decreasing even before the first epoch concludes).

We hypothesize that the reason for this "saturation of scaling laws" occurs for multiple reasons. First, we notice during training on a random distribution of human and AI-generated examples that the loss curves are very spiky. There are several batches in a row with nearly-zero loss followed by single batches with very high loss, causing gradient norms to reach very high values. As a result, low learning rates and aggressive gradient clipping are required for stable convergence. Second, many AI examples follow very simple patterns that make detection very obvious. For example, LLMs responses often begin with "Certainly!" or "Sure, here is a...", which are very obvious tells that a piece of text is LLM-generated. These easy examples flood the training set and cause learning to end prematurely as the model overfits to these simple patterns.

Our intuition is that a naively sampled dataset is flooded with examples that are too easy and have such giveaway patterns. To fix this problem, we resample the dataset with "hard" examples oversampled. To define a hard example, we first train a model on the randomly sampled dataset. We then use this model to mine for high error examples on the RAID dataset. We then take these examples, and their opposite label pairs, and retrain the model, which results in much more stable convergence behavior.

2 Methodology

2.1 Initial Datasets

Our initial dataset is seeded with a wide variety of human-written datasets from prior to 2022. We use datasets from the following domains: reviews, news, general web text, email, student writing/essays, creative writing, question and answers, ELL/ESL (English as a Second Language), scientific/medical papers, Project Gutenberg, and Wikipedia. We do not filter our dataset on language; however we tune the language composition such that English is the primary language used and there is sufficient representation from the top 20 languages used on the Internet. All data is ethically sourced and properly licensed for commercial use. For specifics on dataset composition, please

Proceedings of the 1st Workshop on GenAI Content Detection (GenAIDetect), pages 347–351
January 19, 2025.

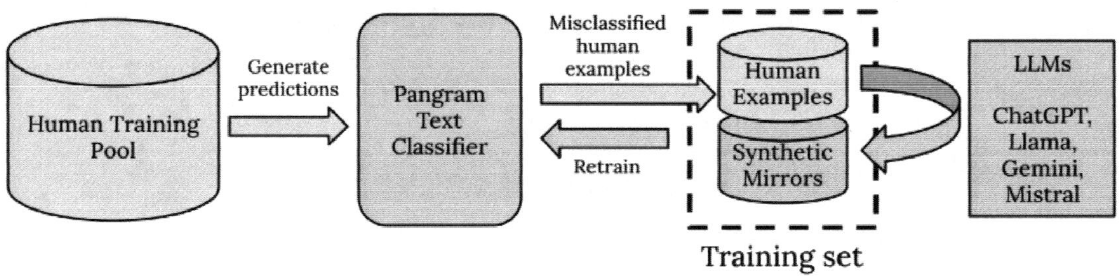

Figure 1: Pangram Active Learning Approach

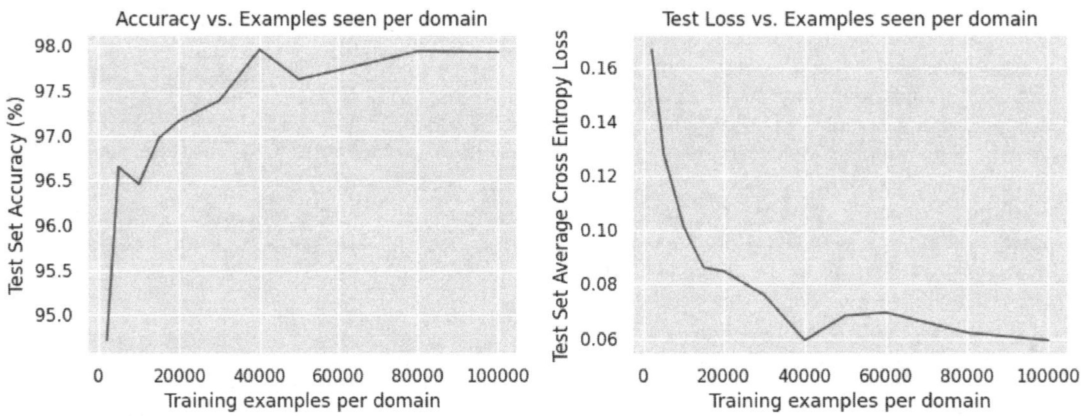

Figure 2: Without active learning, performance saturates as dataset size increases.

contact the authors.

2.2 Synthetic Data Creation

Our initial dataset is sampled randomly and all is labeled as human. To generate the AI side of the dataset, we use synthetic mirror prompts, which we describe in more detail in our technical report (Emi and Spero, 2024).

We define the term "mirror prompt" to be a prompt based on the original example that is used to generated a "synthetic mirror" or "mirror example." The goal of each mirror prompt is to generate an example that matches the topic and length of the original document.

If the original document is "<original review>", then a mirror prompt may look like this:

`[Prompt] Write a <original review star rating> star review for <original review business name>. Make the review around <original review length> words long.`

Another example may be for a student essay. We sometimes use double prompts, such as the following:

`[Prompt] What is a good title for this essay? <original essay> Only give the title in your response.`

`[Assistant] <Title>`

`[Prompt] Write an essay with the following title: <Title>. Make the essay around <original essay length> words long.`

2.3 LLMs used for Synthetic Mirrors

When the initial data is not in English, we translate our prompts to the language of the source data using DeepL's translation API. (DeepL SE, 2024)

For synthetic mirrors in the initial training stage, we use the following LLMs:

- GPT-3.5 (multiple subversions)
- GPT-4, GPT-4-turbo, and GPT-4o (multiple subversions)
- Claude 2 and 3 (multiple subversions and sizes)

- LLaMA 2, 3, and 3.1 (multiple subversions and sizes)
- Mistral (multiple versions and sizes)
- Gemini Pro and Flash (multiple subversions)

It is notable that we only use modern LLMs that are instruction-tuned and post-trained. We do not train on base models because they produce noticeably lower-quality outputs and are substantially less commonly used in real-world applications.

2.4 Preprocessing and Filtering

We employ the following preprocessing strategies prior to tokenization to enhance robustness.

- We remove all zero-width spaces.
- We convert all text to lowercase.
- We collapse all consecutive whitespace into a single whitespace.
- We attempt to remove LLM "headers", such as "Sure! Here is a..." or "Certainly!" or "As an AI language model,", etc.
- We convert all text to unicode standard characters using the `unidecode` package (English text only).

Prior to training, we also filter the dataset using the following criteria:

- We remove all examples that are under 25 words long.
- Sometimes LLMs simply repeat the prompt back to the user and do not say anything else. We attempt to filter out this use case by checking to see if 50 percent or more of the LLM output matches the input prompt exactly and if it does, we filter the example out.

2.5 Augmentation

We also employ two augmentation strategies.

- We randomly machine translate around 20 percent of the English training set to another language using DeepL. We randomly select the language from the top 20 languages on the Internet.
- With 50 percent probability, we randomly mask 15 percent to 75 percent of the input tokens from the model at training time. We find that this improves training stability and helps the model from overfitting to common giveaway phrases and syntactic patterns. This technique is very similar to CutOut which is commonly used in computer vision (DeVries and Taylor, 2017).

2.6 Tokenization, Architecture, and Model Training

We use the Mistral NeMo architecture (Mistral AI Team, 2024) which has approximately 12 billion parameters, with an untrained linear classification head and an LLM classification head (to identify which LLM an AI text came from, as an auxiliary task). Following the usual convention for sequence classification modeling using an autoregressive language model, the hidden state from the final token in the sequence is used as the input to both classification heads. As is common practice in LLM finetuning, we use trainable LoRA (Hu et al., 2022) adapters while keeping the base model frozen. We use the Tekken tokenizer out of the box, which is noted for its strong multilingual performance. We truncate the context window to 512 tokens to constrain the model to using only short-range features. When necessary, we simply crop the input to fit the context window.

We train the model to convergence using 8 A100 GPUs with an effective batch size of 24 using a weighted cross-entropy loss. We use the AdamW optimizer and a linearly decaying learning rate schedule. We train the model for 1 epoch, which took about 9 hours, and select the checkpoint based on a weighted cross-entropy loss with 3 times the weight given to false positives.

2.7 Active Learning

After the initial model is trained, we mine the RAID training set for AI examples that the initial model classifies as human. We then select the 50,000 highest error examples and add them back into the training set with the 50,000 human example pairs corresponding to these highest error examples. We restrict our search to only examples that have no adversarial attack.

This process has several side effects that also improve the underlying data distribution. First, base models and other models that are difficult to detect are introduced into the training set, but only the base model distribution that differs significantly from the instruction-tuned model distributions, and proportionally to how poorly the generalization is to each particular model.

This side effect generalizes to domains, languages, and attacks as well: the worse the initial model is at predicting a particular split of the data, the more that split gets overrepresented in the following training run.

We reintroduce this data into the training set and retrain the model for 1 epoch until convergence.

3 Results

Pangram places first overall in detecting GPT4, ChatGPT, and LLaMA (state-of-the-art models) with no adversarial attacks, second overall in detecting all models without adversarial attacks, and tied for first overall in detecting AI-generated text with adversarial attacks.

The full results are posted publicly on the RAID website. We refer the reader to the leaderboard for full details. (Dugan et al., 2025)

4 Discussion

We believe our method is a general framework for scaling the deep learning approach to detecting AI-generated text, and this prototype model is only a starting point. For example, the framework could be extended beyond the current dataset to even more domains and data and larger models, or customized to private data or domains in which open data is not readily available at scale, such as messaging, email, or other data with high amounts of PII.

4.1 Differences between RAID submission and Pangram's Commercial Model

Our submission uses a similar framework and is otherwise trained in the same way as Pangram's commercial model, but there are some slight differences.

In Pangram's original framework (Emi and Spero, 2024), we perform hard negative mining with synthetic mirrors on large human-written text corpora, to reduce the false positive rate as much as possible. However, when evaluated on RAID, the initial model has excellent precision but poor recall. This is due to the domain shift to the different models used in the RAID benchmark. To reduce our false positive rate, we perform the inverse operation: hard *positive* mining with human mirrors. This is not generally possible in a real-world setting due to the fact that positively labeled examples are not as abundant as negatively labeled examples, but it was possible for the RAID benchmark and so we decided to take advantage.

Because the RAID benchmark contains many lower-quality models, such as MPT, GPT-2, etc., we needed to optimize the model to perform well on these lower quality models, but this required trading off some false positives. For real-world usage, detecting these low-quality model outputs is not important, so our production model does not detect these as well as the RAID model, but has a lower false positive rate.

We also enforce a higher minimum word count for the commercial model, which again lowers our false positive rate but hurts our recall on shorter text. Other researchers have given theoretical and empirical grounding for the relationship between detectability and sequence length (Chakraborty et al., 2023). In practice, for the production model, we choose to prioritize precision, but for the RAID submission, we instead to choose a more balanced approach where we equally prioritize precision and recall on these short texts.

Additionally, we do not use unidecode for the commercial model on non-English languages.

5 Conclusion

In this work, we have demonstrated a general framework for domain and model adaptation of deep-learning based AI detectors based on active learning and mirroring. We further argue that active learning is necessary for scaling performance both in terms of model size and data and present a model larger and more accurate than the other methods in the RAID benchmark, without the need for using perplexity-based features or otherwise handcrafted feature engineering.

References

Souradip Chakraborty, Amrit Singh Bedi, Sicheng Zhu, Bang An, Dinesh Manocha, and Furong Huang. 2023. On the possibilities of ai-generated text detection. *Preprint*, arXiv:2304.04736.

DeepL SE. 2024. Deepl translator. Accessed: 2024-11-12.

Terrance DeVries and Graham W. Taylor. 2017. Improved regularization of convolutional neural networks with cutout. *Preprint*, arXiv:1708.04552.

Liam Dugan, Andrew Zhu, Firoj Alam, Preslav Nakov, Marianna Apidianaki, and Callison-Burch Chris. 2025. GenAI Content Detection Task 3: Cross-domain machine generated text detection challenge. In *Proceedings of the 1st Workshop on GenAI Content Detection (GenAIDetect)*, Abu Dhabi, UAE. International Conference on Computational Linguistics.

Bradley Emi and Max Spero. 2024. Technical report on the pangram ai-generated text classifier. *Preprint*, arXiv:2402.14873.

Edward J Hu, Yelong Shen, Phillip Wallis, Zeyuan Allen-Zhu, Yuanzhi Li, Shean Wang, Lu Wang, and Weizhu Chen. 2022. Lora: Low-rank adaptation of large language models. *arXiv preprint arXiv:2106.09685*.

Mistral AI Team. 2024. Mistral NeMo. Released in collaboration with NVIDIA, July 18, 2024.

LuxVeri at GenAI Detection Task 3: Cross-Domain Detection of AI-Generated Text Using Inverse Perplexity-Weighted Ensemble of Fine-Tuned Transformer Models

Md Kamrujjaman Mobin[1], **Md Saiful Islam**[1, 2]
[1]Computer Science and Engineering, Shahjalal University of Science and Technology, Sylhet, Bangladesh
[2]Computing Science, University of Alberta, Edmonton, Alberta, Canada

Abstract

This paper presents our approach for Task 3 of the GenAI content detection workshop at COLING-2025, focusing on Cross-Domain Machine-Generated Text (MGT) Detection. We propose an ensemble of fine-tuned transformer models, enhanced by inverse perplexity weighting, to improve classification accuracy across diverse text domains. For Subtask A (Non-Adversarial MGT Detection), we combined a fine-tuned RoBERTa-base model with an OpenAI detector-integrated RoBERTa-base model, achieving an aggregate TPR score of 0.826, ranking 10th out of 23 detectors. In Subtask B (Adversarial MGT Detection), our fine-tuned RoBERTa-base model achieved a TPR score of 0.801, securing 8th out of 22 detectors. Our results demonstrate the effectiveness of inverse perplexity-based weighting for enhancing generalization and performance in both non-adversarial and adversarial MGT detection, highlighting the potential for transformer models in cross-domain AI-generated content detection.

1 Introduction

The proliferation of advanced language models such as GPT (Radford et al., 2019) and RoBERTa (Liu et al., 2019), machine-generated content has become prevalent across social media, journalism, and academia, raising concerns about authenticity and misinformation. Detecting AI-generated text is especially challenging across diverse domains, where variations in language and style can hinder detection efforts.

In Task 3 of the COLING 2025 Workshop on Detecting AI-Generated Content (Dugan et al., 2025), we tackle cross-domain Machine-Generated Text (MGT) detection using an ensemble approach that combines fine-tuned RoBERTa-base models (Liu et al., 2019) and OpenAI detection tools (Solaiman et al., 2019). Our method leverages inverse perplexity weighting to enhance the contributions of high-confidence models, yielding a robust detection system.

Our approach achieved an aggregate score of 0.826 in Non-Adversarial Cross-Domain MGT detection (Subtask A), ranking 10th, and 0.801 in Adversarial Cross-Domain MGT detection (Subtask B), ranking 8th. This paper outlines our ensemble-based methodology, dataset considerations, and insights for effective cross-domain AI-generated text detection.

2 Background

2.1 Dataset

The RAID dataset (Dugan et al., 2024), provided for the competition, is designed for evaluating machine-generated text detectors. It contains over 10 million documents across 11 language models, 11 genres, 4 decoding strategies, and 12 adversarial attacks, including both human-written and machine-generated content from 8 different domains like books, news, poetry, and recipes. For training and validation, we used the RAID-train subset (802 million words, 11.8GB) and RAID-test subset (81 million words, 1.22GB). We also utilized the RAID-extra subset, which includes languages like Czech and German (275 million words, 3.71GB). This dataset provides a comprehensive resource for AI-generated text detection.

For the fine-tuning of our model, we reduced the dataset by using about 10% of the publicly available data. This reduction was carried out in a balanced manner across all genres, decoding strategies, attacks, and domains to ensure that each subset was proportionally represented. Specifically, we reduced the data across the following domains: abstracts, books, news, poetry, recipes, reddit, reviews, and wiki. The distribution of this reduced data across models is shown in Table 1, with domain-specific sample sizes for each model. For example, the number of samples for "Chat-

Proceedings of the 1st Workshop on GenAI Content Detection (GenAIDetect), pages 352–357
January 19, 2025.

Model	Domain								Total
	Abstracts	Books	News	Poetry	Recipes	Reddit	Reviews	Wiki	
Human	2119	2137	2136	2125	2126	2135	1132	2135	17109
ChatGPT	4238	4274	4272	4250	4253	4270	2263	4270	34090
Cohere	4238	4274	4272	4250	4253	4270	2263	4270	34090
Cohere-Chat	4238	4274	4272	4250	4253	4270	2263	4270	34090
GPT-2	8477	8549	8544	8501	8506	8540	4526	8540	68183
GPT-3	4238	4274	4272	4250	4253	4270	2263	4270	34090
GPT-4	4238	4274	4272	4250	4253	4270	2263	4270	34090
Llama-Chat	8477	8549	8544	8501	8506	8540	4526	8540	68183
Mistral	8477	8549	8544	8501	8506	8540	4526	8540	68183
Mistral-Chat	8477	8549	8544	8501	8506	8540	4526	8540	68183
MPT	8477	8549	8544	8501	8506	8540	4526	8540	68183
MPT-Chat	8477	8549	8544	8501	8506	8540	4526	8540	68183
Total	62516	63577	63538	63380	63408	63606	37338	63606	518469

Table 1: Data distribution for various models across different domains, with total data per model and summed values for each domain. The values represent domain-specific sample sizes for each model. We used only 10% of the RAID (Dugan et al., 2024) dataset for fine-tuning our models.

GPT" in the "Books" domain is 4274, while for "Human" in the "Reviews" domain, it is 1132. This balanced reduction ensures the data used for training is representative across models and domains, enabling efficient and effective fine-tuning.

2.2 Related Work

The detection of machine-generated text has gained attention with the rise of large language models (LLMs) like GPT (Radford et al., 2019) and BERT (Devlin et al., 2019). Fine-tuned Transformer models have succeeded in binary classification tasks, but challenges remain in cross-domain and multilingual contexts due to data biases (Liu et al., 2019; Solaiman et al., 2019). Ensemble methods combining models like BERT, RoBERTa, GPT variants, and perplexity-based weighting have been explored to improve domain robustness (Schick and Schütze, 2020; Clark et al., 2019).

Recent work in cross-domain detection shows that RoBERTa-based detectors for GPT-2 generated technical text can be transferred with few labeled examples, such as from physics to biomedicine (Rodriguez et al., 2022). Paragraph-level detection is also being explored to address document tampering in mixed-domain texts.

For multilingual detection, models like XLM-RoBERTa (Conneau et al., 2019) and RemBERT (Chung et al., 2021) improve cross-lingual detection, though challenges remain for low-resource languages (Hu et al., 2020). Recent SemEval tasks (Fetahu et al., 2023; Wang et al., 2024) have refined these approaches with task-specific fine-tuning. Our work builds on these methods by using inverse perplexity-weighted ensembles to enhance detection across domains and languages.

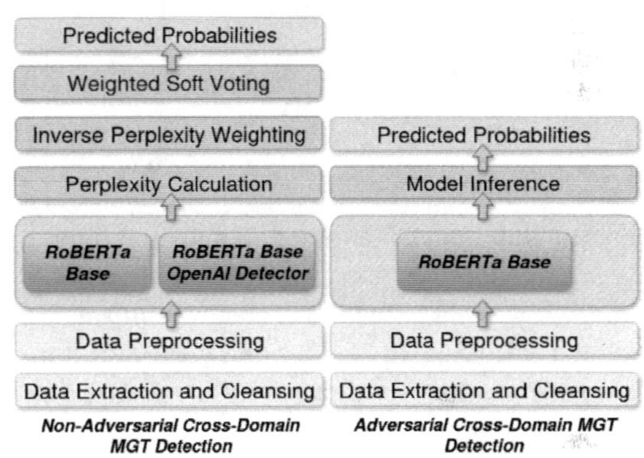

Figure 1: Overall Framework of our Proposed System for both Non-Adversarial and Adversarial Cross-Domain MGT Detection.

3 System Overview

We developed an ensemble approach for AI-generated text detection across multiple domains, using Transformer models with inverse perplexity-based weighted voting for improved accuracy. The system overview is shown in Figure 1.

3.1 Ensemble Model Selection and Justification

For the ensemble model, we selected two Transformer-based models tailored for Non-Adversarial and Adversarial cross-domain text detection, leveraging their strengths in capturing linguistic, syntactic, and semantic patterns essential for AI-generated content detection. For non-adversarial tasks, we employed **RoBERTa-base**, recognized for its strong performance in natural language understanding and robust generalization across text domains (Liu et al., 2019), alongside the **RoBERTa-base OpenAI Detector**, fine-tuned specifically for distinguishing AI-generated text from human-authored content (Solaiman et al., 2019). For adversarial scenarios, **RoBERTa-base** was selected again for its ability to capture subtle linguistic patterns and semantic inconsistencies, making it highly effective in challenging detection tasks (Liu et al., 2019). This strategic selection ensures a balanced approach to handling diverse and adversarial text detection challenges.

3.2 Data Pre-processing

For text classification, the data was preprocessed using model-specific tokenizers, incorporating truncation and padding as required. To enhance memory efficiency and training performance, texts were sorted by word count, reducing unnecessary padding. A fixed random seed was maintained to ensure reproducibility.

3.3 Training Procedure

The models were fine-tuned using the Hugging Face Transformers library [1] for English and multilingual text classification. Tokenization was performed with 'AutoTokenizer', and the architectures were adapted for classification tasks with appropriate label mappings.

Training was conducted for 3 epochs with a learning rate of 2×10^{-5}, batch sizes of 4 for training and 16 for validation, and weight decay of 0.01. Early stopping was applied with a patience of 5 evaluations and a 0.001 improvement threshold. Evaluation checkpoints were saved after each epoch, and the best-performing model was used for testing.

This procedure ensured robust generalization across subtasks. Further training details are provided in Table 2.

3.4 Ensemble Voting Strategy

Our ensemble employs a weighted soft-voting strategy, combining predictions from all fine-tuned models for each subtask. The weights are determined based on inverse perplexity, with lower perplexity values reflecting higher confidence.

[1] Hugging Face Transformers: https://huggingface.co/transformers/

Hyperparameter	**Value**
Number of Epochs	$2 \sim 3$
Learning Rate	$1 \times 10^{-5} \sim 2 \times 10^{-5}$
Training Batch Size	4
Validation Batch Size	16
Early Stopping Patience	5 validation steps
Early Stopping Threshold	0.001
Weight Decay	0.01
Optimizer	AdamW
Loss Function	Binary Cross-Entropy
Evaluation Strategy	Every ¼ epoch
Checkpointing Strategy	Validation loss

Table 2: Training Configuration

3.4.1 Perplexity Calculation

For each model, we compute the perplexity based on its predictions. The perplexity P is computed using the Negative Log Likelihood formula:

$$P = \exp\left(-\frac{1}{N}\sum_{i=1}^{N}\log(p(y_i \mid x_i))\right)$$

where $p(y_i \mid x_i)$ is the predicted probability for the true label y_i, and N is the number of test samples. Lower perplexity values indicate higher confidence.

To compute perplexity, we use each model's logits, apply softmax to obtain probabilities, and then calculate perplexity based on the true labels and these probabilities.

3.4.2 Perplexity-Based Weighting Adjustment

To calculate model weights, each model's perplexity is adjusted by subtracting 1, creating an effective weighting scale. The weight w_i for model i is then computed as the inverse of this adjusted perplexity and normalized across models, giving higher confidence models greater influence.

$$w_i = \frac{1/(P_i - 1)}{\sum_{j=1}^{M}(1/(P_j - 1))}$$

where M represents the total number of models, and P_i is the original perplexity of model i.

3.4.3 Weighted Soft-Voting

Each model's predicted probabilities are scaled by its weight and summed to form the final ensemble prediction. This weighted voting prioritizes models with higher confidence (lower perplexity), giving them greater influence on the final decision. The ensemble's final prediction for each class c is:

Detector	Chat GPT	GPT-4	GPT-3	GPT-2	Mistral	Mistral-Chat	Cohere	Cohere-Chat	Llama-Chat	MPT	MPT-Chat	AGG TPR	Rank
Non-Adversarial Results													
FT RoBERTa + RoBERTa OpenAI	0.960	0.861	0.895	**0.753**	**0.734**	0.936	0.546	0.748	0.891	**0.804**	0.901	**0.826**	10/23
FT RoBERTa + RoBERTa OpenAI + BERT	0.983	**0.934**	0.755	0.730	0.709	**0.960**	0.510	0.747	0.943	0.772	**0.932**	0.825	11/23
FT RoBERTa	0.943	0.836	0.902	0.739	0.719	0.916	0.542	0.737	0.870	0.800	0.891	0.813	12/23
Binoculars	**0.997**	0.907	**0.989**	0.678	0.610	0.914	**0.935**	**0.943**	**0.973**	0.447	0.707	0.790	-
Adversarial Results													
FT RoBERTa	0.911	0.808	**0.873**	**0.730**	**0.720**	0.887	**0.567**	**0.740**	0.855	**0.806**	**0.861**	**0.801**	8/22
FT RoBERTa + RoBERTa OpenAI	0.876	0.777	0.813	0.690	0.681	0.851	0.518	0.696	0.823	0.757	0.817	0.760	10/22
FT RoBERTa + RoBERTa OpenAI + BERT	0.896	0.843	0.675	0.663	0.651	0.874	0.457	0.670	0.857	0.711	0.841	0.749	11/22
SuperAnnotate AI Detector	**0.963**	**0.913**	0.720	0.411	0.342	**0.897**	0.445	0.685	**0.918**	0.314	0.767	0.649	-

Table 3: Cross-domain MGT detection performance under non-adversarial and adversarial conditions. The table shows detector performance across various generator models, with aggregate True Positive Rate (AGG TPR) and rankings. "FT" denotes fine-tuned models, and base models are used for training and evaluation.

$$p_{\text{ensemble}}(c) = \sum_{i=1}^{M} w_i \cdot p_i(c)$$

where $p_i(c)$ is the predicted probability for class c by model i, and w_i is its weight.

This method enhances ensemble accuracy by prioritizing predictions from more confident models, improving overall performance.

4 Results

Table 3 shows cross-domain MGT detection performance for non-adversarial and adversarial testing, with detectors ranked based on aggregate True Positive Rate (TPR).

4.1 Performance

In the non-adversarial setting, the fine-tuned RoBERTa + RoBERTa OpenAI model which was fine-tuned on RAID dataset (Dugan et al., 2024) achieved the highest performance, with an aggregate (AGG) score of 0.826, ranking 10th out of 23 detectors (see Table 3). This model effectively combined fine-tuned RoBERTa Base and RoBERTa Base OpenAI models, with perplexity-based weighting to give more influence to lower-perplexity models, enhancing overall accuracy. It consistently delivered strong results across various generator models, including ChatGPT and GPT-3.

In the adversarial testing, the fine-tuned RoBERTa model outperformed other detectors, achieving an aggregate (AGG) score of 0.801 and ranking 8th out of 22 (see Table 3). This demonstrates the model's robust adaptability in adversarial conditions, achieving top scores with GPT-3 and GPT-4, even under altered input scenarios.

4.2 Model Comparison

The performance of various detectors was evaluated under both non-adversarial and adversarial conditions, revealing key insights into their strengths and limitations.

In the non-adversarial setting, FT RoBERTa + RoBERTa OpenAI emerged as the top performer, achieving an AGG TPR of 0.826 and ranking 10th overall. It demonstrated exceptional performance with models such as ChatGPT (TPR: 0.960) and GPT-4 (TPR: 0.861), outperforming FT RoBERTa (AGG TPR: 0.813, ranked 12th) and the ensemble model FT RoBERTa + RoBERTa OpenAI + BERT (AGG TPR: 0.825, ranked 11th). Interestingly, Binoculars (Hans et al., 2024) showed strong results with specific generators like GPT-3 (TPR: 0.989) and Llama-Chat (TPR: 0.973). However, its inconsistent performance with other generators, such as MPT (TPR: 0.447), limited its reliability. In contrast, FT RoBERTa + RoBERTa OpenAI demonstrated stable results across all generators, including strong performances with Mistral-Chat (TPR: 0.936) and Cohere-Chat (TPR: 0.748), underscoring its robustness and versatility.

Under adversarial conditions, FT RoBERTa proved to be the most robust model, achieving an AGG TPR of 0.801 and ranking 8th overall. It excelled with GPT-3 (TPR: 0.873) and MPT-Chat (TPR: 0.861), outperforming FT RoBERTa + RoBERTa OpenAI (AGG TPR: 0.760, ranked 10th) and FT RoBERTa + RoBERTa OpenAI + BERT (AGG TPR: 0.749, ranked 11th). In comparison, the SuperAnnotate AI Detector (SuperAnnotate, 2024) delivered competitive results with ChatGPT (TPR: 0.963), but its performance was inconsistent, particularly with GPT-2 (TPR: 0.411) and Mistral (TPR: 0.342). These results emphasize the variability of some detectors when faced with adversarial data, highlighting the consistent reliability of FT RoBERTa.

The consistent dominance of FT RoBERTa + RoBERTa OpenAI in non-adversarial settings and FT RoBERTa in adversarial conditions underscores the importance of tailoring architectures to specific scenarios. While models like Binoculars and SuperAnnotate excelled in isolated cases, their lack of stability across diverse generators reinforces the value of robust, well-balanced models like FT RoBERTa. These findings suggest that future efforts should focus on further optimizing architectures to enhance cross-domain robustness and adversarial detection capabilities.

5 Limitations

Our approach, while effective, has several limitations. Focusing on RoBERTa models for fine-tuning and ensemble weighting excluded alternatives like RemBERT (Chung et al., 2021) and XLM-RoBERTa (Conneau et al., 2019), which might better handle longer sequences, noisy data, and multi-label tasks.

Due to computational constraints, we trained on a subset of the RAID dataset, limiting the model's ability to capture its full diversity. Training on the full dataset could greatly improve detection performance, especially for underrepresented domains.

Performance variability across generator models (e.g., GPT-4 vs. Mistral) and limited multilingual capabilities highlight the need for better cross-domain generalization and robust multilingual detection. While the ensemble approach enhanced generalization, it increased computational overhead, warranting exploration of more efficient strategies in future work.

6 Discussion and Conclusion

In this paper, we proposed an ensemble-based approach for cross-domain MGT detection, combining fine-tuned RoBERTa Base and RoBERTa Base OpenAI detectors with inverse perplexity weighting. Our method achieved competitive results, ranking 10th and 8th in non-adversarial and adversarial tasks, respectively, in Task 3 of the GenAI content detection workshop at COLING-2025. Inverse perplexity weighting improved generalization by prioritizing more confident models across diverse domains. For non-adversarial tasks, we explored an inverse perplexity-based ensemble approach. However, the detectors in this ensemble underperformed compared to the fine-tuned RoBERTa model, highlighting the value of fine-tuning on task-specific data and suggesting avenues for refining ensemble techniques.

Our results show that transformer-based models, particularly RoBERTa, are effective for non-adversarial and adversarial MGT detection. For non-adversarial detection (Subtask A), we achieved a score of 0.826, and for adversarial detection (Subtask B), we scored 0.801. However, cross-domain detection remains challenging, especially with varied generator models and multilingual data. Our system performed well with generators like ChatGPT and GPT-4 but struggled with others like Cohere and Mistral, indicating the difficulty of detecting diverse machine-generated content.

Due to limited computational resources, we trained on a subset of the available data. Despite this, our models performed well, demonstrating the potential of our approach even with partial data. This work lays the foundation for further progress in MGT detection, especially in adversarial and cross-lingual settings. Future research can focus on enhancing multilingual capabilities, incorporating more diverse language models, and exploring dynamic ensemble strategies to improve performance across domains and attack scenarios.

References

Hyung Won Chung, Thibault Févry, Henry Tsai, Melvin Johnson, and Sebastian Ruder. 2021. Rethinking embedding coupling in pre-trained language models. In *9th International Conference on Learning Representations, ICLR 2021, Virtual Event, Austria, May 3-7, 2021*. OpenReview.net.

Kevin Clark, Minh-Thang Luong, Quoc V. Le, and Dan So. 2019. Electra: Pre-training text encoders as discriminators rather than generators.

Alexis Conneau, Kartikay Khandelwal, Naman Goyal, Vishrav Chaudhary, Guillaume Wenzek, Francisco Guzmán, Edouard Grave, Myle Ott, Luke Zettlemoyer, and Veselin Stoyanov. 2019. Unsupervised cross-lingual representation learning at scale. *CoRR*, abs/1911.02116.

Jacob Devlin, Ming-Wei Chang, Kenton Lee, et al. 2019. Bert: Pre-training of deep bidirectional transformers for language understanding. In *Proceedings of NAACL-HLT 2019*, pages 4171–4186.

Liam Dugan, Alyssa Hwang, Filip Trhlík, Andrew Zhu, Josh Magnus Ludan, Hainiu Xu, Daphne Ippolito, and Chris Callison-Burch. 2024. RAID: A shared benchmark for robust evaluation of machine-generated text detectors. In *Proceedings of the 62nd Annual Meeting of the Association for Computational Linguistics (Volume 1: Long Papers)*, pages 12463–12492, Bangkok, Thailand. Association for Computational Linguistics.

Liam Dugan, Andrew Zhu, Firoj Alam, Preslav Nakov, Marianna Apidianaki, and Callison-Burch Chris. 2025. Genai content detection task 3: Cross-domain machine generated text detection challenge. In *Proceedings of the 1st Workshop on GenAI Content Detection (GenAIDetect)*, Abu Dhabi, UAE. International Conference on Computational Linguistics.

Besnik Fetahu, Sudipta Kar, Zhiyu Chen, Oleg Rokhlenko, and Shervin Malmasi. 2023. SemEval-2023 task 2: Fine-grained multilingual named entity recognition (MultiCoNER 2). In *Proceedings of the 17th International Workshop on Semantic Evaluation (SemEval-2023)*, pages 2247–2265, Toronto, Canada. Association for Computational Linguistics.

Abhimanyu Hans, Avi Schwarzschild, Valeriia Cherepanova, Hamid Kazemi, Aniruddha Saha, Micah Goldblum, Jonas Geiping, and Tom Goldstein. 2024. Spotting llms with binoculars: Zero-shot detection of machine-generated text. *Preprint*, arXiv:2401.12070.

Xiang Hu, Xuezhe Liu, Peng He, and et al. 2020. Xtreme: A massively multilingual evaluation benchmark.

Y. Liu et al. 2019. Roberta: A robustly optimized bert pretraining approach. *arXiv preprint arXiv:1907.11692*.

Alec Radford, Karthik Narasimhan, Tim Salimans, et al. 2019. Language models are unsupervised multitask learners.

Juan Diego Rodriguez, Todd Hay, David Gros, Zain Shamsi, and Ravi Srinivasan. 2022. Cross-domain detection of GPT-2-generated technical text. In *Proceedings of the 2022 Conference of the North American Chapter of the Association for Computational Linguistics: Human Language Technologies*, pages 1213–1233, Seattle, United States. Association for Computational Linguistics.

Timo Schick and Hinrich Schütze. 2020. Exploiting cloze-style pretraining for few-shot text classification. In *Proceedings of ACL 2020*, pages 255–265.

Irene Solaiman, Miles Brundage, Jack Clark, Amanda Askell, Ariel Herbert-Voss, Jeff Wu, Alec Radford, Gretchen Krueger, Jong Wook Kim, Sarah Kreps, et al. 2019. Release strategies and the social impacts of language models. *arXiv preprint arXiv:1908.09203*.

SuperAnnotate. 2024. Ai detector. Accessed: 2024-11-15.

Yuxia Wang, Jonibek Mansurov, Petar Ivanov, Jinyan Su, Artem Shelmanov, Akim Tsvigun, Osama Mohammed Afzal, Tarek Mahmoud, Giovanni Puccetti, Thomas Arnold, Chenxi Whitehouse, Alham Fikri Aji, Nizar Habash, Iryna Gurevych, and Preslav Nakov. 2024. Semeval-2024 task 8: Multidomain, multimodel and multilingual machine-generated text detection. *Preprint*, arXiv:2404.14183.

A Appendix

Tools & Libraries	**Version**
Python	3.10.14
Pandas	2.2.2
NumPy	1.26.4
PyTorch	2.4.0
Transformers	4.44.2
Evaluate	0.4.3
WandB	0.16.6

Table 4: Main tools and libraries used in our system

Table 4 provide the details about the corresponding libraries, which are beneficial to help replicate our experiments.

BBN-U.Oregon's ALERT system at GenAI Content Detection Task 3: Robust Authorship Style Representations for Cross-Domain Machine-Generated Text Detection

Hemanth Kandula[1] **Chak Fai Li**[1] **Haoling Qiu**[1] **Damianos Karakos**[1]
Hieu Man Duc Trong[2] **Thien Huu Nguyen**[2] **Brian Ulicny**[1]
[1] RTX BBN Technologies [2]University of Oregon
{hemanth.kandula, chak.fai.li, haoling.qiu, damianos.karakos, brian.ulicny}@rtx.com
{hieum,thienn}@uoregon.edu

Abstract

This paper presents BBN-U.Oregon's system, ALERT, submitted to the Shared Task 3: Cross-Domain Machine-Generated Text Detection. Our approach uses robust authorship-style representations to distinguish between human-authored and machine-generated text (MGT) across various domains. We employ an ensemble-based authorship attribution (AA) system that integrates stylistic embeddings from two complementary subsystems: one that focuses on cross-genre robustness with hard-positive and negative mining strategies and another that captures nuanced semantic-lexical-authorship contrasts. This combination enhances cross-domain generalization, even under domain shifts and adversarial attacks. Evaluated on the RAID benchmark, our system demonstrates strong performance across genres and decoding strategies, with resilience against adversarial manipulation, achieving 91.8% TPR at FPR=5% on standard test sets and 82.6% on adversarial sets.

1 Introduction

The rapid advancement of large language models (LLMs) has transformed numerous fields, from natural language processing to automated content generation, enabling machines to generate text that is often indistinguishable from human writing. Models are now capable of producing fluent, coherent, and contextually relevant text, sparking widespread adoption across industries for tasks ranging from content creation to customer service. However, alongside these advancements, the potential for misuse has grown, particularly in areas like disinformation, academic plagiarism, automated phishing attacks, and social media manipulation. New challenges arise in distinguishing between human-authored and machine-generated content.

To address these challenges, we developed the ALERT (Authorship through Learnable and Explainable Rich Transformations) system, which was submitted to the Shared Task on Cross-Domain Machine-Generated Text Detection within the COLING Workshop on Detecting AI Generated Content. The focus of this shared task (Dugan et al., 2025) is on evaluating the cross-domain robustness of MGT detectors across diverse domains, generative models, and decoding strategies. This challenge addresses the critical need for detectors that maintain high accuracy and low false positive rates when applied to MGT in varied real-world contexts.

Traditional approaches for detecting MGT typically rely on supervised learning, where detectors are trained on labeled corpora of human-written and machine-generated documents. However, these methods often struggle with generalization, particularly as new, more sophisticated LLMs emerge (Zellers et al., 2019). Furthermore, these models are highly sensitive to distribution shifts, meaning that performance degrades when applied to LLMs or domains not seen during training (Mitchell et al., 2023). As LLMs become more prevalent and diversified, such approaches become increasingly impractical.

To address these challenges, recent research has focused on learning authorship style representations (Soto et al., 2024). Style, a fundamental characteristic of human authorship, varies across individuals and tasks but tends to be more consistent within a specific LLM. By capturing stylistic nuances, detectors can more effectively identify MGT, even in the face of emerging LLMs or previously unseen content domains. This paper expands on the work of (Rivera-Soto et al., 2021) by proposing an improved Authorship Attribution (AA) system for MGT using authorship style representations. Our models, which generate these representations, are trained using advanced techniques such as GradCache (Gao et al., 2021), various hard-negative mining (Robinson et al., 2021) (Fincke and Boschee, 2024) and hard-positive filter-

Proceedings of the 1st Workshop on GenAI Content Detection (GenAIDetect), pages 358–364
January 19, 2025.

ing strategies, and their embeddings are combined by a fusion module to improve performance. These techniques improve the models' ability to distinguish between the writing styles of humans and MGT, across LLMs and domains. The rest of the paper is organized as follows: Section 2 reviews related work in MGT detection, Section 3 describes our methodology and ensemble-based AA system, Section 4 outlines the experimental setup and results, and Section 5 concludes the paper with future directions.

2 Related Work

Detecting MGT has become an increasingly critical task with the rapid growth of large language models (LLMs) like GPT-3 and -4, LLaMA-2 and -3, which can produce highly fluent and human-like text. Early approaches focused on supervised methods, where models were trained on labeled datasets of humans and MGT. For instance, OpenAI's AI Detector was designed to distinguish between text written by GPT-2 and human authors, but its performance declined with the release of more advanced models like GPT-3 and ChatGPT (Solaiman et al., 2019). These supervised detectors, while effective in their specific settings, often fail to generalize to unseen LLMs due to the constant evolution of model architectures and training paradigms (Zellers et al., 2019). Soto et al. (2024) propose a method based on authorship style representations (Rivera-Soto et al., 2021), which leverages the stylistic features of human-written text to detect machine-generated content in a few-shot scenario, without relying on large amounts of training data from the target LLMs. This method addresses the limitations of supervised learning by focusing on invariant features of writing style. Hans et al. (2024) introduce a zero-shot detection method, "Binoculars", which contrasts the outputs of two closely related LLMs to identify MGT with high accuracy. Recent advances also include adversarial learning approaches like RADAR (Hu et al., 2023), which improve robustness by training detection models to identify adversarially crafted MGT. These methods offer improved performance in challenging scenarios where LLMs are specifically designed to bypass detection systems.

3 Methodology

The core of our detection framework is based on the hypothesis that MGT exhibits consistent stylistic patterns that differ from those of human authors. To capture these stylistic cues effectively, we implement an ensemble-based AA system, combining two complementary subsystems optimized with advanced training techniques for robustness and cross-domain generalization.

Our methodology builds upon the contrastive learning approach used by (Rivera-Soto et al., 2021), with key improvements. The AA system ensemble is designed using a Siamese neural architecture, which captures nuanced stylistic signatures through embeddings that serve as distinctive authorship signatures. The ensemble integrates cues from multiple linguistic and stylistic features, enabling a cohesive detection framework with broad generalization capabilities. While Rivera-Soto et al. (2021) introduced authorship attribution with contrastive learning, our approach extends it by incorporating advanced hard-positive and hard-negative mining strategies (BM25-based and cluster-based), GradCache for larger batch sizes, and fusing embeddings from multiple systems.

The core components of our framework, AA System I and AA System II, each employ unique training strategies. Below, we provide training strategies employed by each system and its specific optimizations.

3.1 AA system I: Cross-Genre Robustness with Hard-Positive and Negative Mining

AA System I employs a training methodology that emphasizes cross-genre robustness through specialized hard-positive filtering and hard-negative mining strategies adopted from (Fincke and Boschee, 2024). For hard-positive examples, the system uses the two most topically distant documents available per author, promoting the learning of stylistic consistency rather than topical similarity. To refine this process, authors with insufficiently dissimilar document pairs are excluded from training, resulting in fewer but more challenging examples that improve performance in both genre-specific and cross-genre contexts. For hard-negatives, the system generates batches containing clusters of authors where each author contributes two documents: one near the cluster center for similarity and the other in the outer reaches for dissimilarity, ensuring stylistic contrast. K-means clustering determines initial centroids, with each centroid representing one author, and documents closest to each centroid are selected to populate clusters. FAISS-based similarity search (Douze et al., 2024)maintains clustering efficiency by capping retrieval to the nearest 2,024 entries. Once clusters are formed, centroids are grouped to fill each batch with a set number of authors, creating more coherent batches and ensuring that each batch offers challenging stylistic contrasts. Further details on these methods, including clustering and selection criteria, are available in Fincke and Boschee (2024). In summary, AA System I focuses on cross-genre robustness by applying hard-positive filtering and a clustering-driven hard-negative mining strategy that relies on topically distant documents. This approach encourages the model to learn stylistic consistency that is not conflated with topic similarity.

3.2 AA System II: Semantic, Lexical, Clustering based Contrastive Learning

System II is designed to capture nuanced stylistic differences across authors through hard-positive filtering and a dual-strategy hard-negative mining approach. The same hard-positive mining strategy from System I Sec 3.1 is used in this system for dataset filtering. This subsystem, while sharing foundational techniques with AA System I, incorporates distinct selection criteria for training examples to improve the model's ability to distinguish stylistic similarities across diverse topics. For mining hard-negative examples, in the first stage, BM25 (Robertson et al., 2009) is applied to retrieve top-k collections, where each "collection" refers to the set of documents written by a single author. By selecting collections that are lexically similar to the anchor documents yet originate from different authors, the model is encouraged to focus on subtle stylistic patterns rather than topical similarities. This process enables the model to focus on subtle stylistic patterns, reducing the influence of the topic. Subsequently, a two-level clustering approach using K-means is adopted, to capture more nuanced semantic content. The first level performs document-level clustering, grouping documents based on their semantic content, primarily capturing topical similarities. The second level implements author-level clustering, organizing author collections based on aggregated embeddings that reveal patterns in authorship style. Within each author-level cluster, collections from different authors are selected as Hard-negative examples, further refined by retaining only documents that fall within the same document-level clusters as the anchor documents. Hard-negative mining (Robinson et al., 2021) is performed on the complete dataset, not limited to training subsets, to ensure a broader range of potential hard-negatives. Document-level and author-level clusters are set to 512, with a balanced distribution of 50% BM25-mined and 50% cluster-mined negative examples. This comprehensive approach supports a variety of negative examples, challenging training instances, and robust model performance. By combining semantic, lexical, and clustering-based approaches, the aforementioned process makes the model focus on the most important features for authorship style discriminability.

Additionally, the GradCache (Gao et al., 2021) technique allows for larger batch sizes, storing intermediate gradients to reduce memory load. This enables the model to handle a higher volume of examples per batch, improving generalization across diverse domains and effectively distinguishing subtle stylistic differences in authorship.

Overall, AA System II builds upon similar concepts but differs notably in its hard-negative mining strategy. While System I relies on clustering and topically distant pairs, System II adopts a dual-strategy method: first, BM25-based retrieval identifies lexically similar yet differently authored documents; second, a two-level clustering approach (document-level and author-level) further refines these candidates. This combination enables System II to pinpoint subtler stylistic discrepancies that persist even among topically and lexically similar texts.

3.3 Machine Style Detection

The MGT Style Detection system uses learned authorship style representations to accurately distinguish between humans and MGT. In the final classification stage, a fully connected layer processes these stylistic embeddings, followed by a binary classification layer specifically trained to detect MGT. The AA (sub-)system produces domain-invariant style representations, thus making the MGT detection system domain/genre-invariant as well. Furthermore, an ensemble system enhances detection capability by combining style embeddings from both AA systems, achieving a robust and comprehensive understanding of stylistic nuances for greater accuracy across diverse domains.

Model	Development Set (20% RAID Train)				Evaluation Set
	Abstracts	Books	News	Average	(RAID Test)
AA System I (Sec: 3.1)	0.790	0.838	0.927	0.852	-
AA System II (Sec: 3.2)	0.975	0.939	0.982	0.965	0.893
Ensemble System	0.966	0.971	0.982	0.973	0.918

Table 1: Performance of Cross-Domain MGT Detection on RAID Dataset (Subtask-A: No Adversarial Attacks)

Model	Development Set (20% RAID Train)				Evaluation Set
	Abstracts	Books	News	Average	(RAID Test)
AA System I (Sec: 3.1)	0.612	0.650	0.912	0.794	-
AA System II (Sec: 3.2)	0.887	0.866	0.937	0.897	0.788
Ensemble System	0.876	0.934	0.978	0.930	0.826

Table 2: Performance of Cross-Domain MGT Detection on RAID Dataset (Subtask-B: with Adversarial Attacks)

4 Experiments and Results

4.1 Data

Both authorship systems are trained on various datasets (see Appendix Table 5) with authorship labels, employing various author contrastive learning objectives—with a focus on authors who have produced at least 100 documents. To increase sample diversity, longer documents are split into shorter segments, augmenting the training pool. The Cross-domain MGT Detection task (Dugan et al., 2025) uses the RAID benchmark (Dugan et al., 2024) which consists of over 10 million documents spanning 11 LLMs, 11 genres, 4 decoding strategies, and 12 adversarial attacks. To evaluate our models, we utilized the training set from RAID. We divided the RAID dataset into 60% train, 20% validation, and 20% development sets, ensuring an equal representation of genres, LLMs, and adversarial attacks. Document source information was used to prevent overlap between training and test sets.

4.2 Experiment Setup

For the AA systems, we use Qwen2 1.5B [1] and E5-mistral-7b-instruct [2] for text embeddings in Systems I and II, respectively. Model optimization was done using the AdamW Optimizer (Loshchilov, 2017), and training was conducted on 4 NVIDIA RTX A6000 GPUs.

To assess cross-domain generalization, we conducted cross-validation experiments by training on two of the three genres in RAID (Abstracts, Books, and News) and testing on the held-out genre. Final classification layers are trained using the 60% of the train set, 20% validation set to select the classification layer weights and results reported in Sec 4.3 are on 20% of the development set. While initial experiments involved domain-specific splits to guide hyperparameter selection, in the final reported model, the final classification layer is trained on the full 60% using all available training domains for maximum coverage.

We use the official evaluation metric, TPR @ FPR=5%, which measures the model's accuracy in detecting MGT at a fixed false positive rate of 5%.

4.3 Results

Table 1 and Table 2 show results with our MGT detection models showing strong cross-domain performance, particularly highlighting the effectiveness of the ensemble-based approach. The cross-validation on the development set reveals that the ensemble system achieves the highest average TPR at FPR=5%, which is also reflected in the evaluation results. Without adversarial attacks, the ensemble system outperforms individual models by capturing more varied stylistic representations, which enabled it to generalize well even when facing domain shifts. In adversarial settings, the ensemble maintained robustness, showing less performance degradation compared to individual systems.

Our results on the Development and Evaluation sets indicate that while both AA System I and AA System II contribute to performance, System II provides a stronger baseline detection accuracy due to its dual-strategy hard-negative mining, which integrates both lexical and semantic constraints. Although System II alone is highly effective, the ensemble capitalizes on System I's cross-genre ro-

[1] https://huggingface.co/Qwen/Qwen2-1.5B

[2] https://huggingface.co/Linq-AI-Research/Linq-Embed-Mistral

bustness and System II's nuanced stylistic discrimination. As a result, combining them leads to more stable and improved performance, particularly in challenging or previously unseen domains.

The results on the Evaluation set further validate the generalizability of our models. The ensemble model (ALERT v1.1 reported in (Dugan et al., 2025)) resulted in a TPR at FPR=5% of 0.918 without adversarial attacks and 0.826 with such attacks, indicating consistent stability across diverse genres and text styles. Although the model was not specifically fine-tuned for adversarial attacks, these results suggest that capturing nuanced authorship styles enhances detection performance across varied content types and adversarial scenarios.

5 Conclusions

We show that our ensemble-based authorship style representations from two complementary subsystems identify MGT across varied domains and adversarial attacks. By integrating advanced training techniques such as GradCache, contrastive learning, and hard-positive/negative mining, the system demonstrates strong cross-domain generalization, achieving reliable MGT detection across various genres, LLMs, and adversarial attacks, thanks to capturing nuanced authorship-style representations. Future work could extend the framework to handle more sophisticated adversarial attacks and support additional languages and low-resource domains, making it adaptable to a wider range of real-world applications. Exploring domain adaptation techniques could improve robustness in detecting MGT by new or unseen models.

Acknowledgments

This research is based upon work supported in part by the Office of the Director of National Intelligence (ODNI), Intelligence Advanced Research Projects Activity (IARPA), via 2022-22072200003. The views and conclusions contained herein are those of the authors and should not be interpreted as necessarily representing the official policies, either expressed or implied, of ODNI, IARPA, or the U.S. Government. The U.S. Government is authorized to reproduce and distribute reprints for governmental purposes notwithstanding any copyright annotation therein.

References

Matthijs Douze, Alexandr Guzhva, Chengqi Deng, Jeff Johnson, Gergely Szilvasy, Pierre-Emmanuel Mazaré, Maria Lomeli, Lucas Hosseini, and Hervé Jégou. 2024. The faiss library. *Preprint*, arXiv:2401.08281.

Liam Dugan, Alyssa Hwang, Filip Trhlík, Andrew Zhu, Josh Magnus Ludan, Hainiu Xu, Daphne Ippolito, and Chris Callison-Burch. 2024. RAID: A shared benchmark for robust evaluation of machine-generated text detectors. In *Proceedings of the 62nd Annual Meeting of the Association for Computational Linguistics (Volume 1: Long Papers)*, pages 12463–12492, Bangkok, Thailand. Association for Computational Linguistics.

Liam Dugan, Andrew Zhu, Firoj Alam, Preslav Nakov, Marianna Apidianaki, and Callison-Burch Chris. 2025. Genai content detection task 3: Cross-domain machine generated text detection challenge. In *Proceedings of the 1st Workshop on GenAI Content Detection (GenAIDetect)*, Abu Dhabi, UAE. International Conference on Computational Linguistics.

Steven Fincke and Elizabeth Boschee. 2024. Separating style from substance: Enhancing cross-genre authorship attribution through data selection and presentation. *arXiv preprint arXiv:2408.05192*.

Luyu Gao, Yunyi Zhang, Jiawei Han, and Jamie Callan. 2021. Scaling deep contrastive learning batch size under memory limited setup. In *Proceedings of the 6th Workshop on Representation Learning for NLP (RepL4NLP-2021)*, pages 316–321, Online. Association for Computational Linguistics.

Abhimanyu Hans, Avi Schwarzschild, Valeriia Cherepanova, Hamid Kazemi, Aniruddha Saha, Micah Goldblum, Jonas Geiping, and Tom Goldstein. 2024. Spotting llms with binoculars: Zero-shot detection of machine-generated text. *arXiv preprint arXiv:2401.12070*.

Xiaomeng Hu, Pin-Yu Chen, and Tsung-Yi Ho. 2023. Radar: Robust ai-text detection via adversarial learning. *Advances in Neural Information Processing Systems*, 36:15077–15095.

I Loshchilov. 2017. Decoupled weight decay regularization. *arXiv preprint arXiv:1711.05101*.

Eric Mitchell, Yoonho Lee, Alexander Khazatsky, Christopher D. Manning, and Chelsea Finn. 2023. Detectgpt: Zero-shot machine-generated text detection using probability curvature. In *International Conference on Machine Learning*.

Rafael A Rivera-Soto, Olivia Elizabeth Miano, Juanita Ordonez, Barry Y Chen, Aleem Khan, Marcus Bishop, and Nicholas Andrews. 2021. Learning universal authorship representations. In *Proceedings of the 2021 conference on empirical methods in natural language processing*, pages 913–919.

Model	Abstracts			Books			News		
	Sys I	Sys II	Ensemble	Sys I	Sys II	Ensemble	Sys I	Sys II	Ensemble
ChatGPT	0.982	1.000	1.000	0.961	0.996	0.999	NA	NA	NA
Cohere	0.103	0.823	0.647	0.355	0.728	0.778	NA	NA	NA
Cohere-Chat	0.780	0.966	0.973	0.667	0.910	0.924	NA	NA	NA
GPT-2	0.710	0.960	0.978	0.843	0.948	0.991	0.916	0.893	0.987
GPT-3	0.773	0.986	0.986	0.879	0.997	0.999	NA	NA	NA
GPT-4	0.966	1.000	0.996	0.527	0.994	0.989	NA	NA	NA
Llama-Chat	0.999	1.000	1.000	0.996	0.996	0.999	0.994	0.996	0.999
Mistral	0.403	0.972	0.953	0.794	0.883	0.967	0.796	0.831	0.926
Mistral-Chat	0.955	0.998	0.999	0.987	0.995	1.000	0.986	0.996	1.000
MPT	0.856	0.967	0.981	0.853	0.869	0.951	0.895	0.942	0.987
MPT-Chat	0.989	0.999	0.999	0.956	0.976	1.000	0.973	0.972	0.993
Aggregate	0.790	0.975	0.966	0.838	0.939	0.971	0.927	0.938	0.982

Table 3: Performance on Various LLMs Detection on Development Set (20% RAID Train). Sys I refers to (Sec: 3.1), Sys II refers to (Sec: 3.2).

Stephen Robertson, Hugo Zaragoza, et al. 2009. The probabilistic relevance framework: Bm25 and beyond. *Foundations and Trends® in Information Retrieval*, 3(4):333–389.

Joshua David Robinson, Ching-Yao Chuang, Suvrit Sra, and Stefanie Jegelka. 2021. Contrastive learning with hard negative samples. In *International Conference on Learning Representations*.

Irene Solaiman, Miles Brundage, Jack Clark, Amanda Askell, Ariel Herbert-Voss, Jeff Wu, Alec Radford, Gretchen Krueger, Jong Wook Kim, Sarah Kreps, et al. 2019. Release strategies and the social impacts of language models. *arXiv preprint arXiv:1908.09203*.

Rafael Alberto Rivera Soto, Kailin Koch, Aleem Khan, Barry Y. Chen, Marcus Bishop, and Nicholas Andrews. 2024. Few-shot detection of machine-generated text using style representations. In *The Twelfth International Conference on Learning Representations*.

Rowan Zellers, Ari Holtzman, Hannah Rashkin, Yonatan Bisk, Ali Farhadi, Franziska Roesner, and Yejin Choi. 2019. Defending against neural fake news. *Advances in neural information processing systems*, 32.

A Detailed Results on MGT Detection

The detailed performance of individual models on the development set (20% of RAID Train) is provided in Table 3, showcasing their performance across specific domains. Similarly, Table 4 highlights the results of each model on the RAID Test set. While the average performance is shown in Table 1 and 2, these results underline the contributions and effectiveness in detecting individual models in various domains.

B Authorship Attribution Model Training, Implementation and Datasets Details

This section provides key implementation details for our Authorship Attribution (AA) systems and the final Machine-Generated Text (MGT) detection classifier.

B.1 Authorship Attribution Models

The architecture leverages pre-trained transformer models, such as `Qwen2-1.5B` and`E5-mistral-7b-instruct` (Sec 4), to process input documents into high-dimensional feature vectors. For longer documents, the text is divided into smaller segments, like paragraphs, to enhance the model's ability to capture local stylistic nuances effectively. These segment embeddings are subsequently aggregated using techniques like self-attention mechanisms and max-pooling to produce a cohesive representation of the author's stylistic signature. The model is optimized with a contrastive loss function, ensuring that embeddings of documents by the same author are positioned closer in the vector space than those of different authors. For a detailed discussion on model training, refer to (Rivera-Soto et al., 2021). Dataset used to train AA System I and System II are shown in Table 5

Hard-Positive and Hard-Negative Mining: For positives, we select each author's two most topically distant documents to emphasize stylistic over topical consistency. For negatives, System I focuses on cluster-based mining, grouping authors via K-means and selecting documents that are both cluster-center and periphery examples. System II integrates BM25 retrieval to find lexically simi-

Model	Subtask-A		Subtask-B	
	ALERT v1.1	ALERT v1.2	ALERT v1.1	ALERT v1.2
ChatGPT	0.976	0.958	0.882	0.854
GPT-4	0.943	0.917	0.834	0.812
GPT-3	0.917	0.932	0.828	0.805
GPT-2	0.919	0.897	0.826	0.787
Mistral	0.862	0.826	0.778	0.740
Mistral-Chat	0.973	0.943	0.874	0.832
Cohere	0.706	0.725	0.629	0.605
Cohere-Chat	0.848	0.823	0.767	0.707
Llama-Chat	0.988	0.952	0.889	0.852
MPT	0.905	0.873	0.825	0.784
MPT-Chat	0.960	0.922	0.859	0.811
Aggregate	0.918	0.893	0.826	0.788

Table 4: Performance of ALERT Detectors for each model on Cross-Domain MGT Detection (RAID Test Dataset) for Subtask-A: no Adversarial Attacks and Subtask-B: with Adversarial Attacks

Dataset Name	# authors	# documents
English Reddit Million User Dataset	7.6K	4.7M
English Pushshift Reddit Dataset	28.9K	2.0M
English Twitter	13	1.9K
English Hackernews	12.3K	1.7M
English StackExchange	19.8K	1.4M
Russian stihi	7.9K	1.4M
English Amazon Review	3.6K	827.2K
Russian proza	1.9K	206.6K
English NYT Comment	1.3K	172.5K
English Blog Authorship Corpus	1223	140.3K
Russian Telegram	2.8K	128.9K
English Yelp Review	485	113.9K
Russian KP	313	43.0K
Russian Pushshift Reddit Dataset	247	37.5K
English IMDb1M/IMDb62	253	3.1K
Russian Stackexchange	122	1.1K

Table 5: Datasets for Authorship Attribution Training

lar but differently authored documents and then refines these candidates via document- and author-level clustering, ensuring that negative pairs are semantically and lexically close but differ in style.

Optimization: We use the AdamW optimizer (Loshchilov, 2017) with a learning rate of 5×10^{-5}. GradCache (Gao et al., 2021) enables an effective batch size of 2048. Each AA system is trained for about 5 epochs, with model selection based on validation performance.

B.2 MGT Detection Classifier

Once AA models are trained, we apply them to produce embeddings for each RAID document. We concatenate embeddings from System I and System II and feed them into a two-layer feed-forward classifier (hidden size 512, ReLU activation, 0.1 dropout) to predict whether the text is machine-generated. The classifier is optimized with AdamW at a 1×10^{-4} learning rate for 3–5 epochs, using a validation set to select the best checkpoint.

Random at GenAI Detection Task 3: A Hybrid Approach to Cross-Domain Detection of Machine-Generated Text with Adversarial Attack Mitigation

Shifali Agrahari
Department of CSE
Indian Institute of Technology Guwahati
a.shifal@iitg.ac.in

Prabhat Mishra
Observe.AI
Bengaluru, India
mrprabhat010@gmail.com

Sujit Kumar
Nanyang Technological University, Singapore
kumar.sujit474@gmail.com

Abstract

Machine-generated text (MGT) detection has gained critical importance in the era of large language models, especially for maintaining trust in multilingual and cross-domain applications. This paper presents Task 3 Subtask B: **Adversarial Cross-Domain MGT Detection** for in the COLING 2025 DAIGenC Workshop. Task 3 emphasizes the complexity of detecting AI-generated text across eight domains, eleven generative models, and four decoding strategies, with an added challenge of adversarial manipulation. We propose a robust detection framework transformer embeddings utilizing Domain-Adversarial Neural Networks (DANN) to address domain variability and adversarial robustness. Our model demonstrates strong performance in identifying AI-generated text under adversarial conditions while highlighting condition scope of future improvement.

1 Introduction

2 Introduction

The advent of large-scale generative language models, such as GPT (Generative Pre-trained Transformer) (Liang et al., 2023) based systems, has revolutionized text generation by producing outputs that closely mimic human writing. These advancements have significantly impacted various fields, including content creation, education, and customer service, by providing highly coherent and contextually relevant text. However, this progress has also introduced new challenges, particularly in detecting MGT across diverse domains and languages. The widespread use of these models has raised concerns in areas like academic integrity, misinformation, and malicious use of AI-generated content.

While there are existing models result mention in Raid[1], still struggle with cross-domain issues and adversarial attacks (manipulations of input data to fool machine learning models).

To tackle these issues, The COLING 2025 Workshop on DAIGenC[2] (Dugan et al., 2025) *"Task 3: Cross-domain Machine-Generated Text Detection"* binary problem formulation as Task 1 however the texts will come from 8 different domains, 11 generative models, and four decoding strategies. This challenge is divided into two sub-tasks: Non-Adversarial and Adversarial. We solve one subtask, Subtask B, which is Adversarial Cross-Domain MGT detection.

Our contributions include a pipeline that integrates XLM-RoBERTa (Liu, 2019) embeddings for enhanced text representation, domain adaptation using Domain-Adversarial Neural Networks (DANN) to minimize domain-specific biases and improve generalization across diverse text domains, and adversarial robustness through incorporating adversarial attack classification to detect and mitigate manipulative techniques. Additionally, we focus on label prediction for improved model accuracy. Experimental results demonstrate strong detection performance, particularly in the same domain and against zero-width space attacks. Our findings from experimental results highlight the strengths of the proposed approach while identifying areas for improvement, such as achieving consistent performance across all domains and all attack types. These results emphasize the importance of balanced datasets, adaptive techniques, and comprehensive evaluation to advance the field of MGT detection.

3 Background

Over the last few years, numerous approaches have been proposed to tackle the task of AI-generated text detection. Detecting machine-generated text

[1]https://gitlab.com/genai-content-detection/genai-content-detection-coling-2025

[2]https://github.com/liamdugan/COLING-2025-Workshop-on-MGT-Detection-Task-3

Proceedings of the 1st Workshop on GenAI Content Detection (GenAIDetect), pages 365–370
January 19, 2025.

is primarily formulated as a binary classification task (Zellers et al., 2019; Gehrmann et al., 2019; Ippolito et al., 2019), naively distinguishing between human-written and machine-generated text. In general, there are three main approaches: the supervised methods (Wang et al., 2023; Uchendu et al., 2021; Zellers et al., 2019; Zhong et al., 2020; Liu et al., 2023, 2022), the unsupervised ones, such as zero-shot methods (Solaiman et al., 2019; Ippolito et al., 2019; Mitchell et al., 2023; Su et al., 2023; Hans et al.; Shijaku and Canhasi, 2023), and Adversarial measures on detection accuracy (Susnjak and McIntosh, 2024; Liang et al., 2023), especially within the education domain. For example, (Antoun et al., 2023) evaluates the robustness of detectors against character-level perturbations or misspelled words, focusing on French as a case study. (Krishna et al., 2024) train a generative model (DIPPER) to paraphrase paragraphs to evade detection. Although supervised approaches yield relatively better results, they are susceptible to overfitting (Mitchell et al., 2023; Su et al., 2023).

There are some techniques like feature-based, fusion, and ensemble methods Neural based or finetuned (Solaiman et al., 2019; Kumarage et al., 2023b; Shah et al., 2023; Mindner et al., 2023; **?**). Therefore, researchers combine statistics-based and deep learning-based techniques to gain adversarial robustness and high performance (Kushnareva et al., 2021; Crothers et al., 2022; Uchendu et al., 2023).Some studies attempt to address the challenges of cross-domain detection and adversarial attacks (Krishna et al., 2024; Kumarage et al., 2023a).

4 System Overview

We present our proposed **Adversarial Cross-Domain MGT Detection** which combines adaptability across diverse domains, attacks and generative models.

4.1 Data

For Task 3, we used the dataset provided by the shared task organizers (Dugan et al., 2025), which consists of a training set with 5,615,820 rows and a test set with 672,000 rows. The training dataset includes the following features: `id`, `adv_source_id`, `source_id`, `model`, `decoding`, `repetition_penalty`, `attack`, `domain`, `title`, `prompt`, and `generation`. Table 1 provides the unique counts for each feature in the training set. The diversity of these features indicates a wide range of model outputs, domains, and text variations, making the dataset well-suited for evaluating model performance in multilingual MGT detection. The test dataset, used only for evaluation, includes the `id` and `generation` fields.

Feature	**Unique Count**
id	5,615,820
adv_source_id	467,985
source_id	13,371
model	12
decoding	2
repetition_penalty	2
attack	12
domain	8
title	13,221
prompt	26,500
generation	4,975,574

Table 1: Unique Counts of Training Dataset Features

4.2 Methodology

4.2.1 Data Preprocessing and Feature Engineering

Use `Tokenizer` (Liu, 2019) to represent text (e.g., `generation`, `title`, `prompt`). Let $X \in \mathbb{R}^{m \times n}$ be the matrix of tokenized sequences, where m is the number of samples and n is the maximum sequence length. Encode categorical features (`domain`, `model`, `decoding`, etc.) using embeddings as $E_{\text{domain}}, E_{\text{model}}, E_{\text{decoding}} \in \mathbb{R}^d$ where d is the embedding dimension. Concatenate embeddings to form a vector representation for each text instance as defined $\mathbf{x}_{\text{features}} = [E_{\text{domain}}, E_{\text{model}}, E_{\text{attack}}, \ldots]$. Final input representation for each sample:

$$\mathbf{x}_{\text{input}} = [X; \mathbf{x}_{\text{features}}] \in \mathbb{R}^{m \times (n+d)} \quad (1)$$

first Feature Extraction Using transformer encoders as G_f to learn domain-invariant representations Eq. 2

$$\mathbf{h} = G_f(\mathbf{x}_{\text{input}}) \in \mathbb{R}^k \quad (2)$$

where k is the latent representation dimensionality.

4.2.2 Domain Adaptation

Domain adaptation refers to the process of enabling machine learning models to generalize well on a target domain that differs from the source domain on which the model was initially trained. To address this, domain adaptation techniques aim to minimize

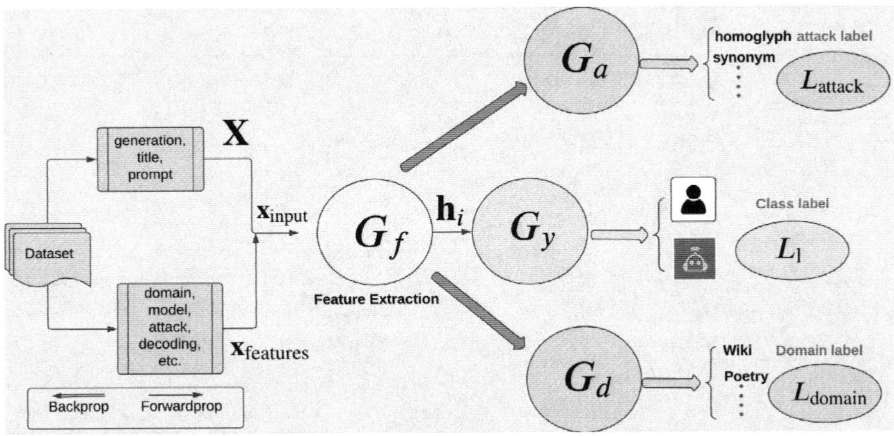

Figure 1: Proposed Detector model architecture: fusing stylometric features with a PLM embedding.

the discrepancy between source and target domain distributions by learning representations that are invariant to domain-specific characteristics while retaining task-relevant features. We use Domain-Adversarial Neural Networks (DANN) to improve cross-domain robustness.

Calculate the Adversarial Loss for Domain Classifier. The domain classifier G_d aims to predict the domain D of the input text. We apply a gradient reversal layer with the following objective:

$$\mathcal{L}_{\text{domain}} = -\frac{1}{m}\sum_{i=1}^{m}\sum_{j=1}^{|\text{domains}|} d_{i,j} \log G_d(\mathbf{h}_i) \quad (3)$$

where $d_{i,j}$ is the true domain label.

4.2.3 Adversarial Attack Classifer for Robuestness

To classify attack types, we introduce an attack classifier G_a, which predicts the specific attack type (e.g., homography, whitespace). The attack types are encoded as categorical labels, and G_a outputs probabilities for each attack type. The cross-entropy loss for attack classification is defined as:

$$\mathcal{L}_{\text{attack}} = -\frac{1}{m}\sum_{i=1}^{m}\sum_{j=1}^{|\text{attacks}|} a_{i,j} \log G_a(\mathbf{h}_i) \quad (4)$$

where $a_{i,j}$ is the true attack label.

4.2.4 Label Classifier and Loss Functions

The MGT classifier G_y is trained to predict whether text is human-Written or machine-generated, using binary cross-entropy (BCE) loss:

$$\mathcal{L}_l = -\frac{1}{m}\sum_{i=1}^{m}(y_i \log(G_y(\mathbf{h}_i)) + (1-y_i)\log(1-G_y(\mathbf{h}_i))) \quad (5)$$

4.2.5 Final Model

The feature extractor G_f is a transformer-based encoder **XLM-RoBERTa** (Liu, 2019) that processes tokenized text and generates domain-agnostic latent representations, capturing high-level semantic information. It produces embedding vector, which is passed through two fully connected (FC) layers.

Each of these FC layers is followed by an activation function such as *ReLU* to introduce non-linearity. The final output layer for the Domain Classifier G_d and Attack Classifier G_a uses the softmax activation to generate a probability distribution over the respective classes. For the Label Classifier G_y, the output layer uses a sigmoid activation function, producing a probability score. The model is trained using a combination of binary cross-entropy loss for classification, adversarial loss for domain adaptation, and attack classification loss. During training, we perform backpropagation to update the weights of the feature extractor, domain classifier, attack classifier, and MGT classifier. The optimizer minimizes the total loss as Equation 6, and we monitor the performance calculating probability that a given text is predicted to be machine-generated.. Early stopping is used to prevent overfitting.

$$\mathcal{L}_{\text{total}} = \mathcal{L}_l + \alpha \cdot \mathcal{L}_{\text{domain}} + \gamma \cdot \mathcal{L}_{\text{attack}} \quad (6)$$

where α and γ control the contributions of attack classification losses. During testing, the trained model is evaluated on a test set, where it provides the probability that a given text is predicted to be machine-generated.

Model	Config 1	Config 2	Config 3	Config 4	Config 5	Config 6
chatgpt	0.361	0.364	0.388	0.319	0.306	0.333
gpt4	0.330	0.325	–	0.300	0.295	–
gpt3	0.307	0.335	–	0.295	0.300	–
gpt2	0.360	0.365	–	0.315	0.285	–
mistral	0.323	0.313	0.340	0.282	0.245	0.295
mistral-chat	0.369	0.378	0.390	0.329	0.325	0.300
cohere	0.386	0.390	0.415	0.359	0.365	0.410
cohere-chat	0.370	0.370	–	0.352	0.335	–
llama-chat	0.372	0.385	–	0.285	0.275	–
mpt	0.350	0.365	0.375	0.305	0.287	0.305
mpt-chat	0.384	0.385	**0.440**	0.369	0.287	0.310

Table 2: Performance metrics for adversarial cross-domain MGT detection across various configurations. **Key:** Config 1: Wiki + All Decoding Strategies + All Repetition Penalties + Zero-width Space, Config 2: Wiki + Greedy Decoding Strategy + All Repetition Penalties + Zero-width Space, Config 3: Wiki + Greedy Decoding Strategy + Yes Repetition Penalty + Zero-width Space, Config 4: Wiki + All Decoding Strategies + All Repetition Penalties + Homoglyph, Config 5: Wiki + Greedy Decoding Strategy + All Repetition Penalties + Homoglyph, Config 6: Wiki + Greedy Decoding Strategy + Yes Repetition Penalty + Homoglyph.

5 Experimental Setup

We utilize the dataset mentioned in Section 4.1 Further details of experimental setup and hyperparameters are presented in the Appendix section A.1. Our model was implemented using PyTorch.

6 Results

As mentioned in Table 2, Our detector performs best on the Wikipedia domain but struggles with other domains. We analyze the data set, revealing that the average generation length in the Wikipedia domain is higher than in different domains, as illustrated in Fig. 2. Similarly, our detector performs better against two adversarial attacks—Homoglyph and Zero-Width Space. However, it struggles to detect text affected by other adversarial attacks. Fig. 3 highlights that Zero-Width Space attacks produce the most extended average text length compared to different attack types.

Among the generated model texts, our detector most effectively identifies the text generated by *mpt-chat*. Further analyses, as shown in Fig. 4 and Fig. 5, indicate that the detector is particularly effective for the Wikipedia domain and the *mpt-chat* model.

In summary, our detector demonstrates optimal performance in the Wikipedia domain, with the greedy decoding strategy, the repetition penalty enabled, the zero-width space adversarial attacks, and text generated by the *mptchat* model. All details of results are mentioned in the Raid cooling shared task leaderboard.

7 Conclusion

This paper introduces a robust approach to **Adversarial Cross-Domain MGT Detection**, leveraging transformer embeddings and domain adaptation to address the challenges of domain variability and adversarial robustness. The proposed architecture, based on Domain-Adversarial Neural Networks, demonstrates strong performance, particularly in detecting machine-generated text from specific domains like Wikipedia and against attacks like homoglyphs and zero-width space manipulations. but still fail to generalization. Future work should focus on curating more balanced datasets, enhancing model adaptability to diverse attack types, and exploring lightweight architectures for real-time applications. These steps are crucial to advance the reliability and scalability of MGT detection systems in multilingual and cross-domain scenarios.

References

Wissam Antoun, Virginie Mouilleron, Benoît Sagot, and Djamé Seddah. 2023. Towards a robust detection of language model-generated text: Is chatgpt that easy to detect? In *Actes de CORIA-TALN 2023. Actes de la 30e Conférence sur le Traitement Automatique des Langues Naturelles (TALN), volume 1: travaux de recherche originaux–articles longs*, pages 14–27.

Evan Crothers, Nathalie Japkowicz, Herna Viktor, and

Paula Branco. 2022. Adversarial robustness of neural-statistical features in detection of generative transformers. In *2022 International Joint Conference on Neural Networks (IJCNN)*, pages 1–8. IEEE.

Liam Dugan, Andrew Zhu, Firoj Alam, Preslav Nakov, and Callison-Burch Chris. 2025. Genai content detection task 3: Cross-domain machine generated text detection challenge. In *Proceedings of the 31st International Conference on Computational Linguistics (COLING)*, Abu Dhabi, UAE. Association for Computational Linguistics.

Sebastian Gehrmann, Hendrik Strobelt, and Alexander M Rush. 2019. Gltr: Statistical detection and visualization of generated text. *arXiv preprint arXiv:1906.04043*.

A Hans, A Schwarzschild, V Cherepanova, H Kazemi, A Saha, M Goldblum, J Geiping, and T Goldstein. Spotting llms with binoculars: Zero-shot detection of machine-generated text, 2024. *URL: https://arxiv.org/abs/2401.12070*.

Daphne Ippolito, Daniel Duckworth, Chris Callison-Burch, and Douglas Eck. 2019. Automatic detection of generated text is easiest when humans are fooled. *arXiv preprint arXiv:1911.00650*.

Kalpesh Krishna, Yixiao Song, Marzena Karpinska, John Wieting, and Mohit Iyyer. 2024. Paraphrasing evades detectors of ai-generated text, but retrieval is an effective defense. *Advances in Neural Information Processing Systems*, 36.

Tharindu Kumarage, Amrita Bhattacharjee, Djordje Padejski, Kristy Roschke, Dan Gillmor, Scott Ruston, Huan Liu, and Joshua Garland. 2023a. J-guard: Journalism guided adversarially robust detection of ai-generated news. *arXiv preprint arXiv:2309.03164*.

Tharindu Kumarage, Joshua Garland, Amrita Bhattacharjee, Kirill Trapeznikov, Scott Ruston, and Huan Liu. 2023b. Stylometric detection of ai-generated text in twitter timelines. *arXiv preprint arXiv:2303.03697*.

Laida Kushnareva, Daniil Cherniavskii, Vladislav Mikhailov, Ekaterina Artemova, Serguei Barannikov, Alexander Bernstein, Irina Piontkovskaya, Dmitri Piontkovski, and Evgeny Burnaev. 2021. Artificial text detection via examining the topology of attention maps. *arXiv preprint arXiv:2109.04825*.

Weixin Liang, Mert Yuksekgonul, Yining Mao, Eric Wu, and James Zou. 2023. Gpt detectors are biased against non-native english writers. *Patterns*, 4(7).

Xiaoming Liu, Zhaohan Zhang, Yichen Wang, Hang Pu, Yu Lan, and Chao Shen. 2022. Coco: Coherence-enhanced machine-generated text detection under data limitation with contrastive learning. *arXiv preprint arXiv:2212.10341*.

Yikang Liu, Ziyin Zhang, Wanyang Zhang, Shisen Yue, Xiaojing Zhao, Xinyuan Cheng, Yiwen Zhang, and Hai Hu. 2023. Argugpt: evaluating, understanding and identifying argumentative essays generated by gpt models. *arXiv preprint arXiv:2304.07666*.

Yinhan Liu. 2019. Roberta: A robustly optimized bert pretraining approach. *arXiv preprint arXiv:1907.11692*, 364.

Lorenz Mindner, Tim Schlippe, and Kristina Schaaff. 2023. Classification of human-and ai-generated texts: Investigating features for chatgpt. In *International Conference on Artificial Intelligence in Education Technology*, pages 152–170. Springer.

Eric Mitchell, Yoonho Lee, Alexander Khazatsky, Christopher D Manning, and Chelsea Finn. 2023. Detectgpt: Zero-shot machine-generated text detection using probability curvature. In *International Conference on Machine Learning*, pages 24950–24962. PMLR.

Aditya Shah, Prateek Ranka, Urmi Dedhia, Shruti Prasad, Siddhi Muni, and Kiran Bhowmick. 2023. Detecting and unmasking ai-generated texts through explainable artificial intelligence using stylistic features. *International Journal of Advanced Computer Science and Applications*, 14(10).

Rexhep Shijaku and Ercan Canhasi. 2023. Chatgpt generated text detection. *Publisher: Unpublished*.

Irene Solaiman, Miles Brundage, Jack Clark, Amanda Askell, Ariel Herbert-Voss, Jeff Wu, Alec Radford, Gretchen Krueger, Jong Wook Kim, Sarah Kreps, et al. 2019. Release strategies and the social impacts of language models. *arXiv preprint arXiv:1908.09203*.

Jinyan Su, Terry Yue Zhuo, Di Wang, and Preslav Nakov. 2023. Detectllm: Leveraging log rank information for zero-shot detection of machine-generated text. *arXiv preprint arXiv:2306.05540*.

Teo Susnjak and Timothy R McIntosh. 2024. Chatgpt: The end of online exam integrity? *Education Sciences*, 14(6):656.

Adaku Uchendu, Thai Le, and Dongwon Lee. 2023. Toproberta: Topology-aware authorship attribution of deepfake texts. *arXiv preprint arXiv:2309.12934*.

Adaku Uchendu, Zeyu Ma, Thai Le, Rui Zhang, and Dongwon Lee. 2021. Turingbench: A benchmark environment for turing test in the age of neural text generation. *arXiv preprint arXiv:2109.13296*.

Zecong Wang, Jiaxi Cheng, Chen Cui, and Chenhao Yu. 2023. Implementing bert and fine-tuned roberta to detect ai generated news by chatgpt. *ArXiv*, abs/2306.07401.

Rowan Zellers, Ari Holtzman, Hannah Rashkin, Yonatan Bisk, Ali Farhadi, Franziska Roesner, and Yejin Choi. 2019. Defending against neural fake news. *Advances in neural information processing systems*, 32.

Wanjun Zhong, Duyu Tang, Zenan Xu, Ruize Wang, Nan Duan, Ming Zhou, Jiahai Wang, and Jian Yin. 2020. Neural deepfake detection with factual structure of text. *arXiv preprint arXiv:2010.07475*.

A Example Appendix

A.1 Details of Experimental Setups

Table 3 lists key hyperparameters: learning rates (1×10^{-5} to 1×10^{-3}), batch sizes (16–64), epochs (50–200), and dropout rates (0.1–0.5), with some parameters experimentally fine-tuned.

Hyperparameter	Typical Values
Learning Rate (η)	$1e-5$ to $1e-3$
Batch Size	16, 32, 64
Number of Epochs	50 to 200
Dropout Rate	0.1 to 0.5
Embedding size	768
First FC & Second FC	512 & 256
Optimizer (Adam)	Beta1: 0.9, Beta2: 0.999, Epsilon: $1e-8$
Learning Rate	Scheduler

Table 3: List of Hyperparameters for the Experiment

A.2 Dataset Analysis Details

As mentioned in Fig. 2, 3, 4, 5, analysis of the distribution of columns over text or other columns.

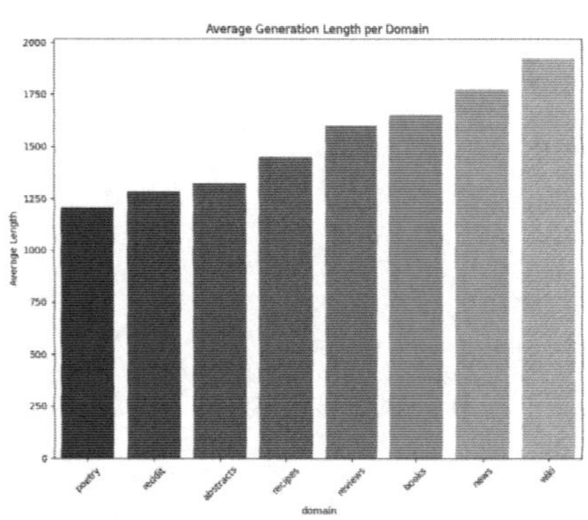

Figure 2: Average Generation Length per Domain

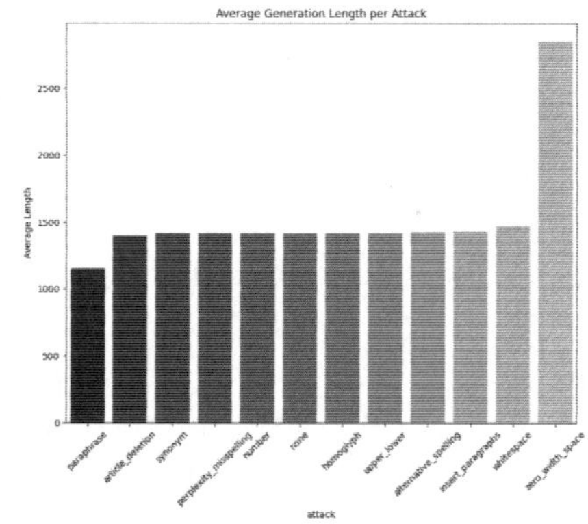

Figure 3: Average Generation Length per attack

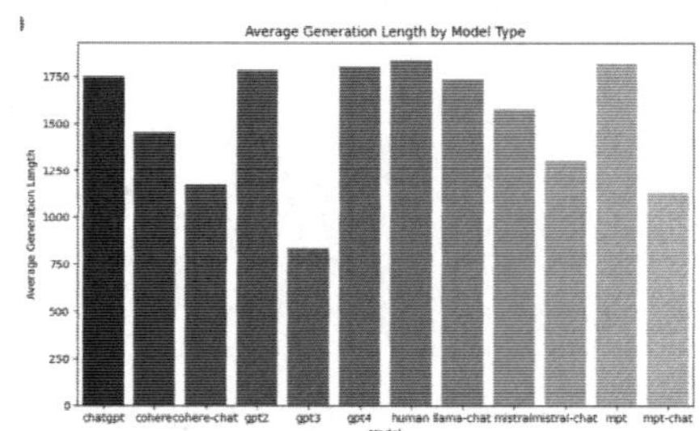

Figure 4: Average Generation Length per model type

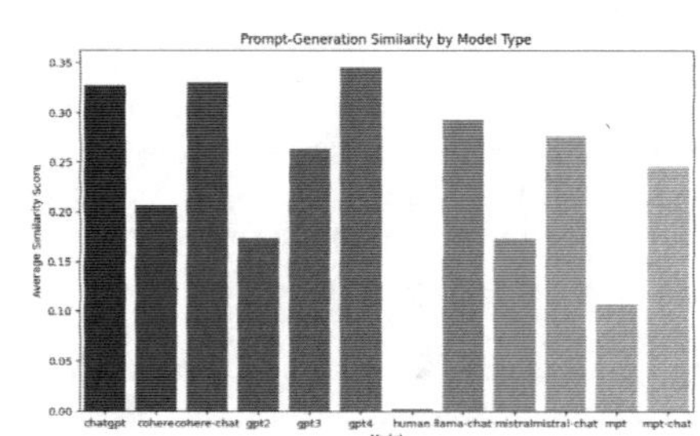

Figure 5: Average similarity score between prompt and text generated by each model.

MOSAIC at GENAI Detection Task 3 : Zero-Shot Detection Using an Ensemble of Models

Matthieu Dubois
Sorbonne Université, CNRS, ISIR
duboism@isir.upmc.fr

François Yvon
Sorbonne Université, CNRS, ISIR
yvon@isir.upmc.fr

Pablo Piantanida
International Laboratory on Learning Systems (ILLS)
Quebec AI Institute (MILA)
CNRS, CentraleSupélec, Université Paris-Saclay
pablo.piantanida@mila.quebec

Abstract

The rapid advancement of Large Language Models (LLMs) has raised issues concerning the misuse of their text generation abilities for creating forged content, fostering the need for reliable detection methods. While most methods are *supervised* and require training samples of human vs. artificial texts, we propose instead to consider *unsupervised detection* approaches. In a nutshell, most unsupervised methods rely on one or several detector model(s), whose (low) perplexity scores serve as a signal of machine-generated contents. Such approaches can be brittle as their performances strongly depend on the choice of a particular detector. To address these limitations, we evaluate a method *for combining multiple detectors* and enhance robustness. In this submission, we report evaluation results on the RAID benchmark, a comprehensive English-centric testbed for machine-generated texts. These results were obtained in the context of the "Cross-domain Machine-Generated Text Detection" shared task. We show that our approach can be competitive for a variety of domains and generator models, but also that it is challenged by adversarial attacks and by changes in the text generation strategy.

1 Introduction

Large Language Models (LLMs) have greatly improved the fluency and diversity of machine-generated texts. The release of ChatGPT and GPT4 by OpenAI has sparked global discussions regarding the effective use of AI-based writing assistants. This progress has also introduced major threats related to the generation of fake news (Zellers et al., 2019), of toxic or dishonest content (Crothers et al., 2023), or more generally regarding misuses of machine generation abilities. In response, the automatic detection of such Machine Generated Texts (MGT) has attracted a lot of recent work.

From a bird's eye view, MGT detection uses *detector* models to discriminate *generator* models' outputs from human writings. Multiple instances of this basic text classification problem have been considered, varying e.g. the number of possible categories to distinguish, the amount of available supervision or the granularity of the task (e.g. at the text, sentence, or even token level). Owing to its large user base and applications, most efforts to date have focused on specifically detecting ChatGPT, for which training and test data is easily obtained. A more difficult problem, that we study here, is **unsupervised generator-agnostic artificial text detection**, where the models to detect are not known in advance, and for which we also assume no training data.

As pointed out e.g., in (Antoun et al., 2024; Hans et al., 2024; Wang et al., 2024), the performance of MGT detection systems varies depending on the choices of the detector(s) / generator(s) pair. The detector may serve to assess probabilities, as in (Mitchell et al., 2023; Bao et al., 2024), or to regenerate content, as e.g., in (Mao et al., 2024; Yang et al., 2024). In most cases, optimal detection performance will require a systematic exploration of the space of possible detectors. As the number and diversity of LLMs keep increasing, such exploration seems not only challenging but also unrealistic. Furthermore, (Dugan et al., 2024) demonstrated that the current detection methods are brittle and easily fooled by changing the generator or altering the associated sampling method, a finding that we reproduce in this study.

In an attempt to increase the robustness of existing detectors, we consider here *ensemble methods*, where a coalition of several models is exploited to build the detector. For this, we generalize perplexity-based approaches, which flag as "artificial" texts having a suspiciously small perplexity,

Proceedings of the 1st Workshop on GenAI Content Detection (GenAIDetect), pages 371–376
January 19, 2025. ©2025 International Conference on Computational Linguistics

As perplexity is also an encoding measure, our ensemble technique will seek to identify time-varying mixture models, in order to minimize the worst-case expected encoding size. The corresponding architecture is in Figure 1. Further details, explanations, and proofs can be found in a companion paper (Dubois et al., 2024). Not only is this method fully unsupervised, it also dispenses with the need to search for the best detector(s). This method nonetheless helps to develop MGT detection systems that can robustly detect multiple generators. In this short contribution, we briefly present the detection task, then our detection algorithms, before discussing and analyzing the experimental results.

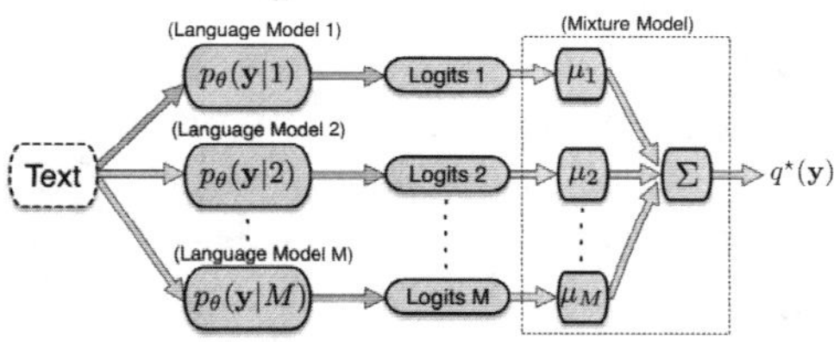

Figure 1: Mixture Model.

2 Data and Task Description

2.1 The Task

The Cross-Domain Machine-Generated Text Detection Task at the COLING 2025 Workshop on Detecting AI-Generated Content (Dugan et al., 2025) aims to challenge detection methods on the RAID test dataset (Dugan et al., 2024), containing samples spanning multiple domains, generators, and decoding methods. The dataset can be split into two parts, each corresponding to a separate subtask:

- Subtask A : Original human-authored texts and MG counterparts, one for each model and decoding method proposed in the RAID dataset;
- Subtask B : The same data with adversarial attacks such as misspellings or paraphrasing.

As our method scores texts in a zero-shot manner, we use the same detection model for both subtasks. The metric used in the competition is the True Positive Rate when the False Positive Rate equals 5% (TPR@5%FPR). For this metric, our method simply outputs one score per text, with larger scores corresponding to natural texts, and lower scores to artificial texts.

2.2 Data Description

Both training and testing sets for this task are described in (Dugan et al., 2024). RAID is a comprehensive benchmark designed to assess the robustness of MGT detection systems. The test set contains about 6 million generated texts produced by 11 models, across 8 domains (Arxiv Abstracts, Book Plot Summaries, BBC News Articles, Poems, Reddit Posts, Recipes, IMDb Movie Reviews and Wikipedia Articles). Each human-written document was paired with a generation prompt used to produce outputs for all models, employing both zero-shot chat and non-chat templates depending on each model's intended usage. When applicable, multiple decoding methods were used, e.g. greedy decoding or ancestral sampling, also varying the repetition penalty for a total of 4 combinations. To further challenge detectors, each text is assigned variations, using 11 types of adversarial attacks such as paraphrasing, alternative spelling, and synonym replacements. As each human entry gets a corresponding version for each model and available decoding strategy, the dataset is mostly comprised of machine generations. When adding the adversarially attacked variations, they make up the majority of the data.

3 Our Method : MOSAIC

Language models predict the probability of a token conditioned on the preceding ones, thus defining a probability distribution over the set of all possible sequences. The probability of generating a sequence $\mathbf{y} = \langle y_0, y_1, \dots, y_T \rangle$ is computed as the product of conditional probabilities for each token, given its preceding context.

A central concept in our method is **information**, which measures the "surprise" of observing a particular token for a model parameterized by θ. This surprisal is quantified as $-\log p_\theta(y_t|\mathbf{y}_{<t})$, where lower values indicate higher predictability. This is akin to compression in information theory: the lower the surprisal, the better the corresponding token can be compressed by the model $p_\theta(.|\mathbf{y}_{<t})$.

Instead of relying on a detector single model, as in most unsupervised methods, our method leverages a diverse set of LLMs, denoted as $\mathcal{P}_\mathcal{M}(\mathcal{Y})$. The key idea is to assign each token in a sequence to the model that best "explains" it, i.e., the model that can compress it most effectively. Given a sequence $\mathbf{y}_{<t}$, we combine the models logits to obtain $q_t^\star$, the distribution minimizing the excess codelength w.r.t

any distribution $p_\theta \in \mathcal{P}_\mathcal{M}$.

$$q^\star(y_t|\mathbf{y}_{<t}) \triangleq \arg \min_{q\in\mathcal{P}(\Omega)} \max_{m\in\mathcal{M}} \mathcal{R}_\theta(m, q, \mathbf{y}_{<t})$$

$$\mathcal{R}_\theta(m, q\ \mathbf{y}_{<t}) \triangleq \mathbb{E}\Big[-\log q(y_t|\mathbf{y}_{<t})\Big] - \mathcal{H}_\theta(Y_t|m, \mathbf{y}_{<t})$$

where Ω is the model vocabulary, $\mathcal{H}_\theta(Y_t|m, \mathbf{y}_{<t})$ is the conditional entropy, and the expectation $\mathbb{E}$ is computed over $y_t \sim p_\theta(y_t|m, \mathbf{y}_{<t})$. It can be shown that the optimal distribution is a mixture distribution, whose weights are computed by the Blahut-Arimoto algorithm (Blahut, 1972; Arimoto, 1972). Our scoring method then evaluates the difference in codelength between the observed text on the one hand, and an averaged equivalent measure for generated texts (for models in $\mathcal{M}$), using:

$$S_{\text{Av}}(\mathbf{w}) = \frac{1}{TM}\sum_{t=1}^{T}\sum_{m\in\mathcal{M}}\Big[\mathcal{L}^\star(w_t|\mathbf{w}_{<t}) - \sum_{y_t\in\Omega} p_\theta(y_t|m, \mathbf{w}_{<t})\mathcal{L}^\star(y_t|\mathbf{w}_{<t})\Big], \quad (1)$$

where $\mathcal{L}^\star(y_t|\mathbf{w}_{<t})$ represents the optimal codelength obtained using a mixture of models. The first term measures how well the optimal model compresses the actual input text, while the second term captures how well the LLMs in the set $\mathcal{M}$ compress typical machine-generated outputs.

A larger score indicates that the text is likely human-written because the observed codelength is significantly larger than what would be expected from AI-generated content. Conversely, a lower score suggests that the text closely resembles outputs from the models in $\mathcal{M}$. Since this competition requires the machine outputs to get higher scores, we simply inverted use a negated version of (1) before submission. More information about MOSAIC can be found in (Dubois et al., 2024).

4 Results and Discussion

4.1 Experimental Setup

For our submission to the shared task, we used two settings: MOSAIC-4 and MOSAIC-5, where the former uses an ensemble of four models (Tower-7b, Tower-13b (Alves et al., 2024), Llama-2-7b and Llama-2-7b-chat (Touvron et al., 2023)), and the latter additionally includes Phi-3-4k-Instruct (Abdin et al., 2024). As the gold labels were not provided, the results discussed below are based on the online leaderboard,[1] reporting the True Positive Rate @ 5% False Positive Rate.

4.2 Results

As our method requires no training at all, we went with the default implementation without ever looking at the training set. This explains why our standings are below other teams who perform tuning on the RAID training set. However, our results are competitive with a similar method evaluated on the RAID leaderboard, the Binoculars approach of Hans et al. (2024). Binoculars obtains a score of 0.790 without adversarial attacks, while MOSAIC-4 and 5 get 0.752 and 0.745 respectively. In the following, unless explicitly specified, we report the results of MOSAIC-4, our default version.

The detailed results for the sampling configurations and various attacks are shown in Figure 2. The values presented for adversarial attacks are averaged across all decoding methods, making them directly comparable to the "all" setting in the table displaying the sampling results.

4.2.1 Impact of the decoding strategy

When **Greedy Decoding** is used, generated texts are very unsurprising, thus our method gets great overall results (over 95% of TPR@5%FPR on average). However, texts generated by GPT2, Mistral, and MPT are harder to reliably detect, getting scores of 0.781, 0.900, and 0.897 respectively. We can only speculate that GPT2 is the furthest from our ensemble's distribution. We notably obtain a perfect score on Llama-chat, which makes sense since our models are Llama-2 variations, the generator in this case is arguably the closest to the probability distribution provided by the models of our ensemble.

In the case of **Ancestral Sampling**, the irregularities added to the text led to a drop in performance for our method, with MOSAIC-4 and MOSAIC-5 scores falling down to 0.785 and 0.799. Not only do the worse generator models (GPT2, Mistral and MPT) become even harder to identify (0.333, 0.571, and 0.609 respectively), but GPT4 generations also join them, as MOSAIC-4 results go from 0.979 to 0.584 when changing the decoding method. Llama-chat texts are still (near)-perfectly identified (TPR@5%FPR=0.999), and so are MPT-chat's. They happen to be the only two open-source models' instruct versions in

[1] https://raid-bench.xyz/shared-task

the generators, allowing us to speculate that either these versions' outputs do not significantly differ when switching from greedy to sampling, or that our ensemble's distribution is very suited to these instruction-tuned models.

Adding **Repetition Penalty** when greedy decoding is used does not change our results much except for MPT generations, the detection score of which drops drastically from 0.897 to 0.343. Similarly, MPT-chat's score goes from near perfect (0.996) to second-to-last (0.621). However, combining sampling and repetition penalty makes the generated text very surprising and completely breaks our detection approach, leading to results close to 0 for GPT2, Mistral, and MPT (0.005, 0.002 and 0.018). Even in this scenario, Llama-chat remains easy to detect, keeping our average results afloat with a score of 0.864.

4.2.2 Adversarial Attacks

As the golden labels are not provided, we can only hypothesize that the test set is constructed in a similar way as the training set. If that is the case, the attacks are also applied to the human texts and thus produce interesting results. While changing the decoding method could only affect the machine-generated outputs, adversarial techniques modify all samples and can sometimes make human texts even more surprising, improving our results. We report scores on average over all decoding techniques, i.e., when decoding strategy and repetition penalty are both set to "all". MOSAIC-4 goes from 0.752 without attacks to 0.693 on average over all of them, while MOSAIC-5 drops from 0.745 to 0.694. Unless otherwise specified, the scores mentioned below correspond to MOSAIC-4.

Most attacks only cause a slight performance decrease, indicating that they add more surprise to machine outputs than human ones. Shuffling numbers, inserting paragraph breaks, switching between the British spelling and American spelling of some words, deleting some articles, and adding common misspellings are adversarial techniques that lead to score drops lower than 0.05. **Swapping the lower or upper case of words and adding spaces between characters** have more impact on our results but these changes remain minor. Both methods decrease our performance by about 0.07.

Swapping tokens with synonyms chosen by BERT is by far the best attack against our detection method. As pointed out in the Detect-GPT paper (Mitchell et al., 2023), synonyms have lower model log-probability on average in machine-generated samples while human-written text does not exhibit this tendency. This heavily disrupts our method's underlying assumptions and makes our TPR@5%FPR drop down to 0.285.

Using Homoglyphs leads to an interesting outcome, as the attack actually improves our performance, making MOSAIC-5 the best performing submission of the competition when only considering homoglyphs attacks for some generators (Chat-GPT, Cohere, Cohere-chat and Llama-chat). We suspect it is due to the Tower models having seen Cyrillic data in their training.

Inserting zero-width space is the most peculiar of the lot, as it leads to a slight MOSAIC-4 deterioration and a MOSAIC-5 improvement. Our interpretation is that Phi-3 saw this Unicode character during its pretraining, while the other models in our ensemble probably did not.

Overall, our method proves to be quite resilient to adversarial attacks even though it was not designed for this purpose as we operate in a completely zero-shot and tuning-free setting. This further demonstrates the robustness of our method.

The detailed results for the sampling configurations and various attacks are shown in Figure 2. The values presented for adversarial attacks are averaged across all decoding methods, making them directly comparable to the "all" setting in the table displaying the sampling results.

5 Conclusion

About our system and its underlying models In this task, we used the MOSAIC scoring algorithm presented in equation 1, using either 4 of 5 models, (Tower-7b, Tower-13b Llama-2-7b and Llama-2-7b-chat with Phi-3-4k-Instruct in the 5 models version). None of these are used as generators in the RAID test set and they are all Llama-2 variants, as mentioned in (Alves et al., 2024). The only Llama model present in the dataset is Llama-chat, and is the easiest generator to detect according to the competition results. Furthermore, the whole test set is in English and 5 of the 11 generator models are chat versions. The assumption behind our score is that the generated texts' distribution are close to our models', considering two of our members are specialized in multilingualism, and only one is a chat version, our ensemble choice was not optimized for this task at all. We believe this showcases the generalization capabilities of the method. Further

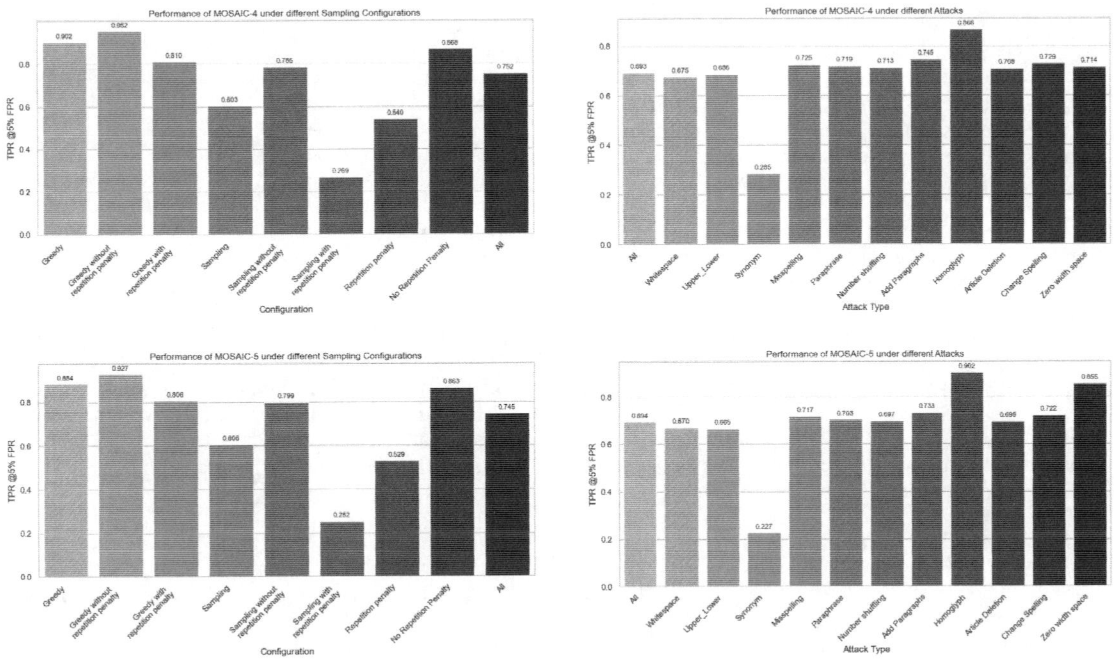

Figure 2: TPR@5% for all Sampling options and Attacks for both MOSAIC configurations

details can be found in the MOSAIC paper (Dubois et al., 2024).

Insights gained from this competition Participating in this shared Task 3 with our MOSAIC method has allowed us to gain valuable insights as to how our method fares against opponents using supervised methods, and take a better look at the effects on detectability of the decoding techniques used to generate the text. Since we underlyingly use language model's probability distribution to identify machine outputs, we expected sampling to affect our performance, and it did. The same observation holds for the use of a repetition penalty and the combination of these generation parameters. However, the adversarial attacks, which were never considered when developing our scoring system, only slightly weaken our results, confirming that our approach is robust to not only changes in the generator model and domain but also resilient to many forms of noise.

Acknowledgements

This work was performed using HPC resources from GENCI–IDRIS (Grant 2023-AD011014903)

References

Marah Abdin, Sam Ade Jacobs, Ammar Ahmad Awan, Jyoti Aneja, Ahmed Awadallah, Hany Awadalla, Nguyen Bach, Amit Bahree, Arash Bakhtiari, Jianmin Bao, Harkirat Behl, Alon Benhaim, Misha Bilenko, Johan Bjorck, Sébastien Bubeck, Qin Cai, Martin Cai, Caio César Teodoro Mendes, Weizhu Chen, Vishrav Chaudhary, Dong Chen, Dongdong Chen, Yen-Chun Chen, Yi-Ling Chen, Parul Chopra, Xiyang Dai, Allie Del Giorno, Gustavo de Rosa, Matthew Dixon, Ronen Eldan, Victor Fragoso, Dan Iter, Mei Gao, Min Gao, Jianfeng Gao, Amit Garg, Abhishek Goswami, Suriya Gunasekar, Emman Haider, Junheng Hao, Russell J. Hewett, Jamie Huynh, Mojan Javaheripi, Xin Jin, Piero Kauffmann, Nikos Karampatziakis, Dongwoo Kim, Mahoud Khademi, Lev Kurilenko, James R. Lee, Yin Tat Lee, Yuanzhi Li, Yunsheng Li, Chen Liang, Lars Liden, Ce Liu, Mengchen Liu, Weishung Liu, Eric Lin, Zeqi Lin, Chong Luo, Piyush Madan, Matt Mazzola, Arindam Mitra, Hardik Modi, Anh Nguyen, Brandon Norick, Barun Patra, Daniel Perez-Becker, Thomas Portet, Reid Pryzant, Heyang Qin, Marko Radmilac, Corby Rosset, Sambudha Roy, Olatunji Ruwase, Olli Saarikivi, Amin Saied, Adil Salim, Michael Santacroce, Shital Shah, Ning Shang, Hiteshi Sharma, Swadheen Shukla, Xia Song, Masahiro Tanaka, Andrea Tupini, Xin Wang, Lijuan Wang, Chunyu Wang, Yu Wang, Rachel Ward, Guanhua Wang, Philipp Witte, Haiping Wu, Michael Wyatt, Bin Xiao, Can Xu, Jiahang Xu, Weijian Xu, Sonali Yadav, Fan Yang, Jianwei Yang, Ziyi Yang, Yifan Yang, Donghan Yu, Lu Yuan, Chengruidong Zhang, Cyril Zhang, Jianwen Zhang, Li Lyna Zhang, Yi Zhang, Yue Zhang, Yunan Zhang, and Xiren Zhou. 2024. Phi-3 Technical Report: A Highly Capable Language Model Locally on Your Phone. *Preprint*, arxiv:2404.14219.

Duarte Miguel Alves, José Pombal, Nuno M Guerreiro, Pedro Henrique Martins, João Alves, Amin Farajian, Ben Peters, Ricardo Rei, Patrick Fernandes, Sweta Agrawal, Pierre Colombo, José G. C. de Souza, and Andre Martins. 2024. Tower: An open multilingual large language model for translation-related tasks. In *First Conference on Language Modeling*.

Wissam Antoun, Benoît Sagot, and Djamé Seddah. 2024. From text to source: Results in detecting large language model-generated content. In *Proceedings of the 2024 Joint International Conference on Computational Linguistics, Language Resources and Evaluation (LREC-COLING 2024)*, pages 7531–7543, Torino, Italia. ELRA and ICCL.

Suguru Arimoto. 1972. An algorithm for computing the capacity of arbitrary discrete memoryless channels. *IEEE Transactions on Information Theory*, 18(1):14–20.

Guangsheng Bao, Yanbin Zhao, Zhiyang Teng, Linyi Yang, and Yue Zhang. 2024. Fast-detectGPT: Efficient zero-shot detection of machine-generated text via conditional probability curvature. In *The Twelfth International Conference on Learning Representations*.

Richard Blahut. 1972. Computation of channel capacity and rate-distortion functions. *IEEE Transactions on Information Theory*, 18(4):460–473.

Evan N. Crothers, Nathalie Japkowicz, and Herna L. Viktor. 2023. Machine-generated text: A comprehensive survey of threat models and detection methods. *IEEE Access*, 11:70977–71002.

Matthieu Dubois, François Yvon, and Pablo Piantanida. 2024. Zero-shot machine-generated text detection using mixture of large language models. *Preprint*, arXiv:2409.07615.

Liam Dugan, Alyssa Hwang, Filip Trhlík, Andrew Zhu, Josh Magnus Ludan, Hainiu Xu, Daphne Ippolito, and Chris Callison-Burch. 2024. RAID: A shared benchmark for robust evaluation of machine-generated text detectors. In *Proceedings of the 62nd Annual Meeting of the Association for Computational Linguistics (Volume 1: Long Papers)*, pages 12463–12492, Bangkok, Thailand. Association for Computational Linguistics.

Liam Dugan, Andrew Zhu, Firoj Alam, Preslav Nakov, Marianna Apidianaki, and Callison-Burch Chris. 2025. Genai content detection task 3: Cross-domain machine generated text detection challenge. In *Proceedings of the 1st Workshop on GenAI Content Detection (GenAIDetect)*, Abu Dhabi, UAE. International Conference on Computational Linguistics.

Abhimanyu Hans, Avi Schwarzschild, Valeriia Cherepanova, Hamid Kazemi, Aniruddha Saha, Micah Goldblum, Jonas Geiping, and Tom Goldstein. 2024. Spotting LLMs with binoculars: Zero-shot detection of machine-generated text. In *Forty-first International Conference on Machine Learning*.

Chengzhi Mao, Carl Vondrick, Hao Wang, and Junfeng Yang. 2024. Raidar: geneRative AI detection viA rewriting. In *The twelfth international conference on learning representations*.

Eric Mitchell, Yoonho Lee, Alexander Khazatsky, Christopher D. Manning, and Chelsea Finn. 2023. DetectGPT: Zero-Shot Machine-Generated Text Detection using Probability Curvature. In *Proceedings International Conference on Machine Learning*, ICML.

Hugo Touvron, Thibaut Lavril, Gautier Izacard, Xavier Martinet, Marie-Anne Lachaux, Timothée Lacroix, Baptiste Rozière, Naman Goyal, Eric Hambro, Faisal Azhar, Aurelien Rodriguez, Armand Joulin, Edouard Grave, and Guillaume Lample. 2023. LLaMA: Open and Efficient Foundation Language Models. *Preprint*, arxiv:2302.13971.

Yuxia Wang, Jonibek Mansurov, Petar Ivanov, Jinyan Su, Artem Shelmanov, Akim Tsvigun, Chenxi Whitehouse, Osama Mohammed Afzal, Tarek Mahmoud, Toru Sasaki, Thomas Arnold, Alham Fikri Aji, Nizar Habash, Iryna Gurevych, and Preslav Nakov. 2024. M4: Multi-generator, multi-domain, and multilingual black-box machine-generated text detection. In *Proceedings of the 18th Conference of the European Chapter of the Association for Computational Linguistics (Volume 1: Long Papers)*, pages 1369–1407, St. Julian's, Malta. Association for Computational Linguistics.

Xianjun Yang, Wei Cheng, Yue Wu, Linda Ruth Petzold, William Yang Wang, and Haifeng Chen. 2024. DNA-GPT: Divergent n-gram analysis for training-free detection of GPT-generated text. In *The twelfth international conference on learning representations*, (ICLR), Vienna, Austria.

Rowan Zellers, Ari Holtzman, Hannah Rashkin, Yonatan Bisk, Ali Farhadi, Franziska Roesner, and Yejin Choi. 2019. Defending Against Neural Fake News. In *Advances in Neural Information Processing Systems*, volume 32. Curran Associates, Inc.

GenAI Content Detection Task 3: Cross-Domain Machine-Generated Text Detection Challenge

Liam Dugan[1], **Andrew Zhu**[1], **Firoj Alam**[3], **Preslav Nakov**[2]
Marianna Apidianaki[1], **Chris Callison-Burch**[1]
University of Pennsylvania[1] MBZUAI[2] Qatar Computing Research Institute[3]
{ldugan, andrz, marapi, ccb}@seas.upenn.edu
preslav.nakov@mbzuai.ac.ae, fialam@hbku.edu.qa

Abstract

Recently there have been many shared tasks targeting the detection of generated text from Large Language Models (LLMs). However, these shared tasks tend to focus either on cases where text is limited to one particular domain or cases where text can be from many domains, some of which may not be seen during test time. In this shared task, using the newly released RAID benchmark, we aim to answer whether or not models can detect generated text from a large, yet fixed, number of domains and LLMs, all of which are seen during training. Over the course of three months, our task was attempted by 9 teams with 23 detector submissions. We find that multiple participants were able to obtain accuracies of over 99% on machine-generated text from RAID while maintaining a 5% False Positive Rate—suggesting that detectors are able to robustly detect text from many domains and models simultaneously. We discuss potential interpretations of this result and provide directions for future research.

1 Introduction

The detection of AI generated text is an increasingly relevant task in the modern age. Such detection can help combat misinformation (Sharevski et al., 2023), phishing attacks (Bethany et al., 2024), and other fraudulent activities (Weiss, 2019; Lund et al., 2023). This is particularly important given that humans struggle to detect generated text reliably (Dugan et al., 2020, 2023) and that generated text is often more persuasive than human-written text (Spitale et al., 2023).

Recently there has been an increase in large scale shared tasks for AI generated text detectors (Wang et al., 2024; Fivez et al., 2024; Bevendorff et al., 2024). These shared tasks tend to either focus on one particular domain or hold out many domains and LLM generators in the final test set. This prevents us from understanding how well a single detector can detect text from a large fixed set of models and domains. Such a setting is important to understand as it helps us to delineate the boundaries of our detector capabilities. For example, it is clear that detectors trained on a single LLM can accurately detect text from that model (Solaiman et al., 2019) but does this extend to arbitrarily many LLMs? What about arbitrarily many domains?

In particular we attempt to answer the following research questions:

- *(RQ1) Can a single detection model be trained to detect generated text from many different known domains and LLMs accurately?*

- *(RQ2) Can a single detection model be robust to many different known adversarial attacks?*

In order to test these research questions, we conduct this shared task using the newly released RAID benchmark (Dugan et al., 2024). RAID is a dataset of over 10 million documents from 11 generative models, 8 textual domains, 4 decoding strategies, and 11 adversarial attacks. We chose RAID as it is one of the largest benchmarks currently available, and it features variation across decoding strategies and adversarial attacks as well as a large variety of textual domains. Crucially, the test set of RAID does not include any held-out models or domains and has yet to be released publicly. Therefore RAID allows us to answer our research questions most effectively.

We received 23 submissions to the shared task from 9 different teams, and 7 system description papers. The results of the evaluation are publicly available.[1] The two best performing teams (Pangram and Leidos) achieved extremely strong performance without adversarial attacks (99.3%) and with adversarial attacks (97.7%). In this paper we will summarize our general takeaways from this re-

[1] https://raid-bench.xyz/shared-task

Proceedings of the 1st Workshop on GenAI Content Detection (GenAIDetect), pages 377–388
January 19, 2025.

Sources in the RAID dataset	
Generative Models ($n = 11$)	GPT2, GPT3, GPT4, Cohere, Cohere Chat, MPT 30B, MPT 30B Chat, Mistral 7B, Mistral 7B Chat, ChatGPT, Llama 70B Chat
Domains ($n = 8$)	Abstracts, Recipes, Books, Reddit, News, Reviews, Poetry, Wiki
Decoding Strategies ($n = 4$)	Greedy (temp=0), Random Sampling (temp=1, top-p=1), Greedy + Repetition Penalty, Sampling + Repetition Penalty
Adversarial Attacks ($n = 11$)	Alternative Spelling, Homoglyph, Article Deletion, Number Swap, Insert Paragraphs, Upper Lower Swap, Paraphrase, Synonym Swap, Zero Width Space, Misspelling, Whitespace Addition

Table 1: The domains, models, decoding strategies and attacks covered by RAID.

Model	Num. Gens	Toks	Self-BLEU	PPL -L7B	PPL -G2X
Human	14971	378.5	7.64	9.09	21.2
GPT 2	59884	384.7	23.9	8.33	8.10
GPT 3	29942	185.6	13.6	3.90	8.12
ChatGPT	29942	329.4	10.3	3.39	9.31
GPT 4	29942	350.8	9.42	5.01	13.4
Cohere	29942	301.9	11.0	5.67	23.7
(+ Chat)	29942	239.0	11.0	4.93	11.6
Mistral	59884	370.2	19.1	7.74	17.9
(+ Chat)	59884	287.7	9.16	4.31	10.3
MPT	59884	379.2	22.1	14.0	66.9
(+ Chat)	59884	219.2	5.39	7.06	56.3
LLaMA	59884	404.4	10.6	3.33	9.76
Total	509k	323.4	13.7	6.61	23.8

Table 2: Statistics for the generations in train and test without adversarial attacks. **PPL-L7B** refers to mean perplexity according to LLaMA 7B and **PPL-G2X** refers to mean perplexity according to GPT 2 XL.

sult and offer future directions for effective benchmarking of generated text classifiers.

2 Related Work

The shared tasks most similar to ours are the SemEval24 Task 8 and GenAI Content Detection Task 1 (Wang et al., 2024, 2025). Both of these tasks include outputs from many generative models and domains in both their train and test set. However, as mentioned in the introduction, these tasks hold out many domains and models in their test set to test the generalization performance of classifiers to new unseen models and domains. In our task we explicitly give all domain and model information to our participants up front and only hold out particular articles within such domains.

Other shared tasks in the past have also evaluated generated text detectors in specific high-risk domains such as academic essays (King et al., 2023; Chowdhury et al., 2025) scientific papers (Kashnitsky et al., 2022) or news articles (Bevendorff et al., 2024). Previous shared tasks have also studied detection in a multilingual context (Shamardina et al., 2022; Sarvazyan et al., 2023; Fivez et al., 2024; Wang et al., 2025; Chowdhury et al., 2025). While such tasks are interesting and valuable, they do not test what we are interested in, namely the ability of single detectors to detect text from many different models and domains.

Finally, the recent Voight-Kampff task (Bevendorff et al., 2024) is particularly noteworthy. In their task they employ a set of builders (who build detectors) and breakers (who create adversarial datasets to fool the detectors). They are the first shared task to explicitly include adversarial constraints into their evaluation—experimenting with homoglyph attacks and different detailed prompt formulations with bullet points and summaries of the original source texts. However, they conduct their task in a pairwise manner, giving each detector two texts, one of which must be human-written, and asking the detector to select the human-written text. While they showed that detectors can do well on this highly adversarial task (96.1 ROC AUC score for the top team), we target the more difficult yet more realistic version of the task, where a single document is given as input.

3 Task Setup

3.1 RAID Benchmark

The RAID benchmark was created by sampling roughly 2000 human-written documents from each of 8 domains. Then, for each human-written document, a machine-written version is generated from each of the 11 LLMs with each of the 4 decoding strategies. Finally, each of the 11 adversarial attacks are applied to all machine-written documents. The test set consists of 200 human-written documents per domain selected from the train set and all generations based on those documents. The documents were then checked to prevent duplication and leakage and to ensure no overlap between train and test data.

In Table 1, we list the domains, models, decoding strategies, and adversarial attacks covered in RAID. In Table 2 we report summary statistics and

		Human	ChatGPT	dav.-003	GPT-4	Cohere	Coh.-C	GPT-2	MPT	MPT-C	Mistral	Mist.-C	Llama2-C
Train	Abstracts	1766	3532	3532	3532	3532	3532	7064	7064	7064	7064	7064	7064
	Books	1781	3562	3562	3562	3562	3562	7124	7124	7124	7124	7124	7124
	News	1780	3560	3560	3560	3560	3560	7120	7120	7120	7120	7120	7120
	Poetry	1771	3542	3542	3542	3542	3542	7084	7084	7084	7084	7084	7084
	Recipes	1772	3544	3544	3544	3544	3544	7088	7088	7088	7088	7088	7088
	Reddit	1779	3558	3558	3558	3558	3558	7116	7116	7116	7116	7116	7116
	Wiki	1779	3558	3558	3558	3558	3558	7116	7116	7116	7116	7116	7116
	Reviews	943	1886	1886	1886	1886	1886	3772	3772	3772	3772	3772	3772
	Total	13371	26742	26742	26742	26742	26742	53484	53484	53484	53484	53484	53484
Test	Abstracts	200	400	400	400	400	400	800	800	800	800	800	800
	Books	200	400	400	400	400	400	800	800	800	800	800	800
	News	200	400	400	400	400	400	800	800	800	800	800	800
	Poetry	200	400	400	400	400	400	800	800	800	800	800	800
	Recipes	200	400	400	400	400	400	800	800	800	800	800	800
	Reddit	200	400	400	400	400	400	800	800	800	800	800	800
	Wiki	200	400	400	400	400	400	800	800	800	800	800	800
	Reviews	200	400	400	400	400	400	800	800	800	800	800	800
	Total	1600	6400	3200	3200	3200	3200	3200	6400	6400	6400	6400	6400

Table 3: Number of documents in the RAID dataset by model and domain. Each human-written document has exactly one machine-written counterpart from each model with each of the decoding strategies listed in Table 1. Due to lack of support for repetition penalty sampling, API-based models have two outputs per human document and open-weight models have four outputs per human document. "-C" in model name indicates the chat fine-tuned version of the model. The adversarial data has an identical distribution but with 12x more documents per cell.

in Table 3 we report the exact distribution of documents from the training set and test set.

3.2 Subtask A: Cross-Domain Detection

For Subtask A, participants were asked to submit detectors that would be robust to all 8 domains in the main RAID dataset without adversarial attacks. In Table 9, we provide a breakdown of the addressed domains, and links to the original data sources for extra training. We provided our teams with these links in order to help them secure as much training data as possible. This is particularly important given that RAID has a roughly 40:1 class imbalance of AI vs. human-written text. We observed that many teams took advantage of this and sampled extra human data from these sources.

3.3 Subtask B: Adversarial Robustness

In Subtask B, the participants had to evaluate their detectors on all data from Subtask A with the addition of 11 adversarial attacks. In Table 10 we list the adversarial attacks applied as well as the source papers that first study them. For this subtask, the participants also had access to the original code[2] used to create the adversarial attacks. This allowed them to adversarially modify any existing piece of data to assist in training.

[2] `https://github.com/liamdugan/raid/tree/main/generation/adversarial/attackers`

3.4 Baselines

We use the following models as baselines:

- **Openai-RoBERTa-large** (Solaiman et al., 2019): RoBERTa-large model fine-tuned on GPT-2 generations.
- **RADAR** (Hu et al., 2023): Vicuna 7B model trained on adversarial paraphrases
- **Binoculars** (Hans et al., 2024): Current SoTA metric-based detection model. Uses perplexity divided by cross-entropy between Falcon 7B and Falcon 7B Instruct.
- **GLTR** (Gehrmann et al., 2019): Baseline metric-based detection model. Uses GPT-2 small and rank=10 for vocabulary cutoff.

We gave our participants access to the code to run these baselines as well as the outputs for these models on the training set.

4 Metrics

4.1 Performance Metric

Due to the class imbalance in the RAID dataset, typical metrics like Accuracy and AUROC are not appropriate for this task. Thus, in keeping with the original RAID paper, we use domain-adjusted TPR@FPR=5% as our metric. This metric represents how much of the generated text we are able to correctly identify while maintaining a 5% false positive rate (where a false positive is defined as incorrectly labeling a human-written text as being machine generated).

4.2 Threshold Search

In order to measure TPR@FPR=5% we need to find a binary classification threshold that results in a 5% false positive rate on the human data for each detector and domain. The search algorithm we use for this purpose is the same algorithm that is described in the RAID paper. We start at the threshold corresponding to the mean score of human data (50% FPR), and approach the desired false positive rate by iteratively incrementing or decrementing the threshold. If we overshoot the target FPR, we divide our increment in half and flip the sign. We continue to do this process until the false positive rate is within $\epsilon = 0.0005$ of the desired false positive rate or until 50 iterations are reached. If 50 iterations are reached without convergence, then we select the threshold corresponding to the FPR that is closest to the target while still being less than the target.

4.3 Robustness Metric

In addition to this performance metric, we also calculate the standard deviation of TPR@FPR=5%. This measures how robust each model is across each domain of comparison. For subtask A, this metric will be measured across domains and for subtask B, this metric will be measured across adversarial attacks.

5 Submissions

We received 23 submissions to the shared task from 9 different teams, and system description papers from 7 of 9 teams. In this section, we describe the systems submitted by each team in detail. In Section 6 we will discuss aggregate results for the teams and in Section 7 we will discuss the broader trends across our participant submissions.

Team LuxVeri [Lx] (Mobin and Islam, 2025): This team fine-tuned both RoBERTa-base and RoBERTa-base-openai-detector on a subset of the RAID training data for 3 epochs, using a learning rate of 2e-5, a batch size of 4, and the AdamW optimizer. These trained models were then used to compute weights for ensembling based on an inverse perplexity weighting technique, which was applied to the ensemble for the adversarial task. For the non-adversarial task, they only used RoBERTa-base with the same hyperparameters.

Team Random [Ra] (Agrahari et al., 2025): This team's contributions include a pipeline that integrates XLM-RoBERTa embeddings for enhanced text representation, domain adaptation using a Domain-Adversarial Neural Network (DANN) (Ganin et al., 2016) to minimize domain-specific biases and improve generalization across diverse text domains, and adversarial robustness through incorporating adversarial attack classification to detect and mitigate manipulative techniques.

Team USTC-BUPT [Us] : This team fine-tuned RoBERTa-Large via focal loss (Lin et al., 2017) on the RAID training set by adding four samples for each human sample using synonym replacement. They then down-sampled the AI-written texts from a 10:1 ratio to a 2:1 ratio of AI to human text to form the training set. In the hyperparameters for focal loss, they set alpha to 0.65 and gamma to 2.5. They used a learning rate of 1e-6 and AdamW as the optimizer. In addition to this, they also had a secondary submission where they simply fine-tuned RoBERTa-base on a subset of the RAID training set with learning rate of 5e-5.

Team ALERT [Al] (Kandula et al., 2025): This team's approach uses robust authorship style representations to distinguish between human-authored and machine-generated text (MGT) across various domains. Their authorship attribution (AA) systems are trained with contrastive learning. They employ an ensemble-based AA system (ALERT v1.1) that integrates stylistic embeddings from two complementary subsystems: One system that focuses on cross-genre robustness with hard positive and negative mining strategies using Linq-Embed-Mistral (Kim et al., 2024) as backbone architecture, and a second system with Semantic, Lexical, Clustering based hard positive and negative mining which uses Qwen2-1.5B.

Team Leidos [Le] (Edikala et al., 2025): This team trained four Distil-RoBERTa-Base detectors to evaluate both binary and multi-class classification, exploring the effects of class weighting to address dataset imbalance, in order to distinguish human-written from machine-generated text. The "Leidos Detector v1.0.1" is a Binary Classifier without Class Weighting (BC): Human vs. Machine, trained without applying class weights. The "Leidos Detector v1.0.3" is a Binary Classifier with

Subtask A: Performance Across Domains (Official Results)									
	News	Wiki	Reddit	Books	Abs.	Reviews	Poetry	Recipes	Total (σ)
[Le] Leidos v1.0.3	**99.9**	99.8	98.3	99.4	99.9	98.6	99.3	**100.0**	**99.4** (0.6)
[Pa] Pangram	99.7	99.1	98.5	99.5	99.3	**99.6**	98.8	99.9	99.3 (**0.4**)
[Le] Leidos v1.0.2	**99.9**	**99.9**	**99.4**	99.5	99.9	95.9	**99.6**	**100.0**	99.3 (1.2)
[Le] Leidos v1.0.4	**99.9**	99.7	99.0	99.3	**100.0**	96.5	99.4	**100.0**	99.2 (1.1)
[Le] Leidos v1.0.1	**99.9**	99.8	98.6	99.4	99.9	96.2	99.4	**100.0**	99.1 (1.2)
[Us] R-L Focal Loss	99.0	97.8	96.1	98.1	99.8	97.0	97.0	99.9	98.1 (1.3)
[Al] ALERT v1.1	99.7	95.4	75.7	**99.9**	99.9	87.2	78.3	98.3	91.8 (9.4)
[Cn] DistilBERT-NITS	89.9	87.7	90.0	93.5	90.9	85.9	90.0	96.0	90.5 (2.9)
[Al] ALERT v1.2	99.5	91.3	87.2	99.2	99.9	89.9	64.9	82.8	89.3 (11.0)
[Lx] R-B & R-Oai	87.5	90.2	62.4	89.5	99.2	83.7	73.5	75.1	82.6 (10.9)
[Lx] R-Oai & BERT	91.8	87.3	75.1	87.1	97.0	86.0	76.3	59.4	82.5 (11.1)
[Lx] Fine-tuned R-B	87.5	89.7	61.7	89.6	98.8	82.5	66.3	74.6	81.3 (11.9)
[Ba] Binoculars	80.7	76.5	81.3	82.8	76.0	78.0	80.1	76.4	79.0 (2.4)
[Mo] MOSAIC-4	79.5	67.6	78.2	79.8	77.1	81.4	63.7	75.8	75.2 (5.9)
[Mo] MOSAIC-5	79.0	65.8	76.7	79.8	76.5	77.2	64.8	75.1	74.5 (5.4)
[Lx] Radar & R-L	91.6	73.7	76.3	78.1	74.2	58.7	45.7	73.5	71.5 (12.8)
[Ba] RADAR	87.4	77.3	73.6	78.1	67.5	6.3	46.0	88.7	65.6 (25.7)
[Ba] GLTR	67.7	63.6	63.2	71.9	60.1	65.0	18.2	67.9	59.7 (16.0)
[80] L3-60 Zero-shot	63.6	36.5	61.5	65.4	55.3	68.9	51.5	53.9	57.1 (9.6)
[80] M3-60 Zero-shot	58.1	58.1	65.8	63.3	44.1	67.1	53.2	50.5	56.5 (7.4)
[Ba] openai-roberta-large	67.8	59.4	60.0	52.5	64.8	52.8	23.3	65.1	55.7 (13.3)
[Cn] Adv.-submission-3	27.1	26.1	52.8	57.1	30.1	48.6	38.0	94.0	46.7 (21.1)
[Cn] Adv.-New-Detector	14.0	16.2	40.4	39.2	34.7	29.4	17.8	91.0	35.3 (23.2)
[Us] Roberta_dataaug.	4.6	3.6	40.5	7.3	83.1	3.1	5.1	98.8	30.8 (36.8)
[Cn] Adv._Data_Detector	10.1	17.5	27.9	24.8	27.7	28.7	13.5	88.0	29.8 (23.0)
[Lx] Radar R-B CGPT-R	20.0	16.0	4.8	2.5	51.1	62.1	4.4	32.9	24.2 (21.1)
[Ra] Adv. CDMGTD	4.2	3.4	2.1	2.1	6.8	2.9	1.7	2.4	3.2 (1.6)
Average Performance	70.7	66.6	68.4	71.8	74.6	67.7	58.1	78.5	69.5 (5.7)

Table 4: TPR at FPR=5% for detectors across different domains on the RAID test set along with their standard deviation (σ). Baselines are given the [Ba] tag. "Abs." is shorthand for Abstracts. Team rankings are determined based on the highest performing submission for each team (see Table 7).

Class Weighting (BW) which is similar to the BC model but trained with class weights to address class imbalance. The "Leidos Detector v1.0.4" is a multi-class classifier without class Weighting (MC): A multi-class classifier that predicts which generator model produced the text or if it was human-written, trained without class weights. Finally the "Leidos Detector v1.0.2" is a Multi-class Classifier with Class Weighting (MW) which is the same as the MC model but trained with class weights to mitigate class imbalance.

Team MOSAIC [Mo] (Dubois et al., 2025): This team submitted a completely unsupervised approach which uses a mixture of models to score the texts. Their ensemble method is grounded in fundamental information-theoretic principles from universal compression in order to optimally combine the strengths of multiple LLMs for machine-generated text detection. The four models used are Tower-7b, Tower-13b, Llama-2-7b and Llama-2-7b-chat.

Team CNLP-NITS-PP [Cn] (Teja et al., 2025): This team submitted a model that first classifies whether the text has been adversarially attacked or not. If an attack is detected, the text undergoes preprocessing to mitigate the attack, after which the preprocessed text proceeds to the model for MGT detection. Finally, their detector works by fine-tuning a DistilBERT model to extract semantic features.

Team 1-800-SHARED-TASKS [80] (Kadiyala, 2024; Kadiyala et al., 2024): This team submitted a model that uses a token classifier for detecting change in authorship within the same text. The data from the current benchmark would be both unseen domain and unseen generators' data. Inference was done without any pre-processing against adversarial methods, nor were those methods present in the training data. The final generated score was based on the proportion of tokens classified as AI generated among the ones within the supported context length.

Subtask B: Performance Across Adversarial Attacks (Official Results)											
	AS	**AD**	**HG**	**IP**	**NS**	**PP**	**MS**	**SY**	**UL**	**WS**	**ZW**	**Total** (σ)
[Le] Leidos v1.0.2	99.2	99.0	**97.3**	98.7	99.2	92.3	98.8	98.6	98.9	99.0	92.7	**97.7 (2.5)**
[Pa] Pangram	99.2	98.7	91.9	**99.3**	99.2	91.6	99.0	96.2	**99.3**	**99.3**	99.3	**97.7** (2.9)
[Le] Leidos v1.0.4	99.1	99.0	94.7	98.7	99.2	94.8	98.8	98.6	98.9	98.8	90.9	97.6 (2.6)
[Le] Leidos v1.0.3	**99.3**	**99.3**	93.6	98.7	**99.4**	**96.3**	**99.2**	**99.1**	99.2	99.2	84.2	97.2 (4.4)
[Le] Leidos v1.0.1	99.0	99.0	86.1	98.1	99.1	94.8	98.9	98.8	98.8	98.5	78.8	95.7 (6.4)
[Us] R-L Focal Loss	97.9	98.2	84.5	93.6	98.1	84.0	97.8	97.4	97.9	97.9	67.1	92.7 (9.5)
[Al] ALERT v1.1	91.8	92.1	68.5	89.7	91.8	57.7	91.0	87.3	91.3	91.2	46.8	82.6 (15.5)
[Lx] Fine-tuned R-B	80.5	78.1	90.4	79.8	79.8	77.9	77.9	74.4	75.0	66.2	**100.0**	80.1 (8.4)
[Al] ALERT v1.2	89.9	89.0	61.9	84.1	88.6	57.1	88.6	84.1	87.2	85.6	40.2	78.8 (16.0)
[Lx] R-B & R-Oai	81.7	79.4	41.7	81.2	81.1	78.1	79.3	75.8	76.1	68.0	86.9	76.0 (11.6)
[Lx] R-Oai & BERT	81.6	79.4	20.9	81.7	82.2	75.8	79.6	77.6	76.7	77.1	83.7	74.9 (17.0)
[Ba] Binoculars	78.2	74.3	37.7	71.7	77.1	80.3	78.0	43.5	73.8	70.1	99.1	71.3 (16.2)
[Ba] Radar	70.8	67.9	59.3	73.7	71.0	67.3	69.5	67.5	70.4	66.1	82.2	69.6 (5.3)
[Mo] MOSAIC-5	72.2	69.5	90.2	73.3	69.7	70.3	71.7	22.7	66.5	67.0	85.5	69.4 (16.3)
[Mo] MOSAIC-4	72.9	70.8	86.6	74.5	71.3	71.9	72.5	28.5	68.6	67.5	71.4	69.3 (13.6)
[Lx] Radar & R-L	70.3	61.2	21.2	73.0	69.9	73.0	63.9	74.9	55.7	60.2	91.3	65.5 (16.6)
[Ba] GLTR	61.2	52.1	24.3	61.4	59.9	47.2	59.8	31.2	48.1	45.8	97.2	53.5 (18.1)
[80] L3-60 Zero-shot	56.6	50.5	3.0	57.4	56.3	50.6	55.6	53.5	57.1	61.9	57.1	51.4 (15.4)
[Ba] openai-roberta-L	52.4	33.2	21.3	55.1	51.7	72.9	39.5	79.4	19.3	40.1	99.9	51.3 (23.6)
[80] M3-60 Zero-shot	55.6	48.6	3.6	56.7	52.2	37.7	53.7	40.2	56.5	59.7	56.5	48.1 (15.4)
[Cn] Adv.-sub.-3	46.7	45.1	20.8	46.7	46.5	18.0	46.8	41.6	46.7	46.7	46.7	41.6 (10.4)
[Cn] Adv.-New-Det.	35.3	35.2	18.9	35.3	35.4	11.9	35.4	31.6	35.3	35.3	35.3	31.7 (7.7)
[Us] Roberta_dataaug.	30.8	31.6	16.4	31.8	30.8	26.8	30.4	30.1	30.8	29.5	11.6	27.6 (6.5)
[Cn] Adv._Data_Det.	29.7	29.4	18.5	29.8	29.6	8.5	29.8	26.9	29.8	29.8	29.8	26.8 (6.5)
[Lx] Radar R-B C-R	22.3	15.2	0.4	4.9	22.0	34.9	18.1	30.0	6.6	4.3	11.0	16.2 (10.6)
[Ra] Adv. CDMGTD	3.2	3.0	24.8	3.2	3.2	3.5	3.2	3.2	3.2	3.2	20.8	6.5 (7.6)
Average Performance	68.4	65.3	49.2	67.4	67.9	60.6	66.8	61.3	64.1	64.2	67.9	64.3 (5.3)

Table 5: TPR at FPR=5% for detectors across different adversarial attacks along with their standard deviation (σ). Baselines are given the [Ba] tag. Abbreviations are: AS: Alternative Spelling, AD: Article Deletion, HG: Homoglyph, IP: Insert Paragraphs, NS: Number Swap, PP: Paraphrase, MS: Misspelling, SY: Synonym Swap, UL: Upper Lower Swap, WS: Whitespace Addition, ZW: Zero-Width Space Addition. Team rankings determined by the highest performing submission (see Table 8).

Team Pangram [Pa] (Emi et al., 2025): This team pretrained an autoregressive LLM-based detector on a wide variety of datasets, domains, languages, prompt schemes, and LLMs used to generate the AI portion of the dataset. They aggressively employed several augmentation strategies and preprocessing strategies to improve robustness. They then mined the RAID train set for the AI examples with the largest error based on the original classifier, mixed those examples and their human-written counterparts back into the training set, and retrained the detector until convergence.

6 Results

6.1 Subtask A: Cross-Domain Detection

In Table 4, we report the official results for Subtask A. Overall, we see that a large fraction of our teams beat our provided baselines and established strong new results. The winning team, Leidos, achieved 99.4% TPR across all 8 domains—a substantial improvement over the prior state of the art result on RAID. This suggests that it is possible to build classifiers that are robust across a finite set of domains and models.

In terms of comparisons between domains, the most difficult domain to classify across all submissions was Poetry (58.1%), and the easiest were Recipes (78.5%) and Abstracts (74.6%). Poems are inherently difficult to identify for machines as they rely on rare and unusual word choice, and are likely to be surprising even to well trained classifiers. On the other hand, both the Recipes and Abstracts domains were unexpectedly easy for the detectors.

6.2 Subtask B: Adversarial Robustness

In Table 5, we report the official results for subtask B. We observe similarly high performance, with the two winning teams (Leidos and Pangram) getting a surprisingly high 97.7% TPR on the dataset. Once again, we see many teams beat our strong baselines and feel that these results validate our intuition that classifiers, when given a finite set of adversarial attacks to defend against, can do quite well.

In addition, while many attacks from the original RAID paper are effective when the defender is not prepared for them (e.g., Whitespace Insertion, Article Deletion), such attacks seem to be relatively easy to defend against. One interesting finding is that the most difficult attacks to defend against were the Homoglyph attack (49.2%), the Paraphrase attack (60.6%), and the Synonym attack (61.3%). Despite having access to the code that generated the Homoglyph attack, it is still difficult to create a model that is robust to this attack without any text preprocessing or normalization. In addition, while many attacks are easy to defend against with good knowledge of the attacker, it seems that both the Paraphrase and Synonym attacks remain difficult to deal with even with perfect knowledge. This is because these attacks are not easily solved with simple preprocessing techniques, and because they require models to learn alternative distributions that are often fairly distinct from generic generated text.

7 Broader Trends

Across all submissions to the shared task we find the following broader trends:

Trend 1: Text Preprocessing The first clear trend we saw was the use of text preprocessing. Team [Cn] and [Ra] both trained classifiers to detect particular adversarial attacks in the dataset in order to apply preprocessing, and team [Pa] simply ran all incoming text to the detector through text normalization. Looking at the results, these methods seemed to be largely effective at neutralizing many of the simpler adversarial attacks such as Zero-Width Space, Upper-Lower Swap, Insert Paragraphs, Whitespace Insertion and Alternative Spelling. However, attacks such as Paraphrasing, Synonym Swap, Article Deletion, and Misspelling seem to be more difficult to preprocess away. Such attacks, which either create or destroy vital information in the text, can be seen as fundamentally different and more difficult to defend against.

Trend 2: Hard Positive and Negative Sampling The second clear trend we found was the active sampling for hard examples in the dataset. Of the top four teams, three reported using this particular technique. Team [Us] used focal loss, which concentrates learning on hard misclassified examples; Team [Al] used pairs of difficult examples to train their contrastive learning objective, and Team [Pa] looked specifically for examples where their classifier had large error and incorporated them into their existing pre-training dataset. While it is difficult to isolate the effect of any one particular method or technique in a study like this, it is clear that sampling particularly hard examples is a promising direction for building robust classifiers.

Trend 3: Diversity of Approach The third and final trend we feel is relevant to mention is the diversity of approaches we witnessed. We saw submissions involving unsupervised methods [Mo], ensemble methods [Lx], token-level models [80], contrastive learning models [Al], and multi-class classification methods [Le]. Each of the submissions differed drastically from the others not only in terms of performance, but also in adversarial and cross-domain robustness properties. For example, we see that the unsupervised approaches [Mo] exhibited lower overall performance but higher cross-domain robustness than ensemble methods [Lx]. This suggests that there is a large potential for novel modeling work to be done in detection.

8 Discussion

In real-world scenarios, API-based detectors can expect a majority of their text to come from a relatively small set of LLMs and domains. The most common frontier models (Gemini Pro, Claude 3.5, GPT-4o) will mostly likely be used to generate text in a set of high-risk domains (academic essays, news articles, scientific papers) with potentially some paraphrasing or synonym changes applied to help avoid detection. In such cases, it is desirable for a detector to focus on optimizing performance as much as possible on this fixed set of models and domains while not caring as much about performance on other less common models. Our results show that detectors can exhibit very strong performance in such constrained settings.

Future work should seek to further target this particular setting and replicate these findings on a much more diverse corpus. Such a study would entail collecting many generations from a core set of models in high risk domains and conduct a heavy adversarial attack circuit. Since prompt-based attacks are likely to be common (e.g. "write in a way that is not detectable") these should be a major focus. In addition, testing a large set of "humanizing" paraphrase models is also desirable. It is unclear whether or not our results will extend to models that have significant prompt and paraphrase

Domain: Abstracts, **Title**: EdgeFlow: Achieving Practical Interactive Segmentation with Edge-Guided Flow	
ChatGPT	EdgeFlow is a novel approach to interactive image segmentation that combines edge detection and flow-based methods to achieve practical and efficient results. The proposed method utilizes an edge-guided flow algorithm to guide the segmentation process, allowing users to interactively refine the segmentation boundaries. The algorithm incorporates both local and global information to accurately capture [...]
Human	High-quality training data play a key role in image segmentation tasks. Usually, pixel-level annotations are expensive, laborious and time-consuming for the large volume of training data. To reduce labelling cost and improve segmentation quality, interactive segmentation methods have been proposed, [...]
Domain: Recipes, **Title**: Olive Spirals	
ChatGPT	Instructions: 1. Preheat your oven to 400°F (200°C) and line a baking sheet with parchment paper. 2. In a bowl, combine the black olives, green olives, sun-dried tomatoes, feta cheese, basil, parsley, olive oil, salt, and pepper. Mix well to combine all the ingredients. 3. Roll out the puff pastry sheet on a lightly floured surface into a rectangle shape, about 1/4 inch thick. 4. Spread the olive mixture evenly over the puff pastry, leaving a small border around the edges. [...]
Human	Mix yeast, sugar& 125ml warm water in a bowl. Cover and set aside in a warm place for 10 minutes, or until frothy. Sift the flour and salt into a bowl and make a well in the centre. Add frothy yeast, oil and 250ml of warm water. Mix to a soft dough and gather into a ball. Turn out on a floured surface and knead for 10 minutes until smooth. Cover loosely with greased plastic wrap and set aside for 1 hour until [...]

Table 6: Comparison of human-written text to chatgpt-written text in the Abstracts and Recipes domain from the RAID dataset. We can see that the human-written abstract has periodic newline characters and the generated text does not. In addition we see that the ChatGPT-written recipe has numbered lists of instructions while the human-written text is written in paragraph form. Artifacts such as these may trivialize the detection task.

variations applied.

Finally, it is worth noting that detectors doing well in constrained settings does not imply generalization to unseen models. Detectors still suffer from poor generalization across unseen models and domains as discussed in Dugan et al. (2024). However, this discrepancy between in-distribution and out-of-distribution performance is something that is worth highlighting as a potential source for future investigation.

Limitations

Test Data Leakage The first thing to note is the potential for test data leakage. Since the human-written documents are sampled from publicly available datasets and we give our participants the links to such datasets, there is a chance that participants models have seen the human-written documents in our test data and have overfit to them, allowing for high performance. In our eyes this is unlikely, as most of the linked datasets have a large amount of documents and the percentage of documents included in test data from those is vanishingly small. In addition, such leakage would only be problematic when searching for thresholds. Since our metric is TPR, we only measure the accuracy of the classifier in identifying machine-written text, all of which is hidden and has never been released publicly. Nonetheless, this is an important caveat to include.

Confounding Factors On manual investigation of the RAID dataset we found instances of confounding factors in the data that would potentially make detection easier (Table 6). For example, all human-written recipes were written without numbered lists of steps whereas all generated recipes included numbered lists of steps. To investigate the effects of these confounds we manually cleaned the data to remove the most egregious examples and trained a RoBERTa-base model on both the original and cleaned RAID. We saw a drop from 92.67 to 89.67 after cleaning the data—a small but significant performance difference. We are continuing to investigate this and do not yet have enough evidence to conclude whether or not this is the source of the high performance. We hope that future studies can help to shed more light on this issue not only in RAID but in other common benchmark datasets as well.

Acknowledgments

This research is supported in part by the Office of the Director of National Intelligence (ODNI), Intelligence Advanced Research Projects Activity (IARPA), via the HIATUS Program contract #2022-22072200005. The views and conclusions contained herein are those of the authors and should not be interpreted as necessarily representing the official policies, either expressed or implied, of ODNI, IARPA, or the U.S. Government. The U.S. Government is authorized to reproduce and distribute reprints for governmental purposes notwithstanding any copyright annotation therein.

References

Shifali Agrahari, Prabhat Mishra, and Sujit Kumar. 2025. Team Random at GenAI Detection Task 3: A Hybrid Approach to Cross-Domain Detection of Machine-Generated Text with Adversarial Attack Mitigation. In *Proceedings of the 1st Workshop on GenAI Content Detection (GenAIDetect)*, Abu Dhabi, UAE.

Mazal Bethany, Athanasios Galiopoulos, Emet Bethany, Mohammad Bahrami Karkevandi, Nishant Vishwamitra, and Peyman Najafirad. 2024. Large Language Model Lateral Spear Phishing: A Comparative Study in Large-Scale Organizational Settings. *Preprint*, arXiv:2401.09727.

Janek Bevendorff, Matti Wiegmann, Jussi Karlgren, Luise Dürlich, Evangelia Gogoulou, Aarne Talman, Efstathios Stamatatos, Martin Potthast, and Benno Stein. 2024. Overview of the "Voight-Kampff" Generative AI Authorship Verification Task at PAN and ELOQUENT 2024. In *Working Notes of CLEF 2024 - Conference and Labs of the Evaluation Forum*, CEUR Workshop Proceedings. CEUR-WS.org.

Meghana Moorthy Bhat and Srinivasan Parthasarathy. 2020. How Effectively Can Machines Defend Against Machine-Generated Fake News? An Empirical Study. In *Proceedings of the First Workshop on Insights from Negative Results in NLP*, pages 48–53, Online. Association for Computational Linguistics.

Shuyang Cai and Wanyun Cui. 2023. Evade chatgpt detectors via a single space. *Preprint*, arXiv:2307.02599.

Shammur Absar Chowdhury, Hind Al-Merekhi, Mucahid Kutlu, Kaan Efe Keleş, Fatema Ahmad, Tasnim Mohiuddin, Georgios Mikros, and Firoj Alam. 2025. GenAI content detection task 2: AI vs. human – academic essay authenticity challenge. In *Proceedings of the 1st Workshop on GenAI Content Detection (GenAIDetect)*, Abu Dhabi, UAE. International Conference on Computational Linguistics.

Matthieu Dubois, François Yvon, and Pablo Piantanida. 2025. MOSAIC at GenAI Content Detection Task 3: Cross-Domain Machine Generated Text Detection. In *Proceedings of the 1st Workshop on GenAI Content Detection (GenAIDetect)*, Abu Dhabi, UAE.

Liam Dugan, Alyssa Hwang, Filip Trhlík, Andrew Zhu, Josh Magnus Ludan, Hainiu Xu, Daphne Ippolito, and Chris Callison-Burch. 2024. RAID: A shared benchmark for robust evaluation of machine-generated text detectors. In *Proceedings of the 62nd Annual Meeting of the Association for Computational Linguistics (Volume 1: Long Papers)*, pages 12463–12492, Bangkok, Thailand. Association for Computational Linguistics.

Liam Dugan, Daphne Ippolito, Arun Kirubarajan, and Chris Callison-Burch. 2020. RoFT: A Tool for Evaluating Human Detection of Machine-Generated Text. In *Proceedings of the 2020 Conference on Empirical Methods in Natural Language Processing: System Demonstrations*, pages 189–196, Online. Association for Computational Linguistics.

Liam Dugan, Daphne Ippolito, Arun Kirubarajan, Sherry Shi, and Chris Callison-Burch. 2023. Real or Fake Text? Investigating Human Ability to Detect Boundaries between Human-Written and Machine-Generated text. In *Proceedings of the Thirty-Seventh AAAI Conference on Artificial Intelligence and Thirty-Fifth Conference on Innovative Applications of Artificial Intelligence and Thirteenth Symposium on Educational Advances in Artificial Intelligence*, AAAI'23/IAAI'23/EAAI'23. AAAI Press.

Abishek R Edikala, Gregorios A Katsios, Noelie V Creaghe, and Ning Yu. 2025. Leidos at GenAI Content Detection Task 3: A Weight-Balanced Transformer Approach for AI Generated Text Detection Across Domains. In *Proceedings of the 1st Workshop on GenAI Content Detection (GenAIDetect)*, Abu Dhabi, UAE.

Bradley Emi, Elyas Masrour, and Max Spero. 2025. Pangram at GenAI Content Detection Task 3: An Active Learning Approach to Machine Generated Text Generation. In *Proceedings of the 1st Workshop on GenAI Content Detection (GenAIDetect)*, Abu Dhabi, UAE.

Pieter Fivez, Walter Daelemans, Tim Van de Cruys, Yury Kashnitsky, Savvas Chamezopoulos, Hadi Mohammadi, Anastasia Giachanou, Ayoub Bagheri, Wessel Poelman, Juraj Vladika, Esther Ploeger, Johannes Bjerva, Florian Matthes, and Hans van Halteren. 2024. The clin33 shared task on the detection of text generated by large language models. *Computational Linguistics in the Netherlands Journal*, 13:233–259.

Rinaldo Gagiano, Maria Myung-Hee Kim, Xiuzhen Zhang, and Jennifer Biggs. 2021. Robustness Analysis of Grover for Machine-Generated News Detection. In *Proceedings of the 19th Annual Workshop of the Australasian Language Technology Association*, pages 119–127, Online. Australasian Language Technology Association.

Yaroslav Ganin, Evgeniya Ustinova, Hana Ajakan, Pascal Germain, Hugo Larochelle, François Laviolette, Mario March, and Victor Lempitsky. 2016. Domain-adversarial training of neural networks. *Journal of Machine Learning Research*, 17(59):1–35.

Ji Gao, Jack Lanchantin, Mary Lou Soffa, and Yanjun Qi. 2018. Black-box Generation of Adversarial Text Sequences to Evade Deep Learning Classifiers. *Preprint*, arXiv:1801.04354.

Sebastian Gehrmann, Hendrik Strobelt, and Alexander Rush. 2019. GLTR: Statistical Detection and Visualization of Generated Text. In *Proceedings of the 57th Annual Meeting of the Association for Computational Linguistics: System Demonstrations*, pages 111–116, Florence, Italy. Association for Computational Linguistics.

Jesus Guerrero, Gongbo Liang, and Izzat Alsmadi. 2022. A Mutation-based Text Generation for Adversarial Machine Learning Applications. *Preprint*, arXiv:2212.11808.

Abhimanyu Hans, Avi Schwarzschild, Valeriia Cherepanova, Hamid Kazemi, Aniruddha Saha, Micah Goldblum, Jonas Geiping, and Tom Goldstein. 2024. Spotting LLMs With Binoculars: Zero-Shot Detection of Machine-Generated Text. *Preprint*, arXiv:2401.12070.

Xiaomeng Hu, Pin-Yu Chen, and Tsung-Yi Ho. 2023. RADAR: Robust AI-Text Detection via Adversarial Learning. In *Proceedings of the 37th International Conference on Neural Information Processing Systems*, NeurIPS 2023, Red Hook, NY, USA. Curran Associates Inc.

Ram Mohan Rao Kadiyala. 2024. RKadiyala at SemEval-2024 Task 8: Black-Box Word-Level Text Boundary Detection in Partially Machine Generated Texts. In *Proceedings of the 18th International Workshop on Semantic Evaluation (SemEval-2024)*, pages 511–519, Mexico City, Mexico. Association for Computational Linguistics.

Ram Mohan Rao Kadiyala, Siddartha Pullakhandam, Kanwal Mehreen, Ashay Srivastava, Subhasya TippaReddy, Arvind Reddy Bobbili, Drishti Sharma, Suraj Chandrashekhar, Modabbir Adeeb, and Srinadh Vura. 2024. mmgtd-corpus (v1).

Hemanth Kandula, Chak Fai Li, Haoling Qiu, Damianos Karakos, Hieu Man Duc Trong, Thien Huu Nguyen, and Brian Ulicny. 2025. BBN-U.Oregon's ALERT system at GenAI Content Detection Task 3: Robust Authorship Style Representations for Cross-Domain Machine-Generated Text Detection. In *Proceedings of the 1st Workshop on GenAI Content Detection (GenAIDetect)*, Abu Dhabi, UAE.

Yury Kashnitsky, Drahomira Herrmannova, Anita de Waard, George Tsatsaronis, Catriona Catriona Fennell, and Cyril Labbe. 2022. Overview of the DAGPap22 shared task on detecting automatically generated scientific papers. In *Proceedings of the Third Workshop on Scholarly Document Processing*, pages 210–213, Gyeongju, Republic of Korea. Association for Computational Linguistics.

Junseong Kim, Seolhwa Lee, Jihoon Kwon, Sangmo Gu, Yejin Kim, Minkyung Cho, Jy yong Sohn, and Chanyeol Choi. 2024. Linq-embed-mistral:elevating text retrieval with improved gpt data through task-specific control and quality refinement. Linq AI Research Blog.

Jules King, Perpetual Baffour, Scott Crossley, Ryan Holbrook, and Maggie Demkin. 2023. Llm - detect ai generated text. `https://kaggle.com/competitions/llm-detect-ai-generated-text`. Kaggle.

Ryuto Koike, Masahiro Kaneko, and Naoaki Okazaki. 2024. How you prompt matters! Even task-oriented constraints in instructions affect LLM-generated text detection. In *Findings of the Association for Computational Linguistics: EMNLP 2024*, pages 14384–14395, Miami, Florida, USA. Association for Computational Linguistics.

Kalpesh Krishna, Yixiao Song, Marzena Karpinska, John Wieting, and Mohit Iyyer. 2023. Paraphrasing evades detectors of ai-generated text, but retrieval is an effective defense. *Preprint*, arXiv:2303.13408.

Yafu Li, Qintong Li, Leyang Cui, Wei Bi, Zhilin Wang, Longyue Wang, Linyi Yang, Shuming Shi, and Yue Zhang. 2024. MAGE: Machine-generated text detection in the wild. In *Proceedings of the 62nd Annual Meeting of the Association for Computational Linguistics (Volume 1: Long Papers)*, pages 36–53, Bangkok, Thailand. Association for Computational Linguistics.

Gongbo Liang, Jesus Guerrero, and Izzat Alsmadi. 2023a. Mutation-based adversarial attacks on neural text detectors. *Preprint*, arXiv:2302.05794.

Weixin Liang, Mert Yuksekgonul, Yining Mao, Eric Wu, and James Zou. 2023b. GPT detectors are biased against non-native english writers. *Patterns*, 4(7):100779.

Tsung-Yi Lin, Priya Goyal, Ross Girshick, Kaiming He, and Piotr Dollar. 2017. Focal Loss for Dense Object Detection . In *2017 IEEE International Conference on Computer Vision (ICCV)*, pages 2999–3007, Los Alamitos, CA, USA. IEEE Computer Society.

Brady D Lund, Ting Wang, Nishith Reddy Mannuru, Bing Nie, Somipam Shimray, and Ziang Wang. 2023. ChatGPT and a new academic reality: Artificial Intelligence-written research papers and the ethics of the large language models in scholarly publishing. *Journal of the Association for Information Science and Technology*, 74(5):570–581.

Md Kamrujjaman Mobin and Md Saiful Islam. 2025. LuxVeri at GenAI Content Detection Task 3: Cross-Domain Detection of AI-Generated Text Using Inverse Perplexity-Weighted Ensemble of Fine-Tuned Transformer Models. In *Proceedings of the 1st Workshop on GenAI Content Detection (GenAIDetect)*, Abu Dhabi, UAE.

Jiameng Pu, Zain Sarwar, Sifat Muhammad Abdullah, Abdullah Rehman, Yoonjin Kim, Parantapa Bhattacharya, Mobin Javed, and Bimal Viswanath. 2023. Deepfake Text Detection: Limitations and Opportunities. In *2023 IEEE Symposium on Security and Privacy (SP)*, pages 1613–1630, Los Alamitos, CA, USA. IEEE Computer Society.

Vinu Sankar Sadasivan, Aounon Kumar, Sriram Balasubramanian, Wenxiao Wang, and Soheil Feizi. 2023. Can AI-Generated Text be Reliably Detected? *Preprint*, arXiv:2303.11156.

Areg Mikael Sarvazyan, José Ángel González, Marc Franco-Salvador, Francisco Rangel, Berta Chulvi, and Paolo Rosso. 2023. Overview of autextification at iberlef 2023: Detection and attribution of machine-generated text in multiple domains. *Preprint*, arXiv:2309.11285.

Tatiana Shamardina, Vladislav Mikhailov, Daniil Chernianskii, Alena Fenogenova, Marat Saidov, Anastasiya Valeeva, Tatiana Shavrina, Ivan Smurov, Elena Tutubalina, and Ekaterina Artemova. 2022. Findings of the RuATD Shared Task 2022 on Artificial Text Detection in Russian. In *Computational Linguistics and Intellectual Technologies*. RSUH.

Filipo Sharevski, Jennifer Vander Loop, Peter Jachim, Amy Devine, and Emma Pieroni. 2023. Talking Abortion (Mis) information with ChatGPT on TikTok. In *2023 IEEE European Symposium on Security and Privacy Workshops (EuroS&PW)*, pages 594–608. IEEE.

Irene Solaiman, Miles Brundage, Jack Clark, Amanda Askell, Ariel Herbert-Voss, Jeff Wu, Alec Radford, Gretchen Krueger, Jong Wook Kim, Sarah Kreps, Miles McCain, Alex Newhouse, Jason Blazakis, Kris McGuffie, and Jasmine Wang. 2019. Release strategies and the social impacts of language models. *Preprint*, arXiv:1908.09203.

Giovanni Spitale, Nikola Biller-Andorno, and Federico Germani. 2023. AI model GPT-3 (dis)informs us better than humans. *Science Advances*, 9(26):eadh1850.

L D M S Sai Teja, Annepaka Yadagiri, M Srikar Vardhan, and Partha Pakray. 2025. CNLP-NITS-PP at Task 3: Cross-Domain Machine-Generated Text Detection Using DistilBERT Techniques. In *Proceedings of the 1st Workshop on GenAI Content Detection (GenAIDetect)*, Abu Dhabi, UAE.

Yuxia Wang, Jonibek Mansurov, Petar Ivanov, Jinyan Su, Artem Shelmanov, Akim Tsvigun, Osama Mohammed Afzal, Tarek Mahmoud, Giovanni Puccetti, and Thomas Arnold. 2024. SemEval-2024 task 8: Multidomain, multimodel and multilingual machine-generated text detection. In *Proceedings of the 18th International Workshop on Semantic Evaluation (SemEval-2024)*, pages 2057–2079, Mexico City, Mexico. Association for Computational Linguistics.

Yuxia Wang, Artem Shelmanov, Jonibek Mansurov, Akim Tsvigun, Vladislav Mikhailov, Rui Xing, Zhuohan Xie, Jiahui Geng, Giovanni Puccetti, Ekaterina Artemova, Jinyan Su, Minh Ngoc Ta, Mervat Abassy, Kareem Elozeiri, Saad El Dine Ahmed, Maiya Goloburda, Tarek Mahmoud, Raj Vardhan Tomar, Alexander Aziz, Nurkhan Laiyk, Osama Mohammed Afzal, Ryuto Koike, Masahiro Kaneko, Alham Fikri Aji, Nizar Habash, Iryna Gurevych, and Preslav Nakov. 2025. GenAI content detection task 1: English and multilingual machine-generated text detection: AI vs. human. In *Proceedings of the 1st Workshop on GenAI Content Detection (GenAIDetect)*, Abu Dhabi, UAE. International Conference on Computational Linguistics.

Max Weiss. 2019. Deepfake Bot Submissions to Federal Public Comment Websites Cannot Be Distinguished from Human Submissions. *Technology Science*, 2019121801.

Max Wolff. 2020. Attacking Neural Text Detectors. *Preprint*, arXiv:2002.11768.

A Team Rankings

Teams are ranked by their highest performing submission. In Table 7 we report the official team ranking for Subtask A and in Table 8 we report the official ranking for Subtask B

B Extra RAID Details

In Table 9 we list the 8 domains present in RAID along with clickable links to the human-written sources from which the data was sampled. These links were given to the participants to assist in curating extra data for training.

In Table 10 we list the 11 adversarial attacks applied to the RAID data along with the relative percentage of attack surface used for the attack and the papers each attack originally came from. We provided participants with the code for these attacks to allow them to train on arbitrarily many examples of each attack at varying attack strengths.

C Recommendations for Future Evaluations

In this section, we will outline recommendations for future robustness studies and shared tasks. These recommendations come not only from our experiences with conducting this shared task, but also from discussions we had with participants about potential areas for future improvements.

Create a common preprocessing script. This should be done with the explicit goal of removing any and all potential confounding factors that

Team Ranking (Subtask A)		
	Best Submission	**Result**
[Le] Leidos	Leidos v1.0.3	**99.4** (0.6)
[Pa] Pangram	Pangram	99.3 (**0.4**)
[Us] USTC	R-L Focal Loss	98.1 (1.3)
[Al] ALERT	ALERT v1.1	91.8 (9.4)
[Cn] CNLP	DistilBERT-NITS	90.5 (2.9)
[Lx] LuxVeri	R-B & R-Oai	82.6 (10.9)
[Ba] **Baseline**	Binoculars	79.0 (2.4)
[Mo] MOSAIC	MOSAIC-4	75.2 (5.9)
[80] 1-800	L3-60 Zero-shot	57.1 (9.6)
[Ra] Random	Adv. CDMGTD	3.2 (1.6)

Table 7: Team ranking for Subtask A ranked by their best submission. Metric used for result is TPR at FPR=5% along with their standard deviation (σ). See Table 4 for full results.

Team Ranking (Subtask B)		
	Best Submission	**Result**
[Le] Leidos	Leidos v1.0.2	**97.7** (**2.5**)
[Pa] Pangram	Pangram	**97.7** (2.9)
[Us] USTC	R-L Focal Loss	92.7 (9.5)
[Al] ALERT	ALERT v1.1	82.6 (15.5)
[Lx] LuxVeri	Fine-tuned R-B	80.1 (8.4)
[Ba] **Baseline**	Binoculars	71.3 (16.2)
[Mo] MOSAIC	MOSAIC-5	69.4 (16.3)
[80] 1-800	L3-60 Zero-shot	51.4 (15.4)
[Cn] CNLP	Adv.-sub.-3	41.6 (10.4)
[Ra] Random	Adv. CDMGTD	6.5 (7.6)

Table 8: Team ranking for Subtask B ranked by their best submission. Metric used for result is TPR at FPR=5% along with their standard deviation (σ). See Table 5 for full results.

do not have to do with the text itself. We suggest making the preprocessing script public so that participants can apply it to existing pre-training data and any other data they have found on the web. This script should include text and character normalization and should standardize whitespace and capitalization rules. Another recommendation would be to restrict the length of text to be identical across all models and domains. A good starting point for such a script would be the punctuation normalizer from the Moses toolkit[3] as this is what was used for the MAGE dataset (Li et al., 2024).

Include more variations across prompts and paraphrasers. Prompts have been shown to wildly alter the stylistic components of generative model outputs even when only given task-oriented constraints—fooling detectors in the process (Koike et al., 2024). In particular, experiments that test robustness to many different prompting strategies, paraphrase models, and synonym replacement methods are likely to give a strong sense of how well detectors will hold up in real-world settings. Strategies such as prefix-based prompting, length-conditioned generation, explicitly adversarial prompting, and others are all valid strategies to incorporate into future work.

Include more human-written text. The imbalanced nature of the RAID dataset required participants to use data augmentation or up-sampling techniques that served only to degrade the quality of the data. Future work should seek to provide participants with a much larger corpus of human written texts from diverse domains.

[3]https://pypi.org/project/mosestokenizer/

Domain	Source	Description
Abstracts	arxiv.org	ArXiv Abstracts
Recipes	allrecipes.com	Ingredients + Recipe
Books	wikipedia.org	Plot Summaries
Reddit	reddit.com	Reddit Posts
News	bbc.com/news	News Articles
Reviews	imbd.com	Movie Reviews
Poetry	poemhunter.com	Poems (Any Style)
Wiki	wikipedia.org	Article Introductions

Table 9: All domains in the RAID dataset alongside a description of where they are from. Clickable source links go directly to the source dataset from which the human samples were taken.

Attack	θ	Source
Alternative Spelling	100%	(Liang et al., 2023b)
Article Deletion	50%	(Liang et al., 2023a; Guerrero et al., 2022)
Homoglyph	100%	(Wolff, 2020; Gagiano et al., 2021)
Insert Paragraphs	50%	(Bhat and Parthasarathy, 2020)
Number Swap	50%	(Bhat and Parthasarathy, 2020)
Paraphrase	100%	(Krishna et al., 2023; Sadasivan et al., 2023)
Misspelling	20%	(Liang et al., 2023a; Gagiano et al., 2021; Gao et al., 2018)
Synonym	50%	(Pu et al., 2023)
Upper Lower	5%	(Gagiano et al., 2021)
Whitespace	20%	(Cai and Cui, 2023; Gagiano et al., 2021)
Zero-Width Space	100%	(Guerrero et al., 2022)

Table 10: The adversarial attacks used in the project. θ represents the manually determined fraction of available attacks carried out. We determine this fraction through manual review.

Author Index

Association for Computational Linguistics
209 N. Eighth Street
Stroudsburg, Pennsylvania 18360

ISBN 979-8-3313-1367-8

CURRAN ASSOCIATES INC.
proceedings.com